MICROECONOMICS

Selected Readings

THIRD EDITION

Companion volumes prepared by Edwin Mansfield

MICROECONOMICS: THEORY AND APPLICATIONS, THIRD EDITION

MICROECONOMIC PROBLEMS: CASE STUDIES AND EXERCISES FOR
REVIEW, THIRD EDITION

MICROECONOMICS
Selected Readings
THIRD EDITION

Edited by
EDWIN MANSFIELD
University of Pennsylvania

W · W · NORTON & COMPANY
New York   **London**

ACKNOWLEDGMENTS

"Consumer Behavior and the 'Dependence Effect'": from *The Affluent Society* by John Kenneth Galbraith. Copyright © 1958 by John Kenneth Galbraith. Reprinted by permission of the publisher, Houghton Mifflin Company, and the author.

"The Non Sequitur of the 'Dependence Effect'" by F. A. Hayek: from *Southern Economic Journal*, April 1961. Reprinted by permission of the publishers and the author.

"Bandwagon, Snob and Veblen Effects in the Theory of Consumer's Demand" by Harvey Leibenstein: from *Quarterly Journal of Economics*, May 1950. Reprinted by permission of the publishers and the author, Harvey Leibenstein, Andelot Professor of Economics and Population, Department of Economics, Harvard University.

"The Meaning of Utility Measurement" by Armen A. Alchian: from *American Economic Review*, March 1953. Reprinted by permission of the publishers and the author.

"The Empirical Determination of Demand Relationships" by William Baumol: from *Economic Theory and Operations Analysis*, Second Edition. Copyright © 1965. Reprinted by permission of Prentice-Hall, Inc., Englewood Cliffs, New Jersey.

"Theories of Decision-Making in Economics and Behavioral Science" by Herbert A. Simon: from *American Economic Review*, June 1959. Reprinted by permission of the publishers and the author.

"Theories of the Firm: Marginalist, Behavioral, Managerial" by Fritz Machlup: from the *American Economic Review*, March 1967. Reprinted by permission of the publisher and author.

"Statistical Cost Functions of a Hosiery Mill" by Joel Dean: from *Journal of Business*, 1941. Reprinted by permission of the University of Chicago Press.

"Economies of Scale: Some Statistical Evidence" by Frederick T. Moore: from *Quarterly Journal of Economics*, May 1959. Reprinted by permission.

"Mathematical or 'Linear' Programming: A Nonmathematical Exposition" by Robert Dorfman: from *American Economic Review*, December 1953. Reprinted by permission of the publishers and author.

"Perfect Competition, Historically Contemplated" by George J. Stigler: from *Journal of Political Economy*, February 1957. Reprinted by permission of the University of Chicago Press.

"Annual Survey of Economic Theory: The Theory of Monopoly" by John Hicks: from *Econometrica*, 1935. Reprinted by permission of the publishers and the author.

"Monopoly and Resource Allocation" by Arnold C. Harberger: from *American Economic Review*, May 1954. Reprinted by permission of the publishers and the author, Arnold S. Harberger, Department of Economics, University of Chicago.

"Allocative Efficiency versus X-Efficiency" by Harvey Leibenstein: from the *American Economic Review*, 1966. Copyright © by the American Economic Association. Reprinted by permission.

"Predatory Price Cutting: The Standard Oil (N.J.) Case" by John S. McGee: from *Journal of Law & Economics*, October 1958. Reprinted by permission of the publishers.

"Price Discrimination in Medicine" by Reuben A. Kessel: from *Journal of Law & Economics*, October 1958. Reprinted by permission of the publishers.

"The Cost of Automobile Model Changes since 1949" by Franklin M. Fisher, Zvi Griliches, and Carl Kaysen: from *Journal of Political Economy*, October 1962. Reprinted by permission of the University of Chicago Press and the authors.

"The Uses of Game Theory in Management Science" by Martin Shubik: from *Management Science*, October 1955. Reprinted by permission of The Institute of Management Science.

"Collusion Among Electrical Equipment Manufacturers": from *Wall Street Journal*, January 1961. Reprinted by permission of the publishers.

"The Monopolistic Competition Revolution" by Paul A. Samuelson: from *Monopolistic Competition Theory*, edited by Robert Kuenne. Copyright © 1967 by John Wiley & Sons. Reprinted by permission of the publishers.

"The Problem of Social Cost" by R. H. Coase: from *Journal of Law & Economics*, October 1960. Reprinted by permission of the publishers.

"The Allocation of Water Supplies" by Jack Hirshleifer, James DeHaven, and Jerome Milliman: from *Water Supply*. Copyright © 1960 by the University of Chicago. Reprinted by permission of the University of Chicago Press, The Rand Corporation, and the authors.

"Some Implications of Marginal Cost Pricing for Public Utilities" by William Vickrey: from *American Economic Review*, May 1955. Reprinted by permission of the publishers and the author.

"Efficiency and Amenity" by Bertrand de Jouvenel. Reprinted by permission of author.

"The Anatomy of Market Failure" by Francis M. Bator: from *Quarterly Journal of Economics*, August 1958. Reprinted by permission of John Wiley & Sons, Inc.

"A Difficulty in the Concept of Social Welfare" by Kenneth J. Arrow: from *Journal of Political Economy*, 1950. Reprinted by permission of the publisher and the author.

"Diagrammatic Exposition of a Theory of Public Expenditure" by Paul A. Samuelson: from *The Review of Economics and Statistics*, Vol. XXXVII, 1955, pp. 350–356. Copyright © the President and Fellows of Harvard College. Reprinted by permission.

"A Theory of Group Organizations" reprinted by permission of the publishers from *The Logic of Collective Action* by Mancur Olson. Cambridge, Mass.: Harvard University Press, copyright © 1965 by the President and Fellows of Harvard College.

Contents

Part Two

PRODUCTION, COSTS, AND THE THEORY OF THE FIRM   83

Part Three

COMPETITION AND MONOPOLY   165

Preface

THIS BOOK, now in its third edition, is designed for use in intermediate courses in microeconomics. It is meant to supplement, not substitute for, a textbook presenting the principles of microeconomic theory. Although intended as a companion to my volume, *Microeconomics: Theory and Applications*, third edition (Norton, 1979), it can be used with any standard textbook. In contrast with other works of this type which concentrate almost entirely on *either* theory *or* applications, this book of readings attempts to present a balanced blend of *both* theory and applications—and to do this within a reasonable length. Judging from the favorable reactions to my text, which stresses the same kind of blend, a great many teachers agree with me about the importance of achieving such a balance.

The papers included in this volume cover the full range of microeconomic theory—consumer behavior and market demand; production, costs, and the theory of the firm; perfect competition and pure monopoly; oligopoly and monopolistic competition; and general equilibrium and welfare economics. In each of these areas, I have included some *classic theoretical papers* that extend and reinforce the student's grasp of the basic theoretical material. (In a few cases, they also give the student some insight into the history of economic thought.) In addition, I have included some well-known papers that illustrate the *measurement* and *application* of these theoretical constructs. And in the sections on the various market structures, I have included *case studies* to illustrate each market structure. The empirical material is derived from and pertains to a wide variety of industries, including—among others—cement, automobiles, textiles, chemicals, metals, agriculture, petroleum, railroads, medicine, electrical equipment, steel, water, and railroads.

In my view, the most effective way to teach microeconomic theory is to demonstrate how microeconomics can be, and has been, used to shed light on important real-world problems. If one takes the time to show students the relevance and power of microeconomic theory, they are usually motivated to learn it more thoroughly. Throughout this volume, articles are included that demonstrate the application and applicability of microeconomic theory. In addition, the final section of the book is devoted primarily to the discussion of some of the major social problems of the eighties—pollution, energy, and law enforcement.

I have tried hard to keep this book at a level commensurate with the abilities and background of the typical student. Of course, there are advantages in including some articles that will appeal to the most capable, and I have done so. But the bulk of the selection can be read and comprehended by those of average competence. Fortunately, it is possible, I believe, to acquaint students with classic papers by many of the great names of present-day economics without expecting them to perform intellectual feats beyond their capacities or training.

In this third edition, I have tried to alter the book's contents in the light of the reactions of the many instructors who have used the book in their courses. Parts Three and Four contain a new article regarding economic regulation and a new report on the steel industry. Parts Five and Six have been changed very considerably. New articles have been included on the nature and causes of market failure, on the provision of public goods, and on externalities. Part Seven, which deals with intertemporal choice and technological change, is entirely new. This part contains classic papers regarding capital budgeting and the evaluation of the social discount rate, as well as discussions of the returns from investments in research and development and of public policy toward civilian technology. In addition, a number of articles have been deleted, often because they had become somewhat dated or because of space limitations. About one-fifth of the articles in this third edition are new.

E. M.

MICROECONOMICS

Selected Readings

THIRD EDITION

Part One

CONSUMER BEHAVIOR AND MARKET DEMAND

The theory of consumer behavior and market demand is of central importance in the study of microeconomics. Typically this is the first area that is taken up in a course on microeconomics; it includes the study of utility, indifference curves, consumer equilibrium, individual demand curves, market demand curves, and related phenomena. A grasp of these topics is essential to an understanding of the nature and workings of the economic system, and significant, too, in promoting better decision-making.

The theory of consumer behavior generally assumes that the preferences, tastes, and wants of the consumer are given data for the economist. The dominance of this assumption is stressed by John Kenneth Galbraith, who argues that it is misleading and incorrect. In his view, "as a society becomes increasingly affluent, wants are increasingly created by the process by which they are satisfied." Because of advertising, salesmanship, and other factors, wants "come to depend on output," with the fundamental result that "it can no longer be assumed that welfare is greater at an all-round higher level of production than at a lower one." This view is not shared by many economists; among those disagreeing is Friedrich Hayek, who attacks Galbraith's distinction between "natural" and "derived" wants. According to Hayek, Galbraith's entire argument is a *non sequitur*.

In the next article, Harvey Leibenstein shows how the theory of consumer demand can be extended to include bandwagon, snob, and Veblen effects. Essentially, what Leibenstein is concerned with "is a reformulation of . . . static theory of consumer's demand while permitting the relaxation of one of the basic implicit assumptions of the current theory—namely, that the consumption behavior of any individual is independent of the consumption of others." In the following paper, Armen Alchian presents a lucid discussion of the extent to which—and the ways in which—utility is measurable. An important feature of this article is its concern with the situation involving choice among uncertain prospects; in elementary accounts of utility theory, it is generally assumed that choices are riskless.

Market demand curves are important tools for decision-making, not merely the playthings of academic economists. To be useful in applied work, demand curves must be measured, not merely conceptualized. William Baumol describes various ways in which firms, government agencies, and academic researchers attempt to measure demand curves—interview approaches, direct market experiments, and various statistical approaches. Also, he presents some modern results concerning the identification problem. The last section in this part of the book deals with the measurement of the price elasticity of demand for automobiles. It presents part of a report by the Senate Subcommittee on Antitrust and Monopoly which summarizes various estimates of the price elasticity of demand for automobiles. The subcommittee finds a substantial measure of agreement among various studies and concludes that "a price elasticity of -1.2 appears to be a minimum estimate."

Consumer Behavior and the Dependence Effect

JOHN KENNETH GALBRAITH

John Kenneth Galbraith is Professor of Economics at Harvard University. This selection is from his well-known book The Affluent Society, *published in 1958.*

The theory of consumer demand, as it is now widely accepted, is based on two broad propositions, neither of them quite explicit but both extremely important for the present value system of economists. The first is that the urgency of wants does not diminish appreciably as more of them are satisfied or, to put the matter more precisely, to the extent that this happens it is not demonstrable and not a matter of any interest to economists or for economic policy. When man has satisfied his physical needs, then psychologically grounded desires take over. These can never be satisfied or, in any case, no progress can be proved. The concept of satiation has very little standing in economics. It is neither useful nor scientific to speculate on the comparative cravings of the stomach and the mind.

The second proposition is that wants originate in the personality of the consumer or, in any case, that they are given data for the economist. The latter's task is merely to seek their satisfaction. He has no need to inquire how these wants are formed. His function is sufficiently fulfilled by maximizing the goods that supply the wants. . . .

The notion that wants do not become less urgent the more amply the individual is supplied is broadly repugnant to common sense. It is something to be believed only by those who wish to believe. Yet the conventional wisdom must be tackled on its own terrain. Intertemporal comparisons of an individual's state of mind do rest on doubtful grounds. Who can say for sure that the deprivation which afflicts him with hunger is more painful than the deprivation which afflicts him with envy of his neigh-

3

bor's new car? In the time that has passed since he was poor his soul may have become subject to a new and deeper searing. And where a society is concerned, comparisons between marginal satisfactions when it is poor and those when it is affluent will involve not only the same individual at different times but different individuals at different times. The scholar who wishes to believe that with increasing affluence there is no reduction in the urgency of desires and goods is not without points for debate. However plausible the case against him, it cannot be proven. In the defense of the conventional wisdom this amounts almost to invulnerability.

However, there is a flaw in the case. If the individual's wants are to be urgent they must be original with himself. They cannot be urgent if they must be contrived for him. And above all they must not be contrived by the process of production by which they are satisfied. For this means that the whole case for the urgency of production, based on the urgency of wants, falls to the ground. One cannot defend production as satisfying wants if that production creates the wants.

Were it so that a man on arising each morning was assailed by demons which instilled in him a passion sometimes for silk shirts, sometimes for kitchenware, sometimes for chamber pots, and sometimes for orange squash, there would be every reason to applaud the effort to find the goods, however odd, that quenched this flame. But should it be that his passion was the result of his first having cultivated the demons, and should it also be that his effort to allay it stirred the demons to ever greater and greater effort, there would be question as to how rational was his solution. Unless restrained by conventional attitudes, he might wonder if the solution lay with more goods or fewer demons.

So it is that if production creates the wants it seeks to satisfy, or if the wants emerge *pari passu* with the production, then the urgency of the wants can no longer be used to defend the urgency of the production. Production only fills a void that it has itself created.

The point is so central that it must be pressed. Consumer wants can have bizarre, frivolous, or even immoral origins, and an admirable case can still be made for a society that seeks to satisfy them. But the case cannot stand if it is the process of satisfying wants that creates the wants. For then the individual who urges the importance of production to satisfy these wants is precisely in the position of the onlooker who applauds the efforts of the squirrel to keep abreast of the wheel that is propelled by his own efforts.

That wants are, in fact, the fruit of production will now be denied by few serious scholars. And a considerable number of economists, though not always in full knowledge of the implications, have conceded the point. In the observation cited at the end of the preceding chapter Keynes noted that needs of "the second class," i.e., those that are the result of efforts to keep abreast or ahead of one's fellow being "may indeed be insatiable; for the higher the general level the higher still are they." And emulation has always played a considerable role in the views of other economists of want creation. One man's consumption becomes his neighbor's wish. This already means that the process by which wants are satisfied is also the process by which wants are created. The more wants that are satisfied the more new ones are born. . . .

The even more direct link between production and wants is provided by the institutions of modern advertising and salesmanship. These cannot be reconciled with the notion of independently determined desires, for their central function is to create desires—to bring into being wants that previously did not exist. This is accomplished by the producer of the goods or at his behest. A broad empirical relationship exists between what is spent on production of consumers' goods and what is spent in synthesizing the desire for that production. A new consumer product must be introduced with a suitable advertising campaign to arouse an interest in it. The path for an expansion of output must be paved by a suitable expansion in the advertising budget. Outlays for the manufacturing of a product are not more important in the strategy of modern business enterprise than outlays for the manufacturing of demand for the product. None of this is novel. All would be regarded as elementary by the most retarded student in the nation's most primitive school of business administration. The cost of this want formation is formidable. In 1956 total advertising expenditure—though, as noted, not all of it may be assigned to the synthesis of wants—amounted to about ten billion dollars. For some years it had been increasing at a rate in excess of a billion dollars a year. Obviously, such outlays must be integrated with the theory of consumer demand. They are too big to be ignored.

But such integration means recognizing that wants are dependent on production. It accords to the producer the function both of making the goods and of making the desires for them. It recognizes that production, not only passively through emulation, but actively through advertising and related activities, creates the wants it seeks to satisfy.

The businessman and the lay reader will be puzzled over the emphasis which I give to a seemingly obvious point. The point is indeed obvious. But it is one which, to a singular degree, economists have resisted. They have sensed, as the layman does not, the damage to established ideas which lurks in these relationships. As a result, incredibly, they have closed their eyes (and ears) to the most obtrusive of all economic phenomena, namely modern want creation.

This is not to say that the evidence affirming the dependence of wants on advertising has been entirely ignored. It is one reason why advertising has so long been regarded with such uneasiness by economists. Here is something which cannot be accommodated easily to existing theory. More pervious scholars have speculated on the urgency of desires which are so obviously the fruit of such expensively contrived campaigns for popular attention. Is a new breakfast cereal or detergent so much wanted if so much must be spent to compel in the consumer the sense of want? But there has been little tendency to go on to examine the implications of this for the theory of consumer demand and even less for the importance of production and productive efficiency. These have remained sacrosanct. More often the uneasiness has been manifested in a general disapproval of advertising and advertising men, leading to the occasional suggestion that they shouldn't exist. Such suggestions have usually been ill received.

And so the notion of independently determined wants still survives. In the face of all the forces of modern salesmanship it still rules, almost undefiled, in the textbooks. And it still remains the economist's mission—and on few matters is the pedagogy so firm—to seek unquestioningly the means for filling these wants. This being so, production remains of prime urgency. We have here, perhaps, the ultimate triumph of the conventional wisdom in its resistance to the evidence of the eyes. To equal it one must imagine a humanitarian who was long ago persuaded of the grievous shortage of hospital facilities in the town. He continues to importune the passers-by for money for more beds and refuses to notice that the town doctor is deftly knocking over pedestrians with his car to keep up the occupancy.

And in unraveling the complex we should always be careful not to overlook the obvious. The fact that wants can be synthesized by advertising, catalyzed by salesmanship, and shaped by the discreet manipulations of the persuaders shows that they are not very urgent. A man who is hungry need never be told of his need for food. If he is inspired by his appetite, he is immune to the influence of Messrs. Batten, Barton, Durstine & Osborn. The latter are effective only with those who are so far removed from physical want that they do not already know what they want. In this state alone men are open to persuasion.

The general conclusion of these pages is of such importance for this essay that it had perhaps best be put with some formality. As a society becomes increasingly affluent, wants are increasingly created by the process by which they are satisfied. This may operate passively. Increases in consumption, the counterpart of increases in production, act by suggestion or emulation to create wants. Or producers may proceed actively to create wants through advertising and salesmanship. Wants thus come to depend on output. In technical terms it can no longer be assumed that welfare is greater at an all-round higher level of production than at a lower one. It may be the same. The higher level of production has, merely, a higher level of want creation necessitating a higher level of want satisfaction. There will be frequent occasion to refer to the way wants depend on the process by which they are satisfied. It will be convenient to call it the Dependence Effect.

The Non Sequitur *of the* *"Dependence Effect"*

FRIEDRICH A. HAYEK

Friedrich A. Hayek, a recent Nobel Laureate in Economics, is Professor of Economics at the University of Freiburg. This article is taken from the Southern Economic Journal, 1961.

For well over a hundred years the critics of the free enterprise system have resorted to the argument that if production were only organized rationally, there would be no economic problem. Rather than face the problem which scarcity creates, socialist reformers have tended to deny that scarcity existed. Ever since the Saint-Simonians their contention has been that the problem of production has been solved and only the problem of distribution remains. However absurd this contention must appear to us with respect to the time when it was first advanced, it still has some persuasive power when repeated with reference to the present.

The latest form of this old contention is expounded in *The Affluent Society* by Professor J. K. Galbraith. He attempts to demonstrate that in our affluent society the important private needs are already satisfied and the urgent need is therefore no longer a further expansion of the output of commodities but an increase of those services which are supplied (and presumably can be supplied only) by government. Though this book has been extensively discussed since its publication in 1958, its central thesis still requires some further examination.

I believe the author would agree that his argument turns upon the "Dependence Effect" explained in [the article which precedes this one]. The argument starts from the assertion that a great part of the wants which are still unsatisfied in modern society are not wants which would be experienced spontaneously by the individual if left to himself, but are wants which are created by the process by which they are satisfied. It is then represented as self-evident that for this reason such wants cannot be urgent or important. This crucial conclusion appears to be a complete *non sequitur* and it would seem that with it the whole argument of the book collapses.

The first part of the argument is of course perfectly true: we would not desire any of the amenities of civilization—or even of the most primitive culture—if we did not live in a society in which others provide them. The innate wants are probably confined to food, shelter, and sex. All the rest we learn to desire because we see others enjoying various things. To say that a desire is not important because it is not innate is to say that the whole cultural achievement of man is not important.

The cultural origin of practically all the needs of civilized life must of course not be confused with the fact that there are some desires which aim, not at a satisfaction derived directly from the use of an object, but only from the status which its consumption is expected to confer. In a passage which Professor Galbraith quotes, Lord Keynes seems to treat the latter sort of Veblenesque conspicuous consumption as the only alternative "to those needs which are absolute in the sense that we feel them whatever the situation of our fellow human beings may be." If the latter phrase is interpreted to exclude all the needs for goods which are felt only because these goods are known to be produced, these two Keynesian classes describe of course only extreme types of wants, but disregard the overwhelming majority of goods on which civilized life rests. Very few needs indeed are "absolute" in the sense that they are independent of social environment or of the example of others, and that their satisfaction is an indispensable condition for the preservation of the individual or of the species. Most needs which make us act are needs for things which only civilization teaches us exist at all, and these things are wanted by us because they produce feelings or emotions which we would not know if it were not for our cultural inheritance. Are not in this sense probably all our esthetic feelings "acquired tastes"?

How complete a *non sequitur* Professor Galbraith's conclusion represents is seen most clearly if we apply the argument to any product of the arts, be it music, painting, or literature. If the fact that people would not feel the need for something if it were not produced did prove that such products are of small value, all those highest products of human endeavor would be of small value. Professor Galbraith's argument could be easily employed, without any change of the essential terms, to demonstrate the worthlessness of literature or any other form of art. Surely an individual's want for literature is not original with himself in the sense that he would experience it if literature were not produced. Does this then mean that the production of literature cannot be defended as satisfying a want because it is only the production which provokes the demand? In this, as in the case of all cultural needs, it is unquestionably, in Professor Galbraith's words, "the process of satisfying the wants that creates the wants." There have never been "independently determined desires for" literature before literature has been produced and books certainly do not serve the "simple mode of enjoyment which requires no previous conditioning of the consumer." Clearly my taste for the novels of Jane Austen or Anthony Trollope or C. P. Snow is not "original with myself." But is it not rather absurd to conclude from this that it is less important than, say, the need for education? Public education indeed seems to regard it as one of its tasks to instill a taste for literature in the young and even employs producers of literature for that purpose. Is this want creation by the producer reprehensible? Or does the fact that some of the pupils may possess a taste for poetry only because of the efforts of their teachers prove that since "it does not arise in spontaneous consumer need and the demand would not exist were it not contrived, its utility or urgency, ex contrivance, is zero"?

The appearance that the conclusions follow from the admitted facts is made possible by an obscurity of the wording of the argument with respect to which it is difficult to know whether the author is himself the victim of a confusion or whether he skillfully uses ambiguous terms to make the conclusion appear plausible. The obscurity concerns the implied assertion that the wants of consumers are determined by the producers. Professor Galbraith avoids in this connection any terms as crude and definite as "determine." The expressions he employs, such as that wants are "dependent on" or the "fruits of" production, or that "production creates the wants" do, of course, suggest determination but avoid saying so in plain terms. After what has already been said it is of course obvious that the knowledge of what is being produced is one of the many factors on which depends what people will want. It would scarcely be an exaggeration to say that contemporary man, in all fields where he has not yet formed firm habits, tends to find out what he wants by looking at what his neighbors do and at various displays of goods (physical or in catalogues or advertisements) and then choosing what he likes best.

In this sense the tastes of man, as is also true of his opinions and beliefs and indeed much of his personality, are shaped in a great measure by his cultural environment. But though in some contexts it would perhaps be legitimate to express this by a phrase like "production creates the wants," the circumstances mentioned would clearly not justify the contention that particular producers can deliberately determine the wants of particular consumers. The efforts of all producers will certainly be directed towards that end; but how far any individual producer will succeed will depend not only on what he does but also on what the others do and on a great many other influences operating upon the consumer. The joint but uncoordinated efforts of the producers merely create one element of the environment by which the wants of the consumers are shaped. It is because each individual producer thinks that the consumers can be persuaded to like his products that he endeavors to influence them. But though this effort is part of the influences which shape consumers' tastes, no producer can in any real sense "determine" them. This, however, is clearly implied in such statements as that wants are "both passively and deliberately the fruits of the process by which they are satisfied." If the producer could in fact deliberately determine what the consumers will want, Professor Galbraith's conclusions would have some validity. But though this is skillfully suggested, it is nowhere made credible, and could hardly be made credible because it is not true. Though the range of choice open to the consumers is the joint result of, among other things, the efforts of all producers who vie with each other in making their respective products appear more attractive than those of their competitors, every particular consumer still has the choice between all those different offers.

A fuller examination of this process would, of course, have to consider how, after the efforts of some producers have actually swayed some consumers, it becomes the example of the various consumers thus persuaded which will influence the remaining consumers. This can be mentioned here only to emphasize that even if each consumer were exposed to pressure of only one producer, the harmful effects which are apprehended from this would soon be offset by the much more powerful example of his fellows. It is of course fashionable to treat this influence of the example of others (or, what comes to the same thing, the learning from the experience made by others) as if it all amounted to an attempt at keeping up with the Joneses and for that reason was to be regarded as detrimental. It seems to me not only that the importance of this factor is usually greatly exaggerated but also that it is not really relevant to Professor Galbraith's main thesis. But it might be worthwhile briefly to ask what, assuming that some expenditure were actually determined solely by a desire of keeping up with the Joneses, that would really prove?

At least in Europe we used to be familiar with a type of persons who often denied themselves even enough food in order to maintain an appearance of respectability or gentility in dress and style of life. We may regard this as a misguided effort, but surely it would not prove that the income of such persons was larger than they knew how to use wisely. That the appearance of success or wealth, may to some people seem more important than many other needs, does in no way prove that the needs they sacrifice to the former are unimportant. In the same way, even though people are often persuaded to spend unwisely, this surely is no evidence that they do not still have important unsatisfied needs.

Professor Galbraith's attempt to give an apparent scientific proof for the contention that the need for the production of more commodities has greatly decreased seems to me to have broken down completely. With it goes the claim to have produced a valid argument which justifies the use of coercion to make people employ their income for those purposes of which he approves. It is not to be denied that there is some originality in this latest version of the old socialist argument. For over a hundred years we have been exhorted to embrace socialism because it would give us more goods. Since it has so lamentably failed to achieve this where it has been tried, we are now urged to adopt it because more goods after all are not important. The aim is still progressively to increase the share of the resources whose use is determined by political authority and the coercion of any dissenting minority. It is not surprising, therefore, that Professor Galbraith's thesis has been most enthusiastically received by the intellectuals of the British Labour Party where his influence bids fair to displace that of the late Lord Keynes. It is more curious that in this country it is not recognized as an outright socialist argument and often seems to appeal to people on the opposite end of the political spectrum. But this is probably only another instance of the familiar fact that on these matters the extremes frequently meet.

Bandwagon, Snob, and Veblen Effects in the Theory of Consumers' Demand

HARVEY LEIBENSTEIN

Harvey Leibenstein is Professor of Economics at Harvard University. The following article, a classic in this area, first appeared in the Quarterly Journal of Economics *in 1950.*

I. The Nature of the Problem

The desire of some consumers to be "in style," the attempts by others to attain exclusiveness, and the phenomena of "conspicuous consumption," have as yet not been incorporated into the current theory of consumers' demand. My purpose, in this paper, is to take a step or two in that direction. ...

1. THE APPROACH AND LIMITS OF THE ENSUING ANALYSIS

It should, perhaps, be pointed out at the outset that the ensuing exposition is limited to statics. In all probability, the most interesting parts of the problem, and also those most relevant to real problems, are its dynamic aspects. However, a static analysis is probably necessary, and may be of significance, in order to lay a foundation for a dynamic analysis. In view of the limitations to be set on the following analysis, it becomes necessary to demarcate clearly the conceptual borderline between statics and dynamics.

There are, unfortunately, numerous definitions of statics and there seems to be some confusion on the matter. In view of this it will not be

12

possible to give *the* definition of statics. All that we can hope to do is to choose *a* definition that will be consistent with and useful for our purposes—and also one that at the same time does not stray too far from some of the generally accepted notions about statics. Because of the fact that we live in a dynamic world most definitions of statics will imply a state of affairs that contradicts our general experience. But this is of necessity the case. What we must insist on is internal consistency but we need not, at this stage, require "realism."

Our task, then, is to define a static situation—a situation in which static economics is applicable. Ordinarily, it is thought that statics is in some way "timeless." This need not be the case. For our purposes, a static situation is not a "timeless" situation, nor is static economics timeless economics. It is, however, "temporally orderless" economics. That is, we shall define a static situation as one in which the order of events is of no significance. We, therefore, abstract from the consequences of the temporal order of events. The above definition is similar to, but perhaps on a slightly higher level of generality than, Hicks's notion that statics deals with "those parts of economic theory where we do not have to trouble about dating."

In order to preserve internal consistency, it is necessary to assume that the period of reference is one in which the consumer's income and expenditure pattern is synchronized. And, we have to assume also that this holds true for all consumers. In other words, we assume that both the income patterns and the expenditure patterns repeat themselves *every* period. There is thus no overlapping of expenditures from one period into the next. This implies, of course, that the demand curve reconstitutes itself every period. The above implies also that only one price can exist during any unit period and that price can change only from period to period. A disequilibrium can, therefore, be corrected only over two or more periods.

II. Functional and Nonfunctional Demand

At the outset it is probably best to define clearly some of the basic terms we are going to use and to indicate those aspects of demand that we are going to treat. The demand for consumers' goods and services may be classified according to motivation. The following classification, which we shall find useful, is on a level of abstraction which, it is hoped, includes most of the motivations behind consumers' demand.

    A. Functional
    B. Nonfunctional
        1. External effects on utility
            (a) Bandwagon effect
            (b) Snob effect
            (c) Veblen effect

2. Speculative

3. Irrational

By functional demand is meant that part of the demand for a commodity which is due to the qualities inherent in the commodity itself. By nonfunctional demand is meant that portion of the demand for a consumers' good which is due to factors other than the qualities inherent in the commodity. Probably the most important kind of nonfunctional demand is due to external effects on utility. That is, the utility derived from the commodity is enhanced or decreased owing to the fact that others are purchasing and consuming the same commodity, or owing to the fact that the commodity bears a higher rather than a lower price tag. We differentiate this type of demand into what we shall call the "bandwagon" effect, the "snob" effect, and the "Veblen" effect. By the bandwagon effect, we refer to the extent to which the demand for a commodity is *increased* due to the fact that others are also consuming the same commodity. It represents the desire of people to purchase a commodity in order to get into "the swim of things"; in order to conform with the people they wish to be associated with; in order to be fashionable or stylish; or, in order to appear to be "one of the boys." By the snob effect we refer to the extent to which the demand for a consumers' good is *decreased* owing to the fact that others are also consuming the same commodity (or that others are increasing their consumption of that commodity). This represents the desire of people to be exclusive; to be different; to dissociate themselves from the "common herd." By the Veblen effect we refer to the phenomenon of conspicuous consumption; to the extent to which the demand for a consumers' good is increased because it bears a higher rather than a lower price. We should perhaps emphasize the distinction made between the snob and the Veblen effect—the former is a function of the consumption of others, the latter is a function of price. This paper will deal almost exclusively with these three types of nonfunctional demand.

For the sake of completeness there should perhaps be some explanation as to what is meant by speculative and irrational demand. Speculative demand refers to the fact that people will often "lay in" a supply of a commodity because they expect its price to rise. Irrational demand is, in a sense, a catchall category. It refers to purchases that are neither planned nor calculated but are due to sudden urges, whims, etc., and that serve no rational purpose but that of satisfying sudden whims and desires.

In the above it was assumed throughout that income is a parameter. If income is not given but allowed to vary, then the income effect on demand may in most cases be the most important effect of all. Also, it may be well to point out that the above is only one of a large number of possible classifications of the types of consumers' demand—classifications that for some purposes may be superior to the one here employed. We therefore suggest the above classification only for the purposes at hand and make no claims about its desirableness, or effectiveness, in any other use.

III. *The Bandwagon Effect*

1. A CONCEPTUAL EXPERIMENT

Our immediate task is to obtain aggregate demand curves of various kinds in those cases where the individual demand curves are nonadditive. First we shall examine the case where the bandwagon effect is important. In its pure form this is the case where an individual will demand more (less) of a commodity at a given price because some or all other individuals in the market also demand more (less) of the commodity.

One of the difficulties in analyzing this type of demand involves the choice of assumptions about the knowledge that each individual possesses. This implies that everyone knows the quantity that will be demanded by every individual separately, or the quantity demanded by all individuals collectively at any given price—after all the reactions and adjustments that individuals make to each other's demand has taken place. On the other hand, if we assume ignorance on the part of consumers about the demand of others, we have to make assumptions as to the nature and extent of the ignorance—ignorance is a relative concept. A third possibility, and the one that will be employed at first, is to devise some mechanism whereby the consumers obtain accurate information.

Another problem involves the choice of assumptions to be made about the demand behavior of individual consumers. Three possibilities suggest themselves: (1) The demand of consumer A (at given prices) may be a function of the total demand of all others in the market collectively. Or, (2) the demand of consumer A may be a function of the demand of all other consumers both separately and collectively. In other words, A's demand may be more influenced by the demand of some than by the demand of others. (3) A third possibility is that A's demand is a function of the number of people that demand the commodity rather than the number of units demanded. More complex demand behavior patterns that combine some of the elements of the above are conceivable. For present purposes it is best that we assume the simplest one as a first approximation.[1] Initially, therefore, we assume that A's demand is a function of the units demanded by all others collectively. This is the same as saying that A's demand is a function of total market demand at given prices, since A always knows his own demand, and he could always subtract his own demand from the total market demand to get quantity demanded by all others.

In order to bring out the central principle involved in the ensuing analy-

[1] As is customary in economic theory the ensuing analysis is carried out on the basis of a number of simplifying assumptions. The relaxation of some of the simplifying assumptions and the analysis of more complex situations must await some other occasion. The present writer has attempted these with respect to some of the simplifying assumptions but the results cannot be included within the confines of an article of the usual length.

sis, consider the following *Gedankenexperiment*. A known product is to be introduced into a well-defined market at a certain date. The nature of the product is such that its demand depends partially on the functional qualities of the commodity, and partially on whether many or few units are demanded. Our technical problem is to compound the nonadditive individual demand curves into a total market demand curve, given sufficient information about the individual demand functions. Now, suppose that it is possible to obtain an accurate knowledge of the demand function of an individual through a series of questionnaires. Since an individual's demand is, in part, a function of the total market demand, it is necessary to take care of this difficulty in our questionnaires. We can have a potential consumer fill out the first questionnaire by having him assume that the total market demand, at all prices, is a given very small amount—say 400 units. On the basis of this assumption the consumer would tell us the quantities he demands over a reasonable range of prices. Subjecting every consumer to the same questionnaire, we add the results across and obtain a market demand curve that would reflect the demand situation if every consumer believed the total demand were only 400 units. This, however, is not the real market demand function under the assumption of the possession of accurate market information by consumers, since the total demand ((at each price) upon which consumers based their replies was not the actual market demand (at each price) as revealed by the results of the survey. Let us call the results of the first survey "schedule No. 1."

We can now carry out a second survey, that is, subject each consumer to a second questionnaire in which each one is told that schedule No. 1 reflects the total quantities demanded, at each price. Aggregating the replies we obtain schedule No. 2. Schedule No. 1 then becomes a parameter upon which schedule No. 2 is based. In a similar manner we can obtain schedules No. 3, No. 4, . . . , No. *n* in which each schedule is the result of adding the quantities demanded by each consumer (at each price), *if each consumer believes that the total quantities demanded (at each price) are shown by the previous schedule*. Now, the quantities demanded in schedule No. 2 will be greater than or equal to the quantities demanded in schedule No. 1 for the same prices. Some consumers may increase the quantity they demand when they note that the total quantity demanded, at given prices, is greater than they thought it would be. As long as some consumers or potential consumers continue to react positively to increases in the total quantity demanded, the results of successive surveys will be different. That is, some or all of the quantities demanded in schedule No. 1 will be less than the quantities demanded, at the same prices, in schedule No. 2, which in turn will be equal to or less than the quantities demanded, at the same prices, in schedule No. 3, and so on.

At this point it is appropriate to introduce a new principle with the intention of showing that this process cannot go on indefinitely. Sooner or later two successive schedules will be identical. If two successive surveys yield the same market demand schedules, then an equilibrium situation exists since the total quantities demanded, at each price, upon which individual consumers based their demand, turn out to be correct. Thus, if schedule No. n is identical with schedule No. $n-1$, then schedule No. n is the actual market demand function for the product on the assumption that consumers have accurate information of market conditions.

The question that arises is whether there is any reason to suppose that sooner or later two successive surveys will yield exactly the same result. This would indeed be the case if we could find good reason to posit a principle to the effect that for every individual there is some point at which he will cease to increase the quantities demanded for a commodity, at given prices, in response to incremental increases in total market demand. Such a principle would imply that beyond a point, incremental increases in the demand for the commodity by others have a decreasing influence on a consumer's own demand; and, further, that a point is reached at which these increases in demand by others have no influence whatsoever on his own demand. It would, of course, also be necessary to establish that such a principle holds true for every consumer. It would not be inappropriate to call this the principle of diminishing marginal external consumption effect. Does such a principle really exist? There are some good reasons for believing that it does. First, the reader may note that the principle is analogous to the principle of diminishing marginal utility. As the total market demand grows larger, incremental increases in total demand become smaller and smaller proportions of the demand. It sounds reasonable, and probably appeals to us intuitively, that an individual would be less influenced, and indeed take less notice of, a one per cent increase in total demand, than of a ten per cent increase in total demand, though these percentage increases be the same in absolute amount. Second, we can probably appeal effectively to general experience. There are no cases in which an individual's demand for a consumers' good increases endlessly with increases in total demand. If there were two or more such individuals in a market then the demand for the commodity would increase in an endless spiral. Last but not least, the income constraint is sufficient to establish that there must be a point at which increases in a consumer's demand must fail to respond to increases in demand by others. Since every consumer is subject to the income constraint, it must follow that the principle holds for all consumers.[2]

Now, to get back to our conceptual experiment, we would find that after administering a sufficient number of surveys, we would sooner or later get two surveys that yield identical demand schedules. The result of the last survey would then represent the true demand situation that would manifest itself on the market when the commodity was offered for sale. We

[2] If the reader should object to our dignifying the diminishing marginal external consumption effect by calling it a principle or a law, we could point out that if it is not a "law," then it must be an equilibrium condition.

may perhaps justly call such a demand function the equilibrium demand function—or demand curve. The equilibrium demand curve is the curve that exists when the marginal external consumption effect for every consumer, but one,[3] at all alternate prices is equal to zero. All other demand curves may be conceived as disequilibrium curves that can exist only because of temporarily imperfect knowledge by consumers of other people's demand. Once the errors in market information were discovered such a curve would move to a new position.

2. THE BANDWAGON EFFECT—DIAGRAMMATICAL METHOD

The major purpose of going through the conceptual experiment with its successive surveys was to illustrate the diminishing marginal external consumption effect and to indicate its role in obtaining a determinate demand curve. There is, however, a relatively simple method for obtaining the market demand function in those cases where external consumption effects are significant. This method will allow us to compare some of the properties of the "bandwagon demand curve" with the usual "functional" demand curve; and, it will also allow us to separate the extent to which a change in demand is due to a change in price, and the extent to which it is due to the bandwagon effect.

Given a certain total demand for a commodity as a parameter,[4] every individual will have a demand function based on this total market demand. Let the alternative total market demands that will serve as parameters for alternate individual demand functions be indicated as superscripts $a, b, \ldots n$ (where $a < b < \ldots n$). Let the individual demand functions be $d_1, d_2, \ldots d_n$; where every subscript indicates a different consumer. Thus d_3^a is the individual demand curve for consumer 3 if the consumer believes that the total market demand is a units. Similarly d_{500}^m is the individual demand curve for the 500th consumer if he believes that the total market demand will be m units. We could now add across $d_1^a, d_2^a, d_3^a, \ldots, d_n^a$ which will give us the market demand curve D^a, which indicates the quantities demanded at alternate prices if all consumers believed that the total demand was a units. In the same manner we can obtain $D^b, D^c, \ldots, D^n$. These hypothetical market demand curves $D^a, D^b, D^c, \ldots, D^n$

---

[3] The fact that the marginal external consumption effect of one consumer is greater than zero can have no effect on the demand schedule since total market demand, at any given price, cannot increase unless there are at least two consumers who would react on each other's demand.

[4] The reader should note that the analysis in the following pages is based on a somewhat different assumption than the *Gedankenexperiment*. In the diagrams that follow, each demand curve (other than the equilibrium demand curve) is based on the assumption that consumers believe that a fixed amount will be taken off the market at all prices. There is more than one way of deriving the equilibrium demand curve. The earlier method helped to bring out the nature of the central principle that is involved, while the method which follows will enable us to separate price effects from bandwagon effects and snob effects, etc.

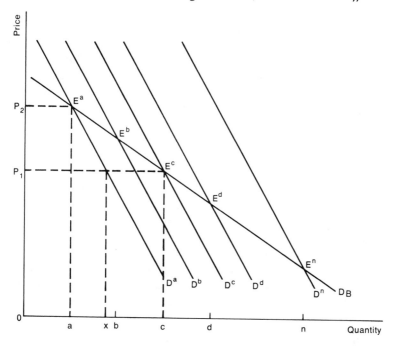

FIGURE 1

are shown in Figure 1. Now, if we assume that buyers have accurate knowledge of market conditions (*i.e.*, of the total quantities demanded at every price) then only one point on any of the curves D^a, D^b, . . . , D^n could be on the real or equilibrium demand curve. These are the points on each curve D^a, D^b, . . . , D^n that represent the amounts on which the consumers based their individual demand curves; that is, the amounts that consumers expected to be the total market demand. These points are labeled in Figure 1 as E^a, E^b, . . . , E^n. They are a series of virtual equilibrium points. Given that consumers possess accurate market information, E^a, E^b, . . . , E^n, are the only points that can become actual quantities demanded. The locus of all these points D_B is therefore the actual demand curve for the commodity.

It may be of interest, at this point, to break up changes in the quantity demanded due to changes in price into a price effect and a bandwagon effect; that is, the extent of the change that is due to the change in price, and the extent of the change in demand that is due to consumers adjusting to each other's changed consumption.[5] With an eye on Figure 1 consider the effects of a reduction in price from P_2 *to* P_1. The increase in

---

[5] We are now really in the area of "comparative statics." It may be recalled that we defined statics and our unit period in such a way that only *one* price holds within any unit period. Thus, when we examine the effects of a change in price we are really examining the reasons for the differences in the quantities demanded at one price in one unit period and another price in the succeeding unit period.

demand after the change in price is *ac*. Only part of that increase, however, is due to the reduction in price. To measure the amount due to the reduction in price we go along the demand curve D^a to P_1 which tells us the quantity that would be demanded at P_1 if consumers did not adjust to each other's demand. This would result in an increase in demand of *ax*. Due to the bandwagon effect, however, an additional number of consumers are induced to enter the market or to increase their demands. There is now an additional increase in demand of *xc* after consumers have adjusted to each other's increases in consumption. Exactly the same type of analysis can, of course, be carried out for increases as well as for decreases in price.

We may note another thing from Figure 1. The demand curve D_B is more elastic than any of the other demand curves shown in the diagram. This would suggest that, other things being equal, the demand curve will be more elastic if there is a bandwagon effect than if the demand is based only on the functional attributes of the commodity. This, of course, follows from the fact that reactions to price changes are followed by additional reactions, *in the same direction*, to each other's changed consumption.

3. SOCIAL TABOOS AND THE BANDWAGON EFFECT

Social taboos, to the extent that they affect consumption, are, in a sense, bandwagon effects in reverse gear. That is to say, some people will not buy and consume certain things because other people are not buying and consuming these things. Thus, there may not be any demand for a commodity even though it has a functional utility, although, apart from the taboo, it would be purchased. Individual A will not buy the commodity because individuals B, C, and D do not, while individuals B, C, and D may refrain from consumption for the same reasons. It is not within the competence of the economist to investigate the psychology of this kind of behavior. For our purposes we need only note that such behavior exists and attempt to analyze how such behavior affects the demand function.

We can proceed as follows. Let d_1^x be the demand curve of the least inhibited individual in the market, where the superscript *x* is the total quantity demanded in the market upon which he bases his individual demand. Suppose that at market demand *x* consumer 1 will demand at some range of prices one unit of the commodity, but at no price will he demand more. If he believes, however, that the total market demand is less than *x* units he will refrain from making any purchases. Since, *ex hypothesi*, consumer 1 is the least inhibited consumer, he will, at best, be the only one who will demand one unit of the commodity if consumers expect the total market demand to be *x* units. It must be clear, then, that *x* units cannot be a virtual equilibrium point, since only points where the total expected quantity demanded is equal to the actual quantity demanded can be points on the real demand curve, and the quantity x cannot at any price be a point where expected total demand is equal to actual total demand. Now, if the total expected demand were $x + 1$ the actual demand might increase, say, to 2 units. At expected total demands $x + 2$ and $x + 3$, more would enter the market and the actual demand would be still greater since the fear of being different is considerably reduced as the expected demand is increased. With given increases in the expected total demand there must, at some point, be more than equal increases in the actual demand, because, if a real demand curve exists at all, there must be some point where the expected demand is equal to the actual demand. That point may exist, say, at $x + 10$. That is, at an expected total demand of $x + 10$ units a sufficient number of people have overcome their inhibitions to being different so that, at some prices, they will actually demand $x + 10$ units of the commodity. Let us call this point "T"—it is really the "taboo breaking point." The maximum bid (the point T^1 in Figure 2) of the marginal unit demanded if the total demand were T units now gives us the first point on the real demand curve (the curve D_B).

How social taboos may affect the demand curve is shown in Figure 2. It will be noted that the price axis shows both positive and negative "prices."

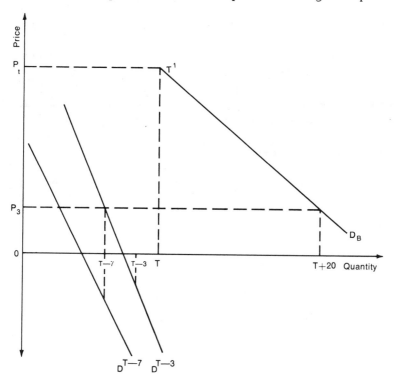

FIGURE 2

A negative price may be thought of as the price it would be necessary to *pay* individuals in order to induce them to consume in public a given amount of the commodity; that is, the price that it would be necessary to pay the consumers in order to induce them to disregard their aversion to be looked upon as odd or peculiar.

As we have already indicated, the point T in Figure 2 is the "taboo breaking point." T represents the number of units at which an *expected* total quantity demanded of T units would result in an *actual* quantity demanded of T units at some *real* price. Now, what has to be explained is why an expected demand of less than T units, say $T - 3$ units, would not yield an actual demand of $T - 3$ units at a positive price but only at a "negative price." Let the curve D^{T-3} be the demand curve that would exist if consumers thought the total demand was $T - 3$. Now, at any positive price, say P_3, the amount demanded would be less than $T - 3$, say $T - 7$. The price P_3 can therefore exist only if there is inaccurate information of the total quantity demanded. Once consumers discovered that at P_3 only $T - 7$ was purchased, and believed that this was the demand that would be sustained, their demand would shift to the D^{T-7} curve. At P_3 the amount purchased would now be less than $T - 7$ and demand would now shift to a curve to the left of the D^{T-7} curve. This procedure would go on until the demand was zero at P_3. We thus introduce a gap into our demand function and focus attention on an interesting psychological phenomenon that may affect demand. What we are suggesting, essentially, is that given "accurate expectations" of the total quantity demanded on the part of consumers, there is a quantity less than which there will not be any quantity demanded at any real price. In other words, this is a case in which a commodity will either "go over big" or not "go over" at all. It will be noted that at P_3 zero units or $T + 20$ units (Figure 2) may be taken off the market given "accurate expectations" of the total quantity demanded. It would seem, therefore, that "accurate expectations" of the total quantity demanded at P_3 can have two values depending upon whether people are generally pessimistic or optimistic about other consumers' demands for the commodity in question. If everybody expects that everybody else would not care much for the commodity, then zero units would be the accurate expectation of the total quantity demanded; if everybody, on the other hand, expects others to take up the commodity with some degree of enthusiasm,[6] then $T + 20$ units would be the accurate expectation of the total quantity demanded. The factors that would determine one set of expectations rather than the other are matters of empirical investigation in the field of social psychology. The factors involved may be the history of the community, the people's conservatism or lack of conserv-

---

[6] If consumers have accurate expectations of the degree of enthusiasm with which others will take up the product, then they will expect demand to be $T + 20$ units.

atism, the type and quantity of advertising about the commodity under consideration, etc.

The really significant point in Figure 2 is T^1, the first point on the real demand curve D_B. As already indicated, it is the point at which the maximum bid of the marginal unit demanded is P_t and the total market demand is T units. If the price were higher than P_t, the Tth unit would not be demanded and all buyers would leave the market because of the effect of the taboo at less than a consumption of T units.[7] By way of summary we might say that the whole point of this section is an attempt to show that in cases where social taboos affect demand, the real demand curve may not start at the price-axis but that the smallest possible quantity demanded may be some distance to the right of the price-axis.

IV. The Snob Effect

Thus far, in our conceptual experiment and diagrammatic analysis, we have considered only the bandwagon effect. We now consider the reverse effect—the demand behavior for those commodities with regard to which the individual consumer acts like a snob. Here, too, we assume at first that the quantity demanded by a consumer is a function of price and of the total market demand, but that the individual consumer's demand is negatively correlated with the total market demand. In the snob case it is rather obvious that the external consumption effect must reach a limit although the limit may be where one snob constitutes the only buyer. For most commodities and most buyers, however, the motivation for exclusiveness is not that great; hence the marginal external consumption effect reaches zero before that point. If the commodity is to be purchased at all, the external consumption effect must reach a limit, at some price, where the quantity demanded has a positive value. From this it follows that after a point the principle of the diminishing marginal external consumption effect must manifest itself. We thus have in the snob effect an opposite but completely symmetrical relationship to the bandwagon effect.

The analysis of markets in which all consumers behave as snobs follows along the same lines as our analysis of the bandwagon effect. Because of the similarity we will be able to get through our analysis of the snob effect in short order. We begin, as before, by letting the alternate total market demands that serve as parameters for alternate individual demand curves be indicated by the superscripts $a, b, \ldots, n$ (where $a < b < n$.) Let the individual demand functions be $d_1, d_2, \ldots d_n$, where there are n consumers in the market. Again, d_3^a signifies the individual demand curve for consumer 3 on the assumption that he expects the total market demand to be "a" units. By adding we obtain the market demand functions on the alter-

[7] This is a "pure" case where *all* buyers are governed by taboo considerations.

nate assumptions of consumers expecting the total market demands to be
$a, b, \ldots, n$. Due to snob behavior the curves $D^a, D^b, \ldots, D^n$ move to the
left as the expected total market demand increases. This is shown in

$$d_1^a + d_2^a + \cdots + d_n^a = D^a$$
$$d_1^b + d_2^b + \cdots + d_n^b = D^b$$
$$\vdots \qquad\qquad \vdots$$
$$d_1^n + d_2^n + \cdots + d_n^n = D^n$$

Figure 3. Using the same procedure as before we obtain the virtual equilibrium points $E^a, E^b, \ldots, E^n$. They represent the only points on the curves
$D^a, D^b, \ldots, D^n$ that are consistent with consumers' expectations (and
hence with the assumption of accurate information). The locus of these
virtual equilibrium points is the demand curve D_s.

Now, given a price change from P_2 to P_1 we can separate the effect of
the price change into a price effect and a snob effect. In Figure 3 we see
that the net increase in the quantity demanded due to the reduction in
price is ab. The price effect, however, is ax. That is, if every consumer
expected no increase in the total quantity demanded then the total quan-

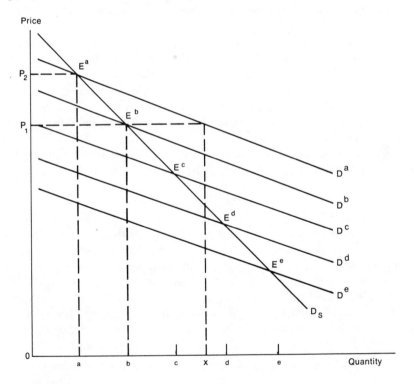

FIGURE 3

tity demanded at P_1 would be Ox. The more extreme snobs will react to this increase in the total quantity demanded and will leave the market.[8] The total quantity demanded will hence be reduced by bx. The net result is therefore an increase in demand of only ab.

It may be of interest to examine some of the characteristics of the curves in Figure 3. First we may note that all the points on the curves other than D_S (except E^a, E^b, . . . , E^n) are theoretical points that have significance only under conditions of imperfect knowledge. Second, we may note from the diagram that the demand curve for snobs is less elastic than the demand curves where there are no snob effects. The reason for this, of course, is that the increase in demand due to a reduction in price is counterbalanced, in part, by some snobs leaving the market because of the increase in total consumption (*i.e.*, the decrease in the snob value of the commodity). It should be clear, however, that the snob effect, as defined, can never be in excess of the price effect since this would lead to a basic contradiction. If the snob effect were greater than the price effect, then the quantity demanded at a lower price would be less than the quantity demanded at a higher price. This implies that some of the snobs in the market at the higher price leave the market when there is a reduction in the total quantity demanded; which, of course, is patently inconsistent with our definition of snob behavior. It therefore follows that the snob effect is never greater than the price effect. It follows, also, that D_S is monotonically decreasing if D^a, D^b, . . . , D^n are monotonically decreasing.[9]

Finally, it may be interesting to note another difference between the usual functional demand curve and the D_S curve. In the usual demand curve the buyers at higher prices always remain in the market at lower prices. That is, from the price point of view, the bids to buy are cumulative downward. This is clearly not the case in the D_S curve. Such terms as intramarginal buyers may be meaningless in snob markets.

V. *The Veblen Effect*

Although the theory of conspicuous consumption as developed by Veblen and others is quite a complex and subtle sociological construct we can, for our purposes, quite legitimately abstract from the psychological and sociological elements and address our attention exclusively to the effects that conspicuous consumption has on the demand function. The essential economic characteristic with which we are concerned is the fact that the utility derived from a unit of a commodity employed for purposes of conspicuous consumption depends not only on the inherent qualities of that unit, but also on the price paid for it. It may, therefore, be helpful to

[8] The other snobs will, of course, reduce their demand but not by an amount large enough to leave the market.
[9] We shall see below however that the snob effect plus the Veblen effect combined can be greater than the price effect.

FIGURE 4   Price effect   =   ST
            Veblen effect = — TR
            Net effect   = — SR

divide the price of a commodity into two categories; the real price and the conspicuous price. By the real price we refer to the price the consumer paid for the commodity in terms of money. The conspicuous price is the price other people think the consumer paid for the commodity[10] and which therefore determines its conspicuous consumption utility. These two prices would probably be identical in highly organized markets where price information is common knowledge. In other markets, where some can get "bargains" or special discounts the real price or conspicuous price need not be identical. In any case, the quantity demanded by a consumer will be a function of both the real price and the conspicuous price.

The market demand curve for commodities subject to conspicuous con-

[10] More accurately, the conspicuous price should be the price that the consumer thinks other people think he paid for the commodity.

sumption can be derived through a similar diagrammatical method (summarized in Figure 4). This time we let the superscripts 1, 2, . . . , n stand for the expected conspicuous prices. The real prices are $P_1, P_2, . . . , P_n$. The individual demand functions are $d_1, d_2, . . . , d_n$. In this way d_6^3 stands for the demand curve of consumer number 6 if he expects a conspicuous price of $P^c{}_3$.[11] We can now add across $d_1', d_2', . . . , d_n'$ and get the market demand curve D^1 which indicates the quantities demanded at alternate prices if all consumers expected a conspicuous price of P . In a similar manner we obtain $D^2, D^3, . . . , D^n$. The market demand curves will, of course, up to a point, shift to the right as the expected conspicuous price increases. Now on every curve $D^1, D^2, . . . , D^n$ in Figure 4 only one point can be a virtual equilibrium point if we assume that consumers possess accurate market information—the point where the real price is equal to the conspicuous price (that is, where $P_1 = P_1^c$, $P_2 = P_2^c$, . . . , $P_n = P_n^c$). The locus of these virtual equilibrium points E^1, E^2, . . . , E^n gives us the demand curve D_{V}.

As before, we can separate the effects of a change in price into two effects—the price effect, and, what we shall call for want of a better term, the Veblen effect. In Figure 4 it will be seen that a change in price from P_4 to P_3 will reduce the quantity demanded by RS. The price effect is to increase the quantity demanded by ST; that is, the amount that would be demanded if there were no change in the expected conspicuous price would be OT. However, at the lower price a number of buyers would leave the market because of the reduced utility derived from the commodity at that lower conspicuous price. The Veblen effect is therefore RT.

It should be noted that unlike the D_S curve, the D_V curve can be positively inclined, negatively inclined, or a mixture of both. It all depends on whether at alternate price changes the Veblen effect is greater or less than the price effect. It is possible that in one portion of the curve one effect may predominate while in another portion another may predominate. It is to be expected, however, that in most cases, if the curve is not monotonically decreasing it will be shaped like a backward S, as illustrated in Figure 5A. The reasons for this are as follows: First, there must be a price so high that no units of the commodity will be purchased at that price owing to the income constraint (among other reasons). This is the price P_n in Figure 5A, and it implies that there must be some point at which the curve shifts from being positively inclined to being negatively inclined as price increases. Second, there must be some point of satiety for the good. This is the point T in Figure 5A. It therefore follows that some portion of the curve must be monotonically decreasing to reach T if there exists some minimum price at which the Veblen effect is zero. It is of course reason-

[11] The expected conspicuous prices are distinguished from the real prices by adding the superscript c to the P's. Thus, to the range of real prices $P_1, P_2, . . . , P_n$, we have a corresponding range of conspicuous prices denoted by $P_1^c, P_2^c, . . . , P_n^c$.

cease to have any value for purposes of conspicuous consumption. If this last assumption does not hold, which is unlikely, then the curve could able to assume that there is some low price at which the commodity would have the shape indicated in Figure 5C. Otherwise, it would have the general shape indicated in Figure 5A, or it might be in two segments as illustrated in Figure 5B.

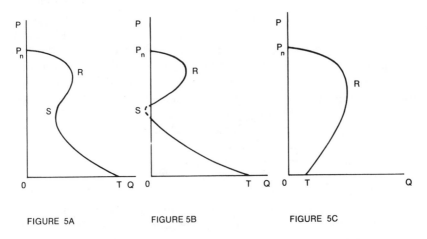

FIGURE 5A   FIGURE 5B   FIGURE 5C

VI. Mixed Effects

Any real market for semi-durable or durable goods will most likely contain consumers that are subject to one or a combination of the effects discussed heretofore. Combining these effects presents no new formal difficulties with respect to the determination of the market demand curve, although it complicates the diagrammatic analysis considerably. The major principle, however, still holds. For any price there is a quantity demanded such that the marginal external consumption effect (or the marginal Veblen effect) for all buyers but one, is zero. This implies that for every price change there is a point at which people cease reacting to each other's quantity changes, regardless of the direction of these reactions. If this is so, then for every price there is a determinate quantity demanded, and hence the demand curve is determinate.

Now, for every price change we have distinguished between the price effect and some other, such as the snob, the Veblen, or the bandwagon effect. In markets where all four effects are present we should be able to separate out and indicate the direction of each of them that will result from a price change. That is, every price change will result in two positive and two negative effects—two which, other things being equal, will increase the quantity demanded, and two which, other things being equal, will decrease it. Which effects will be positive and which will be negative will depend on the relative strength of the Veblen effect as against the price effect. The Veblen and the price effects will depend directly on the direction of the price change. An increase in price will therefore result in price and bandwagon effects that are negative, and in Veblen and snob effects that are positive, provided that the price effect is greater than the Veblen effect; that is, if the net result is a decrease in the quantity demanded at the higher price. If, on the other hand, the Veblen effect is more powerful than the price effect, given a price increase, then the bandwagon effect would be positive and the snob effect negative. The reverse would of course be true for price declines.

The market demand curve for a commodity where different consumers are subject to different types of effects can be obtained diagrammatically through employing the methods developed above—although the diagrams would be quite complicated. There is no point in adding still more diagrams to illustrate this. Briefly, the method would be somewhat as follows: (1) Given the demand curves for every individual, in which the expected total quantity demanded is a parameter for each curve, we can add these curves laterally and obtain a map of aggregate demand curves, in which each aggregate curve is based on a given total quantity demanded. (2) The locus of the equilibrium points on each aggregate demand curve (as derived in Figure 1) gives us a market demand curve that accounts for both bandwagon and snob effects. This last curve assumes that only one conspicuous price exists. For every conspicuous price there exists a separate map of aggregate demand curves from which different market demand curves are obtained. (3) This procedure yields a map of market demand curves in which each curve is based on a different conspicuous price. Employing the method used in Figure 4 we obtain our final market demand curve, which accounts for bandwagon, snob, and Veblen effects simultaneously.

VII. Conclusion

It is not unusual for a writer in pure theory to end his treatise by pointing out that the science is really very young; that there is a great deal more to be done; that the formulations presented are really of a very tentative nature; and the best that can be hoped for is that his treatise may in some small way pave the road for future formulations that are more directly applicable to problems in the real world.[12] This is another way of saying that work in pure theory is an investment in the future state of the science where the returns in terms of applications to real problems are really very

[12] See, for example, Samuelson, *Foundations of Economic Analysis*, p. 350, and Joan Robinson, *Economics of Imperfect Competition*, p. 327.

uncertain. This is probably especially true of value theory, where the investment in time and effort is more akin to the purchase of highly speculative stocks rather than the purchase of government bonds. Since this was only a brief essay on one aspect of value theory, the reader will hardly be surprised if the conclusions reached are somewhat less than revolutionary.

Essentially, we have attempted to do two things. First, we have tried to demonstrate that nonadditivity is not necessarily an insurmountable obstacle in effecting a transition from individual to collective demand curves. Second, we attempted to take a step or two in the direction of incorporating various kinds of external consumption effects into the theory of consumers' demand. In order to solve our problem, we have introduced what we have called the principle of the diminishing marginal external consumption effect. We indicated some reasons for believing that for every individual, there is some point at which the marginal external consumption effect is zero. We have attempted to show that if this principle is admitted, then there are various ways of effecting a transition from individual to collective demand curves. The major conclusion reached is that under conditions of perfect knowledge (or accurate expectations) any point on the demand curve, for any given price, will be at that total quantity demanded where the marginal external consumption effect for all consumers but one, is equal to zero.

In comparing the demand curve in those situations where external consumption effects are present with the demand curve as it would be where these external consumption effects are absent, we made three basic points. (1) If the bandwagon effect is the most significant effect, the demand curve is more elastic than it would be if this external consumption effect were absent. (2) If the snob effect is the predominant effect, the demand curve is less elastic than otherwise. (3) If the Veblen effect is the predominant one, the demand curve is less elastic than otherwise, and some portions of it may even be positively inclined; whereas, if the Veblen effect is absent, the curve will be negatively inclined regardless of the importance of the snob effect in the market.

The Meaning of Utility Measurement

ARMEN A. ALCHIAN

Armen A. Alchian is Professor of Economics at the University of California at Los Angeles. This well-known article appeared in the American Economic Review *in 1953.*

Economists struggling to keep abreast of current developments may well be exasperated by the resurgence of measurability of utility. After all, the indifference curve analysis was popularized little over ten years ago amidst the contradictory proclamations that it eliminated, modified, and strengthened the role of utility. Even yet there is confusion, induced partly by careless reading and exposition of the indifference curve analysis and partly by misunderstandings of the purposes and implications of utility measurement. This paper attempts to clarify the role and meaning of the recent revival of measurement of utility in economic theory and of the meaning of certain concepts and operations commonly used in utility theory.

Measurement in its broadest sense is the assignment of numbers to entities. The process of measurement has three aspects which should be distinguished at the outset. First is the purpose of measurement, second is the process by which one measures something, *i.e.*, assigns numerical values to some aspect of an entity, and the third is the arbitrariness, or uniqueness, of the set of numerical values inherent in the purpose and process. In the first part of this paper we briefly explore the idea of arbitrariness or uniqueness of numbers assigned by a measurement process. In Part II we state some purposes of utility measurement. In Part III we examine a method of measuring utility, the purpose of the measurement, and the extent to which the measurement is unique. In Part IV we look at some implications of the earlier discussion.[1]

[1] The explanation assumes no mathematical background and is on an elementary level. This paper is not original in any of its ideas, nor is it a general review of utility and

31

I. Degree of Measurability

The columns of Table I are sequences of numbers illustrating the concept of the "degree of measurability." The entities, some aspect of which we wish to measure, are denoted by letters. Later we shall discuss the meaning of these entities. Our first task is to explain the difference between monotone transformations and linear transformations.

TABLE I. Illustration of Types of Measurement

Entities	Alternative Measures of "Utility"								
	1	2	3	4	5	6	7	8	9
A	1	2	6	11	2	6	5	6	3
B	2	4	7	12	4	12	7	10	7
C	3	5	8	13	6	18	9	14	13
D	4	8	9	14	8	24	11	18	21
E	5	11	10	15	10	30	13	22	31
F	7	14	12	17	14	42	17	30	43
G	11	22	16	21	22	66	25	46	57
H	14	28	19	24	28	84	31	58	73
I	16	33	21	26	32	96	35	66	91
J	17	34	22	27	34	102	37	70	111

We shall begin with monotone transformations and then come to linear transformations via two of its special cases, additive and multiplicative constants.

MONOTONE TRANSFORMATIONS

Let there be assigned a numerical magnitude (measure) to each entity concerned. For example in Table I, for the ten entities, A–J, listed in the extreme left-hand column, nine different sets of numbers are utilized to assign nine different numbers to each of the entities. If two sets of numbers (measures) result in the same ranking or ordering of the entities (according to the numbers assigned), then the two sets are *monotone transformations* of each other. In Table I it will be seen that all nine measures give the same ranking, thus all nine measures are monotone transformations of each other. If this property holds true over the entire class of entities concerned, then the two measures are monotone transformations of each other for that class of entities. The possible set of monotone transformations obviously is very large.

demand theory. It is merely a statement of some propositions that may help the reader separate the chaff from the wheat. It may even make clear to the reader, as it did to the writer, one meaning of utility. Most of the material presented here is contained in J. Marschak, "Rational Behavior, Uncertain Prospects and Measurable Utility," *Econometrica* (April 1950), XVIII, 111–41, an article written for the mathematically mature.

LINEAR TRANSFORMATIONS: ADDITIVE CONSTANTS

We shall approach the linear transformation by considering two special forms. Look at the numbers in column 3. They are the same as those in 1 except that a constant has been added, in this case 5, *i.e.*, they are the same *"up to"* (except for) an *additive constant*. The measure in column 4 is equivalent to that in column 1 with 10 added. Columns 1, 3, and 4 are *transforms* of each other "up to" (by means of) *additive constants*. This can also be expressed by saying they are equivalent except for an additive constant. The term "up to" implies that we may go through some simpler types. For example, all the transforms up to an additive constant are also contained in the larger, less restricted class of possible transforms known as monotone transforms. An additive constant is a quite strong restriction, even though it may not seem so at first since there is an unlimited number of available constants. But relative to the range of possibilities in the general linear transformations this is very restrictive indeed.

LINEAR TRANSFORMATIONS: MULTIPLICATIVE CONSTANTS

Now look at column 5. It is equivalent to column 1 except for multiplication by a constant, in this case, 2. Column 5 is a monotone transform of column 1, and it is also a "multiplicative by a constant" transform of column 1. Column 6 is column 1 multiplied by 6. Thus, while columns 1, 5, and 6 are monotone transforms of each other, they are also a more particular type of transform. They are transforms up to a multiplicative constant. These are special cases of linear transformations which we shall now discuss.

GENERAL LINEAR TRANSFORMATIONS

The numbers of column 7 are equivalent to column 1 except for multiplication by 2 and addition of 3. Letting y denote the numbers or "measures" in column 7 and x those of column 1, we have $y = 2x + 3$. Column 8 is derived similarly from column 1; the multiplier is 4 and the added constant is 2. Column 8 is given by $4x + 2$, but a little inspection will show that column 8 can be derived from column 7 by the same process of multiplying and adding. In this case column 8 is obtained from column 7 by multiplying by 2 and adding -4. Columns 1, 7, and 8 are thus "linear transforms" of each other. This is also expressed by saying that they are the same measures "up to a linear transformation"; that is, any one of these measures can be obtained from any other one by simply selecting appropriate constants for multiplication and addition.

There is a particular property of the linear transformation that has historical significance in economics. Look at the way the numbers change as one moves from entity to entity. For example, consider columns 1 and 7. The numerical change from entity E to entity F has a value of 2 in the measure of column 1, while in the measure of column 7, it has a numerical value of 4. From F to G the change is 4 in measure 1, and in measure 7 it is 8. If the increment is positive, it will be positive in all sequences which are linear transforms of this particular sequence. But it is true also for all monotone transformations—a much broader class of transformations or measures. Of greater significance, however, is the following attribute of linear transforms: if the differences between the numbers in one of the sequences increases (or decreases) from entity to entity, then the differences between the numbers of these same entities in all of its *linear* transformations will also be increasing (or decreasing). In general, the property of increasing or decreasing increments is not affected by switching from one sequence of numbers to any linear transformation of that given sequence. In mathematical terms, the sign of the second differences of a sequence of numbers is invariant to linear transformations of that sequence.[2] The significance of invariance will be discussed later, but we should note that this property of increasing (or decreasing) differences between the numbers assigned to pairs of entities is nothing but increasing marginal utility—if one christens the assigned numbers "utilities."

II. Purpose of Measurement

ORDER

In the nine columns of Table I are nine "different" measures of some particular aspect of the entities denoted $A, B, C, \ldots J$. How different are they? We have already answered this. Which is the "right" one? This depends upon what one wants to do with the entities and the numbers. It would be more useful to ask which one is a *satisfactory* measure, for then it is clear that we must make explicit for what it is to be satisfactory.[3] For example, if my sole concern were to predict which of the entities would be the heaviest, the next heaviest, etc., I could, by successively comparing pairs in a balancing scale, completely order the entities. [Having done so, I could then assign the numbers in *any* one of the columns 1 through 9] so long as I assign the biggest number to the heaviest, and so on down. This means that for the purpose of indicating *order*, any one of the monotone transforms is acceptable.

The remaining task is to determine whether the order is "correctly" stated; the fact that the order is the same, no matter which one of the above transforms is used, does not imply that the order is correct. What

[2] In monotonic transformations the sign of the *first* differences only are necessarily left undisturbed.

[3] A pause to reflect will reveal that there is a second problem besides that of deciding what "satisfactory" means. This second problem, which we have so far begged, is: "How does one assign numbers to entities?" It is deferred to the following section.

do we mean by "correctly"? We mean that our stated or predicted order is matched by the order revealed by some other observable ordering process. You could put the entities on some new weighing scales (the new scales are the "test"), and then a matching of the order derived from the new scales with our stated order is a verification of the correctness (predictive validity) of our first ordering. Any monotone transform of one valid ordering number sequence is *for the purpose* in this illustration *completely equivalent* to the numbers actually used. That is, any one of the possible monotone transformations is just as good as any other.

We may summarize by saying that, given a method for validly ordering entities, any monotone transformation of the particular numerical values assigned in the ordering process will be equally satisfactory. We may be technical and say that "all measures of order are equivalent up to ((except for being) monotone transformations." Or, in other words, a method of validly denoting *order* only, is not capable of uniquely identifying a particular set of numbers as the correct one. Any monotonic transformation will do exactly as well. The degree of uniqueness of an ordering can also be described by saying it is only as unique as the set of monotone transformations. Thus, we often see the expression that "ordering is unique up to a monotone transformation."

ORDERING GROUPS OF ENTITIES

But suppose our purpose were different. Suppose we want to be able to order *groups* of entities according to their weights. More precisely, suppose we want to assign numbers to each of the component objects so that when we combine the objects into sets or bundles we can order the weights of the composite bundles, knowing only the individually valid numbers assigned to each component, by *merely adding* together the numbers assigned to each component. And we want to be able to do this for any possible combination of the objects. Fortunately, man has discerned a way to do this for weights. The numbers which are assigned by this discovered process are arbitrary up to a multiplicative constant (of proportionality), so that the numbers could express either pounds, ounces, tons, or grams. That is, we can arbitrarily multiply all the numbers assigned to the various components by any constant we please, without destroying the validity of our resulting numbers for this particular purpose. But we can not use any monotone transformation as we could in the preceding case, where our purpose was different.

If we were to add an arbitrary constant to each component's individually valid numerical (weight) value we would not be able to add the resulting numbers of each component in order to get a number which would rank the composite bundles. Thus, the numbers we can assign are rather severely constrained. We can not use any linear transformation, but we can use a multiplicative constant, which is a special type of linear transformation. And if we were to "measure" lengths of items so as to be able simply to "add" the numbers to get the lengths of the items laid end to end, we would again find ourselves confined to sequences (measures) with a multiplicative constant as the one available degree of arbitrariness.

UTILITY AND ORDERING OF CHOICES

The reader has merely to substitute for the concept of weight, in the earlier example about weight orders, the idea of "preference" and he is in the theory of choice or demand. Economics goes a step further and gives the name "utility" to the numbers. Can we assign a set of numbers (measures) to the various entities and predict that the entity with the largest assigned number (measure) will be chosen? If so, we could christen this measure "utility" and then assert that choices are made so as to maximize utility. It is an easy step to the statement that "you are maximizing your utility," which says no more than that your choice is predictable according to the size of some assigned numbers.[4] For analytical convenience it is customary to postulate that an individual seeks to maximize something subject to some constraints. The thing—or numerical measure of the "thing"—which he seeks to maximize is called "utility." Whether or not utility is some kind of glow or warmth, or happiness, is here irrelevant; all that counts is that we can assign numbers to entities or conditions which a person can strive to realize. Then we say the individual seeks to maximize some function of those numbers. Unfortunately, the term "utility" has by now acquired so many connotations, that it is difficult to realize that for present purposes utility has no more meaning than this. The analysis of individual demand behavior is mathematically describable as the process of maximizing some quantitive measures, or numbers, and we assume that the individual seeks to obtain that combination with the highest choice number, given the purchasing power at his disposal. It might be harmless to call this "utility theory."[5]

THREE TYPES OF CHOICE PREDICTIONS

Sure Prospects.   Before proceeding further it is necessary to indicate clearly the types of choice that will concern us. The first type of choice is that of selecting among a set of alternative "riskless" choices. A riskless choice, hereafter called a sure prospect, is one such that the chooser knows exactly what he will surely get with each possible choice. To be able to predict the preferred choice means we can assign numbers to the various

[4] The difficult (impossible?) psychological, philosophical step of relating this kind of utility to some *quantity* of *satisfaction, happiness, goodness,* or *welfare* is not attempted here.

[5] The author, having so far kept his opinions submerged, is unable to avoid remarking that it would seem "better" to confine utility "theory" to attempts to explain or discern why a person chooses one thing rather than another—at equal price.

entities such that the entity with the largest assigned number is the most preferred, the one with the second largest number is the next most preferred, etc. As said earlier, it is customary to christen this numerical magnitude with the name "utility."

An understanding of what is meant by "entity" is essential. An entity denotes any specifiable object, action, event, or set or pattern of such items or actions. It may be an orange, a television set, a glass of milk, a trip to Europe, a particular time profile of income or consumption (*e.g.*, steak every night, or ham every night, or steak and ham on alternate nights), getting married, etc. Identifying an entity exclusively with one single event or action would lead to unnecessary restrictions on the scope of the applicability of the theorem to be presented later.[6]

Groups of Sure Prospects. A second problem of choice prediction would be that of ordering (predicting) choices among riskless *groups* of entities. A riskless group consists of several entities all of which will be surely obtained if that group is chosen. The problem now is to predict the choice among riskless groups knowing only the utilities assigned to the individual entities which have been aggregated into groups. Thus if in Table I we were to assemble the entities A and J into various groups, could we predict the choice among these groups of entities knowing only the utility numbers that were assigned to the component entities for the purpose of the preceding choice problem? Of course we ask this question only on the assumption that the utilities previously assigned to the component entities were valid predictors of choice among the single sure prospects.[7]

Uncertain Prospects. A third type of problem is that of ordering choices among risky choices, or what have been called uncertain prospects. An uncertain prospect is a group of entities, only one entity of which will be realized if that group is chosen. For example, an uncertain prospect might consist of a fountain pen, a radio, and an automobile. If that uncertain prospect is chosen, the chooser will surely get one of the three entities, but which one he will actually get is not known in advance. He is not completely ignorant about what will be realized, for it is assumed that he knows the probabilities of realization attached to each of the component entities in an uncertain prospect. For example, the probabilities might have been .5 for the fountain pen, .4 for the radio and .1 for the automobile. These probabilities sum to 1.0; one and only one of these entities will be realized. An uncertain prospect is very much like a ticket in a lottery. If there is but one prize, then the uncertain prospect consists of two entities, the prize or the loss of the stake. If there are several prizes, the uncertain

[6] For example, see H. Wold, "Ordinal Preferences or Cardinal Utility? (with Additional Notes by G. L. S. Shackle, L. J. Savage, and H. Wold)"; A. S. Manne, "The Strong Independence Assumption-Gasoline Blends and Probability Mixtures (with Additional Notes by A. Charnes)"; P. Samuelson, "Probability, Utility, and the Independence Axiom"; E, Malinvaud, "Note on Neumann-Morgenstern's Strong Independence Axiom," *Econometrica* (Oct. 1952), XX, 661–79.

[7] For an illustration of this problem of rating a composite bundle by means of the ratings of the ratings of the components, see A. S. Manne, *op. cit.*

prospect consists of several entities—the various prizes and, of course, the loss of the stake (being a loser).

But there is another requirement that we want our prediction process to satisfy. Not only must we be able to predict the choices, but we want to do it in a very simple way. Specifically, we want to be able to look at each component separately, and then from utility measures assigned to the elements, as if they were sure prospects, we want to be able to aggregate the component utility measures into a group utility measure predicting choices among the uncertain prospects. For example, suppose the uncertain prospects consisted of a pen, a radio, and an automobile as listed in Table II.

TABLE II. Examples of Uncertain Prospects

Uncertain Prospect	Probabilities of getting		
	Pen	Radio	Automobile
1	.5	.4	.1
2	.58	.30	.12
3	.85	.0	.15
4	.0	.99	.01

Are there utilities which can be assigned to the pen, the radio, and the automobile, so that for the purpose of comparing these four uncertain prospects the same numbers could be used in arriving at utility numbers to be assigned to the uncertain prospects? In particular, can we assign to the pen, the radio, and the automobile numbers such that when multiplied by the associated probabilities in each uncertain prospect they will yield a sum (expected utility) for each uncertain prospect, and such that these "expected utilities" would indicate preference?

Before answering we shall briefly indicate why choices among uncertain prospects constitute an important class of situations. Upon reflection it will be seen to be the practically universal problem of choice. Can the reader think of many cases in which he *knows* when making a choice, the outcome of that choice with absolute certainty? In other words, are there many choices—or actions—in life in which the *consequences* can be predicted with absolute certainty? Even the act of purchasing a loaf of bread has an element of uncertainty in its consequences; even the act of paying one's taxes has an element of uncertainty in the consequences involved; even the decision to sit down has an element of uncertainty in the consequence. But to leave the trivial, consider the choice of occupation, purchase of an automobile, house, durable goods, business investment, marriage, having children, insurance, gambling, etc. ad infinitum. Clearly choices among uncertain prospects constitute an extremely large and important class of choices.

III. Method of Measurement

So far we have discussed the meaning and purpose of measurement. We turn to the method of measurement recognizing that for each type of choice prediction the method of measurement must have a rationale as well as a purpose. For a moment we can concentrate on the rationale which is properly stated in the form of axioms defining rational behavior.

SURE PROSPECTS

Let us start with a rationale for the first type of choice. We postulate that an individual behaves consistently, *i.e.*, he has a consistent set of preferences; that these preferences are transitive, *i.e.*, if B is preferred to A, and C to B, then C is preferred to A; and that these preferences can be completely described merely by attaching a numerical value to each. An implication of these postulates is that for such individuals we can predict their choices by a numerical variable (utility). Asking the individual to make pairwise comparisons, we assign numbers to the sure prospects such that the choice order will be revealed by the size of the numbers attached. The number of pairwise comparisons that the individual must make depends upon how fortunate we are in selecting the pairs for his comparison. If we are so lucky as first to present him a series of pairs of alternatives of sure prospects exactly matching his preference order, the complete ordering of his preferences will be obtained with the minimal amount of pairwise comparisons. Any numbering sequence which gives the most preferred sure prospect the highest number, the second preferred sure prospect the second highest number, etc., will predict his choices according to "utility maximization." But any other sequence of numbers could be used so long as it is a *monotone transformation of* the first sequence. And this is exactly the meaning of the statement that utility is *ordinal* and not cardinal. The transitivity postulate enables this pairwise comparison to reveal the complete order of preferences, and the consistency postulate means he would make his choices according to the prediction. Thus if he were to be presented with any two of ten sure prospects, we would predict his taking the one with the higher utility number. If our prediction failed, then one of our postulates would have been denied, and our prediction method would not be valid. A hidden postulate is that the preferences, if transitive and consistent, are stable for the interval involved.[8] Utility for this purpose and by this method is measurable up to a monotonic transformation, *i.e.*, it is ordinal only.

---

[8] Some problems involved in this assumption and in its relaxation are discussed by N. Georgescu-Roegen, "The Theory of Choice and the Constancy of Economic Laws," *Quart. Jour. Econ.* (Feb. 1950), LXIV, 125–38.

GROUPS OF SURE PROSPECTS

The second type of choice, among *groups* of sure prospects, can be predicted using the same postulates only if we treat each group of sure prospects as a sure prospect. Then by presenting pairs of "groups of sure prospects" we can proceed as in the preceding problem. But the interesting problem here is that of predicting choice among groups of sure prospects (entities) only by knowing valid utility measures for choices among the component sure prospects. Can these utility numbers of the component entities of the group of sure prospects, which are valid for the entities by themselves, be aggregated to obtain a number predicting choice among the groups of sure prospects? In general the answer is "no." Hence, although utility was measurable for the purpose of the kind of prediction in the preceding problem, it is not measurable in the sense that these component measures can be aggregated or combined in any known way to predict choices among *groups* of sure prospects. Utility is "measurable" for one purpose but not for the other.[9]

UNCERTAIN PROSPECTS

We want to predict choices among uncertain prospects. And we want to make these predictions solely on the basis of the utilities and probabilities attached to the elements of the uncertain prospects.

Without going into too many details an intuitive idea of the content of the axioms used in deriving this kind of measurability will now be given.[10] For expository convenience the statement that the two entities A and B are equally desirable or indifferent will be expressed by $A = B$; if however A is either preferred to or indifferent to B, the expression will be $A \geqq B$.

(1) For the chooser there is a transitive, complete ordering of all the

---

[9] It is notable that the usual indifference curve analysis is contained in this case. Any *group* of sure prospects (point in the *xy* plane of an indifference curve diagram) which has more of each element in it than there is in another group of two sure prospects, will be preferred to the latter. And further, if one group of sure prospects has more of one commodity than does the other group of sure prospects, the two groups can be made indifferent by sufficiently increasing the amount of the second commodity in the other group of sure prospects. The indifference curve (utility isoquant) approach does not assign numbers representing utility to the various sure prospects lying along either the horizontal or the vertical axis and then from these numerical values somehow obtain a number which would order choices among the groups of prospects inside the quadrant enclosed by the axes.

[10] This is the method developed by J. von Neumann and P. Morgenstern, *The Theory of Games and Economic Behavior* (Princeton University Press, 1944). A very closely analogous method was suggested in 1926 by F. Ramsey, *The Foundations of Mathematics and Other Logical Essays* (The Humanities Press, N. Y., 1950), pp. 166–90. The neatest, but still very difficult, exposition is by J. Marschak, *op cit.* Still another statement of essentially the same set of axioms is in M. Friedman and L. J. Savage, "The Utility Analysis of Choices Involving Risk," *Jour. Pol. Econ.* (Aug. 1948), LVI, 279–304.

alternative possible choices so far as his preferences are concerned. That is if $C \geqq B$ and $B \geqq A$, then $C \geqq A$.

(2) If among three entities, A, B, and C, $C \geqq B$, and $B \geqq A$, then there is some probability value p, for which B is just as desirable as the uncertain prospect consisting of A and C, where A is realizable with probability p, and C with probability 1-p. In our notation: if $C \geqq B$ and $B \geqq A$, then there is some p for which $B = (A, C; p)$, where $(A, C; p)$ is the expression for the uncertain prospect in which A will be realized with probability p, and otherwise, C will be realized.

(3) Suppose $B \geqq A$, and let C be an entity. Then $(B, C; p) \geqq (A, C; p)$ for any p. In particular, if $A = B$, then the prospect comprising A and C, with probability p for A and 1-p for C, will be just as desirable as the uncertain prospect comprised of B and C, with the same probability p for B, and 1-p for C.

(4) In the uncertain prospect comprising A and B with probability p for A, it makes no difference what the process is for determining whether A or B is received, just so long as the value of p is not changed. Notationally, $((A, B; p_1), B; p_2) = (A, B; p_1 p_2)$.

To help understand what these axioms signify we give an example of behavior or a situation that is inconsistent with each, except that I can think of no totally reasonable behavior inconsistent with the first axiom. Behavior inconsistent with the second axiom would be the following: Suppose C is two bars of candy, B is one bar of candy, and A is being shot in the head. Form an uncertain prospect of C and A with probability p for C. If there is no p, however small or close to zero, which could possibly make one indifferent between the uncertain prospect and B, the one bar of candy, he is rejecting axiom (2). Are such situations purely hypothetical?

The third axiom, sometimes called the "strong independence assumption," has provoked the most vigorous attack and defense. So far no really damaging criticism has been seen. It takes its name from the implication that whatever may be the entity C, it has no effect on the ranking of the uncertain prospects comprised of A or C and B or C. This kind of independence has nothing whatever to do with independence or complementarity among groups of commodities. Here one does not receive both A and C, or B and C. He gets either A or C in one uncertain prospect, or he gets either B or C in the other. Even if A and C were complements and B and C were substitutes, the ordering would not be affected–this is what the postulate asserts.[11]

Axiom (3) is inconsistent with a situation in which the utility of the act of winning itself depends upon the probability of winning, or more generally if probability itself has utility. For example, at Christmas time, one does not want to know what gift his wife is going to give him; he prefers ignorance to any hints or certainty as to what his gift will be. This is a type of love for gambling. Conversely, one may be indifferent to whether

[11] See the literature listed in footnote 6.

he gets roast beef or ham for dinner, but he does want to know which it will be purely for the sake of knowing, not because it will affect any prior or subsequent choices.

Axiom (4) is inconsistent with a concern or difference in feeling about different ways of determining which entity in an uncertain prospect is actually received even though the various systems all have the same probability. For example, suppose an uncertain prospect had a probability of .25 for one of the entities. It should make no difference whether the probability is based on the toss of two successive coins with heads required on both, or whether it is based on the draw of one white ball from an urn containing one white and three black. But consider the case of the slot machine. Why are there three wheels with many items on each wheel? Why not one big wheel, and why are the spinning wheels in sight? One could instead have a machine with covered wheels. Simply insert a coin, pull the handle, and then wait and see what comes out of the machine. Does seeing the wheels go around or seeing how close one came to nearly winning affect the desirability? If observation or knowledge of the number of steps through which the mechanism must pass before reaching the final decision makes any difference, even if the fundamental probability is not subjectively or objectively affected, then axiom (4) is denied.

Implied in the stated axioms is a method for assigning numerical utility values to the various component entities. The method is perhaps explained best by an illustration of the method using the entities of Table I. Take one entity, A, and one other, say B, as the two base entities. Between these two entities you choose B as preferable to A. Now I *arbitrarily* assign (*i.e.*, choose any numbers I wish so long as the number for B exceeds that for A) the number 2 to B and some smaller number, say 1, to A. You then consider entity C, which you assert you prefer to A and to B. The next step is rather involved; I now form an uncertain prospect consisting of C and A. You are now offered a choice between B, a sure prospect, and the uncertain prospect comprised of "A or C", where you get A or C depending upon the outcome of a random draw in which the probability of A is p, otherwise you get C.

You are asked to, and you do, select a value of p which when contained in the uncertain prospect leaves you indifferent between B and the uncertain prospect, "A or C."[12] If p were set at nearly zero, you would choose the uncertain prospect, since C is assumed here to be preferred to A; choosing the uncertain prospect would mean that you would almost surely get C. The converse would be the outcome if p were set at nearly 1. Therefore, some place in between there is a value of p which would leave you indifferent between B and the uncertain prospect of "A or C." After you indicate that value of p, I assign to the uncertain prospect the same

---

[12] It is important to notice that the sure prospect must not be preferred to both of the components of the uncertain prospects, for in that event no probability value would induce indifference.

number, 2, I did to B since they are equally preferred by you.

Now we may determine a number for C by the following procedure. Treat the probability p, and its complement $1-p$, as weights to be assigned to the numbers for A and C such that the weighted sum is equal to the number 2, which has been assigned to the uncertain prospect. If, for example, you were indifferent when p was equal to .6, then we have the following definitional equation, where we let $U(A)$ stand for the number assigned to A, $U(B)$ for the number assigned to B, and $U(C)$ for the number assigned to C:

$$U(B) = p \cdot U(A) + (1-p) \cdot U(C)$$
$$\frac{U(B) - p \cdot U(A)}{(1-p)} = U(C) = 3.5.$$

Using this convenient formula we can assign numbers to the entities D, E, F by appropriately forming uncertain prospects and letting you determine that value of p which produced indifference. These revealed numbers will completely order the entities. If E has a larger number than G, E will be preferred over G. This assignment of numerical value is made without ever comparing E and G directly. Each has been compared with a base entity. A brief pause to reflect will reveal that in this paragraph we have been specifying a convenient method for manipulating, or combining the "utilities" or "choice indicator numbers" as well as specifying a process of attaching numbers (utilities) to the entities.

It happens that if we insist on using the simple formula above, rather than some more complicated one, the numerical magnitudes assigned by this process are unique up to a linear transformation. For example, suppose that by our process of assigning numbers we obtained the set of numbers in column 3 of Table I for entities A to J. Now, instead of assigning 7 and 6 to B and A, had we decided in the first place to assign a value of 7 to entity B and a value of 5 to entity A, we could have obtained instead the sequence in column 7. Column 7 is a linear transformation of column 3. In other words, we may arbitrarily, at our complete discretion, assign numbers to *two* of the entities; once that has been done, our method will determine the remaining unique numbers to be assigned. But all the various *sets* of numbers (utilities) that could have been obtained, depending upon the two initial numerical values, are linear transformations of each other. Thus, our measurement process is unique "up to" a linear transformation.

If the preceding method of assigning numbers does predict correctly the choice a person actually makes among uncertain prospects, then we have successfully assigned numbers as indicators of choice preferences. We have successfully measured utility and have done it with the convenient formula above. Furthermore, every linear transformation of our predicting numbers, "utilities," would be equally valid—or invalid.

In summary, (1) we have found a *way* to assign numbers; (2) for the way suggested, it so happens that the assigned numbers are unique up to linear transformations; (3) the numbers are convenient to manipulate. All this was implicit in our set of postulates. Before asking whether the numbers predict actual behavior, we shall discuss some side issues.

DIMINISHING OR INCREASING MARGINAL UTILITY

Recalling our earlier exposition of the mathematical properties of linear transformations, we see that in all of the columns (except 2 and 9, which are not linear transformations of the others) the pattern of *increments* between the numbers assigned to entities is similar. For example, between pair *H* and *I* on scale 7 the increment is 4 and between pair *I* and *J* it is 2. Moving from *H* through *I* to *J* we have a diminishing increment in the numerical magnitudes assigned. In more familiar terminology we have diminishing marginal utility among *H*, *I*, and *J*.[13] Similarly, all the linear transforms of scale 7 will retain this diminishing marginal utility over the range of entities *H*, *I*, and *J*. And the suggested way of assigning numbers to the component entities assigns numbers (utilities) which are equivalent up to a linear transformation; that is, any one of the linear transformations will be just as good—for our purposes—as any other of them. By implication we can determine whether there is diminishing or increasing marginal utility.

MAXIMIZATION OF EXPECTED UTILITY

By this method of assigning utilities we have ordered all the entities. However, our purpose was more than this; otherwise the uniqueness of the numbers up to a linear transformation would have been an unnecessary restriction. As we know, any monotonic transformation would leave order unaffected. The linear transformation restriction is imposed by our desire to predict choices among uncertain prospects from the utilities and probabilities of the component entities and to do it in a convenient form, *viz.*, according to maximization of expected utility.[14]

Implied in our set of postulates is not only the preceding method of assigning numbers for utilities but also (in fact the two are merely two aspects of the same implication) a method for combining the utilities of the component entities into a utility number for the uncertain prospect.

This method is based on the implication that a person who behaves according to the axioms will choose among uncertain prospects according to expected utility. Expected utility is merely the sum of the weighted util-

---

[13] More strictly we should also have some scale for measuring the amount of *H*, *I*, and *J*, either in weight or volume, etc. While the process for assigning these scales also is a complex one, we may pass over it in order to concentrate upon the "utility" measure.

[14] It is not dictated by any nostalgia for diminishing marginal utility.

ities of the components of the uncertain prospects where the weights are the probabilities associated with each component. In symbolic form

$$U(A \text{ or } B, p) = p\, U(A) + (1\text{-}p)\, U(B)$$

where the expression $U(A \text{ or } B, p)$ denotes the utility of the uncertain prospect of entities A and B in which A will be received with probability p, and B otherwise. For example, we could from any one of our measures in Table I (except columns 2 and 9) predict what one would do when faced with the following choice: he is presented first with an uncertain prospect containing entities B and C. If he chooses this prospect, his probability of getting B is one-half; otherwise, he will get C. The other uncertain prospect which he is offered contains entities A and E, and if he chooses this prospect his probability of getting E is one-fourth—otherwise, he gets A. Our individual will choose the first prospect, no matter which of our acceptable measures we use. We obtain this prediction by multiplying (weighting) the "utility" measures of each entity in each prospect by the probability of that entity. If we use the utility measure of column 8, we have for the first prospect $(\frac{1}{2} \times 14) + (\frac{1}{2} \times 10) = 12$, and for the second prospect, $(\frac{3}{4} \times 6) + (\frac{1}{4} \times 22) = 10$. The first prospect has the larger expected "utility" and will be chosen.[15] How can we justify this procedure of adding the products of probabilities and "measures of utilities" of entities in an uncertain prospect and calling the result "the utility" of the uncertain prospect? The axioms of human behavior on which it is based are those which earlier gave us the procedure for "measuring utility" up to a linear transformation.[16]

Another way to express this implication that a rational person chooses among uncertain prospects so as to maximize expected utility is in terms of the implied shapes of indifference curves in the plane of *probabilities* of the various components of the uncertain prospects.

Suppose that I am indifferent between receiving a watch and receiving $30.00. In Figure 1A, the horizontal scale measures the probability with which I will get $30.00 and the vertical axis measures the probability with which I will get the watch. The origin represents the point at which I am sure to get nothing. The point W on the vertical axis presents the situation in which I am sure to get the watch and not get the $30.00. The

[15] If column 9 had been used, the chooser would have been declared indifferent, *i.e.*, the two combinations have equal utility. This is inconsistent with the utility value and predictions derived from the measures in the other columns.

[16] If our task is merely to order choice among the uncertain prospects, we could, after obtaining the expected utility of the prospect, obviously perform any monotonic transformation on it without upsetting the order of choices among the uncertain prospects. However, there seems little point in doing so, and there is good reason not to do so. In particular one might wish to predict choices among groups of uncertain prospects where, in each group of prospects, the entities are themselves uncertain prospects. This combination of several uncertain prospects into one resultant uncertain prospect is a consistent operation under the preceding postulates, and the utility measures attached to it will have an implied validity if the utility measures attached to the component prospects, derived in the manner indicated earlier, are valid.

point M on the horizontal axis represents the situation in which I am sure
to get the money and am sure not to get the watch. A straight line drawn
from W to M represents all the various uncertain prospects in which I
might get the watch or I might get the money, where the probabilities are
given by the horizontal distance for the money and the vertical distance
for the watch. Thus, the point P represents the prospect in which I will
get the watch with probability ⅔ or otherwise the money (with probability ⅓). The preceding axioms imply that this straight line is an indiffer-

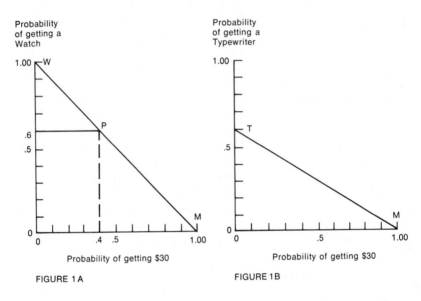

FIGURE 1A

FIGURE 1B

ence line or utility isoquant. In other words, the utility isoquant is a
straight line in the space of probabilities, in this case a straight line from
one sure prospect (the watch with certainty) to the other equally sure
prospect (the $30.00 with certainty).

The straight line utility isoquants need not go from sure prospect to sure
prospect, as can be seen from a second example. Suppose that I am
indifferent between receiving $30.00 with certainty (sure prospect of
$30.00) and the uncertain prospect in which I will get a particular type-
writer with probability .6 and nothing with probability .4. In Figure 1B,
this latter uncertain prospect is T on the vertical axis. Since I am indifferent between this uncertain prospect T and the $30.00 with certainty
(point M) a straight line, TM, is a utility isoquant, and all prospects
represented by the points on that line are indifferent to me—have the
same utility. In summary, in any such figure, a straight line through any
two equally preferred prospects will also contain all prospects (certain and
uncertain) that are equally preferred to the first two. This can be generalized into three and more dimensions in which case the straight line
becomes a plane surface in three or more dimensions.

The additivity of the simple weighted (by probabilities of the components of the entities) "utilities" enables us to call this composite utility function a linear utility function. This means that the measure of "utility" of uncertain prospects (in a probability sense) of entities is the sum of the "expectation" of the "utilities" of the component entities; it does not mean that our numerical numbers (measuring utility) assigned to the entities are linear functions of the physical amounts (*e.g.*, weights or counts) of the magnitude entities. Here linearity means that the utility of the uncertain prospects is a linear function of the utility of the component entities; incidentally the utility function is also a linear function of the probabilities of the entities.

IV. *Validity of Measurement*

Has anyone ever succeeded in assigning numbers in this way and did the sequence based on past observations predict accurately the preferences revealed by an *actual* choice among new and genuinely available prospects? The only test of the validity of this whole procedure, of which the author is aware, was performed by Mosteller and Nogee.[17]

The essence of the Mosteller-Nogee experiment was to subject approximately 20 Harvard students and National Guardsmen to the type of choices (indicated above on pages 39–44) required to obtain a utility measure for different entities. In the experiment, the entities were small amounts of money, so that what was being sought was a numerical value of utility to be attached to different amounts of money. After obtaining for each individual a utility measure for various amounts of money, Mosteller and Nogee predicted how each individual would choose among a set of uncertain prospects, where the entities were amounts of money with associated probabilities. Although some predictions were incorrect, a sufficiently large majority of correct predictions led Mosteller and Nogee to conclude that the subjects did choose among uncertain prospects on the basis of the utilities of the amounts of money involved and the probabilities associated with each, *i.e.*, according to maximized expected utility. Perhaps the most important lesson of the experiment was the extreme difficulty of making a really good test of the validity of the implications of the axioms about behavior.

Whether this process will predict choice in any other situation is still unverified. But we can expect it to fail where there are pleasures of gambling and risk-taking, possibly a large class of situations. Pleasures of gambling refers not to the advantages that incur from the possibility of receiving large gains, but rather to the pleasure of the act of gambling or act of taking on extra risk itself. There may be an exhilaration accompanying

[17] F. Mosteller and P. Nogee, "An Experimental Measurement of Utility," *Jour. Pol. Econ.* (Oct. 1951), LIX, 371–404.

sheer chance-taking or winning per se as distinct from the utility of the amount won. Even worse, the preference pattern may change with experience.

V. *Utility of Income*

We can conclude our general exposition with the observation that although the preceding discussion has referred to "entities" we could have always been thinking of different amounts of income or wealth. The reason we did not was that we wanted to emphasize the generality of the choice problem and to emphasize that utility measures are essentially nothing but choice indicators. However, it is useful to consider the utility of income. How do the numerical values (utilities) assigned by the preceding method vary as income varies? Now this apparently sensible question is ambiguous, even after our preceding discussion which we presume to have eliminated confusion about the meaning of "measurability of utility." For the question still remains as to whether the utility measure assumes (1) a utility curve that stays put and along which one can move up and down as income varies; or, (2) a utility curve whose shape is definable only on the basis of the current income as a reference point for change in levels of income. The former interpretation emphasizes dependence of utility on levels of income, while the latter emphasizes the dependence of utility on the changes in income around one's present position.

The most common type of utility curve has been one whose shape and position is independent of the particular income actually being realized at the time the curve of utility of income is constructed. For example, Friedman and Savage draw a utility curve dependent primarily upon levels of income rather than upon changes in income, and it is presumed that individuals choose as if they were moving along that curve.[18] The generic shape of the curve postulated by Friedman and Savage is shown in Figure 2.[19] This shape is supposed to explain the preference of both gambling and insurance. How does it do this?

Reference back to our method of predicting choices among uncertain prospects reminds us that choices will be made so as to maximize expected utility. A graphic interpretation is very simple. In Figure 2, let the income position now existing be A; let the individual be faced with a choice of staying where he is, or of choosing the uncertain prospect of moving to income position B with probability .999 or of moving to income position C with probability .001. Position A represents paying fire insurance, while positions C and B form the uncertain prospect where C is the position if a fire occurs with no insurance and B is the position if no fire occurs with no insurance. Will he choose the uncertain prospect or the sure position A?

[18] *Op. cit.*
[19] The utility curve is unique up to a linear transformation.

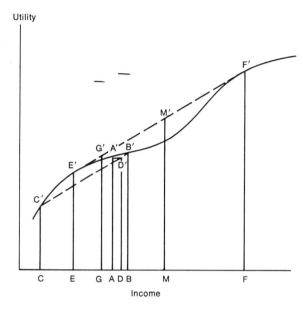

The basis for the choice as implied in our postulates can be described graphically as follows: From point B' draw a straight line to point C'. This straight line gives the expected utility of all uncertain prospects of the incomes B and C as the probability attached to C varies from zero to one. The point on this straight line yielding the expected utility of our uncertain prospect can be found by computing the expected *income*, D, and then rising vertically to point D' on the straight line $B'C'$. The ordinate DD' is the expected utility of the uncertain prospect. If the length of DD' is less than AA', as it is in our example, where AA' denotes the utility of the income after taking insurance, then the person will choose the insurance and conversely.

It is apparent that if the utility curve were always convex as in the first and last part of the curve in Figure 2, a person would never choose an uncertain prospect whose expected income was no greater than the insured income position. And if the curve were concave, a person would always choose the uncertain prospect where the expected income was at least equal to the present insured position.

If the curve has the shape postulated by Friedman and Savage, it is possible to explain why a person will take out insurance and will at the same time engage in a gamble. To see how the latter is possible, suppose a person were at position A. At the same time that he might be willing to take out insurance he may also be willing to gamble by choosing an uncertain prospect of ending up at E or F, despite its lower expected income at G, because the expected utility GG' of the uncertain prospect is larger than the utility AA' of position A. Friedman and Savage tentatively attempt to lend some plausibility to this shape of utility curve by conjecturing that economic society may be divisible into two general income level classes, the lower one being characterized by the first convex part of the curve and the higher one by the upper convex section. An intermediate group is in the concave section.

H. Markowitz has pointed out certain unusual implications of the Friedman-Savage hypothesis.[20] A person at the point M would take a fair bet with a chance to get to F. This seems unlikely to be verified by actual behavior. Secondly, if a person is at a position a little below F, he will not want insurance against small probabilities of large losses. Further, any person with income greater than F will never engage in any fair bet. But wealthy people do gamble. Is it solely the love of risk taking? To overcome these objections, Markowitz postulates that utility is related to *changes* in the level of income and that "the utility function has three inflection points. The middle one is at the person's "customary" income level, which except in cases of recent windfall gains and losses is the present income. The income interval between the inflection points is a nondecreasing function of income. The curve is monotonically increasing but bounded; it is at first concave, then convex, then concave, and finally convex.

Markowitz's hypothesis is consistent with the existence of both "fair" (or slightly "unfair") insurance and lotteries. The same individual will both insure and gamble. The hypothesis implies the same behavior whether one is poor or rich.

Markowitz recognizes that until an unambiguous procedure is discovered for determining when and to what extent current income deviates from customary income, the hypothesis will remain essentially nonverifiable because it is not capable of denying any observed behavior. The Markowitz hypothesis reveals perhaps more forcefully than the Friedman-Savage hypothesis, that utility has no meaning as an indicator of a level of utility. Utility has meaning only for changes in situations. Thus while I might choose to receive an increase in income rather than no increase, there is no implication that after I have received it for a while I remain on a higher utility base—however interpreted—than formerly. It may be the getting or losing, the rising or the falling that counts rather than the actual realized position. In any event Markowitz's hypothesis contains no implications about anything other than changes in income.

Our survey is now completed. We started with developments after the Slutsky, Hicks, Allen utility position in which utility is measured up to monotone transformations only. This meant exactly no more and no less than that utility is ordinal. In other words, the numerical size of the increments in the numbers in any one measure (column of numbers in Table I) is without meaning. Only their signs have significance. Utility transla-

[20] H. Markowitz, "The Utility of Wealth," *Jour. Pol. Econ.* (April 1952), LX, 151–58.

tion: marginal utility has meaning only in being positive or negative, but the numerical value is meaningless, *i.e.*, *diminishing* or *increasing* marginal utility is completely arbitrary since one can get either by using the appropriate column.[21]

The first postwar development was the Neumann and Morgenstern axioms which implied measurable utility up to a linear transformation, thus reintroducing diminishing or increasing marginal utility,[22] and which also implied a hypothesis or maxim about rational behavior. This was followed by the Friedman and Savage article and Marschak's paper. These papers are essentially identical in their postulates and propositions although the presentation and exposition are so different that each contributes to an understanding of the other. The Friedman and Savage paper, however, contains an added element: they attempt to prophesy the shape of the curve of utility of income that would be most commonly revealed by this measurement process. Mosteller and Nogee then made a unique contribution in really trying to verify the validity and applicability of the postulates. Most recently, Markowitz criticized the Friedman and Savage conjecture about the shape of utility of income curve, with his own conjecture about its dependence upon income changes. And that is about where matters stand now.

A moral of our survey is that to say simply that something is, or is not, measurable is to say nothing. The relevant problems are: (1) can numerical values be associated with entities and then be combined according to some rules so as to predict choices in stipulated types of situations, and (2) what are the transformations that can be made upon the initially assigned set of numerical values without losing their predictive powers (validity)? As we have seen, the currently proposed axioms imply measurability up to a linear transformation. Choices among uncertain prospects are predicted by a simple probability-weighted sum of the utilities assigned to the components of the uncertain prospect, specifically from the "expected utility."

And now to provide emotional zest to the reader's intellectual activity the following test is offered. Imagine that today is your birthday; a friend presents you with a choice among three lotteries. Lottery A consists of a barrel of 2,000 tickets of which 2 are marked $1,000 and the rest are blanks. Lottery B consists of another barrel of 2,000 tickets of which 20 are marked $100 and the rest are blanks. Lottery C consists of a barrel of 2,000 tickets of which 1 is marked $1,000 and 10 are marked $100. From the chosen barrel, one ticket will be drawn at random and you will win the amount printed on the ticket. Which barrel would you choose? Remember

---

[21] It is a simple task—here left to the reader—to find current textbooks and articles—which will be left unnamed—stating that the indifference curve analysis dispenses with the concept of utility or marginal utility. Actually it dispenses only with *diminishing* or *increasing* marginal utility.

[22] Incidentally, the *Theory of Games* of Neumann and Morgenstern is completely independent of their utility discussion.

there is no cost to you, this is a free gift opportunity. In barrel A the win of $1,000 has probability .001 and the probability of getting nothing is .999; in barrel B the probability of winning $100 is .01 and getting nothing has probability .99; in barrel C $1,000 has probability .0005, $100 has probability .005 and winning nothing has probability .9945. For each barrel the mathematical expectation is $1.00. The reader is urged to seriously consider and to make a choice. Only after making his choice should he read the footnote.[23]

Conclusion

1. Some readers may be jumping to the conclusion that we really can use *diminishing* or *increasing* marginal utility and that the "indifference curve" or "utility isoquant" technique has been superfluous after all. This is a dangerous conclusion. The "indifference curve" technique is more general in not requiring measurability of utility up to a linear transformation. But its greatest virtue is that unlike the earlier "partial" analysis of demand of a single commodity the indifference curve analysis by using an extra dimension facilitates intercommodity analyses—the heart of price analyses. But does the more "precise" type of measurement give us more than the ordinal measurement gives? Yes. As we have seen, measurability "up to a linear transform" both implies and is implied by the possibility of predicting choices among uncertain prospects, the universal situation.

2. Nothing in the rehabilitation of measurable utility—or choice-indicating numbers—enables us to predict choices among groups of sure

[23] Only the reader who chose C should continue, for his choice has revealed irrationality or denial of the axioms. This can be shown easily. He states he prefers C to A and to B. First, suppose he is indifferent between A and B; he doesn't care whether his friend chooses to give him A or B just so long as he gets one or the other. Nor does he care how his friend decides which to give. In particular if his friend tosses a coin and gives A if heads come up, otherwise B, he is still indifferent. This being so, a 50-50 chance to get A or B is equivalent to C, as one can see by realizing that C is really equivalent to a .5 probability of getting A and a .5 probability of getting B. Thus if A and B are indifferent there is no reason for choosing C.

Second, the reader choosing C may have preferred A over B. We proceed as follows. Increase the prize in B until our new B, call it B', is now indifferent with A. Form the uncertain prospect of A and B' with probability of .5 for A. This is better than C since C is nothing but an uncertain prospect composed of A and the old B, with probability of .5 for A. Where does this leave us? This says that the new uncertain prospect must be preferred to C. But since the new uncertain prospect is composed of .5 probability of A and .5 for B', the chooser of C must be indifferent between the uncertain prospect and A. (In axiom 3 let A and B be indifferent, and let C be identically the same thing as A. In other words, if the two entities in the uncertain prospect are equally preferred, then the uncertain prospect is indifferent to one of the entities with certainty.) The upshot is that A is just as desired as the new uncertain prospect which is better than C. Thus A is preferred to C, but the chooser of C denied this. Why? Either he understood and accepted the axioms and was irrational in making a snap judgment, or else he really did not accept the axioms. He may now privately choose his own escape. This example is due to Harry Markowitz.

prospects. The "utility" of a group of sure prospects is not dependent on *only* the utility (assigned number) of the *entities* in the combination. It is dependent upon the particular *combination of entities; i.e.,* we do not postulate that the utility of one sure element in a group of sure things is independent of what other entities are included. We think it obviously would not lead to valid predictions of actual choices. Therefore, it must be realized that nothing said so far means that we could measure the total utility of a market basket of different entities by merely adding up the utilities of the component entities. No method for aggregating the utilities of the component entities for this purpose has been found; therefore, for this purpose we have to say that utility is not measurable.

3. Is the present discussion more appropriate for a journal in psychology or sociology? If economists analyze the behavior of a system of intereacting individuals operating in a field of action—called the economic sphere—by building up properties of the system from the behavior aspects of the individuals composing the system, then the economists must have some rationale of behavior applicable to the individuals. An alternative approach is to consider the whole system of individuals and detect predictable properties of the system. The classic example of this distinction is in physics. One approach postulates certain laws describing the behavior of individual molecules, or atom particles, while the other starts with laws describing the observable phenomena of masses of molecules. Apparently, most economists have relied upon the former approach, the building up from individuals–sometimes referred to as the aggregation of micro-economic analysis into macro-economic analysis. On the other hand, those who are skeptical of our ability to build from individual behavior find their haven in postulates describing mass behavior. The current utility analyses aid the former approach.

4. The expression "utility" is common in welfare theory. For demand theory and the theory of prediction of choices made by individuals, measurability of the quantity (called "utility") permits us to make verifiable statements about individual behavior, but there is as yet no such happy development in welfare theory. "Measurability up to a linear transformation" does not provide any theorems for welfare theory beyond those derivable from ordinality. I mention this in order to forestall temptations to assume the contrary. The social welfare function as synthesized by Hicks and Scitovsky, for example, does not require the "utility" (choice-ordering numbers) of each individual to be measurable up to a linear transformation. It is sufficient that the individual's utility be measurable up to a monotone transformation—or, in other words, that it have merely ordinal properties. Ordinal utility is adequate in this case because orderings are made of positions or states in which, as between the two states compared, everyone is better off in one state than in the other. The welfare function does not enable a ranking of two states in one of which some people are worse

off.[24] This would require an entirely different kind of measure of utility for each person because of the necessity of making interpersonal aggregations of utilities. As yet no one has proposed a social welfare function acceptable for this purpose, nor has anyone discovered how, even in principle, to measure utility beyond the linear transformation. Even more important, the various elements in the concept of welfare (as distinct from utility) have not been adequately specified. In effect the utility whose measurement is discussed in this paper has literally nothing to do with individual, social, or group welfare, whatever the latter may be supposed to mean.

5. A brief obiter dictum on interpersonal utility comparisons may be appropriate. Sometimes it is said that interpersonal utility comparisons are possible since we are constantly declaring that individual *A* is better off than individual *B*. For example, "a rich man is better off than a poor man." But is this really an interpersonal utility comparison? Is it not rather a statement by the declarer that he would prefer to be in the rich man's position rather than in the poor man's? It does not say that the rich *man* is happier or has more "utility" than the poor *man*. Even if the rich man has a perpetual smile and declares himself to be truly happy and the poor man admits he is sorrowful, how do we know that the rich *man* is happier than the poor *man*, even though both men prefer being richer to being poorer? If I were able to experience the totality of the poor man's situation and the rich man's, and preferred the rich man's, it would not constitute an interpersonal comparison; rather it would be an *intrapersonal*, intersituation comparison.

It is hoped that the reader now has at his command enough familiarity with the meanings of measurability to be able to interpret and evaluate the blossoming literature on utility and welfare, and that this exposition has made it clear that welfare analysis gains nothing from the current utility analysis, and conversely.

[24] Absolutely nothing is implied about taxation. For example, justification of progressive income taxation by means of utility analysis remains impossible. The best demonstration of this is still E. D. Fagan, "Recent and Contemporary Theories of Progressive Taxation," *Jour. Pol. Econ.* (Aug. 1938), XLVI, 457–98.

The Empirical
Determination of
Demand Relationships

WILLIAM BAUMOL

William Baumol is Professor of Economics at Princeton and New York Universities. This piece is taken from his book Economic Theory and Operations Analysis, *which appeared in 1965.*

I. Why Demand Functions?

Demand functions, as they are defined in economic analysis, are rather queer creatures, somewhat abstract, containing generous elements of the hypothetical, and, in general, marked by an aura of unreality. The peculiarity of the concept is well illustrated by the fact that only one point on a demand curve can ever be observed directly with any degree of confidence because by the time we can obtain the data with which to plot a second point, the entire curve may well have shifted without our knowing it. A more fundamental but related source of our discomfort with the idea is the fact that the demand relationship is defined as the answer to the set of hypothetical questions which begin, "What would consumers do if price (or advertising outlay, or some other type of marketing effort) were different than it is in fact?" We are, then, dealing with information about potential consumer behavior in situations which consumers may never have experienced. And, since we have very little confidence in the constancy of consumer tastes and desires, all of these data are taken to refer to possible events at just one moment of time—e.g., consumer reactions to alternative possible prices if any of them were to occur tomorrow at 2:47 P.M.

In view of all this, there should be little wonder that people with an orientation toward applied economics occasionally become somewhat impatient with the economic theorist's demand function. Yet no matter how ingenious the circumlocutions which may have been employed, they have been unable to find an acceptable substitute for the concept. For the demand function must ultimately play a critical role in any probing marketing decision process, and there is really no way to get away from it.

For example, to decide on the number of salesmen which will best serve the interests of the firm, it is first necessary to know what difference in consumer purchases would result from alternative sales force sizes. But this is precisely the sort of odd and hypothetical information which goes to make up the demand relationship. It is for exactly the same reason that many large and reputable firms in diverse fields of industry are conducting ambitious research programs whose aim is the determination of their advertising-demand curves, that is, the relationship between their advertising outlays and their sales. So far, these efforts have met with varying degrees of success, and it must be admitted that many of them have not come up with very meaningful results. For the empirical determination of demand relationships is no simple matter and there are many booby traps for the amateur investigator and the unwary. It is no trick at all, on looking over a small sample of the published demand studies, to come up with horrible examples of just about every available type of misstep.

This chapter is designed primarily to point out some of the pitfalls which threaten the investigator of demand relationships. Its aim is to warn the reader to proceed with extreme caution in any such enterprise. No cut-and-dried solutions are offered to the problems which are discussed. This is true for two reasons. First, because many of the methods for dealing with these difficulties are highly technical matters of specialized econometric analysis and so are completely outside the scope of this volume. Second, and more important, solutions are not listed mechanically because there simply are no panaceas; the problems must be dealt with case by case as they arise, and the effectiveness with which they can be handled is still highly dependent on the skill, experience, and judgment of the specialist investigator.

If after reading the chapter the reader is left somewhat worried and uncomfortable, it will have accomplished its purpose. However, it should be emphasized that the problems which are raised, serious and difficult though they be, are not totally intractable and beyond the power of our statistical techniques.

II. Interview Approaches to Demand Determination

Before turning to statistical methods for the finding of demand functions, it is appropriate to say a few words about a more direct method for dealing with the problem—the consumer interview approach. In its most blatant and naïve form, consumers are simply collared by the interviewer and asked how much they would be willing to purchase of a given product at a number of alternative product price levels.

It should be obvious enough that this is a dangerous and unreliable procedure. People just have not thought out in advance what they would do in these hypothetical situations, and their snap judgments thrown up at the request of the interviewer cannot inspire a great deal of confidence. Even if they attempt to offer honest answers, even if they had thought about their decisions in advance, consumers might well find that when confronted with the harsh realities of the concrete situation, they behave in a manner which belies their own expectations. When we get to the effects of advertising on demand, the problems of such a direct interview approach become even more apparent. What is the consumer to be asked—how much more of the company's product he would buy if it were to institute a 1 per cent increase in its spot announcements to its television budget?

Much more subtle and effective approaches to consumer interviewing are indeed possible. Indirect, but far more revealing questions can be asked. Consumers may, for example, be asked about the difference in price between two competing products, and if it turns out that they simply do not know the facts of the matter, one may be led to infer that a lower product price may have a relatively limited influence on consumer behavior just because few consumers are likely to be aware of its existence. A clever interview designer may in this way build up a strategy of indirect questions which gradually isolates the required facts.

Alternatively, consumers may be placed in simulated market situations, so-called consumer clinics, in which changes in their behavior can be observed as the circumstances of the experiment are varied. An obvious approach to this matter is to get groups of housewives together, give them small amounts of money with which they are offered the opportunity to purchase one of, say, several brands of dishwasher soap which are put on display at the clinic, and observe what happens as the posted prices on the displays are varied from group to group. Here again, much more subtle variants in experimental design are clearly possible.

But even the best of these procedures has its limitations for our purpose, which is the determination of the precise form of a demand relationship. Artificial consumer clinic experiments inevitably introduce some degree of distortion because subjects cannot be kept from realizing that they are in an experimental situation. In any event, such clinics are rather expensive and so the samples involved are usually extremely small—too small for confidence in any inferences which are drawn about the magnitudes of the parameters of the demand relationships for the body of consumers as a whole. And large sample interviews which approach the determination of consumer demand patterns by subtle and indirect questions are often highly revealing, but they rarely can supply the quantitative information required for the estimation of a demand equation.

III. Direct Market Experiments

A second alternative approach which is sometimes considered as a means for finding demand relationship information is the direct market experiment. A company engages in a deliberate program of price or advertising level variation. Suppose it increases its newspaper advertising outlay in one city by 5 per cent, in another city it increases this outlay by 10 per cent, and in still a third metropolis a 10 per cent reduction is undertaken. In some ways such a direct experimental approach must always be the most revealing. It gives real answers to our formerly hypothetical questions and does so without subjecting the consumer to the artificial atmosphere of the interview situation or the consumer clinic.

However, direct experimentation has its serious limitations as well.

1. It can be very expensive or extremely risky for the firm. Customers lost by an experimental price increase may never be regained from competitive products which they might otherwise never have tried, and a 10 per cent increase in advertising outlay for any protracted period may be no trivial matter.

2. Market experiments are almost never *controlled* experiments, so that the observations which they yield are likely to be colored by all sorts of fortuitous occurrences—coincidental changes in consumer incomes or in competitive advertising programs, peculiarities of the weather during the period of the experiment, etc.

3. Because of the high cost of the experiments and because it is often simply physically impossible to try out a large number of variations, the number of observations is likely to be unsatisfactorily small. If, for example, it is desired to determine the effects of varied advertising outlay in a national periodical, the company cannot increase the size of its ads which are seen by Nashville readers and simultaneously reduce those which are seen in Lexington, Kentucky. This difficulty has been eased to some extent by the fact that a number of national magazines now put out several regional editions, but by and large the problem remains: market experiments usually supply information only about a very limited number of alternatives.

4. For similar reasons, market experiments are often of only relatively brief duration. Companies cannot afford to permit them to run long enough to display much more than impact effects. And yet the distinction between impact effects and long-run effects of a change are often extremely significant, as was so clearly demonstrated by the sharp but very temporary drop in cigarette sales when the first announcement was made about the association between smoking and the incidence of cancer. How

often has a rise in the price of a product caused a major reduction in purchases for a few weeks, with customers then gradually but steadily drifting back?

Market experiments do have a role to play in demand relationship determination. They can be important as a check on the results of a statistical study. Or they can provide some critical information about a few points on the demand curve in which past experience is entirely lacking. In some special circumstances experimentation is particularly convenient and has been used in the past, apparently with a considerable degree of success. For example, some mail-order houses have employed systematic programs in which a few special experimental pages were bound inconspicuously into the catalogues distributed to customers within restricted geographic regions, thus permitting observation of the effects of price, product, or even catalogue display variations. However, it should also be clear that market experiments cannot by themselves be relied upon universally to provide the demand information needed by management. Economics is just not a subject which lends itself readily to experimentation, largely because there are always too many elements beyond the control of the investigator and because economic experimentation is often inherently too expensive, risky, and difficult.

IV. Standard Statistical Approaches

The third, and generally most attractive, approach to demand function determination attempts to squeeze its information out of sources such as the accumulated records of the past (a time-series analysis), or a comparative evaluation of the performance of different sectors of the market (a cross-sectional analysis). The available statistics on sales, prices, advertising outlays of the most relevant varieties, and other marketing data are gathered together and then analyzed with the aid of the standard statistical techniques.

The basic procedure is simple enough; in fact, as we shall see presently, it is often far too simple. Suppose, for example, that the following data on company sales and advertising outlays have been accumulated:

TABLE I.

Year	1950	1951	1952	1953	1954	1955	1956	1957
Sales .... (millions of dollars)	67	73	54	62	70	75	79	83
Advertising .... (millions of dollars)	12	15	13	14	18	17	19	15

Once the figures have been plotted, the pattern formed by the dots can be used in an obvious manner to fit a straight line (see Figure 1) or a curve to them. This line is then taken as the desired advertising-demand curve. Its slope can be used as a measure of advertising effectiveness, that is, it measures the marginal sales productivity of an advertising dollar, Δ sales/Δ advertising outlay. This line can be determined impressionistically simply by drawing in a line that appears to fit the dots fairly well, or any one of a variety of more systematic methods can be used.

The most widely employed and best known of these techniques is the method of least squares,[1] in which the object is to find that line which makes the sum of the (squared) vertical deviations between our dots and the fitted line as small as possible, where the deviations are defined as the vertical distances such as AB or CD in Figure 1. The idea is inherently attractive. We wish to minimize deviations because a line which involves very substantial deviations from the dots representing our data surely does not represent the information in a very satisfactory way. But if, in our addition process, a large negative deviation such as AB (that is, a case where the line underestimates the vertical coordinate of our dot) happens to be largely cancelled out by a positive deviation, CD, the sum of the deviations can turn out to be small. This is surely not what we want in looking for a line which does not deviate much from the dots. One can avoid ending up with a line which fits the facts rather badly but in which the positive and negative deviations add up to a rather small number, by squaring all the deviation figures before adding them together. Since the square of a negative real number as well as that of a positive real number is always positive, large, squared negative deviations cannot offset large,

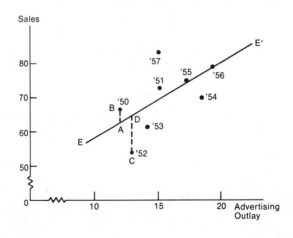

FIGURE 1

[1] The next few paragraphs are a very elementary review of the method of least squares and they should be omitted by the reader who has any acquaintance with the subject.

squared positive deviations, and the sum of squared deviations will never add up to a small number unless our line happens to fit the dots closely.[2]

There exist still more sophisticated techniques for fitting our advertising demand curve from the data. Although it is often too complex and expensive to employ in practice, professional statisticians usually consider the method of maximum likelihood as their ideal. This method requires some information about the probability distribution of the random elements which influence sales. From this probability distribution the statistician determines a likelihood function

$$L = f(x_t, y_t, a, b)$$

where x_t and y_t represent, respectively, advertising expenditures and sales in

[2] Other devices (such as the absolute value or the fourth power of the deviation) might accomplish the objective discussed. The reason one chooses to minimize the sum of the *squares* is that under very simple assumptions such estimates have several extremely desirable technical properties, among them, that these estimated parameter values are "best" in the sense that they minimize variance of the estimate and are unbiased.

To find the straight-line equation which satisfies our least squares requirement we employ the symbol x_t to represent sales in year t and y_t to represent advertising outlay in that year and let the equation of the line to be fitted be written $y_{ct} = a + bx_t$ where the subscript c in y_{ct} is there to remind us that in our equation the y is a figure calculated from the formula rather than observation. Now we proceed as follows:

Step 1. Define a deviation from our line as

$$y_t - y_{ct} = y_t - (a + bx_t) = y_t - a - bx_t.$$

Step 2. Define a squared deviation as

$$(y_t - y_{ct})^2 = y_t^2 + a^2 + b^2 x_t^2 - 2ay_t - 2bx_t y_t + 2abx_t.$$

Step 3. Add the squared deviations

$$\sum (y_t - y_{ct})^2 = \sum y_t^2 + na^2 + b^2 \sum x_t^2 - 2a \sum y_t - 2b \sum x_t y_t + 2ab \sum x_t$$

where, since a *is a constant*, $\sum a^2 = a^2 + a^2 + a^2 \ldots$ (n equal terms) $= na^2$.

Step 4. Find the values of a and b (the parameters of our equation) which minimize the sum of the squared deviations. We do this with the aid of the usual calculus procedure, by taking partial derivatives with respect to a and b and setting them equal to zero, thus:

$$\frac{\partial \sum (y_t - y_{ct})^2}{\partial a} = 2an - 2 \sum y_t + 2b \sum x_t = 0$$

and

$$\frac{\partial \sum (y_t - y_{tc})^2}{\partial b} = 2b \sum x_t^2 - 2 \sum x_t y_t + 2a \sum x_t = 0.$$

These last two equations contain, in addition to a and b, only known statistical figures x_t and y_t. The equations can therefore be solved simultaneously to obtain the desired parameter values, a and b, i.e., they determine for us the least squares line $y_{ct} = a + bx_t$. These two equations are usually referred to as the *normal equations* of the least squares method in this most elementary (two-variable straight line) case. The procedure employed in fitting many variable equations or curvilinear equations is a simple and obvious extension of that which has just been described.

year t, and a and b are the constants in our advertising demand equation $y_t = a + bx_t$. This likelihood function is defined as an answer to the following type of question: "Given any specific values of the parameters in our equation, say $a = 5$ and $b = 63$, how likely is it that the demand situation would have generated the statistics $x_{1950} = 12$, $y_{1950} = 67$, etc.?" (Note that these values of sales and advertising are in fact our observed statistical figures taken from Table I.) Considering all possible values of a and b, we can then employ the differential calculus to find the a and b combination which maximizes the value of the likelihood, L. We will then have found the a and b which provide, in this sense, the best possible explanation of the observed facts, i.e., we will have found that equation $y_t = a + bx_t$ whose parameters a and b are most likely to be the correct values of the true but unknown parameters, given the facts which were actually observed by the data collector.

It is of interest to note that in some special cases the least squares method turns out to be identical with maximum likelihood. That is, in these fortunate circumstances the least squares calculation becomes equivalent to the maximum likelihood procedure. We shall presently discuss one of the things which may go wrong if the least squares method is employed in situations where it does not yield the same results as the maximum likelihood calculation.

Having described now in highly general and impressionistic terms the methods which are most commonly employed by the statistician to determine relationships, let us now see some of the problems to which they give rise.

V. Omission of Important Variables

Clearly, sales are affected by other variables in addition to the company's advertising expenditure. Prices, competitive advertising, consumer income variations, and other variables also play an important role in any demand relationship. If, therefore, we try to extract from our statistics a simple equation relating sales to advertising outlay alone, and in the process we ignore all other variables, our results are likely to be very badly distorted. We may ascribe to the company's advertising outlays sales trends which are really the result of the behavior of other economic changes. The behavior of other variables can thus conceal and even offset the effects of advertising. To show how serious the results can be, consider the illustrative demand equation

$$(1) \qquad\qquad S = 50 + 4A + 0.02Y$$

where S represents sales, A advertising expenditure, and Y consumer income. The values given in Table II can easily be seen to satisfy the equation precisely, and any standard estimation procedure based on such information can be expected to yield the correct equation.

Table II.

Date	1956	1957	1958
Y	3,000	4,000	3,500
A	2	3	2.5
S	118	142	130

But the standard calculation shows that a *two*-variable, straight, least squares line which gives us a (perfect!) correlation between S and A alone (ignoring Y) and which is based on these same values will yield the equation

(2) $$S = 24A + 70.$$

This equation asserts that each added dollar of advertising expenditure brings in $24 in sales, instead of the true $4 return shown by equation (1). In addition, because of the perfect correlation there is, in this case, no residual unexplained variation in S which is left to be accounted for by a subsequent correlation between S and Y, i.e., *this incorrect procedure appears to show that consumer income has absolutely no influence on demand!* This advertising coefficient has been inflated by usurping to itself the influence of Y on sales.

Incidentally, if, instead of proceeding as we just did, we had started off by finding a least squares equation relating sales to consumer income alone, we would have obtained from the same statistics the equation

$$S = 0.024Y + 46$$

which this time overvalues the influence of income on sales and ascribes absolutely no effectiveness to advertising.

It is clear, then, that more than two variables must usually be taken into account in the statistical estimation of a demand relationship. And, in fact, this is ordinarily done, the estimation usually employing what is called a least squares *multiple regression* technique. However, it should be remembered that even if we include five variables in our analysis but omit a sixth rather important variable, precisely the same difficulties will be encountered. That is, the omission of any important variable, however defined, from the statistical procedure can lead to serious distortions in its results.

This might appear to constitute an argument for the inclusion in the analysis of every variable which comes to the statistician's mind as a factor of possible importance, just as a matter of insurance. Unfortunately, however, we are not at liberty to go on adding variables willy-nilly. The more variables whose influence we want to take into account, the more data we require as a basis for the estimation. If we only have statistical information pertaining to three points in time, it is ridiculous to try to disentangle the influence of fifteen variables. In fact, the statistician requires many pieces of information for every variable he includes in his analysis, if he is to estimate his relationship with a clear conscience.

However, large masses of marketing data are not easily come by. Records are often woefully incomplete; additional data can sometimes be acquired only at considerable expense, and in any event, statistics which go too far back in time are apt to be obsolete and irrelevant for the company's current circumstances. We must, therefore, very frequently be contented with skimpy figures which force us to be extremely niggardly in the number of variables which we take into account, despite the very great dangers involved.

VI. Inclusion of Mutually Correlated Variables

Another difficulty which, to some extent, can help to make life easier as far as the problem of the preceding section is concerned arises when a number of the relevant variables are themselves closely interrelated. For example, one encounters advertising effectiveness studies in which income and years of education per inhabitant are both included as variables. Now education is itself very closely related to income level both because higher-income families can afford to provide more education and larger inheritances to their children and because a more educated person is often in a position to earn a higher income.

It may nevertheless be true that education and income do have different consequences for advertising effectiveness. For example, an increase in income without any change in educational level could increase the person's willingness to purchase more in response to an ad, whereas more education not backed up by larger purchasing power might have the reverse effect. But, in general, there is no statistical method whereby these two consequences can be separated, because, for the bulk of the population, whenever one of these variables increases in value, so does the other. Hence, the statistics which can merely exhibit directions of variation might show that, other things remaining equal, whenever sales increased, income also increased, and so (as a consequence?) did education.

In such circumstances if we include both the income and the educational level variables in the statistical demand-fitting procedure, the chances are that the mechanics of the procedure will provide a perfectly arbitrary ascription of the sales changes to our two causal variables. And sometimes the results may turn out completely nonsensical because the standard computational procedure has no way to apply common sense in imputing the total sales change to the separate influences of education and income changes.

Therefore, if in a demand relationship there occur several variables which are themselves highly correlated, it is usually wise to omit all but one of any such set of variables in a statistical study. If this is not done, another powerful source of nonsense results is introduced.

VII. Simultaneous Relationship Problems

The difficulties which have so far been discussed, while they can be extremely important and are often overlooked in practice (with rather sad consequences) may, by and large, be considered rather routine and in retrospect, fairly obvious matters.

We come now to a far more subtle and perhaps a far more serious problem which was only brought to our attention in 1927 by E. J. Working and which has only received serious and systematic attention quite recently, largely as a result of the work of the Cowles Foundation. The problem in question, in a sense, follows from the difficulty which was discussed in the previous section. If there is a close correlation between two variables, it is likely to mean that they are not independent of one another and that there is at least one other relevant equation in the system which expresses the relationship between them. For example, in our illustrative case there might be an equation indicating how income level is ordinarily increased by a person's education. We then end up having to deal with not just a single demand equation, but with a system of several equations in which a number of the variables interact mutually and are determined simultaneously.

Economics is characterized by such simultaneous relationships. The standard example is the price determination process in which a supply equation is involved as well as our demand relationship. Similarly, simultaneous relationships constitute the core of national income analysis. National income depends on the demand for consumers' goods which helps determine the level of profitable production. But the consumption demand equation, in turn, involves national income (as a measure of the public's purchasing power) as a variable. To mention another simultaneous relationship example, the coal mining industry is a customer for steel whose volume of demand depends on coal sales, but the demand for coal itself depends heavily on the amount of coal to be used in producing steel. It is possible to expand the list of simultaneous relationships in economics indefinitely.

The empirical data which are generated by such a set of equations are the information source on which the statistician must base his estimates of the relationships. But since these data are the result of a number of such relationships, the difficult problem arises of separating out the relationships from the observed statistics.

Unless steps are taken to make sure that the influences of the several simultaneous relationships on the data can be and have been separated, there is not the slightest justification for the use of any estimation procedure, such as that depicted in Figure 1, to compute a statistical relationship. Yet it will readily be recognized how frequently this completely fallacious procedure is employed in practice in the form of simple or multiple correlations computed without any attempt to cope with the simultaneous relationship problem. Let us see now how serious are the distortions which can be expected to result.

VIII. *The Identification Problem*

In rather general terms our basic problem can conveniently be divided into two parts:

1. In some circumstances the simultaneous relationships (equations) will be so similar in character that it will be impossible to unscramble them (or at least some of them) from the statistics. Such relationships are said to be *unidentifiable*. Presently it will be shown how such an unhappy situation can arise, and it will be indicated that it is unfortunately not unheard of in marketing problems. Clearly, in such a case, we are wasting our time in a statistical investigation of the equation in question. There do exist some mathematical tests which show whether or not an equation is *identified* (i.e., whether or not it is in principle possible to separate it from the other relationships in the system). These tests should always be applied before embarking on the type of statistical investigation under discussion. It must be emphasized that if an equation happens not to be identified, it is impossible even to approximate the true equation from statistical data alone. Market experiments or other substitute approaches must be employed to obtain this information.

2. Even if an equation turns out to be identified, precautions must be taken to insure that a statistically estimated equation is not distorted by the presence of the simultaneous relationships. We will see in the next section that an ordinary least-squares procedure is likely to lead to precisely this sort of distortion.

In this section we deal with the first of these, the identification problem—the circumstances under which it is, at least in principle, possible to unscramble our simultaneous relationships statistically.

To illustrate, let us consider what is involved in finding statistically an advertising-demand curve such as the one which Figure 1 attempted to construct in a rather primitive fashion. Now while sales are doubtless affected by advertising, as the advertising-demand function assumes, this function is often accompanied by a second relationship in which what we might call the direction of causation is reversed. It is well known that a firm's advertising budget is frequently affected by its sales volume. In fact, many businesses operate on a rule of thumb which allocates to advertising expenditure a fixed proportion of their total revenues. For such a business, then, we will have two advertising expenditure demand relationships: (1) the demand function which shows how quantity demanded, Q, is affected by a firm's advertising budget, $A : Q = f(A)$ and (2) the budgeting equation which shows how the firm's advertising decisions are affected by the demand for its product: $A = g(Q)$.

Both of these relationships may actually be of interest to the businessman. The first, as already stated, is directly relevant to his own optimal expenditure decision. The second, if obtained from industry records, will give him vital information about the behavior patterns of his competitors.

The firm's actual sales and its actual advertising expenditure will, of course, depend on both its advertising budgeting practices (the budgeting equation) and on the demand-advertising relationships. In Figure 2 the graphs of two such hypothetical relationships are depicted.

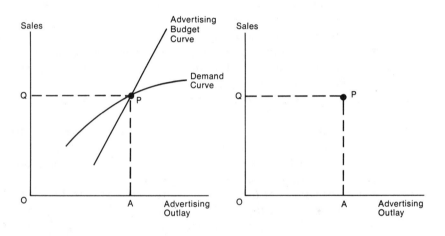

FIGURE 2A   FIGURE 2B

In Figure 2A we show the two curves which the statistician is seeking. We make ourselves, as it were, momentarily omniscient and thus have no difficulty envisioning the true relationships. However, the information available to the statistician is much more restricted, as we shall now see. In our situation the actual advertising expenditure, A, and the volume of sales, Q, are determined, as for any simultaneous equation, by the point of intersection, P, of the two curves.

We now can describe two cases of non-identification:

Case 1. *Neither curve identified.* If the two curves were to retain their shape from year to year, that is, *if neither of them ever shifted*, all the intersection points P would coincide or at least lie very close together (Figure 2B). There would only be a single observed point, as in the figure, or the tightly clustered points would form no discernible pattern, and so the shape of neither curve could even approximately be found from the data. We see then, though it may be a bit surprising, that curves which never shift are from this point of view the worst of all possibilities.

Case 2. *One of the curves not identified* (but the other curve identifiable). This is a case frequently encountered in practice when the demand curve of one firm is investigated. The data form a neat and simple pattern, but what they describe is the firm's inflexible advertising budgeting practices rather than the nature of the demand for its product. In such circumstances what happens is that the budget curve never shifts but the demand curve does. There will then be a number of different intersection points, such as P, P', and P'', but they will always describe only the shape of the advertising budget line (Figure 3). The reader can well imagine how often statistical attempts to find the advertising demand curve have produced neat linear relationships (and spectacularly high correlation coefficients), though what the triumphant investigator has located (without his knowing it) is a totally different curve from the one he was seeking. The situation which we have just examined is really ideal from the point of view of the statistician, *provided the relationship which is not shifting happens to be the one he is seeking.* But the question remains: how is he to know when one relationship is standing still, and even if he somehow knows this, how does he determine which one it is? We will see that in the answers to these questions lies the key to the solution of the identification problem.

It will be shown presently that only where both curves shift over time or from firm to firm or from geographical territory to territory can they ordinarily both be identified. However, in this case the difficult task of unscrambling the two relationships becomes particularly acute. Figure 4 illustrates how three points, A, B, and C, in a diagram similar to Figure 1 might have been generated by three different (shifted) pairs of our curves. It is noteworthy that the negatively sloping (!) "advertising curve" FF' estimated statistically from these points bears not the slightest resem-

FIGURE 3A   FIGURE 3B

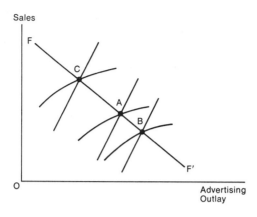

FIGURE 4

blance to any of the true curves. Nor, since it is merely a recording of points of intersection, is there any reason why it should. *The shape of FF' is not even any sort of "compromise" between those of the budget and advertising demand curves!* We conclude that where simultaneous relationships are present the standard curve-fitting techniques described in Section 4 and Figure 1 may well break down completely. *Their results are likely to bear absolutely no resemblance to the equations which are being sought!* Such a naïve approach may therefore well be worse than no investigation because misleading information is usually worse than no information at all.

Let us now see how one can, in principle, test whether the relationship we are seeking is identified (potentially discoverable by statistical means).

First we note that, as the model has so far been described, there is no way of accounting for any shifts in either relationship which, as we have observed, are crucial for our problem. The reason is that only two variables, A and Q, have been considered in the relationships $Q = f(A)$ (the demand relationship) and $A = g(Q)$ (the advertising budget equation).

There must, in fact, be some other influences (other variables) which disturb the relationships between Q and A and produce the shifts in their graphs. These additional variables must be taken explicitly into account. As we know, the demand relationship is likely to involve many variables in addition to A. For example, consumer's disposable income is a variable which affects the volume of sales resulting from a given level of advertising expenditure though, very likely, it does not enter the firm's budget calculation explicitly but only indirectly via the effects of income on the sales of the company's product. Similarly, the firm's budget policy may be affected' by its past dividend payments, which determine how much it can currently spare for advertising expenditure, but this dividend policy will have little or no effect on the demand curve for its products. Suppose, for the sake of simplicity, that the four variables Q, A, Y (the disposable income), and D (the total dividend payments in the preceding year) are the only ones that are relevant to the problem. Our two relationships then become:

(3)   the advertising demand function $Q = f(A, Y)$

and

(4)   the advertising budget equation $A = g(Q, D)$.

Here changes in the value of Y are what produce the shifts in the graph of the demand equation which have been discussed. Similarly, changes in D produce shifts in the advertising budget curve.

Now that we have examined how shifts in the two curves are produced we can return to the question of identification. Let us see, intuitively, how the presence of the shift variables in equations (3) and (4) makes it possible, in principle, to separate the relationships from the statistics (i.e., how the shift variables identify the equations). It will be shown now that Y and D permit the statistician, at least conceptually, to divide up the statistical information in such a way that he is left with situations like that depicted in Figure 3. Such a situation gives him the information that permits him to infer which of the relationships is shifting and which is standing still. That is, he can determine when one graph is not moving while the other shifts around, so that the resulting dots trace out the graph of the equation which is not shifting, the equation he is trying to estimate. The reader should first be warned, however, that the procedure which is about to be described is not usually a practical estimation (curve finding) procedure and that other, more sophisticated measures are normally employed for the purpose.

In Figure 5 we replot the data of Figure 1. Let us, in addition, determine the level of income for each point, Y, for that particular year. Suppose this information is as shown in Table III.

TABLE III.

Advertising Demand point	1950	1951	1952	1953	1954	1955	1956	1957
Disposable Income Y ($ billions)	360	297	295	307	428	381	420	300

We note that the income values for the points representing 1951, 1952, 1953, and 1957 are fairly close together. Hence, if we are convinced that Y is the only variable which makes for sizable shifts in the advertising demand curve, it is reasonable to assume that all four points lie on (or close to) the same curve, that is, among these points there has occurred little or no shift in the curve. We may therefore use these four points (ignoring the others) to locate a demand curve UU' (for income level approximately $300 billion) as shown. Similarly, we can use points for

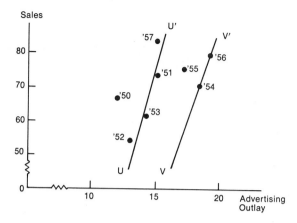

FIGURE 5

years 1954 and 1956 alone to find the shape of the advertising demand curve VV', which pertains to income level approximately $420 billion, etc. In other words, the additional information on the value of Y for each point has permitted us, in principle, to ignore all points which contain information irrelevant to a given advertising demand curve.

We see, then, that if variable Y is present in one equation but not in the other, it permits us, in principle, to discover statistical points over which the budget line has shifted but through which the demand curve remains unchanged. In this same way we were able to trace out a budget line in Figure 3. But it will be remembered that in the situation shown in Figure 3, the demand curve is unidentifiable because the budget curve never shifts. There is no variable such as D in the budget relationship which will move the budget line about and yet permit the demand curve to stay still. This gives us the following result: *one of a pair of simultaneous relationships will be identified if it lacks a variable which is present in the other relationship.*

The relevance of the shift variables Y and D for identification can also be seen in another way. Suppose we use some correlation procedure to find a statistical relationship among variables Q, A, Y, and D. The system is identified if it is possible in principle for this statistical relationship to be an approximation to either equation (3) (the demand function) or to (4) (the budget function) and if it is possible to find out whether the statistical curve represents (3), (4), or neither. There are three possibilities:

1. The statistical relationship turns out to take the form $Q = F(A, Y, D)$ in which all four variables are present (their coefficients are significantly different from zero). In that case we know that the statistics have given us a mongrel function which resembles neither of the relationships which we are seeking, for neither of the relationships contains both variables Y and D.

2. Suppose now that the statistical relationship turns out to have an equation of the form $F(A, Y) = Q$; i.e., D plays no role in the equation. Then the statistical equation cannot involve any advertising budget function component, for if it did, any change in D would have influenced the relationship via its effect on the budget equation. In this case the statistical equation must be an estimate of the demand relationship (3) alone.

3. Similarly, if the form of the statistical equation is $F(A, D) = Q$, it must represent the budget relationship (4) alone.

Thus the two variables Y and D, each of which appears in one and only one of the two relationships, have permitted us to identify both equations. For example, the presence of the variable D, which occurs only in the budget equation, acts as a warning signal which notifies us at once when the budget equation has somehow gotten itself mixed in with our demand information. We conclude, again, that two simultaneous equations are normally identified (they can, at least in principle, be unscrambled from the statistics) if each equation contains at least one variable which is absent from the other.

Of course, some more powerful identification criteria exist. For example, an obvious extension of the preceding result is the theorem that

> In a system of n simultaneous equations, a necessary condition for identification of any one of the equations, say the ith, is that every other equation in the system contain at least one variable which is missing from equation i.

This is hardly the place for a systematic discussion of the identification problem, and most of what has been said on the subject has been intended to be intuitive rather than rigorous. However, the reader should have gathered that it is an extremely serious problem and that inadequate attention on the part of the analyst to this problem can easily invalidate his statistical results in their entirety.

The Price Elasticity of Demand for Automobiles

SENATE SUBCOMMITTEE ON ANTITRUST AND MONOPOLY

This selection is from a report published in 1958 by the Senate Subcommittee on Antitrust and Monopoly.

Durable goods, such as automobiles, have certain characteristics not present in perishable goods which must be taken into account in any analysis of the elasticity of demand. Consumers, at least in the abstract, do not buy commodities for the purpose of just having them around. They buy them for the satisfaction or utility which these commodities will give them. An article of food yields utility only in the eating and disappears in the process, whereas an automobile yields utility over many years. Thus, there is a significant difference between the demand for food and the demand for new automobiles. Price, income, etc., affect the demand for the flow of satisfaction which the commodity yields and not the new purchases of the commodity itself. In the case of food, the correspondence of the flow of satisfaction and new purchases can be made easily, since the act of obtaining utility from a unit of food results in its destruction. But in the case of automobiles no such correspondence can be made. A consumer can obtain a flow of satisfaction or utility by buying a new car, by buying a used car, or by simply holding on to the car he already owns. Though new-car purchases cannot be equated directly with the factors which influence demand, the ownership of automobiles can be so equated, but ownership must be taken in a very special sense. . . .

Automobiles are distinguished from other commodities, both perishable and durable, in the magnitude of expenditure involved. No other commodity except a house requires such a large initial outlay relative to the typical consumer's income or his accumulated savings. Because of the size of the expenditure, and because consumers may have previously committed substantial portions of their incomes, it may not be possible for a consumer to increase his level of ownership as rapidly as he might like to, as a result of a change in income or price. Moreover, most consumers have relatively small savings. Thus even if, because of lower prices or higher incomes, they wish to maintain a higher level of ownership, they cannot do so unless credit is readily available at favorable terms. However, easy credit terms cannot significantly affect new purchases when price has risen or income has fallen and ownership is therefore declining. A consumer does not usually need credit to hold on to his old car. . . .

Six major studies have been made of the elasticity of demand for automobiles which utilize historical data; they are those of: (1) P. de Wolff, (2) M. J. Farrell, (3) C. F. Roos and V. von Szeliski, (4) L. J. Atkinson, (5) G. C. Chow, and (6) D. B. Suits. Neither Mr. de Wolff's study nor Mr. Farrell's study lends itself to easy interpretation in terms of the price elasticity of demand for new cars. Chow and Suits testified before the subcommittee and their testimony will be discussed later. The studies by Roos and Von Szeliski and Atkinson are based entirely on pre-World War II data, and are briefly summarized here.

In 1939 General Motors Corp. published Roos and Von Szeliski's now classic study of automobile demand. Their study is long and quite complicated; however, they have provided a summary which is quoted in full:

> From the demand standpoint, the outstanding characteristic of passenger automobiles and other durable goods is their durability. In consequence, consumption of these goods is dissociated from purchase and ordinarily extends 5 to 15 years beyond the date of acquisition. Consumers' car stocks thus take a prominent part in determining new-car purchases. The demand situation is quite unlike that for perishable goods, in which the part played by consumers' stocks is negligible. Additions to consumers' stocks of automobiles, or new-owner sales, depend chiefly on the difference between the actual car stock and the maximum stock or ownership level attainable under current conditions of income, price, operating costs, and car life.
>
> The concept of a variable maximum ownership level is of primary importance in the automobile industry because when car ownership is near the level of maximum ownership and a decrease in national income occurs, the effect is to make the market suddenly saturated. A consequence is the elimination of new-owner sales, and even the forcing of liquidation of part of the consumers' car stock. It is found by statistical analysis that a 1-percent increase in supernumerary income (national income less direct taxes and necessary living cost) would raise the maximum ownership level by about 0.4 percent. Income changes also affect replacement sales, and a 1-percent increase in supernumerary income would increase replacement sales by about 1.2 percent. The overall effect of income on total new-car sales, new owners as well as replacement, appears to be that a 1-percent change in income causes a 2.5-percent change in sales. When consumer car stocks approach the maximum ownership level and the quality of these stocks is high, new-car sales can be drastically lowered by moderate declines in income.

The influence of price on replacement sales is such that with each 1-percent increase in price, replacement sales tend to decrease by 0.74 percent (without allowance for possible correlation of price with operating costs). The overall effect of price on combined new owners and replacement sales (after allowance for intercorrelation of price with operating costs) appears to be that a 1-percent decrease in price increases sales by between 1 and 2 percent, depending upon the degree of saturation of the market. A figure of 1.5 can be accepted as a fair average value of the elasticity of demand with respect to price under current conditions.

Automobile sales can be explained with an average error of 4.17 percent for the period 1919–37 with the above factors and without taking into account such factors as changes in financing plans, dealers' used-car stocks, hghway carrying capacity and style.

In an article on durable-goods demand published in April 1952, L. Jay Atkinson presents a brief statistical study of the demand for new passenger cars. He obtained a price elasticity of −1.4 and an income elasticity of +2.5. All the studies discussed in this chapter, with the exception of Atkinson's, rest, more or less, on the foundation that ownership is considered as basic, and new purchases are derived from ownership. His analysis relates new private passenger-car registrations per 1,000 households to 4 variables: (1) real disposable income per household in 1939 dollars, (2) percentage of current to preceding year real disposable income in 1939 dollars, (3) ratio of average retail price of new automobiles to the BLS Consumer Price Index, and (4) average scrappage age. For the period 1925–40, Atkinson's analysis explains 98 percent of the variation in new-car purchases. Predictions based on his analysis for recent years in the postwar period are reasonably accurate, as can be seen below:

TABLE I. New Car Registrations in the United States, Actual and Computed by a Formula of Atkinson[1]

Year	Actual	Computed	Percentage difference
	Millions	Millions	
1955	7.2	6.3	−13
1956	6.0	6.5	+ 8
1957	6.0	6.0	0

[1] Calculations made by the subcommittee staff.

The Statistical Investigations of Chow and Suits

The studies of Dr. Gregory C. Chow, of the Massachusetts Institute of Technology, and Dr. Daniel B. Suits, of the University of Michigan, have been singled out for more detailed discussion, principally on the grounds that they are the two most recent analyses and the only studies incorporating post-World War II data.

Professor Chow finds the price elasticity for new-car sales to be −1.2 and the income elasticity to be +3.0. These elasticities are derived from the elasticities between ownership and price and income:

> To understand the mechanism governing sales of automobiles, first of all, we have to understand the mechanism governing automobile ownership.
>
> People buy automobiles because they want to use automobiles, and their wants are satisfied not only by the new cars that they have just bought, but by the total number of automobiles in existence. So that the demand for automobile services actually is a demand for automobile ownership rather than the demand for purchase.
>
> *The demand for purchase is derived from the demand for automobile ownership.*

In obtaining his figure for total car ownership, Chow adjusts for age in the following manner:

> ... the measure of automobile ownership really depends on how much the new car is worth as compared with the used cars, and I have observed the relative prices of automobiles of different age groups at one point in time.
>
> I have found that, historically, approximately 25 percent is depreciated in a year, roughly speaking, so that if we count a new car as 1 unit, we will count a 1-year-old car as one 0.75 unit, and a 2-year-old car as 75 percent of 75 percent, or something like a half unit. ...

In his analysis, which covers the period 1920–41 and 1948–53, Chow relates ownership per capita in this sense to the average price of all cars, new and used, deflated by a general price index, real disposable income per capita, and the ownership of automobiles the preceding year. He thus takes account of four of the major factors affecting the demand for any commodity: its price, the general price level, consumer income, and population. The way in which Chow has allowed for delays in adjustment assumes that such delays are the same, no matter in which direction the adjustment takes place. As indicated above, there are strong reasons for believing that the delays are less marked in a downward direction.

In describing his results on the income and price elasticities of the demand for ownership, Chow said:

> I have estimated that for every percent increase in per capita income, automobile ownership would be increased by 1½ percent.
>
> How about the effect on price? I have also estimated that for every percent increase in price, there will be [a] 0.6 percent drop in automobile ownership; it would decrease people's desire of ownership by 0.6 percent.

Since he assumes that the ownership level depreciates at the rate of 25 percent a year, the elasticities for new-car sales would be 4 times the ownership elasticities, or 2.4 for price and 6 for income. However, for the reasons described earlier (principally other commitments and transactions costs), he assumes that consumers do not fully adjust their level of ownership to changed prices and incomes within a 1-year period. He testified:

The responses of 6 percent to a 1-percent change in income and 2.4 percent to a 1-percent change in price would result if the consumers adjusted their car ownership to the desired [or equilibrium] level at once. But they do not. Time elapses between decision and the act of purchasing. But more important is the cost involved in making a transaction. No one will change his car to a better one the moment his income increases, and to a cheaper one the moment his income drops. If he does that, he will be spending quite a bit of his time and money with the automobile dealers. I have found that about half of the desired change in ownership is achieved in 1 year. This means that a 1-percent change in income, while raising the desired ownership by 1.5 percent to be achieved in due course, will raise actual ownership only by 0.75 percent in the current year. Therefore, the percentage response in sales within 1 year to a 1-percent rise in income during that year will be only 3 percent, and not 6. Similarly, the response of sales to price will only be 1.2 percent, and not 2.4.

This, of course, assumes that delays in adjustment are symmetrical with respect to the direction of adjustment. In a memorandum inserted in the record, Dr. John M. Blair, chief economist of the subcommittee, pointed out that although there are grounds for supposing that delays do exist in both upward and downward adjustments in ownership, there are convincing reasons for believing that these delays are asymmetrical, i.e., that the rates of adjustment differ for upward and downward adjustments. The factor of other commitments is not operative in downward adjustments, while transactions cost is operative to a lesser degree in downward than in upward adjustments. The subcommittee staff did not have the time or the resources necessary to assess the full effects of this possible modification of Chow's results. However, it was possible to make a comparison between the results obtained by Chow's method in which it is assumed that only half of the adjustment is made in 1 year and those secured by an alternative method in which the extreme assumption is made that no delay occurs when new-car purchases are declining. Chow's elasticities of −0.6 and +1.5 for ownership with respect to price and income constituted the underlying basis of the calculations.

Since 1921 there have been nine year-to-year downturns in new-car purchases. The downturns in 1923–24 and 1953–54 were relatively minor, amounting to less than 10 percent, and were accordingly omitted. For each of the downturns, percentage change in price and in income were computed. On the basis of these changes, the percentage changes in new-car purchases were computed by two methods:

(a) A price elasticity of −1.2 and an income elasticity of + 3.0 were applied to the percentage changes in price and income, respectively. The resulting percentage changes were then summed to obtain the calculated value of the percentage change in new-car purchases. The result is carried under the column labeled "Predicted by Chow's method" in the table.

(b) When the direction of price change was upward, an elasticity of −2.4 was applied; when it was downward, an elasticity of −1.2 was applied. When the direction of the income change was downward, an elasticity of $+6.0$ was applied; when it was upward, an elasticity of $+3.0$ was applied. The price and income effects were summed and the result is carried in the last column of the table, labeled "Predicted by alternative method."

TABLE II.   Per capita New-Car Purchases, Actual Percentage Changes, and Predicted by 2 Methods

Years	Actual change	Predicted by Chow's method	Predicted by alternative method
	Percent	Percent	Percent
1926–27	−23.6	− 5.2	−16.7
1929–30	−35.0	− 3.5	−28.4
1930–31	−28.8	−28.6	−72.5
1931–32	−42.7	−48.0	−96.6
1937–38	−44.6	−55.7	−100.0
1950–51	−21.4	− 6.9	−13.8
1951–52	−19.2	− 3.3	−10.5
1955–56	−18.4	+ 1.9	+ .4
1957–58[1]	−29.8	−14.9	−29.8

[1] The 1957–58 estimates were derived by assuming new-car purchases in 1958 of 4,200,000, a decline in real disposable income per capita of 3.4 percent and a price increase of 3.9 percent in real terms.

Of the 9 downturns, the alternative method yielded better results in 6, though in 1, 1955–56, both were in error as to the direction of change. The only downturns in which Chow's method, per se, proved superior were those of 1930–31, 1931–32, and 1937–38. Each of these was a year of extremely depressed economic activity. A possible explanation for the better results yielded by Chow's method for these years, might be that in a period of extreme depression the ownership of automobiles, defined in Chow's terms, would be reduced to relatively low levels. This means that only the hard-core users of transportation services from privately owned automobiles were effectively in the market for cars. Consequently, the basic ownership elasticities of demand must have been lower than the −0.6 price elasticity and the +1.5 income elasticity which Chow obtained over the long-run period of 1921–53. In those years of deep depression Chow offsets his too-high elasticities for ownership with his downward adjustment for new-car purchases. Under the alternative method the overstatement in the elasticity of ownership is not offset, and consequently the decline in car sales during such years is overstated.

There is thus a reasonable basis for assuming that the experience of the deep depression years was atypical (except for downswings of comparable severity), and that the evidence supports the hypothesis that adjustments to changes in price and income are asymmetrical, with the downward adjustments in stock and purchases taking place more rapidly than upward adjustments. The showing for 1957–58 rather strikingly confirms this view. The inference would be that in periods of economic decline (except at the bottom of a severe depression) the elasticities arrived at by Professor Chow are conservative.

His elasticities as well as those of the other students of the problem are conservative for still another reason: they ignore the so-called secondary effects on income of price-induced changes in production—effects which cannot be measured. As was pointed out in the subcommittee's report on steel:

> The automobile workers who lose their jobs because of a price-induced reduction in automobile output lose their ability to purchase cars, as do the workers who would have been employed in making the steel that would have gone into those cars, and so on. Since the production of automobiles is a vast industry, this secondary effect cannot be disregarded.

Dr. Suits' investigation concerns new purchases entirely, although the framework of his analysis does include elements which allow new-car purchases to depend indirectly on ownership. Suits' formulation is basically the same as Chow's, except that population is excluded entirely, some measure of credit terms is introduced, and ownership is treated in absolute numbers rather than in age-comparable units. His analysis covers the period 1929 through 1956, omitting the years 1942–48.

In view of the similarity in the formulation of Suits and Chow it is rather surprising that their statistical results turned out to be so different. Suits obtained a price elasticity of -0.6 and an income elasticity of $+4.2$ for new-car purchases. Thus his price elasticity is only half of that which Chow obtained and his income elasticity is nearly 40 percent greater. The difference appears to be due largely to two factors: (a) the use of different price series and (b) a statistical procedure employed by Suits which has the effect of causing his analysis to ignore the 30 to 40 percent of all cars not sold on credit. With respect to the former, Suits did not use the BLS retail price index for new automobiles, nor did he, as Chow did, use newspaper advertisements. Instead, Suits constructed his own index by multiplying the BLS wholesale index of new car prices by a retailers' margin factor. Suits described his procedure and the rationale behind it to the subcommittee as follows:

> This price index is essentially a markup of the passenger and automobile part of the BLS wholesale price index which is somewhat more inclusive than the consumer price index component—this marked up by an estimate of the gross margin of automobile dealers.
>
> I think I can explain the matter this way: When a dealer sells a car he receives in payment cash or a credit instrument of cash equivalent, and ordinarily, a used car of some value. This used car is then sold and again cash or credit instruments are obtained and generally another used car. This continues down until the cars of course are scrapped out at the bottom.

The sum total of this operation is the way in which the dealer receives his payment for the new car.

So that essentially what I have done is take the ratio of the average value of a new passenger automobile at wholesale, to the average receipts per new car sold of automobile dealers, *receipts of both payments for new and used cars alike.*

Obviously, the price which is relevant to an analysis of the demand for new cars is the price of new cars, not the price of all cars, and certainly not the margins on used cars. Moreover, it matters not at all how an automobile dealer receives the price of a new car; the important factor is the price of a new car, what he gets and what the buyer pays, and the margins on used cars can surely not be relevant to the purchaser of a new car. The whole question thus revolves around how good the price series constructed by Suits is for his purpose. A comparison of this series with the BLS retail price index for new cars raises a number of questions. A memorandum inserted in the record, prepared by Dr. Browne of the subcommittee staff, shows (1) that one of the important series used by Suits is based primarily on the BLS retail price index for new passenger cars; (2) that this same series includes, during certain periods, expenditures on numerous items, such as house trailers, not relevant to the determination of the margins of dealers on new cars; (3) that the BLS wholesale price index which enters Suits' calculation is considered by the Bureau of Labor Statistics itself to be less reliable than the retail price index; and (4) that the BLS series and Suits' series move in different directions in several crucial periods such as 1955. In view of the fact that Suits bases his analysis on year-to-year changes, this last point is especially important.

Thus, Suits does not free himself from the supposed shortcomings of the BLS retail price series, but in the course of his attempt to do so he introduces possibly extensive errors into his price series.

With respect to the second factor, Suits' use of data on average contract duration is unusual. Instead of using average contract duration as a separate variable in his analysis designed to explain year-to-year changes in new-car purchases, Suits divides real retail price by it and uses only the ratio of the two, i.e., he computes what he calls the "real monthly payment" and never introduces contract duration and price as separate variables. In the postwar period only some 50 to 70 percent of all new automobiles purchased have been purchased on credit. Thus, to imply as Suits does that a variable representing the monthly payment for a new automobile is the only effective "price" variable is somewhat misleading because not all purchases of new cars are made on time. Retail price and contract duration should exert separable and possibly different effects on new-car demand.

In order to test whether Suits' procedures had the effect of reducing the price elasticity of demand (which would tend to explain the difference between his elasticities and those of Chow), the subcommittee staff made a statistical analysis which was identical to that made by Suits, except in two respects: (1) The BLS index of retail prices of new automobiles divided by the BLS Consumer Price Index was substituted for Suits' own price series; and (2) average contract duration, as measured by Suits, was treated as a separate variable, i.e., price was not divided by average contract duration, but average contract duration was included in the analysis as a separate variable. The results of this analysis were as follows: The price elasticity of demand obtained was −1.2, identical with that which Professor Chow presented to the subcommittee. The income elasticity obtained was +3.9, which compares to the 3.0 of Chow. The elasticity of new purchases with respect to average contract duration was found to be −0.7. It is thus apparent that Suits' use of a questionable price series and his division of price by contract duration had the effect of reducing the price elasticity which he obtained.

Summary Comparison of Statistical Findings

The investigation of the quantitative effect of price and income upon new-automobile purchases is a complex and difficult subject, about which much more needs to be known. However, there is a substantial measure of agreement among the various authorities, as can be seen below:

TABLE III. Summary Comparison of Several Studies of Automobile Demand

Study	Elasticity of new purchases with respect to—	
	Price	Income
Suits:		
1. As presented	−0.6	+4.2
2. As reworked by the subcommittee staff	−1.2	+3.9
Chow[1]	−1.2	+3.0
Roos and von Szeliski	−1.5	+2.5
Atkinson[1]	−1.4	+2.5

[1] Per capita basis.

Except for Suits' original analysis, the results presented in the table show price elasticities ranging between −1.2 and −1.5 and income elasticities ranging between +2.5 and +3.9. Because of the considerations which have been described above, a price elasticity of −1.2 appears to be a minimum estimate.

Part Two

PRODUCTION, COSTS, AND THE THEORY OF THE FIRM

One of the primary decision-making units in the economy is the business firm. It is appropriate that economists devote a great deal of attention to firms, for the bulk of our goods and services derives from activities in the private sector. After taking up the theory of consumer behavior and market demand, courses in microeconomics generally focus on the firm—its functioning and motivation. In this part of this volume, we present a number of classic papers dealing with production, costs, and the theory of the firm.

The first paper, by Herbert A. Simon, discusses various theories of decision-making in economics. After defining "satisficing" as trying to attain a given sales or profit or other type of goal, Simon argues that "models of satisficing behavior are richer than models of maximizing behavior, because they treat not only of equilibrium but of the method of reaching it as well." He also examines some theories that take account of the limitations of the decision-maker and the complexity of the environment. The following paper, by Fritz Machlup, is concerned with somewhat the same area but is quite different in tone. According to Machlup, the model of the firm in price theory is not "designed to serve to explain and predict the behavior of real firms; instead, it is designed to explain and predict changes in observed prices. . . . [The] firm is only a theoretical link, a mental construct helping to explain how one gets from the cause to the effect."

Cost functions are at the heart of the theory of the firm. The next paper, by Joel Dean, is a pioneering effort to estimate a firm's cost functions. Using statistical techniques, he estimates the cost functions of a hosiery mill, one of his most controversial findings being that marginal cost is constant. The following paper, by Frederick Moore, is concerned with economies of scale. He begins by discussing the ".6 rule" used by engineers to estimate the increases in capital cost resulting from increases in capacity. Then he presents estimates of the relationship between capital cost and capacity for a large number of products in the chemical and metal industries.

Perhaps the most significant recent development in the theory of the firm has been the invention and application of linear programming. Linear programming is the most famous of the mathematical programming methods that have come into existence since World War II. It is a technique that allows decision-makers to solve maximization and minimization problems where there are certain constraints that limit what can be done. In the final paper, Robert Dorfman sets forth clearly the basic ideas of linear programming. Using a simple example of a problem facing an auto producer, he describes the fundamental concepts of this approach and compares these concepts with traditional theory. In addition, he outlines various other applications of linear programming to real-life problems, and discusses several extensions of this method.

Theories of Decision-Making in Economics and Behavioral Science

HERBERT A. SIMON

Herbert A. Simon is Professor of Industrial Administration and Psychology at Carnegie-Mellon University. This article first appeared in the American Economic Review *in 1959.*

The Goals of Firms

Just as the central assumption in the theory of consumption is that the consumer strives to maximize his utility, so the crucial assumption in the theory of the firm is that the entrepreneur strives to maximize his residual share—his profit. Attacks on this hypothesis have been frequent. We may classify the most important of these as follows:

(a) The theory leaves ambiguous whether it is short-run or long-run profit that is to be maximized.

(b) The entrepreneur may obtain all kinds of "psychic income" from the firm, quite apart from monetary rewards. If he is to maximize his utility, then he will sometimes balance a loss of profits against an increase in psychic income. But if we allow "psychic income," the criterion of profit maximization loses all of its definiteness.

(c) The entrepreneur may not care to maximize, but may simply want to earn a return that he regards as satisfactory. By sophistry and adept use of the concept of psychic income, the notion of seeking a satisfactory return can be translated into utility maximizing but not in any operational way. We shall see in a moment that "satisfactory profits" is a concept more meaningfully related to the psychological notion of aspiration levels than to maximization.

(d) It is often observed that under modern conditions the equity owners and the active managers of an enterprise are separate and distinct groups of people, so that the latter may not be motivated to maximize profits.

(e) Where there is imperfect competition among firms, maximizing is an ambiguous goal, for what action is optimal for one firm depends on the actions of the other firms.

In the present section we shall deal only with the third of these five issues. The fifth will be treated in the following section; the first, second, and fourth are purely empirical questions that have been discussed at length in the literature; they will be considered here only for their bearing on the question of satisfactory profits.

SATISFICING VERSUS MAXIMIZING

The notion of satiation plays no role in classical economic theory, while it enters rather prominently into the treatment of motivation in psychology. In most psychological theories the motive to act stems from *drives*, and action terminates when the drive is satisfied. Moreover, the conditions for satisfying a drive are not necessarily fixed, but may be specified by an aspiration level that itself adjusts upward or downward on the basis of experience.

If we seek to explain behavior in the terms of this theory, we must expect the firm's goals to be not maximizing profits, but attaining a certain level or rate of profit, holding a certain share of the market or a certain level of sales. Firms would try to "satisfice" rather than to maximize.

It has sometimes been argued that the distinction between satisficing and maximizing is not important to economic theory. For in the first place, the psychological evidence on individual behavior shows that aspirations tend to adjust to the attainable. Hence in the long run, the argument goes, the level of aspiration and the attainable maximum will be very close together. Second, even if some firms satificed, they would gradually lose out to the maximizing firms, which would make larger profits and grow more rapidly than the others.

However, the economic environment of the firm is complex, and it changes rapidly; there is no *a priori* reason to assume the attainment of long-run equilibrium. Indeed, the empirical evidence on the distribution of firms by size suggests that the observed regularities in size distribution stem from the statistical equilibrium of a population of adaptive systems rather than the static equilibrium of a population of maximizers.

Models of satisficing behavior are richer than models of maximizing behavior, because they treat not only of equilibrium but of the method of reaching it as well. Psychological studies of the formation and change of aspiration levels support propositions of the following kinds:

(a) When performance falls short of the level of aspiration, search behavior (particularly search for new alternatives of action) is induced.

(b) At the same time, the level of aspiration begins to adjust itself downward until goals reach levels that are practically attainable.

(c) If the two mechanisms just listed operate too slowly to adapt aspirations to performance, emotional behavior—apathy or aggression, for example—will replace rational adaptive behavior.

The aspiration level defines a natural zero point in the scale of utility—whereas in most classical theories the zero point is arbitrary. When the firm has alternatives open to it that are at or above its aspiration level, the theory predicts that it will choose the best of those known to be available. When none of the available alternatives satisfies current aspirations, the theory predicts qualitatively different behavior: in the short run, search behavior and the revision of targets; in the longer run, what we have called above emotional behavior, and what the psychologist would be inclined to call neurosis.

STUDIES OF BUSINESS BEHAVIOR

There is some empirical evidence that business goals are, in fact, stated in satisficing terms. First, there is the series of studies stemming from the pioneering work of Hall and Hitch that indicates that businessmen often set prices by applying a standard markup to costs. Some economists have sought to refute this fact, others to reconcile it—if it is a fact—with marginalist principles. The study of Earley belongs to the former category, but its evidence is suspect because the questions asked of businessmen are leading ones—no one likes to admit that he would accept less profit if he could have more. Earley did not ask his respondents how they determined marginal costs and marginal revenue, how, for example, they estimated demand elasticities.

Another series of studies derived from the debate over the Keynesian doctrine that the amount of investment was insensitive to changes in the rate of interest. The general finding in these studies has been that the rate of interest is not an important factor in investment decisions.

More recently, Cyert and March have attempted to test the satisficing model in a more direct way. They found in one industry some evidence that firms with a declining share of market strove more vigorously to increase their sales than firms whose shares of the market were steady or increasing. . . .

ECONOMIC IMPLICATIONS

It has sometimes been argued that, however unrealistic the classical theory of the firm as a profit maximizer, it is an adequate theory for purposes of normative macroeconomics. Mason, for example, in commenting on Papandreou's essay on "Problems in the Theory of the Firm" says, "The writer of this critique must confess a lack of confidence in the marked superiority, *for purposes of economic analysis,* of this newer concept of the firm over the older conception of the entrepreneur." The italics are Mason's.

The theory of the firm is important for welfare economics—e.g., for determining under what circumstances the behavior of the firm will lead to efficient allocation of resources. The satisficing model vitiates all the conclusions about resource allocation that are derivable from the maximizing model when perfect competition is assumed. Similarly, a dynamic theory of firm sizes has quite different implications for public policies dealing with concentration than a theory that assumes firms to be in static equilibrium. Hence, welfare economists are justified in adhering to the classical theory only if: (a) the theory is empirically correct as a description of the decision-making process; or (b) it is safe to assume that the system operates in the neighborhood of the static equilibrium. What evidence we have mostly contradicts both assumptions.

Conflict of Interest

Leaving aside the problem of the motivations of hired managers, conflict of interest among economic actors creates no difficulty for classical economic theory—indeed, it lies at the very core of the theory—so long as each actor treats the other actors as parts of his "given" environment, and doesn't try to predict their behavior and anticipate it. But when this restriction is removed, when it is assumed that a seller takes into account the reactions of buyers to his actions, or that each manufacturer predicts the behaviors of his competitors—all the familiar difficulties of imperfect competition and oligopoly arise.

The very assumptions of omniscient rationality that provide the basis for deductive prediction in economics when competition is present lead to ambiguity when they are applied to competition among the few. The central difficulty is that rationality requires one to outguess one's opponents, but not to be outguessed by them, and this is clearly not a consistent requirement if applied to the actors.

GAME THEORY

Modern game theory is a vigorous and extensive exploration of ways of extending the concept of rational behavior to situations involving struggle, outguessing, and bargaining. Since Luce and Raiffa have recently provided us with an excellent survey and evaluation of game theory, I shall not cover the same ground here. I concur in their general evaluation that, while game theory has greatly clarified the issues involved, it has not provided satisfactory solutions. Not only does it leave the definition of rational conduct ambiguous in all cases save the zero-sum two-person game, but it requires of economic man even more fantastic reasoning powers than does classical economic theory.

POWER AND BARGAINING

A number of exploratory proposals have been put forth as alternatives to game theory—among them Galbraith's notion of countervailing power and Schelling's bargaining theory. These analyses draw at least as heavily upon theories of power and bargaining developed initially to explain political phenomena as upon economic theory. They do not lead to any more specific predictions of behavior than do game-theoretic approaches, but place a greater emphasis upon description and actual observation, and are modest in their attempt to derive predictions by deductive reasoning from a few "plausible" premises about human behavior.

At least four important areas of social science and social policy, two of them in economics and two more closely related to political science, have as their central concern the phenomena of power and the processes of bargaining: the theory of political parties, labor-management relations, international politics, and oligopoly theory. Any progress in the basic theory applicable to one of these is certain to be of almost equal importance to the others....

The Formation of Expectations

While the future cannot enter into the determination of the present, expectations about the future can and do. In trying to gain an understanding of the saving, spending, and investment behavior of both consumers and firms, and to make short-term predictions of this behavior for purposes of policy-making, economists have done substantial empirical work as well as theorizing on the formation of expectations.

EMPIRICAL STUDIES

A considerable body of data has been accumulated on consumer's plans and expectations from the Survey of Consumer Finances, conducted for the Board of Governors of the Federal Reserve System by the Survey Research Center of the University of Michigan. These data, and similar data obtained by others, begin to give us some information on the expectations of consumers about their own incomes, and the predictive value of their expenditure plans for their actual subsequent behavior. Some large-scale attempts have been made, notably by Modigliani and Brumberg and, a little later, by Friedman to relate these empirical findings to classical utility theory. The current empirical research on business men's expectations is of two main kinds:

1. Surveys of businessmen's own forecasts of business and business conditions in the economy and in their own industries. These are obtained by straightforward questionnaire methods that assume, implicity, that businessmen can and do make such forecasts. In some uses to which the data are put, it is also assumed that the forecasts are used as one basis for businessmen's actions.

2. Studies of business decisions and the role of expectations in these decisions—particularly investment and pricing decisions. We have already referred to studies of business decisions in our discussion of the goals of the firm.

EXPECTATIONS AND PROBABILITY

The classical way to incorporate expectations into economic theory is to assume that the decision-maker estimates the joint probability distribution of future events. He can then act so as to maximize the expected value of utility or profit, as the case may be. However satisfying this approach may be conceptually, it poses awkward problems when we ask how the decision-maker actually estimates the parameters of the joint probability distribution. Common sense tells us that people don't make such estimates, nor can we find evidence that they do by examining actual business forecasting methods. The surveys of businessmen's expectations have never attempted to secure such estimates, but have contented themselves with asking for point predictions—which, at best, might be interpreted as predictions of the means of the distributions.

It has been shown that under certain special circumstances the mean of the probability distribution is the only parameter that is relevant for decision—that even if the variance and higher moments were known to the rational decision-maker, he would have no use for them. In these cases, the arithmetic mean is actually a certainty equivalent, the optimal decision turns out to be the same as if the future were known with certainty. But the situations where the mean is a certainty equivalent are, as we have said, very special ones, and there is no indication that businessmen ever ask whether the necessary conditions for this equivalence are actually met in practice. They somehow make forecasts in the form of point predictions and act upon them in one way or another.

The "somehow" poses questions that are important for business cycle theory, and perhaps for other problems in economics. The way in which expectations are formed may affect the dynamic stability of the economy, and the extent to which cycles will be amplified or damped. Some light, both empirical and theoretical, has recently been cast on these questions. On the empirical side, attempts have been made: (a) to compare businessmen's forecasts with various "naïve" models that assume the future will be some simple function of the recent past, and (b) to use such naïve models themselves as forecasting devices.

The simplest naïve model is one that assumes the next period will be exactly like the present. Another assumes that the change from present to next period will equal the change from last period to present; a third, somewhat more general, assumes that the next period will be a weighted average of recent past periods. The term "naïve model" has been applied loosely to various forecasting formulas of these general kinds. There is some affirmative evidence that business forecasts fit such models. There is also evidence that elaboration of the models beyond the first few steps of refinement does not much improve prediction. Arrow and his colleagues have explored some of the conditions under which forecasting formulas will, and will not, introduce dynamic instability into an economic system that is otherwise stable. They have shown, for example, that if a system of multiple markets is stable under static expectations, it is stable when expectations are based on a moving average of past values.

The work on the formation of expectations represents a significant extension of classical theory. For, instead of taking the environment as a "given," known to the economic decision-maker, it incorporates in the theory the processes of acquiring knowledge about that environment. In doing so, it forces us to include in our model of economic man some of his properties as a learning, estimating, searching, information-processing organism.

THE COST OF INFORMATION

There is one way in which the formation of expectations might be reincorporated in the body of economic theory: by treating information-gathering as one of the processes of production, so to speak, and applying to it the usual rules of marginal analysis. Information, says price theory, should be gathered up to the point where the incremental cost of additional information is equal to the incremental profit that can be earned by having it. Such an approach can lead to propositions about optimal amounts of information-gathering activity and about the relative merits of alternative information-gathering and estimating schemes.

This line of investigation has, in fact, been followed in statistical decision theory. In sampling theory we are concerned with the optimal size of sample (and in the special and ingenious case of sequential sampling theory, with knowing when to stop sampling), and we wish to evaluate the efficiencies of alternative sampling procedures. The latter problem is the simpler, since it is possible to compare the relative costs of alternative schemes that have the same sampling error, and hence to avoid estimating the value of the information. However, some progress has been made also toward estimating the value of improved forecast accuracy in situations where the forecasts are to be used in applying formal decision rules to choice situations.

The theory of teams developed by Marschak and Radner is concerned with the same problem. It considers situations involving decentralized and interdependent decision-making by two or more persons who share a common goal and who, at a cost, can transmit information to each other about their own actions or about the parts of the environment with which they are in contact. The problem then is to discover the optimal communication strategy under specified assumptions about communication costs and payoffs.

The cost of communication in the theory of teams, like the cost of observations in sampling theory, is a parameter that characterizes the economic actor, or the relation of the actor to his environment. Hence, while these theories retain, in one sense, a classical picture of economic man as a maximizer, they clearly require considerable information about the characteristics of the actor, and not merely about his environment. They take a long stride toward bridging the gap between the traditional concerns of economics and the concerns of psychology. . . .

Human Cognition and Economics

The developments we have examined have a common theme: they all involve important modifications in the concept of economic man and, for the reasons we have stated, modifications in the direction of providing a fuller description of his characteristics. The classical theory is a theory of a man choosing among fixed and known alternatives, to each of which is attached known consequences. But when perception and cognition intervene between the decision-maker and his objective environment, this model no longer proves adequate. We need a description of the choice process that recognizes that alternatives are not given but must be sought; and a description that takes into account the arduous task of determining what consequences will follow on each alternative.

The decision-maker's information about his environment is much less than an approximation to the real environment. The term "approximation" implies that the subjective world of the decision-maker resembles the external environment closely, but lacks, perhaps, some fineness of detail. In actual fact the perceived world is fantastically different from the "real" world. The differences involve both omissions and distortions, and arise in both perception and inference. The sins of omission in perception are more important than the sins of commission. The decision-maker's model of the world encompasses only a minute fraction of all the relevant characteristics of the real environment, and his inferences extract only a minute fraction of all the information that is present even in his model.

Perception is sometimes referred to as a "filter." This term is as misleading as "approximation," and for the same reason: it implies that what comes through into the central nervous system is really quite a bit like what is "out there." In fact, the filtering is not merely a passive selection of some part of a presented whole, but an active process involving attention to a very small part of the whole and exclusion, from the outset, of almost all that is not within the scope of attention.

Every human organism lives in an environment that generates millions of bits of new information each second, but the bottle neck of the perceptual apparatus certainly does not admit more than 1,000 bits per second, and probably much less. Equally significant omissions occur in the processing that takes place when information reaches the brain. As every mathematician knows, it is one thing to have a set of differential equations, and another thing to have their solutions. Yet the solutions are logically implied by the equations—they are "all there," if we only knew how to get to them! By the same token, there are hosts of inferences that *might* be drawn from the information stored in the brain that are not in fact drawn. The consequences implied by information in the memory become known only through active information-processing, and hence through active selection of particular problem-solving paths from the myriad that might have been followed.

In this section we shall examine some theories of decision-making that take the limitations of the decision-maker and the complexity of the environment as central concerns. These theories incorporate some mechanisms we have already discussed—for example, aspiration levels and forecasting processes—but go beyond them in providing a detailed picture of the choice process.

A real-life decision involves some goals or values, some facts about the environment, and some inferences drawn from the values and facts. The goals and values may be simple or complex, consistent or contradictory; the facts may be real or supposed, based on observation or the reports of others; the inferences may be valid or spurious. The whole process may be viewed, metaphorically, as a process of "reasoning," where the values and facts serve as premises, and the decision that is finally reached is inferred from these premises. The resemblance of decision-making to logical reasoning is only metaphorical, because there are quite different rules in the two cases to determine what constitute "valid" premises and admissible modes of inference. The metaphor is useful because it leads us to take the individual *decision premise* as the unit of description, hence to deal with the whole interwoven fabric of influences that bear on a single decision—but without being bound by the assumptions of rationality that limit the classical theory of choice.

RATIONAL BEHAVIOR AND ROLE THEORY

We can find common ground to relate the economist's theory of decision-making with that of the social psychologist. The latter is particularly interested, of course, in social influences on choice, which determine the *role* of the actor. In our present terms, a role is a social prescription of some, but not all, of the premises that enter into an individual's choices of behavior. Any particular concrete behavior is the resultant of a large number of premises, only some of which are prescribed by the role. In addition to role premises there will be premises about the state of the environment based directly on perception, premises representing beliefs and knowledge, and idiosyncratic premises that characterize the personality. Within this framework we can accommodate both the rational elements in choice, so much emphasized by economics, and the nonrational elements to which psychologists and sociologists often prefer to call attention.

DECISION PREMISES AND COMPUTER PROGRAMS

The analysis of choice in terms of decision premises gives us a conceptual framework for describing and explaining the process of deciding. But so complex is the process that our explanations of it would have remained schematic and hypothetical for a long time to come had not the modern digital computer appeared on the scene. The notion of decision premise can be translated into computer terminology, and when this translation has been accomplished, the digital computer provides us with an instrument for simulating human decision processes—even very complex ones—and hence for testing empirically our explanations of those processes.

A fanciful (but only slightly fanciful) example will illustrate how this might be done. Some actual examples will be cited presently. Suppose we were to construct a robot incorporating a modern digital computer, and to program (i.e., to instruct) the robot to take the role of a business executive in a specified company. What would the program look like? Since no one has yet done this, we cannot say with certainty, but several points are fairly clear. The program would not consist of a list of prescribed and proscribed behaviors, since what an executive does is highly contingent on information about a wide variety of circumstances. Instead, the program would consist of a large number of *criteria* to be applied to possible and proposed courses of action, of routines for *generating* possible courses of action, of computational procedures for *assessing* the state of the environment and its implications for action, and the like. Hence, the program—in fact, a role prescription—would interact with information to produce concrete behavior adapted to the situation. The elements of such a program take the form of what we have called decision premises, and what the computer specialists would call instructions.

The promise of constructing actual detailed descriptions of concrete roles and decision processes is no longer, with the computer, a mere prospectus to be realized at some undefined future date. We can already provide actual examples, some of them in the area of economics.

1. *Management Science.* We have already referred to the use of such mathematical techniques as linear programming and dynamic programming to construct formal decision processes for actual situations. The relevance of these decision models to the present discussion is that they are not merely abstract "theories" of the firm, but actual decision-making devices. We can think of any such device as a simulation of the corresponding human decision-maker, in which the equations and other assumptions that enter into the formal decision-making procedure correspond to the decision premises—including the role prescription—of the decision-maker.

The actual application of such models to concrete business situations brings to light the information-processing tasks that are concealed in the assumptions of the more abstract classical models:

(a) The models must be formulated so as to require for their application only data that are obtainable. If one of the penalties, for example, of holding too small inventories is the loss of sales, a decision model that proposes to determine optimal inventory levels must incorporate a procedure for putting a dollar value on this loss.

(b) The models must call only for practicable computations. For example, several proposals for applying linear programming to certain factory scheduling problems have been shown to be impracticable because, even with computers, the computation time is too great. The task of decision theory (whether normative or descriptive) is to find alternative techniques—probably only approximate—that demand much less computation.

(c) The models must not demand unobtainable forecast information. A procedure that would require a sales department to estimate the third moment of next month's sales distribution would not have wide application, as either description or prescription, to business decision-making.

These models, then, provide us with concrete examples of roles for a decision-maker described in terms of the premises he is is expected to apply to the decision—the data and the rules of computation.

2. *Engineering Design.* Computers have been used for some years to carry out some of the analytic computations required in engineering design—computing the stresses, for example, in a proposed bridge design. Within the past two years, ways have been found to program computers to carry out synthesis as well as analysis—to evolve the design itself. A number of companies in the electrical industry now use computers to design electric motors, transformers, and generators, going from customer specifications to factory design without human intervention. The significance of this for our purpose here is that the synthesis programs appear to simulate rather closely the processes that had previously been used by college-trained engineers in the same design work. It has proved possible to write down the engineers' decision premises and inference processes in sufficient detail to produce workable computer programs.

3. *Human Problem Solving.* The management science and engineering design programs already provide examples of simulation of human deci-

sion-making by computer. It may be thought that, since in both instances the processes are highly arithmetical, these examples are relevant to only a very narrow range of human problem-solving activity. We generally think of a digital computer as a device which, if instructed in painful detail by its operator, can be induced to perform rather complicated and tedious arithmetical operations. More recent developments require us to revise these conceptions of the computer, for they enable it to carry out tasks that, if performed by humans, we would certainly call "thinking" and "learning."

Discovering the proof of a theorem of Euclid—a task we all remember from our high school geometry course—requires thinking and usually insight and imagination. A computer is now being programmed to perform this task (in a manner closely simulating the human geometer), and another computer has been successfully performing a highly similar task in symbolic logic for the past two years. The latter computer is programmed to learn—that is to improve its performance on the basis of successful problem-solving experience–to use something akin to imagery or metaphor in planning its proofs, and to transfer some of its skills to other tasks—for example, solving trigonometric identities—involving completely distinct subject matter. These programs, it should be observed, do not involve the computer in rapid arithmetic—or any arithmetic for that matter. They are basically non-numerical, involving the manipulation of all kinds of symbolic material, including words.

Still other computer programs have been written to enable a computer to play chess. Not all of these programs, or those previously mentioned, are close simulations of the processes humans use. However, in some direct attempts to investigate the human processes by thinking-aloud techniques and to reproduce in computer programs the processes observed in human subjects, several striking simulations have been achieved. These experiments have been described elsewhere and can't be reviewed here in detail.

4. *Business Games.*   Business games, like those developed by the American Management Association, International Business Machines Corporation, and several universities, represent a parallel development. In the business game, the decisions of the business firms are still made by the human players, but the economic environment of these first, including their markets, are represented by computer programs that calculate the environment's responses to the actions of the players. As the games develop in detail and realism, their programs will represent more and more concrete descriptions of the decision processes of various economic actors—for example, consumers.

The games that have been developed so far are restricted to numerical magnitudes like prices and quantitites of goods, and hence resemble the management science and engineering design programs more closely than they do those we have described under the heading of human problem solving. There is no reason, however, to expect this restriction to remain very long.

IMPLICATIONS FOR ECONOMICS

Apart from normative applications (e.g., substituting computers for humans in certain decision-making tasks) we are not interested so much in the detailed descriptions of roles as in broader questions:

(a) What general characteristics do the roles of economic actors have?

(b) How do roles come to be structured in the particular ways they do?

(c) What bearing does this version of role theory have for macroeconomics and other large-scale social phenomena?

Characterizing Role Structure. Here we are concerned with generalizations about thought processes, particularly those generalizations that are relatively independent of the substantive content of the role. A classical example is Dewey's description of stages in the problem-solving process. Another example, of particular interest to economics, is the hypothesis we have already discussed at length: that economic man is a *satisficing* animal whose problem solving is based on search activity to meet certain aspiration levels rather than a *maximizing* animal whose problem solving involves finding the best alternatives in terms of specified criteria. A third hypothesis is that operative goals (those associated with an observable criterion of success, and relatively definite means of attainment) play a much larger part in governing choice than nonoperative goals (those lacking a concrete measure of success or a program for attainment).

Understanding How Roles Emerge. Within almost any single business firm, certain characteristic types of roles will be represented: selling roles, production roles, accounting roles, and so on. Partly, this consistency may be explained in functional terms—that a model that views the firm as producing a product, selling it, and accounting for its assets and liabilities is an effective simplification of the real world, and provides the members of the organization with a workable frame of reference. Imitation within the culture provides an alternative explanation. It is exceedingly difficult to test hypotheses as to the origins and causal conditions for roles as universal in the society as these, but the underlying mechanisms could probably be explored effectively by the study of less common roles—safety director, quality control inspector, or the like—that are to be found in some firms, but not in all.

With our present definition of role, we can also speak meaningfully of the role of an entire business firm—of decision premises that underlie its basic policies. In a particular industry we find some firms that specialize in adapting the product to individual customers' specifications; others that specialize in product innovation. The common interest of economics and psychology includes not only the study of individual roles, but also the explanation of organizational roles of these sorts.

Tracing the Implications for Macroeconomics. If basic professional goals remain as they are, the interest of the psychologist and the economist in role theory will stem from somewhat different ultimate aims. The former will use various economic and organizational phenomena as data for the study of the structure and determinants of roles: the latter will be primarily interested in the implications of role theory for the model of economic man, and indirectly, for macroeconomics.

The first applications will be to those topics in economics where the assumption of static equilibrium is least tenable. Innovation, technological change, and economic development are examples of areas to which a good empirically tested theory of the processes of human adaptation and problem solving could make a major contribution. For instance, we know very little at present about how the rate of innovation depends on the amounts of resources allocated to various kinds of research and development activity. Nor do we understand very well the nature of "know how," the costs of transferring technology from one firm or economy to another, or the effects of various kinds and amounts of education upon national product. These are difficult questions to answer from aggregative data and gross observation, with the result that our views have been formed more by arm-chair theorizing than by testing hypotheses with solid facts.

Theories of the Firm: Marginalist, Behavioral, Managerial

FRITZ MACHLUP

Fritz Machlup is Adjunct Professor of Economics at New York University. This article, part of his Presidential Address to the American Economic Association, appeared in the American Economic Review *in 1967.*

Last year, when it was my task to plan the program for the annual meeting of the American Economic Association, a friend suggested that, with twenty years having passed since the outbreak of the "marginalism controversy," it was appropriate to review what has since happened to the embattled theory of the firm. The topic did not fit the general theme I had chosen for the 1965 meeting, but I reasoned that 1966 would give me a good opportunity to undertake the review myself.

The Battlefield Revisited

So let us recall that literary feud and the warriors, and let us revisit the battlefield. The major battlefield was the *American Economic Review,* with six articles and communications between March 1946 and March 1947. There had been earlier gunfire elsewhere, chiefly in the *Oxford Economic Papers* in 1939. But, since the shooting then was not returned and it takes at least two opponents to join battle, it must be agreed that the real hostilities were the exchanges in the *AER.*

The fight was spirited, even fierce. Thousands of students of economics, voluntary or involuntary readers, have been either shocked or entertained by the violence of some of the blows exchanged and may have thought that the opponents must have become mortal enemies forever. These readers would have been wrong. Even before we came out for the last round of the fight, we exchanged friendly letters (December 1946) assuring each other that we would bear no grudges.

We have remained the best of friends; for several years now Richard Lester and I have been colleagues in the same department; and, as a token of our friendship, he has generously accepted my invitation to share this platform with me today as chairman of the session. Thus the veterans of both sides of the War of 1946 are now joined in revisiting the battlefield. This, incidentally, does not mean that either of us has succeeded in converting the other to the "true faith."

What was the outcome of the controversy? Who won? We could not possibly say if we have not first agreed on precisely what the shooting was about. I have heard it said that Machlup won the battle but Lester won the war. What this means, however, cannot be known unless we know what the issues and objectives of the war had been. Was it merely to make economics safe for or from marginalism? Were there not several other issues being fought over?

Some of the Major Issues

There were no doubt a good many contentions of all sorts—major, minor, essential, incidental, interpretative, factual, methodological, substantive, and all the rest. To present a complete catalogue of the issues involved would be too ambitious a task for this occasion, but a partial listing might be helpful.

The chief issue, of course, was whether marginal analysis was invalid and ought to be discarded, especially as far as the theory of prices, cost, wages, and employment in manufacturing industry is concerned. This issue, however, implied the question of the correct interpretation of marginal analysis, including the tenets of the marginal-productivity principle. In this connection, differences in the models of the firm customarily used in different kinds of analysis became relevant. Involved here was the question of whether the postulate of maximizing money profits led to conclusions very different from those derivable from assumptions of conduct guided by a variety of largely nonpecuniary considerations.

Underlying all these questions were some issues of general scientific methodology; the legitimacy and usefulness of abstract theorizing on the basis of unrealistic assumptions, or perhaps on the basis of assumptions regarded as "reasonable" though not "universally true." These issues, in particular, were whether an assumption of profit maximization as the effective objective of the firm in the theoretical model may be accepted as a tenable hypothesis only if it can be verified that all or a majority of those who actually run business firms in the real world agree that this is their only or major objective, that they are capable of obtaining all the information and of performing all the calculations needed for the realization of that objective, and are really carrying out the actions found to be optimal in this fashion; or, alternatively, whether all these tests may be dispensed with and the assumption of profit maximization nevertheless accepted as a fruitful postulate from which conclusions can be derived which correspond with what can be observed in the records of prices and quantities.

Concerning the empirical testing of theoretical conclusions, there were issues of the validity of surveys through mailed questionnaires and of the proper interpretation of responses to various types of questions about managerial judgment. In the background of the whole controversy, but undoubtedly of pervasive significance, was the comparative acceptability of empirical findings to the effect that the elasticity of demand for labor was virtually zero and of the conventional theoretical inference that the elasticity was normally above zero.

Realizing how manifold were the issues of the controversy, one can appreciate that no clear decision can be made about its outcome. Some of the issues had been raised decades or centuries before 1946 and were not decided in this confrontation one way or the other. Attacks on the assumption of maximizing behavior and on the lack of realism in price theory have occurred with great regularity ever since "economic man" and similar postulates were introduced. The running battles between the classical and the historical schools were largely on these points. The *Methodenstreit* of 1883–84 dealt essentially with the same issues. And in the United States, institutionalism may be seen as a movement animated by the same spirit of protest against abstract theory.

However, the particular form of explicit marginalism (under the name of "theory of the firm") which became the target of the attacks of 1939 and 1946 had only come into being in the 1930's—if one suppresses the memory of the great master of 1838. Ironically, some interpreter of recent history of economic thought—I have forgotten who it was—regarded the 1933–34 versions of the theory of the firm as the theorists' concession to institutionalism, as attempts to supplement the neoclassical model of the firm under atomistic competition with some "more realistic" models allowing for a greater variety of conditions. It was this theory of the profit-maximizing firm in all sorts of market positions, in monopolistic and oligopolistic competition as well as in pure and perfect competition, that was attacked by the researchers in Oxford; and it was the marginal-productivity principle in the explanation of the demand for labor on the part of the individual firm that was the prime target of the attack of 1946.

If the chief aim of the attack was to force the abandonment or subversion of marginalism, and if the chief aim of the defense was to turn back the subversive forces and secure the reign of marginalism once and for all, then, to be sure, the war of 1946 ended in a draw. Look at the textbooks and you will find that marginalism has continued to dominate the teaching of microeconomics, perhaps though with occasional reservations and references to current attempts at greater realism. But look at the journals and monographs and you find that research on alternative approaches to the theory of the firm is regularly reported with the implication that a superior theory may eventually replace marginalism. This replacement, however, according to the proponents of the best-known alternatives to marginalism, is expected chiefly with regard to industries where firms are few and competition is ineffective. The marginalist solution of price determination under conditions of heavy competition is not seriously contested.

In pointing this out, I am not trying to claim that marginal analysis is invincible and forever irreplaceable. If I follow the philosophy of science which, instead of pronouncing theories "false" or "true," distinguishes only between those "rejected" and those "still open to criticism," the only victory that can be claimed for the cause of marginalism is that it is still open to criticism. I must go beyond this and concede that some anti-marginalist suggestions have led in recent years to a number of revisions in the marginal analysis of the firm which amount to the incorporation of other goals besides money profits into expanded marginalist objective functions.

The Alternative Approaches

In their arguments against the profit-maximization model the various alternative approaches to the theory of the firm are very much alike; only their positive programs can distinguish them.

The program of behaviorism is to reject preconceptions and assumptions and to rely only on observation of overt behavior. Thus, behaviorism rejects the assumption of marginal analysis that economic action is directed by the objective to maximize the attainment of ends with given means, and that business action can be deduced from a postulate that firms attempt to maximize money profits. Instead, we are directed to *observe* how businessmen really act and by what processes they reach decisions.

Perhaps it is not entirely fair to suggest here an association between "behaviorism" and the working program of the proponents of a "behavioral theory of the firm." In any case, behavioral research proposes to observe and study the "real processes," in the sense of a "well-defined sequence of behaviors" by which decisions are reached in "actual business organizations." The hope—faithfully inductive—is to develop a theory "with generality beyond the specific firms studied." Such a theory will be based on "four major sub-theories" regarding "organizational *goals*, organizational *expectations*, organizational *choice*, and organizational *control*." It is assumed that five organizational goals—a production goal, an inventory goal, a sales goal, a market-share goal, and the profit goal—become the subject of bargaining among the various members of the "coalition" which make up the business organization but that the goals are continually adapted and are being pressed with varying force. The behavior theory of the firm, with regard to the determination of prices and outputs, will run in terms of a "quasi resolution of conflict" within the organization, of an "adaptively rational, multiple-objective process" with responses to "short-run feedback on performance" and with continuing "organizational learning."

This behavioral approach has been characterized as striving for "realism in process," in contrast to approaches aiming at more "realism in motivation." Such realism in motivation is felt to be needed chiefly because of the separation of ownership and control in the modern corporation, whose managements have great power and wide discretion.

In principle, I could expect three different views to be taken regarding the relative independence of corporation management: (1) Whereas owners would run their business chiefly with a view to a maximum of money profits, managers run it with several supplementary and partly competing goals in mind. (2) Whereas owners, especially wealthy ones, would often allow nonprofit considerations to enter their decision-making, managers have a sense of dedication and identification with the business that makes them the more single-minded seekers of profits. (3) Even if managers are inclined to indulge in seeking other goals as long as profits look satisfactory, they are as professionals, trained in the art and science of management, able to make better profits than the owners could ever hope to make running their own show.

What consequences can be drawn from this? One attitude would be to stick with the assumption of profit maximization because it is the simplest and is applicable with much less detailed information to the largest field. Another attitude would be to insist on starkest realism with a complete catalogue of goals and indices of their effectiveness in each firm. A third attitude would be to select two or three of the most important managerial objectives of a type that can be reduced to quantitative analysis and to combine them in a single manageable "objective function." This third approach merges marginalism with managerialism in that it integrates money profits with other managerial goals within one formula of "maximizing behavior."

The question is whether managerial marginalism is prescribed for general application or only for so-called noncompetitive cases. Its most prominent proponents prefer to use the old formula, based on profit maximization, in situations where competition is effective and managerial discretion therefore narrowly circumscribed. In the next sections we shall discuss matters that at first blush may seem unrelated to this issue but on reflection can shed indirect light on it.

The Analogy of the Theoretical Automobile Driver

One of the best remembered points in my exposition was the use of an analogy designed to warn against mistaking theoretical variables and their links for realistic descriptions of observable processes. This was the analogy of the "theory of overtaking" automobiles on the highways.

Analogies are often misleading, but in this particular case it served its main purpose: to show that the theoretical variables need not be estimated and the theoretical equations need not be solved through actual calculation by the actors in the real world whose idealized types are supposed to perform these difficult operations in the models constructed for the explanation of recorded observations.[1] The critics of marginal analysis believed they had refuted it if they could show that the exact numerical calculations of marginal magnitudes—cost, revenue, productivity—were difficult or impossible to perform by real decision-makers.

Yet, my analogy was only partially successful. An implication which should have been obvious has been widely overlooked: that the type of action assumed to be taken by the theoretical actor in the model under specified conditions need not be expected and cannot be predicted actually to be taken by any particular real actor. The empiricist's inclination is to verify the theoretically deduced action by testing individual behavior, although the theory serves only to explain and predict effects of mass behavior.

We may illustrate this again by means of the same analogy, the theory of overtaking. Assume a change of driving conditions occurs, say, that the roads have become wet and slippery and fog has reduced visibility. Theory enables us to predict that traffic will be slower and accidents more frequent, but it does not enable us to predict that any particular driver will drive more slowly or have an accident. The model of the reactions of the individual driver was not designed to explain the actual driving of any particular operator but only to explain the observable consequences of the observed change of conditions by deducing from the model the theoretical reactions of a hypothetical driver.

Our analogy can also show us the limitations of the model: the prediction will hold only if there is a large number of automobiles on the road. If only a very few cars are around, there may be no accident and there need not be a reduction in their speed. Conceivably, the operators may all be good and self-confident drivers. Marginal analysis of hypothetical driver reaction will suffice for explaining and predicting the consequences of a change in driving conditions if the number of automobiles on the high-

[1] The theoretical automobile driver had to estimate, among other things, the speeds of three vehicles and the distances between them, and to perform calculations involving potential acceleration and a few other things, before he could decide to overtake the truck ahead of him. An actual driver simply "sizes up" the situation and goes ahead.

ways is large. If the number is small, behavioral research will be needed, though it may or may not be worth the cost.

Still another use can be made of our analogy: to show the vast differences in the scope of questions to which answers can be or cannot be expected with the aid of a given theory, for example, from the theory of overtaking as sketched in my article. Compare the following four questions: (1) How fast will traffic move? (2) How fast will the automobile driven by Mr. X move? (3) How will the speed of traffic be affected by fog? (4) How will the speed of Mr. X's driving be affected by fog?

The theory sketched by me offers no answer to the first question, because each of the variables specified may have very different values for different cars and drivers; it has no answer to the second question, and only a suggestion, a rebuttable presumption, for answering the fourth question, because the theory is not really concerned with particular persons or their actions and reactions. The theory is equipped only to answer the third question, regarding the effects of a change in driving conditions on automobile traffic in general, and even this answer will be qualitative only, without good clues to numerical results. It may be interesting to get answers to all four questions, but since Question 3 can be answered with a fraction of the information that would be needed to answer the other questions, it would be foolish to burden the models designed for Question 3 with irrelevant matters, or to reject such models because they cannot do what they are not designed to do.

Confusion of Purposes

The same sort of confusion about the scope of problems and models for their solution has been fostered in recent writings on the theory of the firm: models have been condemned or rejected because they could not be used for purposes for which they had not been designed, and significant differences in the questions to be answered have been obscured or underemphasized.

Let us again pose four typical questions and see which of them we might expect to answer with the aid of "price theory." (1) What will be the prices of cotton textiles? (2) What prices will the X Corporation charge? (3) How will the price of cotton textiles be affected by an increase in wage rates? (4) How will the X Corporation change its prices when wage rates are increased?

Conventional price theory is not equipped to answer any but the third question; it may perhaps also suggest a rebuttable answer to the fourth question. But Questions 1 and 2 are out of reach. We could not obtain all the information that would be required for their answers and there is, therefore, no use burdening the models with variables remaining silent and inactive throughout the show.

We ought to guard against an easy misunderstanding of our denial that conventional price theory can predict actual prices of specified goods. Prediction of future prices of a particular commodity may in fact be quite manageable if we know its present price. It should be obvious, however, that this is Question 3, not Question 1. Or, one may be able to predict prices on the basis of good information on production cost. But this presupposes that we know the demand for the commodity and assume it will remain unchanged; which again comes down essentially to evaluations of changes of some variables with others held constant, that is, to Question 3.

If the number of firms producing cotton textiles is large and the X Corporation does not supply a very large part of the aggregate output of the industry, price theory may suggest an answer to Question 4, although this is not the purpose of the theory and there may be a considerable chance for the suggested answer to be wrong. The point is that a model of a theoretical firm in an industry consisting of a large number of firms can do with a much smaller number of assumptions, provided the model is used to predict, not the actual reactions of any one particular firm, but only the effects of the hypothetical reactions of numerous anonymous "reactors" (symbolic firms). If it were to be applied to predictions of reactions of a particular firm, the model would have to be much more richly endowed with variables and functions for which information could be obtained only at considerable effort and with results that may or may not be worth the cost of the required research.

My charge that there is widespread confusion regarding the purposes of the "theory of the firm" as used in traditional price theory refers to this: The model of the firm in that theory is not, as so many writers believe, designed to serve to explain and predict the behavior of real firms; instead, it is designed to explain and predict changes in observed prices (quoted, paid, received) as effects of particular changes in conditions (wage rates, interest rates, import duties, excise taxes, technology, etc.) In this causal connection the firm is only a theoretical link, a mental construct helping to explain how one gets from the cause to the effect. This is altogether different from explaining the behavior of a firm. As the philosopher of science warns, we ought not to confuse the *explanans* with the *explanandum*.

Misplaced Concreteness

To confuse the firm as a theoretical construct with the firm as an empirical concept, that is, to confuse a heuristic fiction with a real organization like General Motors or Atlantic & Pacific, is to commit the "fallacy of misplaced concreteness." This fallacy consists in using theoretical symbols as though they had a direct, observable, concrete meaning.

In some fields, investigators are protected from committing the fallacy, at least with regard to some of their problems, by the fact that a search for any empirical counterpart to the theoretical construct seems hopeless. Thus, some physicists working on particle theory were able to answer the question "Does the neutrino really exist?" laconically with "Who cares?" and to explain that any belief in the "real existence" of atoms, electrons, neutrinos, and all the rest, would hold up the progress of our knowledge. Some biologists working in genetics warned, after empirical genes were discovered, that these "operational genes" should not be confused with the "hypothetical genes," which had been useful constructs in explanatory models before the discovery of any empirical referents. Economists, however, know for sure that firms exist as empirical entities and, hence, they have a hard time keeping the theoretical firm and the empirical firm apart.

For certain economic problems the existence of the firm is of the essence. For example, if we study the size distribution of firms or the growth of the firm, the organization and some of its properties and processes are the very objects of the investigation. In such studies we insist on a high degree of correspondence between the model (the thought-object) and the observed object. For other problems, however, as for problems of competitive-price theory, any likeness between the theoretical construct of the firm and the empirical firm is purely coincidental.

Economists trained in scientific methodology understand this clearly. I might quote a dozen or more writers, but will confine myself to one quotation, which states that "in economic analysis, the business firm is a postulate in a web of logical connections." Let me add the statement of another writer, who however was plaintiff rather than advocate when he wrote that "It is a fascinating paradox that the received theory of the firm, by and large, assumes that the firm does not exist."

Here is what I wrote on one of the several occasions when I have discussed this problem:

> . . . the firm in the model world of economic micro-theory ought not to call forth any irrelevant associations with firms in the real world. We know, of course, that there are firms in reality and that they have boards of directors and senior and junior executives, who do, with reference to hundreds of different products, a great many things—which are entirely irrelevant for the microtheoretical model. The fictitious firm of the model is a "uni-brain," an individual decision-unit that has nothing to do but adjust the output and the price of one or two imaginary products to very simple imagined changes in data.

I went on, of course, to say that this purely fictitious single-minded firm, helpful as it is in competitive-price theory, will not do so much for us in the theory of monopoly and oligopoly. To explain and predict price reactions under monopoly and oligopoly we need more than the construct of a profit-maximizing reactor. I shall come back to this after discussing the demands for "more realistic" assumptions where they are plainly irrelevant and therefore out of place.

Realistic Models of the Firm Under Competition

Many of the proponents and protagonists of a more realistic theory of the firm are quite aware of the fact that the managerial extension and enrichment of the concept of the firm was not needed except where firms in the industry were large and few, and not under the pressure of competition. There are many very quotable statements to this effect.

Too many students, however, want a realistic model of the firm for all purposes. They forget the maxim of Occam's Razor that unnecessary terms in a theory be kept out (or shaved off). These students seem to miss in a simplified model the realistic trimmings of the observable world; they distrust such a model because it is obviously "descriptively false." In view of this sentimental hankering for realism, it may be helpful to survey some of the inclusions which various writers have proposed in order to meet the demands for greater realism in the "theory of the firm," and to examine their relevance to the theory of competitive price. The following considerations are supposed to supplement, qualify, restrict, or replace the objective of maximizing money profits.

(1) Entrepreneurs and managers cannot be expected to have an inelastic demand for leisure; indeed, one must assume that this demand is income-elastic so that higher profit expectations will cause them to sacrifice some income for the sake of more leisure. (2) Managers are anxious to avoid resentment on the part of their colleagues and subordinates and will, therefore, not enforce their orders with the sternness required for maximization of profits; similarly, minor functionaries do not want to disturb the routines of their superiors and, hence, they often abstain from suggesting improvements which would maximize profits. (3) Managers are more interested in their own salaries, bonuses, and other emoluments, than in the profits of the firm or the income of its owners. (4) The realization of certain asset preferences (for example, liquidity as against inventories and fixed assets) may be in conflict with profit maximization. (5) The flow and biased screening of information through the various levels of management may cause systematic misinformation resulting in earnings far below the maximum obtainable. (6) The objective of maintaining control in the hands of the present control group may require a sacrifice of profit opportunities. (7) The preference for security may be so strong that even relatively conservative ways of making higher profits are eschewed. (8) The striving for status, power, and prestige may be such that it results in conduct not consistent with a maximum of profit. (9) The wish to serve society, be a benefactor, or soothe one's social conscience, may militate against actions or policies that would maximize profits. (10) The instinct of workmanship, a desire to show professional excellence, a pervasive interest in feats of engineering, may lead to performance in conflict with highest possible profits. (11) Compromises among the different goals of execu-

tives with different interests—production, sales, personnel relations, finance, research and development, public relations, etc.—are sure to "compromise" the objective of maximum profits. (12) A variety of influences may be exerted on management decisions, perhaps pulling in different directions and possibly away from maximum profits, as for example influences from labor organizations, suppliers of materials, customers, bankers, government agencies.

I shall not prolong this catalogue even if it is far from complete. Let us admit that each of the possible deviations from maximum profit may be "real" in some circumstances. But how effective and significant are they? If the industry is effectively competitive—and it does not have to be "purely" competitive or "perfectly" competitive—is there much of a chance that the direction in which firms react, through their decisions regarding prices, inputs, and output, to a change in conditions would be turned around by any of the "forces" listed? Before we say apodictically no, we should examine a few of the reservations.

Security and Managerial Coordination

Let us single out two items which have been given especially wide play: the "objective of security" and the question of "managerial coordination."

That there are no business profits without risks and that there is not much point in treating the two quite separately; that it would be silly to call a decision one of profit-maximizing if it increased risk and uncertainty so much as to reduce the chance of survival; that the notion of long-run profits comprises all considerations of risks of loss; that, in terms of my automobile-driving analogies, only a fool would assume that maximization of speed means driving 120 miles an hour regardless of curves and bumps; these are some of the things that have to be said in this connection. But the most essential point to be made is that in the economics of *adjustment to change* the issues of security, survival, and maximum profit are merged. How primitive again to confuse new ventures and daring moves with mere responses to stimuli, obvious reactions to change. If a change in conditions calls for a certain reaction in the name of maximum profits, the very same reaction is called for also in the name of security of survival.

The other matter is of a more "behavioral" nature: the coordination of different goals and judgments on the part of different members of the management and the deviations from profit maximization that may be involved in the process. Frankly, I cannot quite see what great difference organizational matters are supposed to make in the firm's price reactions to changes in conditions. Assume, for example, the import duties on foreign products competing with the products of domestic industry are raised, with a resulting increase in the demand for the products of the firm. Why should the clashes and compromises of divergent opinions reverse the direction of the change that would be "dictated" by the simple rule of profit maximization? Perhaps one vice president wants to raise prices without increasing output, while another wants to increase output without (at least at the moment) raising prices. No matter what their compromise will be, it is likely to conform with what the simple rule suggests. But if not, so what? Remember we are talking about industries with more than a few firms and with free entry.

Other Qualifications to Competitive Price Theory

Substitution between income and leisure looks like the strongest reason for a qualification in cases in which the change in conditions is such that not only the locus of maximum profits is shifted but also the amount of profit obtainable is changed. Take again the example of a tariff increase shutting out foreign competition. The firms in the industry will find that given outputs will now fetch higher prices and that increased outputs can be sold at prices higher than those prevailing before tariffs were raised. And profits will be higher in any case, so that managers—even owner-managers—will be inclined to relax their efforts. Yet would anybody seriously argue that the substitution of leisure (coffee breaks, cocktail parties, golf) for potential profits would be such that total output would be reduced instead of increased? It is not a likely story, and where the industry consists of several or many firms, the small probability vanishes quickly. What remains of the argument is that total output would increase, in reaction to the tariff increase, somewhat less than it would if the managers were eager beavers and did not relax in their efforts when profits increased. Thus, the elasticity of supply of the products in question is a little smaller. But since we do not know how much it would be anyhow, the unknown substraction from an unknown number should not cause the economic theorist any serious anxieties. (And if the politicians who push for the tariff increase decide to push less·hard if we tell them that their friends in the industry will enjoy some of the added protection in the form of more leisure and recreation, we would not really mind.)

Even if formal accuracy demanded that we accept the maximization of the decision-maker's total utility as the basic assumption, simplicity and fruitfulness speak for sticking with the postulate of maximization of money profits for situations in which competition is effective. The question is not whether the firms of the real world will *really* maximize money profits, or whether they even *strive* to maximize their money profits, but rather whether the *assumption* that this is the objective of the theoretical firms in the artificial world of our construction will lead to conclusions— "inferred outcomes"—very different from those derived from admittedly more realistic assumptions.

The second qualification in my list—regarding bosses, colleagues, and subordinates—is quite irrelevant, except perhaps for questions of welfare economics, where it matters whether firms "really" do all they can to maximize efficiency. For theories concerned with *changes* in prices, inputs, and outputs in response to *changes* in conditions (of production, resource availability, and product demand) the strictness with which efficiency is watched in the firm does not matter. The effects of the tariff increase in our illustration, or the effects of changes in wage rates, interest rates, tax rates, and so forth, are, if there is effective competition, essentially independent of the relations among the various levels in the managerial hierarchy of the firm.

It would take too much time here to go through our entire list of reservations. Anybody who makes the effort will find that some of the "realistic assumptions" proposed for inclusion in the theory can affect (by an unknown amount) the magnitude but not the direction of any change that is likely to result from a specified change in conditions; and that other assumptions will not even do that much. In short, they are all irrelevant for purposes of competitive-price theory.

Oligopoly, Monopoly, and Managerial Discretion

I repeat: In the theory of competitive price the "real existence" of firms is irrelevant: imaginary (postulated) agents pursuing a simple (postulated) goal react to assumed changes in conditions and thereby produce (or allow us to infer) changes in prices, inputs, and outputs. The correspondence between these inferences (deduced changes) and actual observations (observed changes in prices, inputs, and outputs, following observed changes in conditions) is close for two reasons: (1) the number of firms in the real world is so large that it suffices if some of them react as posited in the theory; and (2) the profits of firms are only about "normal," that is, excess profits are about zero, because of competitive pressures from newcomers (pliopolistic pressures), so that profits below the maximum obtainable would in fact be net losses in an economic sense.

These two reasons do not hold in the theories of oligopoly and monopoly price. For these theories the real existence of firms (that is, an empirical counterpart to the theoretical construct) is required, because the explanation of changes in prices, inputs, and outputs is at the same time an explanation of decisions of some particular firms, in the sense of organizations of men acting in particular, sometimes unpredictable, ways. Various attempts have been made to develop patterns of oligopolistic and monopolistic conduct and to correlate these patterns with types of organization or with types of personalities exercising ultimate decision-making power. The success has thus far been small; even if the decision-making (say, pricing) in a particular firm was sometimes satisfactorily modeled (for example, in a simulated computer program), the model has usually not been transferable to other cases, to predict decisions in other firms. I do not recall, moreover, that the behavior patterns in these cases were shown to be inconsistent with the postulate of profit maximization.

Under these circumstances, retreat to simpler, less realistic models of firms in oligopoly and monopoly positions is indicated. The first approach is to apply the polypolistic model, in full awareness that the actual facts are entirely different. In many instances the use of the polypolistic model for situations which in our judgment would merit to be labeled as oligopolistic will still yield satisfactory explanations and predictions. Where this is not so, the analyst will resort to the use of models of oligopolistic or monopolistic firms, postulating the simplest possible pattern of action and reaction, dispensing with all peculiar attitudes and "special" strategies. Only where these simple models of oligopolistic and monopolistic firms yield quite unsatisfactory predictions will the analyst need to go further, to more special types of behavior, provided he finds it worth while. It depends on the research interests and on the problems under examination how much effort one wishes to invest in behavioral research where the findings hold little promise of yielding generalizations of wide applicability.

There are, however, some simple models of oligopolistic behavior which seem to be of sufficiently wide applicability. A model that equips the oligopolistic decision-maker not under heavy competitive pressure with an objective of gross-revenue ("sales") maximization, subject to the constraint of satisfactory net-revenue ("profit"), succeeds in explaining the lack of response to some cost-increasing events observed in several instances. There are other simple models explaining the same phenomenon, and one may think of good reasons for finding one model or another more satisfactory. If the sales-maximization hypothesis can explain a greater variety of observed responses or nonresponses than other hypotheses can, and if it seems to correspond better with self-interpretations offered by interviewed businessmen, it merits acceptance, at least for the time being.

An alternative to the maximization of sales is the maximization of the growth rate of sales. This hypothesis is especially interesting because it involves an endogenous relation with profits: while some of the growth of gross revenue may encroach on profits, it does so with an automatic limit in that profits are needed to finance the investment required for the growth of sales.

Another extension of the objective function proposed on the basis of behavioral research combines two managerial preferences for specific expenses of the firm with the usual profit motive. The two additional motives are expenditures for staff personnel and expenditures for managerial emoluments; both figure prominently in the utility functions of executives of companies which, sheltered from competitive pressures, make enough profits to allow management to indulge in these personal desires.

All these "managerial-discretion models" are simple and sufficiently general to allow relatively wide application. We shall have more to say about them later.

Effective Competition and Managerial Discretion

In mapping out the area of applicability for theories of managerial discretion, we have spoken of "oligopoly," "monopoly," and of "firms not under heavy competitive pressure." These are rather vague guideposts, but unfortunately the literature has not been very helpful in ascertaining precisely what it is that allows or restricts the exercise of wide managerial discretion.

Some writers stress the size of the firm, suggesting that it is only in the *large* firm that management can exercise discretion. Others stress the condition of *diffused ownership* as the one that affords management the opportunity of pursuing objectives other than maximization of profits. Those who stress oligopoly as the domain for which objective functions richer than profit maximization are needed are usually not quite specific as to their criterion of an oligopoly position: it may be *fewness of firms* active in the same industry, or the subjective state of awareness of the *interdependence of price making* often characterized as "conjectural variation," or simply the *absence of aggressive competition for increasing shares in the market*. Others again stress *closed entry*, or absence of newcomers' competition, as the essential condition for a profit level sufficiently comfortable to allow managers to indulge in the satisfaction of objectives other than maximization of profits.

To combine all these conditions would probably be far too restrictive; it would confine the application of managerial-discretion models to large firms with diffused ownership, few competitors, full awareness of interdependence in pricing, absence of aggressive efforts by existing competitors to increase their market shares, and little danger of new competitors entering the field. The size of the firm may actually not be relevant, and diffused ownership may not be a necessary condition for some deviations from profit maximization to occur, say, in the interest of larger sales or larger expenditures for staff. Fewness of competitors may be more significant, chiefly because the danger of newcomers' competition is likely to be small where the number of firms has been few and continues to be few; partly also because the few competitors may have learnt that aggressive price competition does not pay. The essential conditions, it seems to me, are these two: that no newcomers are likely to invade the field of the existing firms, and that none of the existing firms tries to expand its sales at such a fast rate that it could succeed only by encroaching on the business of its competitors.

Competition from newcomers, from aggressive expansionists, or from importers is sometimes called "heavy," "vigorous," or "effective." The simplest meaning of these adjectival modifiers is this: a firm is exposed to heavy, vigorous, or effective competition if it is kept under continuing pressure to do something about its sales and its profits position. Under this "competitive pressure" the firm is constantly compelled to react to actual or potential losses in sales and/or reductions in profits, so much so that the firm will not be able to pursue any objectives other than the maximization of profits—for the simple reason that anything less than the highest obtainable profits would be below the rate of return regarded as normal at the time.

I am aware of a defect in this definition: its criterion is lodged in the effect rather than in an independently ascertainable condition. Perhaps, though, "effective" is quite properly defined in this fashion, namely, by whether certain effects are realized: competition is effective if it continually depresses profits to the level regarded as the minimum tolerable. What makes it effective is not part of the definition, but has to be explained by the conditions of entry, aggressive attitudes on the part of existing firms, or imports from abroad.

If my reasoning is accepted, several formulations proposed in the literature will have to be amended. Managerial discretion will be a function, not of the independence of the management from the control of the owners, but chiefly of the independence of the management from urgent worries about the sufficiency of earnings. If one insists, one may still say that all managers are primarily interested in their own incomes. But, since it is clear that their long-term incomes are jeopardized if profits go below the acceptable rate of return, maximization of managerial incomes and maximization of profits come to the same thing if competition is effective.

There can be no doubt about the fact that competition is not effective in many industries and that many, very many, firms are not exposed to vigorous competition. It follows that managerial discretion can have its way in a large enough number of firms to secure wide applicability of well-designed managerial-discretion models—or to invite the use of managerial total-utility models.

I was fully aware, when I wrote my 1946 article, that there were many qualifications and exceptions to the principle of profit maximization. But I considered it hopeless for predictive purposes to work with total-utility maximization and I did not see the possibility of combining a few selected managerial goals with the profit motive.

Statistical Cost Functions of a Hosiery Mill

JOEL DEAN

Joel Dean is Professor of Business Economics at Columbia University. This article, a classic study of a firm's cost functions, appeared in the Journal of Business *in 1941.*

The enterprise whose cost behavior was analyzed is a hosiery knitting mill which is one of a number of subsidiary plants of a large silk-hosiery manufacturing firm. In the particular plant studied, the manufacturing process is confined to the knitting of the stockings; that is, the plant begins with the wound silk and carries the operations up to the point where the stockings are ready to be shipped to other plants for dyeing and finishing. The operations in the mill are, therefore, carried on by highly mechanized equipment and skilled labor.

Cost functions were determined for combined cost and for its components: productive labor cost, nonproductive labor cost, and overhead cost. These functions were derived separately for monthly, quarterly, and weekly data. For the monthly and quarterly observations both simple and partial regressions of the various costs on output were obtained. In this paper the statistical findings for the monthly data alone are presented. . . .

I. Simple Regressions

Scatter diagrams were made between output and combined cost and its three components for the monthly data to indicate the form of the restricted cost function in which output is the only independent variable. The simple regression[1] indicated by the scatter diagrams appeared to be

[1] The "simple" regression referred to should be carefully distinguished from "net" or "partial" regressions.

115

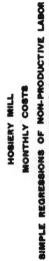

CHART 2

HOSIERY MILL

MONTHLY COSTS

SIMPLE REGRESSIONS OF NON-PRODUCTIVE LABOR
COST AND ITS ELEMENTS ON OUTPUT

Cost (in Hundreds of Dollars)

Total Non-productive Labor

Supervision

Other Indirect Labor

Maintenance

Office

Output (in Thousands of Dozens)

CHART 1

HOSIERY MILL

MONTHLY COSTS

SIMPLE REGRESSIONS OF TOTAL COMBINED COST
AND PRODUCTIVE LABOR COST ON OUTPUT

Total Combined Cost

Total Cost (in Thousands of Dollars)

Output (in Thousands of Dozens)

Productive Labor Cost

Cost (in Thousands of Dollars)

Output (in Thousands of Dozens)

linear, so that a regression equation of the first degree with the general form $X_1 = b_1 + b_2 X_2$ was fitted to the observations for combined cost and its three components.[2] The regression equations derived for the four categories of cost in the form of monthly totals, together with the statistical constants, are shown in Table I.

TABLE I. Hosiery Mill: Simple Regressions of Combined Cost and Its Components on Output

(*Monthly Observations*)

	Combined Cost	Productive Labor Cost	Nonproductive Labor Cost	Overhead Cost
Simple regression equation	$_cX_1 = 2935.59$ $+ 1.998X_2$	$_pX_1 = -1695.16$ $+ 1.780X_2$	$_nX_1 = 992.23$ $+ 0.097X_2$	$_oX_1 = 3638.30$ $+ 0.121X_2$
Standard error of estimate	6109.83	5497.09	399.34	390.58
Correlation coefficient (r)	0.973	0.972	0.952	0.970
Regression coefficient (b)	1.998 ± 0.034	1.780 ± 0.035	0.097 ± 0.045	0.121 ± 0.036

$_cX_1 =$ combined cost in dollars $_oX_1 =$ overhead cost in dollars
$_pX_1 =$ productive labor cost in dollars $X_2 =$ output in dozens of pairs
$_nX_1 =$ nonproductive labor cost in dollars

The results which are expressed in a mathematical form in Table I can also be shown by regression lines or scatter diagrams. The regression equations for combined cost and productive labor cost are illustrated graphically in Chart 1. Chart 2 shows the simple regressions not only of the aggregate nonproductive labor cost but also of its principal elements: supervision, maintenance, labor, office staff, and other indirect labor. In order to show more clearly the nature of the individual cost functions, each of the cost elements and their total are measured from a common base, the X-axis, i.e., they are not cumulated. Simple regressions of total overhead cost and its elements are similarly presented in Chart 3.

II. Partial Regressions

Graphic multiple correlation analysis showed that the deviations from the simple regression functions of cost on output were systematically ordered in time. This indicated that a correction for a time trend might be advisable. A time factor was, therefore, introduced explicitly into the least-squares multiple correlation analysis by the use of the variable X_3, which

[2] Furthermore, statistical examination of the relation of cost and output first differences (an approximation to marginal cost) and of the relation of average cost to output supported the hypothesis of linearity of the total cost function. Despite the support given the linear total cost specification by the analysis of the production techniques and by the distribution of total cost observations and the behavior of average cost and the approximation to marginal cost, a cubic function was also specified and fitted by least-squares regression analysis. The higher-order function did not appear to fit the data significantly better than the linear function.

is a series consisting of the sequential numbering of the months in which observations were taken. In this way it was possible to isolate the systematic variation of cost as a function of time and to determine the net regression of cost on output. By allowing for the influences of changes in conditions through time which had not been taken into account by the rectification of the data, an estimate of the cost-output function which was possibly more accurate was obtained.

The graphic analysis showed a significant time trend for the three major cost components—productive labor, nonproductive labor and overhead—as well as for combined cost. The graphic partial regression of cost and time appeared to be curvilinear in the case of combined cost, productive labor cost, and overhead cost. A curvilinear multiple regression equation of the general form,

$$X_1 = b_1 + b_2 X_2 + b_3 X_3 + b_4 X_3^2$$

was, therefore, selected as the most appropriate specification in these cases. This equation retains the linear specification chosen in the case of the simple regression, since this multiple regression equation is still linear with respect to output. In the remaining instance—nonproductive labor—a linear function, $X_1 = b_1 + b_2 X_2 + b_3 X_3$, was fitted. In these equations X_1 is cost (in the form of totals per month), X_2 is output (in dozens of pairs), and X_3 is time (months numbered sequentially).

The results of the multiple correlation analysis of the monthly data for combined cost and its three principal components are shown mathematically in Table II. These findings are also displayed in graphic form in the accompanying charts (4, 5, 6 and 7), in which the net or partial regressions of the various cost categories on output and time are shown.

In the upper section of Chart 4 the dots represent rectified monthly totals of combined cost that have been adjusted for the curvilinear time trend shown in the lower section of the chart. Although the scatter is considerable, the distribution of the dots appears to substantiate the linearity of the partial regression of total cost over the observed range, from 4,000 dozen to 43,000 dozen pairs of hosiery. Beyond this range there is only one observation. The irregular line in the lower section connects cost observations which have been adjusted for output. They are deviations of the observations from the simple regression of cost on output arranged chronologically. The curved line fitted to these ordered deviations is the partial regression of cost on time, which is assigned a magnitude by the sequential numbering of the months.

A parallel portrayal of variations in productive labor cost with respect to output and time is found in Chart 5. The distribution of adjusted observations of monthly costs plotted against output in the upper section appears to be linear. As in the preceding chart, cost observations have been adjusted for the curvilinear partial regression of cost deviations on time shown in the lower section of the chart.

TABLE II. Hosiery Mill: Multiple and Partial Regressions of Combined Cost and Its Components on Output and on Time

(Monthly Observations)

	Combined Cost	Productive Labor Cost	Nonproductive Labor Cost	Overhead Cost
Multiple regression equation	$_cX_1 = -13,634.83 + 2.068X_2 + 1,308.039X_3 - 22.280X_3^2$	$_pX_1 = -15,832.45 + 1.821X_2 + 1,205.593X_3 - 21.078X_3^2$	$_nX_1 = -343.15 + 0.118X_2 + 27.668X_3$	$_oX_1 = 2451.60 + 0.130X_2 + 65.457X_3 - 0.987X_3^2$
Standard error of estimate*	3,983.31	3572.90	302.87	296.57
Coefficient of multiple correlation $\bar{R}$*	0.988	0.988	0.973	0.983
Coefficient of multiple determination $\bar{R}^2$*	0.977	0.977	0.946	0.966
Partial regression equation for output	$_cX_1 = 762.54 + 2.068X_2$	$_pX_1 = -2993.03 + 1.821X_2$	$_nX_1 = 334.71 + 0.118X_2$	$_oX_1 = 3363.47 + 0.130X_2$
Partial regression coefficient for output	2.068 ± 0.071	1.821 ± 0.064	0.118 ± 0.005	0.130 ± 0.005
Partial regression equation for time	$_cX_1 = -14,397.37 + 1308.039X_3 - 22.280X_3^2$	$_pX_1 = -12,839.42 + 1205.593X_3 - 21.078X_3^2$	$_nX_1 = -677.85 + 27.668X_3$	$_oX_1 = -821.87 + 65.458X_3 - 0.987X_3^2$

$_cX_1$ = combined cost in dollars
$_pX_1$ = productive labor cost in dollars
$_nX_1$ = nonproductive labor cost in dollars

$_oX_1$ = overhead cost in dollars
X_2 = output in dozens of pairs
X_3 = time

CHART 3
HOSIERY MILL
MONTHLY COSTS
SIMPLE REGRESSIONS OF OVERHEAD COST
AND ITS ELEMENTS ON OUTPUT

CHART 4
HOSIERY MILL
MONTHLY COSTS
PARTIAL REGRESSIONS OF
TOTAL COMBINED COST ON OUTPUT AND TIME

Chart 6 shows partial regressions for monthly totals of nonproductive labor cost. In the upper section are plotted corrected cost observations adjusted for time trend. Again the amount of scatter and the character of the distribution of dots does not appear to justify specification of other than a linear partial regression. The deviations from this output regression, which were arranged chronologically and connected by an irregular line in the lower section of the chart, indicate a steady upward trend in nonproductive labor cost after allowance is made for the effect of output.

Chart 7 shows the partial regressions and adjusted observations of total monthly overhead cost. The scatter of adjusted cost observations plotted against output (shown by the dots in the upper section) is so wide and so approximately linear that fitting a cubic or parabolic regression curve does not appear to be justified. The linear partial regression shows that total overhead cost tends to increase with output at a uniform rate over the volume range studied. The lower section shows the time trend in overhead cost behavior, when allowance is made for the effects of output. The irregular line shows chronologically ordered cost deviations from the regression line appearing in the upper section of the chart. The trend is indicated by the curvilinear partial regression. There appeared to be a general tendency for overhead cost to increase during the first part of the period, to level off, and then to decline somewhat in the later months. . . .

III. *Marginal and Average Cost*

Both the simple and the partial regressions on output were determined for costs in the form of monthly totals. Both types of total cost functions were transformed[3] into average and marginal cost functions.[4] The equations for the derived average and marginal cost functions for combined cost and for its major components are found in Table III.

[3] The mathematics of this transformation may be illustrated by the following equations for monthly combined cost, where $_cX_1$ is total combined cost, and X_2 is output. The partial regression equation for combined cost in the form of monthly totals was found to be

$$_cX_1 = 762.54 + 2.068X_2 .$$

By dividing this equation through by X_2, the following equation for the combined cost per dozen was obtained:

$$\frac{_cX_1}{X_2} = 2.068 + \frac{762.54}{X_2} .$$

By differentiating the total cost function with respect to X_2, the output, the resulting first derivative gives the marginal cost function as

$$\frac{d_cX_1}{dX_2} = 2.068 .$$

[4] It should be remembered that these costs do not include raw-material costs.

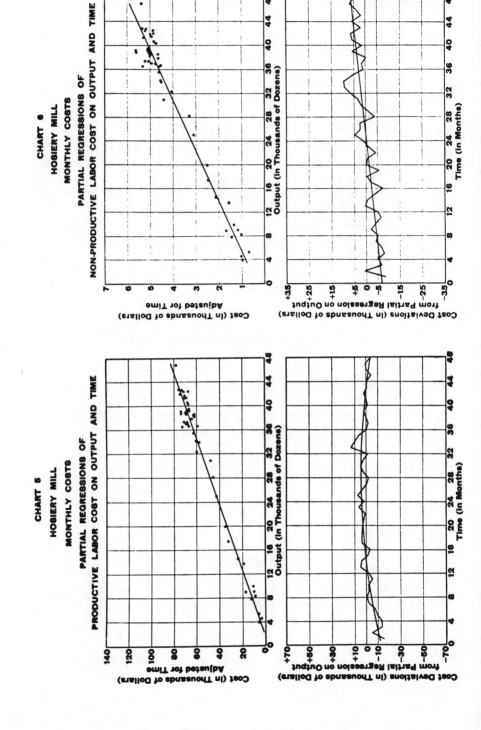

CHART 5
HOSIERY MILL
MONTHLY COSTS
PARTIAL REGRESSIONS OF
PRODUCTIVE LABOR COST ON OUTPUT AND TIME

CHART 6
HOSIERY MILL
MONTHLY COSTS
PARTIAL REGRESSIONS OF
NON-PRODUCTIVE LABOR COST ON OUTPUT AND TIME

The graphic counterparts of the results obtained from the partial regression equation for combined cost expressed in Table III are shown in Chart 8. The upper section shows the partial regression of total monthly cost on output, which is the same as that shown in the upper section of Chart 4. The marginal cost function which is pictured in the lower section is the first derivative of this total cost function. Since the total cost function is linear, its slope obviously remains unchanged; hence marginal cost is con-

TABLE III. Hosiery Mill: Equations for Total, Average, and Marginal Cost-Output Functions Obtained from Simple and Partial Correlation

		Total	Average	Marginal
		Simple Regressions		
Combined cost	$_cX_1 =$	$2935.59 + 1.998X_2$	$_cX_1/X_2 = 1.998 + 2935.59/X_2$	$d_cX_1/dX_2 = 1.998$
Productive labor cost	$_pX_1 =$	$-1695.16 + 1.780X_2$	$_pX_1/X_2 = 1.780 - 1695.16/X_2$	$d_pX_1/dX_2 = 1.780$
Nonproductive labor cost	$_nX_1 =$	$992.23 + 0.097X_2$	$_nX_1/X_2 = 0.097 + 992.23/X_2$	$d_nX_1/dX_2 = 0.097$
Overhead cost	$_oX_1 =$	$3638.30 + 0.121X_2$	$_oX_1/X_2 = 0.121 + 3638.30/X_2$	$d_oX_1/dX_2 = 0.121$
		Partial Regressions		
Combined cost	$_cX_1 =$	$762.54 + 2.068X_2$	$_cX_1/X_2 = 2.068 + 762.54/X_2$	$d_cX_1/dX_2 = 2.068$
Productive labor cost	$_pX_1 =$	$-2993.03 + 1.821X_2$	$_pX_1/X_2 = 1.821 - 2993.03/X_2$	$d_pX_1/dX_2 = 1.821$
Nonproductive labor cost	$_nX_1 =$	$334.71 + 0.118X_2$	$_nX_1/X_2 = 0.118 + 334.71/X_2$	$d_nX_1/dX_1 = 0.118$
Overhead cost	$_oX_1 =$	$3363.47 + 0.130X_2$	$_oX_1/X_2 = 0.130 + 3363.47/X_2$	$d_oX_1/dX_2 = 0.130$

$_cX_1 =$ combined cost in dollars
$_pX_1 =$ productive labor cost in dollars
$_nX_1 =$ nonproductive labor cost in dollars
$_oX_1 =$ overhead cost in dollars
$X_2 =$ output in dozens of pairs

stant. From these results it is seen that the operating cost of producing an additional dozen pairs of hosiery (not including the cost of silk) is approximately $2.00 over the range of output observed.[5]

The average cost function, which lies above the marginal cost line in the lower section, was obtained by dividing the total cost function by output (X_2). This curve shows how cost per dozen varies with the number of dozens produced. Since the fixed cost is relatively small compared to the variable cost, the average cost function is only slightly curved and lies very close to the marginal cost function.

[5] To be more precise, the marginal cost derived from the simple regression function is $1.998, while the estimate of marginal cost obtained from the partial regression function is $2.068.

Economies of Scale:
Some Statistical Evidence

FREDERICK T. MOORE

Frederick T. Moore is an economist at the RAND Corporation. This well-known article appeared in the Quarterly Journal of Economics *in 1959.*

I

Statistical evidence bearing on the existence of economies of scale in industry is, for the most part, sketchy and incomplete, although the logic of the economic and technical origins of such economies has been extensively developed. Reasons for this lack of statistical evidence are not hard to find; detailed cost studies of different sizes of plants are a *sine qua non* for analysis of the problem, yet such studies are difficult to obtain. Of necessity, engineering information on technical possibilities for substitution among inputs must be combined with the mechanism of choice provided by economic calculations of cost. As Chenery has pointed out, the number of combinations of inputs which may be considered feasible by the engineer is much greater than the number observed in operation and studied by the economist; yet changes in relative prices alone will change the range of economically feasible combinations.

In lieu of deriving production functions from technical data (which is what is actually required), engineers—and in particular chemical engineers—have experimented with various "rules of thumb" for estimating the capital cost of plants of different sizes or for estimating process equipment costs. One such rule of thumb which has found some acceptance is the ".6 factor" rule. The uses claimed and achieved for this rule will be summarized in a moment. Although the engineers do not seem to think of it as shedding light on economies of scale of plant, the rule can be so interpreted and will be discussed from that point of view.

Studies of capital coefficients (i.e., the ratio of capital expenditures to increases in capacity) by federal government agencies, universities, and others as part of an interindustry research program provide the statistical material for another evaluation of economies of scale. The methodology and results of these studies can be compared with those above.

II

The envelope cost curve usually serves as the vehicle for a discussion of economies of scale; the succession of plant short-run cost curves may trace out a smooth envelope curve or it may be scalloped in various ways. A discussion along this line overlooks the ways in which plant expansions actually take place, however. Expansions of capacity may occur through: the building of completely new plants at new locations; separate new productive facilities (multiple units) which utilize existing overhead facilities such as office buildings, laboratories, etc.; the addition of new productive facilities which are intermingled with the old (the case of "scrambled" facilities); conversions of plants or processes from one product to another; or the elimination of "bottleneck" areas in a plant (the case of "unbalanced" expansion).

It is conceivable that the elimination of bottleneck areas in a plant will increase the capacity by a large amount (e.g., 50 per cent); if that be the case, it is necessarily implied that in other areas of the plant there is excess capacity which can be utilized once the bottleneck is broken. This in turn implies that the productive units in the plant are not divisible, since, if they were, the plant could have been producing the old output with a smaller scale and lower costs. Thus it is usual to attribute economies of scale primarily—if not solely—to the lack of divisibility of productive units. Economies are realized by moving in the direction of larger common denominators of equipment, i.e., where fewer units are operated at less than capacity.

Size of equipment and indivisibilities therein are significant variables for a study of scale, but they do not necessarily go hand in hand. In a copper smelter capacity may be increased by lengthening or widening the reverberatory furnace by small increments (thus increasing its cubic content). This ability to increase the size of a capital input by small amounts exists for a fairly wide selection of industrial equipment; in fact the usefulness of the ".6 rule" is really predicated on this occurrence. It has been noted by engineers that the cost of an item is frequently related to its surface area, while the capacity of the item increases in accordance with its volume. For that reason alone economies in scale may be achieved.

There is another matter which bears on this topic. Chamberlin has argued that it is not only divisibility but the aggregate amounts of inputs used that explain the existence of economies of scale. As size increases, the inputs change qualitatively as well as quantitatively. Different types of inputs are employed at various scales. Changes in quality mean changes in efficiency. The *form* of the input changes as well as the amount. It will not do to call this a question of classification, and to say that the inputs are really distinct. The functions performed by the inputs are the same; the quality changes do not alter the case.

In general it has been our experience in working with files of information on individual plant expansions in a number of industries, that the complementary character of capital goods in a large expansion is quite marked. A large increase in capacity usually involves the plant in expenditures on all productive equipment, not just on selected items. This does not mean that fixed proportions are the rule; flexibility in the use of particular pieces of equipment is common. However, the isoquants probably tend to be more angular and less flat, as they would be in the case of easy substitution between inputs. (N.B. See the case of pipelines below for the opposite case.) Among other reasons, economies of scale arise because the proportions among inputs change as scale of plant changes, although the proportions are variable within certain limits. In other words, the "scale line" may have "kinks" in it as the size of the plant expands. The kinks indicate the points at which quality and quantity changes in inputs alter the proportions in which they tend to be used.

III

The ".6 rule" derived by the engineers is a rough method of measuring increases in capital cost as capacity is expanded. Briefly stated the rule says that the increase in cost is given by the increase in capacity raised to the .6 power. Symbolically,

$$C_2 = C_1 \left(\frac{X_2}{X_1} \right)^{.6}$$

Here C_1 and C_2 are the costs of two pieces of equipment and X_1 and X_2 are their respective capacities. The rule has been adduced from the fact that for such items of equipment as tanks, gas holders, columns, compressors, etc., the cost is determined by the amount of materials used in enclosing a given volume, i.e., cost is a function of surface area; while capacity is directly related to the volume of the container. Consider a spherical container. The area varies as the volume to the 2/3 power, or in other language, cost varies as capacity to the 2/3 power. If the container is cylindrical, then, by the same analogy, cost varies as capacity to the .5 power, if the volume is increased by changes in diameter, and if the ratio of height to diameter is kept constant, cost varies as capacity to the 2/3 power.

From a consideration of these factors the .6 rule has been developed.

Now consider an alternative and generalized form of the .6 rule

$$E = aC^b$$

where E is capital expenditures, C is capacity and a and b are parameters. So long as $b < 1$, there are economies in capital costs. These economies should not be interpreted as being identical with economies of scale since variable costs must also be considered in the latter case; however, there are some indications that labor, power, and utilities costs also decrease with increased scale while the costs of materials embodied in the final product remain constant. These indications are tentative and not demonstrated by statistical evidence in the cases which follow, so that the ensuing discussion on the evidences of economies of scale must be qualified.

Originally the .6 rule was applied to individual pieces of equipment or processes. A reasonable argument can be made for its validity in those cases; however, the regression line for the formula above cannot be indefinitely extrapolated. There are several reasons for this. In the first place an extrapolation of the line may lead to sizes of equipment which are larger than the standard sizes available or in which stresses beyond the limits of the material are involved. Nelson points out that in building fractionating towers, an economical limit is reached at about 20-foot diameters since beyond that point very heavy beams are necessary in order to keep the trays level. Second, in some industries expansion takes place by a duplication of existing units rather than by an increase in their size, e.g., in aluminum reduction where several pot lines are constructed rather than enlarging individual pots. If the rule is to be applied at all it is safest to limit its use to the range of capacities found in the observations.

The .6 rule when applied to complete plants runs into difficulties not encountered on individual equipment. Some expenditures are relatively fixed for large ranges of capacity, for example the utilities system in the plant, the "overhead" facilities, plant transportation, instruments, etc. Complicated industrial machinery does not necessarily exhibit the same relationships between area (cost) and volume (capacity) as do simple structures like tanks and columns. Furthermore, for both items of equipment and complete plants, the gradations between sizes are not necessarily small. Indivisibilities in size are a real factor in some cases; an illustration from the crude pipeline industry will be discussed later.

In spite of these obvious limitations, estimates of the value of b in the formula

$$\log E = \log a + b \log C$$

have been made for a number of industries or products. These estimates are apt to be best for industries: (1) which are continuous-process rather than batch-operation; (2) which are capital-intensive; and (3) in which a homogeneous, standardized product is produced, so that problems of product-mix do not intrude to muddy the definition of capacity. The industries which best meet these criteria are the chemical industries (including petroleum), cement, and the milling, smelting, refining, and rolling and drawing of metals. These are the industries for which statistical estimates of *b* have been made, and for which some explanation of economies of scale has been supplied.

IV

Chilton has estimated values for *b* for thirty-six products in the chemical and metal industries. In three cases the value was greater than 1 but in only one of the cases was it so much larger as to be suspect. In the other thirty-three cases the values ranged from .48 to .91. The average value of *b* was .68 and the median .66, so that Chilton concluded that the .6 rule was reasonable even when extended to complete plants rather than individual pieces of equipment. Some of the values of *b* which Chilton obtained are shown below. The petroleum industry is well represented in the sample; several processes and one example of complete refineries are shown.

From the point of view of statistical appraisal of these results, it is unfortunate that the error in the regression equation and the standard error of *b* are not shown, although from a visual inspection of a few of the products it would appear that the correlations are very high. Nevertheless, it would be valuable to be able to apply a *t*-test to the *b*'s to determine, for example, whether they differ significantly from 1. If they do not,

Product	Value of b
Magnesium, ferrosilicon process	.62
Aluminum ingot	.90
TNT	1.01
Synthetic ammonia	.81
Styrene	.53
Aviation gasoline	.88
Complete refinery, including catalytic cracking	.75
Catalytic cracking, topping, feed preparation, gas recovery, polymerization	.88
Topping and thermal cracking	.60
Catalytic cracking	.81
Natural gasoline	.51
Thermal cracking	.62
Low-purity oxygen	.47–.59

the evidence on the existence of economies of scale in those industries would be shaky. It is reasonable to suppose that the values of *b* above .85 (approximately) are perhaps the ones most open to question.

The Harvard Economic Research Project directed by Professor Leontief has made estimates of these "scale factors" for a different selection of chemical products. Their results agree in general with those above, although the range of values found is greater (.2 to an aberrational value of 4.2), and the weighted average for fifteen products is also higher than that found by Chilton. A selection of these values is as follows:

Product	Value of b
Aluminum sulfate from bauxite	4.2
Calcium Carbide	.8
Carbon black, furnace process	.6
Carbon black, thermal decomposition	.2
Soda ash, Solvay process	.7
Styrene, from benzene and ethylene	.9
Sulfuric acid, contact process	.8
Synthetic rubber, Buna S	1.1

The average for fifteen products (weighted by the U. S. Census values of shipments in 1947) was .8. The scale factors above were computed from very small samples. Of the fifteen products studied, eight were based on two observations; two were based on three observations; two on four observations; one on five and two on six. On the other hand, most of the observations were derived at least in part from engineering data or were checked for type of process and completeness of design and equipment by engineers conversant with the industry. Nevertheless, the results must be viewed with skepticism. Furthermore, even in the cases in which there were the most observations (e.g., carbon black with six plants), the range of variation of equipment costs was considerable; the correlations do not appear to be very high. It is obvious that there are other factors such as location of the plant, product grade, etc., which affect capital expenditures; the data have not been adjusted to account for these factors so that the test of scale is not without ambiguity.

Under contract to the Bureau of Mines, the Petroleum Research Project, Rice Institute, has made a study of capital coefficients for crude oil and natural gas pipelines; one part of this study involved the derivation of a production function for pipelines and an investigation of economies of scale.

The two basic inputs of importance in the construction of a pipeline are the line pipe and the pumping stations, or, more accurately, the amount of hydraulic horsepower. The two inputs may be combined in a variety of ways to achieve any given capacity (which is defined as barrels per day of "throughput"). Any given throughput can be carried by substituting additional horsepower for a certain number of inches of (inside) diameter of pipe. Obviously, a pipe of smaller diameter involves less line pipe costs but also requires more expenditure on horsepower. For example, a throughput of 125,000 barrels per day (60 SUS oil over 1,000 miles) can be obtained by any of the following combinations of pipe and horsepower:

(Outside) Diameter of pipe	Horsepower (approximate)
30	2,000
26	4,000
22	8,500
18	22,500
16	37,500

Other combinations of pipe diameter and hydraulic horsepower can be derived for throughputs greater or less than 125,000 barrels per day.

The isoquants relating diameter of pipe to hydraulic horsepower are of the usual form, convex to the origin, but they are relatively "flat," indicating a fairly easy substitution of these inputs for each other for any given throughput being considered.

Although the isoquants, in generalized form, appear as continuous curves which indicate that substitution possibilities may be considered in incremental amounts, in fact there are discontinuities because pipe comes in standard sizes only. The most commonly used sizes for crude oil trunk lines have (outside) diameters of 8, 10, 12, 14, 16, 18, 20, 24, 26 and 30 inches. Inside diameters have a greater range of variation since wall thickness is also variable, but the number of sizes is not infinite; consequently, there are discontinuities in the production function.

The study of pipelines indicates clearly that economies of scale exist in the industry. Marginal physical product increases up to about 200,000 barrels per day and for larger throughputs the marginal returns appear to be approximately constant. However, because of the discontinuities in the production function, the line indicating increasing returns to scale may not cut the isoquants at points representing real alternatives in terms of line pipe size and horsepower. Furthermore, as the size of pumps increases, the cost per horsepower definitely decreases so that although the marginal physical product tends to be constant above 200,000 barrels per day, the capital costs per unit may continue to fall if larger pumps are used. Although there are other costs to be considered, many of them are invariant with respect to throughput and are associated only with the length of the line so that they need not be considered for this problem.

V

Some selected industries in the minerals area have been studied using data obtained from records of plants built during World War II and during the mobilization period beginning in 1950. The records of the Defense Plant Corporation ("Plancors") and of applications of firms for rapid tax amortization ("TA's") contain information on specific expenditures for capital equipment and the increase in capacity which was expected. In order to obtain reasonably homogeneous data, observations selected for study were limited to completely new plants and large "balanced additions." Unbalanced expansions (the elimination of bottlenecks) were eliminated from consideration. This increase in sample homogeneity was thus accomplished at the expense of sample size; small samples were the rule rather than the exception. However, in partial compensation, each of the plants was studied intensively; the expenditures were classified by type and compared as between plants and processes within plants; in short, every precaution was taken qualitatively to increase the homogeneity of the data. In final form two statistics were presented for each plant: (1) the total capital expenditure (secured as the sum of individual expenditures on equipment and facilities); and (2) the capacity increase secured. These were then correlated using a linear function of the logarithms (i.e., in the form indicated above in this paper). The results in general corroborated those discussed above. In almost all cases the scale factor was less than 1. The industries covered are as follows:

A. *Alumina.*   Complete and detailed information was available on only two plants, both using the combination Bayer process for production of alumina; on both of the plants (Baton Rouge, Louisiana, and Hurricane Creek, Arkansas) the engineering designs and flow sheets as well as the engineering rated capacities were available. Scale factors for the complete plants and for particular process equipment in the plant were computed.

Plant or Equipment	*Values of* b
Total plant and equipment	.95
Total equipment	.93
Boiler shop products	.85
Construction and mining machinery	.24
Industrial furnaces and ovens	.98
Pipe and fittings	1.13

The value of *b* for the total plant corresponds closely to that secured by Harvard. The range of values secured for the process equipment is particularly interesting. The chief machinery complex in the plant exhibits very marked economies of scale, while the value for pipe and fittings indicates diseconomies of scale. It appears that the larger size plant (which has a yearly capacity of 778,000 tons compared with 500,000 tons for the other) can use machinery more efficiently but the connections among the units (piping, etc.)must become substantially more expensive in order, for example, to utilize fully a group of evaporators, mills, or filter presses. An analysis of the engineering flow diagram of the plant tends to confirm this deduction.

It also appears that short-run costs fall as output is expanded. Operating costs, including raw materials, operating labor, allocable share of overhead, and interest on working capital, for the Baton Rouge plant have been estimated for three different levels of output.

Output	Operating Cost ($ ton)
1,000 tons/day	$27.28
500 tons/day	29.63
300 tons/day	32.43

B. *Aluminum Reduction.* The sample consisted of eight plants comprising a little less than half of the total in existence. Some of the results of the calculations are summarized in the following table.

Item	b	Sy	$\bar{r}$	σ_b
Total plant and equipment	.93	.038	.98	.06
Total equipment	.95	.021	.99	.03

A t-test applied to the values of b, testing it against the hypothesis $b = 1$, gave values of 1.17 for total plant and equipment and 1.67 for equipment. Using a 5 per cent critical probability level, neither of the values of b can be regarded as significantly different from 1, so that there is reason for questioning whether these values are really indicative of economies of scale in the industry.

This industry expands by introducing multiple pot lines rather than by expansion in the size of individual process equipment so that it is possible that the results would be improved if samples stratified according to number of pot lines were used. This suggests, of course, that there is a "lowest common denominator" for total equipment in the plant, and that the equipment is simply duplicated in any expansion, so that economies of scale cease once the lowest common denominator has been reached.

In this industry there are two basic processes of production which are basically similar but which have different capital expenditures in certain process areas. In a pre-baked carbon plant the carbon anodes are manufactured separately and then used in the pots; in Soderberg plants the carbon anodes are continuously replenished in the pot, so that expenditures on pot lines are larger. A Soderberg plant substitutes larger initial costs on equipment for lower operating costs; therefore a consideration of scale necessarily involves an attention to short-run operating costs in deciding on the type of plant to be built.

C. *Aluminum Rolling and Drawing.* The sample in this industry consisted of four plants making rolled products and four making extrusions. The two types of operations were kept separate in the analysis. The results are summarized below:

Process	b	r̄	σb
Aluminum rolling			
Total plant	.88	.95	.16
Equipment	.81	.93	.18
Aluminum extrusions			
Total plant	1.00	.99	—
Equipment	.92	.97	.13

The *t*-test applied to these results also fails to reveal values of *b* significantly different from 1; however, it is true here as in aluminum reduction, that there are limits to the size of rolls or dies and that multiple units are the usual way in which capacity is expanded.

D. *Cement.* The sample consisted of seven plants with a range in yearly capacity from 450,000 tons to 1,400,000 tons. For total plant the value of *b* was .77 and for equipment 1.06; the former value was not significantly different from 1 according to the *t*-test.

The major variable in the construction of a cement plant is the size (length and diameter) of the kiln. Fuel economy in firing the kilns is a prime objective, since fuel constitutes a large part of operating costs. Kilns and allied furnace equipment may be almost infinitely varied in size; however, since the primary purpose of the kiln is the holding of a cubic charge it was interesting to see if the .6 rule applied to kilns and to allied machinery in the cement plant.

Construction and mining machinery	.60
Furnaces and ovens (including kilns)	.73

These values accord well with the logic of the .6 rule.

E. *Tonnage Oxygen.* The sample consisted of five plants ranging in capacity from 50 to 500 tons per day, and producing 95 per cent oxygen. The value for *b* was .63. There are significant changes in capital inputs and costs in one process area (air compression) as scale increases. The major cost item in this ●rea is compressors. For plants of up to 100 tons per day it is most economical to use reciprocating compressors, while between 100 and 200 tons, there is a choice of reciprocating or centrifugal compressors, and above 300 tons axial flow compressors are more economical. Not only the size, but, more particularly, the character of the capital input changes as the scale increases, and, since the horsepower-hours required per ton decrease as scale increases, there are distinct economies of scale in this process area of the plant. A value of $b = .54$ was computed for compressor costs; this bears out the deductions made from the information on compressor types used in various sizes of plants.

VI

All of the above is but a smattering of evidence on the existence of economies of scale or the lack thereof. From a purely statistical point of view it is discouraging to find no scale factors which test out significantly against the hypothesis of constant returns; yet the samples are small, and above all it is not clear that a lack of homogeneity in the data does not vitiate the results. These are complex plants usually with a number of process areas. Some areas may be deliberately built with capacities larger than necessary in order to make easier any future expansion. If such is the case, the results are biased.

Although the formula may be applied to complete plants with useful result, it is clear that its application to particular pieces of equipment or process areas is apt to provide better results. The statistical evidence is amply buttressed by engineering information on this point. By adhering strictly to processes rather than complete plants, modifications in the formula can be made to account for individual capacity-cost relationships. For example, although a linear function of the logarithms seems to fit most of the data well, there is some process equipment for which a curvilinear function is required. For equipment such as cyclone separators, centrifugals, and towers, a function which is concave upward seems to fit the data better. In most cases these curves indicate the existence of economies of scale up to a certain capacity (i.e., slope less than 1) and diseconomies beyond that point (i.e., slope greater than 1); hence an average cost curve for these items would turn up eventually but in general would tend to be flat-bottomed over a considerable range in capacity.

Let us outline a general simple procedure for analyzing the behavior of economies of scale using this process analysis. Suppose that plants in industry X can be divided into four main process areas and one "cooperating" area (e.g., the plant utilities system, piping, or transportation); further let us assume that application of the formula to each area has produced the following values for b_1:

Process area A	.25
Process area B	.60
Process area C	.80; 1.20
Process area D	1.00
Cooperating area E	1.10

From the above it is evident that there are economies of scale in areas A, B, and C, although in the last the economies exist only up to a certain point and then are replaced by diseconomies (e.g., the fractioning tower mentioned previously). Area E contains no possibilities for economies and area D provides constant returns to scale.

It would now be possible to investigate the behavior of economies of scale for different sizes of plant. Eventually the cost curve may turn up. It depends on the importance (from the standpoint of the per cent of total expenditure) of areas C and E. If 75 per cent of total capital expenditures normally occur in area C, or if the per cent of expenditures in that area increases for larger sizes of plants, diseconomies of scale may occur fairly rapidly. If, on the other hand, area A is the most important in the plant, then economies of scale may continue over the whole observable range.

In order to assess the problem we should also know whether the scale of effort in each area can be expanded in small increments or whether the capacities of equipment increase by discrete amounts. In the latter case, economies of scale are limited to specific congeries of equipment. The qualitative characteristics of the equipment must also be investigated, since proportions may be affected thereby.

This would appear to be a relatively simple method of analyzing economies of scale in industry and one which is capable of use without an elaborate study of production functions. The engineers have compiled a good bit of information which can be used immediately and catalogues of equipment can provide more. This information is not in the form which can be used directly; usually it specifies the cost of an item which can perform a certain job such as grinding a certain number of tons a day, or conveying a certain charge per hour, etc. But these data can be utilized with only small changes; three steps are normally involved:

(1) The engineering data in technical journals and catalogues give cost relative to some engineering or physical magnitude (*e.g.*, diameter of tank, square feet of heating surface, peripheral area, etc.).

(2) The physical or engineering magnitude can be related to capacity by an appropriate formula (e.g., the capacity of a tank can be related to the diameter). Chenery has suggested some ways this can be done for whole processes, but what is suggested here is on a much simpler level; it may involve nothing more than an application of simple formulas of area and volume, for example. Of course, in the process some of the elements may be omitted, but rough justice can usually be done to the relationship.

(3) From (1) and (2) it is then possible to express the relationship between cost and capacity and to analyze the behavior of economies of scale.

It would be interesting to apply this procedure, process by process, to plants in several industries, to go through, in short, a simplified version of design of a plant including an analysis of the changes to be made in equipment as size varies. It would not be necessary to consider the whole range of substitutions among capital inputs which are possible; sufficient indications of economies of scale could be obtained from perhaps three or four typical sizes, so that the amount of analysis necessary would be smaller than for a complete production function analysis. It is hoped that others may find in this method much to commend as a simple procedure for evaluating the evidences of economies of scale.

Mathematical, or "Linear," Programming: A Nonmathematical Exposition

ROBERT DORFMAN

Robert Dorfman is Professor of Economics at Harvard University. This well-known expository article appeared in the American Economic Review *in 1953.*

This paper is intended to set forth the leading ideas of mathematical programming[1] purged of the algebraic apparatus which has impeded their general acceptance and appreciation. This will be done by concentrating on the graphical representation of the method. While it is not possible, in general, to portray mathematical programming problems in two-dimensional graphs, the conclusions which we shall draw from the graphs will be of general validity and, of course, the graphic representation of multidimensional problems has a time-honored place in economics.

The central formal problem of economics is the problem of allocating scarce resources so as to maximize the attainment of some predetermined objective. The standard formulation of this problem—the so-called marginal analysis—has led to conclusions of great importance for the under-

---

[1] The terminology of the techniques which we are discussing is in an unsatisfactory state. Most frequently they are called "linear programming" although the relationships involved are not always linear. Sometimes they are called "activities analysis," but this is not a very suggestive name. The distinguishing feature of the techniques is that they are concerned with programming rather than with analysis and, at any rate, "activities analysis" has not caught on. We now try out "mathematical programming"; perhaps it will suit.

137

standing of many questions of social and economic policy. But it is a fact of common knowledge that this mode of analysis has not recommended itself to men of affairs for the practical solution of their economic and business problems. Mathematical programming is based on a restatement of this same formal problem in a form which is designed to be useful in making practical decisions in business and economic affairs. That mathematical programming is nothing but a reformulation of the standard economic problem and its solution is the main thesis of this exposition.

The motivating idea of mathematical programming is the idea of a "process" or "activity." A process is a specific method for performing an economic task. For example, the manufacture of soap by a specified formula is a process. So also is the weaving of a specific quality of cotton gray goods on a specific type of loom. The conventional production function can be thought of as the formula relating the inputs and outputs of all the processes by which a given task can be accomplished.

For some tasks, *e.g.*, soap production, there are an infinite number of processes available. For others, *e.g.*, weaving, only a finite number of processes exist. In some cases, a plant or industry may have only a single process available.

In terms of processes, choice in the productive sphere are simply decisions as to which processes are to be used and the extent to which each is to be employed. Economists are accustomed to thinking in terms of decisions as to the quantities of various productive factors to be employed. But an industry or firm cannot substitute factor A for Factor B unless it does some of its work in a different way, that is, unless it substitutes a process which uses A in relatively high proportions for one which uses B. Inputs, therefore, cannot be changed without a change in the way of doing things, and often a fundamental change. Mathematical programming focuses on this aspect of economic choice.

The objective of mathematical programming is to determine the optimal levels of productive processes in given circumstances. This requires a restatement of productive relationships in terms of processes and a reconsideration of the effect of factor scarcities on production choices. As a prelude to this theoretical discussion, however, it will be helpful to consider a simplified production problem from a commonsense point of view.

I. An Example of Mathematical Programming

Let us consider a hypothetical automobile company equipped for the production of both automobiles and trucks. This company, then, can perform two economic tasks, and we assume that it has a single process for accomplishing each. These two tasks, the manufacture of automobiles and that of trucks, compete for the use of the firm's facilities. Let us assume that the company's plant is organized into four departments: (1) sheet metal stamping, (2) engine assembly, (3) automobile final assembly, and (4) truck final assembly—raw materials, labor, and all other components being available in virtually unlimited amounts at constant prices in the open market.

The capacity of each department of the plant is, of course, limited. We assume that the metal stamping department can turn out sufficient stampings for 25,000 automobiles or 35,000 trucks per month. We can then calculate the combinations of automobile and truck stampings which this department can produce. Since the department can accommodate 25,000 automobiles per month, each automobile requires 1/25,000 or 0.004 per cent of monthly capacity. Similarly each truck requires 0.00286 per cent of monthly capacity. If, for example, 15,000 automobiles were manufactured they would require 60 per cent of metal stamping capacity and the remaining 40 per cent would be sufficient to produce stampings for 14,000 trucks. Then 15,000 automobiles and 14,000 trucks could be produced by this department at full operation. This is, of course, not the only combination of automobiles and trucks which could be produced by the stamping department at full operation. In Figure 1, the line labeled "Metal Stamping" represents all such combinations.

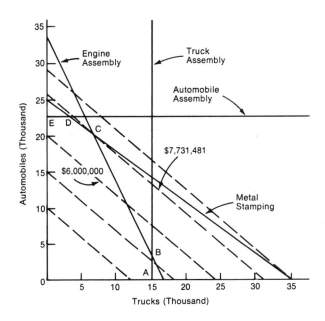

FIGURE 1. CHOICES OPEN TO AN AUTOMOBILE FIRM

Similarly we assume that the engine assembly department has monthly capacity for 33,333 automobile engines or 16,667 truck engines or, again, some combination of fewer automobile and truck engines. The combinations which would absorb the full capacity of the engine assembly department are shown by the "Engine Assembly" line in Figure 1. We assume also that the automobile assembly department can accommodate 22,500 automobiles per month and the truck assembly department 15,000 trucks. These limitations are also represented in Figure 1.

We regard this set of assumptions as defining two processes: the production of automobiles and the production of trucks. The process of producing an automobile yields, as an output, one automobile and absorbs, as inputs, 0.004 per cent of metal stamping capacity, 0.003 per cent of engine assembly capacity, and 0.00444 per cent of automobile assembly capacity. Similarly the process of producing a truck yields, as an output, one truck and absorbs, as inputs, 0.00286 per cent of metal stamping capacity, 0.006 per cent of engine assembly capacity, and 0.00667 per cent of truck assembly capacity.

The economic choice facing this firm is the selection of the numbers of automobiles and trucks to be produced each month, subject to the restriction that no more than 100 per cent of the capacity of any department can be used. Or, in more technical phraseology, the choice consists in deciding at what level to employ each of the two available processes. Clearly, if automobiles alone are produced, at most 22,500 units per month can be made, automobile assembly being the effective limitation. If only trucks are produced, a mximum of 15,000 units per month can be made because of the limitation on truck assembly. Which of these alternatives should be adopted, or whether some combination of trucks and automobiles should be produced, depends on the relative profitability of manufacturing trucks and automobiles. Let us assume, to be concrete, that the sales value of an automobile is $300 greater than the total cost of purchased materials, labor, and other direct costs attributable to its manufacture. And, similarly, that the sale value of a truck is $250 more than the direct cost of manufacturing it. Then the net revenue of the plant for any month is 300 times the number of automobiles produced plus 250 times the number of trucks. For example, 15,000 automobiles and 6,000 trucks would yield a net revenue of $5,000,000. There are many combinations of automobiles and trucks which would yield this same net revenue; 10,000 automobiles and 12,000 trucks is another one. In terms of Figure 1, all combinations with a net revenue of $6,000,000 lie on a straight line, to be specific, the line labeled $6,000,000 in the figure.

A line analogous to the one which we have just described corresponds to each possible net revenue. All these lines are parallel, since their slope depends only on the relative profitability of the two activities. The greater the net revenue, of course, the higher the line. A few of the net revenue lines are shown in the figure by the dashed parallel lines.

Each conceivable number of automobiles and trucks produced corresponds to a point on the diagram, and through each point there passes one member of the family of net revenue lines. Net revenue is maximized when the point corresponding to the number of automobiles and trucks produced lies on the highest possible net revenue line. Now the effect of the capacity restrictions is to limit the range of choice to outputs which correspond to points lying inside the area bounded by the axes and by the broken line *ABCDE*. Since net revenue increases as points move out from the origin, only points which lie on the broken line need be considered. Beginning with Point *A* and moving along the broken line we see that the boundary of the accessible region intersects higher and higher net revenue lines until point *C* is reached. From there on, the boundary slides down the scale of net revenue lines. Point *C* therefore corresponds to the highest attainable net revenue. At point *C* the output is 20,370 automobiles and 6,481 trucks, yielding a net revenue of $7,731,481 per month.

The reader has very likely noticed that this diagram is by no means novel. The broken line *ABCDE* tells the maximum number of automobiles which can be produced in conjunction with any given number of trucks. It is therefore, apart from its angularity, a production opportunity curve or transformation curve of the sort made familiar by Irving Fisher, and the slope of the curve at any point where it has a slope is the ratio of substitution in production between automobiles and trucks. The novel feature is that the production opportunity curve shown here has no defined slope at five points and that one of these five is the critical point. The dashed lines in the diagram are equivalent to conventional price lines.

The standard theory of production teaches that profits are maximized at a point where a price line is tangent to the production opportunity curve. But, as we have just noted, there are five points where our production opportunity curve has no tangent. The tangency criterion therefore fails. Instead we find that profits are maximized at a corner where the slope of the price line is neither less than the slope of the opportunity curve to the left of the corner nor greater than the slope of the opportunity curve to the right.

Diagrammatically, then, mathematical programming uses angles where standard economics uses curves. In economic terms, where does the novelty lie? In standard economic analysis we visualize production relationships in which, if there are two products, one may be substituted for the other with gradually increasing difficulty. In mathematical programming we visualize a regime of production in which, for any output, certain factors will be effectively limiting but other factors will be in ample supply. Thus, in Figure 1, the factors which effectively limit production at each point can be identified by noticing on which limitation lines the point lies. The rate of substitution between products is determined by the limiting factors alone and changes only when the designation of the limiting factors changes. In the diagram a change in the designation of the limiting factors is represented by turning a corner on the production opportunity curve.

We shall come back to this example later, for we have not exhausted its significance. But now we are in a position to develop with more generality some of the concepts used in mathematical programming.

II. The Model of Production in Mathematical Programming

A classical problem in economics is the optimal utilization of two factors of production, conveniently called capital and labor. In the usual analysis, the problem is formulated by conceiving of the two factors as cooperating with each other in accordance with a production function which states the maximum quantity of a product which can be obtained by the use of stated quantities of the two factors. One convenient means of representing such a production function is an "isoquant diagram," as in Figure 2. In this familiar figure, quantities of labor are plotted along the horizontal axis and quantities of capital along the vertical. Each of the arcs in the body of the diagram corresponds to a definite quantity of output, higher arcs corresponding to greater quantities.

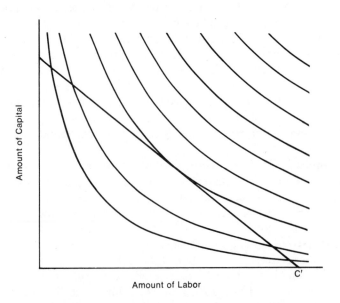

FIGURE 2. AN ISOQUANT DIAGRAM

If the prices per unit of capital and labor are known, the combinations of labor and capital which can be purchased for a fixed total expenditure can be shown by a sloping straight line like *CC'* in the figure, the slope depending only on the relative prices. Two interpretations follow immediately. First, the minimum unit cost of producing the output represented by any isoquant can be achieved by using the combination of labor and capital which corresponds to the point where that isoquant is tangent to a price line. Second, the greatest output attainable with any given expenditure is represented by the isoquant which is tangent to the price line corresponding to that expenditure.

This diagram and its analysis rest upon the assumption that the two factors are continuously substitutable for each other in such wise that if the amount of labor employed be reduced by a small amount it will be possible to maintain the quantity of output by a *small* increase in the amount of capital employed. Moreover, this analysis assumes that each successive unit decrement in the amount of labor will require a slightly larger increment in the amount of capital if output is to remain constant. Otherwise the isoquants will not have the necessary shape.

All this is familiar. We call it to mind only because we are about to develop an analogous diagram which is fundamental to mathematical programming. First, however, let us see why a new diagram and a new approach are felt to be necessary.

The model of production which we have just briefly sketched very likely is valid for some kinds of production. But for most manufacturing industries, and indeed all production where elaborate machinery is used, it is open to serious objection. It is characteristic of most modern machinery that each kind of machine operates efficiently only over a narrow range of speeds and that the quantities of labor, power, materials, and other factors which cooperate with the machine are dictated rather inflexibly by the machine's built-in characteristics. Furthermore, at any time there is available only a small number of different kinds of machinery for accomplishing a given task. A few examples may make these considerations more concrete. Earth may be moved by hand shovels, by steam or diesel shovels, or by bulldozers. Power shovels and bulldozers are built in only a small variety of models, each with inherent characteristics as to fuel consumption per hour, number of operators and assistants required, cubic feet of earth moved per hour, etc. Printing type may be set by using hand-fonts, linotype machines, or monotype machines. Again, each machine is available in only a few models and each has its own pace of operation, power and space requirements, and other essentially unalterable characteristics. A moment's reflection will bring to mind dozens of other illustrations: printing presses, power looms, railroad and highway haulage, statistical and accounting calculation, metallic ore reduction, metal fabrication, etc. For many economic tasks the number of processes available is finite, and each process can be regarded as inflexible with regard to the ratios among factor inputs and process outputs. Factors cannot be substituted for each other except by changing the levels at which entire technical processes are used, because each process uses factors in fixed characteristic ratios. In mathematical programming, accordingly, process substitution plays a role analogous to that of factor substitution in conventional analysis.

We now develop an apparatus for the analysis of process substitution. For convenience we shall limit our discussion to processes which consume two factors, to be called capital and labor, and produce a single output. Figure 3 represents such a process. As in Figure 2, the horizontal axis is scaled in units of labor and the vertical axis in units of capital. The process is represented by the ray, OA, which is scaled in units of output. To each output there corresponds a labor requirement found by locating the appropriate mark on the process ray and reading straight down. The capital requirement is found in the same manner by reading straight across from the mark on the process line. Similarly, to each amount of labor

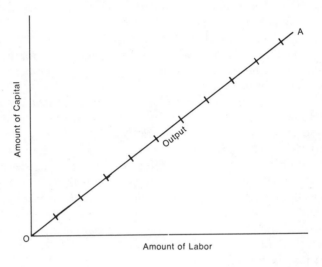

FIGURE 3. A PROCESS

there corresponds a quantity of output, found by reading straight up, and a quantity of capital, found by reading straight across from the output mark.

It should be noted that the quantity of capital in this diagram is the quantity used in a process rather than the quantity owned by an economic unit; it is capital-service rather than capital itself. Thus, though more or less labor may be combined with a given machine—by using it more or fewer hours—the ratio of capital to labor inputs, that is, the ratio of machine hours to labor hours—is regarded as technologically fixed.

Figure 3 incorporates two important assumptions. The fact that the line OA is straight implies that the ratio between the capital input and the labor input is the same for all levels of output and is given, indeed, by the slope of the line. The fact that the marks on the output line are evenly spaced indicates that there are neither economies or diseconomies of scale in the use of the process, *i.e.*, that there will be strict proportionality between the quantity of output and the quantity of either input. These assumptions are justified rather simply on the basis of the notion of a process. If a process can be used once, it can be used twice or as many times as the supplies of factors permit. Two linotype machines with equally skilled operators can turn out just twice as much type per hour as one. Two identical mills can turn out just twice as many yards of cotton per month as one. So long as factors are available, a process can be duplicated. Whether it will be economical to do so is, of course, another matter.

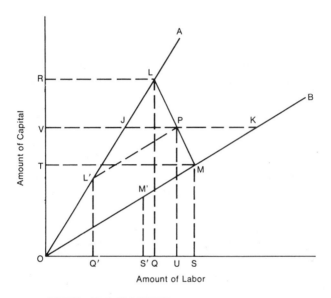

FIGURE 4. TWO PROCESSES

If there is only one process available for a given task there is not much scope for economic choice. Frequently, however, there will be several processes. Figure 4 represents a situation in which two procedures are available, Process A indicated by the line OA and Process B indicated by OB. We have already seen how to interpret points on the lines OA and OB. The scales by which output is measured on the two rays are not necessarily the same. The scale on each ray reflects the productivity of the factors when used in the process represented by that ray and has no connection with the output scale on any other process ray. Now suppose that points L and M represent production of the same output by the two processes. Then LM, the straight line between them, will represent an isoquant and each point on this line will correspond to a combination of Processes A and B which produces the same output as OL units of Process A or OM units of Process B.

To see this, consider any point P on the line LM and draw a line through P parallel to OB. Let L′ be the point where this line intersects OA. Finally mark the point M′ on OB such that OM′ = L′P. Now consider the production plan which consists of using Process A at level OL′ and Process B at level OM′.[2] It is easy to show that this production plan uses OU units of labor, where U is the labor coordinate of point P, and OV units of capital, where V is the capital coordinate of point P.[3]

Since the coordinates of point P correspond to the quantities of factors consumed by OL′ units of Process A and OM′ units of Process B, we interpret P as representing the combined production plan made up of the specified levels of the two processes. This interpretation implies an important economic assumption, namely, that if the two processes are used simultaneously they will neither interfere with nor enhance each other, so that the inputs and outputs resulting from simultaneous use of two processes at any levels can be found by adding the inputs and outputs of the individual processes.

In order to show that P lies on the isoquant through points L and M it remains only to show that the sum of the outputs corresponding to points L′ and M′ is the same as the output corresponding to point L or point M. This follows at once from the facts that the output corresponding to any point on a process ray is directly proportional to the length of the ray up to that point and that the triangles LL′P and LOM in Figure 4 are similar.[4] Thus if we have two process lines like OA and OB and find points L and M on them which represent producing the same output by means of the two processes, then the line segment connecting the two equal-output points will be an isoquant.

We can now draw the mathematical programming analog of the familiar isoquant diagram. Figure 5 is such a diagram with four process lines shown. Point M represents a particular output by use of Process A and points L, K, J represent that same output by means of Processes B, C, D,

---

[2] An alternative construction would be to draw a line through point P parallel to OA. It would intersect OB at M′. Then we could lay off OL′ equal to M′P on OA. This would lead to exactly the same results as the construction used in the text. The situation is analogous to the "parallelogram of forces" in physics.

[3] Proof: Process A at level OL′ uses OQ′ units of labor, Process B at level OM′ uses OS′ units of labor, together they use OQ′ + OS′ units of labor. But, by construction, L′P is equal and parallel to OM′. So Q′U = OS′. Therefore, OQ′ + OS′ = OQ′ + Q′U = OU units of labor. The argument with respect to capital is similar.

[4] Proof: Let Output (X) denote the output corresponding to any point, X, on the diagram. Then Output (M′)/Output (M) = OM′/OM and Output (L′)/Output (L) = OL′/OL. By assumption: Output (L) = Output (M). So Output (M′)/Output (L) = OM′/OM. Adding, we have:

$$\frac{\text{Output (M')} + \text{Output (L')}}{\text{Output (L)}} = \frac{OM'}{OM} + \frac{OL'}{OL} = \frac{L'P}{OM} + \frac{OL'}{OL} = \frac{L'L}{OL} + \frac{OL'}{OL} = 1.$$

respectively. The succession of line segments connecting these four points is the isoquant for that same output. It is easy to see that any other succession of line segments respectively parallel to those of *MLKJ* is also an isoquant. Three such are shown in the figure. It is instructive to compare Figure 5 with Figure 2 and note the strong resemblance in appearance as well as in interpretation.

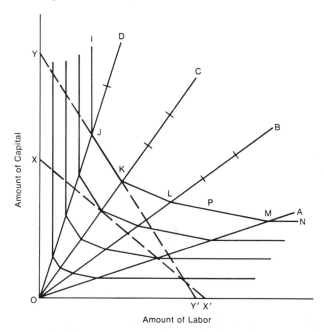

FIGURE 5. FOUR PROCESSES

We may draw price lines on Figure 5, just as on the conventional kind of isoquant diagram. The dashed lines XX′ and YY′ represent two possible price lines. Consider XX′ first. As that line is drawn, the maximum output for a given expenditure can be obtained by use of Process C alone, and, conversely, the minimum cost for a given output is also obtained by using Process C alone. Thus, for the relative price regime represented by XX′, Process C is optimal. The price line YY′ is drawn parallel to the isoquant segment *JK*. In this case Process C is still optimal, but Process D is also optimal and so is any combination of the two.

It is evident from considering these two price lines, and as many others as the reader wishes to visualize, that an optimal production program can always be achieved by means of a single process, which process depending, of course, on the slope of the price line. It should be noted, however, that the conventional tangency criterion is no longer applicable.

We found in Figure 5 that an optimal economic plan need never use more than a single process for each of its outputs.[5] That conclusion is valid for the situation depicted, which assumed that the services of the two factors could be procured in any amounts desired at constant relative prices. This assumption is not applicable to many economic problems, nor is it used much in mathematic programming. We must now, therefore, take factor supply conditions into account.

III. Factor Supplies and Costs

In mathematical programming it is usual to divide all factors of production into two classes: unlimited factors, which are available in any amount desired at constant unit cost, and limited or scarce factors, which are obtainable at constant unit cost up to a fixed maximum quantity and thereafter not at all. The automobile example illustrates this classification. There the four types of capacity were treated as fixed factors available at zero variable cost; all other factors were grouped under direct costs which were considered as constant per unit of output.

The automobile example showed that this classification of factors is adequate for expressing the maximization problem of a firm dealing in competitive markets. In the last section we saw that when all factors are unlimited, this formulation can be used to find a minimum average cost point.

Both of these applications invoked restrictive assumptions, and, furthermore, assumptions which conflict with those conventionally made in studying resource allocation. In conventional analysis we conceive that as the level of production of a firm, industry, or economy rises, average unit costs rise also after some point. The increase in average costs is attributable in part to the working of the law of variable proportions,[6] which operates when the inputs of some but not all factors of production are increased. As far as the consequences of increasing some but not all inputs are concerned, the contrast between mathematical programming and the marginal analysis is more verbal than substantive. A reference to Figure 4 will show how such changes are handled in mathematical programming. Point J in Figure 4 represents the production of a certain output by the use of Process A alone. If it is desired to increase output without increasing the use of capital, this can be done by moving to the right along the dotted line JK, since this line cuts successively higher isoquants. Such a movement would correspond to using increasingly more of Process B and increasingly less of Process A and thus, indirectly, to substituting labor for capital. If, further,

[5] Recall, however, that we have not taken joint production into account nor have we considered the effects of consideration from the demand side.
[6] *Cf.* J. M. Cassels, "On the Law of Variable Proportions," in W. Fellner and B. F. Haley, eds., *Readings in the Theory of Income Distribution* (Philadelphia, 1946), pp. 103–18.

we assume that unit cost of production is lower for Process A than for Process B this movement would also correspond to increasing average cost of production. Thus both marginal analysis and mathematical programming lead to the same conclusion when factor proportions are changed: if the change starts from a minimum cost point the substitution will lead to gradually increasing unit costs.

But changing input proportions is only one part of the story according to the conventional type of analysis. If outputs is to be increased, any of three things may happen. First, it may be possible to increase the consumption of all inputs without incurring a change in their unit prices. In this case both mathematical programming and marginal analysis agree that output will be expanded without changing the ratios among the input quantities, and average cost of production will not increase.[7] Second, it may not be possible to increase the use of some of the inputs. This is the case we have just analyzed. According to both modes of analysis the input ratios will change in this case and average unit costs will increase. The only difference between the two approaches is that if average cost is to be plotted against output, the marginal analyst will show a picture with a smoothly rising curve while the mathematical programmer will show a broken line made up of increasingly steep line segments. Third, it may be possible to increase the quantities of all inputs but only at the penalty of increasing unit prices or some kind of diseconomies of scale. This third case occurs in the marginal analysis, indeed it is the case which gives long-run cost curves their familiar shape, but mathematical programming has no counterpart for it.

The essential substantive difference we have arrived at is that the marginal analysis conceives of pecuniary and technical diseconomies associated with changes in scale while mathematical programming does not.[8] There are many important economic problems in which factor prices and productivities do not change in response to changes in scale or in which such variations can be disregarded. Most investigations of industrial capacity, for example, are of this nature. In such studies we seek the maximum output of an industry, regarding its inventory of physical equipment as given and assuming that the auxiliary factors needed to cooperate with the equipment can be obtained in the quantities dictated by the characteristics of the equipment. Manpower requirement studies are of the same nature. In such studies we take both output and equipment as given and calculate the manpower needed to operate the equipment at the level which will

[7] *Cf.* F. H. Knight, *Risk, Uncertainty and Profit* (Boston, 1921), p. 98.
[8] Even within the framework of the marginal analysis the concept of diseconomies of scale has been challenged on both theoretical and empirical grounds. For examples of empirical criticism see Committee on Price Determination, Conference on Price Research, *Cost Behavior and Price Policy* (New York, 1943). The most searching theoretical criticism is in Piero Sraffa, "The Laws of Returns under Competitive Conditions," *Econ. Jour.*, Dec. 1926, XXXVI, 535–50.

yield the desired output. Studies of full employment output fall into the same format. In such studies we determine in advance the quantity of each factor which is to be regarded as full employment of that factor. Then we calculate the optimum output obtainable by the use of the factors in those quantities.

These illustrations should suffice to show that the assumption made in mathematical programming can comprehend a wide variety of important economic problems. The most useful applications of mathematical programming are probably to problems of the types just described, that is, to problems concerned with finding optimum production plans using specified quantities of some or all of the resources involved.

IV. Analysis of Production with Limited Factors

The diagrams which we have developed are readily adaptable to the analysis of the consequences of limits on the factor supplies. Such limits are, of course, the heart of Figure 1, where the four principal lines represent limitations on the process levels which result from limits on the four factor quantities considered. But Figure 1 cannot be used when more than two processes have to be considered. For such problems diagrams like Figures 3, 4, and 5 have to be used.

Figure 6 reproduces the situation portrayed in Figure 5 with some additional data, to be explained below. Let *OF* represent the maximum

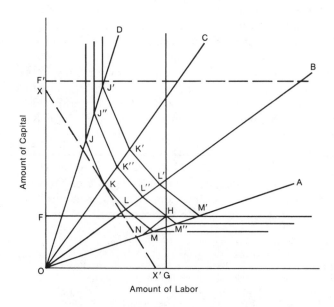

FIGURE 6. FOUR PROCESSES, WITH LIMITATIONS

amount of capital which can be used and thus show a factor limitation. The horizontal line through *F* divides the diagram into two sections: all points above the line correspond to programs which require more capital than is available; points on and below the line represent programs which do not have excessive capital requirements. This horizontal line will be called the capital limitation line. Points on or below it are called "feasible," points above it are called "infeasible."

The economic unit portrayed in Figure 6 has the choice of operating at any feasible point. If maximum output is its objective, it will choose a point which lies on the highest possible isoquant, *i.e.*, the highest isoquant which touches the capital limitation line. This is the one labeled *J'K'L'M'*, and the highest possible output is attained by using Process A.

Of course, maximum output may not be the objective. The objective may be, for example, to maximize the excess of the value of output over labor costs. We shall refer to such an excess as a "net value." The same kind of diagram can be used to solve for a net value provided that the value of each unit of output is independent of the number of units produced[9] and that the cost of each unit of labor is similarly constant. If these provisos are met, each point on a process ray will correspond to a certain physical output but also to a certain value of output, cost of labor, and net value of output. Further, along any process ray the net value of output will equal the physical output times the net value per unit and will therefore be proportional to the physical output. We may thus use a diagram similar to Figure 6 except that we think of net value instead of physical output as measured along the process rays and we show isovalue lines instead of isoquants. This has been done on Figure 7, in which the maximum net value attainable is the one which corresponds to the isovalue contour through point *P*, and is attained by using Process C.

It should be noted in both Figures 6 and 7 that the optimal program consisted of a single process, that shifts in the quantity of capital available would not affect the designation of the optimal process though they would change its level, and that the price lines, which are crucial in Figure 5, played no role.

The next complication, and the last one we shall be able to consider, is to assume that both factors are in limited supply. This situation is portrayed in Figure 6 by adding the vertical line through point G to represent a labor limitation. The available quantity of labor is shown, of course, by the length OG. Then the points inside the rectangle OFHG represent programs which can be implemented in the sense that they do not require more than the available supplies of either factor. This is the rectangle of feasible programs. The greatest achievable output is the one which corresponds to the highest isoquant which touches the rectangle of feasible pro-

[9] This is a particularly uncomfortable assumption. We use it here to explain the method in its least complicated form.

grams. This is the isoquant $J''K''L''M''$, and furthermore, since the maximum isoquant touches the rectangle at H, H represents the program by which the maximum output can be produced.

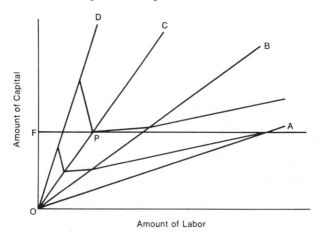

FIGURE 7. FOUR PROCESSES WITH ISOVALUE LINES

This solution differs from the previous ones in that the solution point does not lie on any process ray but between the rays for Processes A and B. We have already seen that a point like H represents using Process A at level ON and Process B at level NH.

Two remarks are relevant to this solution. First: with the factor limitation lines as drawn, the maximum output requires two processes. If the factor limitation lines had been drawn so that they intersected exactly on one of the process rays, only one process would have been required. If the factor limitation lines had crossed to the left of Process D or to the right of Process A, the maximizing production plan would require only one process. But, no matter how the limitation lines be drawn, at most two processes are required to maximize output. We are led to an important generalization: maximum output may always be obtained by using a number of processes which does not exceed the number of factors in limited supply, if this number is greater than zero. The conclusions we drew from Figures 6 and 7 both conform to this rule, and it is one of the basic theorems of mathematical programming.

Second: although at most two processes are required to obtain the maximum output, which two depends on the location of the factor limits. As shown, the processes used for maximum output were Processes A and B. If somewhat more capital, represented by the amount OF', were available, the maximizing processes would have been Processes C and D. If two factors are limited, it is the ratio between their supplies rather than the absolute supplies of either which determines the processes in the optimum program. This contrasts with the case in which only one factor is limited. Just

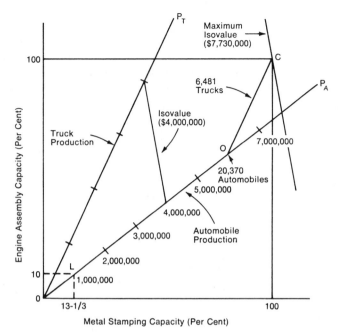

FIGURE 8. AUTOMOBILE EXAMPLE, OPTIMAL PLAN

as the considerations which determine the optimum set of processes are more complicated when two factors are limited than when only one is, so with three or more limited factors the optimum conditions become more complicated still and soon pass the reach of intuition. This, indeed, is the *raison d'être* of the formidable apparatus of mathematical programming.

We can make these considerations more concrete by applying them to the automobile example. Referring to Figure 1, we note that the optimum production point, *C*, lay on the limitation lines for engine assembly and metal stamping, but well below the limits for automobile and truck assembly. The limitations on automobile and truck assembly capacity are, therefore, ineffective and can be disregarded. The situation in terms of the two effectively limiting types of capacity is shown in Figure 8.

In Figure 8 the ray P_A represents the process of producing automobiles and P_T the process for producing trucks. These two processes can be operated at any combination of levels which does not require the use of more than 100 per cent of either metal stamping or engine assembly capacity. Thus the rectangle in the diagram is the region of feasible production programs. The optimal production program is the one in the feasible region which corresponds to the highest possible net revenue.[10] Thus it will be helpful to construct isorevenue lines, as we did in Figure 7. To do this,

[10] Since the objective of the firm is, by assumption, to maximize revenue rather than physical output, we may consider automobile and truck production as two alternative processes for producing revenue instead of as two processes with disparate outputs.

consider automobile production first. Each point on P_A corresponds to the production of a certain number of automobiles per month. Suppose, for example, that the scale is such that point L represents the production of 3,333 automobiles per month. It will be recalled that each automobile yields a net revenue of $300. Therefore, 3,333 automobiles yield a revenue of $1,000,000. Point L, then, corresponds to a net revenue of $1,000,000 as well as to an output of 3,333 automobiles per month. Since (see Figure 1), 3,333 automobiles require 13⅓ per cent of metal stamping capacity and 10 per cent of engine assembly capacity, the coordinates of the $1,000,000 net revenue point on P_A are established at once. By a similar argument, the point whose coordinates are 26⅔ per cent of metal stamping capacity and 20 per cent of engine capacity is the $2,000,000 net revenue point on P_A. In the same manner, the whole ray can be drawn and scaled off in terms of net revenue, and so can P_T, the process ray for truck production. The diagram is completed by connecting the $4,000,000 points on the two process lines in order to show the direction of the isorevenue lines.

The optimum program is at point C, where the two capacity limits intersect, because C lies on the highest isorevenue line which touches the feasible region. Through point C we have drawn a line parallel to the truck production line and meeting the automobile production line at D. By our previous argument, the length OD represents the net revenue from automobile production in the optimal program and the length DC represents the net revenue from trucks. If these lengths be scaled off, the result, of course, will be the same as the solution found previously.

V. *Imputation of Factor Values*

We have just noted that the major field of application of mathematical programming is to problems where the supply of one or more factors of production is absolutely limited. Such scarcities are the genesis of value in ordinary analysis, and they generate values in mathematical programming too. In fact, in ordinary analysis the determination of outputs and the determination of prices are but two aspects of the same problem, the optimal allocation of scarce resources. The same is true in mathematical programming.

Heretofore we have encountered prices only as data for determining the direct costs of processes and the net value of output. But of course the limiting factors of production also have value although we have not assigned prices to them up to now. In this section we shall see that the solution of a mathematical programming problem implicitly assigns values to the limiting factors of production. Furthermore, the implicit pricing problem can be solved directly and, when so solved, constitutes a solution to the optimal allocation problem.

Consider the automobile example and ask: how much is a unit (1 per cent) of each of the types of capacity worth to the firm? The approach to this question is similar in spirit to the familiar marginal analysis. With respect to each type of capacity we calculate how much the maximum revenue would increase if one more unit were added, or how much revenue would decrease if one unit were taken away. Since there is a surplus of automobile assembly capacity, neither the addition nor the subtraction of one unit of this type would affect the optimum program or the maximum net revenue. Hence the value of this type of capacity is nil. The analysis and result for truck assembly are the same.

We find, then, that these two types of capacity are free goods. This does not imply that an automobile assembly line is not worth having, any more than, to take a classic example, the fact that air is a free good means that it can be dispensed with. It means that it would not be worth while to increase this type of capacity at any positive price and that some units of these types could be disposed of without loss.

The valuation of the other types of capacity is not so trivial. In Figure 9 possible values per per cent of engine assembly capacity are scaled along the horizontal axis and values per per cent of metal stamping capacity are scaled along the vertical axis. Now consider any possible pair of values, say engine assembly capacity worth $20,000 per unit and metal stamping worth $40,000. This is represented by point A on the figure. Applying these values to the data on pages 139–140, the values of capacity required for producing an automobile is found to be $(0.004 \times \$40,000) + (0.003 \times \$20,000) = \$220$ which is well under the value of producing an automobile, or $300.[11] In the same way, if engine assembly capacity is worth $60,000 per per cent of capacity and metal stamping capacity is valued at $30,000 per unit (point B), the cost of scarce resources required to produce an automobile will be exactly equal to the value of the product. This is clearly not the only combination of resource values which will precisely absorb the value of output when the resources are used to produce automobiles. The automobile production line on the figure, which passes through point B, is the locus of all such value combinations. A similar line has been drawn for truck production to represent those combinations of resource values for which the total value of resources used in producing trucks is equal to the value of output. The intersection of these two lines is obviously the only pair of resource values for which the marginal resource cost of producing an additional automobile is equal to the net value of an automobile and the same is true with respect to trucks. The pair can be found by plotting or, with more precision, by algebra. It is found that 1 per cent of engine assembly capacity is worth $9,259 and 1 per cent of metal stamping capacity is worth $68,056.

To each pair of values for the two types of capacity, there corresponds a value for the entire plant. Thus to the pair of values represented by point A there corresponds the plant value of $(100 \times \$20,000) + (100 \times$

---

[11] These unit values are also marginal values since costs of production are constant.

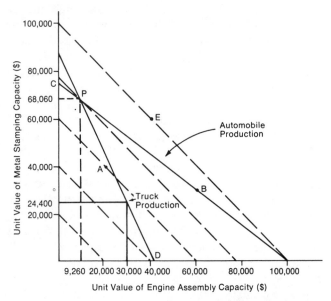

FIGURE 9. AUTOMOBILE EXAMPLE, IMPLICIT VALUES

$40,000) = $6,000,000. This is not the only pair of resource values which give an aggregate plant value of $6,000,000. Indeed, any pair of resource values on the dotted line through A corresponds to the same aggregate plant value. (By this stage, Figure 9 should become strongly reminiscent of Figure 1.) We have drawn a number of dotted lines parallel to the one just described, each corresponding to a specific aggregate plant value. The dotted line which passes through the intersection of the two production lines is of particular interest. By measurement or otherwise this line can be found to correspond to a plant value of $7,731,500 which, we recall, was found to be the maximum attainable net revenue.

Let us consider the implications of assigning values to the two limiting factors from a slightly different angle. We have seen that as soon as unit values have been assigned to the factors an aggregate value is assigned to the plant. We can make the aggregate plant value as low as we please, simply by assigning sufficiently low values to the various factors. But if the values assigned are too low, we have the unsatisfactory consequence that some of the processes will give rise to unimputed surpluses. We may, therefore, seek the lowest aggregate plant value which can be assigned and still have no process yield an unimputed surplus. In the automobile case, that value is $7,731,500. In the course of finding the lowest acceptable plant value we find specific unit values to be assigned to each of the resources.

In this example there are two processes and four limited resources. It turns out that only two of the resources were effectively limiting, the others being in relatively ample supply. In general, the characteristics of the solution to a programming problem depend on the relationship between the number of limited resources and the number of processes taken into consideration. If, as in the present instance, the number of limited resources exceeds the number of processes it will usually turn out that some of the resources will have imputed values of zero and that the number of resources with positive imputed values will be equal to the number of processes.[12] If the number of limited resources equals the number of processes all resources will have positive imputed values. If, finally, the number of processes exceeds the number of limited resources, some of the processes will not be used in the optimal program. This situation, which is the usual one, was illustrated in Figure 6. In this case the total imputed value of resources absorbed will equal net revenue for some processes and will exceed it for others. The number of processes for which the imputed value of resources absorbed equals the net revenue will be just equal to the number of limited resources, and the processes for which the equality holds are the ones which will appear at positive levels in the optimal program. In brief, the determination of the minimum acceptable plant value amounts to the same thing as the determination of the optimal production program. The programming problem and the valuation problem are not only closely related, they are basically the same.

This can be seen graphically by comparing Figures 1 and 9. Each figure contains two axes and two diagonal boundary lines. But the boundary lines in Figure 9 refer to the same processes as the axes in Figure 1, and the axes in Figure 9 refer to the same resources as the diagonal boundary lines in Figure 1. Furthermore, in using Figure 1 we sought the net revenue corresponding to the highest dashed line touched by the boundary; in using Figure 9 we sought the aggregate value corresponding to the lowest dashed line which has any points on or outside the boundary; and the two results turned out to be the same. Formally stated, these two figures and the problems they represent are *duals* of each other.

The dualism feature is a very useful property in the solution of mathematical programming problems. The simplest way to see this is to note that when confronting a mathematical programming problem we have the choice of solving the problem or its dual, whichever is easier. Either way we can get the same results. We can use this feature now to generalize our discussion somewhat. Up to now when dealing with more than two processes we have had to use relatively complicated diagrams like Figure 6 because straightforward diagrams like Figure 1 did not contain enough axes to represent the levels of the processes. Now we can use diagrams modeled on Figure 9 to depict problems with any number of processes so long as they do not involve more than two scarce factors. Figure 10 illus-

[12] We say "usually" in this sentence because in some special circumstances the number of resources with positive imputed values may exceed the number of processes.

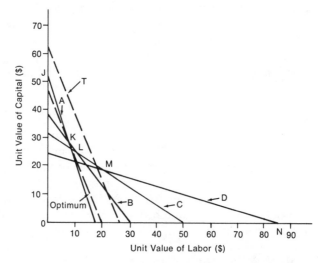

FIGURE 10. THE VALUATION PROBLEM, FOUR PROCESSES

trates a diagram for four processes and is, indeed, derived from Figure 6. In Figure 10, line A represents all pairs of factor values such that Process A would yield neither a profit nor a loss. Lines B, C, and D are similarly interpreted. The dashed line T is a locus along which the aggregate value of the labor and capital available to the firm (or industry) is constant. Its position is not relevant to the analysis; its slope, which is simply the ratio of the quantity of available labor to that of capital, is all that is significant. The broken line *JKLMN* divides the graph into two regions. All points on or above it represent pairs of resource values such that no process gives rise to an unimputed surplus. Let us call this the acceptable region. For each point below that broken line there is at least one process which does have an unimputed surplus. This is the unacceptable region. We then seek for that point in the acceptable region which corresponds to the lowest aggregate plant value. This point will, of course, give the set of resource values which makes the accounting profit of the firm as great as possible without giving rise to any unimputed income. The point which meets these requirements is K, and a dotted line parallel to T has been drawn through it to indicate the minimum acceptable aggregate plant value.

At point K, Processes A and B yield zero profits, and Processes C and D yield losses. Hence Processes A and B are the ones which should be used, exactly as we found in Figure 6. To be sure, this diagram does not tell the levels at which A and B should be used, any more than Figure 6 tells the valuations to be placed on the two resources. But finding the levels after the processes have been selected is a comparatively trivial matter. All that is necessary is to find the levels which will fully utilize the resources which are not free goods. This may be done algebraically or by means of a diagram like Figure 8.

VI. Applications

In the first section we asserted that the principal motivation of mathematical programming was the need for a method of analysis which lent itself to the practical solution of the day-to-day problems of business and the economy in general. Immediately after making that claim we introduced a highly artificial problem followed by a rather extended discussion of abstract and formal relationships. The time has now come to indicate the basis for saying that mathematical programming is a practical method of analysis.

The essential simplification achieved in mathematical programming is the replacement of the notion of the production function by the notion of the process. The process is a highly observable unit of activity and the empirical constants which characterize it can be estimated without elaborate analysis. Furthermore in many industries the structure of production corresponds to operating a succession of processes, as we have conceived them. Many industrial decisions, like shutting down a bank of machines or operating an extra shift, correspond naturally to our concept of choosing the level of operation of a process. In brief, mathematical programming is modeled after the actual structure of production in the hope that thereby it will involve only observable constants and directly controllable variables.

Has this hope been justified? The literature already contains a report of a successful application to petroleum refining.[13] I have made a similar application which, perhaps, will bear description. The application was to a moderate-sized refinery which produces premium and regular grades of automotive gasoline. The essential operation studied was blending. In blending, ten chemically distinct kinds of semirefined oil, called blending stocks, are mixed together. The result is a salable gasoline whose characteristics are approximately the weighted average of the characteristics of the blending stocks. For example, if 500 gallons of a stock with octane rating of 80 are blended with 1,000 gallons of a stock with octane rating of 86 the result will be $500 + 1,000 = 1,500$ gallons of product with octane rating of $(\frac{1}{3} \times 80) + (\frac{2}{3} \times 86) = 84$.

The significant aspect of gasoline blending for our present purposes is that the major characteristics of the blend—its knock rating, its vapor pressure, its sulphur content, etc.—can be expressed as linear functions of the quantities of the various blending stocks used. So also can the cost of the blend if each of the blending stocks has a definite price per gallon. Thus the problem of finding the minimum cost blend which will meet given quality specifications is a problem in mathematical programming.

[13] A. Charnes, W. W. Cooper, and B. Mellon, "Blending Aviation Gasolines," *Econometrica*, Apr. 1952, XX, 135–59.

Furthermore, in this refinery the quantities of some of the blending stocks are definitely limited by contracts and by refining capacity. The problem then arises: what are the most profitable quantities of output of regular and premium gasoline, and how much of each blending stock should be used for each final product? This problem is analogous to the artificial automobile example, with the added complication of the quality specifications. The problem is too complicated for graphic analysis but was solved easily by arithmetical procedures. As far as is known, mathematical programming provides the only way for solving such problems. Charnes and Cooper have recently published the solution to a similar problem which arose in the operations of a metal-working firm.[14]

An entirely different kind of problem, also amenable to mathematical programming, arises in newsprint production. Freight is a major element in the cost of newsprint. One large newsprint company has six mills, widely scattered in Canada, and some two hundred customers, widely scattered in the United States. Its problem is to decide how much newsprint to ship from each mill to each customer so as, first, to meet the contract requirements of each customer, secondly, to stay within the capacity limits of each mill, and third, to keep the aggregate freight bill as small as possible. This problem involves 1,200 variables (6 mills $\times$ 200 customers), in contrast to the two- or four-variable problems we have been discussing. In the final solution most of these variables will turn out to be zero—the question is which ones. This problem is solved by mathematical programming and, though formidable, is not really as formidable as the count of variables might indicate.

These few illustrations should suffice to indicate that mathematical programming is a practical tool for business planning. They show, also, that it is a flexible tool because both examples deviated from the format of the example used in our expansion. The petroleum application had the added feature of quality specification. In the newsprint application there were limits on the quantity of output as well as on the quantities of the inputs. Nevertheless mathematical programming handled them both easily.

On the other hand, it should be noted that both of these were small-scale applications, dealing with a single phase of the operation of a single firm. I believe that this has been true of all successful applications to date. Mathematical programmers are still a long way from solving the broad planning problems of entire industries or an entire economy. But many such broad problems are only enlarged versions of problems which have been met and solved in the context of the single firm. It is no longer premature to say that mathematical programming has proved its worth as a practical tool for finding optimal economic programs.

[14] A. Charnes, W. W. Cooper, and Donald Farr and Staff, "Linear Programming and Profit Preference Scheduling for a Manufacturing Firm," *Jour. Operations Research Society of America*, May 1953, I, 114–29.

VII. Conclusion

Our objective has been only to introduce the basic notions of mathematical programming and to invest them with plausibility and meaning. The reader who would learn to solve a programming problem—even the simplest—will have to look elsewhere,[15] though this paper may serve as a useful background.

Although methods of solution have been omitted from this exposition, we must emphasize that these methods are fundamental to the whole concept of mathematical programming. Some eighty years ago Walras conceived of production in very much the same manner as mathematical programmers, and more recently A. Wald and J. von Neumann used this view of production and methods closely allied to those of mathematical programming to analyze the conditions of general economic equilibrium.[16] These developments, however, must be regarded merely as precursors of mathematical programming. Programming had no independent existence as a mode of economic analysis until 1947 when G. B. Dantzig announced the "simplex method" of solution which made practical application feasible.[17] The existence of a method whereby economic optima could be explicitly calculated stimulated research into the economic interpretation of mathematical programming and led also to the development of alternative methods of solution. The fact that economic and business problems when formulated in terms of mathematical programming can be solved numerically is the basis of the importance of the method. The omission of methods of solution from this discussion should not, therefore, be taken to indicate that they are of secondary interest.

We have considered only a few of the concepts used in mathematical programming and have dealt with only a single type of programming problem. The few notions we have considered, however, are the basic ones; all the rest of mathematical programming is elaboration and extension of

[15] The standard reference is T. C. Koopmans, ed., *Activity Analysis of Production and Allocation* (New York, 1951). Less advanced treatments may be found in A. Charnes, W. W. Cooper, and A. Henderson, *An Introduction to Linear Programming* (New York, 1953); and my own *Application of Linear Programming to the Theory of the Firm* (Berkeley, 1951).

[16] Walras' formulation is in *Eléments d'économie politique pure ou théorie de la richesse sociale*, 2d ed. (Lausanne, 1889), 20ᵉ Leçon. The contributions of A. Wald and J. von Neumann appeared originally in *Ergebnisse eines mathematischen Kolloquiums*, Nos. 6, 7, 8. Wald's least technical paper appeared in *Zieitschrift für Nationalökonomie*, VII (1936) and has been translated as "On some Systems of Equations of Mathematical Economics," *Econometrica*, Oct. 1951, XIX, 368–403. Von Neumann's basic paper appeared in translation as "A Model of General Economic Equilibrium," *Rev. Econ. Stud.*, 1945–46, XIII, 1–9.

[17] G. B. Dantzig, "Maximization of a Linear Function of Variables Subject to Linear Inequalities," T. C. Koopmans, ed., *op. cit.*, pp. 339–47.

them. It seems advisable to mention two directions of elaboration, for they remove or weaken two of the most restrictive assumptions which have here been imposed.

The first of these extensions is the introduction of time into the analysis. The present treatment has dealt with a single production period in isolation. But in many cases, successive production periods are interrelated. This is so, for example, in the case of a vertically integrated firm where the operation of some processes in one period is limited by the levels of operation in the preceding period of the processes which supply their raw materials. Efficient methods for analyzing such "dynamic" problems are being investigated, particularly by George Dantzig.[18] Although the present discussion has been static, the method of analysis can be applied to problems with a time dimension.

The second of these extensions is the allowance for changes in the prices of factors and final products. In our discussion we regarded all prices as unalterable and independent of the actions of the economic unit under consideration. Constant prices are, undeniably, a great convenience to the analyst, but the method can transcend this assumption when necessary. The general mathematical theory of dealing with variable prices has been investigated[19] and practical methods of solution have been developed for problems where the demand and supply curves are linear.[20] The assumption of constant prices, perhaps the most restrictive assumption we have made, is adopted for convenience rather than from necessity.

Mathematical programming has been developed as a tool for economic and business planning and not primarily for the descriptive, and therefore predictive, purposes which gave rise to the marginal analysis. Nevertheless it does have predictive implications. In so far as firms operate under the conditions assumed in mathematical programming it would be unreasonable to assume that they acted as if they operated under the conditions assumed by the marginal analysis. Consider, for example, the automobile firm portrayed in Figure 1. How would it respond if the price of automobiles were to fall, say by $50 a unit? In that case the net revenue per automobile would be $250, the same as the net revenue per truck. Diagrammatically, the result would be to rotate the lines of equal revenue until their slope was 45 degrees. After this rotation, point C would still be optimum and this change in prices would cause no change in optimum output. Mathematical programming gives rise, thus, to a kinked supply curve.

On the other hand, suppose that the price of automobiles were to rise by $50. Diagrammatically this price change would decrease the steepness

[18] "A Note on a Dynamic Leontief Model with Substitution" (abstract), *Econometrica*, Jan. 1953, XXI, 179.

[19] See H. W. Kuhn and A. W. Tucker, "Non-Linear Programming," in J. Neyman, ed., *Proceedings of the Second Berkeley Symposium on Mathematical Statistics and Probability* (Berkeley, 1951), pp. 481–92.

[20] I reported one solution of this problem to a seminar at the Massachusetts Institute of Technology in September 1952. Other solutions may be known.

of the equal revenue lines until they were just parallel to the metal stamping line. The firm would then be in a position like that illustrated by the YY′ line in Figure 5. The production plans corresponding to points on the line segment DC in Figure 1 would all yield the same net revenue and all would be optimal. If the price of automobiles were to rise by more than $50 or if a $50 increase in the price of automobiles were accompanied by any decrease in the price of trucks, the point of optimal production would jump abruptly from point C to point D.

Thus mathematical programming indicates that firms whose choices are limited to distinct processes will respond discontinuously to price variations: they will be insensitive to price changes over a certain range and will change their levels of output sharply as soon as that range is passed. This theoretical deduction surely has real counterparts.

The relationship between mathematical programming and welfare economics is especially close. Welfare economics studies the optimal organization of economic effort; so does mathematical programming. This relationship has been investigated especially by Koopmans and Samuelson.[21] The finding, generally stated, is that the equilibrium position of a perfectly competitive economy is the same as the optimal solution to the mathematical programming problem embodying the same data.

Mathematical programming is closely allied mathematically to the methods of input-output analysis or interindustry analysis developed largely by W. W. Leontief.[22] The two methods were developed independently, however, and it is important to distinguish them conceptually. Input-output analysis finds its application almost exclusively in the study of general economic equilibrium. It conceives of an economy as divided into a number of industrial sectors each of which is analogous to a process as the term is used in mathematical programming. It then takes either of two forms. In "open models" an input-output analysis starts with some specified final demand for the products of each of the sectors and calculates the level at which each of the sector-processes must operate in order to meet this schedule of final demands. In "closed models" final demand does not appear but attention is concentrated on the fact that the inputs required by each sector-process must be supplied as outputs by some other sector-processes. Input-output analysis then calculates a mutually compatible set of output levels for the various sectors. By contrast with mathematical programming the conditions imposed in input-output analysis are sufficient to determine the levels of the processes and there is no scope for finding an optimal solution or a set of "best" levels. To be sure, input-output analysis can be regarded as a special case of mathematical program-

---

[21] T. C. Koopmans, "Analysis of Production as an Efficient Combination of Activities," in T. C. Koopmans, ed., *op. cit.*, pp. 33–97; P. A. Samuelson, "Market Mechanisms and Maximization" (a paper prepared for the Rand Corp., 1949).
[22] W. W. Leontief, *The Structure of American Economy 1919–1939*, 2nd. ed. (New York, 1951).

ming in which the number of products is equal to the number of processes. On the other hand, the limitations on the supplies of resources which play so important a role in mathematical programming are not dealt with explicitly in input-output analysis. On the whole it seems best to regard these two techniques as allied but distinct methods of analysis addressed to different problems.

Mathematical programming, then, is of significance for economic thinking and theory as well as for business and economic planning. We have been able only to allude to this significance. Indeed, apart from the exploration of welfare implications, very little thought has been given to the consequences for economics of mathematical programming because most effort has been devoted to solving the numerous practical problems to which it gives rise. The outlook is for fruitful researches into both the implications and applications of mathematical programming.

Part Three

COMPETITION AND
MONOPOLY

Microeconomics is vitally concerned with the determination of price and output in various kinds of markets. Two of the most important types of market structure are perfect competition and monopoly. Although these two are polar cases that do not often turn up in the real world, they are very useful models that have permitted economists to shed considerable light on the functioning of actual markets in the American economy. In this part of the book, we present a number of classic papers dealing with perfect competition and pure monopoly.

The first paper, by George Stigler, is an interesting description of the evolution of the concept of perfect competition. It is of some importance that the student acquire at least a minimal familiarity with the great names of economics in the past and some insight into the history of economic thought. This paper is a useful introduction to this topic. The following paper, by J. R. Hicks, is a famous survey of the theory of monopoly, including a discussion of monopolistic competition (discussed further in Part Four below). This paper requires more mathematical sophistication than others in this book, but it should be within the reach of students who have some familiarity with elementary calculus.

Whereas Hicks is concerned with the purely theoretical analysis of monopoly (and related market structures), Arnold Harberger, in the next article, goes a step further: he makes an attempt to measure—in dollars and cents—the cost of monopoly in the United States in the 1920's. On the basis of assumptions that admittedly are very imprecise, Harberger comes to the following conclusion: "Elimination of resource misallocations in American manufacturing in the late twenties would bring with it an improvement in consumer welfare of just a little more than a tenth of a per cent. In present values, this welfare gain would amount to about $2.00 per capita." This conclusion is surprising—and controversial, many economists having taken issue with some of the assumptions.

Harvey Leibenstein, in the following article, discusses the importance of what he calls "X-efficiency," as contrasted with the allocative efficiency Harberger is concerned with. Leibenstein concludes that "in a great many instances the amount to be gained by increasing allocative efficiency is trivial while the amount to be gained from increasing X-efficiency is frequently significant."

Case studies are extremely valuable in illustrating and extending theoretical principles and results. In the next paper, Kenneth Boulding presents a case study of perfect competition. As he points out, agriculture "is one place in the economy where the economist's beau ideal of perfect competition is found." He analyzes the cyclical and long-term behavior and problems of agriculture, using many of the theoretical concepts of microeconomics. The following paper, by John McGee, is a case study of unregulated monopoly. McGee is interested in determining whether the Standard Oil Company used predatory price cutting to achieve or maintain its monopoly in the early 1900's. His conclusion is that "Standard Oil did not use predatory price discrimination to drive out competing refiners, nor did its pricing practice have that effect." Of course, as McGee points out, this in no way acquits Standard Oil; it merely sets the record straight concerning the way in which the monopoly was achieved.

The next paper, by the Council of Economic Advisers, describes the reasons for economic regulation in the United States, and presents brief case studies of the effects of regulation in several major industries: trucking, railroads, air travel, and financial institutions. According to the Council, the costs of regulation are high in these industries. In the last paper in this part of the book, Reuben Kessel presents a case study of price discrimination. He argues that the economist's model of the discriminating monopolist is "valid for understanding the pricing of medical services, and that each individual buyer of medical services that are produced jointly with hospital care constitutes a unique, separable market."

Perfect Competition, Historically Contemplated

GEORGE J. STIGLER

George J. Stigler is Walgreen Professor of American Institutions at the University of Chicago. This article appeared in the Journal of Political Economy, 1957.

No concept in economics—or elsewhere—is ever defined fully, in the sense that its meaning under every conceivable circumstance is clear. Even a word with a wholly arbitrary meaning in economics, like "elasticity," raises questions which the person who defined it (in this case, Marshall) never faced: for example, how does the concept apply to finite changes or to discontinuous or stochastic or multiple-valued functions? And of course a word like "competition," which is shared with the whole population, is even less likely to be loaded with restrictions or elaborations to forestall unfelt ambiguities.

Still, it is a remarkable fact that the concept of competition did not begin to receive explicit and systematic attention in the main stream of economics until 1871. This concept—as pervasive and fundamental as any in the whole structure of classical and neoclassical economic theory—was long treated with the kindly casualness with which one treats of the intuitively obvious. Only slowly did the elaborate and complex concept of perfect competition evolve, and it was not until after the first World War that it was finally received into general theoretical literature. The evolution of the concept and the steps by which it became confused with a perfect market, uniqueness of equilibrium, and stationary conditions are the subject of this essay.

The Classical Economists

"Competition" entered economics from common discourse, and for long it connoted only the independent rivalry of two or more persons. When Adam Smith wished to explain why a reduced supply led to a higher price, he referred to the "competition [which] will immediately begin" among buyers; when the supply is excessive, the price will sink more, the greater "the competition of the sellers, or according as it happens to be more or less important to them to get immediately rid of the commodity."[1] It will be noticed that "competition" is here (and usually) used in the sense of rivalry in a race—a race to get limited supplies or a race to be rid of excess supplies. Competition is a process of responding to a new force and a method of reaching a new equilibrium.

Smith observed that economic rivals were more likely to strive for gain by under- or overbidding one another, the more numerous they were:

> The trades which employ but a small number of hands, run most easily into such combinations.
>
> If this capital [sufficient to trade in a town] is divided between two different grocers, their competition will tend to make both of them sell cheaper, than if it were in the hands of one only; and if it were divided among twenty, their competition would be just so much the greater, and the chance of their combining together, in order to raise the price, just so much the less.[2]

This is all that Smith has to say of the number of rivals.

Of course something more is implicit, and partially explicit, in Smith's treatment of competition, but this "something more" is not easy to state precisely, for it was not precise in Smith's mind. But the concept of competition seemed to embrace also several other elements:

1. The economic units must possess tolerable knowledge of the conditions of employment of their resources in various industries. "This equality [of remuneration] can take place only in those employments which are well known, and have been long established in the neighborhood."[3] But the necessary information was usually available: "Secrets . . . , it must be acknowledged, can seldom be long kept; and the extraordinary profit can last very little longer than they are kept."[4]

2. Competition achieved its results only in the long run: "This equality in the whole of the advantages and disadvantages of the different employments of labour and stock, can take place only in the ordinary, or what may be called the natural state of those employments."[5]

---

[1] *The Wealth of Nations* (Modern Library ed.), pp. 56–57.
[2] *Ibid.*, pp. 126 and 342.
[3] *Ibid.*, p. 114.
[4] *Ibid.*, p. 60.
[5] *Ibid.*, p. 115.

3. There must be freedom of trade; the economic unit must be free to enter or leave any trade. The exclusive privileges of corporations which exclude men from trades, and the restrictions imposed on mobility by the settlement provisions of the poor law, are examples of such interferences with "free competition."

In sum, then, Smith had five conditions of competition:

1. The rivals must act independently, not collusively.

2. The number of rivals, potential as well as present, must be sufficient to eliminate extraordinary gains.

3. The economic units must possess tolerable knowledge of the market opportunities.

4. There must be freedom (from social restraints) to act on this knowledge.

5. Sufficient time must elapse for resources to flow in the directions and quantities desired by their owners.

The modern economist has a strong tendency to read more into such statements than they meant to Smith and his contemporaries. The fact that he (and many successors) was willing to call the ownership of land a monopoly—although the market in agricultural land met all these conditions—simply because the total supply of land was believed to be fixed is sufficient testimony to the fact that he was not punctilious in his language.[6]

Smith did not state how he was led to these elements of a concept of competition. We may reasonably infer that the conditions of numerous rivals and of independence of action of these rivals were matters of direct observation. Every informed person knew, at least in a general way, what competition was, and the essence of this knowledge was the striving of rivals to gain advantages relative to one another.

The other elements of competition, on the contrary, appear to be the necessary conditions for the validity of a proposition which was to be associated with competition: the equalization of returns in various directions open to an entrepreneur or investor or laborer. If one postulates equality of returns as the equilibrium state under competition, then adequacy of numbers and independence of rivals are not enough for equilibrium. The entrepreneur (or other agents) must know what returns are obtainable in various fields, he must be allowed to enter the fields promising high rates of return, and he must be given time to make his presence felt in these fields. These conditions were thus prerequisites of an analytical theorem, although their reasonableness was no doubt enhanced by the fact that they corresponded more or less closely to observable conditions.

This sketch of a concept of competition was not amplified or challenged

[6] *Ibid.*, p. 145. Perhaps this is not the ideal illustration of the laxness of the period in the use of the competitive concept, for several readers of this paper have sympathized with this usage. But, to repeat, competition is consistent with a zero elasticity of supply: the fact of windfall gains from unexpected increases in demand is characteristic of all commodities with less than infinitely elastic supplies.

in any significant respect for the next three-quarters of a century by any important member of the English school. A close study of the literature, such as I have not made, would no doubt reveal many isolated passages on the formal properties or realism of the concept, especially when the theory was applied to concrete problems. For example, Senior was more interested in methodology than most of his contemporaries, and he commented:

> But though, under free competition, cost of production is the regulator of price, its influence is subject to much occasional interruption. Its operation can be supposed to be perfect only if we suppose that there are no disturbing causes, that capital and labour can be at once transferred, and without loss, from one employment to another, and that every producer has full information of the profit to be derived from every mode of production. But it is obvious that these suppositions have no resemblance to the truth. A large portion of the capital essential to production consists of buildings, machinery, and other implements, the results of much time and labour, and of little service for any except their existing purposes. ... Few capitalists can estimate, except upon an average of some years, the amounts of their own profits, and still fewer can estimate those of their neighbours.[7]

Senior made no use of the concept of perfect competition hinted at in this passage, and he was wholly promiscuous in his use of the concept of monopoly.

Cairnes, the last important English economist to write in the classical tradition, did break away from the Smithian concept of competition. He defined a state of free competition as one in which commodities exchanged in proportion to the sacrifices (of labor and capital) in their production.[8] This condition was amply fulfilled, he believed, so far as capital was concerned, for there was a large stock of disposable capital which quickly flowed into unusually remunerative fields.[9] The condition was only partly fulfilled in the case of labor, however, for there existed a hierarchy of occupational classes ("non-competing industrial groups") which the laborer found it most difficult to ascend.[10] Even the extra rewards of skill beyond those which paid for the sacrifices in obtaining training were a monopoly return.[11] This approach was not analytically rigorous—Cairnes did not tell how to equate the sacrifices of capitalists and laborers—nor was it empirically fruitful.

Cairnes labeled as "industrial competition" the force which effects the proportioning of prices to psychological costs which takes place to the extent that the products are made in one noncompeting group, and he called on the reciprocal demand theory of international trade to explain exchanges of products between noncompeting groups. Hence we might

---

[7] N. W. Senior, *Political Economy* (New York, 1939), p. 102.
[8] *Some Leading Principles of Political Economy Newly Expounded* (London, 1874), p. 79.
[9] *Ibid.*, p. 68.
[10] *Ibid.*, p. 72.
[11] *Ibid.*, p. 85. Thus Cairnes tacitly labeled all differences in native ability as "monopolistic."

call industrial competition the competition within noncompeting groups, and commercial competition that between noncompeting groups. But Sidgwick and Edgeworth attribute the opposite concepts to Cairnes: commercial competition is competition within an industry, and industrial competition requires the ability of resources to flow between industries.[12] Their nomenclature seems more appropriate; I have not been able to find Cairnes's discussion of commercial competition and doubt that it exists.[13]

The Critics of Private Enterprise

The main claims for a private-enterprise system rest upon the workings of competition, and it would not have been unnatural for critics of this system to focus much attention on the competitive concept. They might have argued that Smith's assumptions were not strong enough to insure optimum results or that, even if perfect competition were formulated as the basis of the theory, certain deviations from optimum results (such as those associated with external economies) could occur. The critics did not make this type of criticism, however, possibly simply because they were not first-class analysts; and for this type of development we must return to the main line of theorists, consisting mostly of politically conservative economists.

Or, at another pole, the critics might simply have denied that competition was the basic form of market organization. In the nineteenth century, however, this was only a minor and sporadic charge.[14] The Marxists did not press this point: both the labor theory of value and the doctrine of equalization of profit rates require competition.[15] The early Fabian essayists were also prepared to make their charges rest upon the deficiencies in the workings of competition rather than its absence.[16] The charge that competition was nonexistent or vanishing did not become commonplace until the end of the nineteenth century.

[12] Henry Sidgwick, *Principles of Political Economy* (London, 1883), p. 182; F. Y. Edgeworth, *Papers Relating to Political Economy* (London, 1925), II, 280, 311.

[13] Karl Marx once distinguished interindustry from intraindustry competition in *Theorien über den Mehrwert* (Stuttgart, 1905), II, Part 2, 14 n.

[14] For example, Leslie repeatedly denied that resource owners possessed sufficient knowledge to effect an equalization of the rates of return (see T. E. Cliffe Leslie, *Essays in Political and Moral Philosophy* [London, 1888], pp. 47, 48, 81, 158–59, 184–85).

[15] See especially Volume III of *Das Kapital* and also F. Engels, *The Condition of the Working-Classes in England*, reprinted in Karl Marx and Friedrich Engels, *On Britain* (London, 1954), pp. 109 ff. The Marxian theory of the increasing concentration of capital was a minor and inconsistent dissent from the main position (see *Capital* [Modern Library ed.], pp. 684 ff.).

[16] See *Fabian Essays* (Jubilee ed.; London, 1948), especially those by Shaw and Webb. But the attention devoted to monopoly was increasing, and the essay by Clarke argued that "combination is absorbing commerce" (*ibid.*, p. 84). A few years later the Webbs used a competitive model in their celebrated discussion of "higgling in the market" and then went on to describe the formation of monopolistic structures as defenses erected against the competitive pressures the Webbs did not quite understand (see *Industrial Democracy* [London, 1920], Part III, chap. ii).

The critics, to the extent that they took account of competition at all, emphasized the evil tendencies which they believed flowed from its workings. It would be interesting to examine their criticisms systematically with a view to their treatment of competition; it is my impression that their most common, and most influential, charge was that competition led to a highly objectionable, and perhaps continuously deteriorating, distribution of income by size.[17] In their explanations of the workings of a competitive economy the most striking deficiency of the classical economists was their failure to work out the theory of the effects of competition on the distribution of income.

The Mathematical School

The first steps in the analytical refinement of the concept of competition were made by the mathematical economists. This stage in the history of the concept is of special interest because it reveals both the types of advances that were achieved by this approach and the manner in which alien elements were introduced into the concept.

When an algebraically inclined economist seeks to maximize the profits of a producer, he is led to write the equation

$$\text{Profits} = \text{Revenue} - \text{Cost}$$

and then to maximize this expression; that is, to set the derivative of profits with respect to output equal to zero. He then faces the question: How does revenue (say, pq) vary with output (q)? The natural answer is to *define* competition as that situation in which p does not vary with q—in which the demand curve facing the firm is horizontal. This is precisely what Cournot did:

> The effects of competition have reached their limit, when each of the partial productions D_k [the output of producer k] is *inappreciable*, not only with reference to the total production $D = F(p)$, but also with reference to the derivative $F'(p)$, so that the partial production D_k could be subtracted from D without any appreciable variation resulting in the price of the commodity.[18]

This definition of competition was especially appropriate in Cournot's system because, according to his theory of oligopoly, the excess of price

[17] A second main criticism became increasingly more prominent in the second half of the nineteenth century: that a private-enterprise system allowed or compelled large fluctuations in employment. For some critics (e.g., Engels), competition was an important cause of these fluctuations.

[18] *Mathematical Principles of the Theory of Wealth* (New York, 1929), p. 90. It is sufficient to assume that D_k is small relative to D if one assumes that the demand function is continuous, for then "the variations of the demand will be sensibly proportional to the variations in price so long as these last are small fractions of the original price" (*ibid.*, p. 50).

over marginal cost approached zero as the number of like producers became large.[19] Cournot believed that this condition of competition was fulfilled "for a multitude of products, and, among them, for the most important products."[20]

Cournot's definition was enormously more precise and elegant than Smith's so far as the treatment of numbers was concerned. A market departed from unlimited competition to the extent that price exceeded the marginal cost of the firm, and the difference approached zero as the number of rivals approached infinity. But the refinement was one-sided: Cournot paid no attention to conditions of entry and so his definition of competition held also for industries with numerous firms even though no more firms could enter.

The role of knowledge was made somewhat more prominent in Jevons' exposition. His concept of competition was a part of his concept of a market, and a perfect market was characterized by two conditions:

[1]. A market, then, is theoretically perfect only when all traders have perfect knowledge of the conditions of supply and demand, and the consequent ratio of exchange; ...

[2] ... there must be perfectly free competition, so that anyone will exchange with anyone else upon the slightest advantage appearing. There must be no conspiracies for absorbing and holding supplies to produce unnatural ratios of exchange.[21]

One might interpret this ambiguous second condition in several ways, for the pursuit of advantages is not inconsistent with conspiracies. At a minimum, Jevons assumes complete independence of action by every trader for a corollary of the perfect market is that "in the same market, at any moment, there cannot be two prices for the same kind of article."[22] This

[19] Let the revenue of the firm be $q_i p$, and let all firms have the same marginal costs, MC. Then the equation for maximum profits for one firm would be

$$p + q_i \frac{dp}{dq} = \text{MC}.$$

The sum of n such equations would be

$$np + q \frac{dp}{dq} = n\text{MC},$$

for $nq_i = q$. This last equation may be written,

$$p = \text{MC} - \frac{p}{nE},$$

where E is the elasticity of market demand (*ibid.*, p. 84).

[20] *Ibid.*, p. 90.

[21] *Theory of Political Economy* (1st ed.; London, 1871), pp. 87 and 86.

[22] *Ibid.*, p. 92. This is restated as the proposition that the last increments of an act of exchange (i.e., the last exchange in a competitive market) must be proportional to the total quantities exchanged, or that dy exchanges for dx in the same proportion that y exchanges for x, or

$$\frac{dy}{dx} = \frac{y}{x}.$$

(Footnote Continued)

rule of a single price (it is called the "law of indifference" in the second edition) excludes price discrimination and probably requires that the market have numerous buyers and sellers, but the condition is not made explicit. The presence of large numbers is clearly implied, however, when we are told that "a single trader . . . must buy and sell at the current prices, which he cannot in appreciable degree affect."[23]

The merging of the concepts of competition and the market was unfortunate, for each deserved a full and separate treatment. A market is an institution for the consummation of transactions. It performs this function efficiently when every buyer who will pay more than the minimum price for any class of commodities succeeds in buying the commodity, and every seller who will sell for less than the maximum realized price succeeds in selling the commodity. A market performs these tasks more efficiently if the commodities are well specified and if buyers and sellers are fully informed of their properties and prices. Possibly also a perfect market allows buyers and sellers to act on differing expectations of future prices. A market may be perfect and monopolistic or imperfect and competitive. Jevons' mixture of the two has been widely imitated by successors, of course, so that even today a market is commonly treated as a concept subsidiary to competition.

Edgeworth was the first to attempt a systematic and rigorous definition of perfect competition. His exposition deserves the closest scrutiny in spite of the fact that few economists of his time or ours have attempted to disentangle and uncover the theorems and conjectures of the *Mathematical Psychics*, probably the most elusively written book of importance in the history of economics. For his allegations and demonstrations seem to be the parents of widespread beliefs on the nature of perfect competition.

The conditions of perfect competition are stated as follows:

> The *field of competition* with reference to a contract, or contracts, under consideration consists of all individuals who are willing and able to recontract about the articles under consideration. . . .
> There is free communication throughout a *normal* competitive field. You might suppose the constituent individuals collected at a point, or connected by telephones—an ideal supposition [1881], but sufficiently approximate to existence or tendency for the purposes of abstract science.
> A *perfect* field of competition professes in addition certain properties peculiarly favourable to mathematical calculation; . . . The conditions of a *perfect* field are four; the first pair referrible to the heading *multiplicity* or continuity, the second *dividedness* or fluidity.

It would have been better for Jevons simply to assert that, if x_i exchanges for y_i, then for all i

$$\frac{x_i}{y_i} = \frac{P_y}{P_x}.$$

[23] *Ibid.*, p. 111. In the Preface of the second edition, where on most subjects Jevons was farseeing, the conceptual treatment of competition deteriorated: "Property is only another name for monopoly . . . Thus monopoly is limited by competition . . ." (*Theory* [4th ed.], pp. xlvi–xlvii).

I. An individual is free to *recontract* with any out of an indefinite number, ...

II. Any individual is free to *contract* (at the same time) with an indefinite number; ... This condition combined with the first appears to involve the indefinite divisibility of each *article* of contract (if any X deal with an indefinite number of Ys he must give each an indefinitely small portion of x); which might be erected into a separate condition.

III. Any individual is free to *recontract* with another independently of, *without the consent* being required of, any third party, ...

IV. Any individual is free to *contract* with another independently of a third party; ...

The failure of the first [condition] involves the failure of the second, but not *vice versa*; and the third and fourth are similarly related.[24]

The natural question to put to such a list of conditions of competition is: are the conditions necessary and sufficient to achieve what intuitively or pragmatically seems to be a useful concept of competition? Edgeworth replies, in effect, that the conditions are both necessary and sufficient. More specifically, competition requires (1) indefinitely large numbers of participants on both sides of the market; (2) complete absence of limitations upon individual self-seeking behavior; and (3) complete divisibility of the commodities traded.[25]

The rationale of the requirement of indefinite numbers is as follows. With bilateral monopoly, the transaction will be indeterminate—equilibrium can be anywhere on the contract curve.[26] If we add a second buyer and seller, it is shown that the range of permissible equilibrium (the length of the tenable contract curve) will shrink.[27] By intuitive induction, with infinitely many traders it will shrink to a single point; a single price must rule in the market.[28]

Before we discuss this argument, we may take account also of the condition that individual traders are free to act independently. Edgeworth shows that combinations reduce the effective number of traders and that "combiners *stand to gain*."[29] In effect, then, he must assume that the individual trader not only is free to act independently but will in fact do so.

The proof of the need for indefinite numbers has serious weaknesses. The range of indeterminacy shrinks only because one seller or buyer tries to cut out the other by offering better terms.[30] Edgeworth fails to show that such price competition (which is palpably self-defeating) will occur

[24] *Mathematical Psychics* (London, 1881), pp. 17–19.
[25] Edgeworth's emphasis upon recontract, the institution which allows tentative contracts to be broken without penalty, is motivated by a desire to assure that equilibrium will be achieved and will not be affected by the route by which it is achieved. It will not be examined here.
[26] *Ibid.*, pp. 20 ff.
[27] *Ibid.*, pp. 35 ff.
[28] *Ibid.*, pp. 37–39.
[29] *Ibid.*, p. 43.
[30] "... It will in general be possible for *one* of the Ys (without the consent of the other) to *recontract* with the two Xs, so that for all those three parties the recontract is more advantageous than the previously existing contract" (*ibid.*, p. 35).

or why, if it does occur, the process should stop before the parties reach a unique (competitive) equilibrium. Like all his descendants, he treated the small-numbers case unsatisfactorily.

It is intuitively plausible that with infinite numbers all monopoly power (and indeterminacy) will vanish, and Edgeworth essentially postulates rather than proves this. But a simple demonstration, in case of sellers of equal size, would amount only to showing that

$$\text{Marginal revenue} = \text{Price} + \frac{\text{Price}}{\text{Number of sellers} \times \text{Market elasticity}}$$

and that this last term goes to zero as the number of sellers increases indefinitely.[31] This was implicitly Cournot's argument.

But why do we require divisibility of the traded commodity?

> Suppose a market, consisting of an equal number of masters and servants, offering respectively wages and service; subject to the condition that no man can serve two masters, no master employ more than one man; or suppose equilibrium already established between such parties to be disturbed by any sudden influx of wealth into the hands of the masters. Then there is no *determinate*, and very generally *unique*, arrangement towards which the system tends under the operation of, may we say, a law of Nature, and which would be predictable if we knew beforehand the real requirements of each, or of the average, dealer; . . .[32]

Consider the simple example: a thousand masters will each employ a man at any wage below 100; a thousand laborers will each work for any wage above 50. There will be a single wage rate: knowledge and numbers are sufficient to lead a worker to seek a master paying more than the going rate or a master to seek out a worker receiving less than the market rate. But any rate between 50 and 100 is a possible equilibrium.[33]

It is not the lack of uniqueness that is troublesome, however, for a market can be perfectly competitive even though there be a dozen possible stable equilibrium positions.[34] Rather, the difficulty arises because the

[31] Let one seller dispose of q_i, the other sellers each disposing of q. Then the seller's marginal revenue is

$$\frac{d(pq_i)}{dq_i} = p + q_i \frac{dp}{dQ} \frac{dQ}{dq_i},$$

where Q is total sales, and $dQ/dq_i = 1$. Letting $Q = nq_i = nq$, and writing E for

$$\frac{dQ}{dp} \frac{p}{Q},$$

we obtain the expression in the text.

[32] *Mathematical Psychics*, p. 46.

[33] Of course, let there be one extra worker, and the wage will be 50; one extra master, and it will be 100.

[34] Since chance should operate in the choice of the equilibrium actually attained, it is not proper to say, as Edgeworth does (in a wider context), that the dice will be "loaded with villainy" (*ibid.*, p. 50).

demand (or supply) functions do not possess continuous derivatives: the withdrawal of even one unit will lead to a large change in price, so that the individual trader—even though he has numerous independent rivals —can exert a perceptible influence upon price.

The element of market control arising out of the non-continuity is easily eliminated, of course. If the article which is traded is divisible, then equalities replace inequalities in the conditions of equilibrium: the individual trader can no longer influence the market price. A master may employ a variable amount of labor, and he will therefore bid for additional units so long as the wage rate is below his marginal demand price. A worker may have several employers, and he will therefore supply additional labor so long as any employer will pay more than his marginal supply price. "If the labour of the assistants can be sold by the hour, or other sort of differential dose, the phenomenon of determinate equilibrium will reappear."[35] Divisibility was introduced to achieve determinateness, which it fails to do, but it is required to eliminate monopoly power.

Divisibility had a possible second role in the assumptions, which, however, was never made explicit. If there are infinitely many possessors of a commodity, presumably each must have only an infinitesimal quantity of it if the existing total stock is to be finite. But no economist placed emphasis upon the strict mathematical implications of concepts like infinity, and this word was used to convey only the notion of an indefinitely large number of traders.

The remainder of the mathematical economists of the period did not extend, or for that matter even reach, the level of precision of Edgeworth. Walras gave no adequate definition of competition.[36] Pareto noticed the possible effects of social controls over purchases and sales.[37] Henry Moore, in what may have been the first article on the formal definition of competition,[38] listed five "implicit hypotheses" of competition:

I. Each economic factor seeks a maximum net income.

II. There is but one price for commodities of the same quality in the same market.

III. The influence of the product of any one producer upon the price per unit of the total product is negligible.

IV. The output of any one producer is negligible as compared with the total output.

[35] *Collected Papers Relating to Political Economy* (London, 1925), I. 36. One might also seek to eliminate the indeterminateness by appeal to the varying demand-and-supply prices of individual traders; this is the path chosen by Hicks in "Edgeworth, Marshall, and the Indeterminatenes of Wages," *Economic Journal*, XL (1930), 45–31. This, however, is a complicated solution; one must make special hypotheses about the distribution of these demand-and-supply prices.

[36] *Elements of Pure Economics*, trans. Jaffé (Homewood, Ill., 1954), pp. 83 and 185. It is indicative that the word "competition" is not indexed.

[37] *Cours d'économie politique* (Lausanne, 1896, 1897), §§ 46, 87, 705, 814; *cf.* also *Manuel d'économie politique* (2d ed.; Paris, 1927), pp. 163, 210, 230.

[38] "Paradoxes of Competition," *Quarterly Journal of Economics*, XX (1905–6), 209–30. Most of the article is concerned with duopoly.

V. Each producer orders the amount of his product without regard to the effect of his act upon the conduct of his competitors.[39]

This list of conditions is noteworthy chiefly because it marked an unsuccessful attempt to revert to the narrower competitive concept of Jevons.

Marshall

Marshall as usual refused to float on the tide of theory, and his treatment of competition was much closer to Adam Smith's than to that of his contemporaries. Indeed, Marshall's exposition was almost as informal and unsystematic as Smith's in this area. His main statement was:

> We are investigating the equilibrium of normal demand and normal supply in their most general form: we are neglecting those features which are special to particular parts of economic science, and are confining our attention to those broad relations which are common to nearly the whole of it. Thus we assume that the forces of demand and supply have free play in a perfect market; there is no combination among dealers on either side, but each acts for himself: and there is *free competition*; that is, buyers compete freely with buyers, and sellers compete freely with sellers. But though everyone acts for himself, his knowledge of what others are doing is supposed to be sufficient to prevent him from taking a lower price and paying a higher price than others are doing; . . .[40]

If this quotation suggests that Marshall was invoking a strict concept of competition, we must remember that he discussed the "fear of spoiling the market" and the firms with negatively sloping demand curves in the main chapters on competition[41] and that the only time perfect competition was mentioned was when it was expressly spurned.[42]

Soon he yielded a bit to the trend toward refinement of the concept. Beginning with the third (1895) edition, he explicitly introduced the horizontal demand curve for the individual firm as the normal case and gave it the same mathematical formulation as did Cournot.[43] But these were patchwork revisions, and they were not carried over into the many passages where looser concepts of competition had been employed.

Marshall's most significant contribution was indirect: he gave the most powerful analysis up to his time of the relationship of competition to optimum economic organization (Book V, chap. xiii, on the doctrine of maximum satisfaction). There he found the competitive results to have not only the well-known qualification that the distribution of resources must

[39] *Ibid.*, pp. 213–14. The fifth statement is held to be a corollary of III and IV; but see below.
[40] *Principles of Economics* (1st ed.; London, 1890), p. 402. A comparison with the corresponding passage in the eighth edition (*op. cit.*, p. 341) will reveal the curious changes which were later made in the description of competition.
[41] *Principles* (8th ed.; London, 1929), pp. 374 and 458.
[42] *Ibid.*, p. 540.
[43] *Ibid.*, pp. 517 and 849–50.

be taken as a datum, and the precious exception that only one of several multiple stable equilibriums could be the maximum,[44] but also a new and possibly extremely important exception, arising out of external economies and diseconomies. The doctrine of external economies in effect asserts that in important areas the choices of an individual are governed by only part of the consequences, and inevitably the doctrine opens up a wide range of competitive equilibriums which depart from conventional criteria of optimum arrangement. It was left for Pigou to elaborate, and exaggerate, the importance of this source of disharmonies in *Wealth and Welfare*.

The Complete Formulation: Clark and Knight

Only two new elements needed to be added to the Edgeworth conditions for competition in order to reach the modern concept of perfect competition. They pertained to the mobility of resources and the model of the stationary economy, and both were presented, not first,[45] but most influentially, by John Bates Clark.

Clark, in his well-known development of the concept of a static economy, ascribed all dynamic disturbances to five forces:

1. Population is increasing.
2. Capital is increasing.
3. Methods of production are improving.
4. The forms of industrial establishments are changing: . . .
5. The wants of consumers are multiplying.[46]

The main purpose of his treatise was to analyze the stationary economy in which these forces were suppressed, and for this analysis the assumption of competition was basic:

> There is an ideal arrangement of the elements of society, to which the force of competition, acting on individual men, would make the society conform. The producing mechanism actually shapes itself about this model, and at no time does it vary greatly from it.
>
> We must use assumptions boldly and advisedly, making labor and capital absolutely mobile, and letting competition work in ideal perfection.[47]

Although the concepts of a stationary economy and of competition are completely independent of each other, Clark somehow believed that compeition was an element of static analysis:

> The statement made in the foregoing chapter that a static state excludes true entrepreneurs' profits does not deny that a legal monopoly

[44] Both of these qualifications were of course recognized by predecessors such as Walras and Edgeworth.
[45] In the mathematical exposition of theory it was natural to postulate stable supply and demand functions, and therefore stable technologies and tastes, so one could trace a gradually expanding concept of the stationary economy in Walras, Auspitz and Lieben, and Irving Fisher.
[46] *The Distribution of Wealth* (New York, 1899), p. 56.
[47] *Ibid.*, pp. 68 and 71.

might secure to an entrepreneur a profit that would be permanent as the law that should create it—and that, too, in a social condition which, at first glance, might appear to be static. The agents, labor and capital, would be prevented from moving into the favored industry, though economic forces, if they had been left unhindered, would have caused them to move in. This condition, however, is not a true static state, as it has been defined. . . . Industrial groups are in a truly static state when the industrial agents, labor and capital, show a *perfect mobility, but no motion.* A legal monopoly destroys at a certain point this mobility. . . .[48]

I shall return to this identification of competition with stationary equilibrium at a later point.

The introduction of perfect mobility of resources as an assumption of competition was new, and Clark offers no real explanation for the assumption. One could simply eliminate his five dynamic influences, and then equilibrium would be reached after a time even with "friction" (or less than instantaneous mobility). Clark was aware of this possible approach but merely said that "it is best to assume" that there is no friction.[49] The only gain in his subsequent work, of course, is the avoidance of an occasional "in the long run."

Mobility of resources had always been an implicit assumption of competition, and in fact the conditions of adequate knowledge of earning opportunities and absence of contrived barriers to movement were believed to be adequate to insure mobility. But there exist also technological limitations to the rate at which resources can move from one place or industry to another, and these limitations were in fact the basis of Marshall's concept of the short-run normal period. Once this fact was generally recognized, it became inevitable that mobility of resources be given an explicit time dimension, although of course it was highly accidental that instantaneous mobility was postulated.

The concept of perfect competition received its complete formulation in Frank Knight's *Risk, Uncertainty and Profit* (1921). It was the meticulous discussion in this work that did most to drive home to economists generally the austere nature of the rigorously defined concept[50] and so prepared the way for the widespread reaction against it in the 1930's.

Knight sought to establish the precise nature of an economy with complete knowledge as a preliminary step in the analysis of the impact of uncertainty. Clark's procedure of eliminating historical changes was shown to be neither necessary nor sufficient: a stationary economy was not necessary to achieve complete competitive equilibrium if men had complete foresight; and it was not sufficient to achieve this equilibrium, because

[48] *Ibid.,* p. 76; *cf.* also p. 78.
[49] *Ibid.,* p. 81.
[50] Although Pigou was not concerned with the formal definition of competition, he must also be accounted an influential figure in the popularization of the concept of perfect competition. In his *Wealth and Welfare* (1912), he devoted individual chapters to the effects of immobility (with incorrect knowledge as one component) and indivisibility upon the ability of a resource to receive an equal rate of return in all uses (*ibid.,* Part II, chaps. iv and v).

there might still be non-historical fluctuations, owing, for example, to drought or flood, which were imperfectly anticipated.[51] Complete, errorless adjustments required full knowledge of all relevant circumstances, which realistically can be possessed only when these circumstances do not change; that is, when the economy is stationary.

The assumptions necessary to competition are presented as part of a list that describes the pure enterprise economy, and I quote those that are especially germane to competition:

2. We assume that the members of the society act with complete "rationality." By this we do not mean that they are to be "as angels, knowing good from evil"; we assume ordinary human motives . . . ; but they are supposed to "know what they want" and to seek it "intelligently." . . . They are supposed to know absolutely the consequence of their acts when they are performed, and to perform them in the light of the consequences. . . .

4. We must also assume complete absence of physical obstacles to the making, execution, and changing of plans at will; that is, there must be "perfect mobility" in all economic adjustments, no cost involved in movements or changes. To realize this ideal all the elements entering into economic calculations—effort, commodities, etc.—must be continuously variable, divisible without limit. . . . The exchange of commodities must be virtually instantaneous and costless.

5. It follows as a corollary from number 4 that there is perfect competition. There must be perfect, continuous, costless intercommunication between all individual members of the society. Every potential buyer of a good constantly knows and chooses among the offers of all potential sellers, and conversely. Every commodity, it will be recalled, is divisible into an indefinite number of units which must be separately owned and compete effectually with each other.

6. Every member of the society is to act as an individual only, in entire independence of all other persons. . . . And in exchanges between individuals, no interests of persons not parties to the exchange are to be concerned, either for good or for ill. Individual independence in action excludes all forms of collusion, all degrees of monopoly or tendency to monopoly. . . .

9. All given factors and conditions are for the purposes of this and the following chapter and until notice to the contrary is expressly given, to remain absolutely unchanged. They must be free from periodic or progressive modification as well as irregular fluctuation. The connection between this specification and number 2 (perfect knowledge) is clear. Under static conditions every person would soon find out, if he did not already know, everything in his situation and surroundings which affected his conduct. . . .

The above assumptions, especially the first eight, are idealizations or purifications of tendencies which hold good more or less in reality. They are the conditions necessary to perfect competition. The ninth, as we shall see, is on a somewhat different footing. Only its corollary of perfect knowledge (specification number 2) which may be present even when change takes place is necessary for perfect competition.[52]

This list of requirements of perfect competition is by no means a state-

---

[51] *Risk, Uncertainty and Profit* (New York, 1921), pp. 35–38.
[52] *Ibid.*, pp. 76–79; *cf.* also p. 148.

ment of the *minimum* requirements, and in fact no one is able to state the minimum requirements.

Consider first complete knowledge. If each seller in a market knows any *n* buyers, and each seller knows a different (but overlapping) set of buyers, then there will be perfect competition if the set of *n* buyers is large enough to exclude joint action. Or let there be indefinitely many brokers in any market, and let each broker know many buyers and sellers, and also let each buyer or seller know many brokers—again we have perfect competition. Since entrepreneurs in a stationary economy are essentially brokers between resource owners and consumers, it is sufficient for competition if they meet this condition. That is, resource owners and consumers could dwell in complete ignorance of all save the bids of many entrepreneurs. Hence knowledge possessed by any one trader need not be complete; it is sufficient if the knowledge possessed by the ensemble of individuals in the market is in a sense comprehensive.

And now, mobility. Rigid immobility of every trader is compatible with perfect competition if we wish to have this concept denote only equilibrium which is not affected by the actions of individual traders: large numbers (in any market) and comprehensive knowledge are sufficient to eliminate monopoly power. If we wish perfect competition to denote also that a resource will obtain equal returns in all possible uses, mobility becomes essential, but not for all resources. If one resource were immobile and all others mobile, clearly the returns of all resources in all uses could be equalized. Even if all resources were immobile, under certain conditions free transport of consumers' goods lead to equalization of returns.[53] Even in the general case in which mobility of resources is required, not all the units of a resource need be mobile. If some units of each resource are mobile, the economic system will display complete mobility for all displacements up to a limit that depends upon the proportion of mobile units and the nature of the displacement.

The condition that there be no costs of movement of resources is not necessary in order to reach maximum output for an economy; under competition only those movements of resources will take place for which the additional return equals or exceeds the cost of movement. But costless movement is necessary if equality is to obtain in the return to a resource in all uses: if the movement between *A* and *B* costs $1.00 (per unit of time), the return to a resource at *A* can vary within $1.00 of either direction of its return at *B*. Equilibrium could be reached anywhere within these limits (but would be uniquely determined), and this equilibrium would depend upon the historical distribution of resources and consumers.

Next, divisibility. It is not enough to have a large number of informed traders in a market: price must change continuously with quantity if an

[53] See P. A. Samuelson, "International Factor-Price Equalization Once Again," *Economic Journal*, LIX (1949), 181–97; and S. F. James and I. F. Pierce, "The Factor Price Equalization Myth," *Review of Economic Studies*, XIX (1951–52), 111–22.

individual trader is to have only an imperceptible influence upon the market rate, and this will generally require divisibility of the commodity traded. Infinite divisibility, however, is not necessary to eliminate significant control over price by the individual trader, and divisibility of time in the use of a resource is a substitute for divisibility in its quantity. Divisibility, however, is not sufficient to insure uniqueness of equilibriums; even in the simpler problems one must also require that the relevant economic functions display strict monotonicity, but this has nothing to do with competition.

And homogeneity. The formal condition that there be many producers of *a* commodity assumes homogeneity of this commodity (Knight's assumption 5). Certain forms of heterogeneity are of course unimportant because they are superficial: potatoes need not be of the same size if they are sold by the pound; laborers do not have to be equally efficient if the differences in their productivity are measurable. As these examples may suggest, heterogeneity can be a substitute for divisibility.

The final assumption, concerning collusion, is especially troublesome. If one merely postulates the absence of collusion, then why not postulate also that even two rivals can behave in such a way as to reach competitive equilibrium? Instead, one usually requires that the number of traders be large enough so that collusion will not appear. To determine this number, one must have a theory of the conditions under which collusion occurs. Economists have generally emphasized two barriers to collusion. The first is imperfect knowledge, especially of the consequences of rivalry and of the policy which would maximize profits for the group, and of course neither of these difficulties would arise in the stationary economy with perfect knowledge. The second barrier is the difficulty of determining the division of profits among colluders, and we simply do not know whether this difficulty would increase with the number of traders under the conditions we are examining. Hence it seems essential to assume the absence of collusion as a supplement to the presence of large numbers: one of the assumptions of perfect competition is the existence of a Sherman Act.

It is therefore no occasion for complaint that Knight did not state the minimum requirements for perfect competition; this statement was impossible in 1921, and it is impossible today. The minimum assumptions for a theoretical model can be stated with precision only when the complete theory of that model is known. The complete theory of competition cannot be known because it is an open-ended theory; it is always possible that a new range of problems will be posed in this framework, and then, no matter how well developed the theory was with respect to the earlier range of problems, it may require extensive elaboration in respects which previously it glossed over or ignored.

The analytical appeal of a definition of competition does not depend upon its economy of assumptions, although gratuitously wide assumptions are objectionable.[54] We wish the definition to specify with tolerable clarity—with such clarity as the state of the science affords—a model which can be used by practitioners in a great variety of theoretical researches, so that the foundations of the science need not be debated in every extension or application of theory. We wish the definition to capture the essential general content of important markets, so the predictions drawn from the theory will have wide empirical reliability. And we wish a concept with normative properties that will allow us to judge the efficiency of policies. That the concept of perfect competition has served these varied needs as well as it has is providential.

Concluding Reflections

If we were free to redefine competition at this late date, a persuasive case could be made that it should be restricted to meaning the absence of monopoly power in a market. This is an important concept that deserves a name, and "competition" would be the appropriate name. But it would be idle to propose such a restricted signification for a word which has so long been used in a wide sense, and at best we may hope to denote the narrower concept by a suggestive phrase. I propose that we call this narrower concept *market competition.*

Perfect market competition will prevail when there are indefinitely many traders (no one of which controls an appreciable share of demand or supply) acting independently in a perfect market. A perfect market is one in which the traders have full knowledge of all offer and bid prices. I have already remarked that it was unfortunate that a perfect market was made a subsidiary characteristic of competition, for a perfect market may also exist under monopoly. Indeed, in realistic cases a perfect market may be more likely to exist under monopoly, since complete knowledge is easier to achieve under monopoly.

Market competition can exist even though resources or traders cannot enter or leave the market in question. Hence market competition can rule in an industry which is not in long-run competitive equilibrium and is compatible with the existence of large profits or losses.

It is interesting to note that Chamberlin's definition of "pure" competition is identical with my definition of market competition: "competition unalloyed with monopoly elements."[55] But Chamberlin implied that pure competition could rule in an imperfect market; the only conditions he postulated were large numbers of traders and a standardized commodity. The conditions are incomplete: if one million buyers dealt with one million

[54] They are objectionable chiefly because they mislead some user or abusers of the concept as to its domain of applicability. That dreadful list of assumptions of perfect competition which textbooks in labor economics so often employ to dismiss the marginal productivity theory is a case in point.
[55] *The Theory of Monopolistic Competition* (1st ed.; Cambridge, Mass., 1933), p. 6.

sellers of a homogeneous product, each pair dealing in ignorance of all others, we should simply have one million instances of bilateral monopoly. Hence pure competition cannot be contrasted with perfect competition, for the former also requires "perfect" knowledge (subject to qualifications I have previously discussed), and for this reason I prefer the term "market competition."

The broad concept of perfect competition is defined by the condition that the rate of return (value of the marginal product) of each resource be equal in all uses. If we wish to distinguish this concept from market competition, we may call it (after the terminology attributed to Cairnes) *industrial competition.* Industrial competition requires (1) that there be market competition within each industry; (2) that owners of resources be informed of the returns obtainable in each industry; and (3) that they be free to enter or leave any industry. In addition, the resources must be infinitely divisible if there is to be strict equality in the rate of return on a resource in all uses.

An industrial competitive equilibrium will obtain continuously if resources are instantaneously mobile or in the long run if they move at a finite time rate. Since the concept of long-run competitive equilibrium is deeply imbedded in modern economic theory, it seems most desirable that we interpret industrial competition as a long-run concept. It may be noticed that a time period did not have to figure explicitly in the pre-Marshallian theory because that theory did not separate and devote special attention to a short-run normal period in which only a portion of the resources were mobile: the basic classical theory was a long-run theory.

The concept of industrial competition has a natural affinity to the static economy even though our definition does not pay any explicit attention to this problem. Rates of return on resources will be equalized only if their owners have complete knowledge of future returns (in the case of durable resources), and it seems improper to assume complete knolwdege of the future in a changing economy. Not only is it misleading to endow the population with this gift of prophecy but also it would often be inconsistent to have people foresee a future event and still have that event remain in the future.

One method by which we might seek to adapt the definition to a historically evolving economy is to replace the equalization of rates of return by *expected* rates of return. But it is not an irresistibly attractive method. There are troublesome questions of what entrepreneurs seek to maximize under these conditions and of whether risk or uncertainty premiums also enter into their calculations. A more important difficulty is that this formulation implies that the historically evolving industry is in equilibrium in long-run normal periods, and there is no strong reason to believe that such long-run normal periods can be defined for the historically evolving industry. If all economic progress took the form of a secularly smooth development, we could continue to use the Marshallian long-run normal period, and indeed much progress does take this form. But often, and sooner or later always, the historical changes come in vast surges, followed by quiescent periods or worse, and it is harder to assume that the fits and starts can be foreseen with tolerable confidence or that they will come frequently enough to average out within economically relevant time periods.

It seems preferable, therefore, to adapt the concept of competition to changing conditions by another method: to insist only upon the absence of barriers to entry and exit from an industry in the long-run normal period; that is, in the period long enough to allow substantial changes in the quantities of even the most durable and specialized resources. Then we may still expect that some sort of expected return will tend to be equalized under conditions of reasonably steady change, although much work remains to be done before we can specify exactly what this return will be.[56]

The way in which the competitive concept loses precision when historically changing conditions are taken into account is apparent. It is also easily explained: the competitive concept can be no better than the economic theory with which it is used, and until we have a much better theory of economic development we shall not have a much better theory of competition under conditions of non-repetitive change.

The normative role of the competitive concept arises from the fact that the equality of rate of return on each resource in all uses which defines competition is also the condition for maximum output from given resources. The outputs are measured in market prices, and the maximum is relative to the distribution of ownership of resources. This well-known restriction of the competitive optimum to production, it may be remarked, should be qualified by the fact that the effects of competition on distribution have not been studied. A competitive system affects the distribution of the ownership of resources, and—given a stable distribution of human abilities—a competitive system would probably lead eventually to a stable income distribution whose characteristics are unknown. The theory of this distribution might have substantial normative value.

The vitality of the competitive concept in its normative role has been remarkable. One might have expected that, as economic analysis became more precise and as the range of problems to which it was applied widened, a growing list of disparities between the competitive allocation of resources and the maximum-output allocation would develop. Yet to date there have been only two major criticisms of the norm.[57] The first is that

[56] It is worth noticing that even under static conditions the definition of the return is modified to suit the facts and that mobility of resources is the basic competitive requirement. Thus we say that laborers move so that the net advantages, not the current money return, of various occupations are equalized. The suggestion in the text is essentially that we find the appropriate definition of net advantages for the historically evolving economy.

[57] In a wider framework there have of course been criticisms of the competitive norm with respect to (i) the ability of individuals to judge their own interests and (ii) the ability of a competitive system to achieve a continuously high level of employment of resources.

the competitive individual ignores external economies and diseconomies, which—rightly or wrongly—most economists are still content to treat as an exception to be dealt with in individual cases. The second, and more recent, criticism is that the competitive system will not provide the right amount (and possibly not the right types) of economic progress, and this is still an undocumented charge. The time may well come when the competitive concept suitable to positive analysis is not suitable to normative analysis, but it is still in the future.

Finally, we should notice the most common and the most important criticism of the concept of perfect competition—that it is unrealistic. This criticism has been widespread since the concept was completely formulated and underlies the warm reception which the profession gave to the doctrines of imperfect and monopolistic competition in the 1930's. One could reply to this criticism that all concepts sufficiently general and sufficiently precise to be useful in scientific analysis must be abstract: that, if a science is to deal with a large class of phenomena, clearly it cannot work with concepts that are faithfully descriptive of even one phenomenon, for then they will be grotesquely undescriptive of others. This conventional line of defense for all abstract concepts is completely valid, but there is another defense, or rather another form of this defense, that may be more persuasive.

This second defense is that the concept of perfect competition has defeated its newer rivals in the decisive area: the day-to-day work of the economic theorist. Since the 1930's, when the rival doctrines of imperfect and monopolistic competition were in their heyday, economists have increasingly reverted to the use of the concept of perfect competition as their standard model for analysis. Today the concept of perfect competition is being used more widely by the profession in its theoretical work than at any time in the past. The vitality of the concept is strongly spoken for by this triumph.

Of course, this is not counsel of complacency. I have cited areas in which much work must be done before important aspects of the definition of competition can be clarified. My fundamental thesis, in fact, is that hardly any important improvement in general economic theory can fail to affect the concept of competition. But it has proved to be a tough and resilient concept, and it will stay with us in recognizable form for a long time to come.

Annual Survey of Economic Theory: The Theory of Monopoly

J. R. HICKS

Sir John Hicks is Professor of Economics at Oxford University. This famous article appeared in Econometrica *in 1935.*

I propose in this survey to confine attention to the progress which has recently been made in one particular part of economic theory. Such a limitation has obvious advantages in facilitating more detailed discussion; and when one has decided to confine oneself to a particular field, it is obvious that monopoly has the best claim to be chosen. The last five or six years have seen the appearance of at least four important works specially devoted to this subject—those of Dr. Zeuthen, Dr. Schneider, Professor Chamberlin, and Mrs. Robinson;[1] while there is, I think, no theoretical subject which has received more attention in the recent volumes of most of the chief economic journals than the theory of monopoly and imperfect competition. To most of these articles we shall refer as we proceed; but the names of Mr. Harrod, Mr. Shove, Dr. von Stackelberg, and Professor Hotelling, cannot be omitted from even a preliminary bibliography.[2]

The preoccupation of contemporary theorists with problems of monopoly does not appear to be due, as might perhaps be expected, to their consciousness of the increased urgency of these problems in the modern world. It may very well be that monopoly is more important today than it was fifty years ago, though it is not so obvious as it appears at first sight. It is certain, however, that the phenomena of monopolistic competition to

---

[1] F. Zeuthen, *Problems of Monopoly and Economic Warfare*, London 1930; Schneider, *Reine Theorie monopolistischer Wirtschaftsformen*, Tübingen 1932; E. H. Chamberlin, *Theory of Monopolistic Competition*, Harvard 1933; J. Robinson, *Economics of Imperfect Competition*, London 1933.
[2] R. F. Harrod, "Notes on Supply," *Econ. Jour.*, 1930; "Law of Decreasing Costs," *Econ. Jour.*, 1931; "Doctrines of Imperfect Competition," *Q.J.E.*, 1934; G. F. Shove, "The Imperfection of the Market," *Econ. Jour.*, 1933; H. Hotelling, "Stability in Competition," *Econ. Jour.*, 1929.

which attention has so particularly been directed are not new phenomena; they were observed and analysed, however imperfectly, by older economists, by Cairnes and Wicksell, if by no others.[3]

The widespread interest in monopoly theory is much easier to account for on grounds inherent in the development of economic theory itself, though here an element of coincidence is present. On the one hand, the generally increased interest in mathematical economics during the last few years (of which this journal is itself a symptom) has naturally turned attention back to the work of Cournot, the great founder of the subject, and still one of its best teachers. It was Cournot's creation of elementary monopoly theory which was the first great triumph of mathematical economics; yet Cournot had left much undone, and it is not surprising that the endeavor to complete his work should have been an attractive occupation for his successors.

But if some modern monopoly theorists have been seeking to fill the gaps in Cournot, others have been more concerned with the gaps in the work of Marshall. These gaps were more skillfully passed over, and it was not until after many years' criticism that they were clearly discerned. But the controversy on the "Laws of Returns," begun by Mr. Sraffa in 1926, and carried on more or less continuously in the *Economic Journal* for some years afterward,[4] made it increasingly evident to the most convinced Marshallians that the device of "external economies," by which Marshall sought to reconcile the postulate of perfect competition with the observed facts of increasing returns, would not bear the weight that had been imposed upon it. A tendency therefore developed away from the postulate of perfect competition. The participants in the discussion began to assume as the normal case that a firm can influence to some extent the prices at which it sells, that it is confronted with a downward sloping demand curve for its products, though this demand curve may have a high elasticity. With this assumption, the cardinal difficulty of increasing returns disappeared, since a firm might still be in equilibrium under conditions of diminishing cost. But numerous other difficulties started up, and it became necessary for these writers, like those mentioned before, to make a detailed examination of the theory of monopoly.

From each line of approach a substantially similar theory has emerged though there are important points which still remain controversial. It remains convenient for us to discuss the modern theory under the old headings: (1) *Simple Monopoly*, where the individual firm is confronted with given demand functions for its products, and given supply functions for its factors; (2) *Monopolistic Competition*, the relations of a group of firms producing similar products, i.e., an industry; (3) *Bilateral Monopoly*, where one firm is selling to another.

[3] Cairnes, *Political Economy*, pp. 115–116 (quoted in Chamberlin, *op. cit.*, p. 106); Wicksell, *Lectures on Political Economy*, I, pp. 87–88.
[4] See bibliography in *Econ. Jour.*, 1930, p. 79.

I. Simple Monopoly

As far as simple monopoly is concerned, the improvement on Cournot is mainly a matter of exposition, although there has been some further inquiry into the effect of monopoly on the demand for factors of production.

1. If the prices at which the monopolist hires his factors are fixed, his cost of production can be taken as a simple function of output. Let $\phi(x)$ be the total cost of producing an output x.

If the monopolist's selling price is p, and $p = f(x)$ is the demand curve confronting him, his profit on selling an output x will be

$$xf(x) - \phi(x)$$

which is maximized when

$$xf'(x) + f(x) = \phi'(x).$$

So much has been familiar since Cournot; the principal recent innovation has been to give the expression on the left of the last equation a name, "Marginal Revenue."[5] The equation can then be written

Marginal Revenue = Marginal Cost

which is certainly a convenient way of expressing the first condition of monopolistic equilibrium.

Since the elasticity of the demand curve $= \eta = -\dfrac{f(x)}{xf'(x)}$, marginal revenue

$$= \text{price} \left(1 - \frac{1}{\eta} \right).$$

The second condition of maximum profits is that

$$\frac{d}{dx} \left\{ xf'(x) + f(x) - \phi'(x) \right\}$$

should be negative. This can be written

$$\frac{d}{dx}\,(MR) < \frac{d}{dx}\,(MC).$$

Monopolistic equilibrium is therefore stable, so long as the marginal revenue curve slopes downward more steeply than the marginal cost curve. All cases where the marginal revenue curve slopes downward and the marginal cost curve upward are therefore stable, but instability may occur if either

[5] So Mrs. Robinson. It seems the most convenient of the names which have been suggested.

of these conditions is not fulfilled. Upward sloping marginal revenue curves, though possible, are unlikely to be very important, since the demand curve from which a marginal revenue curve is derived may be taken to be always downward sloping. Much more important is the fact that stable equilibrium with a downward sloping marginal cost curve is possible, so long as the downward slope is less than that of the marginal revenue curve, and so long, also, as total receipts exceed total costs by an amount sufficient to keep the monopolist in business.

The question of stability once settled, it becomes possible to apply the apparatus in the ordinary manner, familiar in elementary theory, to simple problems of change. A rise in the marginal cost curve will reduce output, a rise in the marginal revenue curve will increase it; but a rise in the demand (average revenue) curve may not increase output, unless it is such as to cause a rise in the marginal revenue curve. Similarly a rise in average costs will not contract output, unless it is associated with a rise in marginal costs, or is otherwise large enough to drive the monopolist out of business.

2. *The monopolist and the factors of production.*[6] It is convenient, for the analysis of this problem, to conceive of the monopolist as owning certain factors of production (his *private factors,* we may call them) and hiring others. If he is unable to vary the supply of these private factors, then it is strictly correct to suppose him endeavoring to maximize his profits, that is to say, to maximize the net earnings of these private factors. If this assumption cannot be made, difficulties emerge, which had better be examined later.

If the quantities of factors hired are $a, b, c, \ldots$, their prices $\pi_a, \pi_b, \pi_c, \ldots$, and their supply curves to the monopolist are given, then

$$\text{Monopoly profit} = xp - a\pi_a - b\pi_b - c\pi_c - \cdots.$$

This is maximized when

$$\left(p + x\frac{dp}{dx} \right) dx - \left(\pi_a + a\frac{d\pi_a}{da} \right) da - \left(\pi_b + b\frac{d\pi_b}{db} \right) db - \cdots = 0$$

which becomes

$$MRdx - MC_a da - MC_b db - \cdots = 0,$$

if we write MC_a for $\pi_a + a\dfrac{d\pi_a}{da}$, and so on.

Taking $x = \phi(a, b, c, \ldots)$ as the production function, technically given, then

$$dx = \frac{\partial x}{\partial a} da + \frac{\partial x}{\partial b} db + \cdots.$$

---

[6] Robinson, *op. cit.,* Books vii–ix; Schneider, "Bemerkungen zur Grenzproduktivitäts-theorie," *Zeitschrift für Nationalökonomie,* 1933. See also Dr. Schneider's *Theorie der Produktion,* 1934, pp. 57, 76.

Substituting in the above, we have

$$\left(\text{MR} \frac{\partial x}{\partial a} - \text{MC}_a \right) da + \left(\text{MR} \frac{\partial x}{\partial b} - \text{MC}_b \right) db + \cdots = 0.$$

Since this equation must hold for all values of $da, db, \ldots$, it follows that

$$\text{MR} \frac{\partial x}{\partial a} = \text{MC}_a, \quad \text{MR} \frac{\partial x}{\partial b} = \text{MC}_b, \cdots$$

for all factors.

$\text{MC}_a, \text{MC}_b, \ldots$, are the *marginal costs to the monopolist* of hiring an additional unit of the factors, $a, b, \ldots$ If the supply curves of the factors slope upward, these marginal costs will exceed the prices of the factors by $a \frac{d\pi_a}{da}$ etc., respectively, that is to say, by the additional amounts which have to be paid on earlier units in order to keep their prices on a level with that of the marginal unit of the factor. $\text{MR} \frac{\partial x}{\partial a}$ is conveniently described as the "marginal value product" of the factor a; it is the increment in the total value of the product which results from the application of an additional unit of a. The condition of factor equilibrium is thus that the marginal value product of a factor should equal its marginal cost.

The stability conditions for factor equilibrium do not appear to have been fully investigated; but a cursory examination suggests that there are several ways in which the presence of monopoly brings into the possible range of stable equilibria positions which would not be stable under perfect competition.

If the supply curve of any factor to the monopolist is horizontal, so that the monopolist is unable to affect the price of that factor, then even so his demand for that factor will be reduced below what it might have been, if the product demand curve confronting him is imperfectly elastic. Monopolistic exploitation of the consumer therefore brings about a directly consequent reduction in the demand for factors. And if a number of monopolists are employing a particular factor, they may each be unable by isolated action to influence the price of the factor; and yet, in their efforts to exploit the consumer, they will each reduce their demand for the factor, and the price of the factor may, in consequence, be reduced. But this is a different thing from the additional reduction in demand which comes about if a monopolist is able to influence the price of a factor directly, so that he takes into account the saving on other units which he gets by reducing his demand at the margin. The first type of reduction would be called by Mrs. Robinson "monopolistic exploitation" of the factors, while she has invented the term "monopsonistic" to describe exploitation of the second type.

3. *Simple monopoly and joint production.* Nearly all the writers here discussed have confined their analysis of simple monopoly to the case

where the monopolist produces only one product.[7] For reasons which will appear later, this limitation seems rather unfortunate. A brief but illuminating discussion of the problem has, however, been given by Dr. von Stackelberg, which we may here reproduce.[8]

It is convenient, in order to isolate the problem, to assume that the prices of the factors are now given to the monopolist; we can then introduce a cost function expressing the total cost of production of quantities x_1, x_2, . . . , of the different products. Let $\phi(x_1, x_2, \ldots)$ be the cost function. Then

$$\text{Monopoly profit} = p_1 x_1 + p_2 x_2 + p_3 x_3 + \cdots - \phi(x_1, x_2, \cdots).$$

If we assume that the demand curves for the various products are independent, so that p_1 depends upon x_1 only, not on x_2, x_3 . . . , then the conditions of equilibrium are

$$\frac{d}{dx_1}(p_1 x_1) = \frac{\partial \phi}{\partial x_1}, \frac{d}{dx_2}(p_2 x_2) = \frac{\partial \phi}{\partial x_2}, \cdots.$$

The ordinary "marginal revenue–marginal cost" condition still holds.

If, however, the demand curves are not independent, then the conditions become

$$p_1 + x_1 \frac{\partial p_1}{\partial x_1} + x_2 \frac{\partial p_2}{\partial x_1} + \cdots = \frac{\partial \phi}{\partial x_1}$$

$$p_2 + x_1 \frac{\partial p_1}{\partial x_2} + x_2 \frac{\partial p_2}{\partial x_2} + \cdots = \frac{\partial \phi}{\partial x_2}$$

and so on. That is to say, the monopolist has to take into account, when fixing the output of any particular product, not only the reaction of an increased supply upon the price of that product, but also its reaction upon the prices of all other products which he is selling. If the cross-coefficients $\left(\frac{\partial p_2}{\partial x_1} \text{ etc.}\right)$ are negative (roughly speaking, the case when the different products are competitive in consumption),[9] these reactions will lower the marginal revenue curve for any particular product, and so tend to restrict output. But in the opposite case, when the cross-coefficients are positive, the marginal revenue curve will be raised; so that here the restriction of output under monopoly will be less than we should have at first expected.

If $x_2 \dfrac{\partial p_2}{\partial x_1} + x_3 \dfrac{\partial p_3}{\partial x_1} + \cdots$ is positive, and greater than $\dfrac{\partial \phi}{\partial x_1}$, it may pay the

[7] Professor Chamberlin gives us an interesting account of the factors which determine what that one product shall be (*op. cit.*, ch. 4 and 5).
[8] H. von Stackelberg, *Grundlagen einer reinen Kostentheorie*, Vienna 1932, p. 68. See also Hotelling, "Edgeworth's Taxation Paradox," *Journal of Political Economy*, 1932.
[9] I say "roughly speaking," for it is becoming apparent that the terms *competitive* and *complementary* conceal a great many ambiguities. (See Hicks and Allen, "A Reconsideration of the Theory of Value," *Economica*, 1934.)

monopolist to produce a finite output of x_1, even if he has to give it away. And such a phenomenon is surely not uncommon; a very considerable part of what are usually described as "selling costs" comes very conveniently under this head. The subject of selling costs has been analyzed at considerable length and with much insight by Professor Chamberlin, who maintains, however, the single-product firm as the foundation of his analysis. It may be suggested that the subject could be further illuminated, and brought closer into relation with fundamentally analogous cases where the "bait" is not actually given away, if a start had been made from Dr. von Stackelberg's more general case.[10]

4. *Discrimination*. From one point of view, discrimination is a limiting case of joint production. When we say that a single commodity is sold by a monopolist at various different prices, the singleness of the commodity consists solely in its various units being perfect substitutes on the supply side. We can introduce this condition of being perfect substitutes in production, and so go over from joint production to discrimination.

But this line of approach, although it has conveniences, and brings discrimination into a very satisfactory relation with general monopoly theory, is not that which has traditionally been adopted. Of recent writers, Mrs. Robinson is the only one who has added anything substantial to the traditional theory of discrimination. She has devoted to it what is probably the best, as it is certainly the most ingenious, part of her book; there can be no question that these chapters will find their place along with Dupuit and Pigou on the very select bibliography of discriminatory theory.

5. *The "private" factors*. Most modern writing on monopoly, as we have said, has been content to assume a monopolist simply seeking to maximize his profits, that is to say, it neglects possible changes in the supply of private factors. This omission seems to me unfortunate, though it must be confessed that the subject presents grave difficulties.[11] On the one hand, unless we assume that the marginal utility of money to the monopolist is constant, we cannot unambiguously express in monetary terms the subjective cost to the monopolist of producing additional units of output; we are therefore unable to introduce the private factors into the "marginal revenue=marginal cost" equation, and are obliged to fall back upon Paretian indifference curves, more cumbrous, and in this case decidedly less informative. The second difficulty is even more formidable. Under conditions of monopoly, there is no reason to suppose any particular connection between subjective cost and *output*, since it is probable that a considerable part of the monopolist's efforts and sacrifices will be devoted, not to increasing his output, but finding to what precise point he should restrict it. Now, as Professor Bowley[12] and others have pointed out, the variation in monopoly profit for some way on either side of the highest profit output

[10] The same foundation might be used for an analysis of monopolistic exploitation by "compulsory joint supply."

[11] *Cf.* Robinson, "Euler's Theorem and the Problem of Distribution," *Econ. Jour.*, 1934.

[12] *Mathematical Groundwork of Economics*, pp. 25, 60.

may often be small (in the general case, it will depend on the difference between the slopes of the marginal revenue and marginal cost curves); and if this is so, the subjective costs involved in securing a close adaptation to the most profitable output may well outweigh the meager gains offered. It seems not at all unlikely that people in monopolistic positions will very often be people with sharply rising subjective costs; if this is so, they are likely to exploit their advantage much more by not bothering to get very near the position of maximum profit, than by straining themselves to get very close to it. The best of all monopoly profits is a quiet life.

II. *Monopolistic Competition*

1. We come now to the "group problem," the equilibrium of a group of firms producing similar but not identical products. The treatment of this problem by Professor Chamberlin and by Mrs. Robinson (the same applies, though with some qualification, to Mr. Harrod) is based upon a very neat geometrical proposition.[13] Since the products of the various firms are not identical, the demand curve which confronts each individual firm will not be horizontal, but will slope downward.[14] On the other hand, if entry into the industry is free, it will be impossible for the firms in the industry to earn more than "normal profits." On the basis of the first assumption, it is concluded that the output of each firm will have to satisfy the condition of monopolistic equilibrium, marginal revenue=marginal cost. On the basis of the second, it is concluded that the price of each product will have to equal average cost, when average cost is calculated in such a way as to include "normal profits."

If then we write π_x=average cost (in the above sense) of producing an output x, and p_x=the price at which the firm can sell that output, the second condition gives us

$$p_x = \pi_x \qquad (1)$$

while we have from the first condition

$$\frac{d}{dx}(xp_x) = \frac{d}{dx}(x\pi_x)$$

$$\therefore \quad p_x + x\frac{dp_x}{dx} = \pi_x + x\frac{d\pi_x}{dx}$$

$$\therefore \text{ from } (1), \frac{dp_x}{dx} = \frac{d\pi_x}{dx}. \qquad (2)$$

[13] Chamberlin, *op. cit.*, p. 84; Robinson, pp. 94–95; Harrod, "Doctrines of Imperfect Competition," *Q.J.E.*, 1934, p. 457.
[14] Professor Chamberlin constructs this individual demand curve on the assumption that the prices of the rival commodities remain unchanged (p. 75). Mrs. Robinson's formulation seems distinctly ambiguous (p. 21).

From (1) and (2) it follows that the demand curve and the average cost curve must touch at a point of equilibrium.

Since the demand curve is downward sloping, the average cost curve must also be downward sloping at the equilibrium point. Equilibrium under monopolistic competition is only possible when average costs are diminishing; that is to say, the equilibrium output of a firm will be less than the output which would give minimum average costs—the output which would actually be reached under conditions of perfect competition. From this Professor Chamberlin proceeds to the conclusion that analysis based on perfect competition makes "the price always too low, the cost of production too low, the scale of production too large, and the number of producers too small."

In order for us to estimate the importance of this result, we must begin by examining the premises on which it is based. To take first the "average cost curve." When Walras and Pareto reckoned profits into costs, they were thinking of conditions of perfect competition, and their conclusion that price=average cost, so that the entrepreneur makes "ni bénéfice ni perte," meant nothing else than that the private factors of the entrepreneur could get no other return in the static equilibrium of perfect competition than would have accrued to them if they had been directly hired out on the market. But is it possible to transfer this conception to the theory of monopolistic competition? So far as the private factors are to some extent unique, so that there are no perfect substitutes for them (and this seems the most likely case in which monopolistic competition might arise), they can have no market price which is not to some extent monopolistically determined. If there are perfect substitutes for them, why are those perfect substitutes not being employed in making perfect substitutes for the product?

There is only one way out of this dilemma, and I can only suppose that it is this which the writers in question have in mind. The factors of production, private or hired, may be sufficiently divisible, and sufficiently scattered in ownership, to ensure that there is a perfect market for them, or something sufficiently perfect for the imperfections to be negligible. But there may still be a range of increasing returns in the production of any particular product, due to indivisibilities in the production function, not in the factors themselves.[15] If this is the case, substantially homogeneous factors may be put together by a limited number of firms into a limited number of different products, each of which is unique, and the demand curve for each of which is downward sloping.

This is the only state of affairs of which the Chamberlin-Robinson apparatus seems to be an exact description; it is probable that it does correspond with a certain region of reality. But I cannot help feeling that the application of the apparatus is implicitly much exaggerated. This is only

[15] Kaldor, "The Equilibrium of the Firm," *Econ. Jour.*, March 1934, p. 65n. On the general question of indivisibilities and costs, see also the appendix to Mrs. Robinson's book; also Schneider, *Theorie der Produktion*, ch. 1.

partly because of the actual heterogeneity of factors—both writers accept this difficulty, and at the worst it only means that the technical apparatus is over-rigid. They can still claim to have shown that monopolistic restriction of output is compatible with earnings in no way out of the ordinary. A much more serious objection arises from the variability of the product.

There are two relevant sorts of product variation. One, the only kind which has been much discussed, is where each firm produces a single product, but the nature of that product is capable of being changed. This problem has been dealt with mostly in terms of location; a product available in a different place is economically a different product, and a change in the location of the firm is one of the ways of varying the product. (Professor Chamberlin's discussion of location is, however, reinforced by a discussion of the same problem in more general terms.)

In his paper, "Stability in Competition,"[16] Professor Hotelling had demonstrated that there is a tendency, when two firms are competing for a given market, for them to get together in the center of the market. This tendency in itself would thus be favorable to the establishment of conditions of approximately perfect competition, if it could be shown to hold for more firms than two.

Unfortunately, as Professor Chamberlin shows, this is not so.[17] Once there are more than two firms in the market, they will tend to scatter, since any firm will try to avoid being caught between a pair of others. It seems evident that this general tendency to dispersion will be present when it is a question of quality competition as well as of competition in location, though of course the possible kinds of variation are even more complex.

Thus, so long as we retain the "one firm one product" assumption, variability of the product is not sufficient to prevent an appreciable degree of imperfection in the elasticity of the demand curve confronting any particular firm. The position seems, however, to be different once we drop this assumption.

In fact, when "product" is interpreted in the strict economic sense of a collection of articles that are to the consumer perfect substitutes, almost every firm does produce a considerable range of different products. It does so largely because there are economies to be got from producing them together,[18] and these economies consist largely in the fact that the different products require much the same overheads. Further, at any time the products it is actually producing will probably not exhaust the list of products it could produce from approximately the same plant. Thus it will have various potential products which it could produce in small quantities at quite a low marginal cost.

Now when other producers are able to supply small quantities of highly

---

[16] *Op. cit.* See also Zeuthen, "Theoretical Remarks on Price Policy," *Q.J.E.*, 1933.
[17] *Theory of Monopolistic Competition*, Appendix C.
[18] In the sense that it costs less to produce outputs x_1 and x_2 in a single firm, than it would cost (in total) to produce output x_1 in one firm and output x_2 in another.

competitive products at low prices, this is at last an effective force tending to keep the demand curve for a particular product of a particular firm very highly elastic. Of course, it will probably not be perfectly elastic; for in fact any degree of specialization on a particular line offers a *prima facie* case that the specializing firm has some particular facilities for that line, and it may be able to carry out a certain degree of restriction before it tempts other firms to follow it. Further, a firm is always likely to be on the lookout for a line in which it is relatively safe from such competition. Nevertheless, this consideration does seem to go a good way to justify the traditional practice of economists in treating the assumption of perfect competition as a satisfactory approximation over a very wide field.[19]

A considerable degree of the sort of market imperfection we have been discussing seems likely to arise in two cases only: (1) where the producer has command of some specialized "factor," such as patent, legal privilege, site, or business capacity, for which no clear substitute is available; (2) where economies of scale are narrowly specialized, so that it would be impossible for another firm to produce commodities highly competitive with these produced by the first firm excepting at much greater marginal cost. There is no doubt that such conditions as these are fairly frequent, but they are, after all, precisely the cases which have been traditionally treated under the heading of monopoly.

2. *Duopoly.* There is, however, one further difficulty of greater importance. We have suggested that the demand curve for a particular product of a particular firm will usually be kept highly elastic by the incursion of other producers selling small quantities of highly competitive products, if the first firm raises its price. But if they do so, will not the first firm retaliate on them?

Two cases have thus to be distinguished. The first is when the other potential producers are fairly numerous. In this case, they are not likely to be much deterred by the fear of retaliation. For although the first firm may find it profitable to turn its attention to some other product if it meets with competition in the line it had first chosen, the chance of that other product being highly competitive with the products of any particular other producer is small.

In the other case, when the other potential producers are few, the fear of retaliation is likely to be more serious, and it may very well stop poaching.

The difficult problem which arises from the relations of a very small number of competing firms has been much studied in recent years, but there has not yet developed any very close agreement on the solution. Largely owing to the difficulty of the problem, it has been chiefly studied in its most simple case, that of two firms producing an identical product—duopoly.[20]

[19] *Cf.* Shove, "The Imperfection of the Market," *Econ. Jour.*, 1933, pp. 115–116.
[20] Chamberlin, however, has made at any rate a preliminary investigation of the more complex cases where several firms are involved. See his sections on "oligopoly" (*Theory*, pp. 100, 170).

The theory of duopoly has a long history; and here we can do no more than allude to the classical theory of Cournot, and the displacement of Cournot's theory by the criticisms of Bertrand and Edgeworth, which form the ancient history of the subject. Edgeworth's solution, based on "the characteristic freedom of the monopolist to vary price," involved such peculiar assumptions about costs that it could hardly have held the field forever. The postwar period therefore saw a renaissance of Cournotism, led by Amoroso and Wicksell;[21] this movement is represented also by the chapter on "Mehrfaches Monopol" in Dr. Schneider's book.[22] In the next stage, criticism of both the Cournot and Edgeworth solutions were offered by Dr. Zeuthen and by Professor Chamberlin;[23] it then became clear that each of the rivals had pointed the way toward a possible solution, but that even together they did not exhaust the list.

A very convenient line of approach, which sets these alternative solutions in their places, and so opens a path toward a general theory, can be developed from a hint given in Professor Bowley's *Mathematical Groundwork*.[24] It is this approach which appears to be gaining ground at present. Its main principle can be expressed as follows.[25]

The marginal revenue, which a duopolist endeavors to equate to his marginal cost,

$$= \frac{d}{dx_1} (px_1)$$

where x_1 is his output, and $p = f(x_1 + x_2)$ being the output of his rival. Thus

$$MR_1 = \frac{d}{dx_1} (px_1) = p + x_1 f'(x_1 + x_2) + x_1 f'(x_1 + x_2) \frac{\delta x_2}{\delta x_1}.$$

The marginal revenue curve which confronts the duopolist is thus in part dependent upon a quantity $\frac{\delta x_2}{\delta x_1}$, which we can only interpret as the degree to which the duopolist expects his rival to expand (or contract) output, if he himself expands his output by an increment dx_1. Since $f'(x_1 + x_2)$ is negative, a negative value of $\frac{\delta x_2}{\delta x_1}$ will raise the adjusted marginal revenue curve of the duopolist, and thus be favorable to an expansion of output; a positive value will favor a contraction.

---

[21] Amoroso, *Lezioni d'economia matematica*; Wicksell, Review of Bowley's *Mathematical Groundwork*, Archiv für Sozialwissenschaft, 1927.
[22] Schneider, *Reine Theorie*, ch. 4.
[23] Zeuthen, *Problems of Monopoly*, ch. 2; Chamberlin, *Theory*, ch. 3, which substantially reproduces his article on "Duopoly," Q.J.E., 1929.
[24] P. 38.
[25] The following owes much to some yet unpublished work by Mr. W. M. Allen, of Oxford.

The conception of these "conjectural variations," $\dfrac{\delta x_2}{\delta x_1}$ etc., has been

analyzed in very general terms by Professor Frisch.[26] There is, in the short period, no need for any particular degree of consistency between the con-

jecture of the first duopolist $\dfrac{\delta x_2}{\delta x_1}$, and that of the second $\dfrac{\delta x_1}{\delta x_2}$.

The equation of marginal revenue and marginal cost thus determines the output of the first duopolist, once the output of the second duopolist, and the first duopolist's conjecture as to the variation of this output, are given. For any particular type of conjecture, we can thus construct a "reaction curve," similar to that employed by Cournot, giving the preferred output of the first duopolist, corresponding to each possible output of the second. A similar reaction curve can be constructed for the second duopolist, and the intersection of the two will give the point of equilibrium.

In the majority of cases, these reaction curves will be negatively inclined;[27] and in the majority of these cases, the inclination will be such that an increased output by the other duopolist will react on the first in such a way as to increase the total output of both together. If we confine our attention to these *normal* cases, which are much the most likely to yield stable solutions, the more interesting assumptions about conjectures which have been made by recent writers fall into their places very simply.

(1) If the conjectural variations are both zero, we have of course the Cournot case. (2) If one of the conjectural variations is zero, but the other duopolist takes as his conjectural variation the actual slope of the reaction curve of his rival, we have the case of an "active" policy by one duopolist.[28] In *normal* conditions, this will make the conjectural varia-

[26] "Monopole—Polypole—La Notion de Force dans l'économie," *Nationaløkonomisk Tidsskrift*, 1933.

[27] The condition for negative inclination is that $1 + \dfrac{hx_1}{x}\left(1 + \dfrac{\delta x_2}{\delta x_1}\right)$ should be positive;

where h is the "adjusted concavity" of the market demand curve. (That is to say, $h = \dfrac{(x_1 + x_2)\, f''\,(x_1 + x_2)}{f'\,(x_1 + x_2)}$. *Cf.* Robinson, *Economics of Imperfect Competition*, p. 40.) Since we may assume that in all sensible cases, $1 + \dfrac{\delta x_2}{\delta x_1}$ is positive, it follows that the reaction curve will be negatively inclined in all cases when h is positive (when the demand curve is convex upward) and also for a considerable number of cases when h is negative. It has been further shown by Mr. Allen that in such cases of negative inclination, the slope of the reaction curve will also (for reasons of stability) be numerically less than 1, excepting when there is a high degree of asymmetry between the positions of the two duopolists. "Normal cases" are defined as satisfying these two conditions, so that dx_1/dx_2, taken along the reaction curve of the first duopolist, lies between 0 and −1.

[28] von Stackelberg, "Sulla teoria del duopolio e del polipolio," *Rivista italiana di statistica*, June 1933. This article also contains an important and ingenious extension of the theory to the case of several producers.

tion of the active duopolist negative; thus, as compared with the Cournot case, it will raise his marginal revenue curve, increase his output, and (again in normal conditions) lead to an increased total output, and so a lower price. (3) If both duopolists act in this manner, each calculating conjectural variations from the other's Cournotian reaction curve, we have a curious case which has been investigated by Dr. von Stackelberg and Mr. Harrod.[29] In normal conditions, once more, this will lead to a further expansion of total output, and a further fall in price. (4) There does not seem to be any reason why we should stop here. One duopolist may become doubly "active," and calculate a conjectural variation from the reaction curve of his rival on the assumption that the rival is active. In most, though not (it appears) quite all, *normal* cases, this would lead to a further fall in price. The process becomes similar to one of price-cutting.

But once we are on the road of competitive price-cutting, it is reasonable to suppose that, sooner or later, one duopolist or the other would perceive that his conjecture that an increase in his output was leading to a contraction of his rival's was proving wrong. Once he acted on this, and constructed a conjectural variation based on this experience (and consequently a *positive* variation) the whole situation would be transformed. Price-cutting would give place to "tacit combination"; positive conjectures, again in normal conditions, would give a higher price than that given by the Cournot equilibrium.[30]

The method just described is capable of extension to the case where the product of one duopolist is not a perfect substitute for that of the other. We have only to write $p_1 = f_1(x_1, x_2)$, $p_2 = f_2(x_1, x_2)$; the two sellers will now of course usually sell at different prices. We then have

$$\text{Adjusted marginal revenue of first seller} = \frac{d}{dx_1}(p_1 x_1) = p_1 + x_1 \frac{\partial p_1}{\partial x_1} + x_1 \frac{\partial p_1}{\partial x_2}\left(\frac{\delta x_2}{\delta x_1}\right),$$

from which we proceed much as before. This highly general solution can be applied whatever is the relation between the demands for the products; it can thus be applied to cases where the products are complementary instead of competitive.[31] Here $\dfrac{\partial p_1}{\partial x_2}$ will probably be positive, so that it is an anticipated consequential expansion of the other's output which will raise the marginal revenue curve of the first duopolist, and *vice versa*.[32]

[29] von Stackelberg, *ibid.* Harrod, "The Equilibrium of Duopoly," *Econ. Jour.*, June 1934.
[30] Nicoll, "Professor Chamberlin's Theory of Limited Competition," *Q.J.E.*, February 1934. Mr. Nicoll's case of tacit combination emerges if we write $\dfrac{\delta x_2}{\delta x_1} = \dfrac{x_2}{x_1}$, $\dfrac{\delta x_1}{\delta x_2} = \dfrac{x_1}{x_2}$.

[31] *Cf.* Edgeworth, "The Pure Theory of Monopoly," *Papers*, II, pp. 122–126.
[32] See further, on the subject of duopoly, Professor Divisia's paper to the Leyden meeting of the Econometric Society, summarized in *Econometrica*, June 1934, and also in the *Revue d'Economie politique*, May 1934.

III. *Bilateral Monopoly*

"Bilateral Monopoly" is a phrase which has been applied to two different problems, and it is well to keep them distinct. The first is the case of isolated exchange, or of exchange between a group of buyers and a group of sellers, each acting in combination. Now so far as this problem is concerned, when the exchange is studied *in vacuo*, without reference to other people (outside the two groups) who may be indirectly concerned, I think one may say that there is complete agreement among economists. It has been evident since the days of Edgeworth that isolated exchange leads to "undecidable opposition of interests,"[33] and that therefore the problem is indeterminate, in the sense that the mere condition of each party seeking its maximum advantage is not sufficient to define an equilibrium.

The second problem is a more complex one. It arises when the commodity sold is a raw material or factor of production; so that we have also to take into account the relation of the buyer of the raw material to another market—that in which he sells his finished product. For this problem there existed a solution alternative to Edgeworth's, that of Cournot; Cournot had concluded that this more general problem is determinate. Here, as in the question of duopoly, Cournot has his modern followers; his position is defended by Dr. Schneider, and also, though with considerable qualifications, by Dr. Zeuthen.[34]

It must be confessed, however, that the reader of their works finds it very difficult to see just how the presence of a consumers' market makes any difference to the opposition of interests deduced by Edgeworth; and we have the authority of Professor Bowley in support of the view that there is indeterminateness also in the more general case.[35] Personally, I find myself in agreement with Professor Bowley; but I think it may be worth while to restate Professor Bowley's argument in terms of the *marginal revenue* concept, since this seems to make the crux of the dispute clearer than it has been made up to the present.

A, a monopolist producer of raw material (iron ore), is selling to B, a monopolist producer of finished product (steel). Now, as we have seen, B's demand curve for iron ore (DD') is given by the marginal value product of iron ore (i.e., marginal physical product of iron ore in steel production × marginal revenue from the sale of steel); while A's supply curve of iron ore will be given by his ordinary marginal cost curve (CC'). That is to say, if a particular price OH is fixed by some external authority, A would be willing to supply HM units, B would be willing to take HL units; the amount actually sold will be whichever of these is the less. Now, within limits, the higher the price fixed, the greater will be A's profits, the lower the price fixed, the greater will be the profit of B. There is thus an

---

[33] *Mathematical Psychics*, p. 29.
[34] Schneider, *Reine Theorie*, ch. 2; Zeuthen, *Problems of Monopoly*, pp. 65 ff.
[35] "Bilateral Monopoly," *Econ. Jour.*, 1928.

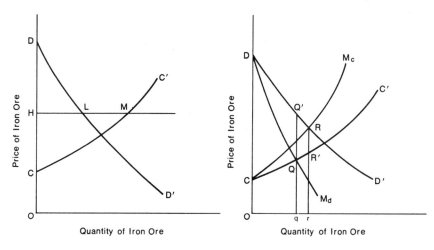

Quantity of Iron Ore   Quantity of Iron Ore

opposition of interests. But this only within limits; for after a point it would not pay A to push up the price any further. The output which maximizes A's profits will be given by the intersection of the curve marginal to *DD'* with *CC'*. *DD'* is the demand curve confronting A; we can draw a marginal revenue curve (DM_d) corresponding to it, to cut *CC'* at Q. A vertical line through Q cuts the horizontal axis in *q*, and *DD'* in *Q'*. Then the most profitable position for A is when his output is *Oq* and his price *Q'q*.

If on the other hand, B can fix the price, what is the point where his profits are maximized? This is found by drawing a curve marginal to *CC'* (CM_c), to intersect *DD'* in R. Draw *RR'r* perpendicular to the horizontal axis. The output most favorable to B will then be *Or*, and the price *R'r*.

Thus there does seem to be an "opposition of interests"; how did Cournot and his followers come to an opposite view? They would hold that there is an equilibrium with the price at *Q'q*, for in this case both producers are earning a maximum monopoly profit, B from the consumers of steel, A from B. That is perfectly true; no monopoly action by A can stop B earning a monopoly profit from the consumers. But B is not only a monopoly seller with regard to the consumers; he is also a monopoly buyer with respect to A. If he is allowed to do so, he will also extract a monopsony profit from A; it was this that Cournot left out of account.

As we have said, this indeterminateness does not mean that the law of causality is suspended; it only means that the static assumptions of fixed demand and cost curves do not suffice to determine the price. Attempts have been made by Dr. Zeuthen and myself to reach a determinate solution by introducing more "dynamic" factors.[36] Dr. Zeuthen's solution proceeds by examining the probability of each side breaking off relations,

[36] Zeuthen, *op. cit.*, ch. 4; "du Monopole Bilatéral," *Revue d'Economie politique*, 1933; Hicks, *Theory of Wages*, ch. 7; A treatment somewhat similar to Dr. Zeuthen's is to be found in G. di Nardi, "L'Indeterminazione nel Monopolio bilaterale," *Archivo Scientifico*, Bari 1934.

which correspond to each set of terms; mine by considering the length of time for which either party would be willing to "strike" in order to get any particular price. The two methods appear to be complementary.

IV. Conclusion

I have so far confined my remarks to the purely formal aspect of recent work on monopoly; but in conclusion something ought to be said about the applicability of this now well-developed technique. It is evidently the opinion of some of the writers under discussion that the modern theory of monopoly is not only capable of throwing considerable light on the general principles underlying an individualistic economic structure, but that it is also capable of extensive use in the analysis of particular practical economic problems, that is to say, in applied economics. Personally, I cannot but feel skeptical about this.

We have already seen, in the case of duopoly, that the marginal revenue of a duopolist depends upon a term which can properly be called "conjectural." It is not the actual degree to which the second seller's output would change—it is the estimate of this degree on the part of the first seller. But once we have seen this, why mark this term only as conjectural? Is not the slope of the individual demand curve confronting a simple monopolist conjectural too? There does not seem to be any reason why a monopolist should not make a mistake in estimating the slope of the demand curve confronting him, and should maintain a certain output, thinking it was the position which maximized his profit, although he could actually have increased his profit by expanding or contracting.[37]

It is this subjective character of the individual demand curve which leads one to skepticism about the applicability of the apparatus. For what are the objective grounds from which we can deduce the existence of a significant degree of imperfect competition? It may be said that as soon as we find firms concerning themselves with a price policy, or undertaking selling costs, some degree of imperfect competition must be present. This may be granted;[38] but what degree? Is it important or negligible? There is no means of finding out but to ask the monopolist, and it will be kind of him to tell us.

Whether competition is perfect or imperfect, the expansion of the individual firm will be stopped by factors which are purely subjective estimates; in the one case by rising subjective costs or costs of organization;[39]

[37] This argument is fortified if the demand curve is interpreted (as for most purposes it probably ought to be) as a fairly "long-period" demand curve.

[38] Professor W. H. Hutt, "Economic Method and the Concept of Competition," *Economic Journal of South Africa*, June 1934, disputes this as far as selling costs are concerned. His argument would appear to be valid so long as advertisement and product are sold in fixed proportions, but it ceases to be so if the "coefficients of consumption" are variable.

[39] *Cf.* E. A. G. Robinson, "The Problem of Management and the Size of Firms," *Econ. Jour.*, June 1934, and the same author's *Structure of Competitive Industry*. Also Kaldor, *op. cit.*

in the other by an estimated downward slope of the marginal revenue curve. Objective facts give us no means of distinguishing between them.

The new theories seem to make little difference to the laws of change as they are exhibited in the traditional analysis; usually they do no more than suggest new reasons why we should get certain familiar effects, and there is very little means of distinguishing between the new reasons and the old. Whether an industry is monopolized, or duopolized, or polypolized, or operates under conditions of perfect competition, we shall expect a rise in demand to lead to a rise in output (though in all cases there are possible, but highly improbable, exceptions); and it is still likely that the rise in demand will be accompanied either by no change in price, or by a rise. New reasons are indeed adduced why a rise in output may be accompanied by a fall in price; it may be due to a rise in the elasticity of demand to the individual firm, rather than to economies of the Marshallian type. But the new explanation is not overwhelmingly convincing, and does not drive the Marshallian from the field.[40]

It does indeed now become possible that a rise in supply—if it takes the form of an influx of new firms—may actually lead to a rise in price, as would not be possible under perfect competition. Yet the conditions for this to happen, that the influx of firms should make the demand curve confronting each firm in the industry *less elastic*, is so peculiar, that it is hard to attach very much importance to this case—at least, as analyzed.

It is therefore hard to see that the new analysis does much to displace Marshallian methods. Marshall's assumptions are simpler, and if we are unable to tell which of two hypotheses is more appropriate, the simpler has the obvious claim to be chosen. But of course this is not to say that in strong cases—cases, for example, where discrimination is practiced—we are not obliged to assume monopoly conditions, and to make what use we can of the elaborations here described.

From this point of view, substantial gains have certainly been made; we are now in the possession of a much more complete theory of monopoly than was the case a very few years ago. If, when we have it, it seems less use than had been hoped, this is not an uncommon experience in the history of human thought.

---

[40] It is tempting to propose a rehabilitation of Marshall on the basis of these recent developments. Since it has become clear that "increasing returns" are mainly a matter of indivisibilities and discontinuities, it is very possible that a firm may be in perfect competitive equilibrium with its (conjectured) demand curve horizontal, at the point of equilibrium, although it knows that a considerable increase in output would enable it to diminish average costs (of hired factors) considerably. But it is uncertain whether so large an increase in sales could be brought about without a considerable reduction in price, and refrains from expansion because it is unwilling to take the risk. This seems at least as plausible a construction as the other, and better suited to a world of very imperfect knowledge.

On the general question of discontinuity in cost, see M. Joseph, "A Discontinuous Cost Curve," *Econ. Jour.*, Sept. 1933.

Monopoly and Resource Allocation

ARNOLD C. HARBERGER

Arnold C. Harberger is Professor of Economics at the University of Chicago. This well-known, and controversial, paper appeared in the American Economic Review *in 1954.*

One of the first things we learn when we begin to study price theory is that the main effects of monopoly are to misallocate resources, to reduce aggregate welfare, and to redistribute income in favor of monopolists. In the light of this fact, it is a little curious that our empirical efforts at studying monopoly have so largely concentrated on other things. We have studied particular industries and have come up with a formidable list of monopolistic practices: identical pricing, price leadership, market sharing, patent suppression, basing points, and so on. And we have also studied the whole economy, using the concentration of production in the hands of a small number of firms as the measure of monopoly. On this basis we have obtained the impression that some 20 or 30 or 40 per cent of our economy is effectively monopolized.

In this paper I propose to look at the American economy, and in particular at American manufacturing industry, and try to get some quantitative notion of the allocative and welfare effects of monopoly. It should be clear from the outset that this is not the kind of job one can do with great precision. The best we can hope for is to get a feeling for the general orders of magnitude that are involved.

I take it as an operating hypothesis that, in the long run, resources can be allocated among our manufacturing industries in such a way as to yield roughly constant returns. That is, long-run average costs are close to constant in the relevant range, for both the firm and the industry. This hypothesis gives us the wedge we need to get something from the data. For as is well known, the malallocative effects of monopoly stem from the difference between marginal cost and price, and marginal costs are at first glance terribly difficult to pin down empirically for a wide range of firms and industries. But once we are ready to proceed on the basis of constant average costs, we can utilize the fact that under such circumstances marginal and average costs are the same, and we can easily get some idea of average costs.

But that does not solve all the problems, for cost and profit to the economist are not the same things as cost and profit to the accountant, and the accountants make our data. To move into this question, I should like to conjure up an idealized picture of an economy in equilibrium. In this picture all firms are operating on their long-run cost curves, the cost curves are so defined as to yield each firm an equal return on its invested capital, and markets are cleared. I think it is fair to say that this is a picture of optimal resource allocation. Now, we never see this idyllic picture in the real world, but if long-run costs are in fact close to constant and markets are cleared, we can pick out the places where resources are misallocated by looking at the rates of return on capital. Those industries which are returning higher than average rates have too few resources; and those yielding lower than average rates have too many resources. To get an idea of how big a shift of resources it would take to equalize profit rates in all industries, we have to know something about the elasticities of demand for the goods in question. In Figure 1, I illustrate a hypothetical case. The indus-

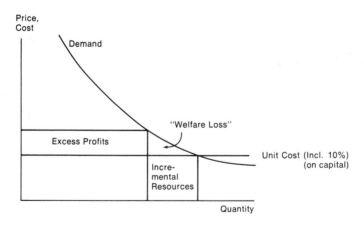

FIGURE 1

try in question is earning 20 per cent on a capital of 10 million dollars, while the average return to capital is only 10 per cent. We therefore build a 10 per cent return into the cost curve, which leaves the industry with 1 million in excess profits. If the elasticity of demand for the industry's product is unity, it will take a shift of 1 million in resources in order to expand supply enough to wipe out the excess profits.

The above argument gives a general picture of what I have done empirically. The first empirical job was to find a period which met two conditions. First, it had to be reasonably close to a long-run equilibrium period; that is, no violent shifts in demand or economic structure were to be in process. And second, it had to be a period for which accounting values of capital could be supposed to be pretty close to actual values. In particular, because of the disastrous effect of inflation and deflation on book values of capital, it had to be a period of fairly stable prices, which in turn had been preceded by a period of stable prices. It seemed to me that the late twenties came as close as one could hope to meeting both these requirements.

The late twenties had an additional advantage for me—because my choice of this period enabled me to use Professor Ralph C. Epstein's excellent study, *Industrial Profits in the United States* (National Bureau of Economic Research, 1934), as a source of data. Professor Epstein there gives, for the years 1924–28, the rates of total profit to total capital for seventy-three manufacturing industries, with total capital defined as book capital plus bonded indebtedness and total profit defined as book profit plus interest on the indebtedness. To get rid of factors producing short-period variations in these rates of return, I average the rates, for each industry, for the five-year period. The results are given in column 1 of Table I. The differences among these profit rates, as between industries, give a broad indication of the extent of resource malallocation in American manufacturing in the late twenties.

Column 2 presents the amount by which the profits in each industry diverged from what that industry would have obtained if it had gotten the average rate of profit for all manufacturing industry. In column 3, these excesses and shortages of profit are expressed as a per cent of sales in the industry. By analogy with Figure 1, you can see that this column really tells by what percentage prices in each industry were "too high" or "too low" when compared with those that would generate an optimal resource allocation.

Now suppose we ask how much reallocation of resources it would take to eliminate the observed divergences in profit rates. This depends, as you can see in Figure 1, on the demand elasticities confronting the industries in question. How high are these elasticities? It seems to me that one need only look at the list of industries in Table I in order to get the feeling that the elasticities in question are probably quite low. The presumption of low elasticity is further strengthened by the fact that what we envisage is not the substitution of one industry's product against all other products, but rather the substitution of one great aggregate of products (those yielding high rates of return) for another aggregate (those yielding low rates of return). In the light of these considerations, I think an elasticity of unity is about as high as one can reasonably allow for, though a somewhat higher elasticity would not seriously affect the general tenor of my results.

Returning again to Figure 1, we can see that once the assumption of unit elasticity is made the amount of excess profit measures the amount of resources that must be called into an industry in order to bring its profit rate into line. When I say resources here I mean the services of labor and capital plus the materials bought by the industry from other industries. In many ways it seems preferable to define resources as simply the services of labor and capital. This could be done by applying to the value added in the industry the percentage of excess profits to sales. The trouble here is that adding to the output of industry X calls resources not only into that industry but also into the industries that supply it. And by the time we take all the increments in value added of all these supplying industries that would be generated by the initial increase in output of industry X, we come pretty close to the incremental value of sales in industry X. Of course, the movement to an optimal resource allocation entails some industries expanding their output, like X, and others, say Y, contracting their output. If we really traced through the increments to value added which are required in their supplying industries, say Z, we would often find that there was some cancellation of the required changes in the output of Z. Hence by using sales rather than value added as our measure of resource transfer, we rather overstate the necessary movement.

Keeping this in mind, let us return to the data. If we add up all the pluses and all the minuses in column 2, we find that to obtain equilibrium we would have to transfer about 550 million dollars in resources from low-profit to high-profit industries. But this is not the end. Those of you who are familiar with Epstein's study are aware that it is based on a sample of 2,046 corporations, which account for some 45 per cent of the sales and capital in manufacturing industry. Pending a discussion of possible biases in the sample a little later, we can proceed to blow up our 550 million figure to cover total manufacturing. The result is 1.2 billion. Hence we tentatively conclude that the misallocations of resources which existed in United States manufacturing in the period 1924–28 could have been eliminated by a net transfer of roughly 4 per cent of the resources in manufacturing industry, or 1½ per cent of the total resources of the economy.

Now let us suppose that somehow we effected these desired resource transfers. By how much would people be better off? This general question was answered in 1938 for an analogous problem by Harold Hotelling.[1] His

[1] Harold Hotelling, "The General Welfare in Relation to Problems of Taxation and of Railway and Utility Rates," *Econometrica*, July, 1938, pp. 242–269. The applicability of Hotelling's proof to the present problem can be seen by referring to pp. 252 ff. He there indicates that he hypothecates a transformation locus which is a hyperplane. This is given us by our assumption of constant costs. He then inquires what will be the loss in moving from a point Q on the hyperplane, at which the marginal conditions of competitive equilibrium are met, to a point Q' at which these conditions of competitive equilibrium are not met. At Q' a nonoptimal set of prices P' prevails. These are, in our

TABLE I.

Industry	(1) Rate of Profit on Capital (1924–28)	(2) Amount by which Profits Diverged from "Average" (Millions)	(3) Column (2) as Per Cent of Sales	(4) Welfare Cost of Divergence in Column (2) (Millions)
Bakery products	17.5%	$17	5.3%	$.452
Flour	11.9	1	0.4	.002
Confectionery	17.0	7	6.1	.215
Package foods	17.9	7	3.3	.116
Dairying	11.8	3	0.7	.010
Canned goods	12.4	1	0.6	.003
Meat packing	4.4	−69	−1.7	.596
Beverages	5.8	−2	−4.0	.080
Tobacco	14.1	27	0.3	.373
Miscellaneous foods	8.1	−13	−2.4	.164
Cotton spinning	10.0	−0	0	0
Cotton converting	8.0	−1	−0.6	.008
Cotton weaving	4.7	−15	−5.5	.415
Weaving woolens	2.6	−16	−9.5	.762
Silk weaving	7.9	−3	−2.3	.035
Carpets	9.8	−1	−1.3	.006
Men's clothing	11.4	1	0.5	.002
Knit goods	12.9	3	1.9	.028
Miscellaneous clothing	13.1	1	1.1	.006
Miscellaneous textiles	9.2	−2	−0.9	.008
Boots and shoes	15.8	9	3.8	.172
Miscellaneous leather products	7.7	−3	−2.1	.032
Rubber	7.6	−23	−2.5	.283
Lumber manufacturing	7.8	−6	−3.9	.118
Planing mills	13.1	1	3.2	.016
Millwork	7.3	−1	−2.9	.014
Furniture	13.4	2	2.2	.022
Miscellaneous lumber	12.9	4	1.7	.034
Blank paper	6.6	−17	−6.2	.524
Cardboard boxes	13.6	2	3.1	.031
Stationery	7.5	−2	−3.0	.030
Miscellaneous paper	9.3	−1	−1.1	.005
Newspapers	20.1	37	8.5	1.570
Books and music	14.6	2	4.3	.042
Miscellaneous printing and publishing	18.6	1	5.6	.028
Crude chemicals	10.2	−0	0	0
Paints	14.6	5	3.3	.082
Petroleum refining	8.4	−114	−3.6	2.032
Proprietary preparations	20.9	25	11.7	1.460
Toilet preparations	30.4	3	15.0	.225
Cleaning preparations	20.8	15	5.5	.413
Miscellaneous chemicals	15.6	45	8.8	.197
Ceramics	10.8	1	1.0	.005

TABLE I.—(cont'd.)

Industry	(1) Rate of Profit on Capital (1924–28)	(2) Amount by which Profits Diverged from "Average" (Millions)	(3) Column (2) as Per Cent of Sales	(4) Welfare Cost of Divergence in Column (2) (Millions)
Glass	13.5%	$ 4	2.6%	$.052
Portland cement	14.3	10	8.4	.420
Miscellaneous clay and stone	17.6	14	8.0	.560
Castings and forgings	5.6	−234	−7.7	8.994
Sheet metal	10.5	0	0	0
Wire and nails	11.6	1	1.2	.006
Heating machinery	13.3	3	1.6	.024
Electrical machinery	15.7	48	5.3	1.281
Textile machinery	13.6	3	6.1	.092
Printing machinery	9.7	−0	0	0
Road machinery	17.3	10	6.8	.374
Engines	13.7	2	5.9	.059
Mining machinery	11.0	1	0.7	.004
Factory machinery	11.7	33	3.0	.045
Office machinery	16.1	7	5.6	.194
Railway equipment	6.0	−24	−9.6	1.148
Motor vehicles	18.5	161	4.4	3.878
Firearms	12.9	1	2.0	.010
Hardware	12.8	8	2.3	.092
Tools	11.6	1	1.1	.006
Bolts and nuts	15.4	1	3.1	.016
Miscellaneous machinery	12.6	3	2.2	.032
Nonferrous metals	11.9	15	1.4	.106
Jewelry	10.6	0	0	0
Miscellaneous metals	12.5	14	2.0	.140
Scientific instruments	21.2	20	11.6	1.163
Toys	15.0	1	3.2	.016
Pianos	9.9	−0	0	0
Miscellaneous special manufacturing	12.0	4	1.4	.027
Job printing	13.8	4	2.2	.044

Col. (1)—from Ralph C. Epstein, *Industrial Profits in the United States* (N.B.E.R., 1934), Tables 43D through 53D. Entries in column (1) are the arithmetic means of the annual entries in the source tables.

Col. (2)—divergences in the profit rates given in column (1) from their mean (10.4) are here applied to the 1928 volume of capital in each industry. Total capital is the sum of book capital (Epstein, Appendix Table 6C) plus bonded debt (Epstein, Appendix Table 6D).

Col. (3)—1928 figures were used for sales (Epstein, Appendix Table 6A).

Col. (4)—measures the amount by which consumer "welfare" fell short of the level it would have attained if resources had been so allocated as to give each industry an equal return on capital. It assumes that the elasticity of demand for the products of each industry is unity and approximates the area designated as "welfare loss" in Figure 1.

general formula would be strictly applicable here if all our industries were producing products for direct consumption. The question thus arises, how to treat industries producing intermediate products. If we neglect them altogether, we would be overlooking the fact that their resource shifts and price changes do ultimately change the prices and amounts of consumer goods. If, on the other hand, we pretend that these intermediate industries face the consumer directly and thus directly affect consumer welfare, we neglect the fact that some of the resource shifts in the intermediate sector will have opposing influences on the prices and quantities of consumer goods. Obviously, this second possibility is the safer of the two, in the sense that it can only overestimate, not underestimate, the improvement in welfare that will take place. We can therefore follow this course in applying the Hotelling formula to our data. The results are shown in column 4 of Table I. This gives, opposite each industry, the amount by which consumer welfare would increase if that industry either acquired or divested itself of the appropriate amount of resources. The total improvement in consumer welfare which might come from our sample of firms thus turns out to be about 26.5 million dollars. Blowing up this figure to cover the whole economy, we get what we really want: an estimate of by how much consumer welfare would have improved if resources had been optimally allocated throughout American manufacturing in the late twenties. The answer is 59 million dollars—less than one-tenth of 1 per cent of the national income. Translated into today's national income and today's prices, this comes out to 225 million dollars, or less than $1.50 for every man, woman, and child in the United States.

Before drawing any lessons from this, I should like to spend a little time evaluating the estimate. First let us look at the basic assumption that long-run costs are constant. My belief is that this is a good assumption, but that if it is wrong, costs in all probability tend to be increasing rather than decreasing in American industry. And the presence of increasing costs would result in a lowering of both our estimates. Less resources would have to be transferred in order to equalize profit rates, and the increase in consumer welfare resulting from the transfer would be correspondingly less.

---

example, actual prices, while the equilibrium price-vector P is given by costs, defined to include normal profits. Hotelling's expression for the welfare loss in shifting from Q to Q' is $\frac{1}{2}\sum dp_i dq_i$ where p_i and q_i are the price and quantity of the i-th commodity. We obtain this by defining our units so that the cost of each commodity is $1.00. The equilibrium quantity of each commodity under the assumption of unit elasticities is then equal to the value of sales of that commodity. If we call r_i the percentage divergence of actual price from cost, we may write the total welfare loss due to monopoly as $\frac{1}{2}\sum r_i^2 q_i$ if the elasticities of demand are unity, and as $\frac{1}{2}\sum r_i^2 q_i k_i$, if the elasticities of demand are k_i. In column 4 of Table I, I attribute to each commodity a welfare loss equal to $\frac{1}{2}r_i^2 q_i$. This measure of the welfare loss due to monopoly abstracts from distributional considerations. Essentially it assumes that the marginal utility of money is the same for all individuals. Alternatively, it may be viewed as measuring the welfare gain which would occur if resources were shifted from producing Q' to producing Q, and at the same time the necessary fiscal adjustments were made to keep everybody's money income the same.

On the other hand, flaws in the data probably operate to make our estimate of the welfare loss too low. Take for example the question of patents and good will. To the extent that these items are assigned a value on the books of a corporation, monopoly profits are capitalized, and the profit rate which we have used is an understatement of the actual profit rate on real capital. Fortunately for us, Professor Epstein has gone into this question in his study. He finds that excluding intangibles from the capital figures makes a significant difference in the earnings rates of only eight of the seventy-three industries. I have accordingly recomputed my figures for these eight industries.[2] As a result, the estimated amount of resource trans-

Industry	Adjusted Profit Rate*	Adjusted Rate of Excess Profit	Adjusted Amount of Excess Profits (Millions)	Adjusted Welfare Loss (Millions)
Confectionery	21.1%	10.7%	$11	$.530
Tobacco	19.0	8.6	66	2.225
Men's clothing	14.9	4.5	5	.068
Stationery	8.8	—	—	—
Newspaper publishing	27.9	17.5	67	5.148
Proprietary preparations	27.8	17.4	42	4.121
Toilet preparations	50.8	40.4	6	1.400
Printing machinery	12.9	2.5	2	.064
			199	13.556
Less previous amount of excess profit or welfare loss			−100	−3.845
Net adjustment			99	9.711

* Epstein, *op. cit.*, p. 530.

fer goes up from about 1½ per cent to about 1¾ per cent of the national total. And the welfare loss due to resource misallocations gets raised to about 81 million dollars, just over a tenth of 1 per cent of the national income.

There is also another problem arising out of the data. Epstein's sample of firms had an average profit rate of 10.4 per cent during the period I investigated, while in manufacturing as a whole the rate of return was 8 per cent. The reason for this divergence seems to be an overweighting of high-profit industries in Epstein's sample. It can be shown, however, that a correct weighting procedure would raise our estimate of the welfare cost of equalizing profit rates in all industries by no more than 10 million dollars.[3]

[2] Following is a breakdown of the adjustment for the eight industries in question.
[3] Epstein's results in samples from small corporations (not included in his main sample) indicate that their earnings rates tend to be quite close, industry by industry, to the earnings rates of the large corporations in the main sample. This suggests that the average rate of profit in the main sample (10.4 per cent) was higher than the average for all industry (8 per cent) because high-profit industries were overweighted in the sample rather than because the sampled firms tended to be the high-profit firms within each industry. The overweighting of high-profit industries affects our estimate of the welfare cost of resource misallocations in two ways. First, quite obviously, it tends to overstate

Finally, there is a problem associated with the aggregation of manufacturing into seventy-three industries. My analysis assumes high substitutability among the products produced by different firms within any industry and relatively low substitutability among the products of different industries. Yet Epstein's industrial classification undoubtedly lumps together in particular industries products which are only remote substitutes and which are produced by quite distinct groups of firms. In short, Epstein's industries are in some instances aggregates of subindustries, and for our purposes it would have been appropriate to deal with the subindustries directly. It can be shown that the use of aggregates in such cases biases our estimate of the welfare loss downward, but experiments with hypothetical examples reveal that the probable extent of the bias is small.[4]

Thus we come to our final conclusion. Elimination of resource misallocations in American manufacturing in the late twenties would bring with it an improvement in consumer welfare of just a little more than a tenth of a per cent. In present values, this welfare gain would amount to about $2.00 per capita.

Now we can stop to ask what resource misallocations we have measured. We actually have included in the measurement not only monopoly misallocations but also misallocations coming out of the dynamics of economic growth and development and all the other elements which would cause divergent profit rates to persist for some time even in an effectively competitive economy. I know of no way to get at the precise share of the total welfare loss that is due to monopoly, but I do think I have a reasonable way of pinning our estimate down just a little more tightly. My argument here is based on two props. First of all, I think it only reasonable to roughly identify monopoly power with high rates of profit. And secondly, I think it quite implausible that more than a third of our manufacturing

the cost by pretending that the high-profit industries account for a larger share of the aggregate product of the economy than they actually do. Second, and perhaps not so obviously, it tends to understate the cost by overstating the average rate of profit in all manufacturing, and hence overstating the amount of profit which is "built in" to the cost curves in the present analysis. The estimated adjustment of 10 million dollars presented in the text corrects only for this second effect of overweighting and is obtained by imputing as the normal return to capital in the Epstein sample only 8 per cent rather than 10.4 per cent and recomputing the welfare costs of resource misallocations by the method followed in Table I. It takes no account of the first effect of overweighting, mentioned above, and thus results in an overstatement of the actual amount of welfare cost.

[4] The extent of the bias is proportional to the difference between the average of the squares of a set of numbers and the square of the average, the numbers in question being the rates of excess profit in the subindustries. Consider an industry composed of three subindustries, each of equal weight. Assume, for an extreme example, that the rates of excess profit (excess profit expressed as a per cent of sales) are 10 per cent, 20 per cent, and 30 per cent in the three subindustries. The average rate of excess profit of the aggregate industry would then be 20 per cent, and, by our procedure, the estimate of the welfare loss due to that industry would be 2 per cent of its sales. If we had been able to deal with the hypothetical subindustry data directly, we would have estimated the welfare loss associated with them at 2⅓ per cent of the aggregate sales.

profits should be monopoly profits; that is, profits which are above and beyond the normal return to capital and are obtained by exercise of monopoly power. I doubt that this second premise needs any special defense. After all, we know that capital is a highly productive resource. On the first premise, identifying monopoly power with high profits, I think we need only run down the list of high-profit industries to verify its plausibility. Cosmetics are at the top, with a 30 per cent return on capital. They are followed by scientific instruments, drugs, soaps, newspapers, automobiles, cereals, road machinery, bakery products, tobacco, and so on. But even apart from the fact that it makes sense in terms of other evidence to consider these industries monopolistic, there is a still stronger reason for making this assumption. For given the elasticity of demand for an industry's product, the welfare loss associated with that product increases as the square of its greater-than-normal profits. Thus, granted that we are prepared to say that no more than a third of manufacturing profits were monopoly profits, we get the biggest welfare effect by distributing this monopoly profit first to the highest profit industries, then to the next highest, and so on. When this is done, we come to the conclusion that monopoly misallocations entail a welfare loss of no more than a thirteenth of a per cent of the national income. Or, in present values, no more than about $1.40 per capita.

Before going on, I should like to mention a couple of other possible ways in which this estimate might fail to reflect the actual cost of monopoly misallocations to the American consumer. First, there is the possibility that book capital might be overstated, not because of patents and good will, but as a result of mergers and acquisitions. In testing this possibility I had recourse to Professor J. Fred Weston's recent study of mergers. He found that mergers and acquisitions accounted for only a quarter of the growth of seventy-odd corporations in the last half-century (*The Role of Mergers in the Growth of Large Firms*, pages 100–102). Even a quite substantial overstatement of the portion of their capital involved in the mergers would thus not seriously affect the profit rates. And furthermore, much of the merger growth that Weston found came in the very early years of the century; so that one can reasonably expect that most of the assets which may have been overvalued in these early mergers were off the books by the period that I investigated.

The second possibility concerns advertising expenditures. These are included as cost in accounting data, but it may be appropriate for our present purpose to include part of them as a sort of quasi-monopoly profit. I was unable to make any systematic adjustment of my data to account for this possibility, but I did make a cursory examination of some recent data on advertising expenditures. They suggest that advertising costs are well under 2 per cent of sales for all of the industries in Table I. Adjustment of our results to allow for a maximal distorting effect of advertising expenditures would accordingly make only a slight difference, perhaps raising our estimate of the welfare cost of monopoly in present values to $1.50 per capita, but not significantly higher.[5]

I should like now to review what has been done. In reaching our estimate of the welfare loss due to monopoly misallocations of resources we have assumed constant rather than increasing costs in manufacturing industry and have assumed elasticities of demand which are too high, I believe. On both counts we therefore tend to overstate the loss. Furthermore, we have treated intermediate products in such a way as to overstate the loss. Finally, we have attributed to monopoly an implausibly large share—33⅓ per cent—of manufacturing profits, and have distributed this among industries in such a way as to get the biggest possible welfare loss consistent with the idea that monopolies tend to make high profits. In short, we have labored at each stage to get a big estimate of the welfare loss, and we have come out in the end with less than a tenth of a per cent of the national income.

I must confess that I was amazed at this result. I never really tried to quantify my notions of what monopoly misallocations amounted to, and I doubt that many other people have. Still, it seems to me that our literature of the last twenty or so years reflects a general belief that monopoly distortions to our resources structure are much greater than they seem in fact to be.

Let me therefore state the beliefs to which the foregoing analysis has led me. First of all, I do not want to minimize the effects of monopoly. A tenth of a per cent of the national income is still over 300 million dollars,

[5] I was unable similarly to take account of selling costs other than advertising expenditures, even though some of such costs may be the price paid by firms to enhance market control or monopoly position. In principle, clearly, some share of selling costs should be taken into account, and it is a limitation of the present study that no adjustment for such costs was possible. Scrutinizing Table I, however, I should suggest that such selling costs are important in only a few of the industries listed, and that an allowance for them would almost certainly not alter the general order of magnitude of the estimates here presented. It should be pointed out, also, that the general conclusions reached in this paper are not closely dependent on the precise data used. Suppose, for example, that we had observed the following situation: industries accounting for half the output of American manufacturing were charging prices which yielded them a 10 per cent "monopoly profit" on sales, while the remainder of industries earned a constant rate of profit on capital (here called normal profit) but no more. If we were, in this situation, to reallocate resources so as to equalize profit rates in all industries, the prices of competitive products would rise and those of monopolistic products would fall. If demand for the product of each sector were assumed to be of unit elasticity, we would estimate the gain in welfare incident upon the reallocation of resources at .125 per cent of total industrial sales. This would be just about a tenth of a per cent of the national income if the ratio of manufacturing sales to national income approximated its 1924–28 figure. The estimated welfare gain is obtained as follows: Under our elasticity assumption, prices would rise by 5 per cent in the competitive sector and fall by 5 per cent in the monopolistic sector, and quantities would change inversely by an equal percentage. Taking 100 as the aggregate sales of manufacturing, the change in output in each sector will be 2.5, and taking 1 as the index of initial prices in each sector, the change in price in each sector will be .05. According to the Hotelling formula, the welfare gain coming from each sector will be ½(2.5)(.05), and when these gains are added together the aggregate gain turns out to be .125.

so we dare not pooh-pooh the efforts of those—economists and others—who have dedicated themselves to reducing the losses due to monopoly. But it seems to me that the monopoly problem does take on a rather different perspective in the light of present study. Our economy emphatically does not seem to be monopoly capitalism in big red letters. We can neglect monopoly elements and still gain a very good understanding of how our economic process works and how our resources are allocated. When we are interested in the big picture of our manufacturing economy, we need not apologize for treating it as competitive, for in fact it is awfully close to being so. On the other hand, when we are interested in the doings of particular industries, it may often be wise to take monopoly elements into account. Even though monopoly elements in cosmetics are a drop in the bucket in the big picture of American manufacturing, they still mean a lot when we are studying the behavior of this particular industry.

Finally I should like to point out that I have discussed only the welfare effects of resource misallocations due to monopoly. I have not analyzed the redistributions of income that arise when monopoly is present. I originally planned to discuss this redistribution aspect as well, but finally decided against it. All I want to say here is that monopoly does not seem to affect aggregate welfare very seriously through its effect on resource allocation. What it does through its effect on income distribution I leave to my more metaphysically inclined colleagues to decide. I am impelled to add a final note in order to forestall misunderstandings arising out of matters of definition. Resource misallocations may clearly arise from causes other than those considered here: tariffs, excise taxes, subsidies, trade-union practices, and the devices of agricultural policy are some obvious examples. Some of these sources of misallocation will be discussed in a forthcoming paper. Suffice it to say here that the present paper is not concerned with them.

Allocative Efficiency vs. "X-Efficiency"

HARVEY LEIBENSTEIN

Harvey Leibenstein is Professor of Economics at Harvard University. This article appeared in the American Economic Review *in 1966.*

At the core of economics is the concept of efficiency. Microeconomic theory is concerned with allocative efficiency. Empirical evidence has been accumulating that suggests that the problem of allocative efficiency is trivial. Yet it is hard to escape the notion that efficiency in some broad sense is significant. In this paper I want to review the empirical evidence briefly and to consider some of the possible implications of the findings, especially as they relate to the theory of the firm and to the explanation of economic growth. The essence of the argument is that microeconomic theory focuses on allocative efficiency to the exclusion of other types of efficiencies that, in fact, are much more significant in many instances. Furthermore, improvement in "nonallocative efficiency" is an important aspect of the process of growth.

In Section I the empirical evidence on allocative efficiency is presented. In this section we also consider the reasons why allocation inefficiency is frequently of small magnitude. Most of the evidence on allocative inefficiency deals with either monopoly or international trade. However, monopoly and trade are not the focus of this paper. Our primary concern is with the broader issue of allocative efficiency versus an initially undefined type of efficiency that we shall refer to as "X-efficiency." The magnitude and nature of this type of efficiency is examined in Sections II and III. Although a major element of "X-efficiency" is motivation, it is not the only element, and hence the terms "motivation efficiency" or "incentive efficiency" have not been employed.

As he proceeds, the reader is especially invited to keep in mind the sharp contrast in the magnitudes involved between Tables 1 and 2.

I. Allocative Inefficiency: Empirical Evidence

The studies that are of interest in assessing the importance of allocative efficiency are summarized in Table 1. These are of two types. On the one side we have the studies of Harberger and Schwartzman on the "social welfare cost" of monopoly. On the other side we have a number of studies, among them those of Johnson, Scitovsky, Wemeslfelder, Janssen, and others, on the benefits of reducing or eliminating restrictions to trade. In both cases the computed benefits attributed to the reallocation of resources turn out to be exceedingly small.

TABLE I. Calculated "Welfare Loss" as Percentage of Gross or Net National Product Attributed to Misallocation of Resources

Study	Source	Country	Cause	Loss
A. C. Harberger	A.E.R.	U.S.A. 1929	Monopoly	.07 percent
D. Schwartzman	1954	U.S.A. 1954	Monopoly	.01 percent
T. Scitovsky	J.P.E. 1960 (1)	Common Market 1952	Tariffs	.05 percent
J. Wemelsfelder	E.J. 1960	Germany 1958	Tariffs	.18 percent
L. H. Janssen	(2)	Italy 1960	Tariffs	max. .1 percent
H. G. Johnson	Manchester School 1958	U. K. 1970	Tariffs	max. 1.0 percent
A. Singh	(3)	Montevideo Treaty Countries	Tariffs	max. .0075 percent

Let us look at some of the findings. In the original Harberger study the benefits for eliminating monopoly in the United States would raise income no more than $\frac{1}{13}$ of 1 percent. Schwartzman's study which recomputes the benefits of eliminating monopoly by comparing Canadian monopolized industries as against counterpart competitive U.S. industries, and vice versa in order to determine the excess price attributable to monopoly, ends up with a similar result. Similarly, the benefits attributed to superior resource allocation as a consequence of the Common Market or a European Free Trade Area are also minute—usually much less than 1 percent.

The calculations made by Scitovsky of the benefits to the Common Market (based on Verdoorn's data) led him to the conclusion that ". . . the most striking feature of these estimates is their smallness. The one that is really important (for reasons to appear presently), the gain from increased specialization . . . which is less than one-twentieth of one percent of the gross social product of the countries involved. This is ridiculously small. . . ." J. Wemelsfelder has calculated that the welfare gain of reducing import duties and increasing imports and exports accordingly amounts to .18 of 1 percent of national income. Harry Johnson in an article on England's gain in joining a Free Trade Area calculates the net gain from trade at less than 1 percent. That is, Johnson arrives at the conclusion that 1 percent of the national income would be the absolute maximum gain for Britain from entering the European Free Trade Area.

A recent study by L. H. Janssen calculates that the gains from increased specialization for the different countries of the European Economic Community would be largest for Italy, but even here the amount is only $\frac{1}{10}$ of 1 percent of total production. Janssen points out that, if the production gain for Italy due to specialization were calculated by Scitovsky's method, which he believes involves an overestimation, "the production gain in the most extreme case is still less than .4 percent." Janssen concludes, as have others, that the welfare effects of a customs union based on the superior allocation of resources are likely to be trivial. He does, however, point to the possibility "that the mere prospect of the frontiers opening would infuse fresh energy into entrepreneurs." He recognizes that certain qualitative factors may be highly important and that the consequences of growth are certainly more significant than those of allocative welfare.

My research assistant, A. Singh, has calculated the gains from trade (following the Scitovsky method) for the Montevideo Treaty Countries (Argentina, Brazil, Chile, Mexico, Paraguay, Peru, and Uruguay) and found it to be less than $\frac{1}{150}$ of 1 percent of their combined GNP. Even if we double or triple this result to allow for such factors as the effect of failing to take account of quantitative restrictions in the analysis, the outcome is still trivial.

Harberger's study on Chile which involves the reallocation of both labor and capital yields a relatively large estimate. Harberger intends to obtain as large an estimate as possible of the consequences of reallocating resources by using what I believe to be (and what he admits to be) rather extreme assumptions in order to obtain maximum outer bounds. Despite this he comes up with a number that is between 9 and 15 percent. However, no actual data are employed. What are used are outer-bound estimates based on personal impressions. I expect that a careful study similar to the Verdoorn-Scitovsky study would probably come up with numbers that would be no larger than 1 or 2 percent.

The empirical evidence, while far from exhaustive, certainly suggests that the welfare gains that can be achieved by increasing *only* allocative efficiency are usually exceedingly small, at least in capitalist economies. In all but one of the cases considered all of the gains are likely to be made up in one month's growth. They hardly seem worth worrying about.

Let us see briefly why these gains are usually small. We cannot prove that we would expect them to be small on purely theoretical grounds. If we combine our theory with what we would agree are probably reasonable estimates of some of the basic magnitudes, then it appears likely that in many cases (but certainly not all *possible* cases) the welfare loss of allocative inefficiency is of trivial significance. The idea could be developed with the aid of the diagram employed by Harberger. (See Figure 1.) In Figure I we assume that costs are constant within the relevant range. D is the demand function. Under competition price and quantity are determined at the intersection C. The monopoly price is above the competitive price equal to AB in the figure. The monopoly output is determined at the point A. The welfare loss due to monopoly, which is the same as the welfare gain if we shifted to competition, is equal to the triangle ABC. We obtain an approximation to this amount by multiplying the price differential AB by the quantity differential BC by one-half and multiplying this by the proportion of national income in industries involving the misallocation.

FIGURE 1

Let us play around with some numbers and see the kind of results we get as a consequence of this formulation. Suppose that half of the national output is produced in monopolized industries and that the price differential is 20 percent and that the average elasticity of demand is 1.5. Now the outcome will turn out to be 1½ percent. But we really used enormous figures for the misallocation. And yet the result is small. Monopoly prices, according to estimates, appear to be only about 8 percent on the average above competitive prices. We can substitute some reason other than monopoly for the misallocation and still come out with similar results.

Consider the cases of subsidized industries under some sort of governmental inducements to growth; and that of governmentally run industries. In the subsidy case the calculation would be similar. Suppose that as much as 50 percent of the industries are subsidized to the extent of a 20 percent difference in cost and that the output point on the demand function is where elasticity is unity. This last point may be reasonable since the operators of subsidized industries might want gross revenue to be as large as possible. If, on the other hand, we assume that they are profit maximizers and restrict output to a greater extent, then we might assume a price elasticity of two. This later, however, is unlikely because monopoly profits are inconsistent with subsidized industries. Those who receive the subsidy would have the legitimate fear that the subsidy would be lowered if unusual profits were earned. Hence, behavior in the direction of revenue maximization appears reasonable and the calculated welfare loss is less than 2 percent.

A similar result could be achieved in the case in which the government runs industries that affect 50 percent of the national income of an economy. In all the cases we have considered, the magnitudes chosen appear to be on the large side and the outcome is on the small side.

Of course, it is possible that the magnitude of allocative inefficiency would be large if there are large discontinuities in productivity between those industries where inputs are located and those industries to which the same inputs could be moved. This, in effect, is the basic assumption that Harberger made in his study of Chile. But if it turns out that there is a reasonable degree of continuity in productivity, and that the only way shifts could be made is by simultaneously increasing either social overhead capital or direct capital in order to make the shifts involved, then, of course, a great deal of the presumed gains would be eaten up by the capital costs and the net marginal gains would turn out to be rather small. My general impression is that this is likely to be the case in a great many underdeveloped countries where differential productivities appear to exist between the agricultural sector and the industrial sector. One cannot go beyond stating vague impressions since there is a lack of hard statistical evidence on this matter.

Why are the welfare effects of reallocation so small? Allocational inefficiency involves only the net marginal effects. The basic assumption is that every firm *purchases and utilizes* all of its input "efficiently." Thus, what is left is simply the consequences of price and quantity distortions. While some specific price distortions might be large it seems unlikely that all relative price distortions are exceptionally large. This implies that most quantity distortions must also be relatively small since for a given aggregate output a significant distortion in one commodity will be counterbalanced by a large number of small distortions in the opposite direction in quantities elsewhere. While it is possible to *assume* relative price distortions and quantity distortions that would be exceedingly high, it would be difficult to believe that, without intent, the sum of such distortions should be high. However, it is not *necessarily* so on purely *a priori* grounds.

There is one important type of distortion that cannot easily be handled by existing microeconomic theory. This has to do with the allocation of managers. It is conceivable that in practice a situation would arise in which managers are exceedingly poor, that is, others are available who do not obtain management posts, and who would be very much superior. Managers determine not only their own productivity but the productivity of all cooperating units in the organization. It is therefore possible that the actual loss due to such a misallocation might be large. But the theory does not allow us to examine this matter because firms are presumed to exist as entities that make optimal input decisions, apart from the decisions of its managers. This is obviously a contradiction and therefore cannot be handled.

II. X-Efficiency: *The Empirical Evidence*

We have seen that the welfare loss due to allocational inefficiency is frequently no more than $\frac{1}{10}$ of 1 percent. Is it conceivable that the value of X-inefficiency would be larger than that? One way of looking at it is to return to the problem of the welfare loss due to monopoly. Suppose that one-third of the industries are in the monopolized sector. Is it possible that the lack of competitive pressure of operating in monopolized industries would lead to cost $\frac{3}{10}$ of a percent higher than would be the case under competition? This magnitude seems to be very small, and hence it certainly seems to be a possibility. The question essentially, is whether we can visualize managers bestirring themselves sufficiently, if the environmen forced them to do so, in order to reduce costs by more than $\frac{3}{10}$ of 1 percent. Some of the empirical evidence available suggests that not only is this a possibility, but that the magnitudes involved are very much larger. As we shall see, the spotty evidence on this subject does not prove the case but it does seem to be sufficiently persuasive to suggest the possibility that X-efficiency exists, and that it frequently is much more significant than allocational efficiency.

Professor Eric Lundberg in his studies of Swedish industries points to the case of the steel plant at Horndal that was left to operate without any new capital investment or *technological change*, and furthermore maintenance and replacement were kept at a minimum, and yet output per man hour rose by 2 percent per annum. Professor Lundberg asserts that according to his interviews with industrialists and technicians "sub-optimal disequilibrium in regard to technology and utilization of existing capital stock is a profoundly important aspect of the situation at any time." (This according to Gorin Ohlin's summary of Lundberg's findings.) If a sub-optimal disequilibrium exists at any time, then it would seem reasonable that under the proper motivations managers and workers could bestir themselves to produce closer to optimality, and that under other conditions they may be motivated to move farther away from optimality.

Frederick Harbison reports visiting two petroleum refineries in Egypt less than one-half mile apart. "The labor productivity of one had been nearly double that in the other for many years. But recently, under completely new management, the inefficient refinery was beginning to make quite spectacular improvements in efficiency with the same labor force." We may inquire why the management was changed only recently whereas the difference in labor productivity existed for many years. It is quite possible that had the motivation existed in sufficient strength, this change could have taken place earlier.

In a recent book on the firm, Neil Chamberlain visualizes his firms reacting to variances between forecasted revenues and expenditures and actual. He quotes from the president of a corporation: "Actual sales revenue for the fiscal year varied one percent from the original forecast. Expenditures varied 30 percent. The reasons were practically entirely due to manufacturing problems of inefficiency and quality. . . . The only actions specifically taken were in attempted changes in methods of production . . . [and] the use of an engineering consulting firm. . . ." One would have thought that the cost-reducing activities mentioned could be carried out irrespective of the variance. Nevertheless, the quotation clearly implies that, in fact, they would not have been motivated to attempt the changes were it not that they were stimulated by the variance.

Before proceeding to present more empirical evidence on the possible magnitude of X-efficiency it is of importance to say something about the nature of the data. The empirical evidence does not present many unambiguous cases. Most of the evidence has to do with specific firms or, at best, industries, and not for the economy as a whole. In the evidence presented on allocative efficiency the entire economy was considered. It is quite possible that the cases considered are entirely atypical and could not be duplicated in large segments of the economy. In addition, the cases do not always deal with X-efficiency in a pure sense. Some additional inputs or reallocations are sometimes involved. Also uncertainty elements and accidental variations play a role. Nevertheless, it seems that the magnitudes involved are so large that they suggest that the conjecture that X-efficiency is frequently more significant than allocative efficiency must be taken seriously.

Now let us turn to Tables 1 and 2. In contrast to Table 1 where the misallocation effects are small, we see in Table 2 that the X-efficiency effects, at least for specific firms, are usually large. Table 2 abstracts (in the interest of conserving space) from a much more comprehensive table developed by Kilby that summarizes the results of a number of International Labor Organizations (ILO) productivity missions. (I usually picked for each country the first three and the last items contained in Kilby's table.)

TABLE II. ILO Productivity Mission Results

Factory or Operation	Method*	Increase in Labor Productivity %	Impact on the Firm (Unit Cost Reduction)	
			Labor Savings %	Capital† Savings %
India				
Seven textile mills	n.a.	5-to-250	5–71	5–71
Engineering firms				
All operations	F, B	102	5,0	50
One operation	F	385	79	79
One operation	F	500	83	83
Burma				
Molding railroad brake shoes	A, F, B	100	50	50
Smithy	A	40	29	29
Chair assembly	A, B	100	50	50
Match manufacture	A, F	24	19	—
Indonesia				
Knitting	A, B	15	13	—
Radio assembly	A, F	40	29	29
Printing	A, F	30	23	—
Enamel ware	F	30	23	—
Malaya				
Furniture	A, D	10	9	9
Engineering workshop	A, D	10	9	9
Pottery	A, B	20	17	17
Thailand				
Locomotive maintenance	A, F	44	31	31
Saucepan polishing	E, D	50	33	—
Saucepan assembly	B, F	42	30	—
Cigarettes	A, B	5	5	—
Pakistan				
Textile plants	C, H, G			
Weaving		50	33	33
Weaving		10	9	9
Bleaching		59	37	37
Weaving		141	29	29
Israel				
Locomotive repair	F, B, G	30	23	23
Diamond cutting and polishing	C, B, G	45	31	—
Refrigerator assembly	F, B, G	75	43	43
Orange picking	F	91	47	—

* A = plant layout reorganized
  B = machine utilization and flow
  C = simple technical alterations
  D = materials handling
  E = waste control
  F = work method
  G = payment by results
  H = workers training and supervision
† Limited to plant and equipment, excluding increased depreciation costs.

It is to be observed that the cost-reducing methods used do not involve additional capital nor, as far as one can tell, any increase in depreciation or obsolescence of existing capital. The methods usually involve some simple reorganizations of the production process, e.g., plant-layout reorganization, materials handling, waste controls, work methods, and payments by results. It is of interest that the cost reductions are frequently about 25 percent and that this result is true for a technically advanced country such as Israel as well as for the developing countries considered· in other parts of the table. If the firms and/or operations considered are representative, then it would appear that the contrast in significance between X-efficiency and allocative efficiency is indeed startling. Representativeness has not been established. However, the reports of the productivity missions do not suggest that they went out of their way to work only on cases where large savings in costs could be obtained. By comparative standards (with other producticity missions) some of the results were modest, and in some cases Kilby reports that when some members of the missions returned to some of the firms they had worked on previously (e.g., in Pakistan) they found a reversion to previous methods and productivities.

There are of course a number of other studies, in addition to those by Lundberg and Harbison just mentioned which present results similar to the ILO reports. L. Rostas in his study of comparative productivity in British and American industry points to the finding that differences in amount and quality of machinery per worker and the rates of utilization and replacement do not account for the entire difference in output per worker in the two countries. He further states that ". . . in a number of industries (or firms) where the equipment is very largely identical in the U.S. and U.K., eggs, boots and shoes, tobacco, strip steel (or in firms producing both in the U.K. and U.S. . . . .), there are still substantial differences in output per worker in the U.K. and the U.S." Clearly there is more to the determination of output than the obviously observable inputs. The nature of the management, the environment in which it operates, and the incentives employed are significant.

That changes in incentives will change productivity per man (and cost per unit of output) is demonstrated clearly by a wide variety of studies on the effects of introducing payments by results schemes. Davison, Florence, Gray, and Ross review the literature in this area for British industry, survey the results for a number of manufacturing operations, and present illustrative examples of their findings from a number of firms. The summary of their findings follows: "The change in output per worker was found to vary among the different operations all the way from an increase of 7.5 percent to one of 291 percent, about half the cases falling between 43 percent and 76 percent. Such increases in output, most of them large, from our 'first-line' case histories, and from additional evidence, were found not to be just a 'flash in the pan' but were sustained over the whole period of study."

Roughly similar findings were obtained for the consequences of introducing payments by results in Australia, Belgium, India, the Netherlands, and the United States. In Victoria it was found that "soundly designed and properly operated incentive plans have in practice increased production rate in the reporting firms from 20 to 50 percent." In the Netherlands labor efficiency increases of 36.5 percent were reported. It seems clear that with the same type of equipment the working tempo varies considerably both between different workers and different departments. Appropriate incentives can obviously change such tempos considerably and reduce costs, without any changes in purchasable inputs per unit.

The now-famous Hawthorne Studies suggest that the mere fact that management shows a special interest in a certain group of workers can increase output. That is, management's greater interest in the group on whom the experiments were tried, both when working conditions were improved and when they were worsened, created a positive motivation among the workers. (The magnitudes were from 13 to 30 percent.) In one of the ILO missions to Pakistan an improvement in labor relations in a textile mill in Lyallpur resulted in a productivity increase of 30 percent. Nothing else was changed except that labor turnover was reduced by one-fifth.

Individual variations in worker proficiency are probably larger than plant differences. Frequently the variation between the best to poorest worker is as much as four to one. Certainly improved worker selection could improve productivity at the plant level. To the extent that people are not working at what they are most proficient, productivity should rise as a consequence of superior selection methods.

Although there is a large literature on the importance of psychological factors on productivity, it is usually quite difficult to assess this literature because many psychologists work on the basis of high- and low-productivity groups but do not report the actual numerical differences. In general, it seems that some of the psychological factors studied in terms of small-group theory can account for differences in productivity of from 7 to 18 percent. The discoveries include such findings as (1) up to a point smaller working units are more productive than larger ones; (2) working units made up of friends are more productive than those made up of nonfriends; (3) units that are generally supervised are more efficient than those that are closely supervised; and (4) units that are given more information about the importance of their work are more proficient than those given less information. A partial reason for these observed differences is probably the likelihood that individual motivation towards work is differently affected under the different circumstances mentioned.

The shorter-hours movement in Western Europe and in the United States, especially up to World War I, has some interesting lessons for productivity differentials without capital changes. Economists frequently assume that for a given capital stock and quality of work force, output will be proportional to number of hours worked. Experiments during World War I and later showed that not only was the proportionality law untrue, but that frequently *absolute* output actually increased with reductions in hours—say from a ten-hour day to an eight-hour day. It was also found that with longer hours a disproportionate amount of time was lost from increased absenteeism, industrial accidents, and so on. In many cases it would obviously have been to a firm's interest to reduce hours below that of the rest of the industry. Firms could have investigated these relations and taken advantage of the findings. For the most part, governments sponsored the necessary research on the economics of fatigue and unrest under the stimulus of the war effort, when productivity in some sectors of the economy was believed to be crucial. The actual reduction of hours that took place was a consequence of the pressure of labor unions and national legislation.

In this connection it is of interest to note that Carter and Williams in their study of investment in innovations found that a high proportion (over 40 percent) was of a "passive" character—i.e., either in response to the "direct pressure of competition" or "force of example of firms (etc.) other than immediate rivals." Unfortunately it is difficult to find data that would represent the obverse side of the coin; namely, data that would suggest the degree to which firms do not innovate for lack of a sufficient motivating force, such as a lack of competitive pressure. However, there is a great deal of evidence that the delay time between invention and innovation is often exceedingly long (sometimes more than 50 years), and the lag time between the use of new methods in the "best practice" firms in an industry and other firms is also often a matter of years. Salter in his study on *Productivity and Technical Change* points to the following striking example. "In the United States copper mines, electric locomotives allow a cost saving of 67 percent yet although first used in the mid-twenties, by 1940 less than a third of locomotives in use were electric." Other similar examples are mentioned by Salter and others. A survey of industrial research undertaken by 77 companies showed that one-third were carrying on research for "aggressive purposes," but that two-thirds were "forced into research for defensive purposes."

The relation between the "cost" of advice or consulting services and the return obtained has not been worked out for the ILO productivity missions as a whole. In one case (in Pakistan) the savings affected in three textile mills as a consequence of the work of the mission during the year that the mission was there "represented about 20 times the entire cost of the mission in that year." While the study does not indicate how representative this result was, the impression one gets is that rates of return of rather large magnitudes are not entirely unusual.

J. Johnston studied the return to consulting services in Great Britain. For the class of jobs where it was possible to make a quantitative assessment of the results (600 jobs were involved), it was found that on the average the rate of return was about 200 percent on consulting fees. Johnston's study is of special interest for our purposes because (a) it is a very careful study, and (b) the magnitudes of increases in productivity are of the same order (although the variations are less extreme) as those obtained in underdeveloped countries. The nature of the consulting work was not too dissimilar to that carried out by the ILO teams. On the whole they involved improvements in general management, plant layout, personnel, production procedures, selling organization, management and budgeting and accounting systems. For the consulting jobs whose consequences were quantitatively assessed, the average increase in productivity was 53 percent, the lowest quartile showed an increase of 30 percent, and the highest quartile 70 percent.

The studies mentioned deal with examples that are more or less of a microeconomic nature. In recent years we have had a number of studies that are their *macro*economic complements. The work of Solow, Aukrust, Denison, and others show that only a small proportion of increase in GNP is accounted for by increases in inputs of labor or capital. The "unexplained residual" covers about 50 percent to 80 percent of growth in advanced countries. The residual comprehends a greater range of "noninput" growth factors (e.g., technological change, education of the labor force) than was covered in the examples we considered, but the motivational efficiency elements may account for some fraction of the residual. (E.g., Johnston estimates that one-quarter of the annual increase in product is accounted for by consulting services.)

What conclusions can we draw from all of this? First, the data suggest that there is a great deal of possible variation in output for similar amounts of capital and labor and for similar techniques, in the broad sense, to the extent that technique is determined by similar types of equipment. However, in most of the studies the nature of the influences involved are mixed, and in some cases not all of them are clear to the analyst. In many instances there appears to have been an attempt to impart knowledge, at least of a managerial variety, which accounts for *some* of the increase in output. But should this knowledge be looked upon as an increase in inputs of production in all instances? Although the first reaction might be that such attempts involve inputs similar to inputs of capital or labor, I will want to argue that in many instances this is not the case.

It is obvious that not every change in technique implies a change in knowledge. The knowledge may have been there already, and a change in circumstances induced the change in technique. In addition, knowledge may not be used to capacity just as capital or labor may be underutilized. More important, a good deal of our knowledge is vague. A man may have nothing more than a sense of its existence, and yet this may be the critical element. Given a sufficient inducement, he can then search out its nature in detail and get it to a stage where he can use it. People normally operate within the bounds of a great deal of intellectual slack. Unlike underutilized capital, this is an element that is very difficult to observe. As a result, occasions of genuine additions to knowledge become rather difficult to distinguish from those circumstances in which no new knowledge has been added, but in which existing knowledge is being utilized to greater capacity.

Experience in U.S. industry suggests that adversity frequently stimulates cost-reducing attempts, some of which are successful, within the bounds of existing knowledge. In any event, some of the studies suggest that motivational aspects are involved entirely apart from additional knowledge. The difficulty of assessment arises because these elements are frequently so intertwined that it is difficult to separate them.

Let us now consider types of instances in which the motivational aspect appears fairly clearly to play a role. The ILO studies discuss a number of cases in which there had been a reversion to previous less efficient techniques when demonstration projects were revisited after a year or more. This seems to have occurred both in India and in Pakistan. Clearly, the new knowledge, if there were such knowledge, was given to the management by the productivity mission at the outset, and the new management methods were installed at least for the period during which the productivity mission was on hand, but there was not a sufficient motivational force for the management to maintain the new methods. The "Hawthorne Effects" are of a more clear-cut nature. Here an intentional reversion to previous methods still led to some increases in output simply because the motivational aspects were more important than the changes in the work methods. The ILO mission reports also mention with regret the fact that techniques applied in one portion of a plant, which led to fairly large increases in productivity, were not taken over by the management and applied to other aspects of the production process, although they could quite easily have done so. In a sense we may argue that the knowledge was available to the management, but that somehow it was not motivated to transfer techniques from one portion of a plant to another.

Studies which showed increases in output as a consequence of introducing payment by results clearly involve motivational elements. For the men subjected to the new payment scheme economic motivations are involved. For the management the situation is less clear. It is possible that in many instances the firms were not aware of the possible advantages of payment by results until they obtained the new knowledge that led to the introduction of the scheme. However, it seems most likely that this scheme is so well known that this is not the case in all, or in many instances. Management quite likely had to be motivated to introduce the scheme by some factors either within the firm or within the industry. In any event, these studies clearly suggest that for some aspects of production, motivational elements are significant.

Both the ILO studies and the Johnston study speak of the need to get the acceptance of top management for the idea of obtaining and implementing consulting advice. In addition, the ILO studies make the point that low productivity is frequently caused by top management's concern with the commercial and financial affairs of the firm rather than with the running of the factory. The latter was frequently treated as a very subordinate task. Whether this last aspect involves a lack of knowledge or a lack of motivation is difficult to determine. However, it seems hard to believe that if some top-management people in some of the firms in a given industry were to become concerned with factory management and achieve desirable results thereby, some of the others would not follow suit. Johnston makes the point that, "without the willing cooperation of management the consultant is unlikely to be called in the first instance or to stay for long if he does come in." The ILO missions make similar remarks.

It is quite clear that consulting services are not only profitable to consultants but also highly profitable to many of the firms that employ them. But it is rather surprising that more of these services are not called for. Part of the answer may be that managements of firms are not motivated to hire consultants if things appear to be going "in any reasonably satisfactory rate." There are, of course, numerous personal resistances to calling for outside advice. If the motivation is strong enough, e.g., the threat of the failure of the firm, then it is likely that such resistances would be overcome. But these are simply different aspects of the motivational elements involved.

III. The Residual and X-Efficiency: An Interpretation

The main burden of these findings is that X-inefficiency exists, and that improvement in X-efficiency is a significant source of increased output. In general, we may specify three elements as significant in determining what we have called X-efficiency: (1) intra-plant motivational efficiency, (2) external motivational efficiency, and (3) nonmarket input efficiency.

The simple fact is that neither individuals nor firms work as hard, nor do they search for information as effectively, as they could. The importance of motivation and its association with degree of effort and search arises because the relation between inputs and outputs is *not* a determinate one. There are four reasons why given inputs cannot be transformed into predetermined outputs: (a) contracts for labor are incomplete, (b) not all factors of production are marketed, (c) the production function is not completely specified or known, and (d) interdependence and uncertainty lead competing firms to cooperate tacitly with each other in some respects, and to imitate each other with respect to technique, to some degree.

The conventional theoretical assumption, although it is rarely stated, is that inputs have a fixed specification and yield a fixed performance. This ignores other likely possibilities. Inputs may have a fixed specification that yields a variable performance, or they may be of a variable specification and yield a variable performance. Some types of complex machinery may have fixed specifications, but their performance may be variable depending on the exact nature of their employment. The most common case is that of labor services of various kinds that have variable specifications and variable performance—although markets sometimes operate as if much of the labor of a given class has a fixed specification. Moreover, it is exceedingly rare for all elements of performance in a labor contract to be spelled out. A good deal is left to custom, authority, and whatever motivational techniques are available to management as well as to individual discretion and judgment.

Similarly, the production function is neither completely specified nor known. There is always an experimental element involved so that something may be known about the current state; say the existing relation between inputs and outputs, but not what will happen given changes in the input ratios. In addition, important inputs are frequently not marketed or, if they are traded, they are not equally accessible (or accessible on equal terms) to all potential buyers. This is especially true of management knowledge. In many areas of the world managers may not be available in well-organized markets. But even when they are available, their capacities may not be known. One of the important capacities of management may be the degree to which managers can obtain factors of production that in fact are not marketed in well-organized markets or on a universalistic basis. In underdeveloped countries the capacity to obtain finance may depend on family connections. Trustworthiness may be similarly determined. Some types of market information may be available to some individuals but not purchasable in the market. For these and other reasons it seems clear that it is one thing to purchase or hire inputs in a given combination; it is something else to get a predetermined output out of them.

Another possible interpretation of the data presented is in connection with the "residual" in economic growth analysis. The residual manifests itself in three basic ways: (1) through cost reduction in the production of existing commodities without inventions or innovations; (2) the introduction of innovations in processes of production; and (3) the introduction of new commodities or, what is the same thing, quality improvements in consumer goods or inputs. We have ignored the introduction of new commodities, but the other two elements are pertinent here. The data suggest that cost reduction that is essentially a result of improvement in X-efficiency is likely to be an important component of the observed residual in economic growth. In addition, there is no doubt that, in some of the cases of reduced cost, new knowledge was conveyed to the firms involved, and this too is part of the residual. It is of special interest that such new knowledge involves knowledge dissemination rather than invention. The detailed studies suggest that the magnitudes are large, and hence a significant part of the residual does not depend on the types of considerations that have been prominent in the literature in recent years, such as those that are *em-*

bodied in capital accumulation or in invention. We have considered the problem in terms of decreasing real costs per unit of output. It is clear that for a given set of resources, if real costs per unit of output are decreased, then total output will grow, and output per unit of input will also rise. Such efforts to reduce cost are part of the contribution of the residual to economic growth.

Both competition and adversity create some pressure for change. Even if knowledge is vague, if the incentive is strong enough there will be an attempt to augment information so that it becomes less vague and possibly useful. Where consulting advice is available it is significant that relatively few firms buy it. Clearly, motivations play a role in determining the degree that consulting advice is sought. The other side of the coin is that, where the motivation is weak, firm managements will permit a considerable degree of slack in their operations and will not seek cost-improving methods. Cyert and March point to cases in which costs per unit are allowed to rise when profits are high. In the previous sections we have cited cases in which there was a reversion to less efficient methods after the consultants left the scene. Thus we have instances where competitive pressures from other firms or adversity lead to efforts toward cost reduction, and the absence of such pressures tends to cause costs to rise.

Some of the essential points made in the previous paragraphs can be illustrated diagramatically, if (in the interest of simplicity) we allow for abstraction from some of the realities of the situation. The main ideas to be illustrated are as follows: (1) Some firms operate under conditions of nonminimum costs, and it is possible for an industry to have a nonminimal cost equilibrium. (2) Improvements in X-efficiency are part of the process of development, and probably a significant proportion of the "residual." In what follows we assume that there are many firms, and that each firm's output is sufficiently small so as not to affect the output, costs, or prices set by other firms. For simplicity we also assume that for each firm there is an average total unit cost (ATUC) curve that has a significant horizontal segment at its trough, and that the output selected will be on that segment. When we visualize a firm's costs reacting to competitive conditions in the industry we imply that the entire ATUC curve moves up or down. Some firms are presumed to react to changes in the unit cost of production of the industry as a whole, i.e., to the weighted average of the unit costs of all the firms, in which each firm's weight is in proportion to its contribution to the output of the industry. Here we posit a one-period lag relation. Each firm's expectations of current industry unit costs depends on actual industry unit cost in the previous period. If we choose sufficiently small periods, then this seems to be reasonable relation.

In Figure 2 each curve represents the "reaction cost line" of a firm. The ordinate shows the actual unit cost of any firm determined by that firm's reaction to what it believes or expects to be the unit cost performance of the industry as a whole. The alternate expected unit cost performance of the industry is shown on the abscissa. Thus each point on line $C_t{}^i$ associates the unit cost for firm i in period t, given the average unit cost in the industry in period t-1. The lines are drawn in such a way that they reflect the idea that if the unit cost that is the average for the industry is higher, then the firm's unit cost will also be higher. As average industry unit costs fall, some firms are motivated to reduce their unit costs accordingly. The higher the industry unit cost, the easier it is for any firm to search and successfully *find* means for reducing its own cost. Therefore, for a given incentive toward cost reduction, the firm is likely to find more successful ways of reducing its cost when industry costs are high compared to what they might find when they are low. As a consequence the typical reaction unit cost lines are more steeply sloped where industry unit costs are high compared to when they are low. Indeed, at very low industry unit costs the firm reaction cost lines approach an asymptote. It is not necessary for our analysis to assume that all firms are nonminimizers. Therefore some firms may have reaction cost lines that are horizontal.

FIGURE 2

The curve C^A is the average of the unit costs of all the firms in question, where the weight for any firm's cost is the proportion of its output to the total industry output. C^A is the average reaction cost line for all the firms. The basic assumption is that a firm's costs will be higher if the average industry costs are expected to be higher, and vice versa. Beyond some point, where expected average industry costs are very low, every reaction cost line will be above the 45° line.

In Figure 3 the line P is a locus of equilibrium prices. Each point on the line associates an equilibrium price with a level of industry unit cost in the previous period, which in turn determines the unit costs level of the various firms in the current period. Thus, given the industry unit cost in period *t-1*, this determines the unit cost level for each firm in period *t*. Each firm in turn will pick that output that maximizes its profits. The sum of all the outputs determines the industry output, and given the demand function for the product, the industry output determines the price. The price will be an equilibrium price if at that price no additional firms are induced to enter the industry or to withdraw from it. Thus the price for each industry unit cost is determined in accordance with conventional price theory considerations. If the price at the outset is above equilibrium

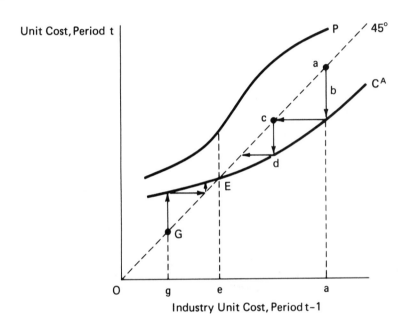

FIGURE 3

price, then the entry of firms will bring that price down toward equilibrium, and if the price is below equilibrium, marginal firms will be forced to leave the industry, which in turn will cause the price to rise. Thus at every level of industry unit cost in period *t-1* there is a determinate number of firms, that number consistent with the associated equilibrium price.

The point *E* in Figure 3, the intersection between curve C^A and the 45° line, is an equilibrium point for all the firms. The process envisioned is that each firm sets its cost in period *t* in accordance with its expectation of the industry cost, which by assumption is what the industry cost was in period *t-1*. This is a one-period lag relation. Each firm finds out what all of its competitors were doing as a group in terms of cost and reacts accordingly in the next period. If the industry cost is equal to *Oe* then in the subsequent period each firm would set its cost so that the weighted average unit cost of all the firms would be equal to *Oe*. Hence E is an equilibrium point.

But suppose that the initial industry costs were equal to *Oa*. We want to show that this sets up a movement that leads eventually to the point E. The firms' unit costs will average out at *ab*, which generates a process shown by the set of arrows *abcd*, etc., toward the point E. In a similar fashion, if we start with an industry cost of *Og*, a process is set in motion so that costs move from G toward the point E. Clearly E is a stable equilibrium point. It is to be noted that every point on curve C^A need not presume that the same number of firms exist in the industry. At higher costs more firms exist, but as costs decline, some firms are forced out and fewer firms exist. In terms of the weighted average indicated by the points on the curve C^A, this simply means that some of the outputs will be zero for some of the firms as we get to lower and lower industry costs.

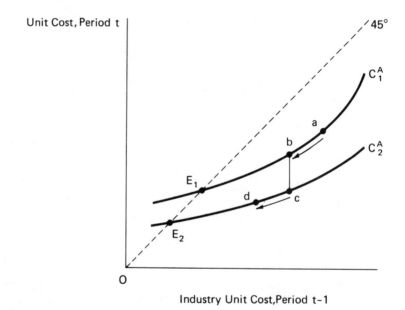

FIGURE 4

Figure 4 is intended to illustrate the cost reduction aspect of the residual in growth. When we begin the process the average reaction cost line is C_1^A. Firms start at point *a* and reduce costs along the arrow shown by *ab*. At this point additional information is introduced into the industry which is reflected in a diagram by the shift in the reaction cost line from C_1^A to C_2^A. Once firms are on C_2^A they then proceed with the cost reduction process as shown by the arrow *cd*. This illustrates two basic elements involved in the residual, the process of cost reduction in response to the motivation created by competitive pressures, as well as that part of cost reduction that is reflected in actual innovations, and is illustrated by downward shifts in the reaction cost lines.

IV. Conclusions

We have suggested three reasons for X-inefficiency connected with the possibility of variable performance for given units of the inputs. These are: (a) contracts for labor are incomplete, (b) the production function is not completely specified or known, and (c) not all inputs are marketed or, if marketed, are not available on equal terms to all buyers. These facts lead us to suggest an approach to the theory of the firm that does not depend on the assumption of cost-minimization by all firms. The level of unit cost depends in some measure on the degree of X-efficiency, which in turn depends on the degree of competitive pressure, as well as on other motivational factors. The responses to such pressures, whether in the nature of effort, search, or the utilization of new information, is a significant part of the residual in economic growth.

One idea that emerges from this study is that firms and economies do not operate on an outer-bound production possibility surface consistent with their resources. Rather they actually work on a production surface that is well within the outer bound. This means that for a variety of reasons people and organizations normally work neither as hard nor as effectively as they could. In situations where competitive pressure is light, many people will trade the disutility of greater effort, of search, and the control of other peoples' activities for the utility of feeling less pressure and of better interpersonal relations. But in situations where competitive pressures are high, and hence the costs of such trades are also high, they will exchange less of the disutility of effort for the utility of freedom from pressure, etc. Two general types of movements are possible. One is along a production surface towards greater allocative efficiency and the other is from a lower surface to a higher one that involves greater degrees of X-efficiency. The data suggest that in a great many instances the amount to be gained by increasing allocative efficiency is trivial while the amount to be gained by increasing X-efficiency is frequently significant.

Agriculture: Problems of a Competitive Industry

KENNETH E. BOULDING

Kenneth E. Boulding is Professor of Economics at the University of Colorado. The following discussion was presented as his testimony before the Joint Economic Committee in 1957.

Agriculture is rightly regarded as the last great area of small business. Even the 100,000 farms which are classified in the census as "large" are tiny compared with even a medium-sized manufacturing company, and the 3 million or 4 million "family farms" are, of course, still small. The only other large areas of economic life which compare with agriculture in the average size of the firm are retailing and the service industries, and even here the income per enterprise is 3 or 4 times what it is in agriculture.[1]

The problem of the relation of the size of the firm to the nature of the market which it faces is one of the most difficult in economics, both theoretically and empirically. We cannot assume, offhand, that, just because a firm is small, there are no elements of monopoly in its market situation. The village barber, the small specialized manufacturing concern, may have an effective degree of monopoly. Nor is there a necessary connection between large size and monopoly power; many large corporations are effectively hemmed in by the competition of similar firms, of substitute products, and by the pressures of public opinion and Government regulation.

Nevertheless, where we have a situation with small firms producing for the most part a standard commodity for a large national market, as we do

[1] Income per enterprise (1950 census) was $2,521 in agriculture, $7,846 in retail trade, and $8,408 in service industries. The disparity would be much less, of course, if subsistence agriculture were excluded. By comparison, income per enterprise was $49,179 in mining and quarrying, and $83,149 in manufacturing. (See Ronald H. Mighell, *American Agriculture*, p. 47.)

in commercial agriculture, we can feel confident that the element of monopoly in this situation is practically nil, and that here is one place in the economy where the economist's beau ideal of perfect competition is found. One may hesitate to claim, with Adam Smith, that "Country gentlemen and farmers are, to their great honor, of all people, the least subject to the wretched spirit of monopoly," but the most jaundiced antiagrarian cannot deny that, of all people, farmers have the least opportunity for monopoly. Indeed, I am aware of only one agricultural product in which there has been any really successful exercise of monopoly power; this is the California lemon, where a relatively small number of growers, concentrated in one area and protected by climate and the tariff, have succeeded in organizing themselves sufficiently to exert a true monopolistic control over the output and price of lemons.

Is this, however, an occasion for rejoicing; that, in the midst of so many who have bowed the knee to the Baal of monopoly, there are the faithful remnant who preserve the practice, if not the faith, of competition in its purest form on which our society supposedly rests, or is it an occasion for lamenting the injustice involved to the faithful remnant, who do not, or cannot, avail themselves of the monopolistic defenses of the rest of the economy, and who, therefore, merit the special protection and support of government? One wishes there were some nice, simple answers to these questions.

There are really two distinct problems. One is the short-run problem of the effects of the distribution of monopoly and competition on the behavior of the economic system during the business cycle. The other is the long-run problem of the effects on the broad course of economic progress. Of these two problems the first is the easiest to answer. The record makes it clear that agriculture behaves very differently from manufacturing industry over the course of a business fluctuation, and especially in severe depressions. A depression is characterized by a general decline in money income and in the money value of output. This decline is fairly uniform, industry by industry. That is to say, when the money value of national income is about halved, as it was from 1929 to 1932, the money income of each major industry likewise is approximately halved. The money income of an industry however is the money value of its annual product, and this in turn is equal to the quantity of product multiplied by its price. If wheat farmers for instance produce 500 million bushels of wheat in a year, and sell it at an average price of $2 per bushel, the value of their product, and therefore their gross money income, is $1 billion. In agriculture a decline in money income is brought about almost wholly by a decline in the prices of agricultural produce. In manufacturing industry by contrast much of the decline in money income is brought about by a decline in employment and output, while prices stay up or decline much less. There is no doubt that the reason for this difference lies in the different market structures: in agricultural markets unsalable stocks of goods produce an almost immediate downward pressure on the price. In the markets for industrial goods unsalable stocks of goods produce not so much a fall in the price as a cutback in output and employment. These different market structures are again related to the size of the firm in proportion to the total output of its product: if an individual wheat farmer reduces his output this will have no perceptible effect on the price of wheat; if a manufacturer of some specialized and brand-named article cuts back his output, he can maintain his price without difficulty in the face of falling money demand.

From the point of view of society as a whole the inability of agriculture to reduce output in a depression is an almost unmixed blessing. If it were not for this fortunate characteristic of agriculture we would starve in a depression as well as suffer from unemployment and from diminished outputs of industrial goods. As it is, even in the severe depression of 1929–32, average food consumption in the United States did not appreciably decline, though there is no doubt that the distribution of food consumption worsened—that is, some people ate very little and some too well. Food consumption did not decline because food production did not decline. If the farmers had been able to protect their prices by restricting their outputs, as manufacturers are so frequently able to do, we would not merely have suffered loss of real income and unemployment, we might have starved as well.

The question must be raised however whether this support of the rest of the economy in depression by the farmer does not involve him in a real sacrifice, so that in a sense he is exploited by the rest of society. It is true that a depression invariably involves the worsening of the farmer's "terms of trade" or "parity ratio," and this is undoubtedly one reason why parity has become an important symbol for the farm groups. The reason for this is found basically in the different responses of agriculture and industry in regard to output. The farmer's terms of trade are what he gets (in real goods) for one unit of what he sells. In a depression he has just about as much to sell as before, as his production stays up. What industry has to offer to him, however, has sharply diminished in quantity. He can buy less industrial goods with his wheat, simply because there are fewer industrial goods being produced. It is the bathtubs and paint and clothing and automobiles which are not being produced because of unemployment that the farmer cannot buy, because they are not there to buy. This is the "real" phenomenon behind the relative price changes—the greater fall in agricultural prices than in industrial prices.

The farmer, of course, is not the only person who is affected adversely by a depression, and it may be doubted whether he is affected more adversely than the industrial worker, the stockholder, or the small-business man. Indeed, the fact that there is a slight drift back to the farms in a severe depression indicates that in spite of the worsened terms of trade of agriculture, the fact that it offers employment opportunities more than outweighs the disadvantages, and that as compared with the combination of high real wages for the employed and a large chance of unemployment in industrial occupations, and full employment at low real wages in agriculture there seems to be some pull toward the latter. We really know very little about the incidence of depression on the distribution of personal incomes by occupations and by regions and by large industrial groups. The only groups which clearly gain from depression are the receivers of interest, pensions, and annuities, and those who are in "protected" employment positions, with tenure and seniority. Thus the proportion of national income going to interest rose sharply from 7 percent in 1929 to 13 percent in 1932; the proportion going to wages and salaries likewise rose from 58 percent to 73 percent. We may be pretty sure that this represents a shift from youth to age—a depression almost certainly shifts income markedly from the young to the old. Just how it shifts income from urban to rural populations we do not really know. It would not be surprising, however, if we discovered that there was a shift away from rural areas; more interest receivers and pensioners proportionally may live in urban areas, and certainly more people with "protected" jobs live in urban areas.

The farmer may not be the most disadvantaged group in a depression, but he is certainly on the disadvantaged side of the line. The answer to this problem, however, is not to improve the relative position of the farmer by a still further decline in the national product. The answer is clearly to prevent depressions. The worsening of the terms of trade of agriculture in a depression is not a result of something that is wrong with agriculture, but is a result of something that is wrong with industry. We could, of course, improve the terms of trade of agriculture by diminishing its output, as the worsening of the terms of trade are simply a reflection of the fact that agricultural output declines less than the output of industry. But this would be sheer madness: the sensible thing to do is obviously to improve agricultural terms of trade by increasing industrial output, not by diminishing agricultural output—assuming here that we are not talking of a shift in output between agriculture and industry, but simply of unemployed capacity.

One further point in connection with the depression experience is relevant to this discussion. There is not much relation between the distribution of monopoly power in the economy and the ability to protect profits. A depression is marked by a great shift away from profits into almost all other forms of income, for reasons which we cannot go into here. The monopolist can protect his price in a depression better than the firm in highly competitive markets, but this does not mean that he can protect his profits. The decline in output which the monopolist suffers is just as destructive to his profits as the decline in price which the competitve firm suffers. Indeed that broad division of national income which suffers the greatest decline in a depression is corporation profits. The fact that so large a proportion of total farm income is labor income probably protects farm income very substantially in a depression. Thus in the face of sharp deflationary movements it is by no means clear that monopoly gives any advantage. Indeed, there is evidence to show that firms which are in a monopoly position are too reluctant to cut prices in a depression, even from the point of view of their own profits, and that the inertia and lack of sensitivity to price policy which seems inevitably to be the outcome of monopoly is a detriment to the monopolist himself in times of sharp monetary changes, whether of deflation or inflation. The monopolist even from the point of view of his own interest does not lower his prices fast enough·in a deflation, nor does he raise them fast enough in an inflation. In these short-run problems, then, the view that a monopolistic market situation gives a great advantage to its possessor may be severely questioned.

We now turn to the much more difficult question of the long-run effects of the distribution of monopoly power, especially as between industry and agriculture. Here we must take a look for a moment at the broad dynamics of the historical relation between agriculture and the rest of the economy. In a society in which agricultural techniques are improving there is a constant decline in the proportion of the national economy which is occupied by agriculture, whether this is measured by labor force, by value of output, or any other measure. This is basically because of the nature of agricultural commodities as "necessities"—goods of low-income elasticity. As income rises a smaller and smaller proportion of income is spent on food and fibers. Improvements in agriculture therefore result ultimately in an increase in the proportion of the total product which is contributed by industry, rather than an expansion of agricultural production. If the total population is rising rapidly enough of course there may not be an absolute decline in the agricultural population, but there will always be a relative decline. In the United States for instance the agricultural population has declined from something over 90 percent in colonial times to about 15 percent today. It is the resources released from agriculture, moreover, which have enabled the United States and similar countries to build up their industrial systems. If it had not been for the technical improvement in agriculture the effectiveness of industrial improvements would have been much less. In a very real sense therefore the American standard of life and economic power rests on the base of agricultural improvement, in the sense of constantly increasing output per agricultural worker.

Paradoxically enough, however, it has been precisely this high rate of improvement in the productivity of agriculture which has led to the relative disadvantage of agriculture in the distribution of income. One may put the matter crudely by saying that the only way to get people out of a declining industry is to squeeze them out—that is, to make the declining industry less attractive than the expanding ones. This is accomplished very neatly through the price system; the declining industry has a chronic tendency toward overproduction, as it never declines quite fast enough; this overproduction leads to relatively low prices for its products and therefore to relatively low incomes for its workers and its capitalists. The differential in incomes between the declining and the expanding industries depends on the mobility of resources between them—that is, on the ease with which labor and capital can move out of the declining and into the expanding industry. If resources are mobile a very slight disadvantage of incomes in the declining industry is enough to induce people to make the requisite transfers to the expanding industries; if resources are immobile it will take a large disadvantage in the declining industry to induce enough people to transfer out of it.

Mobility has two aspects: one is the ease in getting out and the other the ease of getting in. Resources in agriculture may be immobile either because there are customs, habits, or laws which tie people to the land and prevent them from leaving agriculture, or because there are obstacles to people entering industry. The question at issue here, and it is a difficult one to which no very positive answer can be given in the present state of knowledge, is the importance of the distribution of monopolistic and competitive markets, and the related distribution of sizes of firms, among the various factors which affect the mobility of resources between agriculture and industry.

About the best we can do is to outline the various elements in the situation which contribute toward the mobility of resources out of agriculture, in order to try to make some rough assessment of the possible importance of the element of monopoly power. Historically one of the principal obstacles to exit from agriculture has been the geographical and cultural isolation of the rural population. In all previous civilizations there has been a sharp cultural division between urban and rural people; the very word "civilization" means literally something that happens only in cities, and the overtones of words like civil, urban, rustic, and so on testify to the past differentiation between urban and rural life. Insofar as the cities have maintained themselves by the exploitation of the rural population they have usually tried to justify themselves by the denigration of rural culture as crude, primitive, and uncivilized. It is to the very great credit of our own society that to a large extent, at least in the field of commercial agriculture, we have overcome this geographical and cultural isolation of rural people. For the first time in history we have built a civilization in which the farmer also is part of the "civis." Part of this is due to the revolution in transportation and communications which has removed the geographical and communicational isolation of the farmer—the automobile, the radio and television, and so on. Part of it is due to the high technology of commercial agriculture itself, which demands a level of education and skill of the farmer at least equal, if not superior to his urban equivalent. Whatever the reason, it is clear that in the area of commercial agriculture at any rate the farmer is no longer isolated from the rest of society, and that this factor no longer can be invoked as an explanation of the failure of resources to leave commercial agriculture in sufficient amount. In the area of subsistence agriculture, which represents the main problem of agricultural poverty, pockets of cultural and geographical isolation still are found though even here better roads, radios, buses, and so on are breaking down the old isolation.

A dynamic factor which used to be of considerable importance in explaining the continuing surplus of the agricultural population is the differential birthrate in rural areas. A marked feature of earlier periods was the much greater reproduction rate in the country than in the towns. This meant that even if agriculture maintained a constant proportion of the labor force it would still be necessary for people to move from agriculture into industry in order to feed the population increase of the country into the population deficiencies of the towns. Even if there were no forces making for relative decline in the proportion of people engaged in agriculture, it would still be necessary for agricultural incomes to be somewhat less than urban incomes in order to move the excess population of rural areas into industrial occupations. This factor again is of considerable importance in the area of subsistence agriculture; it is of much less importance in the area of commercial agriculture, where birthrates are no longer greatly different from urban birthrates—perhaps because of the profound urbanization of rural life.

Another factor which may be of some importance in preventing the exodus from agriculture is found in the institutions of land tenure and ownership. If farmers are bound to the land by feudal ties, or if land ownership and tenure are in forms which freeze existing arrangements, and make consolidation or extension of holdings difficult, or if credit arrangements are so primitive that it is difficult for able and active farmers to extend their operations beyond what chance or inheritance has given them in the way of land and equipment, or so that children are encouraged to stay on the land and farm tiny, scattered, and inadequate plots, then the difficulties of migration from agriculture are accentuated. In many parts of the world these factors are of great importance; it is hard to believe that they are of much importance in the commercial agriculture of the United States, where credit facilities are generally good, where farms have been growing in size rather than being fractionated, and where it does not seem to be too difficult for an able farmer to acquire more land and equipment.

One is left with the conclusion that the cultural and institutional factors are not of great importance in holding people in commercial agriculture in this country; the exit gate is pretty wide and easy to open. The one criticism of existing institutions which might be made on this score is of the rural school, which might perhaps do more to equip its pupils for the urban lives which a considerable proportion of them will face. Where the difference between urban and rural culture is so small, however, as it is in this country this factor cannot be of very great importance.

Is then the difficulty with the entrance into industrial occupations rather than with exit from agriculture, and if so, is this at least partly to be explained by the prevalence of monopoly or large-scale organization in industry? This is a question to which I frankly do not know the answer, and which deserves very serious study. I can think of no more valuable research project in this field than a good study of farmers who have left agriculture in the past generation. Unfortunately it is nobody's business to study these people: having left agriculture, they have passed out of the heavily subsidized intellectual area, and they do not form an easily recognizable class of people or a pressure group. Nevertheless the key to understanding what is the matter with agriculture may very well lie in the study of the experiences of those who have left it. We do not really know where they go, what they go into, what fields are open to them, and most important, what fields are closed to them. It might turn out that one difficulty is that of fitting a small capital into the current industrial structure. It may not be too difficult for farm laborers without capital to enter the industrial working force. It may be quite difficult for a farm operator, who is a laborer-plus-capital, to find an equivalent niche in industrial society. This may or may not have anything to do with the existence of large-scale industry. We do not expect, of course, a farmer to start a steel mill or an automobile plant. There are, however, many areas of industry where small capitalists are important—in retailing, in construction, in personal services, and in the professions. If, however (as one suspects), in the overall distribution of enterprise by size there is a disproportionate number of small enterprises in agriculture, this may present a real obstacle to the transfer of small worker-capitalists from agriculture to industrial employment.

One further question needs to be asked, though here also a definite answer is hard to give. It is sometimes argued that the farmer is peculiarly disadvantaged because he sells to large concerns with monopolistic control over their markets, whereas he buys in the general competitive market, or even worse, buys from large, monopolistic concerns also. According to this view he is subject to monopolistic exploitation from his suppliers, and to what economists call monopsonistic exploitation from the purchasers of his products, squeezed between big buyers on the one hand and big sellers on the other. We certainly cannot deny the possibility of such exploitation. For it to be effective, however, there would have to be an almost total absence of competition among the firms supplying or buying from farmers, and it is probable that there would also have to be price discrimination—the purchasers, for instance, paying a smaller price to farmers with lower costs or with lower mobility. Otherwise, given sufficient mobility, any attempt to exploit farmers would simply result in their leaving the occupation in numbers sufficient to force the purchasers to raise their prices in order to get an adequate supply. It is to mobility, rather than to simple market monopoly, that we must look for an explanation of the farmer's difficulties.

In the past, and in particular places, this element of monopolistic or monopsonistic exploitation may have been important. Today however there are two important safeguards against it. One is the Robinson-Patman amendment to the Clayton Act, which seems to have been at least modestly effective in preventing price discrimination. The other, and perhaps the most important, is the rise of the marketing cooperative. If there are any unusual profits in the wholesaling, processing, or even retailing of farm produce it will not be difficult for farmers to cash in on these profits for themselves through the device of the marketing cooperative.

If there are unusual profits in the business of selling to farmers, farmers should be able to cash in on these through the device of the purchasing cooperative. The rise of the farm cooperative in the past fifty years or more is evidence that a problem of exploitation by middlemen may have existed. The relative stability of the cooperative sector of the market now however is evidence that the problem is no longer serious, and that there are no longer any large areas of unusual profit for the cooperatives to undermine. This does not preclude the possibility of local situations where exploitation of this kind continues, especially where it may be combined with racial or other forms of group discrimination. As a large general problem, however, I think we may claim that whatever its importance in the past, it is no longer a major concern.

A final word might be added on the peculiar position of the landowner in agriculture, for although this is not a problem of size of enterprise, it may well be a problem in monopoly. It is a long established principle in economics that an increase in agricultural income tends to be absorbed eventually by the landowner either in rise in rents or in the value of property. This is especially likely to be the case where the location of the farm gives it an advantage, whether natural or artificial, and whether geographic location or social location. A striking illustration of this principle is the impact on land values of tobacco marketing quotas. These are attached to the farm rather than to the farmer. Insofar as they enable the tobacco grower to get monopoly gains (which apparently they do) these gains are soon capitalized in the value of the farms to which quotas are attached. Thus the benefits of the scheme to the tobacco growers tend to accrue to those fortunate individuals who own the farms which received quotas at the beginning of the scheme.

Anyone wishing to come into tobacco growing now has to pay what amounts to a tax to the present owners of these farms in the shape of higher land prices. A plan therefore which was devised to help growers simply amounts to a free gift from society to landowners—a gift which is hard to defend on any rational or moral grounds. There is a somewhat weaker tendency for all subsidies to agriculture to be captured by the landowner. Where—as is frequently and increasingly the case in this country—the landowner and the farm operator are combined in the same person the problem may not be serious. There still may be substantial inequities involved, however, and as the poorer farmers are the least likely to be the landowners, subsidies to agriculture (as opposed to subsidies to the poor) are all the more likely to aggravate the existing inequalities within agriculture. Our agricultural policy has not inaptly been described as a "charity racket": in order to help the 25 percent or so of farmers who really need it, we scatter largess broadcast over the 75 percent who do not. Any program designed to help agriculture is bound to produce scandalous inequities, because agriculture is not a homogeneous industry, and farmers are not a homogeneous group of people. Programs of redistribution should be designed to deal with poverty, not with agriculture. There is nothing in the mere fact of a man being a farmer which entitles him to special consideration from society. We should be particularly on guard against the argument that because some farmers may be in a disadvantaged position, whether because of their situation in the market network or for any other cause, therefore all farmers should be subsidized.

Predatory Price Cutting:
The Standard Oil (N. J.) Case

JOHN S. McGEE

John S. McGee is Professor of Economics at the University of Washington. This well-known article appeared in the Journal of Law and Economics *in 1958.*

He [Rockefeller] applied underselling for destroying his rivals' markets with the same deliberation and persistency that characterized all his efforts, and in the long run he always won.—IDA TARBELL.

I. Introduction

The purpose of this paper is to determine whether the pre-dissolution Standard Oil Company actually used predatory price cutting to achieve or maintain its monopoly. This issue is of much more than antiquarian or theoretic interest. Settling it is of direct importance to present antitrust policy. At the very least, finding the facts should aid in defining certain hazy notions that now figure in discussions of monopoly and its control.

The *Standard Oil* case of 1911[1] is a landmark in the development of antitrust law. But it is more than a famous law case: it created a legend. The firm whose history it relates became the archetype of predatory monopoly.

It is sometimes said that *Standard Oil* was influential because it revealed deadly and reprehensible techniques by which Monopoly on a heroic scale could be achieved and, probably more important, perpetuated. Historians tell us that the facts revealed in *Standard Oil* were in good part responsible for the emphasis that the antitrust laws came to place upon unfair and monopolizing business practices.

Perhaps the most famous of all of the monopolizing techniques that

[1] Standard Oil Co. of New Jersey v. United States, 221 U.S. 1 (1911).

Standard is supposed to have used is local price cutting. Given the bad repute in which monopoly has long been officially held in this country, and the prominence of predatory pricing in *Standard Oil*, it is not surprising that the practice received special attention in the law. Monopoly was not new in 1911, but a predatory giant may have seemed novel. The vision of a giant firm that used a brutally scientific, and completely effective, technique for acquiring and maintaining monopoly must have aroused uncommon concern. Standard was invincible. Anything economists could say about the transience of monopoly must have seemed hopelessly unrealistic in view of the vigor and success with which Standard was said to have prevented entry.

In any case, by 1914, in the Clayton Act, predatory price discrimination was included among a select group of business practices the character or effect of which called for explicit statutory prohibition. The Robinson-Patman amendment of 1936 lengthened the list, but certainly did not weaken the hostility toward local price cutting. Indeed, its legislative history and subsequent interpretation reveal a continuing dread of the device.

Predatory discrimination thus occupies a special and almost unquestioned place in law and economics. This has led to a certain amount of difficulty, especially in connection with the Robinson-Patman Act. Some critics claim that this statute unnecessarily restricts rivalry, thereby softening competition. Yet even the critics apparently fear that if we permit the helpful kind of discrimination we will encourage the lethal kind. Most are obliged to rely on the tenuous standard of intent to distinguish one kind from the other.

This fearful ambivalence, in which the specter of *Standard Oil* figures prominently, may be responsible for the continuing, and somewhat fruitless, arguments about the proper role of a "good faith" defense under Section 2(B) of the Robinson-Patman Act. It may also account for the popular view that disciplinary price cutting makes cartelization easier and its benefits more lasting. It surely has influenced thinking about small firms that face large rivals.

For these reasons, a reexamination of *Standard Oil* may be worthwhile.

II. Predatory Price Cutting: Some Hypotheses

According to most accounts, the Standard Oil Co. of New Jersey established an oil refining monopoly in the United States, in large part through the systematic use of predatory price discrimination. Standard struck down its competitors, in one market at a time, until it enjoyed a monopoly position everywhere. Similarly, it preserved its monopoly by cutting prices selectively wherever competitors dared enter. Price discrimination, so the story goes, was both the technique by which it obtained its dominance and the device with which it maintained it.

The main trouble with this "history" is that it is logically deficient, and I can find little or no evidence to support it.[2]

A brief examination of the logic of predatory price discrimination is helpful in interpreting the facts. In the beginning, oil refining in the United States apparently was competitive. Necessary capital was relatively slight, because of the modest quality demands imposed by consumer preferences and the primitive technological character of the refining process itself. The number of refiners was evidently large, since the Standard interests bought out more than a hundred of them. Standard Oil was not born with monopoly power: as late as 1870 it had only 10 per cent of the refining business.

The usual argument that local price cutting is a monopolizing technique *begins* by assuming that the predator has important monopoly power, which is his "war chest" for supporting the unprofitable raids and forays. Evidently the technique could not be used until the Standard interests achieved the necessary monopoly power. Similarly, advantages from monopsonistic bargaining[3] would not be available until the buyer attained considerable stature.

A simpler technique did exist, and Standard used it. Unless there are legal restraints, anyone can monopolize an industry through mergers and acquisitions, paying for the acquisitions by permitting participation of the former owners in the expected monopoly gains. Since profits are thus expanded, all of the participants can be better off even after paying an innovator's share to the enterpriser who got the idea in the first place.

Under either competition or monopoly, the value of a firm is the present worth of its future income stream. Competitive firms can be purchased for competitive asset values or, at worst, for only a little more. Even in the case of important recalcitrants, anything up to the present value of the future monopoly profits from the property will be a worthwhile exchange to the buyer, and a bountiful windfall to the seller.

It is conceivable that Standard did not merge to the full size it wanted, but did achieve whatever size was necessary to use predatory techniques to grow the rest of the way. How would it go about using them? Assume that Standard had an absolute monopoly in some important markets, and was earning substantial profits there. Assume that in another market there are several competitors, all of whom Standard wants to get out of the way. Standard cuts the price below cost. Everyone suffers losses. Standard

---

[2] I am profoundly indebted to Aaron Director, of the University of Chicago Law School, who in 1953 suggested that this study be undertaken. Professor Director, without investigating the facts, developed a logical framework by which he predicted that Standard Oil had not gotten or maintained its monopoly position by using predatory price cutting. In truth, he predicted, on purely logical grounds, that they never systematically used the technique at all. I was astounded by these hypotheses, and doubtful of their validity, but was also impressed by the logic which produced them. As a consequence, I resolved to investigate the matter, admittedly against my better judgment; for, like everyone else, I knew full well what Standard had really done.

[3] Example: railroad rebates. Although this subject lies outside the present inquiry, I am convinced that the significance of railroad rebates has also been misunderstood.

would, of course, suffer losses even though it has other profitable markets: it could have been earning at least competitive returns and is not. The war could go on until average variable costs are not covered and are not expected to be covered; and the competitors drop out. In the meanwhile, the predator would have been pouring money in to crush them. If, instead of fighting, the would-be monopolist bought out his competitors directly, he could afford to pay them up to the discounted value of the expected monopoly profits to be gotten as a result of their extinction. Anything above the competitive value of their firms should be enough to buy them. In the purchase case, monopoly profits could begin at once; in the predatory case, large losses would first have to be incurred. Losses would have to be set off against the prospective monopoly profits, discounted appropriately. Even supposing that the competitors would not sell for competitive value, it is difficult to see why the predator would be unwilling to take the amount that he would otherwise spend in price wars and pay it as a bonus.

Since the revenues to be gotten during the predatory price war will always be less than those that could be gotten immediately through purchase, and will not be higher after the war is concluded, present worth will be higher in the purchase case. For a predatory campaign to make sense the direct costs of the price war must be less than for purchase. It is necessary to determine whether that is possible.

Assume that the monopolizer's costs are equal to those of his competitors. The market has enough independent sellers to be competitive. Otherwise the problem of monopolizing it ceases to concern us. This implies that the monopolist does not now sell enough in the market to control it. If he seeks to depress the price below the competitive level he must be prepared to sell increasing quantities, since the mechanism of forcing a lower price compels him to lure customers away from his rivals, making them meet his price or go without customers. To lure customers away from somebody, he must be prepared to serve them himself. The monopolizer thus finds himself in the position of selling more—and therefore losing more—than his competitors. Standard's market share was often 75 per cent or more. In the 75 per cent case the monopolizer would sell three times as much as all competitors taken together, and, on the assumption of equal unit costs, would lose roughly three times as much as all of them taken together.[4]

Losses incurred in this way are losses judged even by the standard of competitive returns. Since the alternative of outright purchase of rivals would have produced immediate monopoly returns, the loss in view of the alternatives can be very great indeed.[5] Furthermore, at some stage of the

[4] Any assumption that the monopolizer's size gives him sufficient cost advantages rapidly takes us away from a predatory price cutting example and into the realm of so-called natural monopolies.

[5] It must not be supposed that, just because he enjoys profits elsewhere, anyone will be so stupid as to assume that it is costless to use them for anything but the best alternatives.

game the competitors may simply shut down operations temporarily, letting the monopolist take all the business (and all the losses), then simply resume operations when he raises prices again. At prices above average variable costs, but below total unit costs, the "war" might go on for years.

Purchase has an additional marked advantage over the predatory technique. It is rare for an industrial plant to wear out all at once. If price does not cover average variable costs, the operation is suspended. This will often leave the plant wholly intact. In the longer run, it may simply be the failure of some key unit, the replacement of which is uneconomic at the present price level, that precipitates shutdown. In either case, physical capacity remains, and will be brought back into play by some opportunist once the monopolizer raises prices to enjoy the fruits of the battle he has spent so much in winning.

All in all, then, purchase would not be more expensive than war without quarter, and should be both cheaper and more permanent. It may at first be thought that predatory pricing more than makes up for its expense by depressing the purchase price of the properties to be absorbed. In effect, this requires that large losses reduce asset values less than smaller losses. This is not at all likely. Furthermore, assuming that the properties in question are economic,[6] it is unlikely that their long-run market value will be much reduced by an artificially low price that clearly will not be permanent. The owners can shut down temporarily, allowing the monopolist to carry all of the very unprofitable business, or simply wait for him to see the error of his ways and purchase. Even if there is widespread bankruptcy, wise men will see the value to the monopolist of bringing the facilities under his control, and find it profitable to purchase them at some price below what the monopolist can be expected to pay if he must. Since the monopolist is presumably interested in profits, and has a notion of the effect of discount factors upon future income, he cannot afford to wait forever. Properties that a would-be monopolist needs to control can be an attractive investment.

Predation would thus be profitable only when the process produces purchase prices that are so far below competitive asset figures that they more than offset the large losses necessary to produce them. One empirical test, for those who suspect the logic, would be to examine prices paid for properties in cases where predatory pricing is alleged to have been practiced.

Some of the most strategic factors to be monopolized may be the skilled managerial and technical personnel of competitors. Reproducing them can be a much more formidable and longer job than the construction of physical facilities. But short of murder, the cost of which can also be expected to be high if undertaken in any quantity, the only feasible way of preventing their embarrassing and costly reappearance is to hire, retire, or share

---

[6] If they are not, they need not concern us, since their extinction might be expected or welcomed under competition.

with them. None of these things can be accomplished well or permanently if these people are too much badgered in the process.[7]

There are two other crucial issues that must be examined, the first dealing with the extent to which monopolization is profitable; the second, with the necessary conditions for its success. Monopolization as such will be carried only so far as is necessary to maximize profits, since it inevitably involves certain expenses of planning, purchase, and rationalization. In the case of a vertically integrated industry the would-be monopolist will choose to monopolize the level that will produce the largest net profit. This requires choosing that one which is both cheapest to control and over which control is likely to endure. If a monopoly can be achieved at the refining level, for example, there is little sense trying to achieve one at the crude oil producing level, or marketing. Standard Oil of New Jersey achieved a refinery monopoly; anything more would have been redundant.[8]

This should not be taken to mean that the monopolist will not care what happens to the other levels; for he has every interest in seeing to it that the other levels are not monopolized by someone else. In marketing, for example, he would prefer that the product be distributed as cheaply as possible, since he can then extract full monopoly revenues from the level in his control. This point is important in interpreting the facts of the *Standard Oil* case.

Obstacles to entry are necessary conditions for success. Entry is the nemesis of monopoly. It is foolish to monopolize an area or market into which entry is quick and easy. Moreover, monopolization that produces a firm of greater than optimum size is in for trouble if entry can occur even over a longer period. In general, monopolization will not pay if there is no special qualification for entry, or no relatively long gestation period for the facilities that must be committed for successful entry.

Finally, it is necessary to examine certain data that are often taken to be symptomatic of predatory price cutting, when in fact they may be nothing of the sort. Assume that a monopolist·sells in two markets, separated effectively by transport costs or other impediments to free interchange, and that he has a complete monopoly in both. Elasticity of demand is assumed

---

[7] "[A]s Mr. Rockefeller and Mr. Archbold testified, most of the concerns which were brought together continued to be operated and managed by the former owners." Brief for the U.S., Vol. 1, at 19.

Further, "There are only a few cases in which the Standard interests, during this period [1872–80], acquired stock in concerns without taking the former owners in as stockholders of the Standard, or bringing them into the combination by leaving them a minority interest in the original concern." Id., at 32.

[8] This abstracts from any cost reductions that integration may make possible. These have nothing to do with the problem at hand.

See Bork, "Vertical Integration and the Sherman Act," *U. of Chi. L. Rev.*, XXII (1954), 157. Standard began producing crude oil in 1889, and by 1898 produced 33 per cent of the total. By 1906, its share declined to 11.11 per cent. Transcript of Record Vol., 19, at 626 (Def. Exh. 266).

to be the same in both markets, and monopoly prices are identical. Assume that, for some unknown reason, entry occurs in one market but not in the other. Supplies are increased in the first and price falls; price in the second remains unchanged. There are now two different prices in the two markets, reflecting the existence of alternative supplies in the first. The theory of the dominant firm, maximizing by taking into account the outputs of his lesser rivals at various prices, appears to fit the case. An objective fact-finder discovers that the monopolist is discriminating in price between the two markets. A bad theorist then concludes that he is preying on somebody. In truth, the principle established is only that greater supplies bring lower prices.

Compare this example with another. Assume that we have two separate markets, and that each is in short-run competitive equilibrium with firms earning supernormal returns. Assume that, for some reason, entry takes place in one market but not in the other. Supply increases and price falls in one but not in the other. From this evidence of price changes in both the monopoly and competition examples, the inference is simply that greater supplies lower prices. We should not infer from the price data that either case has anything to do with predatory price cutting.

To sum up: (1) Predatory price cutting does not explain how a seller acquires the monopoly power that he must have before he could practice it. (2) Whereas it is *conceivable* that someone might embark on a predatory program, I cannot see that it would pay him to do so, since outright purchase is both cheaper and more reliable. (3) Because monopolization by any technique always involves some expense, a firm *qua* monopolizer will carry it to the one securest level in an integrated industry, not to all. (4) Actual variations in prices among markets may be accounted for in terms of variations in demand elasticities, but do not imply or establish that anybody is preying on anybody else. . . .

III. Conclusions

Judging from the Record, Standard Oil did not use predatory price discrimination to drive out competing refiners, nor did its pricing practice have that effect. Whereas there may be a very few cases in which retail kerosene peddlers or dealers went out of business after or during price cutting, there is no real proof that Standard's pricing policies were responsible. I am convinced that Standard did not systematically, if ever, use local price cutting in retailing, or anywhere else, to reduce competition. To do so would have been foolish; and, whatever else has been said about them, the old Standard organization was seldom criticized for making less money when it could readily have made more.

In some respects it is too bad that Standard did not employ predatory price cutting to achieve its monopoly position. In doing so it would surely have gotten no greater monopoly power than it achieved in other ways, and during the process consumers could have bought petroleum products for a great deal less money. Standard would thereby not only have given some of its own capital away, but would also have compelled competitors to donate a smaller amount.[9]

It is correct that Standard discriminated in price, but it did so to maximize profits given the elasticities of demand of markets in which it sold. It did not use price discrimination to change those elasticities. Anyone who has relied upon price discrimination to explain Standard's dominance would do well to start looking for something else.[10] The place to start is merger.

It should be quite clear that this is not a verdict of acquittal for the Standard Oil Company; the issue of monopoly remains. What this study says is that Standard did not achieve or maintain a monopoly position through price discrimination. The issue of whether the monopoly should have been dissolved is quite separate.

I think one further observation can tentatively be made. If the popular interpretation of the *Standard Oil* case is at all responsible for the emphasis that antitrust policy places on "unfair" and "monopolizing" business practices, that emphasis is misplaced.[11] This limited study suggests that what businessmen do *to* one another is much less significant to monopoly than what they find it useful to do together to serve their common interest.

[9] This, of course, ignores certain moral issues. Economics is not a particularly useful tool for dealing with them.

[10] In arguing against the Defendant's motion for adjournment to prepare its case, Government Counsel may have admitted what I have concluded: "What is there, then, to prepare for in this case? Simply the question of unfair competition. The Examiner can see from the testimony that has already been taken that that is not a great task; that it won't take any particular time for them to prepare to meet that testimony." Vol. 6, at 3333.

[11] The Standard Legend may also be responsible for the strained analogy often drawn between business and war. Analogies to chess strike me as being equally weak. Chess is a competitive game which one player wins, while the other loses. Successful quasi-monopoly seeks to avoid the competitive game, since all players lose as soon as they begin playing it.

Regulation of Monopoly and Competition

COUNCIL OF ECONOMIC ADVISERS

This is an excerpt from the 1975 Annual Report *of the Council of Economic Advisers.*

Regulation of Monopoly

As mentioned earlier, some industries are characterized by economies of scale over relevant ranges of output. Among the examples frequently cited are local distribution systems for telephone service and electric power transmission, where the high fixed costs associated with fixed facilities tend to preclude viable competition. Under such circumstances, it is argued, the establishment of a regulated monopolist would be a more efficient way of organizing the market. Such regulation, however, is inherently limited in its ability to promote efficient production and resource allocation.

Effective regulation depends on a great deal of information which is often difficult to obtain and interpret. In practice, neither the judgment nor the information of those responsible for regulation can be perfect. For example, even under the best of conditions it is difficult to ascertain the true cost base of a regulated monopolist, and often it is not very easy to determine the firm's cost of capital for the purpose of regulating its return on investment.

Idealized regulation also presumes that firms are passive with respect to the restraints imposed by the regulations. Recent studies suggest that a regulated monopolist will overcapitalize or undercapitalize, depending on the relation between the regulator's "guaranteed" return on investment and the firm's perceived cost of capital. Moreover, by forbidding the regulated firm to raise prices during times of excess demand, regulation reduces the incentive for the monopolist to maintain sufficient excess capacity. On the other hand, the assurance that regulation will shelter the firm from the costs associated with scheduling too much excess capacity will act in the opposite direction, so the net effect is open to question.

During times of rapidly rising or falling prices, strict adherence to historical costs may have significant adverse effects. The delays necessary in regulatory proceedings frequently cause regulated prices to be held down unduly during times of rapidly rising costs. Unless the firm has a considerable degree of flexibility in altering production costs by reducing the quality of service—and even here demand must not respond too negatively to this diminution in quality—relying on historical costs may erode the firm's cash flow position and possibly even lead to bankruptcy. Although the results are seldom so severe, regulatory delays often cause deterioration of service and costly deferments in investment and maintenance expenditures.

Regulation of Competition

Most governmental regulation is now concerned with the regulation of competition rather than with the regulation of monopoly. This change has come partly as a result of historical and technological evolution. For example, the ICC was understandably concerned with railroad monopoly power during the first years of its existence. In the first part of this century, however, technological advances brought about considerable competition for the railroads from trucking. Because of cross-subsidy, some railroad rates were unduly high, and truckers tended to concentrate on this kind of traffic. If the system of regulation were to be preserved, there had to be ways of administering it without bankrupting the railroads. Therefore, in 1935 the ICC and the railroads were successful in bringing most trucking under the regulatory umbrella, despite objections at that time from some truckers. In 1940, coverage was extended to inland water carriers. Thus, an opportunity to deregulate railroads made possible by new competition was sacrificed, and the scope of regulation was expanded.

As opposed to monopoly, markets with significant competition present the regulator with a slightly different set of problems. Although as a matter of law the regulator must still determine the rate base and the "fair" profit element, the more important problem is to understand and assess the way rate changes affect service under these quasi-competitive conditions, and how policies regarding price, entry, and exit affect the financial viability of the regulated firms.

In regard to financial viability, although exit from an industry via bankruptcy is a normal characteristic of efficient competitive markets, the bankruptcy of a regulated firm tends to be viewed as a sign of regulatory failure. To prevent bankruptcies, regulators are thus prone to protect firms from competition—frequently to the detriment of efficient service. For example, since the establishment of the Civil Aeronautics Board (CAB) in 1938, not a single trunk air carrier has gone bankrupt, although several trunk airlines at the brink of bankruptcy have merged with stronger carriers. For the purpose of limiting institutional failures, the Federal Reserve Board (FRB), the Federal Deposit Insurance Corporation (FDIC) and the Federal Home Loan Bank Board (FHLBB) have set maximum rates of interest that may be paid on deposits and on savings and loan shares. A policy of protection can lead to knotty problems when the competitors employ different production techniques—as, for example, with trucking and railroading. ICC regulation has not been able to prevent (and probably has contributed significantly toward) the bankruptcy of several rail carriers in the northeastern part of the country. Protection is also difficult when technology changes. Thus, some regulated competitive industries are slow in introducing innovations.

The second major problem for the regulator of a quasi-competitive industry derives from the fact that, depending on technical feasibility and how firms view the response patterns of their rivals, there will be a tendency for changes in the extent of nonprice competition to raise or lower costs to match the regulated price. In such cases, cost tends to be determined by price, rather than the other way around, and the regulator's control over price amounts to regulating the extent of nonprice competition in the industry—and thus the quality and price choices available to buyers. Since higher quality will be associated with higher costs, a broad range of combinations of price and quality is often consistent with reasonably competitive returns to the individual firms, or at least to the firms as a group. In these circumstances the regulatory commission, in effect, serves as a surrogate for the general public, choosing the price and quality option which will be offered.

One ramification of this behavior among regulated competitive industries is that explicit regulation of the industry's rate of return may not be possible without additional controls, such as direct restraints on the extent of non-price competition. Another aspect is that, whatever its justification, cross-subsidy may not be feasible. Purported "high-profit" markets will realize more costly, higher-quality service rather than excess profits; in alleged "losing" markets firms will restrict the quality of service to where average cost is in line with the low price.

Examples of Economic Regulation

Each regulated industry has different economic characteristics and ways of behaving under regulation. In several areas the economic costs of regulation have become apparent and are indeed significant.

TRANSPORTATION

Of all sectors of the American economy, few are more important than transportation, and none is more affected by Federal economic regulation.

Trucking. In interstate trucking an antitrust exemption allows carriers to agree upon rates in secret, through rate-bureau negotiations. Although these rates are subject to review by the ICC, they are seldom challenged except in cases of general across-the-board increases. For example, during fiscal 1974, only 5 percent of motor common carrier rates were even challenged, and fewer than one-third of those challenged were ultimately disapproved. As a result of this process, rates tend to be set so as to cover the costs of less efficient carriers. The consequences are windfall profits to more efficient truckers and higher prices to consumers. In trucking markets with two or more carriers, service competition—for example, providing more frequent schedules or larger trucks—tends to eliminate the potential excess profits. However, the reduction in profits results not from lower rates but from the creation of excess capacity which has a lower value to the shipper than the extra price paid. In those markets where only one trucker has a certificate to serve, this process of rate setting helps the carrier to earn excess profits by offering poorer service, at the regulated price, than would be the case if other firms were allowed to compete.

The problems of excess capacity in "competitive" markets and of poor service in "monopoly" markets would both be eliminated if entry into the trucking industry were not restricted and if the ICC encouraged meaningful price competition. A monopolist earning excess profits would attract new firms; the result, in turn, would be lower rates and improved service. In those previously regulated competitive markets which had excess capacity, incumbent carriers would offer lower rates consistent with higher average loads. If they did not, new carriers would enter and force rates downward; the incumbent carriers would then have to respond with rate reductions or else lose out to the new competition. The ICC, however, has stringently controlled entry and price competition in trucking. Opportunities for profits attract many potential entrants, and during fiscal 1974 more than 70 percent of the Commission's case workload consisted of processing motor carrier operating permits.

Railroads. In railroad freight transportation, the problem is exit rather than entry. As outlying areas of the country gained access to good highways, and especially interstate highways, firms began to utilize trucks for much of their transport. This meant that low-density rail lines were used less and less, until many of them were no longer economical to operate. Nevertheless, regulation has prevented the railroads from discontinuing such services as fast as would seem warranted. The losses on unprofitable lines have impaired the overall financial position of the railroads and have reduced needed maintenance and capital investments elsewhere.

The structure of railroad rates often provides incentives that are inconsistent with an efficiently organized transport sector. Regulation enforces a considerable amount of cross-subsidy among commodities—to the point where certain high-valued items, such as machinery and equipment, are hauled at rates greatly exceeding their transport costs, while the rates for other items, such as crude ores, are much less than their transport costs. Similarly, regulation attempts to maintain an elaborate system of discriminatory rate "equalizations" which tend to favor certain regions over others.

Rates that rail carriers pay for the use of other carriers' cars (called per diem) and the rates shippers pay carriers when they hold freight cars for extended periods (demurrage) are maintained at levels far below the opportunity cost on rail cars. As a result, freight cars are retained by carriers and are used excessively by shippers for warehousing. On average, a rail boxcar moves only 1 hour in 8, and its average speed while moving is less than 20 miles per hour.

Air Travel. In the domestic airline industry, regulation has served primarily to bring about a nonoptimal choice of price and quality. Because the CAB had a fairly liberal policy during the 1950's and 1960's toward the entry of existing carriers into city-pair markets, the principal markets are now served by two or more airlines. However, since their fares are regulated by the CAB, the airlines tend to compete on the basis of scheduling, over which the Board does not exercise direct control. The result is "excess capacity," and efforts to raise the regulated fares in order to assure a return on investment greater than the industry's perceived cost of capital serve only to set the stage for further capacity augmentation.

Carriers as a group have consequently tended to earn neither excess profits nor losses, but the traveling public has paid higher fares because of the regulation-induced excess capacity. While excess capacity does yield some benefit in the form of more frequent departures, less crowding, and a better chance of obtaining a seat on the preferred departure, the value of this excess capacity is almost surely less than its cost. As evidence, in the relatively unregulated California and Texas intrastate markets the competitively determined (higher-load factor) service has historically been sold at prices some 40 percent below the prices of comparable interstate (CAB-regulated) services. Moreover, a recent study reports that in 1969 domestic air passengers paid "excess fares" ranging between $366 million and $538 million, for which they received service quality improvements valued at between $118 and $182 million. The difference, between $248 million and $356 million, represents a deadweight loss to society.

In its recent Domestic Passenger Fare Investigation the CAB established target load factors of 55 percent. Since the prevailing load factors were around 50 percent, this policy had the effect of reducing excess capacity and lowering fares. However, it would appear that a much higher load factor standard is justified, especially in view of the recent increases in fuel prices. The Board's new policy of encouraging agreements among carriers to limit capacity is not an appropriate way of dealing with this problem. In markets covered by agreements, the passenger's total cost of service is increased because of increased delays, but the fare is not reduced.

Airline regulation imposes other costs, which are not generally well perceived. For instance, through the regulatory process, fares have tended to be set at levels and with a structure that maximizes total seat capacity, as opposed to maximizing total passenger traffic, the result being added congestion and environmental costs, as well as increased costs of airports and airways. By restricting the entry of new firms into trunk carrier service in order to protect less efficient incumbent firms, regulation has also penalized potentially more efficient firms and has resulted in higher fares for a given quality of service.

These costs of airline regulation could be reduced substantially or even eliminated if entry into and exit from markets were made easier and if control over fares were liberalized so as to encourage price competition. Under such circumstances an individual airline could attract more passengers by lowering its price rather than increasing its total capacity.*

FINANCIAL INSTITUTIONS

Banks and thrift institutions are among the most highly regulated businesses in the United States. The FRB, the FDIC, and the FHLBB, together with a host of other Federal and State agencies, regulate virtually every aspect of financial intermediation: entry, expansion, and exit, as well as pricing practices and allowable assets and liabilities. Opening a new bank, for instance, requires a charter that can be obtained from the appropriate State or Federal agency only if the applicant can demonstrate that a new bank would be in the public interest. Opening a new branch of an existing bank requires similar evidence in those States which permit branch banking. Comparable entry tests exist for thrift institutions.

Financial institutions are subject to a number of regulations when they issue liabilities (deposits) or buy assets. Banks, for example, are required to hold cash reserves for their deposits, and they are precluded from holding certain assets, including common stocks. Thrift institutions are subject to similar restrictions; in addition they are not permitted to issue checking accounts. Finally, and perhaps most importantly, except on large certificates of deposit, financial institutions may not pay interest to their depositors at rates that exceed maximums imposed by law or by regulation.

Although the rationale for regulating financial institutions is to safeguard deposits and assure market stability, in recent years the desirability of some

* *Editor's note:* In the late 1970s, the Civil Aeronautics Board, under the chairmanship of Alfred E. Kahn, deregulated the airlines in a variety of ways and promoted a greater degree of price competition among them. The Deregulation Act of 1978 made formal the swing to more freedom for fare reductions and route competition. Thus, the recommendations in the text pertaining to the airlines now have been accepted in considerable measure.

forms of financial regulation has been increasingly questioned. This is particularly true of those regulations that were established before the 1930's, when Federal insurance of deposits greatly increased the security of banks and thrift institutions. One suggested reform is to reduce the restriction on the types of assets that banks and thrift institutions may hold and to allow thrift institutions to issue checking accounts. These changes would make financial institutions more flexible in their adjustments to changing market conditions and would also make the industry more competitive. An even more important proposed reform would eliminate interest rate ceilings on all deposits. Depositors could then enjoy competitive rates of return (especially during high interest rate periods like 1969 and 1973–74), and the flow of loanable funds for such purposes as housing would increase.

Price Discrimination
in Medicine

REUBEN A. KESSEL

Reuben A. Kessel is Professor of Business Economics at the Graduate School of Business at the University of Chicago. This article appeared in the Journal of Law and Economics *in 1958.*

Many distinguished economists have argued that the medical profession constitutes a monopoly, and some have produced evidence of the size of the monopoly gains that accrue to the members of this profession.[1] Price discrimination by doctors, i.e., scaling fees to the income of patients, has been explained as the behavior of a discriminating monopolist.[2] Indeed this has become the standard textbook example of discriminating monopoly.[3] However this explanation of price discrimination has been incomplete. Economists who have subscribed to this hypothesis have never indicated why competition among doctors failed to establish uniform

[1] M. Friedman and S. Kuznets, *Income from Independent Professional Practice* (1945); M. Friedman in *Impact of the Trade Union*, p. 211, edited by D. M. Wright (1951); also K. E. Boulding, *Conference on the Utilization of Scientific and Professional Manpower*, p. 23 (1944).
   The results of the Friedman-Kuznets study, at p. 133, using pre-war data, indicate that the costs of producing doctors are seventeen per cent greater than the costs of producing dentists, while the average income of doctors is thirty-two per cent greater.
[2] J. Robinson, *Economics of Imperfect Competition*, p. 180 (1933). For example, the world famed Mayo Clinic discriminates in pricing. Albert Deutsch, "The Mayo Clinic," *Consumer Reports*, XXII (Jan. 1957), 37, 40. A finance department makes inquiries into the patient's economic status and scales the bills accordingly. Fees are not discussed in advance.
[3] E. A. G. Robinson, *Monopoly*, p. 77 (1941); C. E. Daugherty and M. Daugherty, *Principles of Political Economy*, p. 591 (1950); T. Scitovsky, *Welfare and Competition*, p. 408 (1941); K. E. Boulding, *Economic Analysis*, p. 662 (1955); S. Enke, *Intermediate Economic Theory*, p. 42 (1950); G. Stigler, *The Theory of Price*, p. 219 (1952).

prices for identical services. For any individual doctor, given the existing patterns of price discrimination, income from professional services would be maximized if rates were lowered for affluent patients and increased for poor patients. However, if many doctors engaged in such price policies, a pattern of prices for medical services would be established that would be independent of the incomes of patients. Yet despite this inconsistency between private interests and the existing pattern or structure of prices based on income differences, this price structure has survived. Is this a contradiction of the law of markets? Why is it possible to observe in a single market the same service sold at different prices?

The primary objective of this paper, which is an essay in positive economics, is to show by empirical evidence that the standard textbook rationalization of what appears to be a contradiction of the law of markets is correct. It will be argued that the discriminating monopoly model is valid for understanding the pricing of medical services, and that each individual buyer of medical services that are produced jointly with hospital care constitutes a unique, separable market. In the process of presenting evidence supporting this thesis, other closely related phenomena will be considered. These are (1), why the AMA favors medical insurance prepayment plans that provide money to be used to buy medical services, but bitterly opposes comparable plans that provide instead of money, the service itself and (2), why the AMA has opposed free medical care by the Veterans Administration for veterans despite the enormous increase in the quantity of medical services demanded that would result from the reduction to zero of the private costs of medical care for such a large group. . . .

I. A Hypothesis Alternative to the Discriminating Monopoly Model

The standard position of the medical profession on price discrimination is in conflict with what might be regarded as the standard position of the economics profession. Economists argue that price discrimination by doctors represents the profit maximizing behavior of a discriminating monopolist; the medical profession takes the contrary position[*] that price discrimination exists because doctors represent a collection agency for medical charities.[4] The income of these charities is derived from a loading charge imposed upon well-to-do patients. This income is used to finance the costs of hiring doctors to provide medical care for the poor who are sick. The doctor who is hired by the medical charity and the medical charity itself are typically the same person. Since the loading charge that is

---

[*] However, there is not a unanimity of views either among economists or medical men. Means, a retired professor of clinical medicine at Harvard and a former president of the American College of Surgeons, takes the point of view of the economists. He describes this price policy as charging what the traffic will bear. J. H. Means, *Doctors, People and Government*, p. 66 (1953).

imposed upon non-charity patients to support the activities of medical charities is proportional to income or wealth, discriminatory prices result. The following quotation from an unnamed but highly respected surgeon presents the position of the medical profession.

> I don't feel that I am robbing the rich because I charge them more when I know they can well afford it; the sliding scale is just as democratic as the income tax. I operated today upon two people for the same surgical condition—one a widow whom I charged $50, the other a banker whom I charged $250. I let the widow set her own fee. I charged the banker an amount which he probably carries around in his wallet to entertain his business friends.[5]

It is relevant to inquire, why have we had the development of charities operated by a substantial fraction of the non-salaried practitioners of a profession in medicine alone? Why hasn't a parallel development occurred for such closely related services as nursing and dental care? Why is it possible to observe discrimination by the Mayo Clinic but not the A and P? Clearly food is as much of a "necessity" as medical care. The intellectual foundation for the existence of price discrimination and the operation of medical charities by doctors appears to rest upon the postulate that medicine is in some sense unlike any other commodity or service. More specifically, the state is willing to provide food, clothing, and shelter for the indigent but not medical care.[6] Since medical care is so important, doctors do not refuse to accept patients if they are unable to pay. As a consequence, discrimination in pricing medical services is almost inevitable if doctors themselves are not to finance the costs of operating medical charities.

The foregoing argument in defense of price discrimination in medicine implies that a competitive market for the sale of medical services is inconsistent with the provision of free services to the indigent. This implication is not supported by what can be observed elsewhere in our economy. Clearly there exist a number of competitive markets in which individual practitioners provide free goods or services and price discrimination is absent. Merchants, in their capacity of merchants, give resources to charities yet do not discriminate in pricing their services. Similarly many busi-

---

[5] Seham, "Who Pays the Doctor?" *New Republic*, CXXXV (July 9, 1956), 10, 11. Those who favor price discrimination for this reason ought to be in favor of a single price plan with a system of subsidies and taxes. Such a scheme, in principle, could improve the welfare of both the poor and the well-to-do relative to what it was under price discrimination.

The equity of a tax that is imposed upon the sick who are well-to-do as contrasted with a tax upon the well-to-do generally has not troubled the proponents of this method of taxation.

[6] H. Cabot contends that the community is unwilling to provide for the medical care of the indigent. Therefore the system of a sliding scale of fees has evolved; pp. 123, 266 ff. He estimates that the more opulent members of the community pay ". . . from five to thirty times the average fee . . ." p. 270, *The Doctor's Bill* (1935).

Robinson has defended discriminatory pricing of medical services in sparsely populated areas by using an argument based on indivisibilities. "A Fundamental Objection to Laissez-Faire," *Economic Journal*, XLV (1935), 580. For a refutation of this position see Hutt, "Discriminating Monopoly and the Consumer, *Economic Journal*, XLVI (1936), 61, 74.

nesses give huge sums for educational purposes. Charity is consistent with non-discriminatory pricing because the costs of charity can be and are paid for out of the receipts of the donors without recourse to price discrimination.

However the fact that non-discriminatory pricing is consistent with charity work by doctors doesn't imply that discriminatory pricing of medical services is inconsistent with the charity hypothesis. Clearly what can be done without discrimination can, *a fortiori*, be done with discrimination. Therefore, it is pertinent to ask, is there any evidence that bears directly on the validity of the charity interpretation of price discrimination? The maximizing hypothesis of economics implies that differences in fees can be explained by differences in demand. The charity hypothesis propounded by the medical profession implies that differences in fees result from income differences. The pricing of medical services to those who have medical insurance provides what might be regarded as a crucial experiment for discriminating between these hypotheses. Whether or not one has medical insurance affects the demand for medical service but does not affect personal income. Consequently if the charity hypothesis is correct, then there should be no difference in fees, for specified services, for those who do and those who do not have medical insurance. On the other hand, if the maximizing hypothesis of economics is correct, then fees for those who have medical insurance ought to be higher than for those who do not have such insurance. Existing evidence indicates that if income and wealth differences are held constant, people who have medical insurance pay more for the same service than people who do not have such insurance. Union leaders have found that the fees charged have risen as a result of the acquisition of medical insurance by their members; fees, particularly for surgery, are higher than they would otherwise be if the union member were not insured.[7] Members of the insurance industry have found that ". . . the greater the benefit provided the higher the surgical bill. . . ."[8] This suggests that the principle used for the determinations of fees is, as Means pointed out, what the traffic will bear. Obviously fees determined by this principle will be highly correlated with income, although income will have no independent predictive content for fees if the correlation between income and what the traffic will bear is abstracted.[9]

Other departures from the implications of the hypothesis that price dis-

[7] E. A. Schuler, R. J. Mowitz, and A. J. Mayer, *Medical Public Relations* (1952), report the attitude of lay leaders of the community toward the medical profession. For the attitudes of union leaders and why they have these attitudes, see pp. 97 ff.
[8] Lorber in *Hearings Before the House Committee on Interstate and Foreign Commerce on Health Inquiry*, 83d Cong. 2d Sess. pt. 7, p. 1954 (1954); also Joanis, "Hospital and Medical Costs," *Proceedings of the Fourth Annual Group Meeting of the Health and Accident Underwriters Conference*, p. 18 (Feb. 19–20, 1952).
[9] The principle of what the traffic will bear and the indemnity principle of insurance are fundamentally incompatible and in principle make medical care uninsurable. This has been a real problem for the insurance industry and in part accounts for the relative absence from the market of major medical insurance plans. See the unpublished doctoral dissertation of A. Yousri, *Prepayment of Medical and Surgical Care in Wisconsin*, p. 438, University of Wisconsin Library (1956).

crimination results from the desires of the medical profession to finance the cost of medical care for the indigent exist. These are: (1) Doctors typically do not charge each other for medical care when clearly inter-physician fees ought to be relatively high since doctors have relatively high incomes. (2) The volume of free medical care, particularly in surgery, has declined as a result of the rise in real per capita income in this country in the last twenty years. Yet there has been no change in the extent of price discrimination. As real per capita income rises, price discrimination ought to fade away. There is no evidence that this has been the case.[10] (3) There exists no machinery for matching the receipts and disbursements of medical charities operated by individual doctors. There are no audits of the receipts and the expenditures of medical charities and well-to-do patients are not informed of the magnitude of the loading charges imposed. Moreover one study of medical care and the family budget reported "... no relation in the case of the individual doctor between the free services actually rendered and this recoupment, the whole system is haphazard any way you look at it."[11]

II. History of the Development of the Medical Monopoly

A necessary condition for maintaining a structure of prices that is inconsistent with the maximization by doctors of individual income is the availability and willingness to use powerful sanctions against potential price cutters. When one examines the problems that have been encountered in maintaining prices that are against the interests of individual members of a cartel composed of less than fifteen members, one cannot help being impressed with the magnitude of the problem confronting a monopoly composed of hundreds of thousands of independent producers. Yet despite the fact that medicine constitutes an industry with an extraordinarily large number of producers, the structure of prices for a large number of medical services nevertheless reflects the existence of discrimination based on income. This implies that very strong sanctions must be available to those empowered to enforce price discipline. Indeed, *a priori* reasoning suggests that these sanctions must be of an order of magnitude more powerful than anything we have hitherto encountered in industrial cartels. What are the nature of these sanctions? How are they employed? In order to appreciate fully the magnitude of the coercive measures available to organized medicine, it is relevant to examine the history of medicine to understand how these sanctions were acquired.

Medicine, like the profession of economics today, was until the found-

---

[10] Berger, "Are Surgical Fees Too High?" *Medical Economics*, XXXII (June 1955), 97, 100 ff.

[11] Deardorff and Clark, *op. cit. supra* note 8, pt. 6, p. 1646.

ing of the AMA a relatively competitive industry. With very few exceptions, anyone who wanted to practice was free to hang out a shingle and declare himself available. Medical schools were easy to start, easy to get into, and provided, as might be expected in a free market, a varied menu of medical training that covered the complete quality spectrum. Many medical schools of this time were organized as profit making institutions and had stock outstanding. Some schools were owned by the faculty.

In 1847, the American Medical Association was founded and this organization immediately committed itself to two propositions that were to lead to sharp restrictions upon the freedom of would-be doctors to enter the medical profession and the freedom of patients to choose doctors whom the AMA felt were not adequately qualified to practice medicine. These propositions were (1) that medical students should have acquired a "suitable preliminary education" and (2) that a "uniform elevated standard of requirements for the degree of M.D. should be adopted by all medical schools in the United States.[12]

These objectives were achieved in two stages. During the first stage, the primary concern of the AMA was licensure. In the second, it was accrediting schools of medicine. During the first stage, which began with the founding of the AMA and lasted until the turn of the century, organized medicine was able by lobbying before state legislatures to persuade legislators to license the practice of medicine. Consequently the various states set up boards of medical examiners to administer examinations to determine whether or not applicants were qualified to practice medicine and to grant licenses to those the State Board deemed qualified to practice. Generally speaking, organized medicine was very successful in its campaign to induce states to license physicians. However, the position of organized medicine was by no means unopposed. William James, in testimony offered before the State House in Boston in 1898 when legislation concerned with licensing of non-medically trained therapists was being considered, adopted a nineteenth century liberal position. To quote from this testimony:

> One would suppose that any set of sane persons interested in the growth of medical truth would rejoice if other persons were found willing to push out their experience in the mental healing direction, and to provide a mass of material out of which the conditions and limits of such therapeutic methods may at last become clear. One would suppose that our orthodox medical brethren might so rejoice; but instead of rejoicing they adopt the fiercely partisan attitude of a powerful trade union, they demand legislation against the competition of the "scabs." . . . The mind curers and their public return the scorn of the regular profession with an equal scorn, and will never come up for the examination. Their movement is a religious or quasi-religious movement; personality is one condition of success there, and impressions and intuitions seem to accomplish more than chemical, anatomical or physiological information. . . . Pray, do not fail, Mr. Chairman, to catch my point. You are not to ask yourselves whether

[12] A. Flexner, *Medical Education in the U.S. and Canada,* Bull. No. 4, Carnegie Foundation for the Advancement of Teaching, p. 10 (1910).

these mind-curers do really achieve the successes that are claimed. It is enough for you as legislators to ascertain that a large number of our citizens, persons whose number seems daily to increase, are convinced that they do achieve them, are persuaded that a valuable new department of medical experience is by them opening up. Here is a purely medical question, regarding which our General Court, not being a well-spring and source of medical virtue, not having any private test of therapeutic truth, must remain strictly neutral under penalty of making the confusion worse. ... Above all things, Mr. Chairman, let us not be infected with the Gallic spirit of regulation and regimentation for their own abstract sakes. Let us not grow hysterical about law-making. Let us not fall in love with the enactments and penalties because they are so logical and sound so pretty, and look so nice on paper.[13]

However, it was not until the second stage that economically effective power over entry was acquired by organized medicine. This stage began with the founding in 1904 of the Council on Medical Education of the AMA. This group dedicated itself to the task of improving the quality of medical education offered by the medical schools of the day. In 1906, this committee undertook an inspection of the 160 medical schools then in existence and fully approved of the training in only 82 schools. Thirty-two were deemed to be completely unacceptable. As might be expected, considerable resentment developed in the medical colleges and elsewhere as a result of this inspection. Consequently the council withheld publication of its findings, although the various colleges were informed of their grades.[14] In order to gain wider acceptance of the results of this study, the Council solicited the aid of the Carnegie Foundation. "If we could obtain the publication and approval of our work by the Carnegie Foundation for the Advancement of Teaching, it would assist materially in securing the results we were attempting to bring about."[15] Subsequently Abraham Flexner, representing the Carnegie Foundation, with the aid of N. P. Colwell, secretary of the Council on Medical Education, repeated the AMA's inspection and grading of medical schools. In 1910, the results of the labors of Flexner and Colwell were published.[16] This report, known as the Flexner report, recommended that a substantial fraction of the existing medical schools be closed, standards be raised in the remainder, and admissions sharply curtailed. Flexner forcefully argued that the country was suffering from an overproduction of doctors and that it was in the public interest to

[13] *Letters of W. James* II, 66–72 (edited H. James, 1920). Dollard reports that James took this position at the risk of being drummed out of the ranks of medicine. Dollard, "Monopoly and Medicine," speech delivered at Medical Center, UCLA, to be published by the University of California Press as one of a series of papers presented in celebration of Robert Gordon Sproul's 25th anniversary as President of the University of California. The significance of consumers' sovereignty has been recognized by at least one other maverick doctor. Means, *op. cit. supra* note 4, at p. 72.

[14] Johnson in Fishbein, *A History of the American Medical Association*, pp. 887 ff. (1947).

[15] Bevan, "Cooperation in Medical Education and Medical Service," *Journal of the American Medical Association*, XC (1928), 1175.

[16] Flexner, *op. cit. supra* note 12.

have fewer doctors who were better trained. In effect, Flexner argued that the public should be protected against the consequences of buying medical services from inadequately trained doctors by legislating poor medical schools out of business.[17]

If impact on public policy is the criterion of importance, the Flexner report must be regarded as one of the most important reports ever written. It convinced legislators that only the graduates of first class medical schools ought to be permitted to practice medicine and led to the delegation to the AMA of the task of determining what was and what was not a first class medical school. As a result, standards of acceptability for winning a license to practice medicine were set by statute or by formal rule or informal policy of state medical examining boards, and these statutes or rules provided that boards consider only graduates of schools approved by the AMA and/or the American Association of Medical Colleges, whose lists are identical.[18]

The Flexner report ushered in an era, which lasted until 1944, during which a large number of medical schools were shut down. With its new found power, the AMA vigorously attacked the problem of certification of medical schools. By exercising its power to certify, the AMA reduced the number of medical schools in the United States from 162 in 1906 to 85 in 1920, 76 in 1930 and 69 in 1944.[19] As a result of the regulation of medical schools, the number of medical students in school in the United States today is 28,500, merely 5,200 more than in 1910 when Flexner published his report.[20]

[17] Flexner, *op. cit. supra* note 12, at p. 14. Two errors in economic reasoning are crucial in helping Flexner establish his conclusions. One is an erroneous interpretation of Gresham's Law. This law is used to justify legislation to keep low quality doctors out of the medical care market by interpreting it to mean that second-class doctors will drive first-class doctors out of business. The other is that raising the standards of medical education is necessarily in the public interest. Flexner fails to recognize that raising standards implies higher costs of medical care. This argument is on a par with arguing that we should keep all cars of a quality below Cadillacs, Chryslers, and Lincolns off the automobile market.

[18] Hyde and Wolff, "The American Medical Association: Power, Purpose, and Politics in Organized Medicine," *Yale L. J.*, LXIII (1954), 969.

[19] These figures are from R. M. Allen, *Medical Education and the Changing Order*, p. 16 (1946). Allen imputes this decline in the number of medical schools to a previous error in estimating the demand for doctors. The decline in the number of schools in existence represented an adjustment to more correctly perceived demand conditions for medical care.

[20] Dollard, *op. cit. supra* note 13. This result was far from unanticipated. Bevan, the head of the AMA's Council on Medical Education, clearly anticipated a decline in both medical students and schools. "In this rapid elevation of the standard of medical education with the increase in preliminary requirements and greater length of course, and with the reduction of the number of medical schools from 160 to 80, there occurred a marked reduction in the number of medical students and medical graduates. We had anticipated this and felt that this was a desirable thing. We had an over-supply of poor mediocre practitioners." Bevan, *op. cit.* note 15, at p. 1176. Friedman and Kuznets state, "Initially, this decline in the number of physicians relative to total population was an unplanned by-product of the intensive drive for higher standards of medical education." *Op. cit supra* note 1 at pp. 10–11. It may have been a by-product, and there are some grounds for doubts on this count, but it surely was not unanticipated.

The AMA, by means of its power to certify what is and what is not a class A medical school, has substantial control over both the number of medical schools in the United States and the rate of production of doctors.[21] While the control by the AMA over such first class schools as, say, Johns Hopkins is relatively weak because it would be ludicrous not to classify this institution as a class A school, nevertheless control over the aggregate production rate of doctors is great because of its more substantial power over the output of less distinguished medical schools.

The delegation by the state legislatures to the AMA of the power to regulate the medical industry in the public interest is on a par with giving the American Iron and Steel Institute the power to determine the output of steel. This delegation of power by the states to the AMA, which was actively sought and solicited, placed this organization in a position of having to serve two masters who in part have conflicting interests. On the one hand, the AMA was given the task of providing an adequate supply of properly qualified doctors. On the other hand, the decision with respect to what is adequate training and an adequate number of doctors affects the pocketbooks of those who do the regulating as well as their closest business and personal associates. It is this power that has been given to the AMA that is the cornerstone of the monopoly power that has been imputed by economists to organized medicine.[22]

III. Evidence Supporting the Discriminating Monopoly Model

The preceding analysis tells us nothing about the mechanism for controlling the price policies of individual doctors; it only implies that the rate of return on capital invested in medical training will be greater than the rate of return on capital invested in other classes of professional training. This difference in returns is imputable as a rent on the power of the AMA to control admissions to the profession by means of control over medical education. Here it will be argued that control over the pricing policies of doctors is directly and immediately related to AMA control of medical education. The relationship is that control over medical education is the primary instrumentality for control over individual price policies. More

[21] Dr. Spahr contends that there is a "... widespread but erroneous belief that the AMA governs the profession directly and determines who may practice medicine." "Medicine's Neglected Control Lever," *Yale Rev.*, XL (1950), 25. She correctly contends that this power belongs to the state but fails to recognize that it has been delegated to the AMA by the state. Mayer on the other hand recognizes both the power in the hands of the AMA and its source. He argues that the AMA has life and death powers over both medical schools and hospitals. *Harpers*, CLXXX (Dec. 1939), 27.

[22] Dollard, *op. cit. supra* note 20, concedes that medicine is a monopoly but argues that the AMA has used its power, by and large, in the public interest. Therefore, he implies that the monopoly power of the AMA has been unexploited, and the profession has acted against its own self interest.

specifically, control over postgraduate medical training—internship and residency, and control over admission to specialty board examinations—is the source of the power over the members of the medical profession by organized medicine.

A. THE CONTROL MECHANISM

Part of nearly every doctor's medical education consists of internship and for many also a period of hospital service known as residency. Internship is a necessary condition for licensure in most states. This training is administered by hospitals. However, hospitals must be approved by the AMA for intern and residency training, and most non-proprietary, i.e., nonprofit, hospitals in this country are in fact approved for at least intern training. Each approved hospital is allocated a quota of positions that can be filled by interns as part of their training. Hospitals value highly participation in internship and residency training programs. These programs are valued highly because at the prevailing wage for intern services, it is possible to produce hospital care more cheaply with interns than without them. Interns to hospitals are like coke to the steel industry: in both cases, it is perfectly possible to produce the final product without these raw materials; in both cases, the final product can be produced more cheaply by using these particular raw materials.

There exist some grounds for suspecting that the wages of interns are maintained at an artificially low level, i.e., that interns receive compensation that is less than the value of their marginal product: (1) Hospitals are reporting that there is a "shortage" of interns and have been known to send representatives to Europe and Asia to invite doctors to serve as interns.[23] (2) University hospitals are more aggressive bidders for intern services than non-university hospitals. The fraction of the available intern positions that are filled by university hospitals is greater than by non-university hospitals.[24] If controls are exercised over what hospitals can offer in wages to interns, university hospitals are apt to be less vulnerable to the threat of loss of their class A hospital ratings than non-university hospitals. This would be true for the same reason that Johns Hopkins would have a freer hand in determining the size of its freshman class. The status of university hospitals is stronger because these hospitals are likely to be among the better hospitals in the country. Therefore, if controls over intern wages exist then it seems reasonable to suspect they would be relatively weaker over the wages of interns in university hospitals. For this reason, one would expect university hospitals to be more aggressive in bidding for interns.

However, whether or not interns are underpaid, the AMA has control over the supply of a vital, in an economic sense, agent of production for

---

[23] "Congress to Probe Doctor Shortage," *Medical Economics*, XXXIII (June 1956), 141.
[24] *Journal of the American Medical Association*, CLXII (1956), 281.

producing hospital care. Revocation of a hospital's class A rating implies the loss of interns. In turn, the loss of interns implies higher costs of production. Higher costs of production result in a deterioration of the competitive position of any given hospital vis-à-vís other hospitals in the medical care market. This control over hospitals by the AMA has been used to induce hospitals to abide by the Mundt Resolution.[25] This resolution advises hospitals that are certified for intern training that their staff ought to be composed solely of members of local medical societies.[26] As a result of this AMA control over hospitals, membership in local medical societies is a matter of enormous importance to practicing physicians. Lack of membership implies inability to become a member of a hospital staff.[27]

County medical societies are for all practical purposes private clubs with their own rules concerning eligibility for membership and grounds for expulsion. A system of appeals from the rulings of county medical societies with respect to their members is provided. On the other hand, for non-members attempting to obtain membership in county medical societies, there is no provision for appeal. The highest court in the medical judicial system is the Judicial Council of the AMA. Between this council and the county medical societies are state medical societies. Judicial review is bound by findings of fact made at the local level.[28] For doctors dependent upon hospitals in order to carry out their practice, and presumably this constitutes the bulk of the profession, being cut off from access to hospitals constitutes a partial revocation of their license to practice medicine. Consequently, more doctors belong to their county medical associations than is true of lawyers with respect to local bar associations. More significantly, doctors are subject to very severe losses indeed if they should be expelled from their local county medical associations or be refused admission to membership. It is this weapon, expulsion from county medical associations, that is probably the most formidable sanction employed to keep doctors from maximizing their personal incomes by cutting prices to high income patients. "Unethical" doctors, i.e., price cutters, can be in large part removed as a threat to a structure of prices that discriminates in terms of income by the use of this weapon.[29] For potential unethical physicians,

[25] "By a long record of authoritative inspection and grading of facilities, organized medicine has placed itself in a position to deny alternatively the services of doctor and hospital to each other." O. Garceau, *Political Life of the American Medical Association*, p. 109 (1941).

[26] Hyde and Wolff, *op. cit. supra* note 18, at 952. The certification of hospitals for nursing training and the value of nursing training programs to hospitals may be on a par with intern training.

[27] The strike is another instrument for control over hospitals by the AMA. Doctors have refused to work in hospitals that have admitted osteopaths to their staff. Hyde and Wolff, *op. cit. supra* note 18 at 966; M. M. Belli, *Ready for the Plaintiff*, p. 115 (1956). The threat of a strike has also been used to induce hospitals to refuse staff membership to "unethical" doctors.

[28] Hyde and Wolff, *op. cit. supra* note 18, at 949–950.

[29] "Ethics has always been a flexible, developing, notion in medicine, with a strong flavor of economics from the start." Garceau, *op. cit. supra* note 25, at p. 106. Also consult the Hippocratic Oath.

it pays not to cut prices if cutting prices means being cut off from hospitals.

Thus far we have argued that control over the individual price policies of the members of the medical profession has been achieved by the AMA through its control over postgraduate medical education. By means of its power to certify a hospital for intern training, the AMA controls the source of supply of a crucial agent for the production of hospital care. Control over the supply of interns has been used to induce hospitals to admit to their staffs only members of county medical associations. Since membership in the county medical associations is in the control of organized medicine, and membership in a hospital staff is extremely important for the successful practice of most branches of medicine, the individual doctor can be easily manipulated by those who control membership in county medical associations.

Members of the medical profession are also subject to another type of control derived from AMA control over postgraduate medical education, that is particularly effective over younger members. Membership in a county medical society is a necessary condition for admission to specialty board examinations for a number of specialties, and passing these examinations is a necessary condition for speciality ratings.[30] Non-society members cannot win board membership in these specialties. This is a particularly important form of control over newcomers to the medical profession because newcomers tend to be young doctors who aspire to specialty board ratings.[31] Consequently the AMA has particularly powerful sanctions over those who are most likely to be price cutters. These are young doctors trying to establish a practice.[32]

B. THE EVIDENCE

Just as one would expect an all-out war to reveal a country's most powerful weapons, substantial threats to the continued existence of price discrimination ought to reveal the strongest sanctions available to organized medicine. For this reason, the opposition or lack of opposition to prepaid medical plans that provide medical service directly to the patient ought to be illuminating.

Generally speaking, there exist two classes of medical insurance. One is the cash indemnity variety. Blue Cross and Blue Shield plans fall within this class.[33] Under cash indemnity medical insurance, the doctor and

---

[30] Hyde and Wolff, *op. cit. supra* note 18, at p. 952.

[31] A statement of sanctions similar to that noted above appears in *Restrictions on Free Enterprise in Medicine*, p. 9 (April 1949), pamphlet, Committee on Research in Medical Economics.

[32] "Other things being equal, old well-established concerns tend to be more hostile to price cutting than younger concerns." G. Stocking and M. Watkins, *Monopoly and Free Enterprise*, p. 117 (1951).

[33] Most of these plans have services provisions; that is, they agree to provide the service required to treat particular ailments only if the subscriber's income is below some pre-

patient are able to determine fees jointly at the time medical service is sold just as if there were no insurance. Therefore, this class of medical insurance leaves unaffected the power of doctors to discriminate between differences in demand in setting fees. If anything, doctors welcome insurance since it improves the ability of the patient to pay. On the other hand, for non-indemnity type plans, plans that provide medical services directly as contrasted with plans that provide funds to be used to purchase desired services, payments are typically independent of income. Costs of membership in such prepayment plans are a function of family size, age, coverage, quality of service, etc., but are independent of the income of the subscriber. Consequently, such plans represent a means for massive price cutting to high income patients. For this reason, the reception of these plans by organized medicine constitutes an experiment for testing the validity of the discriminating monopoly model. If no opposition to these plans exists, then the implication of the discriminating monopoly model—that some mechanism must exist for maintaining the structure of prices—is invalid. On the other hand, opposition to these plans by organized medicine constitutes observable phenomena that support this implication. If such opposition exists, then it supports the discriminating monopoly hypothesis in addition to providing evidence of the specific character of the sanctions available to organized medicine.

A number of independent observers have found that a systematic pattern of opposition to prepaid medical service plans, as contrasted with cash indemnity plans, exists. "In many parts of the country, organized medical bodies have been distinctly hostile to group practice. This is particularly true where the group is engaged in any form of prepaid medical care."[34] "Early groups were disparaged as unethical. But within recent years active steps have been taken only against those groups offering a plan for some type of flat-fee payment."[35] "There is reason to believe that the Oregon, the San Diego, and the District of Columbia cases exemplify a nationwide pattern of behavior by the American Medical Association and its state and county subsidiaries. What has come into the open here is working beneath the surface in other states and counties."[36] This systematic pattern of opposition to single price medical plans has taken two distinct courses. These are (1) using sanctions in an effort to terminate the life of prepaid medical plans already in existence and (2) lobbying for legislation that would abort their birth.

---

assigned level. Of the 78 plans approved by organized medicine, 58 have service provisions. Of these, only 3 provide service to all income classes. The remainder provide a cash indemnity to subscribers whose income exceeds the relevant pre-assigned income levels. Therefore, these plans do not interfere with the discriminatory pricing policies of doctors. Consult *Voluntary Prepayment Medical Benefit Plans*, American Medical Association (1954).

[34] *Building America's Health*, report to the President by the Commission on the Health Needs of the Nation, V. I, p. 34 (1952).

[35] Hyde and Wolff, *op. cit. supra* note 18, at p. 977.

[36] *Op. cit. supra* note 31, at p. 14.

There have been a number of dramatic battles for survival by prepaid non-price-discriminatory medical plans resulting from the efforts of organized medicine to destroy them. These struggles have brought into action the most powerful sanctions available to organized medicine for use against price cutters. Consequently, the history of these battles provides valuable evidence of the character of the weapons available to the participants. For this purpose, the experiences of the following organizations are particularly illuminating: Farmers Union Hospital Association of Elk City, Oklahoma, the Kaiser Foundation of San Francisco and Oakland, Group Health of Washington, Group Health Cooperative of Puget Sound, Civic Medical Center of Chicago, Complete Service Bureau of San Diego, and the medical cooperatives in the state of Oregon. These plans are diverse, from the point of view of location, organization, equipment, sponsorship, and objective. However, they all have one crucial unifying characteristic—fees or service charges are independent of income.[37] Similarly, the experiences of Ross-Loos in Los Angeles and the Palo Alto Clinic in California are illuminating because these organizations both operate prepayment single price medical plans and nevertheless continue to stay within the good graces of organized medicine.

The founder and director of the cooperative Farmers Union Hospital in Elk City, Oklahoma, Dr. Michael A. Shadid, was harassed for a number of years by his local county medical association as a consequence of founding and operating this price cutting organization. He was ingeniously thrown out of the Beckham County Medical Society; this organization was dissolved and reconstituted apparently for the sole purpose of not inviting Shadid to become a member of the "new" organization. Before founding the cooperative, Shadid had been a member in good standing in his county medical association for over a decade.

The loss of hospital privileges stemming from non-county-society membership was not sufficient for the task of putting Shadid out of business, because his organization had its own hospital. Therefore, organized medicine turned to its control over licensure to put the cooperative out of business. Shadid was equal to this challenge. He was shrewd enough to draw members of the politically potent Farmers Union into his organization.

---

[37] The Health Insurance Plan of New York is not included in the foregoing enumeration because charges are not completely independent of income. For determining premiums, families are divided into two groups, those with incomes above $6,500 are assessed premiums twenty per cent greater than those applicable to the lower income group. Consult M. M. Davis, *Medical Care for Tomorrow*, p. 237 (1955). However, as a threat against the structure of prices for medical services based on income, this plan is almost as potent as those listed. Consequently, the opposition to it ought to be just about as severe and the weapons employed just as interesting for gaining insights into the nature of the sanctions over the behavior of individual doctors by organized medicine.

Available evidence suggests that HIP is under attack. See the testimony of G. Baehr, President and Medical Director of HIP in *Hearings*, op. cit. note 8, at pp. 1604, 1642, and 1663. Legislation that would outlaw such plans as HIP has been sponsored by organized medicine. Consult *N. Y. Times*, p. 15, col. 5 (Feb. 21, 1954).

Therefore, in the struggle to take away Shadid's license to practice medicine, the farmers were pitted against the doctors. The doctors came out of this political battle the losers because the state governor at the time, Murray, sided with the farmers.[38] However, the Beckham County Medical Society has been powerful enough to keep doctors who were known to be coming to Oklahoma to join Shadid's organization from getting a license to practice, powerful enough to frighten and cause the departure of a doctor who had been associated with Shadid's organization for a substantial period of time, powerful enough to keep Shadid out of a two-week postgraduate course on bone fractures at the Cook County Graduate School of Medicine (the course was open only to members in good standing of their local county medical societies), and was able to get enough of Shadid's doctors drafted during the war to endanger the life of his organization.[39] In recent years, the tide of battle has turned. The Hospital Association brought suit against the Beckham County Medical Society and its members for conspiracy in restraint of trade. This case was settled out of court. As part of this settlement, the county medical association agreed to accept the staff of the cooperative as members.

The experience of the Kaiser Foundation Plan is parallel to that of the Farmers Union. Both were vigorously opposed by organized medicine. The medical staff in each case could not obtain membership in local county medical societies. In both cases, the plans were able to prosper despite this obstacle, since they operated their own hospitals. In both cases, the doctor draft was used as a tool in an attempt to put these plans out of business.[40]

Control by organized medicine over licensure was used as a weapon in an attempt to kill the Kaiser Plan. Dr. Sidney Garfield, the plan's medical director, was tried by the State Board of Medical Examiners for unprofessional conduct. Garfield's license to practice was suspended for one year and he was placed on probation for five years. However, the suspension was withheld pending good behavior while on probation. This ruling by the State Board of Examiners was not supported in court. Superior Court Judge Edward P. Murphy ordered the board to rescind all action against Garfield. The judge ruled that the board was arbitrary in denying Garfield a fair trail. Subsequently the appellate court reversed the decision of the trial court on one count but not the second. Nevertheless the judgment of the trial court in rescinding the decision of the board of examiners was

[38] Davis argues that Shadid would have lost his license to practice if he had not had the powerful political support of the farmers. *Op. cit supra* note 37 at p. 229.

[39] The story of Shadid and his organization may be found in M. A. Shadid, *A Doctor for the People* (1939), and *Doctors of Today and Tomorrow* (1947). In Two Harbors, Minnesota, doctors associated with a medical society disapproved plan could not win admission to their local county medical society and a doctor associated with this plan could not get into the same school from which Shadid had been barred—the Cook County Graduate School of Medicine. *Christian Century*, LXXI (Feb. 10, 1954), 173.

[40] For evidence on this point for the Kaiser Plan, see *Hearings before a Subcommittee of the Senate Committee on Education and Labor*, pt. 1, p. 338 ff., 77th Cong. 2nd Sess. on S. Res. 291 (1942).

upheld. The entire matter was sent back to the board for reconsideration of penalty.[41]

Subsequently, Garfield was tried by the county medical association for unethical practices, namely advertising, and found guilty. However, he came away from this trial with only a reprimand and not the loss of his license.[42] By virtue of having its own hospitals and legal intervention by the courts against the rulings of organized medicine, the Kaiser Foundation has been able to resist the onslaughts of its foes. However, the battle is not over yet. Although Kaiser Foundation doctors are now admitted to the Alameda County Society, the San Francisco County Society still excludes them.[43]

Group Health in Washington was not as fortunate as Kaiser or Farmers Union with respect to hospitals. Unlike these other two organizations, Group Health did not have its own hospital and therefore was dependent upon the existing hospitals in the community. Consequently, when Group Health doctors were ejected from the District Medical Society, Group Health was seriously crippled. Nearly all the hospitals in the district were coerced into denying staff privileges to Group Health doctors and bed space to their patients. Moreover, many doctors were deterred from becoming members of the Group Health staff because of fear of punitive action by the District Medical Society. Still other doctors who were members of the Group Health medical staff suddenly discovered attractive employment possibilities elsewhere and resigned their Group Health positions.[44]

It was fortunate for Group Health that it was located in Washington, D. C. and therefore under the jurisdiction of federal laws, in particular the Sherman Act. The tactics of the District Medical Society and the AMA came to the attention of the Justice Department. This led to the successful criminal prosecution of organized medicine under the Sherman Act. The opinion of the Supreme Court delivered by Mr. Justice Roberts pinpoints the primary concern of the petitioners, the District Medical Society and the AMA. "In truth, the petitioners represented physicians who desired that they and all others should practice independently on a fee for service basis, where whatever arrangement for payment each had was a matter that lay between him and his patient in each individual case of service or treatment."

As a result of this victory, consumer sovereignty with respect to Group Health was restored. As might be suspected from the intense opposition of

---

[41] P. DeKruif, *Life Among the Doctors*, p. 416 (1949). The last two chapters of this book deal with the activities of organized medicine against the Kaiser Plan.

[42] Mayer reports that Dr. Louis Schmidt, the urologist, was expelled from organized medicine for advertising his venereal disease clinic. *Harpers*, CLXXX (Dec. 1939), 27.

[43] Means, *op. cit. supra* note 4, at p. 131. Opposition to Kaiser also exists in Los Angeles area where this plan also operates. *Bulletin of the Los Angeles County Medical Society*, LXXXIII (1953), 501, contains a condemnation of the Kaiser Plan and a call-to-arms.

[44] Hyde and Wolff, *op. cit. supra* note 18, at p. 990.

the AMA and the District Medical Society, Group Health has shown unusual survival properties and flourishes in competition with fee-for-service medical care. Since its victory at court, good relations with the District Medical Society have been achieved by the Group Health staff.[45]

If price discrimination is in fact highly valued by organized medicine and prepayment direct service medical plans have been opposed in order to maintain a structure of discriminating prices, doesn't the existence of the prepayment plans unopposed by the AMA constitute an anomaly?[46]

How can the Ross-Loos and Palo Alto Clinic cases be explained?[47] The Ross-Loos plan in Los Angeles is a prepaid medical plan that is a profit-seeking organization. It was started in 1929 and by the end of 1952 had 127,000 members.[48] The Ross-Loos plan does not have hospitals of its own and is therefore forced to rely on the existing hospitals of the community. Consequently, the condemnation of this plan by organized medicine which occurred after it won acceptance from consumers in the medical care market, represented an enormous threat to its continued existence. The Ross-Loos plan doctors were expelled from the Los Angeles County Medical Association. Among the doctors to lose their county society membership was a former President of the Los Angeles County Medical Society. As a result of a number of appeals to higher courts, all within the judicial machinery of organized medicine, the decision that would have crippled if not destroyed this plan was reversed.

An excellent reason for thie reversal is suggested by the testimony of Dr. H. Clifford Loos, a co-founder of Ross-Loos. In response to the question, "Are you handicapped to any extent by the fact that you are not able to advertise," Dr. Loos replied:

> As far as that goes, we do not care to be big, or bigger. If I had accepted all of the groups who applied to us, we would need our city hall to house us. We have put the brakes on. We can't accept too many. We feel we can't be too big.[49]

[45] Becker, President, Group Health Association, *Hearings before Senate Committee on Education and Labor*, pt. 5, p. 2528, 79th Cong. 2nd Sess. on S. Res. 1606 (1946).

[46] Evidence of opposition to price cutting on a more modest scale exists. Individuals who have cut prices have either encountered the sanctions of organized medicine or a threat to employ these sanctions. Consult, "Medical Group's Protest Stops Polio Shot Project in Brooklyn," *N. Y. Times*, p. 33M (Sept. 12, 1956). The Los Angeles *Times* reports that Dr. Sylvan O. Tatkin filed a complaint in the Superior Court of Los Angeles charging that the local association was engaging in unlawful rate fixing. Tatkin charged that he was refused membership in the local society and therefore dropped from the staff of Behrens Memorial Hospital in Glendale as a result of price cutting. L. A. *Times*, sec. 2, p. 30, col. 4 (June 29, 1956).
Economic theory implies that there would be no point for a monopolist that has control over supply being concerned with prices directly. For a non-discriminating monopolist, control over supply implies control over prices.

[47] There is evidence that opposition to prepayment plans is not merely local society policy. In Logan County, Arkansas, the entire county society was expelled from the state society by means of charter revocation. The local society was dominated by physicians participating in a disapproval plan. *Journal of the Arkansas Medical Society*, XXVII (1930), 29.

[48] *Hearings, op. cit. supra* note 8, at p. 1451.

[49] *Ibid.*, at p. 1469.

This constitutes strange behavior indeed for a profit-seeking institution that certainly ought to have no fears of Justice Department action for either being too large or monopolizing an industry. One cannot help suspecting that the amicable relations with the Los Angeles County Medical Society may have been acquired at the cost of a sharply curtailed rate of expansion.[50]

The Palo Alto Clinic in California provides prepaid medical care that is non-income discriminating to the students, employees, and faculty of Stanford University. This constitutes a small fraction of the clinic's business. Eighty-five per cent of the receipts of the clinic are attributable to conventional fee-for-service practice that lends itself to discriminatory pricing. This clinic continues to stay within the good graces of organized medicine. When questioned about extending the prepaid nondiscriminatory service, Dr. Russel V. Lee, Director of the Clinic and Professor of Medicine in the School of Medicine of Stanford University, threw some light upon this apparent anomaly. "Several of the industries in the area have come to us for such service. We have been trying to get our county medical society approval before we go into these things, and we are doing a little job of county medical education because in general the county medical society will not approve of anything that smacks of a closed panel."[51] This suggests that the Palo Alto Clinic is in the position of having to go to its principal competitors for permission to sell its services to new customers. This is comparable to a requirement that a Ford dealer must first obtain the permission of his competing Chevrolet dealer before he can sell Fords to non-Ford owners who have asked for the opportunity to buy them. Probably the county medical society that includes the Palo Alto Clinic does not feel that the present level of sales of prepaid medical services by this clinic is high enough to justify the costs and risks of punitive action.

Organized medicine, i.e., the AMA and its political subdivisions, has opposed prepaid non-price-discriminatory medical plans not only directly by fighting against them but also indirectly by lobbying for legislation that would make such plans illegal. State medical societies have achieved a fair degree of success in sponsoring legislation designed to prevent price cutting in the medical care market caused by prepaid medical plans. As of 1954, "there are at least 20 states that have had such laws passed at the instigation of medical societies, which are designed to prevent prepaid group practice and to keep medical practice on a fee-for-service solo basis."[52] Another source says: "Most of the states now have restrictive statutes per-

---

[50] Loos has also served as an expert witness for the San Diego County Society during its struggle with another prepayment plan. Hyde and Wolff, *op. cit supra* note 18, at p. 985 impute the tolerance of Ross-Loos by organized medicine to the fact that it is physician sponsored as contrasted to being lay or non-physician sponsored. The theory outlined in this paper implies that this is not a relevant distinction.

[51] *Hearings, op. cit. supra* note 8, at p. 1559.

[52] Baehr, *Hearings, op. cit. supra* note 8, at p. 1594. Very unorthodox lobbying tactics have been successfully employed by distinguished doctors to achieve the legislative goals of organized medicine. See Osler's forthright description in H. Young, *A Surgeon's Autobiography*, p. 407 (1940).

mitting only the medical profession to operate or to control prepayment medical care plans."[53] Hansen lists as one of the primary objectives of this legislation "to preserve the fee-for-service system as far as possible by controlling the financial administration of the plans."[54] . . .

IV. Conclusion

If different prices for the same service exist, then economic theory implies that there must also exist some means for enjoining producers of this service from acting in their own self-interest and thereby establishing uniform prices. Observable phenomena abundantly support this implication. Available evidence suggests that the primary control instrument of organized medicine is the ability to cut off potential price cutters from the use of resources complementary to doctors' service for producing many classes of medical care. However, techniques other than the withdrawal of staff privileges in hospitals are also employed to maintain discipline in the medical profession. These include *no-criticism rules*, professional courtesy or the free treatment by doctors of other doctors and their families, prohibition of advertising that might reallocate market shares among producers, preventing doctors from testifying against one another in malpractice suits, and the selection of candidates for medical schools and postgraduate training in the surgical specialities that have a relatively low probability of being price cutters. All of these sanctions can be rationalized as means for maintaining price discrimination. Therefore the use of these sanctions is consistent with the hypothesis that the medical profession constitutes a discriminating monopoly.

If being cut off from the use of a complementary agent of production, hospital services, is the chief means of disciplining the existing members of the medical profession, then there ought to be a difference in the price discipline maintained in the surgical and non-surgical specialities. Consequently there ought to be a significant difference between the surgical and the non-surgical specialities in the frequency of discriminatory pricing. There are no grounds for believing that there is any difference between the surgical and non-surgical specialities with respect to the effectiveness of the more subtle means of control. Therefore as a result of the relatively weaker impact on the non-surgical specialities of the loss of hospital staff privileges, it should be possible to observe that the non-surgical specialities have not only more price cutters in their midst but also are relatively freer

[53] Hansen, "Laws Affecting Group Health Plans," *Iowa L. Rev.*, XXXV (1950), 209, 225.
[54] *Ibid.*, at p. 209. Yet in his conclusion, Hansen argues that "Farsighted medical societies should find no valid reason for opposing group health enabling legislation. Instead they should welcome experimentation in the field of medical economics with the same spirit they welcome it in the field of medical science." pp. 235–36. It is one of the implications of this paper that the more farsighted medical societies provide the strongest opposition to experimentation in the field of medical economics.

in criticizing other members of the profession, serving as expert witnesses, and violating professional courtesy. Similarly this analysis implies that before the turn of the century, price discrimination in medicine was less pervasive, doctors criticized each other more freely, were more willing to act as expert witnesses against one another, did not as readily provide free medical care to other members of the profession, and did not discriminate against potential price cutters in admission to medical training.

This economic interest of the medical profession in maintaining price discrimination has led to opposition directed against new techniques for marketing medical services that offer promise of utilizing the existing stock of physicians more efficiently than heretofore. Consequently the opposition by organized medicine to prepaid service type medical plans probably has resulted in higher economic costs of medical care for the community than would otherwise have been the case. Similarly the incompatibility of the indemnity principle of insurance and the "what the traffic will bear" principle of pricing medical services has inhibited the development of major, medical catastrophe insurance in this country and consequently has limited the ability of individuals to insure themselves against these risks. Insofar as freer criticism by the members of the medical profession of one another before the public is of value to consumers in helping them distinguish between better and poorer practitioners and in raising standards within the profession, the public has obtained a lower quality of medical service than would otherwise have been obtainable at existing costs. And insofar as being a potential price cutter weeds out candidates from medical schools and postgraduate training in the surgical specialities who were better potential doctors than those accepted, then the quality of the medical services that could have been achieved at existing costs was reduced.

Economic theory implies that prepaid medical service plans imperil the existence of price discrimination. Consequently theory also implies that in geographical areas where such plans exist, price discrimination ought to be relatively less prevalent. In California, the Kaiser Plan has captured a substantial fraction of the medical care market and is the largest single producer in the state. In an effort to meet this competition, service-type plans have been offered by orthodox members of the medical profession that are non-discriminatory with respect to income. Competition has had the effect of reducing the extent of discriminatory pricing in the area. This has been true in a number of counties in California where the Kaiser Plan is particularly strong. Therefore both economic theory and empirical evidence suggest that if there were more competition among doctors in the sale of medical services, i.e, if doctors were individually freer to pursue their self-interest, there would be less discrimination in the pricing of medical services.

Part Four

OLIGOPOLY AND MONOPOLISTIC COMPETITION

Most markets in the United States fall between the polar extremes of perfect competition and pure monopoly. In many markets there are a few sellers, not just one (as in monopoly). Such markets are called oligopolies. Examples of oligopolies are the markets for steel, petroleum, automobiles, cans, and electrical equipment in the United States. In other markets, there are a great many sellers, but the products that they sell are differentiated. (That is, the products differ somewhat.) Such markets are said to be characterized by monopolistic competition. Examples of monopolistically competitive markets are clothing stores and gasoline stations. In this part of this book, we present a number of well-known papers and reports dealing with oligopoly and monopolistic competition.

Oligopoly is often characterized by an emphasis on style change, one firm trying to gain business from the others through changes in its product. In the first article, Franklin Fisher, Zvi Griliches, and Carl Kaysen estimate the cost of automobile model changes during the 1950's, concluding that these costs were about five billion dollars a year—a very substantial sum. As the authors point out, it is not easy to decide whether these costs were socially worthwhile. Oligopoly is also characterized by interdependence among firms, each firm being aware that the effects of its own decisions depend on how its competitors respond. In the next article, Martin Shubik describes the nature and uses of game theory, a method for the study of decision-making in situations of this sort.

Oligopoly sometimes results in collusion, even though collusion is illegal in the United States. The following article, taken from the *Wall Street Journal* of January 10 and 12, 1962, is an interesting case study of collusion in the electrical-equipment industry. In 1961, the electrical-equipment manufacturers—General Electric, Westinghouse, and others—pleaded guilty to charges of violating the antitrust laws. The next article, taken from hearings before the Senate Subcommittee on Antitrust and Monopoly, is also a study of collusion, but it describes the case of an international cartel. Beginning in 1959, practically all of the world's producers of quinine entered into a series of agreements to control prices, distribution, and production in the quinine industry. This article describes the negotiation and the resulting arrangements among the members of the cartel.

The modern petroleum industry is an example of an oligopoly. In the following article the staff of the Federal Trade Commission, in a 1973 preliminary report, characterizes the structure and functioning of the petroleum industry. According to this report, the major oil companies "seek to consolidate market power by various exclusionary tactics," and "the federal and state governments with the force of law do for the major companies that which would be illegal for the companies to do themselves." Another industry that is oligopolistic is the steel industry. The next article, which describes the pricing behavior in the steel industry, is part of a staff report of the Federal Trade Commission, published in 1977. It deals with changes in concentration in the industry, and the role of imports and foreign pricing, as well as the pricing behavior of American steel producers. Needless to say, both of these articles discuss and contain numerous controversial points.

The theory of monopolistic competition dates back to the early 1930's, when Edward Chamberlin and Joan Robinson published their famous books on the subject. In the next paper, Paul Samuelson attempts to put this theory into historical perspective. Samuelson's article is wide-ranging and witty, his conclusion being that, despite the shortcomings of the theory of monopolistic competition, "Chamberlin, Sraffa, Robinson, and their contemporaries have led economists into a new land from which their critics will never evict us."

The Costs of Automobile Model Changes since 1949

FRANKLIN M. FISHER, ZVI GRILICHES, AND
CARL KAYSEN

*Franklin M. Fisher is Professor of Economics at Massachusetts In-
stitute of Technology, Zvi Griliches is Professor of Economics at
Harvard University, and Carl Kaysen is Professor of Political
Science at the Massachusetts Institute of Technology. This paper
appeared in the* Journal of Political Economy, *1962.*

Aims of the Study

This paper reports estimates of the costs to the consumer of the changes
in private automobile specifications that took place during the 1950's.
Throughout we concentrate on the costs that would not have been
expended if cars with the 1949 model lengths, weights, horsepowers, transmissions, and other specifications had been produced in every year. As
there was technological change in the industry, we are thus assessing not
the expenditure that would have been saved had the 1949 models themselves been continued, but rather the expenditure that would have been
saved had such cars been continued but been built with the developing
technology.

We count as costs not only the costs to the automobile manufacturers
themselves of special retooling for new models, but also the direct costs of
producing larger, heavier, and more powerful cars, plus the costs of automatic transmissions, power brakes, and the like. Finally, we include the
secondary costs not paid out by the automobile companies but paid nevertheless by the consuming public in the form of increased expenditures
for gasoline necessitated by the "horsepower race."

This procedure clearly counts as "changes" *all* changes in those specifications which directly relate to the appearance or performance of the automobile. We do not count alterations in design of the car that do not *directly* change the package the consumer thinks he is buying. Thus, we assume that horsepower is a dimension of the car that enters directly into the utility function of the car-buyer, but that engine displacement is not. This is not to say that changes in engine displacement are not relevant; it is to say that such changes are relevant only insofar as they influence one of the performance or appearance variables under consideration.

We have mentioned a consumer's utility function. The use of this concept carries with it the clear implication that the changes we consider may all have been desired by the car-buying public. The question thus naturally arises: why not cost only those changes which were essentially "frills"? Why include in the estimates such things as automatic transmissions that were quite arguably improvements? The answer is that there is always a presumption of consumer sovereignty in the market economy and that it would be wholly arbitrary for us to say "this change was an improvement, and this was unnecessary" without detailed information on the utility functions of consumers. If tailfins were a frill, what about increased horsepowers? What about *extremely* increased horsepowers? Where there are costs, there are likely to be benefits as well, and, while the automobile market is not perfectly competitive, it seems likely to us that for most of the period in question the car manufacturers were giving the public what it wanted, save perhaps for overshooting in some respects.

We thus wish to avoid having this study taken as an indictment of the automobile companies. We are rather in the position of one who observes another man drinking various liquors. We do not blame the bartender for anything save that he occasionally gives the man more than he asks for of some expensive drink; nor do we question the man's right to drink; nor do we distinguish between "good" liquors and "bad." We do, however, present the bar bill. Since the argument is sometimes advanced that the resources spent on automobile model changes could be put to better use in the public sector, it is clearly worth investigating the order of magnitude of the resources involved. . . .

Total Costs and Conclusions

The various components of costs estimated in previous sections are brought together in Table I and graphed in Figure 1.

What can we say about these figures?

First, let us ask whether our estimates are likely to overstate or understate the costs to the economy of model changes since 1949. The answer seems to be that our estimates understate the cost. Aside from items previously discussed, we have not attempted to estimate such possibly important secondary costs as the added traffic and parking problems due to greater car length, or the costs in human life and property damage that

TABLE I. Total Estimated Costs of Model Changes Since 1949

(Millions of Current Dollars)

Year*	Total Direct Cost (1)	Retooling Costs (2)	Gasoline Costs (3)	Total Costs† (4)
1950	−27	20	13	6
1951	267	45	36	348
1952	460	82	102	644
1953	436	246	161	844
1954	1,072	264	240	1,576
1955	2,425	469	372	3,266
1956	3,040	336	590	3,966
1957	4,048	772	806	5,626
1958	2,354	626	949	3,924
1959	3,675	532	1,147	5,354
1960	3,456	537	1,346	5,339
1956–60 average	—	—	—	4,843
Present value in 1961 of future gasoline costs already committed‡	—	—	—	7,110

* We have combined model-year and calendar-year figures. The actual timing of the various elements of the total is slightly different.

† Total may not equal sum of components due to rounding.

‡ Due to lack of data at time of writing, we do not present complete estimates for 1961. Preliminary estimates using 1961 figures presented in earlier sections indicate that costs in that year (including gasoline costs) continue well above $5 billion.

may have resulted from higher horsepowers. Further, newer model cars (especially as automatic transmissions became more and more widespread) tended to have higher repair costs than would presumably have been the case with 1949 specifications. None of these items has been included in our estimates.

Moreover, while we [have] argued that the exclusion of design and research and development costs was in part an avoidance of double counting, it is clear that large elements of such design and research and development costs hardly contributed to the technological change involved in our estimates. One need only mention the expenditures that Ford must have incurred in the introduction of the short-lived Edsel to realize that we have failed to include some sizable items in our analysis.

Next, we have assumed throughout that the number of cars would have been unchanged had 1949 specifications been continued. This may or may not be a good assumption, but it is difficult to argue that *more* cars would have been sold. It follows that, if anything, our results fail to cost the extra cars that were in fact produced.

Finally, in choosing the 1949 model year as a standard for specifications, and in resting our analyses on the actual costs and gasoline consumption of domestically produced cars, we have not asked whether a more stringent

FIGURE 1.—TOTAL ESTIMATED COSTS OF MODEL
CHANGES SINCE 1949.

standard could not be derived from the experience of various European car producers. Our cost estimates rest on the historical experience of the domestic industry. Had we chosen a European small-car standard, estimated costs clearly would have been higher.

For all these reasons, it seems to us that our estimates must err considerably on the low side, even after the greatest benefit of the doubt is given to the stochastic nature of our estimates. The order of magnitude of the cost of model changes is clearly greater than that indicated in our figures. On the other hand, we have not attempted to assess monetary benefits. For example, the increases in horsepower and in the use of power steering and automatic transmissions may have led to an increase in the average speed of automobile travel of about 10 per cent. Assuming that in the base period the average speed was about 30 miles per hour, that approximately 9,000 miles were traveled by a car per year, and that on the average there were about 1.5 passengers per car, we get an estimate of 45 man-hours saved per new car year. Valuing these hours at $1.00 per hour leads us to a guess of $45 as the annual per car benefit from the time saving aspects of higher speeds. This is a large figure, of the same order of magnitude as our estimate of the costs of increased gasoline consumption per car, and would similarly persist throughout the life of the car. It is hard to think of many additional "benefits" of this sort. Their existence, however, is indicated by the apparent willingness of consumers to pay for at least some of these changes.

The costs of model changes since 1949 were thus a substantial part of expenditures on automobiles, especially in the last half of the 1950's, our estimates running about $5 billion a year. Were such costs worthwhile? It is difficult to say. There is a presumption that consumer purchases are worth the money paid, yet one might argue that the fact that our figures for the late 1950's (about $700 in the purchase price per car, or more than 25 per cent, and $40 per year in gasoline expenses) will probably seem surprisingly high to consumers is an indication that the costs in question were not fully understood by the consuming public.

On the other hand, one must not press such an argument too far. We have repeatedly stated that, in every model year considered, the *average* 1949 specifications lay inside the actual range of specifications encountered. The clear implication is that consumers could have bought such cars had they wished. Moreover, such items as automatic transmissions, power brakes, and power steering were separately available and had prices of their own. It is thus extremely hard to claim that at least some of the costs of model changes were not explicitly reflected in the prices set before consumers. Indeed, the only elements of such costs that were obviously not explicitly stated were the costs of retooling and advertising and (possibly) gasoline costs. Thus consumers knowingly purchased more costly cars than those with 1949 specifications, even in the presence of *some* explicit cost differential in favor of the latter.

All in all, save for the understatement of costs involved and the possibility that such costs were not fully understood by car-buyers, the model changes of the last decade seem to have been largely those desired by the consuming public, at least until the last years of the horsepower race. There are thus grounds for believing that car owners (at the time of purchase) thought model changes worth most of the cost. The general presumption of consumer sovereignty thus implies that these model changes *were* worth their cost. How heavily that presumption is to be weighted in the presence of some cost understatement or in the presence of advertising directed at the formation or changing of tastes is not a question that can be readily decided. Nor, indeed, is it obvious in retrospect that a referendum among the same car owners on the desirability of model changes would now reveal (or would have revealed in 1949) the same preferences for model change that seem to have been revealed in the historical market place.

It is thus not easy to decide whether the costs reported in this paper were worth incurring. Unlike some other examples of product change, the issue seems difficult enough to be worth raising. No one would deny that the shift from the horse and buggy to the automobile and the change from the kerosene lamp to the electric light were worth their respective costs. Such improvements were so large and obvious that the issue is easy to decide. Whether this is true of some or all of the changes from the 1949 automobile specifications seems to us to be at least an open question.

The Uses of Game Theory in Management Science

MARTIN SHUBIK

Martin Shubik is Professor of Industrial Administration at Yale University. This paper appeared in Management Science *in 1955.*

I. What Is Game Theory?

Game theory is a method for the study of decision-making in situations of conflict. It deals with problems in which the individual decision-maker is not in complete control of the factors influencing the outcome. A general whose forces face the enemy, an industrialist whose products must compete with those of another industrialist, a player in a poker game, duelists, politicians fighting for a nomination, bandits, and bridge players are all involved in struggles which we may classify as game situations.

The essence of a game problem is that it involves individuals with different goals or objectives whose fates are interlocked. There are many examples of decision-making where this is not so. An architect who has been allotted a specified sum of money in order to carry out a given building program or an engineer engaged in redesigning an industrial process in order to cut cost of production is not involved in a game situation. The engineer and architect face direct minimization or maximization problems in which they are in control of the relevant variables and do not have to contend with anti-engineers or anti-architects who try to destroy their work. The architect may try to maximize certain features of the quality and quantity of building that he can get done for the amount of money at his disposal. The engineer tries to minimize costs for the output of goods required. There may be forces which they do not control, such as the weather; but in most cases some physical law of prediction can be found for estimating the effect of outside influences.

Although it may appear that the Weather wants to rain every time we go on a picnic; unless our pessimism and religion are such, it is not always reasonable to assume that the Weather is a human or super-human agency whose desires are consciously opposed to ours. On the battlefield we may assume that the opposing general is consciously trying to thwart our purposes. The rival firm in business may be actively engaged in taking our customers away from us. In the first case we do not have a game situation; in the other cases we do.

The problem of game theory is more difficult than that of simple maximization. The individual has to work out how to achieve as much as possible, taking into account that there are others whose goals are different and whose actions have an effect on all. A decision-maker in a game faces a cross-purposes maximization problem. He must plan for an optimal return, taking into account the possible actions of his opponents.

II. The Elements of Game Theory

The elements which describe a poker game are the players, money, a pack of cards, a set of rules describing how the games are played, which hands win in any situation that can arise, and what information conditions there are at any state of the game. The elements which describe the situation of two firms in an advertising campaign are the two sets of individuals in control of the decisions of both firms, the amounts of money available, the information state, the market forecasts of the effect of different types of advertising, and the various laws and physical conditions which delineate which actions are legally or physically possible. The situation in which two opposing field commanders may find themselves can be described in terms of the number of men at their disposal, the amount of equipment, their information and intelligence service, the terrain of the battlefield, and weather conditions, and their valuation of the importance of various objectives.

All the above examples obviously have a common core. A game is described in terms of the players, or individual decision-makers, the rules of the game, the payoffs or outcomes of the game, the valuations that the players assign to various payoffs, the variables that each player controls, and the information conditions that exist during the game.

These elements, common to all situations of conflict, are the building blocks of game theory. They play the same role in this theory as do particles and forces in a theory of mechanics. The players and the rules of the game provide a description of the physical situation and the attempt of the players to maximize or to achieve some individual goal provides the motivation or force.

A *player* in a game is an autonomous decision-making unit. A player is not necessarily one person; it may be a group of individuals acting in an organization, a firm, or an army. The feature that distinguishes a player is that it has an objective in the game and operates under its own orders in an attempt to obtain its objective.

Each player is in control of some set of resources. In poker these resources are cards and money; in business corporations they are various assets; in war, men, armaments, and resources. These resources, together with the *rules of the game*, describing how they can be utilized, enable us to work out every alternative that is available to a player. In chess we start with a set of pieces placed on the board in a certain manner; the rules tell us how each piece can be moved. Given that information, we can work out every possible first move that is feasible in a chess game. As we know the initial distribution of the enemy's men and the rules concerning their movement, we can also work out every alternative that he can choose for his first move. In fact, it is theoretically possible to work out the whole game of chess without ever playing it because we could calculate every possible way of playing the game beforehand. Practically, the computation problem is too immense to carry out, but we can imagine a game of chess being played in which each player goes up to the referee, hands him a book containing his complete *strategy* for the game, and then leaves. The referee then works out the game according to these instructions. A strategy for a chess game is a complete set of instructions which states how a player will make every *move* until the end of the game, taking into account all information concerning the enemy's moves. A strategy in war or in business is the same. It is a general plan of action containing instructions as to what to do in every contingency. Thus, the commanding general may tell his subordinates how he wants the attack to begin, then he may tell them what he wants done after the first part of the attack, depending upon what the enemy's actions have been up to that point.

The outcome of a game will depend upon the strategies employed by every player. Let us call the set of possible strategies that the i-th player can use S_i. This is the set of every possible plan of action that the i-th player can have, taking into account his resources, what he can do with them, and also taking into account every possible act by his opponents. Suppose that the i-th player selects a strategy s_i out of all his available strategies S_i. The outcome of the game to him will depend upon what he did and what his opponents did. His *payoff* is a function of the strategies employed by all the players. We can denote the payoff to the i-th player by the *payoff function* $P_i(s_1, s_2, s_3, \ldots, s_n)$. The possible payoffs in chess are win, lose, or draw; in poker they are various sums of money; in business, profits and growth. In every case each player must have a method of valuation or a utility function which enables him to decide whether or not one payoff is better than another. In business and in games the payoff may be in money and there may be no difficulty in distinguishing between a payoff of $1,000 or one of $100. However, in many cases the payoff can be complicated by other factors. For instance, the payoff arising from following one line of action in battle may result in 1,000 enemy casualties at a cost of 200 men lost; another line of action could result in 5,090 enemy casualties at a cost of 2,000 men lost. It is difficult to say which is preferable.

In general, a player has a valuation scheme by which he can evaluate the worth of any set of *prospects* with which he is confronted. For instance, we assume that a player knows whether or not he would rather make a profit of $1 billion or $10 million. The game in which he is playing may be such that he can never obtain a profit of $1 billion. This amounts to saying that the *prospect* of a profit of $1 billion to a player is not a possible *payoff* in this game.

We may now reformulate the problem of game theory. An N-person game consists of a set of N players, each in control of a set of strategies S_i, $i = 1, 2, \ldots, N$; each player has a payoff function $P_i(s_1, s_2, \ldots, s_n)$ which tells him what prospect he receives as his payoff if each player has chosen his strategy s_i. The object of every player is to attempt to obtain a payoff which yields him a prospect of maximal value.

The technical terms described above give us a method whereby we can formalize any sort of situation involving conflict. For the general purposes of the game theorist this is very desirable. However, those of us interested in management science must ask: Can the general scheme be applied to areas of specific interest to us? It turns out that the simplest sort of game we can discuss has several useful applications.

III. The Two-Person Zero-Sum Game

The two-person zero-sum game is a game in which the amount that one player loses is precisely the amount that the other player wins. Two-person poker, matching pennies, and most other two-person games are of this variety. Competition between two large firms may not be of this type. A price war may damage both of them; collusion may help both of them. However, there are situations in business and war which can be approximated by a zero-sum model.

We can display the relevant features of a two-person zero-sum game by making use of a *payoff matrix*. A whimsical example serves as an illustration. A bootlegger has two possible routes over the border: one is down the highway and the other through the mountains. If he could go down the highway unhampered, he could take a fully loaded truck and make a tidy profit. If there is a light police guard on the main road, he can avoid arrest but will not be able to get his load through and will have to lose the expense of the journey. If there is a heavy police guard on the road, he will be caught and will be arrested and lose his load. The mountain road is such that he can only take a small load. If it is unguarded, he will have no trouble. If it is lightly or heavily guarded, then he will still get through but will have to bribe the peasants to get him by the police. The police have three alternatives: they can put a heavy guard on the main highway, leaving the mountain route unpatrolled; a heavy watch on the mountain route, leaving the highway unpatrolled; or to split their forces and put a light guard on both.

We can display the bootlegger's values for the six possibilities as follows:

	Guard only highway	Guard both routes lightly	Guard only mountain road
Highway	—5	—2	5
Mountain road	2	1	1

The police's preferences are diametrically opposed to those of the bootlegger; thus, their valuation for any outcome is the negative of his. We call this type of game *strictly determined* because, upon examination of the payoffs, there is a definite optimal choice for the bootlegger which is to take always the mountain road, while there is also an optimal choice for the police which is to guard both roads lightly. Both sides can work out that they can always enforce this compromise on the other but can enforce nothing better. The bootlegger knows that if he chose the highway, the police would try to minimize his gain and could guard it heavily; if he chose the mountains, the police would try to minimize his gain and guard the mountains; but even if they did so, the worst that could happen to him is that he would be able to get a small shipment in after having bribed the peasants. The police argue that if they decided to guard the highway only, the bootlegger would use the mountains; if they guarded the mountains only, he would use the highway; if they guarded both lightly, he would use the mountains but would only be able to get a small shipment by them, no matter what he did. We can illustrate these computations by adding a column giving the minimum of each row in the matrix, and a row giving the maximum of each column:

	Strategy of Police			
Strategy of Bootlegger	1	2	3	row minima
1	—5	—2	5	—5
2	2	1	1	①
column maxima	2	①	5	

The column represents the computation done by the bootlegger which tells him what the police could do to him if he chose strategy 1 or 2. The row represents the computation done by the police on the assumption that the bootlegger would try to maximize against their actions. By choosing the mountains, the bootlegger guarantees for himself the maximum of the minima. By putting a light guard on both roads the police guarantee that the bootlegger can never get more than the minimum of his maxima. But we observe that here the

$$Minimax. = Maximin. = 1$$

The bootlegger can guarantee a small trade for himself, and the police can guarantee that it stays a small trade, no matter what the other side does. A game which has the property that each side has a strategy which results in the maximin. being equal to the minimax. is said to possess a *saddlepoint*. An economic interpretation can be given to this value. When the bootlegger decides to retire, the market value of his trade should be that amount which yields an income of 1 in the same period as it takes per trip.

Not all games possess saddlepoints and, in those which do not, it is not possible for one side blithely to pick a strategy which guarantees very much. For instance, suppose that there had been a general overhauling of both bootlegging and police techniques. The bootlegger had obtained better trucks, and the police managed to stop bribery in the mountains. The effect of the better trucks is that the bootlegger can get by a light police guard at the cost of some breakage and personal strain. He now can carry a bigger load both on the highway and in the mountains. The effect of the police improvement is that a strong patrol could catch the bootlegger if he were in the mountains. The new payoff matrix is:

Strategy of Bootlegger	Strategy of Police 1	2	3	row minima
1	—5	3	6	—5
2	6	3	—5	—5
column maxima	6	3	6	

If the bootlegger persists in sticking to the mountain route, he will be lost; if he keeps to the highway, he will be lost. There is no longer a simple decision to which he can commit himself which will yield him a guaranteed profit, even though his techniques seem to have improved more than those of the police. He still has a profitable trade, however, and there is a way for him to guarantee himself an expected profit by following the actions and precepts of most decision-makers in competitive trades, and that is to take a calculated risk. His problem is to decide how to calculate the risk he should take. He is a prudent man and has no false illusions about the stupidity of the police. He knows, for instance, that the police will never split their forces because this would amount to handing him an income of 3 per period, no matter what happened. The bootlegger wishes to calculate what is the biggest expected income that he can guarantee for himself, regardless of what the police try to do. At the very worst, they could find out his plans and maximize their return, i.e., minimize his return given this information. If he definitely commits himself to one action and plays a *pure strategy*, he stands to lose 5. He may, however, decide not to commit himself directly but to choose between his two pure strategies according to some probability weighting. We call the use of such a device, which attaches probability weightings to a set of pure strategies, a *mixed strategy*. By using a mixed strategy he can guarantee an expected profit, even if the police were to find out his strategy.

Suppose he decides to take the highway with a probability of x_1 and the mountains with a probability of x_2, where $x_1 + x_2 = 1$. He wishes to pick these numbers in such a manner that he can make his expected return, which we call V, as large as possible under all circumstances. If the police employed their strategy 1 against him, his expected return would be: $-5x_1 + 6x_2$. This must be greater than, or equal to, V. Similarly, for the other strategies, we can write down an inequality. We find that we must solve the following set of equations and inequalities:

$$-5x_1 + 6x_2 \geqq V$$
$$3x_1 + 3x_2 \geqq V$$
$$6x_1 - 5x_2 \geqq V \quad \text{and} \quad x_1 + x_2 = 1.$$

Similarly, the police wish to make sure that no matter how shrewd the bootlegger becomes they will be able to restrict his expected gains as much as possible. In fact, they can make sure that he never can get more than an expectation of V. The police decide to guard the highway with probability y_1, split forces with probability y_2, and guard the mountains with probability y_3 where $y_1 + y_2 + y_3 = 1$. The police must solve the following set of equations and inequalities:

$$-5y_1 + 3y_2 + 6y_3 \leqq V$$
$$6y_1 + 3y_2 - 5y_3 \leqq V \quad \text{and} \quad y_1 + y_2 + y_3 = 1.$$

The general method for the solution of such systems can be found in McKinsey's book;[1] we present a graphical method for this 2 x 3 game.

If the first player uses the probabilities of x_1 and $1 - x_1$ and if the second player uses his first pure strategy, then the expected payoff for the first player is $-5x_1 + 6(1 - x_1) = 6 - 11x_1$; similarly, we get two other expressions if the second player uses his second or third pure strategies. We now draw a diagram with the three lines: $v = 6 - 11x_1$; $v = 3$; and $v = 11x_1 - 5$ represented over the interval $(0, 1)$. For any x_1 chosen by the bootlegger he can guarantee for himself the minimum value of the three lines at x_1; thus, we see here that the optimal choice for x_1 is ½. Hence, his mixed strategy uses each of his pure strategies with probability of ½ and can be expressed as $(½, ½)$. It is clear that the police will never use their second strategy; thus, we need only investigate the probability

[1] McKinsey, J. C. C., *Introduction to the Theory of Games*, RAND Corporation, Santa Monica, 1952, Chapters 2 and 3.

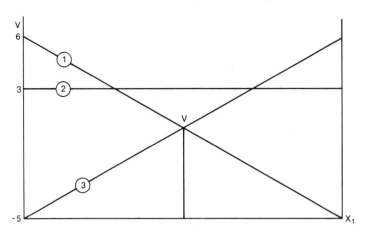

Graph I

weighting of the police to guard the highway or the mountain road. Their optimal strategy is ($\frac{1}{2}$, 0, $\frac{1}{2}$). Using these strategies, we can see that the value of the game is $V = \frac{1}{2}$. Even with better equipment, his business is now worth less than before.

We note that the use of probability in a mixed strategy is a *strategic* use. Any mixture other than an optimal one leaves the player open to damage that he could have avoided, regardless of his opponent's actions.

IV. Applications of Two-Person Zero-Sum Games

1. BUSINESS PROBLEMS

The type of problem to which this theory has a direct application is one which has some of the aspects of a duel. A duel has the property that the goals of the opponents are diametrically opposed. In any market in which the size of the demand is more or less fixed by the government or by habits, the extra customers that one firm can attract must have been lost by another firm. The firms are in pure opposition in such a situation. What one gains, the other loses. An advertising campaign in a market for detergents may be of this nature. A highly simplified example is given below. Charnes and Cooper have written a more detailed paper on this topic.[2]

1a) The Advertising Campaign. Two firms, A and B, each have a million dollars to spend on advertising their products in a certain market area. They can use the media of radio, television, newspapers, magazines, and billboards. For simplicity, we will group these five alternatives into radio,

[2] Charnes, A., and Cooper, W. W., "An Example of Constrained Games in Industrial Economics" (abstract), *Econometrica*, 22, October 1954, p. 526.

television, and printed media. The marketing research sections of each firm work out the expected effect of any contingency. We will discuss the decision-making at firm A only. A payoff matrix of 4 x 4 is drawn up. This contains information on the 16 contingencies that might arise if either firm spent all its money advertising solely by means of radio, television, or printed media, or decided to save the million dollars and not advertise at all. Each entry in the payoff matrix represents the amount of extra revenue above cost estimated under these circumstances (in millions of dollars).

	Radio	Television	Printed Media	No Advertising
Radio	0	− .5	0	2.5
Television	2	0	1.5	5
Printed Media	1	− .5	0	3.5
No Advertising	−2	−4	−3	0

We can see immediately that in this case the alternative of no advertising can be rejected. Any pure strategy, which can be rejected by comparing it with the other pure strategies and finding that there are others which are always better under every circumstance, is a *dominated* strategy and will not enter into a solution. In this simple example, where we have assumed that the firms must put all their money into one advertising medium, we can see by inspection that all the other strategies are dominated by television. This game has a saddlepoint at which both firms put their money into television advertising with the net result that they make the same as they would if neither advertised, but neither can risk not advertising.

A more complicated and slightly more realistic example is obtained if we list a series of advertising campaigns involving different integrated programs using more than one medium. Consider each firm to have the choice of three types of campaigns:

	Program 1	Program 2	Program 3
Program 1	2	4	−2
Program 2	4	2	−2
Program 3	−2	−2	3

The problem for firm A is to find three numbers, x_1, x_2, x_3, such that

$$2x_1 + 4x_2 - 2x_3 \geqq V$$
$$4x_1 + 2x_2 - 2x_3 \geqq V$$
$$-2x_1 - 2x_2 + 3x_3 \geqq V$$

where the

$$x_i \geqq 0 \quad \text{and} \quad x_1 + x_2 + x_3 = 1$$

The example above has a solution of $x_1 = \frac{1}{4}$, $x_2 = \frac{1}{4}$ $x_3 = \frac{1}{2}$, and $V = \frac{1}{2}$. Two interpretations can be given to the x_i. They can be regarded as probabilities which should be attached to the decision to adopt any specific program. Or, if it is possible to spend varying sums on the programs (with approximately constant returns), then the x_i give information as to how firm A should split up its advertising budget between the three different programs. It should spend $250,000 on each of programs 1 and 2 and $500,000 on program 3.

The more satisfactory way to treat the advertising problem is as one of a series of games being played every period. Charnes and Cooper suggest this approach in their analysis of Constrained Games in their article noted above.

1b) A Distribution Problem. Competition between two refineries sharing a market with relatively fixed demand has been set up and treated as a two-person zero-sum game by G. H. Symonds in his examination of game theory uses in problems of petroleum refining.[3]

2. MILITARY PROBLEMS

Considerable work has been done in the application of the game theory of "duels" to problems of weapons evaluation for tactical weapons. These applications are, for the most part, of more interest to those whose scope is confined to operations research than to management science. Much of the work in this area is classified. Search theory has, however, been applied to marketing.

3. PRODUCTION PROBLEMS INDIRECTLY USING GAME THEORY

3a) Linear Programming. Gale, Kuhn, and Tucker[4] have discussed the mathematical analogy that exists between the solution of a linear program and the solution of a two-person zero-sum game. It is always possible to formulate a two-person zero-sum game from a linear program in such a manner that the solution of this game amounts to a solution of the linear program.

3b) The Optimal Assignment Problem. Suppose that we have n people available and n jobs to be filled. Suppose further that we have an evaluation a_{ij} which tells us the worth of the i-th person doing the j-th job.

[3] Symonds, G. H., "Applications to Industrial Problems, Including Scheduling and Technological Research" (abstract), *Econometrica*, 22, October 1954, p. 526.
[4] Gale, D., Kuhn, H. W., and Tucker, A. W., "Linear Programming and the Theory of Games," in Koopmans, T. C., ed., *Activity Analysis of Production and Allocation*, John Wiley and Sons, Inc., New York, 1951.

The optimal assignment problem concerns itself with the distribution of personnel in a maximal manner. There is a related two-person zero-sum game whose solution gives us a solution of this problem. The difficulty in the application of this comes in the evaluation of the suitability of the attributes of various individuals in the performance of different tasks; although use has been made of this method by the Army.

3c) Statistical Decision. Situations in which sampling or gathering extra information costs money, yet cuts down on the possibility of making a wrong decision which may, in itself, be very costly, lead to the formulation of statistical games. In essence, the problem amounts to working out how much one should be willing to pay for information, the value of which will not be known until it is obtained. An example of importance to industry is the design of a decision process to be followed in sequential sampling of a batch of goods where the cost of sampling is high and the loss incurred by sending out a batch with above a certain number of defective items is great.

V. *Non-Zero-Sum Games*

Many of the more interesting problems of competition are not zero-sum. The goals of a group of large firms in a market are not necessarily diametrically opposed. There may be "room for all" if instead of fighting among themselves they follow a policy of live and let live. A period of cut-throat competition might hurt all of them. When pure opposition of all interests is no longer the case, the computations of the two-person zero-sum game theory no longer apply. No completely satisfactory theory for general N-person games exists at this time. However, the two theories of von Neumann and Morgenstern[5] and of Nash[6] provide much insight into, and useful models of, many situations. It is possible to set up simplified models of some non-zero-sum game situations which merit consideration for application.

1. BUSINESS PROBLEMS

1a) Contract Bidding. A firm wishes to bid on some government contracts. It has a certain amount of information concerning the previous behavior of its competitors. Its productive capacity is limited in such a manner that it cannot possibly fulfill orders for more than 25 per cent of the contracts. This N-person non-zero-sum bidding game can be approxi-

[5] von Neumann, J., and Morgenstern, O., *Theory of Games and Economic Behavior*, Princeton: Princeton University Press, 1944, Chapter VI.
[6] Nash, J. F., "Non-Cooperative Games," *Annals of Mathematics*, LIV, September 1951, pp. 286–295.

mated by a maximization problem which involves picking bids in such a manner that the firm expects to lose 75 per cent of its bids by having named too high a price. This is an example in which it may very easily be to the advantage of the firm involved to go actually to the trouble of randomizing to decide upon certain prices.

1b) The Cost of Price Wars. A very important feature of business life which has not received very much stress in economic theory, as it is taught in most institutions, concerns the asset position of a firm and its ability to weather bad times or long fights in its industry. Given information on the asset position of a firm and its major competitors, the expected state of demand for its products, and certain other economic data, it is possible to make some basic computations concerning the advisability and profitability of price wars and the introduction of new lines of goods. The major drawback to this work is that few firms have enough information available to make many involved calculations worthwhile at this time.

1c) Checkerboard Land Buying. A problem amenable to a certain amount of game analysis may arise when a mining company discovers a tract of land which has promising mineral deposits. The company knows more or less what the land contains and decides that it does not want to develop it immediately. It knows that if it does not buy it, then, sooner or later, the knowledge will leak out and competitors will buy the land. The cost of carrying the land when not using it for anything may involve a tying up of considerable capital. The company needs to work out a maximal strategy of "checkerboard buying" of the land in such a manner that it cuts down on the financing costs by leaving strips unbought, but these strips are unworkable by themselves. It is possible that small competitors step in, buy the strips, and then try to hold up the company when it is ready to develop the land. The company must design its buying strategy in such a manner as to make the holding of these marginal strips as unprofitable as possible to any newcomer. Under certain circumstances it is easy to see that it may pay the company to incur the carrying charges and purchase the whole tract of land. However, if its competitors are financially weak, then they may not be in a position to tie up capital while waiting for the first company to buy them out.

VI. *Topics in Social Theory and Organization Theory*

Almost everything that has been discussed in this article so far has referred to situations involving competition and individualistic struggle. Many of the interesting problems of game theory are concerned with the nature of cooperation between competitors whose aims are not diametrically opposed. The von Neumann and Morgenstern definition of the solution of a game in which cooperation takes place[7] is a first attempt to arrive

[7] von Neumann, J., and Morgenstern, O., *op. cit.*

at a comprehensive theory of coalition formation in society. In an article of this length, space does not permit a detailed discussion of the concepts of cooperative games. However, several problems and areas of application can be noted without having to go into a detailed technical discussion.

1. LAWS CONCERNING COMPETITION

Words such as competition, collusion, implicit collusion, cooperation, "fair trade," and unfair practices have an important role in much of the legislation dealing with the bounds placed upon the actions of individual enterprises in an enterprise economy. The words above are used in an attempt to define a set of concepts which are extremely hard to define, but the concepts involved happen to be at the very basis of game theory. It has become increasingly evident in the past two decades that the antitrust and cartel laws are in need of a reconsideration which must take into account the advances in economic theory. Although work in this application of game theory is only in its infancy, it may well become an area of application of primary importance to industry.

2. DESIGN OF COMMITTEES AND VOTING POWER

It is well known that when an individual is given more than one vote on a committee his power does not go up in direct proportion to the number of votes he controls. In most cases it increases faster. Thus, in corporation voting, an individual who controls half of the stock plus one, has complete power over the corporation. The study of a certain set of games known as "Simple Games" has enabled Shapley[8] to construct an *a priori* index which measures the amount of power given to an individual as a function of the number of votes he controls. This index can be applied to problems in the design of voting structure in committees.

A simple example evaluates the power of a man who has two votes in a committee where three others have one vote each. We can represent this committee symbolically by (2, 1, 1, 1). The index is computed by finding out how many times out of all possible orders of voting the man with two votes could be vital to the securing of a majority. We call a man pivotal if the addition of his votes to a group converts it from a losing coalition into a winning coalition. We give a man credit of 1 whenever he is pivotal. Below we demonstrate the number of times the man with two votes is pivotal. In the arrangements below a dot above the number indicates that that man is pivotal.

There are 6 arrangements of the form: 1, $\dot{2}$, 1, 1

There are 6 arrangements of the form: 1, 1, $\dot{2}$, 1

[8] Shapley, L. S., "A Value for N-Person Games," in Kuhn, H. W., and Tucker, A. W., eds., *Contributions to the Theory of Games*, Vol. II, Princeton: Princeton University Press, 1952, pp. 307–318.

There are 6 arrangements of the form: 2, İ, 1, 1
There are 6 arrangements of the form: 1, 1, İ, 2

We see that there are 24 possible voting line-ups and the man with two votes is pivotal in 12 of them. Although he has only 2/5ths of the votes, a reasonable index of his power is ½.

The above index is constructed so that all possible coalitions have the same chance of being formed. This is usually not the case. Special features such as greater chances for certain types of coalitions and special quorum rules must be introduced in the application of this method to actual committee design.

3. DESIGN OF SELF-POLICING SYSTEMS

There is an old story about two individuals who argued about how to divide a fish between them. A passing lawyer was asked to settle the dispute. He did so by awarding the head to one, the tail to the other, while he took the body of the fish as his fee. This may be a slander on the legal profession, but it illustrates a basic problem faced in organizations. Can a mechanism be designed that will guarantee that certain aims can be achieved without destroying the very goals for which it was designed? A company may decide to put in a secret detective force in order to cut down on losses due to theft and carelessness. The net result may be that the cost of the service is greater than the amount of theft prevented and that production drops due to a lowering of the morale among the workers. As soon as a tourist guide or hotel listing becomes so well known that it has a large influence on many tourists, a problem arises concerning its susceptibility to deals and bribes from the places it lists. If an enforcement agency consists of individuals whose desires are not necessarily coincident with the perceived or defined desires of the organization which uses the agency, an evaluation of how the difference in goals will affect the operation of the agency must be made. It may pay to hire a weak and honest night-watchman to guard a warehouse more than it would pay to hire a strong crook; although technically the latter could be a better watchman. Who or what keeps the referee, the watchman, the police force, the judge, or the impartial expert honest is always a part of the problem in the design of a self-policing organization.

The type of cooperative game situation in which there is a self-policing—hence, stable—mechanism is one in which everyone can see that any betrayal will do more harm to the betrayer than it will do him good. For instance, if each firm in a cartel is forced to put a very considerable amount of gold into a common fund to protect against doublecross, then the motivation for doublecrossing will be weakened considerably. It is obvious that in our society the phenomenon of doublecrossing or betraying is of great complexity and often involves the paying of psychic or sociological rather than monetary penalties when an individual acts against his conditioning.

4. THE THEORY OF TEAMS

An area of research closely related to game theory and information theory deals with the formalization of the basic concepts of a team or organization. Such a study involves setting up a structure which delineates the group or organizational goals, the individual goals, the communication and action system, and the environment. If the group goals coincide identically with the individual goals, then the game aspects of the problem need not be considered. However, this is not usually the case. This subject is possibly one of the most important to those interested in sociology, economic organization, and management science, and is the least developed, although recently there has been much active research going on as can be seen from the works of Marschak, Radner, and Simon.[9, 10, 11]

5. SMALL GROUP INTERACTION AND EXPERIMENTAL GAMES

The growth of game theory, information theory, and the study of communication networks has stimulated several groups of researchers to construct games and experiment with them in order to isolate and study certain aspects of group behavior. Members of the RAND Corporation have carried out several experimental studies[12] along these lines. One of the major drawbacks to work in the behavioral sciences has been the inability to perform experiments. Although the scope is somewhat restricted, direct experimentation with games played by small groups offers a new avenue of research.

VII. Conclusions: Problems and Prospects in the Use of Game Theory Methods in Management Science

Since the war, there has been a great growth in interest in the theory of organization. The size of many modern organizations has brought to the surface problems of communication and decision-making of a very different

---

[9] Marschak, J., "Elements for a Theory of Teams," *Management Science*, I, January 1955, pp. 127–137.

[10] Marschak, J., and Radner, R., "The Firm as a Team," *Cowles Commission Discussion Paper* Economics 2093 (hectographed).

[11] Simon, H., "Two Papers on Organization Problems and Economic Theory," *Cowles Commission Papers*, No. 47, 1952.

[12] Flood, M. M., "On Game-Learning Theory and Some Decision-Making Experiments," in Thrall, R. M., Coombs, C. H., and Davis, R. L., eds., *Decision Processes*, New York: John Wiley and Sons, Inc., 1954, pp. 139–157.

nature to those confronted by smaller groups. A large organization appears to be both quantitatively and qualitatively different from a small one. Information flows and decisions that could be comfortably handled by one "jack-of-all-trades" executive in a small organization or in a dictatorial system, where wastage may be no problem, must be broken down and handled by many specialists. In many cases they may never reach the one-man decision level but are finally acted upon by groups. The need to understand these vital processes of decision-making has impelled us to lay emphasis upon the gathering and study of information, the evaluation of goals, and the role of the individual decision-maker.

The new methods of game theory appear to provide an important approach to many of the problems of decision-making. In this survey of areas of application of game theory some problems which have been completely formulated, solved, and are of immediate practical value have been discussed in Sections IV and V. However, for those interested in the deeper and more important long-range problems which confront the researcher in the behavioral sciences, Section VI indicates where some of the work of yesterday has taken place and where much of the work of tomorrow must lie.

Collusion Among Electrical Equipment Manufacturers

WALL STREET JOURNAL

The following article, from the Wall Street Journal *of January 10 and 12, 1962, is an interesting case study of collusion in the electrical equipment industry.*

The term "organization man" may well be looked on with suspicion as a too simple, too pat summation of a personality that is complex as any. But the term is meaningful. And while Judge Ganey and some of the attorneys involved in the Government's criminal antitrust cases against various members of the electrical equipment industry sought to dodge the word, they found it a useful one in referring to some individual defendants.

Here were men of substance in their communities and in the business world who were pleading guilty or "no contest" to serious charges of conspiracy. From the court record and from some of the pleas it can hardly be argued that most of them did not know what they were doing. Yet the overwhelming impression is that these men hardly fit the stereotype of law evaders. Almost as pervasive as the almost undisputed evidence of wrong-doing was the question of why. And the simplest, if not the complete, answer goes back to the organization man.

It would seem that in these cases the term not only concerned solid and respectable businessmen, however, but also the whole mores and what was taken for the mores of an entire industry. One charge sometimes leveled against the organization man is that he is strong on conformity. If, in the case of the individuals in the electrical cases, what was to be conformed to was a large-scale system of law evasion, they evidently conformed to that too.

Potentials for Trouble. Certainly the climate in which the individuals and companies in the heavy electrical equipment industry operated was

306

loaded with potentials for trouble, and these may well have been the genesis of the legal difficulties which came to afflict a large segment.

The industry is a relatively compact one. Its members range from very large enterprises to relatively small ones. For example, among those indicted in the case were General Electric with $4 billion annual sales and Joslyn Manufacturing and Supply Co. of Chicago with annual sales of less than $2 million and only 45 production employees.

The industry is tightly-knit with many friendships among executives of competing firms; indeed, officials of smaller firms sometimes are former General Electric or Westinghouse Electric executives. The men involved oftentimes had similar educational backgrounds also—college graduates in engineering with a rise through technical ranks into the world of sales. There sometimes existed on the part of the men with the bigger companies an almost protective, big brother attitude toward the smaller companies; this was reciprocated.

And the friendships were not only professional but often quite personal. Trade association meetings fostered these. It was perhaps easy in the camaraderie of these meetings at upper bracket hotels, amid speeches typical of any association lauding the industry's members and "mission," to draw even closer than business and background indicated. It was perhaps easy, with wives and children present, and acquainted from past conventions, to drift into the belief that nothing could be very wrong in such an atmosphere.

Darkening Grays. Indeed, many of the meetings took place at the conventions of the National Electrical Manufacturers Association and other trade groups. Rather typically, after a conventional and perfectly lawful meeting of some kind, certain members would adjourn for a rump session and a few drinks in someone's suite. It seemed natural enough that mutual business problems would be discussed—specifications, for example—and like as not prices would come up. In time it was easy enough to drift from general talk about prices into what should be done about them—and finally into separate meetings to fix them for everyone's mutual benefit.

Thus purely legal gatherings might have drifted into ones with increasingly dark shades of gray and finally into ones that were pretty black; more than one moralist has noted that it isn't the blacks and whites of situations that get initially law-abiding citizens into trouble; rather it is a progressive inability to distinguish between shades of gray.

It was especially easy in this industry to get into price discussions.

The economic position of the various companies has often been one of feast or famine—large orders or none at all for the gigantic pieces of equipment manufactured. Widespread overcapacity after World War II brought intermittent price warring. In 1955, for example, there occurred a price war, known throughout the industry as the "white sale," which saw some prices cut as much as 50% Profit losses resulted and in some cases red ink. Again in 1957 there was a lesser wave of competitive cutting. At least during the "white sale" General Electric and Westinghouse wound up with most of the business. By reports then current some smaller companies were seeking Government intervention under the Sherman Act's anti-monopoly provisions.

The case has a number of ironic aspects but one of the great ones is that men in the large companies believed they had to protect the position of the smaller companies or run the risk of antitrust prosecution. Another is that much of the overcapacity underlying the "need" to fix prices was Government spurred. Fast tax write-offs, growing out of two wars in two decades, brought the greater capacity for defense that the Government wanted, but they also left the manufacturers with an embarrassing amount of plant.

As a result of this industry makeup, the friendships, and the price-capacity situation, there evidently developed in wide segments the philosophy that collusive activity was ethical, illegal though it might be.

Perhaps an extreme exponent of this view, though expressing a widespread one, is F. F. Loock, president, general manager, and sales manager of Allen-Bradley Co. of Milwaukee, who has pleaded guilty.

Looking back on what happened, he says: "No one attending the gatherings [in the electrical controls industry] was so stupid he didn't know [the meetings] were in violation of the law. But it is the only way a business can be run. It is free enterprise."

Price fixing is not usually associated with the idea of free enterprise, with the idea that the market mechanism is to be the ultimate controlling factor, and that this mechanism must remain unimpaired either by individuals or governments. But there is a rationale for the cartel system which permits the general type of collusive activity the electrical men were engaged in. According to it, markets are divided and prices fixed so everyone involved can "get along." Even the consumer is supposed to benefit because stable markets aid stable production and supposedly costs can thus be stabilized.

"*Protection Against Buyers.*" Price competition is anathema to such a setup. Mr. Loock says one reason for the gatherings in his industry was "we also need protection against buyers" and the "illegal meetings gave us such protection."

Elaborating on the need for "protection," Mr. Loock cites one instance in which the purchasing agent of a major Detroit manufacturer told the electrical manufacturer another one had offered a lower price. "By discussing the matter, which was not true, among ourselves, we were able to iron out the problem." He concludes: "I believe that in an industry where money is necessary to continue research and development of products we should have some protection against the crookedness of some buyers."

There was also a feeling in the industry that the antitrust laws were unjust. With a rationale developed of friendly live and let live among competitors, laws designed to force competition seemed "Government interference." The question was also asked in the industry: If such getting together was all right under the old N.R.A. why isn't it all right now? Of course the N.R.A. of the 1930's was declared unconstitutional by the Supreme Court, but some say the industry's philosophy of "getting together" has roots in that era.

But if illegal "stabilization" was an industry way of life, it should not be assumed that relations were continually rosy among competitors, or that all authority in the industry was bent on collusive activity.

Getting together to fix prices did not alter the basically competitive situation prevailing in the industry's markets. Indeed, it often seems some attendance at the collusive meetings was with tongue in cheek as to stabilizing prices, with a real reason of finding out what the rest of the industry was up to in order to get the jump in the next price cutting wave. Too, some of the conspirators pretty much inherited their roles from predecessors, older men who may have felt more of a tug from the industry's "way of life" than they did. In fact there was personal dislike among some of the individual conspirators; perhaps an individual who did not like himself for conspiring had little respect for others also so engaged. . . .

It is plain that many of the individuals involved in the conspiracy were under, or felt they were under, heavy pressure to produce and basically believed their meetings, however clandestine, were ethically justifiable.

An attorney for one company sums it up: "Most of the businessmen and attorneys involved don't think there's a moral issue. This isn't a blind spot in American business. These people honestly think they were getting a fair profit and weren't hurting their customers. An unenforced law isn't respected. The Government should have given the companies a warning before cracking down. Now either the companies will conform to the law or the law will be changed."

A look at some individual stories, and at some of these meetings, illustrates the pressures and difficulties—the law aside—that these organization men ran into.

The Problems of Price Fixing. For a number of years various electrical companies and individuals successfully evaded the antitrust laws. They periodically met to fix prices, divide up markets, and otherwise cartelize their industry.

But examination of court records of the case indicates the conspiracy was not a very successful one. Prices were not fixed except temporarily—some one of the conspirators was forever evading the intent of conspiracy.

Markets were divided somewhat more successfully, but here again the planners of the market were always running afoul of new circumstances which did not fit into the master plan. Certainly the attempt to evade the give and take of the market place meant for the people and companies involved a good deal of unforeseen trouble—the law aside. Red tape flourished; bureaucracy, unofficial and perhaps illegal though it may have been, grew apace. The need for conspiratorial gatherings mounted, all as man-made rules were substituted for competition.

For example, the circuit breaker conspiracy involving General Electric, Westinghouse, Allis-Chalmers, and Federal Pacific ran into this problem in 1958—what to do about the entrance onto the scene of a new company? While a new competitor is never an easy matter for an individual company, it was also quite complex for the conspirators.

What happened was that I-T-E Circuit Breaker Co., a factor in other aspects of the electrical equipment business, in 1958 bought out a small company and wanted to enter the circuit breaker field, where prices were being fixed and markets allotted on a percentage basis.

"Now, room had to be made for I-T-E," Antitrust Chief Bicks noted in remarks at the arraignment of the defendants. "So a series of meetings began in January of 1958, at which I-T-E indicated its desire for some business. I-T-E had bought a company; it wanted to get into the business.

"The knowledge by I-T-E that it was entering into a preexisting conspiracy is clear beyond doubt from the pattern of events in early 1958. I-T-E began meeting with the four conspirators that had been going, going more or less smoothly, it's true, with greater or less success, with greater or less mutual confidence that each of the conspirators was living up to his part of the deal, but, nonetheless, one constant conspiracy I-T-E sought to get in."

Over-all Policy. "In early 1958 I-T-E secured an agreement as to the over-all pricing policy leaving the allocation aside.

"The nature of that agreement arrived at in early 1958 at a series of meetings was roughly this, that general pricing would be tied to G.E.'s book price, that I-T-E in the southern part of California would be allowed 15% off, that I-T-E nationally would be allowed 5% off . . . Remaining to be finalized was I-T-E's allocation share of the sealed bid business. This was discussed . . . I-T-E was cut in for a share of 4% following a series of conferences, and so from 1958 on everybody cut back a bit except Federal Pacific . . .

"The three big companies, G.E., Westinghouse, Allis-Chalmers . . . cut down their percentage. Federal Pacific came up from 10 to 15. I-T-E was cut in for 4. That was roughly the pattern of the conspiracy that kept on until the date of the indictment."

I-T-E, seeking to plead no contest in this case, said among other things that it was charged with being only a small factor in the industry for a short period of time. It has told its men to stay away from competitors, that if they're caught in such activities again they'll be fired.

It was one thing, as in the circuit breaker case, to agree that a certain company would get a specific piece of sealed-bid business. It was something else again to see that the designated company actually got the job. Here, again according to Mr. Bicks' statement to the court, is how that worked, amid burgeoning red tape.

"At a working level meeting where a particular big job was up for discussion the percentages initially would be reviewed in light of what was known as the ledger list, which had on it recent sealed-bid jobs given to the other defendants. In light of that ledger list it was decided which of the companies, to keep the percentages constant, would get the job. Now if that company was prepared to say the price at which it was going to bid, then the other companies could discuss among themselves what they would bid, add on for accessories, to make sure to give . . . the company . . . whose turn it was to get the job, the best shot at it."

Numbers Code. "If the company whose job the particular rigged job was supposed to be did not know the price, there would be later communication, either by phone to homes with just the first names used, or by letter to homes with just first names of senders, with no return address, and this wonderful code. . . . The numbers were 1, General Electric; 2, Westinghouse; 3, Allis-Chalmers; and 7, Federal Pacific. What happened to 4 or 5 and 6 until I-T-E came in remains a mystery."

One of the great ironies of the conspiracies was that no matter how hard the participants schemed, no matter how friendly their meetings and communications might be, there was an innate tendency to compete. Someone was always violating the agreements to get more business and this continually called for new illegal plans. For example, price-cutting in sales of power switching equipment to Government agencies was getting out of hand in late 1958. This led to the "quadrant" system of dividing markets.

"So," declared Baddia Rashid, chief of the trial section of the antitrust division, "at a meeting in November of 1958 at Philadelphia . . . they decided that the best way to handle the sealed-bid market was to allocate the business; however, since there were sixteen companies involved in this particular conspiracy it would have been difficult to try to allocate the business as in other cases on a percentage basis, and therefore it was decided that it would be best to divide the country into four separate geographical areas which were called quadrants—the northwest quadrant, the southwest quadrant, the southeast quadrant, and the northeast quadrant.

"Four companies were assigned to participate in each quadrant, and one of the company representatives in that quadrant was designated as a secretary for the purpose of handling the allocation within the particular quadrant. [For example,] in the northeast quadrant . . . meetings were held and it was decided that the business within that quadrant would be allocated in an alphabetical rotation. . . ."

This plan did not work to everyone's satisfaction, but rather than fall back on the give and take of the market place which the law requires, the conspirators formulated another plan.

"In September of 1959, however, there were some complaints that had arisen because some companies felt they were not getting a sufficient share of the business . . . it appeared that certain of the quadrants were obtaining more sealed-bid business than other quadrants. Therefore, they held a meeting in Pittsburgh ... in September, 1959 ... and they discussed this situation. . . . After some discussion it was finally decided that perhaps the best way to do it would be to go back to a national allocation scheme at which every company would be allotted a certain percentage of the business. They all agreed to that plan and each company was then asked to indicate what percentage of the sealed-bid market it felt it should obtain. . . . An individual from one of the . . . companies was designated to act as secretary. . . ."

But the basic problem, in this industry where price fluctuations were sometimes drastic, was "stabilizing" prices and efforts to bring this about spawned many a difficulty. . . . No matter how diligently plans and schemes were laid, they somehow could not defeat the basic economic factors, which insisted on responding to the inherent forces of the free market.

Quinine: An International Cartel

SENATE SUBCOMMITTEE ON ANTITRUST AND MONOPOLY

The following article is taken from testimony by John Blair before the Senate Subcommittee on Antitrust and Monopoly in 1967.

Beginning in November 1959 all of the world's producers of quinine, with the sole exception of the Bandoeng factory of the Indonesian Government, entered into a series of restrictive agreements designed to control prices, distribution, and production in every aspect of the quinine industry. A key objective was the elimination of competition among the various producers in securing the U.S. stockpile. This grouping of producers, referred to by its members as a "convention," had been preceded by an earlier cartel agreement between the two largest producers, the Dutch firm, N.V. Nederlandsche Combinatie voor Chemische Industrie (referred to as "Nedchem" or "Combinatie") and the German company, C. F. Boehringer & Soehne G. m. b. H. (referred to as "Boehringer" or "Waldhof"). When the Dutch brought the "convention" to an end in November 1962, the earlier cartel agreement appears to have continued in effect.

This is only the latest chapter in a history of cartel control of quinine and quinidine prices which extends over a period of three-quarters of a century. The first agreement was recorded in 1892 between Dutch and German quinine processors. In 1913 a full-fledged cartel was organized by agreement between the European quinine manufacturers and producers of Javanese bark, largely at the instigation of the Netherlands Indies Government. A secretariat, the Kina Bureau, was established at Amsterdam to implement the agreement. The Kina Bureau had "full power to allot supplies of cinchona bark and fix prices of quinine in all the markets of the world."

At a series of meetings starting late in 1959 a new "convention" was

313

formed which wove a web of restrictions, made up of four different agreements:

1. a stockpile agreement,
2. an export agreement,
3. a gentlemen's agreement, and
4. a barkpool agreement.

The first provided that the Dutch member, Nedchem, would be the sole bidder on behalf of the group for the U.S. stockpile, which would then be shared among them on a pro rata basis in terms of previously established quotas. The second fixed prices and imposed other restraints in world markets outside the U.S. and the countries of the European Economic Community (Germany, Holland, France, Belgium, and Italy). The third, which applied to countries within the EEC as well as the United Kingdom, fixed prices, reserved for each of the producers their home markets (except Great Britain), fixed sales quotas for each member, established a regularized system by which those who undersold their quotas would receive adjustments from those who had oversold, designated certain favored buyers to receive specified rebates or discounts, limited the right to manufacture quinidine to the Dutch and German producers, put into effect a method of eliminating competition (though not its appearance) on government bids, and imposed a variety of other restrictions. Finally, the barkpool agreement, which represented an effort to hold the price for the raw material, set selling prices for cinchona bark and made some efforts toward pooling purchases. . . .

The "convention" held a series of meetings beginning on December 2, 1959 and ending at Brussels in October 1962. Detailed minutes of these meetings were kept and circularized to the various members, one of whom was the British concern, Carnegies of Welwyn Limited. In recent months the Subcommittee learned that during the life of the "convention" this firm was a wholly-owned subsidiary of Rexall Drug Company Limited of Great Britain, which in turn is a wholly-owned subsidiary of Rexall Drug and Chemical Company of the United States. The minutes of these meetings, as well as related correspondence and memorandums, were produced pursuant to a subpoena served on the U.S. parent corporation.

To facilitate understanding, there is presented below the names of the participating companies and of their officials who customarily attended the meetings.

England:	Rexall Drug Co. Ltd.	Mr. J. R. Lumley
	Carnegies of Welwyn Ltd.	Mr. F. Chapman
	Lake & Cruickshank Ltd.	Mr. G. M. Cruickshank
France:	Société Nogentaise de Produits Chimiques	M. L. Augustins and M. P. Jacob
	Pointet and Girard	M. L. Girard, M. A. Pointet, and M. J. R. Roques
Germany:	C. F. Boehringer & Sœhne G.m.b.H.	Mr. G. Tessmar
	Buchler & Co.	Dr. W. Buchler
Holland:	N. V. Nederlandsche Combinatie voor Chemische Industrie	Mr. C. N. van der Spek and Mr. C. W. van Heeckeren van der Schoot

Early in the "convention's" history the members began to grapple with [a] dilemma concerning the stockpile, which was to plague them for months to come. Should they raise the world price of quinine, thereby increasing their immediate profits, or should they keep it at its existent and relatively low level, thereby making it possible for them to purchase the stockpile at a lower price? To the Dutch one of the great advantages of a "convention" was that they could immediately raise the price—an objective fervently supported by the British:

> *Mr. van der Spek:* Now if we make a convention and put up the price to say Hfl. 3,— that means a million guilders a year, which we let go if we do not make a convention to better our chances to get the stockpile. To quote the immortal Omar: "I'll take the cash and let the profit go."
> *Dr. Buchler* says . . . that it is not wise to make a convention just now. We must wait for the stockpile to be disposed of.
> *Mr. van der Spek* asks when this will be; the stockpile came up in 1956 and only now a decision has been taken. It may be a long time before anything is decided. There is much truth in *Dr. Buchler*'s argument, but *Mr. van der Spek* should prefer to agree with Omar: the price increase is the certain "cash", getting the stockpile is uncertain, therefore hardly "the profit."[1]

At their meeting in Paris on July 19, 1962 all members joined in applauding the Dutch for their success in securing more than four-fifths of the stockpile at an average price of slightly over 21 cents. . . .

The heart of the price-fixing arrangements of the "convention" is to be found in two documents—the export agreement and the gentlemen's agreement—which, by their nature, must be considered together. The first of these agreements was to serve, in effect, as a cover for the "convention's" activities, while the second provides a much more comprehensive picture of its real operations.

The export agreement was a contract of dubious but possible legality. Originally negotiated between the Dutch and Boehringer in July 1959, it was extended to include Buchler in March 1960 and the British and French producers on April 7, 1960. With its implementing Rules ("Richtlinen"), it established for export markets only a quota for each member and a uniform system of prices, delivery conditions, and payment terms binding on all members. There was also some reservation of export markets, e.g., East Germany to the German producers, Dutch overseas territories to the Dutch, and certain French colonies and former colonies to the French firms. . . .

An essential feature of any cartel can be found in the market-sharing arrangements accepted by the membership. Some system of marketing quotas, whether overt or carefully hidden, mut underlie any price-fixing agreement. The price level for any given product can be maintained above the competitive market level only if the producers are willing to restrict their own sales to a point where the supply offered by the group as a whole is not so great as to depress prices.

[1] Minutes of meeting, February 4, 1960, pp. 2–3.

The importance of a quota arrangement inevitably makes it one of the major areas of bargaining and contention among the member firms.... In quinine, as in most international cartels, certain geographic markets were made the exclusive preserve of one or more producers. For example, the various producers were usually granted an exclusive monopoly in their home countries. In this way the "deterioration" of markets resulting from sales by outsiders was brought to an end. The English had been exporting to West Germany and, along with Buchler, to France. The Boehringer representative complained that "since the English sell to Germany, the German home-market price has deteriorated...."

[In the gentlemen's agreement, the] parties agree to work together in the spirit outlined above and in particular to be guided by their conviction that their cooperative intention can only have effect if all parties, each of its own accord, strive to overcome the practical and legal difficulties that are going to arise. This applies most especially to the punctual fulfillment of the obligation to effect egalisation and *the protection of the national markets.*

In addition to reserving geographic markets for designated producers, the "convention" also imposed restraints on the manufacture of designated products. Thus, a plant in the Congo originally built by Belgian interests to process Kivu bark and owned by Boehringer was prohibited from exporting quinine and quinidine; in exchange the Congolese market for these products was reserved for Boehringer....

Sales below the established price by "outsiders" can doom any cartel or pricefixing arrangement. Since each of the producers abiding by the price agreement fears that the other parties may reduce their price to meet the outsider's competition and that, therefore, he had better do likewise, the quantities involved need not be very large. As Dr. Buchler put it, "... one outsider can ruin the entire market."[2]

At the first meeting of the "convention" Dr. Buchler remarked on the impossibility of a price agreement while "outsiders" existed; he was reassured by the representative of Boehringer:

> Mr. *Tessmar* is of opinion that this is a consequence of concluding a cartel while there still are outsiders, but if the manufacturers assembled around this table come to an agreement, he does not see any outsiders.[3]

There were, nevertheless, three potential sources of market disturbance from "outside" sources of supply. One consisted of the U.S. stockpile. A first order of business of the "convention" was to eliminate competitive rivalry, both among themselves and from outsiders, for this huge source of bulk quinine. A second potential source was the Pharmakina plant in the Belgian Congo, which enjoyed preferred access to Congolese bark; Pharmakina was successfully neutralized through its acquisition by Boehringer.

There still remained, however, the large—though old—quinine factory

[2] Minutes of meeting on December 2, 1959, p. 8.
[3] *Ibid.,* p. 7.

at Bandoeng, Indonesia. Originally established by cinchona planters in 1894 to counteract the efforts of the earliest (1892) Dutch-German cartel, Nederlandsche Bandoengsche Kininefabriek provided effective competition to the European firms until it, too, was brought into the cartel in 1913 and later acquired by Nedchem. For years the Dutch plant had deliberately. refrained from exploiting the potential capacity of the plant—which, according to van der Spek, was far more than enough to supply the entire world—and resisted efforts of the Indonesian Government to develop export markets for native quinine. . . .

By limiting the output of the Bandoeng plant, the Dutch were also limiting its input of cinchona bark, leaving that much more available for export to the Netherlands. Throughout the "convention," Dutch strategy was to prevent the Bandoeng factory from exporting finished quinine in order to free up bark supplies for export. To this end members were not to purchase quinine from Indonesia.

From the very outset the members of the "convention" were fully aware of the existence of antitrust statutes in most of the major industrialized countries. They were fully aware that what they were doing was in violation of the antitrust laws of the United States, West Germany, and the European Economic Community; they also devised various stratagems to avoid detection by the various antitrust agencies. . . .

The members were most circumspect with regard to the U.S. antitrust laws, using a variety of strategies to avoid the appearance of collusion. The Dutch, in particular, always had in mind their experience as a defendant in the Sherman Act case of 1928 and their inclusion in the resultant permanent consent order. Thus, in the "convention's" third meeting on February 4, 1960 the representative of Nedchem described one of the devices by which the U.S. order had been evaded, proffering the necessary information to the others so that they ". . . can export to the U.S. at the same basis."

On November 2, 1962 the life of the "convention" was terminated by unilateral action on the part of the Dutch. . . . One possible explanation is that the Dutch had undergone a conversion to the righteousness of competition. . . . Another possible explanation is that the "convention" had already served its primary purpose, which was to eliminate competition by other producers for the U.S. stockpile. . . . Certainly the facts are that the Dutch did end up with physical possession of the stockpile, while the British gave up their right to compete for their large amount of low-cost material.

The Petroleum Industry: Structure and Conduct

FEDERAL TRADE COMMISSION

This article is an excerpt from the Preliminary Federal Trade Commission Staff Report on its investigations of the petroleum industry. This report was published in 1973 by the Senate Committee on Government Operations. The report has stirred considerable controversy, many of its conclusions having been challenged by the oil industry.

The petroleum industry is functionally divided into four basic levels: crude oil production, refining, marketing and transportation. While varying numbers of independent companies operate at each level, the industry is dominated by 18 vertically integrated companies that operate at all levels. These firms are large and generally have leading market positions at each level vis-a-vis independents. All 18, according to the *Fortune* 500 sales ranking, are among the 200 largest industrial corporations. Ten are within the top 40, and seven are within the top 20. Industry concentration has resulted both from the dominant positions of these firms and from institutional constraints peculiar to this industry. In order to examine the industry, each level of activity and each relevant institutional factor on a national basis will be discussed.

Crude Oil Production

Concentration in crude oil production by the majors has increased markedly since 1960. While it has been estimated that the number of oil producers in the United States is somewhere between 10,000 to 12,000, the Top 4, 8 and 20 oil producing companies in 1969 accounted respectively for 31, 51 and 70 percent of the average daily barrels of crude produced domestically. (See Table 1.) In 1960, the Top 4, 8 and 20 firms accounted for 26, 43 and 62 percent respectively. A clear trend toward even greater concentration is thus borne out by these comparative statistics.

TABLE I. Company Share of Domestic Net Crude Production, 1969 and 1960

Production Rank in 1969	Company	Company Share 1969 (percent)	Company 1960
1	Standard (New Jersey)	9.76	6.53
2	Texaco	8.47	8.93
3	Gulf	6.78	5.13
4	Shell	6.08	4.78
5	Standard (California)	5.31	4.75
6	ARCO	5.11	5.92
7	Standard (Indiana)	5.09	4.30
8	Mobil	3.94	3.42
9	Getty	3.38	2.92
10	Union	2.88	2.32
11	Sun	2.47	2.65
12	Continental	2.21	2.54
13	Marathon	1.64	1.38
14	Phillips	1.55	1.79
15	Cities Service	1.28	1.29
16	Amerada Hess	1.04	1.22
17	Tenneco	.99	NA
18	Skelly	.88	.94
19	Superior	.74	1.39
20	Louisiana Land & Exploration Co.	.61	.45
	Top 4	31.09	26.51
	Top 8	50.54	43.76
	Top 20	70.21	63.02

NOTE: Individual company production data obtained from the estimates of Rice, Kerr & Co., Engineers. Universe data obtained from *Report on Crude Oil and Gasoline Price Increases of November, 1970: A Background Study*, Nov. 3, 1971, p. 48.

While average daily oil production data may yield short-run insight into the structure of the crude producing industry, it is not particularly relevant for long-run considerations. As oil is pumped from a well, its technically efficient rate of production falls. Eventually it becomes a "stripper well" and is operated until the pumping costs make it uneconomic to do so. A more relevant long-run measure of concentration at the crude level is the amount of domestic proven reserves owned by firms in the industry.

While considerable difficulty has been encountered in obtaining proved reserve data, our best estimates, presented in Table 2, indicate that in

1970, the Top 4, 8 and 20 firms had approximately 37, 64 and 94 percent respectively of domestic crude proven reserves. On the basis of these data, the industry structure viewed in a long-run sense is even more concentrated than short-run statistics have indicated.

The structure of this industry, and hence its conduct and performance, is strongly influenced by certain institutional factors. Basically, these are the import quota, prorationing and special tax regulations.

The single most important federal intervention into the petroleum industry was through mandatory oil import quotas. In order to exercise monopoly power, a firm or firms must be able to control the supply of the industry's product. In the traditional tight oligopoly case, that control is

TABLE II.　Company Shares of Proved Domestic Crude Reserves, 1970

Rank	Company	Share of Domestic Proved Reserves (percent) 1970
1	Standard (N.J.)	9.92
2	Texaco	9.31
3	Gulf	8.97
4	Standard (Calif.)	8.97
5	Standard (Ind.)	8.46
6	ARCO	7.48
7	Shell	5.90
8	Mobil	4.87
9	Getty	3.85
10	Phillips	3.55
11	Signal	3.28
12	Union	3.18
13	Continental	2.77
14	Sun	2.67
15	Amerada Hess	2.49
16	Cities Service	2.49
17	Marathon	2.37
18	Skelly	1.09
19	Superior	1.03
20	Tenneco	.90
	Top 4	37.17
	Top 8	63.88
	Top 20	93.55

NOTE: Individual company reserves obtained from estimates of Rice, Kerr & Co., Engineers. Universe data obtained from *Report on Crude Oil and Gasoline Price Increases.* This figure was taken as approximately 39,000,000,000 barrels, including Alaska. Concentration data would be lower the more this figure understates actual proven reserves. Concentration data should be taken to be, at best, only rough estimates. It is not known to what extent both the universe estimate and the individual company reserve data include crude production from secondary recovery techniques.

exercised through a combination of few sellers acting in an interdependent fashion and effectively erecting barriers to entry against new suppliers. In the petroleum industry, however, that control of supply is importantly influenced by public policy. Between 1959 when the import quota system became mandatory and May 1, 1973 when the quotas were removed, the entry of foreign produced crude oil was severely limited in the United States. Thus, one of the chief sources of competitive supply was curtailed, and domestic integrated firms were operating in an environment where their domestic prices were protected against large scale alternative sources of supply, namely, imports.

It is interesting to observe that the mandatory quotas were enacted at a time when events had conspired to cause some of the previous methods of supply control to break down. Until the 1950's control of supply of crude oil was maintained largely by a system of state prorationing. Under that system the states that had enacted prorationing legislation would limit supply with the goal of maintaining crude prices. Such legislation was particularly effective when imports were unimportant and when states with prorationing (Texas, Louisiana, and Oklahoma) accounted for almost all domestic production. But, in the 1950's foreign supplies from the Middle East and domestic supplies from nonprorationed states became increasingly important. In 1957 voluntary import-controls were initiated, and in 1959 the mandatory controls were imposed. Thus, at a time when supply was becoming increasingly loose, new controls to the advantage of the existing petroleum oligopoly were imposed. It is noteworthy that complaints of financial distress from independent refiners and marketers became more prevalent after the imposition of quotas and that many of those firms trace their difficulties to the international arrangement.

The major oil firms have had the advantage of other federal provisions which have served to buttress their control over the supply of crude oil available in domestic markets. The impact of quotas on the price of domestic crude oil was substantial. The domestic price of crude has in recent years averaged $1.25 to $1.50 per barrel above the world price, and most of the difference is attributable to the import quota. The import quota clearly contributed to profits earned in producing crude oil by elevating prices, but the quota increased profits to the majors in another way. The right to import went only to existing refineries. Thus, the major companies through import tickets were able to purchase oil at the world price as an input for their refineries, which produced final products at elevated domestic prices. A further benefit accruing to the majors was that they were able frequently to obtain profits by trading at favorable terms domestic crude for the independents' allotted foreign crude because some independents located inland were not in a position to economically utilize imports.

While the import quota was in effect, it was an important source of control of crude oil supply, but there are others that must be considered.

The states, with an assist from the federal government, also placed limits on the production of domestic crude oil through prorationing.

Prorationing was originally instituted as a means of conserving the supply of domestic petroleum reserves and avoiding "wasteful" practices such as those that resulted from the rule of capture. However, it functions as a means of controlling supply and setting price. Essentially, the technologically maximum efficient rate of recovery (MER) is determined for each well. Then, demand forecasts for crude oil are examined, and each well is permitted to pump as much crude (subject to its MER) as will clear the market in the aggregate at the market price.

In the U.S. today, prorationing is used in the states of Texas, Louisiana, Oklahoma, New Mexico and Kansas (although these states now claim that they are permitting 100 percent well production during the present shortage). Each state has its own prorationing agency to make state supply determinations. Together, these five states accounted for approximately 74 percent of domestic crude production in 1970. Texas alone accounted for approximately 36 percent. Hence, the supply and price of the vast majority of domestic crude are determined by forces outside the marketplace.

The Federal Government gave teeth to prorationing with the passage of the Connally "Hot Oil" Act in 1935. This act prohibits interstate shipments of crude oil produced in violation of state prorationing laws. However, the Federal Government has the power to "suspend its operation—presumably both enforcement activity as well as basic consent legalizing state action—if state action should unduly burden interstate commerce." The Attorney General is responsible for an annual review, under the Interstate Oil Compact, to determine if such legislation is consistent with its intent, and if not, to suspend it. Its intent is set forth in Article V of the Interstate Oil Compact:

> It is not the purpose of this compact to authorize the states joining herein to limit the production of oil and gas for the purpose of stabilizing or fixing the price thereof, or create or perpetuate monopoly, or to promote regimentation, but is limited to the purpose of conserving oil and gas and preventing the avoidable waste thereof within reasonable limitations.

Thus far, Article V has not been invoked.

The set of federal laws remaining to be discussed are those pertaining to the effect of certain tax regulations on industry incentives.

Special tax provisions permit oil companies to expense many of their exploration and drilling costs rather than depreciating them over an extended period. These provisions tend to lead to an understatement of gross income and to a reduction in tax liability. In addition, the oil companies are permitted to treat royalties paid to foreign governments for drilling rights as an income tax. These "taxes" may then be used as a dollar for dollar offset against U.S. corporate income tax liability. These measures act as a subsidy to crude oil production and, therefore, stimulate increased allocation of resources to the discovery and recovery of crude oil. Hence, it is not surprising that the oil firms seek to integrate backwards to take advantage of the favorable tax provisions. It is, however, the oil depletion allowance that has had the greatest impact upon resource allocation among production stages and relative price structure in the petroleum industry in past years.

Oil depletion allowances were passed originally as a method of encouraging oil exploration. It was argued that since oil was a scarce and valuable natural resource, it would not be advisable to permit national reserves to be depleted. Therefore an incentive was granted to oil producers through a special tax deduction in the hope that more resources would be devoted to the discovery of additional crude oil sources. A crude oil producing firm is permitted to subtract from its gross income before taxes an amount equal to 22 percent of its total revenues from crude production (i.e., actual production times posted price at the wellhead) up to 50 percent of the firms net pretax income. Under this system, the major integrated firms have an incentive to seek high crude prices. The high crude prices are, however, a cost to the major firms' refineries. Thus, an increase in crude prices implies an increase in crude profits but a decrease in refinery profits. The integrated oil companies gain because the depletion allowance reduces the tax on crude profits, while refinery profits are not subject to the same advantageous depletion deduction. A simple model developed by the FTC suggests that for American integrated firms that typically produce between 40 and 80 percent of their crude needs, it pays to raise crude prices up to a point where refinery profits have been reduced to zero. Beyond that point, net income after taxes for the integrated oil firm begins to fall.

Thus, the major integrated oil companies have been able to capitalize upon the existence of import quotas, state prorationing, and oil depletion allowances to limit effectively the supply of crude oil to a point which reduces their refinery profits to zero. Clearly, such a system creates a hazardous existence for independent refiners, who have little or no crude production. In such an environment, only those independent refiners who have: (1) lower costs through locational or other advantages; (2) some monopoly power in a local market; or (3) sufficient access to inexpensive imported oil, can survive.

It is important to note that no technological imperative renders crude production inherently profitable and refinery and marketing operations inherently unprofitable. Rather, the tax laws have made it highly remunerative for integrated firms to artificially shift profits away from downstream activities toward the crude end of integrated business. This goal is accomplished by raising crude prices through various controls on supply.

Refining

The petroleum refining industry is the pivotal point in the petroleum industry. It is virtually the sole buyer of crude and it transforms crude into more efficient particular energy products. In 1969, the domestic refinery yield was as follows:

	Percent
Gasoline	45.5
Distillate fuel oil	21.6
Jet fuel	8.2
Residual fuel oil	6.8
Kerosene	2.6
Lubricants	1.7

TABLE III.   Company Share of Domestic Crude Oil and Gasoline Refining Capacity, 1970

Rank in Crude Oil Capacity	Company	Share of Crude Oil Capacity (percent)	Share of Gasoline Capacity (percent)
1	Standard (N.J.)	8.59	9.22
2	Standard (Ind.)	8.22	7.94
3	Texaco	8.13	9.19
4	Shell	7.99	7.69
5	Standard (Calif.)	7.66	6.72
6	Mobil	6.28	6.30
7	Gulf	5.78	6.47
8	ARCO	5.42	6.25
9	Sun	3.60	4.54
10	Union	3.51	3.24
11	Standard (Ohio)	3.47	3.09
12	Phillips	3.14	4.24
13	Ashland	2.51	2.11
14	Continental	2.36	2.03
15	Cities Service	2.22	2.26
16	Getty	1.64	1.76
17	Marathon	1.12	1.92
18	Coastal States	1.06	.73
19	Amerada Hess	.98	.79
20	Champlin	.97	.63
	Top 4	32.93	34.04
	Top 8	58.07	58.78
	Top 20	86.15	87.38

NOTE: Data obtained from Mineral Industry Surveys, Bureau of Mines, "Crude Oil Capacity," Jan. 1, 1971.

As of January 1, 1972, there were 282 domestic refineries and approximately 129 refining companies. The 1970 crude oil refining capacity as shown in Table 3, accounted for by the leading 4, 8 and 20 firms, was 33, 58 and 86 percent respectively. These same firms accounted for 34, 59 and 87 percent of gasoline refining capacity.

A comparison of firm rankings in refining and production (Table 4) yields some interesting results. While there are some minor deviations, three of the top four refiners are among the top four crude producers and the top eight refiners are also the top eight crude producers. Further, 16 of the top 20 refiners are among the top 16 crude producers. Hence, independent monopsonistic purchasing power conducive to downward pressure on crude prices is virtually absent.

TABLE IV. A Comparison of Company Ranking in Crude Production and Crude Refining Capacity

Company	Rank in Crude Production	Rank in Crude Oil Refining Capacity
Standard (New Jersey)	1	1
Texaco	2	3
Gulf	3	7
Shell	4	4
Standard (California)	5	5
ARCO	6	8
Standard (Indiana)	7	2
Mobil	8	6
Getty	9	16
Union	10	10
Sun	11	9
Continental	12	14
Marathon	13	17
Phillips	14	12
Cities Service	15	15
Amerada Hess	16	19
Tenneco	17	—
Skelly	18	—
Superior	19	—
Louisiana Land and Exploration	20	—
Standard (Ohio)	—	11
Ashland	—	13

There could, of course, still be some downward pressure on crude prices, despite the integration of the leading firms, if there were a mismatch between a company's crude production and its refining capacity. The extent of this would depend upon the degree of self-sufficiency and the marginal effect of higher crude prices on total revenue due to the interrelationship of self-sufficiency and the marginal effect of higher crude prices on total revenue due to the interrelationship of self-sufficiency and the oil depletion allowance. De Chazeau and Kahn developed a simple model to examine this relationship. They determined that a company with a self-sufficiency greater than 77 percent would benefit from a crude price increase even if this increase were not passed on in the price of products at all. If 50 percent of the price increase were passed on, a company with a degree of self-sufficiency in excess of 38.5 percent would benefit from a price increase. Their estimates were based on the 27½ percent depletion allowance which was in effect at that time.

Using the identical model and substituting the present 22 percent depletion allowance only alters their conclusions slightly. If the price increase is not passed on, a company with a self-sufficiency in excess of 40.4 percent would benefit from a price increase. The greater the percentage of the price increase passed on, the lower the self-sufficiency required to benefit from a crude price increase.

As can be seen from Table 5, all of the Top 8 and 15 of the Top 17 refining companies have self-sufficiency greater than 40 percent. Three of the Top 8 and 5 of the Top 17 have self-sufficiency greater than 81 percent. Thus, vertical integration combined with the depletion allowance places upward pressure on crude prices.

TABLE V. Domestic Self-Sufficiency of the 17 Leading Refiners 1969

	Self-Sufficiency (percent of runs to stills)
Company:	
Standard (New Jersey)	87.4
Standard (Indiana)	50.5
Texaco	81.0
Shell	62.1
Standard (California)	68.8
Mobil	42.2
Gulf	87.6
ARCO	64.9
Sun	46.7
Union	64.3
Standard (Ohio)	6.7
Phillips	51.8
Ashland	12.6
Continental	64.0
Cities Service	49.9
Getty	137.2
Marathon	88.1

NOTE: Obtained from estimates of Kerr, Rice and Co., Engineers.

It is vitally important to keep in mind that while the recent removal of the oil import quota may to some extent exert slight downward pressure on crude prices as the U.S. price reaches an equilibrium with world prices, it will not necessarily substantially alter the structure of the refining level of the petroleum industry. This is true for two reasons. First, the major integrated companies have substantial interests in crude oil production world-wide. Second, and most important, it is questionable that new independent refiners would enter the market, even with available supplies of foreign crude. The reason is quite simple—the uncertainty of the continual availability of foreign crude. Just as the federal government first restricted imports and then removed them, they may be restored at a moment's notice. And since refining is the pivotal point in the petroleum industry, the implications are that removal of the import quotas alone may not be sufficient to cure the present ills of the industry or alter its noncompetitive performance significantly.

TABLE VI. Worldwide Self-Sufficiency of the 17 Leading U.S. Refiners 1969 and 1959

U.S. Rank in Crude Refining Capacity	Company	Self-Sufficiency 1969 (percent)	Self-Sufficiency 1959 (percent)
1	Standard (New Jersey)	88.3	77.1
2	Standard (Indiana)	66.4	51.5
3	Texaco	106.7	92.4
4	Shell Group	72.5	74.2
5	Standard (California)	138.1	105.4
6	Mobil	75.5	69.5
7	Gulf	193.0	172.7
8	ARCO	96.7	64.6
9	Sun	87.4	55.7
10	Union	85.6	50.0
11	Standard (Ohio)	28.9	28.1
12	Phillips	65.4	71.3
13	Ashland	13.9	8.8
14	Continental	158.4	104.0
15	Cities Service	89.5	44.6
16	Getty	241.1	71.8
17	Marathon	163.2	109.0
	Top 4	84.8	76.5
	Top 8	96.2	84.2
	All 17	97.1	96.8
	5 largest United States international companies.	108.9	93.5

NOTE: Ratios obtained from the "Oil and Gas Journal," Jan. 18, 1971, pp. 22–23. Multicompany measures were computed from production and capacity data contained in the same source.

Gasoline Marketing

Gasoline marketing is the most competitive area of the petroleum industry and has the largest number of independent companies. Marketing consists primarily of jobbers purchasing refined gasoline and supplying retail gasoline stations. These jobbers may be completely independent, may own their own retail stations, or may be vertically tied to refinery operations. They also may carry branded or unbranded products.

The 1970 gasoline market shares of the Top 20 companies are presented in Table 7. The top 4, 8 and 20 companies accounted for approximately 31, 55 and 79 percent, respectfully, of domestic gasoline sales. The Top 4 and 8 gasoline marketers correspond with the Top 4 and 8 refiners, and the Top 8 crude producers are identical with the Top 8 marketers and refiners. (See Table 8.)

TABLE VII. Company Gasoline Market Shares 1970

Rank	Company	Market Share (percent of)
1	Texaco	8.13
2	Shell	7.87
3	Standard (New Jersey)	7.42
4	Standard (Indiana)	7.30
5	Gulf	7.12
6	Mobil	6.60
7	ARCO	5.55
8	Standard (California)	5.02
8	Sun	4.15
10	Phillips	3.97
11	Union	3.29
12	Continental	2.35
13	Cities Service	1.96
14	Marathon	1.73
15	Standard (Ohio)	1.46
16	BP	1.41
17	Ashland	1.27
18	Tenneco	.93
19	Kerr-McGee	.77
20	Murphy	.75
	Top 4	30.72
	Top 8	55.01
	Top 20	79.05

NOTE: Market shares obtained from *National Petroleum News*, "Factbook Issue," mid-May 1971, p. 127.

The distinction between the major branded retail gasoline stations and the independent stations is one of the primary reasons for price competition at this level.

TABLE VIII.   A Comparison of Company Ranking in Crude Production, Crude Refining Capacity, and Gasoline Sales

Company	Rank in Crude Oil Refining Production	Rank in Crude Capacity	Rank in Gasoline Sales
Standard (New Jersey)	1	1	3
Texaco	2	3	1
Gulf	3	7	5
Shell	4	4	2
Standard (California)	5	5	8
ARCO	6	8	7
Standard (Indiana)	7	2	4
Mobil	8	6	6
Getty	9	16	—
Union	10	10	11
Sun	11	9	9
Continental	12	14	12
Marathon	13	17	14
Phillips	14	12	10
Cities Service	15	15	13
Amerada Hess	16	19	—
Tenneco	17	—	18
Skelly	18	—	—
Superior	19	—	—
Louisiana Land & Exploration	20	—	—
Standard (Ohio)	—	11	15
Ashland	—	13	17
BP	—	—	16
Kerr-McGee	—	—	19
Murphy	—	—	20

The major branded stations differentiate their products and convey a national image. These retail stations generally offer a full line of services, including credit cards, automobile repair, etc. The independents, on the other hand, differentiate their products primarily on a price basis and offer few services other than pumping gasoline. This, of course, gives the consumer a choice between purchasing gasoline and services at a higher price, and purchasing only gasoline at a lower price. If, in a given area, consumers show a strong preference for the latter, and/or if independents move into a market, vigorous price competition between the majors and independents may result.

Of course some price competition may result directly from the major companies themselves. This may occur when a major company decides to move into a market area dominated by other majors or possibly independents. As a new entrant, this major company may begin as a vigorous price cutter; but, as his price cuts are matched by other companies, the retail gasoline price will eventually stabilize somewhere near the old level. If he is strong enough, he may achieve his desired market share. But, in doing so, he will have obtained it at the expense of the weakest segment of the market, the independent portion. If independents are diversified geographically, however, they may withstand price competition. If not, they will be the first to be eliminated.

However, today a price war is unnecessary for the elimination of the independent marketer. Because the major oil companies control the lion's share of domestic crude oil and refinery capacity under conditions of excess demand, they have been able to direct the flow of gasoline to their own service stations first, thus denying to the independent marketer access to a substantial portion of the gasoline supply. In fact, independent gasoline marketers receive only about 2 percent of their supply of product from the eight largest oil companies.

Transportation

Because crude oil is low in value relative to its weight and the refinery process requires a relatively constant flow of crude and product, pipelines are generally the most economical form of bulk land transportation in this industry. Approximately 75 percent of crude and 27 percent of refinery product are carried by pipeline.

Gathering pipelines collect crude from the wells and transport it to a main trunkline station. From the trunkline station, it flows through a larger diameter pipeline to the refinery. Product pipelines carry gasoline and other products from the refinery to local or regional storage facilities from which jobbers and ultimately retailers purchase their product.

These pipelines form a vast, complex intrastate and interstate transportation network. Because of the high construction costs, most of the pipelines are owned directly by individual major petroleum companies or by several of these companies through joint venture. However, the nature of the interstate lines causes them to come under the "common carrier" regulatory jurisdiction of the Interstate Commerce Commission.

Our investigation disclosed charges leveled against these pipeline owners by nonowners who claim that they have been excluded from using the common-carrier lines. The inherent technological nature of the pipeline system and the petroleum industry provides the basis for such exclusionary practices.

Through the pipeline system, crude oil is transported more or less on a constant flow-pressure basis. Trunkline stations can pump-in a batch of crude only when there is a slot in the flow for it and then line pressure must be increased or decreased to adjust for the desired flow speed. The scheduling of pipeline input is very complex and must be worked out in advance of the shipment. Because of this process, an independent crude producer may have great difficulty in securing a place in the flow, especially if he does not have storage tanks at the trunkline station and/or ships a relatively small amount of crude. The result of this pipeline system is to place the major firms who own the pipelines in an excellent position to discriminate against the independent producer. The opportunity to require the independent to enter into an agreement to sell his product at the well head in order to obtain regular sale and transportation of crude clearly exists for the majors.

Barriers to Entry

In addition to being a highly integrated industry, the petroleum industry, and refining in particular, is also characterized by high barriers to entry. Without such barriers, excess profits would attract new firms into the market, increasing the supply, and eliminating the excess profits.

Because of the lack of substantial entry by new independent refiners over the last 20 years, we turn our attention to factors in the petroleum industry which tend to act as barriers to entry. In most instances, the factors leading to further concentration, e.g. import quotas, prorationing, depletion allowances, also serve to inhibit new entrants into the industry or component segments of the industry.

The most obvious barrier is the high capital cost of entering the refining industry. A refinery large enough to achieve maximum scale economies in the production of gasoline costs approximately $250 million. The operation of the capital market is such that the number of firms which can borrow that amount of money is relatively small. Even for those firms which have access to the required capital, the risks which they face vis-a-vis the major petroleum companies are such as to discourage entry.

Several of those risks are associated with the ability of the refiner to obtain a dependable source of supply of its major input, crude oil. In the past, refiners have had to depend on their major oil company competitors for access to this crucial input. This has occurred because the major oil companies directly own substantial amounts of the crude oil, and because they control the vast majority of the remainder of the crude (primarily through control of pipeline transportation). Thus, in any short supply situation, the independent refiner would be the first firm to lose access to crude oil and the last to regain access. Having refinery output subject to great variation because of variation in crude inputs imposes substantial costs upon nonintegrated refiners. The alternative of entering the petroleum industry as a vertically integrated firm raises capital costs to even greater proportions.

The plight of the would-be entrant at the refining stage has to some extent been alleviated through the recent Presidential removal of the oil import quotas. However, this does not eliminate the problems faced by the independent refiners in this context. All students of the petroleum industry (surely anyone planning to expend $250 million as a capital investment would become a serious student of the industry) are well aware that the major firms have always turned to governmental entities to help them rationalize excess supply situations. They would have to assume that if the inflow of foreign crude became sufficient to cause a reduction in the current price of domestic crude, the major companies would again turn to the government to request limitations on imports. Their past success in obtaining such actions is such that one might infer a high probability of future success. Thus, a firm which had built a $250 million refinery might suddenly find that its access to crude oil was greatly reduced. The nature of refinery cost functions, i.e., sharply declining average costs as a refinery nears capacity operation, would make any reduction in the availability of crude oil a traumatic and possibly bankrupting experience for the new entrant.

Since pipelines transporting crude oil across state lines are common carriers subject to Interstate Commerce Commission regulation, it might seem strange to classify pipeline control as a barrier to entry to new refinery capacity. However, there are two reasons to suppose that pipeline control does, in fact, constitute a legitimate barrier. First, the owners of pipelines seek approval from the ICC of rates that provide sufficient returns from their pipeline investment. However, the rate approved may be well above the competitive cost of transporting crude oil. For the vertically integrated owners the excessive rate is no burden. Those firms simply transfer funds from the Refinery Department to the Pipeline Department; a bookkeeping transaction of no moment is made. Nonintegrated independent refiners, though, must pay the excessive pipeline charge. For these firms a real cost is incurred. To the extent that major-firm owners of pipelines earn greater than competitive returns on investments, the independent refiners are put at a cost disadvantage relative to their major competitors, and a barrier to entry is imposed. To a lesser extent control of product pipelines can be used to erect a barrier to entry.

Second, pipelines can be employed as a barrier to entry if the owners can exclude or limit flows of crude oil to independents. In fact, this can be done by (1) requiring shipments of minimum size, (2) granting independents irregular shipping dates, (3) limiting available storage at the pipeline terminal, (4) imposing unreasonable product standards upon independent customers of pipelines, and (5) employing other harassing or delaying tactics.

A barrier of substantial importance in the past existed because of the vertical integration in the industry and the federal tax laws. The depletion allowance worked to encourage vertically integrated firms to report all profits at the crude oil stage rather than at later stages such as refining or marketing. The effect was to raise the price of crude oil for refining operations, whether vertically integrated or not. For the vertically integrated concern the price was simply a bookkeeping one and raising it resulted in decreasing refining profits, increasing profits on crude, reducing tax payments, and increasing total profit. For the independent refiner the result was to decrease refining profits which were total profits.

The system contained all the elements essential to a squeeze on refining profits and could be overcome only if the potential refining entrant could enter on a vertically integrated basis. However, entry on this basis substantially increases the already high capital cost of entry. Even with the freeing of imports the system will still work to the disadvantage of independent refiners unless the world price of petroleum settles to a competitive level.

A final barrier to entry results from the recent emphasis on environmental impact. Even firms who can overcome the high barriers may find either that they cannot obtain government permission to build at the optimal location or that additional capital is required to eliminate possible adverse environmental impacts. In any case they may be at a disadvantage relative to existing plants which were located without respect to such constraint.

Pricing Behavior in the American, European and Japanese Steel Industries

FEDERAL TRADE COMMISSION

This is an excerpt from the Federal Trade Commission Staff Report on The United States Steel Industry and Its International Rivals, *published in 1977.*

There are many theories of the pricing behavior of the U.S. steel industry. Adams and Dirlam have argued that:

> Cost movements and target returns—more so than demand—are prime determinants of price policy. . . . Pricing policy of the steel industry, and of its price leaders, includes therefore, not only the achievement of goals set for individual prices, but also maintenance of the proportions, ratios and margins between prices at successive levels of production that seem to be in the best interest of the industry. . . . When a strategic price is threatened, however, the threat must be dealt with at almost any cost not simply because of the necessity for re-evaluating the specific price, but because of the danger to the market structure dependent upon it.

They conclude that import erosion of domestic markets, especially wire rods, was directly attributable to the industry pricing policies. The pricing policy is in turn attributable to the oligopolistic and vertically integrated nature of the industry.

The Council on Wage and Price Stability's "A Study of Steel Prices" has presented a model of steel pricing similar to Adams and Dirlam. The report claims:

Prices are set by industry leaders in an effort to cover full costs and generate a desired rate of return at a level of output less than capacity. . . .
The customary situation is price leadership by larger mills, and following by the other major mills.

The report by the Council on Wage and Price Stability, however, qualifies the above theory by stating that limitations such as imports and alternate suppliers, including minimills, might cause the industry to fail to achieve its goals.

On the other hand, in analyzing the historical position of the U.S. steel industry (the first quarter of the 20th century and possibly later), Stigler has concluded that the U.S. Steel Corporation was a dominant firm, whereas Parsons and Ray have characterized the industry as a "dominant cartel." However, the Gaskins model of limit pricing implies that even if U.S. Steel were a dominant firm (or the industry a dominant cartel or group of joint profit maximizing oligopolists) it would still price in a manner to slow the import erosion of its markets. Moreover, there are authors such as Rowley and Mancke who regard the pricing practices of the U.S. steel industry as quasi-competitive; i.e., the observed pricing pattern is similar to that which would occur in a competitive industry.

Change in the Pricing Behavior of the U.S. Steel Corporation

Data on the market shares of each of the top eight U.S. steel companies are reported in [Table 1] . . . to provide background for the pricing behavior discussion which follows. These data reveal that since 1962, U.S. Steel Corporation's market share has eroded slightly. This is in contrast to the 1951–61 period, in which U.S. Steel's share declined 6.9 percentage points from 32.6 percent to 25.7 percent. Simultaneously, the four-firm concentration ratio declined 7.1 percentage points, while the eight-firm concentration ratio declined just 2.8 percentage points.

Thus, in the decade preceding 1962, virtually the entire erosion of four-firm concentration ratios came at the expense of U.S. Steel. Moreover, during this period, the share of firms two through eight increased by 4.1 percentage points, the principal gainer being Armco Steel. On the other hand, U.S. Steel's share has been eroding at a slower rate since 1961, while the four- and eight-firm shares were buttressed by the National-Granite City merger.

The 1961–76 period is also in contrast with the longer 1902–61 period in the table. There U.S. Steel's share declined 39.7 percentage points from 65.4 percent to 25.7 percent. The longrun trend was arrested before, during, and after the World War II years. Simultaneously, the four- and eight-firm concentration ratios declined only 24.2 percentage points and 8.0 percent-

Table I Concentration of Raw Steel Production Shares (percent)

Company	1902	1904	1908	1920	1938	1947	1951	1961	1976	1961–1902	1961–1951	1976–1961
U.S. Steel Corporation	65.4	60.8	56.0	45.8	33.1	33.7	32.6	25.7	22.1	−39.7	−6.9	−3.6
Four Largest Firms	78.8	74.2[a]	68.2[a]	58.5	62.0	63.5	61.7	54.6	52.8	−24.2	−7.1	−1.8
Eight Largest Firms	N.A.	83.5[a]	76.3[b]	65.7[b]	79.0[b]	79.9[b]	78.3[b]	75.5	73.4	−8.0[c]	−2.8	−2.1

[a] The shares of firms two through eight for the years 1904 and 1908 were computed from data for estimated capacity.
[b] National Steel Corporation's share of production was estimated from its share of capacity for the years 1920, 1938, 1947, and 1951.
[c] Computed by subtracting the 1904 eight-firm share from the 1961 eight-firm share.

SOURCES: The American Iron and Steel Institute and the *Iron Age* Annual Financial Survey for the years 1920 forward; U.S. Department of Commerce, Bureau of the Census, *Historical Statistics of the United States, Colonial Times to 1970, Part 2*; and D. Parsons, and E. Ray, "The United States Steel Consolidation: The Creation of Market Control," *Journal of Law and Economics*, April 1975, pp. 209, 210, for the years 1902, 1904, and 1908.

age points. Thus, the share of the second through fourth largest firms *increased* by 15.5 percentage points, and the share of the second through eighth largest firms *increased* by 31.8 percentage points while U.S. Steel experienced its secular decline. The four- and eight-firm concentration ratios were buttressed by mergers, especially the acquisitions by Bethlehem and Republic.

Compared to earlier periods, the decline of U.S. Steel's market share has slowed. On the basis of these data, one should suspect a change in the pricing policy of the U.S. Steel Corporation following 1961. The suspicions raised by the market share data are strongly supported by accounts in the trade press. On the basis of these accounts, Scherer has found that, by 1962, U.S. Steel had abandoned its strong price leadership role. He states that "When U.S. did exercise leadership, it announced cuts mixed with increases, displaying a new diplomacy which contrasted vividly with the 'bludgeon' approach employed up to 1962 . . . [and by 1968] . . . U.S. Steel abandoned its traditional policy of holding list prices inviolate and joined the 'chiselers' offering substantial secret concessions to a number of buyers. The once rigid steel price structure began to crumble." This chapter will present extensive data from the trade press which support these conclusions by Scherer.

A new development since 1968 is that Bethlehem Steel Corporation has on occasion been the industry price disciplinarian. When steel companies, including U.S. Steel, have offered price cuts off list prices, Bethlehem has cut the list price to stop "chiseling." . . . In addition, there were a number of other incidents in the early 1970's, where Bethlehem cut or refused to raise list prices because of clandestine discounts.

On August 2, 1971, U.S. Steel announced an eight percent price hike on practically all mill products to take effect on a staggered schedule from August 5 to December 1, 1971; within hours the move was followed by Bethlehem, Armco, Republic, and Youngstown. On August 11, Bethlehem postponed its price hike on cold rolled sheets, until February 1, 1972. Because of softness in the economy, the growth of steel imports, and increasing resistance of purchasing agents, analysts questioned whether the industry could actually realize these higher prices or would be forced to continue making the discounts prevalent on some product categories for the last 18 months. On April 13, 1972, Bethlehem announced it would raise prices on virtually none of its steel mill products before January 1, 1973. Similarly, in February 1970, Bethlehem guaranteed it would not raise prices more than once a year. The 1972 action was apparently motivated by the fact that some small companies, notably Alan Wood Company and Phoenix Steel Corporation, had been offering price discounts. Moreover, foreign steel producers were seeking fall orders by offering buyers current prices. Bethlehem's senior vice-president for sales, Edward D. Bickford, stated, "We absolutely do not make deals. We say, 'This is our price to everybody. If a competitor wants to make it lower, then that will be our price to everybody.' "

The analysis of Gaskins has shown that in the static demand case when a dominant firm (or dominant cartel or group of joint profit maximizers) enjoys no cost advantage over rivals:

> . . . in response to optimal pricing by the dominant firm the output of the competitive fringe will asymptotically approach . . . the total industry output. *The dominant firm in this case prices itself out of the market in the long run.* While it is acknowledged that our model will lose its validity at some point as the dominant firm's market share declines, the conclusion remains that dominant firms with little or no cost advantage decline if they strive to maximize their present value. [Emphasis added.]

The relevant point is (as the Gaskins analysis has shown in the case quoted above) that, if the dominant firm continues to price lead, absent a cost advantage, above competitive levels, it prices itself out of the market. It appears United States Steel recognized that it had virtually lost its ability to maintain prices at monopolistic levels, ceased doing so, and thereby slowed its market share decline.

The Role of Imports

Table 2 contains data on world and United States steel trade. It is apparent that the United States has moved from a net exporter of steel mill products to a significant net importer. In an effort to determine if the longrun pricing policy has been responsible for this change, three selected steel mill products are examined: hot rolled carbon sheet (HRS), cold rolled carbon sheet (CRS), and wire rod (WR).

HRS and CRS were selected because they are representative of flat rolled products, generally produced by major steel mills and because together they account for one-third of net industry shipments. WR was chosen because it is representative of the non-flat type product which the minimills are capable of producing . . . Clearly, comparative cost considerations are crucial in determining if pricing policy contributed to the observed erosion of domestic markets. The pricing policy hypothesis of import erosion argues that domestic producers maintained prices above competitive levels, thereby forming a price umbrella under which competitively priced imports were free to erode domestic markets. However, if costs for foreign producers fell relative to domestic producers during the 1955–71 period, that would significantly contribute to the observed pattern of import erosion.

TABLE II. Growth Trends in Production, Shipments, Imports and
Exports of Steel Mill Products: 1950–76

Year	Raw steel production	Net industry shipments	Imports	Exports	Apparent consumption	Imports relative to apparent consumption	Exports relative to net industry shipments
1976	128,000	89,447	14,285	2,654	101,078	14.1	3.0
1975	116,642	79,957	12,012	2,953	89,016	13.5	3.7
1974	145,720	109,472	15,970	5,833	119,609	13.4	5.3
1973	150,799	111,430	15,150	4,052	122,528	12.4	3.6
1972	133,241	91,805	17,681	2,873	106,613	16.6	3.1
1971	120,443	87,038	18,304	2,827	102,515	17.9	3.2
1970	131,514	90,798	13,364	7,062	97,100	13.8	7.8
1969	141,262	93,877	14,034	5,229	102,682	13.7	5.6
1968	131,462	91,856	17,960	2,170	107,646	16.7	2.4
1967	127,213	83,897	11,455	1,685	93,667	12.2	2.0
1966	134,101	89,995	10,753	1,724	99,024	10.9	1.9
1965	131,462	92,666	10,383	2,496	100,553	10.3	2.7
1964	127,076	84,945	6,440	3,442	87,943	7.3	4.1
1963	109,261	75,555	5,452	2,180	78,827	6.9	2.9
1962	98,328	70,552	4,100	2,013	72,639	5.6	2.9
1961	98,014	66,126	3,163	1,990	67,299	4.7	3.0
1960	99,282	71,149	3,359	2,977	71,531	4.7	4.2
1959	93,446	69,377	4,396	1,677	72,096	6.1	2.4
1958	85,255	59,914	1,707	2,823	58,798	2.9	4.7
1957	112,715	79,895	1,155	5,348	75,702	1.5	6.7
1956	115,216	83,251	1,341	4,348	80,244	1.7	5.2
1955	117,036	84,717	973	4,061	81,629	1.2	4.8
1954	88,312	63,153	788	2,659	61,282	1.3	4.2
1953	111,610	80,152	1,674	2,907	78,919	2.1	3.6
1952	93,168	68,004	1,186	3,918	65,272	1.8	5.8
1951	105,200	78,929	2,178	3,051	78,056	2.8	3.9
1950	96,836	72,232	1,016	2,639	70,609	1.4	3.7

(Thousands of short tons)

NOTE: Apparent consumption equals domestic shipments plus imports less exports. It differs from actual consumption to the extent that inventories are built up and drawn down by steel users.

SOURCE: American Iron & Steel Institute, *Annual Statistical Report*, various years.

As mentioned above, the Gaskins model implies that even if the U.S. steel industry were characterized by dominant firm or joint profit maximizing pricing, it would be optimal to price to retard entry by imports. That is, a price less than the shortrun profit maximizing price (but above the price at which no imports enter) is optimal in view of the threat of market erosion by imports. A qualification to the preceding conclusion is that the dominant firm will price below the level at which no imports enter (i.e., price to drive out imports and other competitors) if its market share is less than its longrun equilibrium share. In view of the secular decline of the U.S. Steel Corporation and the rise of imports in the late 1950's and 1960's, this qualification is evidently irrelevant to the steel industry. Thus, with respect to the domestic steel industry, the Gaskins model implies that (1) prices are lower than they would be without imports but (2) some import erosion is permitted.

However, it is fundamental to the limit pricing model that the dominant firm does not suffer a cost disadvantage. As Gaskins states: "While there may be examples of dominant firms with cost disadvantage, their fate is obvious with or without optimal pricing." They will decline.

In both the HRS and CRS markets, the longrun trend of the ratio of imports to apparent consumption rose as the relative costs of the U.S. rose. However, as the U.S. enjoyed a favorable cost advantage in the years 1973 and 1974, the import share of HRS declined to the lowest level since 1964; and in CRS the import share experienced a significant drop from 1971. Corresponding to the trend in costs is the trend in profits . . . The long-run trend in profits as a percentage of revenues declined from 1955 through 1971 but was reversed during 1972–74. Thus, with respect to the basic flat rolled products, it appears that imports have been eroding the domestic share and squeezing profit margins in accordance with longrun trends in relative costs. As relative costs began to shift in favor of the U.S. in the past few years, the domestic industry saw its market share of these products and its profit margins improve. . . .

In the wire rod market, the European producers enjoyed a significant cost advantage for all years from 1957 to 1969, inclusive. Thus, it is not surprising to find the import share increasing during these years. We do not attribute the longrun market erosion to the longrun pricing policy but, rather, to cost differences. . . .

European Pricing

The historical list (base) prices of steel products of the countries in the original European Community (EC) and recent list price data of the countries in the enlarged community were examined. These data reveal a remarkable degree of list price stability. *The overall tendency is for prices not to decline, and occasionally to increase.* This pattern is exhibited to an extreme degree by the Luxembourg producers. The data reveal absolutely no price change on many steel products for a 10-year period between 1958 and 1968, after which list prices tended to increase, never to decline.

Although not as marked, the non-decreasing pattern of list prices is also true of the German and French producers. During the worldwide recession of 1958, the major producers of West Germany and France raised their list prices for virtually all products. The next most serious recession for the

EC was in 1965; again, the major producers of West Germany and France held their list prices unchanged. The years 1961–63 are years of below average growth in apparent steel consumption for the EC. Yet the West German producers held their list prices fixed, while the French producers raised their list prices on Thomas quality steel. Again, in the 1971 recession, German list prices rose, while the French remained constant. During the 1975 recession, list prices did not decline. However, most producers listed "temporary rebates" on carbon steel products.

Unlike the major producers of the EC, the smaller Belgian steel producers exhibited aggressive list price cutting during recessions. Stegemann concluded that during the years of depressed growth in steel demand in the EC—1963, 1965, 1966, and 1967:

> . . . aggressive price cutting (by the Belgians) which reduced the price floor did take place . . . Whereas in the case of the other countries the VDMA data for each product generally reflect the pricing behavior of one major national producer or a coherent group of national producers, the lowest Belgian list prices for certain products are the result of considerably diverse pricing policies of individual firms or subgroups.

During the 1963–68 period, the Belgian list prices became the lowest in the EC for wire rod, merchant bars and heavy plate.

Although not to the same extent as the Belgians, the producers of The Netherlands and Italy have also exhibited some list price flexibility. For example, list prices were lowered in both Italy and The Netherlands during the 1958 recession. During the recent recession of 1975, "temporary rebates" off list prices were granted by both Dutch and Italian producers on products such as hot rolled hoop and strip, merchant bars, and concrete reinforcing bars.

However, one must look beyond the monotonic non-decreasing list prices in the EC to transactions prices if one is to discern the pattern of EC pricing. Legally, no EC steel firm may sell steel at a given place for a price lower than the lowest delivered list price that has been quoted by any firm for that place. For example, if a French firm has quoted the lowest delivered price for Paris, a German firm may legally sell at a price below its own published delivered price, provided it is not below the French firm's quotation. Such sales are termed "alignment" sales. An EC steel firm may sell below its own quoted price by aligning on another EC firm's quoted price or on the delivered price of a firm from outside the EC. Selling at prices lower than the lowest quoted delivered price is illegal under the terms of the Treaty of Paris.

During the 1963 recession in the European Coal and Steel Community (ECSC), steel producers made significant use of their alignment rights. The weighted average of the price reductions for all alignment sales by Community producers in 1963 is estimated at 30 to 35 percent . . . Moreover, price cutting below legal EC levels has occurred. The major German steel producers aligned themselves into joint sales agencies in 1966–67, after which the share of imports into the German market rose from the 15 to 20 percent level to over 30 percent in 1968. There were widespread reports of illegal price cutting in the German market; especially accused of price cutting were the Belgian and Italian producers. These illegal price cuts led to the issuance of a series of "temporary rebates" by the German joint sales agencies.

During the recession of 1975, deep and significant price cutting developed. Alignments on imports from Japan, Spain, and Eastern Europe permitted significant legal price reductions, and the price competition was depicted by some as severe. The French steel leader, Jacques Ferry, led a move to have the European Community declare a "manifest crisis" and establish minimum prices along with production cuts and import controls. However, the Germans maintained strong opposition to Ferry's proposal and finally the market began to improve in 1976.

Japan

In Japan, as in Europe and the United States, there is a significant difference between list prices and transactions prices of steel products. However, unlike the situation in the other countries, list prices until recently were arrived at jointly by 43 steel producers under the guidance of the Japanese Ministry of International Trade and Industry (MITI). These companies met monthly with their trading companies and, except for slight variations, announced uniform prices. This system, known as the "kokai hanbai seido" or "kohan" system, for short, was first established in June 1958 in an effort to reduce price cutting during recessions. These prices are termed "joint open sales prices" (JOSP). Prices for large users such as the automobile industry are given separately. In addition, the industry quotes "joint open sales standard prices" (JOSSP). The JOSSP are intended to represent the prices steelmakers consider necessary for longrun industry growth. *However, these JOSP and JOSSP have shown extreme inflexibility and are above transactions prices except during periods of strong demand.*

It should be understood that the Japanese distribution system differs markedly from that of the U.S. In the U.S., approximately 80 percent of the steel is sold directly by the steel company to the end user. Japanese steel companies sell approximately 90 percent of their steel products indirectly through middlemen.

Virtually all of these indirect sales are made through intermediary companies known as trading companies. Trading companies market almost all Japanese steel exports and the bulk of domestic sales. The trading companies actually take possession and reship to the end user about 20 to 25 percent of the steel which they purchase. In addition, there are small steel service centers for local demand who usually purchase their steel from the trading companies. The f.o.b. prices at which the steel service centers purchase their steel from the trading companies are called "market prices." It is estimated that about 5 percent of total transactions occur at these "market prices," with such transactions rising as a percentage of the market during contractions. Sales not made through trading companies are generally those of the Big Five steel producers to a large buyer of steel; e.g., sales to a Japanese automobile manufacturer like Nissan.

The major functions of the trading company, as intermediary between steel producer and domestic end user, are threefold: finance, delivery, and product finishing. Generally speaking, trading companies are involved most frequently in transactions between steel producer and end user when the consuming firm has a high debt-equity ratio. These consuming firms find the credit extended by the trading companies attractive.

Most contracts between steel producers and trading companies involve the use of the so-called "uchikosen" system, by which the price of the steel is first determined through direct negotiation, and then the commission of the trading company follows as a predetermined proportion of the sales price. Trading companies claim that competition among them prevents the commission from exceeding competitive rates; the commission is currently about three percent. The nature of contracts between trading companies and steel consuming companies changes substantially with cyclical fluctuations in the economy. During recessions, particularly in times of tight credit, trading companies frequently extend the financing period under which end users may pay for the steel. Trading companies usually pay steel producers cash for products received and sell them on credit to end users.

Thus, Japanese steel producers are selling steel either to large end users or to trading companies (who are even larger buyers); one would surmise, then, that the kohan system of prices does not generally characterize the transactions prices at which the Japanese steel producers sell their products. In fact, it is known that the prices at which steelmakers sold their steel to the trading companies were arrived at privately outside the large monthly meetings.

The Monopolistic Competition Revolution

PAUL A. SAMUELSON

Paul A. Samuelson is Institute Professor at Massachusetts Institute of Technology. This article is taken from a book, Monopolistic Competition Theory, edited by Robert Kuenne and published in 1967.

Some Sociology of Knowledge

No historian of science would be surprised to learn that Edward Chamberlin and Joan Robinson[1] had written in the same year separate books that break definitively with the assumptions of perfect competition. Newton and Leibniz both discovered the calculus because that subject was then in the air, waiting to be discovered. Similarly, 1933, the year of *The Theory of Monopolistic Competition* and of *The Economics of Imperfect Competition*, followed a decade of intense discussion concerning the nature of competition, the so-called "cost controversy" initiated by Clapham's famous complaint about the "empty boxes" of economic theory.

Many of the great names of the day were involved in that controversy: Allyn Young, Knight, J. M. Clark, Dennis Robertson, Robbins, Viner, Shove, Harrod, Schumpeter, Yntema, Hotelling, Sraffa, Pigou, J. Robinson, Kahn, and many others.[2] In retrospect I judge it to have been rather

[1] E. H. Chamberlin, *The Theory of Monopolistic Competition*, Harvard University Press, Cambridge, Mass., first edition, 1933; eighth edition, 1962; J. Robinson, *Economics of Imperfect Competition*, Macmillan, London, 1933.

[2] For a sampling, see G. J. Stigler and K. E. Boulding, eds., *Readings in Price Theory*, Irwin, Homewood, Ill., 1952, which contains articles by J. H. Clapham (1922), A. C. Pigou (1922), D. H. Robertson (1924), F. H. Knight (1924), P. Sraffa (1926), and J. Viner (1931); cf. also J. M. Clark, *Economics of Overhead Costs*, University of Chicago Press, Chicago, 1923. Aside from preparing the way for theories of monopolistic and imperfect competition, the cost controversy did result in a better understanding of competitive theory.

344

a sterile debate, as will appear from what follows. But experience with the history of science amply testifies that the journey between two points is not a straight line. Having made detours and been caught in *culs-de-sac*, a subject must make progress by the negative act of dumping ballast.

The keen historian of science will not be surprised, either, to learn that simultaneous discoveries that appear to be substantially similar turn out, on careful examination, to be substantively different. In our own field of economics, it is customary to bracket Jevons, Menger, and Walras as independent discoverers of the subjective theory of value and of utility; but with the hindsight of a century we see that Walras's formulation of general equilibrium quite overshadows the brilliant work of his contemporaries and he might have been spared the pain of discovery that Jevons had beaten him to what both thought was the important Pole.

With cogency and pertinacity, Chamberlin has always insisted on differentiating his product from that of Mrs. Robinson. Posterity will agree. But in its typical wayward manner, posterity will amalgamate into an optimal package what it conceives to be the best of the various systems. Thus, when Chamberlin tells us that his work did not find its inspiration in the cost controversy, we find strong corroboration in the historical documents denoting his journey along the road to Damascus, from 1921 through 1927 and beyond, as well as in the structure and texture of his 1933 classic. But, again, as the sociologist of science knows, there is a feedback reaction between the readers of a seminal work and its author. Most of Chamberlin's readers, in America as well as in England, were exercised by the cost controversy. Allyn Young, Chamberlin's thesis supervisor and teacher of Frank Knight, who in turn taught Chamberlin, was an important participant in the controversy. Although we have abundant evidence, after 1933 as well as before, that Edward Chamberlin was a lone-wolf scholar with infinite capacity for formulating and pushing a problem to solution in his own way, still, no man is an island unto himself. If A has any sort of communication with B who has any communication with C, . . . , there is no way to rule out mutual interaction between A and Z even if they have never met or had any direct contact.

As an illustration of mutual dependence, consider Mrs. Robinson and J. M. Clark's *Economics of Overhead Costs*. There is no reason to think she had ever heard of this stimulating 1923 book. But if Robertson, Pigou, Shove, Austin Robinson, Kahn, or any other member of the Cambridge set had ever read the work, then some degree of influence cannot be ruled out by the historian of science even though he can never hope to measure its degree. Or consider Sraffa's December 1926 article. Without doubting that an April 1927 thesis could have been written completely independently of it, we are still not surprised that Chamberlin's 1933 book should take notice of the great similarity between the *Weltanschauung* of Sraffa's final part with the perfected theory of monopolistic competition. In rereading Sraffa for the present essay, I was struck by, and marked, certain lines that seemed to me to be in the Chamberlin spirit; and it was, therefore, with interest that I subsequently noted some of them quoted at the beginning of Chamberlin's book.

A final illustration of the virtual impossibility of ruling out truly independent simultaneous scientific discovery can be taken from the combined field of international trade and welfare economics. At the London School of Economics in the 1930's, brilliant young economists such as Lerner, Hicks, and Kaldor worked out graphical models of international exchange and what we would today call Pareto-optimality necessary conditions for welfare. References to Vilfredo Pareto will be sought in vain, even though his books were known to the more widely-read members of that circle. The reason? Pareto is an obscure enough writer, the subject is a sufficiently subtle one, and the men involved are sufficiently creative and self-stimulating for me to think that Pareto's influence was at best subconscious. But a quite different influencing is that which I would associate with the name of Viner. In January 1931, Viner gave a public lecture at L.S.E. on international trade, in which he married Haberler's production-possibility frontier to consumer indifference curves. Everyone, including the lecturer, may have forgotten the very fact that the lecture was given. But nothing can change the fact that independent rediscovery of this bit of analysis became impossible in that environment after that date. Even if only Victor Edelberg understood Viner . . .[3]

The Theoretical Shortcomings of Perfect Competition

My purpose in this essay is not to isolate the peculiar contributions to price theory made by Edward Chamberlin. He has done that job superlatively well and we can take it for granted. Indeed the time has come when we may permit ourselves to use the terms monopolistic competition and imperfect competition interchangeably, emancipating them from their first associations with the different conceptions of Chamberlin and Mrs. Robinson, and using them as convenient names for the best current models of price theory.[4]

My purpose here is to discuss some of the *theoretical* reasons why perfect competition provides an empirically inadequate model of the real world. This forces us to work with some versions of monopolistic or imper-

[3] That the compensation principle as applied to losers from free trade should have been enunciated in the late 1930's using the same kind of example that Viner had used earlier shows a similar indirect influence of Viner on the London School, but it would take a more tedious detective operation to trace through its unconscious contracts. See J. Viner, *Studies in the Theory of International Trade*, Harper, New York, 1937, p. 521.
[4] Admittedly, impure competition might be a better name than imperfect competition, in consideration of Chamberlin's point that denying perfect knowledge can still leave the firm a pure competitor facing a price at which it can sell all it wishes; but impure competition sounds dirty, just as monopolistic competition sounds evil, and so we find convenience in the label *imperfect competition*.

fect competition. Chicago economists can continue to shout until they are blue in the face that there is no elegant alternative to the theory of perfect competition.[5] If not, the proper moral is, "So much the worse for elegance" rather than, "Economists of the world, unite in proclaiming that the Emperor has almost no clothes, and in pretending that the model of perfect competition does a good enough job in fitting the real world." More than once I shall have to report that we theorists, quite removed from Cook County, have retrogressed in the last quarter of a century, taking the coward's way of avoiding the important questions thrown up by

[5] G. J. Stigler, *Five Lectures on Economic Problems*, Macmillan, London, 1950, in particular Lecture 2, "Monopolistic Competition in Retrospect"; M. Friedman, *Essays in Positive Economics*, University of Chicago Press, Chicago, 1953, Ch. 1; E. H. Chamberlin, *Toward a More General Theory of Value*, Oxford University Press, New York, 1957, Ch. 15; G. C. Archibald, "Chamberlin *versus* Chicago," *Review of Economic Studies*, XXIX (1961), pp. 2–28; G. J. Stigler, "Archibald *versus* Chicago," *Review of Economic Studies*, XXX (1963), pp. 63–64; M. Friedman, "More on Archibald *versus* Chicago," *Review of Economic Studies*, XXX (1963), pp. 65–67; G. C. Archibald, "Reply to Chicago," *Review of Economic Studies* XXX (1963), pp. 68–71. First, I must emphasize that, despite some ambiguity in Chamberlin's own writing, the symmetric large group of Chamberlin must not be taken to be the content of the words "monopolistic competition" or even to constitute the significant content of the theoretical revolution. Second, although I personally emphasized in my *Foundations of Economic Analysis*, Harvard University Press, Cambridge, Mass., 1947, the importance of the empirically testable implications of second-order maximization inequalities, I must dissociate myself from Archibald's criticism of the Chicago criticism, which consists of Archibald's demonstration that the Chamberlin theory has few unambiguously signed implications of my *Foundations* type. If the real world displays the variety of behavior that the Chamberlin-Robinson models permit—and I believe the Chicago writers are simply wrong in denying that these important empirical deviations exist—then reality will falsify *many* of the important qualitative and quantitative *predictions* of the competitive model. Hence, by the pragmatic test of prediction adequacy, the perfect-competition model fails to be an adequate approximation. When Friedman claims (*Essays*, pp. 36–37) that a tax will have the type of incidence on the cigarette industry that it would on a competitive industry, he is at most showing that *some* predictions of the latter theory are adequate. To the degree that other predictions are falsified— consumer price approximately equal to marginal cost, advertising cost equal to zero—the competitive model fails the pragmatic predictive test.

The fact that the Chamberlin-Robinson model is "empty," in the sense of ruling out few empirical configurations and being capable of providing only formalistic descriptions, is not the slightest reason for abandoning it in favor of a "full" model of the competitive type *if reality is similarly* "empty" and "non-full." In 1960, elementary particle theory was similarly "empty" and Newtonian mechanics similarly "full"; but only an idiot would have tried in 1960 to use Newton's model to describe high-energy physics. To reach retroactively into the urn of monopoly to explain advertising expense and into that of the competitive model to explain some case of tax incidence is to advance not a step, and, as the wastes of free entry under imperfectly competitive conditions cannot be predicted by any blend of items selected from each urn, illustrates the indispensability of the 1933 revolution. *Cf.* R. L. Bishop, "Monopolistic Competition after Thirty Years: The Impact on General Theory," *American Economic Review, Papers and Proceedings.* LIV (1964), pp. 33–43.

As a final instance, consider the notion that many business firms set price on some kind of a "full-cost mark-up" over some kind of cost (R. L. Hall and C. J. Hitch. "Price Theory and Business Behavior," *Oxford Economic Papers*, II (1939), pp. 12–45). It might be argued that this is an empty formulation, because, depending on alternative estimates of demand elasticity and alternative specifications of entry of rivals, this model can lead to price above marginal cost to any percentage degree. Granted, but by what logic does that permit anyone to replace the vacuum by asserting the competitive outcome of P equals one times $M.C.$, or P equals one-plus epsilon times $M.C.$?

the real economic world and fobbing off in their place nice answers to less interesting easy questions.

Exorcising the Marshallian Incubus

The ambiguities of Alfred Marshall paralyzed the best brains in the Ango-Saxon branch of our profession for three decades. By 1930 the profession had just about reattained the understanding of the pure theory of monopoly that Cournot had achieved in 1838; and it had yet to reattain the understanding of the theory of competitive general equilibrium that Walras had achieved by 1878 or 1896.

Although Marshall was a great economist, we must remember in appraising his originality that he knew well the work of Mill, Cournot, Dupuit, and Mangoldt. Even if we accept at face value his claim that he owed little or nothing to such contemporaries as Jevons and Walras—and I for one think the only appropriate answer to that claim is: the more fool he—we must realize that there was precious little in the theory of partial equilibrium under perfect competition to be developed by anyone unlucky enough to have been born as an economist *after* Cournot, Mill, Dupuit, and Mangoldt.[6]

Unfortunately, because of his unwillingness to make sharp distinctions between perfect and less-than-perfect competition, Marshall managed to set back the clock both on competitive theory and on the theory of monopoly. Edgeworth was almost an exact contemporary of Marshall, but seems to have been scared to death of that eminent Victorian. The profound researches of Edgeworth on bilateral monopoly and various forms of oligopoly received little attention from the Marshallian tradition. And it was not until 1934 with the work of Von Stackelberg, and indeed 1944 with the *Theory of Games* of von Neumann and Morgenstern, that the modern literature reattained the depth of Edgeworth's analysis.[7]

Let us make no mistake about it. The theory of simple monopoly is

[6] Testifying to the cogency of my *a priori* reasoning on this point is the fact that both Fleeming Jenkin (1870) and Auspitz and Lieben (1889) developed partial-equilibrium theory in all of its fundamentals before Marshall's 1890 *Principles of Economics;* neither could have been helped in this regard by Marshall's 1879 tract, *The Pure Theory of Domestic and International Values,* which deals hardly at all with partial equilibrium and deserves high praise thereby.

[7] H. von Stackelberg, *Marktform und Gleichgewicht,* Springer, Berlin, 1934; W. Fellner, *Competition Among the Few,* Knopf, New York, 1949; J. von Neumann and O. Morgenstern, *Theory of Games and Economic Behavior,* Princeton University Press, Princeton, New Jersey, 1944. Chamberlin's Chapter 23 and Appendix A provide a valuable but far-from-adequate history and analysis of the problems of bilaterial monopoly, duopoly, and general game-theoretic problems. In particular the 1929 notion that Edgeworth was principally to be known for his "oscillatory" solution to duopoly is a sad understatement. By 1897 Edgeworth already had a full appreciation of the game-theoretic interminacy: his Arctic explorers already trace out 1934 von Stackelberg solutions and much else. F. Y. Edgeworth, *Papers Relating to Political Economy,* Royal Economic Society, London, 1925. Indeed, in his *Mathematic Psychics,* Paul, London, 1881, pp. 35–39, 139–148, Edgeworth had already anticipated the modern concept of the "core" of a game, in its relation to large numbers of sellers.

child's play. That grown men argued seriously in 1930 about who had first used or named the curve that we now call "marginal revenue" is a joke. Cournot had settled all that a century earlier and in a completely modern manner, so that the reader who picks up the English translation of his book and has to guess at the date of its authorship merely on the basis of an understanding of the cost-controversy literature ought to guess 1927 or 1933. Chamberlin always used to insist that the essence of his contribution to the subject had nothing particularly to do with the rediscovery and naming of the simple marginal curves. We can readily agree with him. Whether it is correct to go and say, as some have said, that Mrs. Robinson's book differs from his in that hers is primarily a book on monopoly, I find a more difficult question to answer. To a considerable extent her book is that, and we feel that the reviewer of it had a small point when he said that the time spent in reading her work might with better profit be spent on studying Irving Fisher's little textbook on the infinitesimal calculus.[8] For it is true that simple monopoly theory consists of little other than elementary calculus, in which ordinary and partial derivatives are to be set equal to zero whereas higher derivatives are required to be nonpositive. Marshall was so enamored of his silly little unitary-elasticity hyperbolas that he omitted a straightforward treatment of simple monopoly, leaving room in the first third of this century for quasi-independent rediscovery by literary economists of these rudiments.

Retrogression in Monopoly Theory

But where Marshall threw off two generations of scholars was in his insistence on having his cake and eating it too. He would try to treat at the same time cases of less-than-perfect and of perfect competition. He would try to achieve a spurious verisimilitude by talking about vague biological dynamics, and by failing to distinguish L veen reversible and irreversible developments. He would insist on confusing the issue of external economies and diseconomies—which played an important role in the work of such pre-Marshallian writers as Henry Sidgwick—with the entirely separable (and separate!) issue of varying laws of returns. Marshall was so afraid of being unrealistic that he merely ends up being fuzzy and confusing—and confused.

Although harsh, these are my well-considered judgments on the matter, and I mention them only because no one can understand the history of the subject if he does not realize that much of the work from 1920 to 1933 was merely the negative task of getting Marshall out of the way. I shall not document these opinions but shall merely give single examples of what I have in mind.

[8] A. J. Nichols, "Robinson's Economics of Imperfect Competition," *Journal of Political Economy*, XLII (1934), pp. 257–259. Actually, when Mrs. Robinson comes to discuss a world of monopolies and other issues, she does go far beyond simple monopoly theory.

First, that part of simple monopoly theory which consists of neat theorems—such as that a lump-sum tax or a tax on net profits will have no effect on monopoly output, whereas a tax on gross revenues or on output will lower output and raise prices—was well known to any reader of Cournot and involves little more than the calculus of a single variable.

Second, which of us has not been brought up short in his reading of Marshall when suddenly, in the midst of what was thought to be a discussion of "competition," it turns out that some entrepreneur fails to do something because of his "fear of spoiling the market," a sure sign of some kind of imperfection of competition? Such aberrations as these, to which I point in horror, are taken by some modern writers as signs of Marshall's genius and erudite wisdom about the facts of life. "It's all in Marshall," they say, failing to add, "All the words of economics are in Webster's dictionary or in the fingertips of monkeys in the British Museum." But just as it takes more than monkeys to find the Michaelangelo statues that lurk in any old cube of marble, so it takes more than can be learned in Marshall to isolate the good sense that is embalmed therein. Marshall's crime is to pretend to handle imperfect competition with tools only applicable to perfect competition.

Third, Marshall was a victim of what the modern Freudians call self-hate. He was a good chess player who was ashamed of playing chess, a good analytical economist who was ashamed of analysis. He well understood Cournot's insistence that the marginal cost curve must not be falling for any maximizing pure competitor, but balked at simple acceptance of the fact. All of his prattle about the biological method in economics—and the last decades' genuine progress in biology through the techniques of physics has confirmed my dictum of 20 years ago that talk of a unique biological method does mostly represent prattle—cannot change this fact: any price taker who can sell more at the going price than he is now selling and who has falling marginal cost will not be in equilibrium. Talk of birds and bees, giant trees in the forest, and declining entrepreneurial dynasties is all very well, but why blink at such an elementary point?

Fourth, this leads to the further confusion by Marshall of *external* effects with increasing *returns* phenomena. Because Marshall [9] made an elementary mistake in his graphical reckoning of consumers' surplus, forgetting to take into account producers' surplus—an odd omission for a chap who always insisted correctly that there are two blades in the scissors of supply and demand—he came up with what seems like an exciting policy theorem: *Tax to contract increasing cost industries; subsidize to expand decreasing cost industries.*

As we congratulate ourselves that commonsense economics has for once produced fruit, we are brought up short by the realization that this is quite wrong. It merely sounds like a couple of other things that are right. Increasing returns industries are likely to be somehow monopolized, and a

[9] *Principles*, Book V, Ch. XIII, pp. 467–470.

monopoly markup of price over marginal cost does create a *prima facie* case for public expansion of that industry. Furthermore, under increasing returns, marginal cost is below average cost; and hence marginal cost pricing would require a state subsidy. But wait: it was a *competitive* decreasing cost industry we were talking about, a contradiction in terms if the increasing returns are *internal* to the firm. So Marshallians hasten to say that it must be, of course, decreasing cost due to *external economies* that was meant, and which ought to be subsidized. Subsidizing external economies is indeed correct but, unfortunately for the false theorem of Marshall, external economies ought to be subsidized even when they occur in industries strongly subject to increasing cost; and external diseconomies require penalty even when they occur in decreasing cost industries. The point is that Marshall was simply wrong in focusing on the effect of external diseconomies and economies on the trend of industry *unit* costs. It took Pigou years to extricate his welfare economics from their Marshallian origins and misconceptions.[10]

Retrogression in Perfect Competition Theory

At the same time that Marshall was doing a disservice to the theory of monopoly and less-than-perfect competition, he was inadvertently delaying the understanding of general equilibrium. (I might have written Walrasian general equilibrium but there is only one general equilibrium, whatever its name.) Ironically, it was not until after World War II that economists generally began to think in terms of general equilibrium. As will be seen in a moment, this represents an advance in logical clarity but something of a retreat in terms of realistic appraisal of actual imperfectly competitive market structures.

If there is a proper understanding of general equilibrium, it is posssible to attain for the first time an understanding of partial equilibrium. The studies by Chamberlin and the contemporaries involved in the cost controversy had, along with the task of developing an analysis of monopolistic or imperfect competition, the task of developing for the first time a proper analysis of the relationship between firms and industry. This task, neglected by Marshall, was not needed by Walras for his ideal model of general equilibrium. For, as we shall see, perfect competition proceeds most smoothly when the extreme assumption of *constant returns to scale* is

[10] Allyn Young in his original review of Pigou's 1912 *Wealth and Welfare* pointed out Pigou's error in thinking that the upward bidding of rents in an industry whose output expands represents anything other than a transfer item that ought to be allowed to take place. Later Knight and Robertson made the same point and Pigou finally capitulated. For a historical recapitulation and summary, see H. S. Ellis and W. Fellner, "External Economies and Diseconomies," *American Economic Review*, XXXIII (1943), pp. 493–511, reprinted in Stigler and Boulding eds., *op. cit.*, pp. 242–263. My generally critical view of Marshall is not universally shared, but a trend is discernible, and it is significant that Marshall's remaining defenders among theorists tend to be those satisfied with perfect competition as an approximation to reality.

firmly adhered to. And yet it is precisely under strict constant returns to scale that the theory of the firm evaporates.

If scale does not matter it is immaterial where we draw the boundaries of the firm or whether we draw them at all. So to speak, the proportions of labor and fertilizer to land are determined at the same ratio everywhere on the homogeneous Iowa plain; and it is industry demand that sets the total output to be produced with these factor proportions. Or as Wicksell so well put the matter, under constant returns to scale and statical conditions of certainty, it is immaterial which factor hires which. Like Topsy, they all spontaneously come together under Darwinian competition in the proper amounts, with any deviations lacking survival value. Labor as much hires capital goods and land as capital hires labor and land. (As we shall see, the situation is a little changed if strict constant returns to scale is relaxed in favor of replicable quanta of least-unit-cost combinations.)

This euthanasia of the concept of the firm under most-perfect competition—which is actually an odd way of putting the matter since what need never exist cannot very well be said to wither away—paradoxically bothered writers of the 1920's and 1930's. Writers like Kaldor and Hicks seemed to agree with Schumpeter that pushing perfect competition to its extreme assumptions led ultimately to the blowup of perfect competition. Thus a constant unit cost curve coinciding with a horizontal firm demand curve would make each pure competitor's output quite indeterminate. (The mathematical economists encountered the same phenomenon in the shape of a singular Hessain matrix associated with homogeneous functions and semidefinite quadratic forms.) My example of the Iowa plain shows that this concern over the firm's indeterminacy was misplaced, for the reason that it is inessential under strict constant returns just how industry's (determinate!) output is allocated among firms. These writers erred in supposing that with every firm in neutral equilibrium, there would be no penalty to having one expand indefinitely until it "monopolized" the industry. Actually, as pointed out elsewhere,[11] even if a firm has 99 or 100 percent of the output, it has under the stipulated returns condition *zero* long-run monopoly power: the net long-run demand curve to it is derived by subtracting from the industry curve the horizontal supply curve of actual and *potential* suppliers, leaving it with a horizontal long-run personal demand curve; like a constitutional monarch, it is left to reign only so long as it does not rule.[12]

---

[11] P. A. Samuelson, *Foundations of Economic Analysis*, Harvard University Press, Cambridge, Mass., 1947, pp. 78–79.

[12] Even within the constant returns technology, we shall see that there are possible advantages (and no disadvantages!) to be derived from having the owners of any unique factor of production, e.g., land suitable for mulberry growing, form a coalition that exploits its monopoly power. We should not wonder that the calculating self-interest on which Adam Smith relies to move the Invisible Hand of perfect competition should motivate people to utilize the ballot box of democracy to institute crop control and other public programs interfering with perfect competition. To a psychologist, Bentham's individualism and Webb's Fabianism are one in motive and appeal.

The Revolution Beckons

The empty boxes that Clapham should have been asking to be filled in the 1920's were thus not the Marshallian categories of increasing, constant, and diminishing cost under competition. The empty boxes were those of market description and classification, involving all the possible patterns of oligopoly, monopoly, duopoly, differentiation of products with numbers large and numbers small, and so forth. But Chamberlin had not yet created this new theoretical vision of the economic world.

Piero Sraffa's justly famous 1926 article takes on a new light in terms of this analysis of the Marshallian influence. Truly reversible decreasing cost industries associated with external economies are perhaps a *curiosum*. If a competitive industry is small, and to the degree that it uses no specialized factors in intensities different from that of the bulk of the rest of industry, it does tend to fall in the category of *constant* costs. We can agree with Sraffa on this.

But this constant cost case is of no intrinsic difference for policy or other purposes from the case that Sraffa needlessly plays down—the case in which the industry uses some factors of special advantage to it alone or in which it uses the various factors of production of society in proportions significantly different from the rest of industry. In this case, and particularly where we add the realistic consideration that almost any product you can name is something of a joint product produced along with and in partial competition with certain by-products, increases in demand for the products of the industry *will* result in increasing costs and relative prices. Such cases create absolutely no complications for general equilibrium, even though Sraffa may be right in thinking they do for partial equilibrium (in which case, so much the worse for partial equilibrium analysis, Marshallian or otherwise!). The point needing emphasis for Sraffa's readers is that *these* phenomena and complications do not themselves create a need for monopolistic competition theory. Where that theory is needed is in handling genuine empirical deviations from perfect competition. Mere interdependence of essentially competitive industries should have led Sraffa merely to a plea for abandonment of Marshallian partial-equilibrium models in favor of Walrasian general-equilibrium models.

Today, as a result of quite other historical influences and developments, general-equilibrium thinking has swept the field of analytical economics. A modern theorist would say that the box diagram analysis of optimal allocation of inputs among industries is just the tool to handle this standard instance of increasing cost. The production possibility frontier, or so-called opportunity cost transformation frontier, captures the essence of the phenomena. But remember that this frontier was first introduced, and then in connection with Haberler's analysis of international trade, only in

1930. It was *after* the 1930's that Stolper and Samuelson, Joan Robinson, and Viner clarified the increasing cost case by considering it in its general-equilibrium context by use of the factor box diagram or equivalent verbal reasonings.[13]

Fortunately, Sraffa's failure to realize that the Walrasian model would supply many of the deficiencies of the Marshallian partial equilibrium served the useful function of pushing him down the road toward Chamberlinian monopolistic competition theory. Because of realistic market conditions that standard theory had been forced to gloss over, ignore, or deny, economics was long overdue for a movement in that direction. If anyone doubts that Sraffa, Mrs. Robinson, and Chamberlin had a useful task to perform, let him only compare the contribution to the cost controversy by Dennis Robertson in 1924[14] with the Sraffa contribution of 1926. Robertson was one of the world's leading economists, a Marshallian expert if ever there was one, and at the prime of his scholarly life. Yet he still enmeshed himself in mystical falling cost curves of a competitive industry, conjuring up group identities that have no existence, and failed completely to relate the behavior of the trees to that of the forest. Robertson's realistic instinct was right—costs do *not* behave as if generated by constant-returns-to-scale production functions—but he failed to follow through and drop the incompatible assumption of perfect competition, thereby forcing himself into logical contradiction and ambiguity. In Sraffa's world of monopolies, each with its own market but checked by overlapping substitutes, we are clearly on the way to Robert Triffin's 1940 *Monopolistic Competition and General Equilibrium Theory*, and hence on the way to *The Theory of Monopolistic Competition*. . . .

Conclusion

In speaking of theories of monopolistic or imperfect competition as "revolutions," I know in advance that I shall provoke dissent. There are minds that by temperament will define away every proposed revolution. For them it is enough to point out that Keynes in 1936 had some partial

[13] See W. F. Stolper and P. A. Samuelson, "Protection and Real Wages," *Review of Economic Studies*, IX (1941), pp. 58–74, reprinted in H. S. Ellis and L. A. Metzler, eds., *Readings in the Theory of International Trade*, Irwin, Homewood, Ill., 1949; J. Robinson, "Rising Supply Price," *Economica*, VIII (1941), pp. 1–8, reprinted in Stigler and Boulding, *Readings in Price Theory*, pp. 233–241; J. Viner, Supplement to 1931 *Zeitschrift für Nationalökonomie*, appearing in *Readings in Price Theory*, pp. 198–232. For Haberler's first paper using the frontier, see G. Haberler, "Die Theorie der komparativen Kosten und ihre Auswertung für die Begründung des Freihandels," *Weltwirtschaftliches Archiv*, XXXII (1930), which gave rise to the well-known expository articles by A. P. Lerner in the 1932 and 1934 *Economica* and by W. W. Leontief in the 1934 *Quarterly Journal of Economics*. Irving Fisher had used a transformation curve in connection with the trade-off between present and future consumption early in this century; Frederic Benham and R. F. Harrod had anticipated in the 1930's a number of the critical relationships involved in the factor-price box diagrams.
[14] Stigler and Boulding, *op. cit.*, pp. 143–149.

anticipator in 1836. Newton is just a guy getting too much credit for the accretion of knowledge that covered centuries. A mountain is just a high hill; a hill, merely a bulging plain. Such people remind me of the grammar-school teacher we all had, who would never give 100 to a paper on the ground that "No one is perfect."

With such semantics, I have no quarrel—provided its rules-of-the-game are clearly understood. However, to those familiar with the history of sciences—how they develop, the role of new and altered modes of thinking in marking their growth, the role even of myth in the autobiography of a science—revolutions are a useful way of describing accelerations in the path of growth. An old theory—or model; or, to use Kuhn's terminology,[15] "paradigm"—is never killed off, as it should be, by a new set of facts. Being prisoners of their own *Gestalts*, scientists (like lovers) abandon an old theory only when they have found a new theory in which to clothe their beliefs. Chamberlin, Sraffa, Robinson, and their contemporaries have led economists into a new land from which their critics will never evict us.

[15] T. S. Kuhn, *The Anatomy of Scientific Revolutions*, University of Chicago Press, Chicago, 1962.

Part Five

WELFARE ECONOMICS

Many of the most important, and most interesting, questions in micro-economics fall under the heading of welfare economics, which is concerned with the nature of the policy recommendations that economists can make. In this part of the book, we present a number of classic articles dealing with welfare economics. Welfare economists have long been interested in the distinctions between private and social costs and benefits. In the first paper, Ronald Coase argues that the traditional treatment of this topic is wrong and "that the suggested courses of action are inappropriate, in that they lead to results which are not necessarily, or even usually, desirable." Welfare economists have also been fascinated for a long time by marginal-cost pricing. In the following paper, Jack Hirshleifer, James DeHaven, and Jerome Milliman describe some of the basic principles underlying marginal-cost pricing and discuss the implications of these principles for the allocation of water supplies. In the next paper, William Vickrey discusses the role of marginal-cost pricing in promoting efficiency in public utilities.

The next two articles are concerned with other aspects of welfare economics. Bertrand de Jouvenel points out that "If the children now being born can, when reaching the age of 32, find themselves two or three times better off than their parents are now, it is worth thinking what to make of this opportunity." His paper is a wide-ranging essay on this topic. In the final paper of this section, Francis Bator describes and analyzes the causes of market failure, which he defines as "the failure of a more or less idealized system of price-market institutions to sustain 'desirable' activities or to stop 'undesirable' activities. The desirability of an activity, in turn, is evaluated relative to the solution values of some explicit or implied maximum-welfare problem." He suggests a comprehensive ordering of types of market failure, "with generalized indivisibility, public goods, and, last and least, nonappropriability as the villains of the piece."

The Problem of Social Cost

RONALD H. COASE

Ronald H. Coase is Professor of Economics at the University of Chicago. This paper is taken from his well-known piece in the Journal of Law and Economics in 1960.

I. The Problem to Be Examined[1]

This paper is concerned with those actions of business firms which have harmful effects on others. The standard example is that of a factory the smoke from which has harmful effects on those occupying neighboring properties. The economic analysis of such a situation has usually proceeded in terms of a divergence between the private and social product of the factory, in which economists have largely followed the treatment of Pigou in *The Economics of Welfare*. The conclusions to which this kind of analysis seems to have led most economists is that it would be desirable to make the owner of the factory liable for the damage caused to those injured by the smoke, or alternatively, to place a tax on the factory owner varying with the amount of smoke produced and equivalent in money terms to the damage it would cause, or finally, to exclude the factory from residential districts (and presumably from other areas in which the emission of smoke would have harmful effects on others). It is my contention that the suggested courses of action are inappropriate, in that they lead to results which are not necessarily, or even usually, desirable.

[1] This article, although concerned with a technical problem of economic analysis, arose out of the study of the Political Economy of Broadcasting which I am now conducting. The argument of the present article was implicit in a previous article dealing with the problem of allocating radio and television frequencies ("The Federal Communications Commission," *J. Law & Econ.*, II [1959]) but comments which I have received seemed to suggest that it would be desirable to deal with the question in a more explicit way and without reference to the original problem for the solution of which the analysis was developed.

II. *The Reciprocal Nature of the Problem*

The traditional approach has tended to obscure the nature of the choice that has to be made. The question is commonly thought of as one in which A inflicts harm on B and what has to be decided is: how should we restrain A? But this is wrong. We are dealing with a problem of a reciprocal nature. To avoid the harm to B would inflict harm on A. The real question that has to be decided is: should A be allowed to harm B or should B be allowed to harm A? The problem is to avoid the more serious harm. I instanced in my previous article[2] the case of a confectioner the noise and vibrations from whose machinery disturbed a doctor in his work. To avoid harming the doctor would inflict harm on the confectioner. The problem posed by this case was essentially whether it was worth while, as a result of restricting the methods of production which could be used by the confectioner, to secure more doctoring at the cost of a reduced supply of confectionery products. Another example is afforded by the problem of straying cattle which destroy crops on neighboring land. If it is inevitable that some cattle will stray, an increase in the supply of meat can only be obtained at the expense of a decrease in the supply of crops. The nature of the choice is clear: meat or crops. What answer should be given is, of course, not clear unless we know the value of what is obtained as well as the value of what is sacrificed to obtain it. To give another example, Professor George J. Stigler instances the contamination of a stream.[3] If we assume that the harmful effect of the pollution is that it kills the fish, the question to be decided is: is the value of the fish lost greater or less than the value of the product which the contamination of the stream makes possible. It goes almost without saying that this problem has to be looked at in total *and* at the margin.

III. *The Pricing System with Liability for Damage*

I propose to start my analysis by examining a case in which most economists would presumably agree that the problem would be solved in a completely satisfactory manner: when the damaging business has to pay for all damage caused *and* the pricing system works smoothly (strictly this means that the operation of a pricing system is without cost).

A good example of the problem under discussion is afforded by the case of straying cattle which destroy crops growing on neighboring land. Let us suppose that a farmer and a cattle-raiser are operating on neighboring properties. Let us further suppose that, without any fencing between the prop-

[2] Coase, "The Federal Communications Commission," *J. Law & Econ.*, II (1959), 26–27.
[3] G. J. Stigler, *The Theory of Price*, p. 105 (1952).

erties, an increase in the size of the cattle-raiser's herd increases the total damage to the farmer's crops. What happens to the marginal damage as the size of the herd increases is another matter. This depends on whether the cattle tend to follow one another or to roam side by side, on whether they tend to be more or less restless as the size of the herd increases, and on other similar factors. For my immediate purpose, it is immaterial what assumption is made about marginal damage as the size of the herd increases.

To simplify the argument, I propose to use an arithmetical example. I shall assume that the annual cost of fencing the farmer's property is $9 and that the price of the crop is $1 per ton. Also, I assume that the relation between the number of cattle in the herd and the annual crop loss is as follows:

Number in Herd (Steers)	Annual Crop Loss (Tons)	Crop Loss per Additional Steer (Tons)
1	1	1
2	3	2
3	6	3
4	10	4

Given that the cattle-raiser is liable for the damage caused, the additional annual cost imposed on the cattle-raiser if he increased his herd from, say, two to three steers is $3 and in deciding on the size of the herd, he will take this into account along with his other costs. That is, he will not increase the size of the herd unless the value of the additional meat produced (assuming that the cattle-raiser slaughters the cattle) is greater than the additional costs that this will entail, including the value of the additional crops destroyed. Of course, if, by the employment of dogs, herdsmen, airplanes, mobile radio, and other means, the amount of damage can be reduced, these means will be adopted when their cost is less than the value of the crop which they prevent being lost. Given that the annual cost of fencing is $9, the cattle-raiser who wished to have a herd with four steers or more would pay for fencing to be erected and maintained, assuming that other means of attaining the same end would not do so more cheaply. When the fence is erected, the marginal cost due to the liability for damage becomes zero, except to the extent that an increase in the size of the herd necessitates a stronger and therefore more expensive fence because more steers are liable to lean against it at the same time. But, of course, it may be cheaper for the cattle-raiser not to fence and to pay for the damaged crops, as in my arithmetical example, with three or fewer steers.

It might be thought that the fact that the cattle-raiser would pay for all crops damaged would lead the farmer to increase his planting if a cattle-raiser were to occupy the neighboring property. But this is not so. If the crop was obviously sold in conditions of perfect competition, marginal cost was equal to price for the amount of planting undertaken and any expansion would have reduced the profits of the farmer. In the new situation, the existence of crop damage would mean that the farmer would sell less on the open market but his receipts for a given production would remain the same, since the cattle-raiser would pay the market price for any crop damaged. Of course, if cattle-raising commonly involved the destruction of crops, the coming into existence of a cattle-raising industry might raise the price of the crops involved and farmers would then extend their planting. But I wish to confine my attention to the individual farmer.

I have said that the occupation of a neighboring property by a cattle-raiser would not cause the amount of production, or perhaps more exactly the amount of planting, by the farmer to increase. In fact, if the cattle-raising has any effect, it will be to decrease the amount of planting. The reason for this is that, for any given tract of land, if the value of the crop damaged is so great that the receipts from the sale of the undamaged crop are less than the total costs of cultivating that tract of land, it will be profitable for the farmer and the cattle-raiser to make a bargain whereby that tract of land is left uncultivated. This can be made clear by means of an arithmetical example. Assume initially that the value of the crop obtained from cultivating a given tract of land is $12 and that the cost incurred in cultivating this tract of land is $10, the net gain from cultivating the land being $2. I assume for purposes of simplicity that the farmer owns the land. Now assume that the cattle-raiser starts operations on the neighboring property and that the value of the crops damaged is $1. In this case $11 is obtained by the farmer from sale on the market and $1 is obtained from the cattle-raiser for damage suffered and the net gain remains $2. Now suppose that the cattle-raiser finds it profitable to increase the size of his herd, even though the amount of damage rises to $3; which means that the value of the additional meat production is greater than the additional costs, including the additional $2 payment for damage. But the total payment for damage is now $3. The net gain to the farmer from cultivating the land is still $2. The cattle-raiser would be better off if the farmer would agree not to cultivate his land for any payment less than $3. The farmer would be agreeable to not cultivating the land for any payment greater than $2. There is clearly room for a mutually satisfactory bargain which would lead to the abandonment of cultivation.[4] But the same argu-

---

[4] The argument in the text has proceeded on the assumption that the alternative to cultivation of the crop is abandonment of cultivation altogether. But this need not be so. There may be crops which are less liable to damage by cattle but which would not be as profitable as the crop grown in the absence of damage. Thus, if the cultivation of a new crop would yield a return to the farmer of $1 instead of $2, and the size of the herd which would cause $3 damage with the old crop would cause $1 damage with the new crop, it would be profitable to the cattle-raiser to pay any sum less than $2 to induce the farmer to change his crop (since this would reduce damage liability from $3 to $1) and it would be profitable for the farmer to do so if the amount received was more than $1 (the reduction in his return caused by switching crops). In fact, there would be

ment applies not only to the whole tract cultivated by the farmer but also to any subdivision of it. Suppose, for example, that the cattle have a well-defined route, say, to a brook or to a shady area. In these circumstances, the amount of damage to the crop along the route may well be great and if so, it could be that the farmer and the cattle-raiser would find it profitable to make a bargain whereby the farmer would agree not to cultivate this strip of land.

But this raises a further possibility. Suppose that there is such a well-defined route. Suppose further that the value of the crop that would be obtained by cultivating this strip of land is $10 but that the cost of cultivation is $11. In the absence of the cattle-raiser, the land would not be cultivated. However, given the presence of the cattle-raiser, it could well be that if the strip was cultivated, the whole crop would be destroyed by the cattle. In which case, the cattle-raiser would be forced to pay $10 to the farmer. It is true that the farmer would lose $1. But the cattle-raiser would lose $10. Clearly this is a situation which is not likely to last indefinitely since neither party would want this to happen. The aim of the farmer would be to induce the cattle-raiser to make a payment in return for an agreement to leave this land uncultivated. The farmer would not be able to obtain a payment greater than the cost of fencing off this piece of land nor so high as to lead the cattle-raiser to abandon the use of the neighboring property. What payment would in fact be made would depend on the shrewdness of the farmer and the cattle-raiser as bargainers. But as the payment would not be so high as to cause the cattle-raiser to abandon this location and as it would not vary with the size of the herd, such an agreement would not affect the allocation of resources but would merely alter the distribution of income and wealth as between the cattle-raiser and the farmer.

I think it is clear that if the cattle-raiser is liable for damage caused and the pricing system works smoothly, the reduction in the value of production elsewhere will be taken into account in computing the additional cost involved in increasing the size of the herd. This cost will be weighed against the value of the additional meat production and, given perfect competition in the cattle industry, the allocation of resources in cattle-raising will be optimal. What needs to be emphasized is that the fall in the value of production elsewhere which would be taken into account in the costs of the cattle-raiser may well be less than the damage which the cattle would cause to the crops in the ordinary course of events. This is because it is possible, as a result of market transactions, to discontinue cultivation of the land. This is desirable in all cases in which the damage that the cattle would cause, and for which the cattle-raiser would be willing to pay, exceeds the amount which the farmer would pay for the use of land. In

room for a mutually satisfactory bargain in all cases in which a change of crop would reduce the amount of damage by more than it reduces the value of the crop (excluding damage)—in all cases, that is, in which a change in the crop cultivated would lead to an increase in the value of production.

conditions of perfect competition, the amount which the farmer would pay for the use of the land is equal to the difference between the value of the total production when the factors are employed on this land and the value of the additional product yielded in their next best use (which would be what the farmer would have to pay for the factors). If damage exceeds the amount the farmer would pay for the use of the land, the value of the additional product of the factors employed elsewhere would exceed the value of the total product in this use after damage is taken into account. It follows that it would be desirable to abandon cultivation of the land and to release the factors employed for production elsewhere. A procedure which merely provided for payment for damage to the crop caused by the cattle but which did not allow for the possibility of cultivation being discontinued would result in too small an employment of factors of production in cattle-raising and too large an employment of factors in cultivation of the crop. But given the possibility of market transactions, a situation in which damage to crops exceeded the rent of the land would not endure. Whether the cattle-raiser pays the farmer to leave the land uncultivated or himself rents the land by paying the land-owner an amount slightly greater than the farmer would pay (if the farmer was himself renting the land), the final result would be the same and would maximize the value of production. Even when the farmer is induced to plant crops which it would not be profitable to cultivate for sale on the market, this will be a purely short-term phenomenon and may be expected to lead to an agreement under which the planting will cease. The cattle-raiser will remain in that location and the marginal cost of meat production will be the same as before, thus having no long-run effect on the allocation of resources.

IV. The Pricing System with No Liability for Damage

I now turn to the case in which, although the pricing system is assumed to work smoothly (that is, costlessly), the damaging business is not liable for any of the damage which it causes. This business does not have to make a payment to those damaged by its actions. I propose to show that the allocation of resources will be the same in this case as it was when the damaging business was liable for damage caused. As I showed in the previous case that the allocation of resources was optimal, it will not be necessary to repeat this part of the argument.

I return to the case of the farmer and the cattle-raiser. The farmer would suffer increased damage to his crop as the size of the herd increased. Suppose that the size of the cattle-raiser's herd is three steers (and that this is the size of the herd that would be maintained if crop damage was not taken into account). Then the farmer would be willing to pay up to $3 if the cattle-raiser would reduce his herd to two steers, up to $5 if the herd were reduced to one steer and would pay up to $6 if cattle-raising was abandoned. The cattle-raiser would therefore receive $3 from the farmer if he kept two steers instead of three. This $3 foregone is therefore part of the cost incurred in keeping the third steer. Whether the $3 is a payment which the cattle-raiser has to make if he adds the third steer to his herd (which it would be if the cattle-raiser was liable to the farmer for damage caused to the crop) or whether it is a sum of money which he would have received if he did not keep a third steer (which it would be if the cattle-raiser was not liable to the farmer for damage caused to the crop) does not affect the final result. In both cases $3 is part of the cost of adding a third steer, to be included along with the other costs. If the increase in the value of production in cattle-raising through increasing the size of the herd from two to three is greater than the additional costs that have to be incurred (including the $3 damage to crops), the size of the herd will be increased. Otherwise, it will not. The size of the herd will be the same whether the cattle-raiser is liable for damage caused to the crop or not.

It may be argued that the assumed starting point—a herd of three steers—was arbitrary. And this is true. But the farmer would not wish to pay to avoid crop damage which the cattle-raiser would not be able to cause. For example, the maximum annual payment which the farmer could be induced to pay could not exceed $9, the annual cost of fencing. And the farmer would only be willing to pay this sum if it did not reduce his earnings to a level that would cause him to abandon cultivation of this particular tract of land. Furthermore, the farmer would only be willing to pay this amount if he believed that, in the absence of any payment by him, the size of the herd maintained by the cattle-raiser would be four or more steers. Let us assume that this is the case. Then the farmer would be willing to pay up to $3 if the cattle-raiser would reduce his herd to three steers, up to $6 if the herd were reduced to two steers, up to $8 if one steer only were kept and up to $9 if cattle-raising were abandoned. It will be noticed that the change in the starting point has not altered the amount which would accrue to the cattle-raiser if he reduced the size of his herd by any given amount. It is still true that the cattle-raiser could receive an additional $3 from the farmer if he agreed to reduce his herd from three steers to two and that the $3 represents the value of the crop that would be destroyed by adding the third steer to the herd. Although a different belief on the part of the farmer (whether justified or not) about the size of the herd that the cattle-raiser would maintain in the absence of payments from him may affect the total payment he can be induced to pay, it is not true that this different belief would have any effect on the size of the herd that the cattle-raiser will actually keep. This will be the same as it would be if the cattle-raiser had to pay for damage caused by his cattle, since a receipt foregone of a given amount is the equivalent of a payment of the same amount.

It might be thought that it would pay the cattle-raiser to increase his herd above the size that he would wish to maintain once a bargain had been made in order to induce the farmer to make a larger total payment. And this may be true. It is similar in nature to the action of the farmer (when the cattle-raiser was liable for damage) in cultivating land on which, as a result of an agreement with the cattle-raiser, planting would subsequently be abandoned (including land which would not be cultivated at all in the absence of cattle-raising). But such maneuvers are preliminaries to an agreement and do not affect the long-run equilibrium position, which is the same whether or not the cattle-raiser is held responsible for the crop damage brought about by his cattle.

It is necessary to know whether the damaging business is liable or not for damage caused since without the establishment of this initial delimitation of rights there can be no market transactions to transfer and recombine them. But the ultimate result (which maximizes the value of production) is independent of the legal position if the pricing system is assumed to work without cost. . . .

V. *The Cost of Market Transactions Taken into Account*

The argument has proceeded up to this point on the assumption that there were no costs involved in carrying out market transactions. This is, of course, a very unrealistic assumption. In order to carry out a market transaction it is necessary to discover who it is that one wishes to deal with, to inform people that one wishes to deal and on what terms, to conduct negotiations leading up to a bargain, to draw up the contract, to undertake the inspection needed to make sure that the terms of the contract are being observed, and so on. These operations are often extremely costly, sufficiently costly at any rate to prevent many transactions that would be carried out in a world in which the pricing system worked without cost.

In earlier sections, when dealing with the problem of the rearrangement of legal rights through the market, it was argued that such a rearrangement would be made through the market whenever this would lead to an increase in the value of production. But this assumed costless market transactions. Once the costs of carrying out market transactions are taken into account it is clear that such a rearrangement of rights will only be undertaken when the increase in the value of production consequent upon the rearrangement is greater than the costs which would be involved in bringing it about. When it is less, the granting of an injunction (or the knowledge that it would be granted) or the liability to pay damages may result in an activity being discontinued (or may prevent its being started) which would be undertaken if market transactions were costless. In these conditions the initial delimitation of legal rights does have an effect on the efficiency with which the economic system operates. One arrangement of rights may bring about a greater value of production than any other. But unless this is the arrangement of rights established by the legal system, the costs of reaching the same result by altering and combining rights through the market may be so great that this optimal arrangement of rights, and the greater value of production which it would bring, may never be achieved. The part played by economic considerations in the process of delimiting legal rights will be discussed in the next section. In this section, I will take the initial delimitation of rights and the costs of carrying out market transactions as given.

It is clear that an alternative form of economic organization which could achieve the same result at less cost than would be incurred by using the market would enable the value of production to be raised. As I explained many years ago, the firm represents such an alternative to organizing production through market transactions. Within the firm individual bargains between the various cooperating factors of production are eliminated and for a market transaction is substituted an administrative decision. The rearrangement of production then takes place without the need for bargains between the owners of the factors of production. A landowner who has control of a large tract of land may devote his land to various uses taking into account the effect that the interrelations of the various activities will have on the net return of the land, thus rendering unnecessary bargains between those undertaking the various activities. Owners of a large building or of several adjoining properties in a given area may act in much the same way. In effect, the firm would acquire the legal rights of all the parties and the rearrangement of activities would not follow on a rearrangement of rights by contract, but as a result of an administrative decision as to how the rights should be used.

It does not, of course, follow that the administrative costs of organizing a transaction through a firm are inevitably less than the costs of the market transactions which are superseded. But where contracts are peculiarly difficult to draw up and an attempt to describe what the parties have agreed to do or not to do (e.g., the amount and kind of a smell or noise that they may make or will not make) would necessitate a lengthy and highly involved document, and, where, as is probable, a long-term contract would be desirable; it would be hardly surprising if the emergence of a firm or the extension of the activities of an existing firm was not the solution adopted on many occasions to deal with the problem of harmful effects. This solution would be adopted whenever the administrative costs of the firm were less than the costs of the market transactions that it supersedes and the gains which would result from the rearrangement of activities greater than the firm's costs of organizing them. I do not need to examine in great detail the character of this solution since I have explained what is involved in my earlier article.

But the firm is not the only possible answer to this problem. The administrative costs of organizing transactions within the firm may also be high, and particularly so when many diverse activities are brought within the control of a single organization. In the standard case of a smoke nuisance, which may affect a vast number of people engaged in a wide variety of activities, the administrative costs might well be so high as to make any attempt to deal with the problem within the confines of a single firm impossible. An alternative solution is direct government regulation. Instead of instituting a legal system of rights which can be modified by transactions on the market, the government may impose regulations which state what people must or must not do and which have to be obeyed. Thus, the government (by statute or perhaps more likely through an administrative agency) may, to deal with the problem of smoke nuisance, decree that certain methods of production should or should not be used (e.g., that smoke preventing devices should be installed or that coal or oil should not be burned) or may confine certain types of business to certain districts (zoning regulations).

The government is, in a sense, a super-firm (but of a very special kind) since it is able to influence the use of factors of production by administrative decision. But the ordinary firm is subject to checks in its operations because of the competition of other firms, which might administer the same activities at lower cost and also because there is always the alternative of market transactions as against organization within the firm if the administrative costs become too great. The government is able, if it wishes, to avoid the market altogether, which a firm can never do. The firm has to make market agreements with the owners of the factors of production that it uses. Just as the government can conscript or seize property, so it can decree that factors of production should only be used in such-and-such a way. Such authoritarian methods save a lot of trouble (for those doing the organizing). Furthermore, the government has at its disposal the police and the other law enforcement agencies to make sure that its regulations are carried out.

It is clear that the government has powers which might enable it to get some things done at a lower cost than could a private organization (or at any rate one without special governmental powers). But the governmental administrative machine is not itself costless. It can, in fact, on occasion be extremely costly. Furthermore, there is no reason to suppose that the restrictive and zoning regulations, made by a fallible administration subject to political pressures and operating without any competitive check, will necessarily always be those which increase the efficiency with which the economic system operates. Furthermore, such general regulations which must apply to a wide variety of cases will be enforced in some cases in which they are clearly inappropriate. From these considerations it follows that direct governmental regulation will not necessarily give better results than leaving the problem to be solved by the market or the firm. But equally there is no reason why, on occasion, such governmental administrative regulation should not lead to an improvement in economic efficiency.

This would seem particularly likely when, as is normally the case with the smoke nuisance, a large number of people are involved and in which therefore the costs of handling the problem through the market or the firm may be high.

There is, of course, a further alternative, which is to do nothing about the problem at all. And given that the costs involved in solving the problem by regulations issued by the governmental administrative machine will often be heavy (particularly if the costs are interpreted to include all the consequences which follow from the government engaging in this kind of activity), it will no doubt be commonly the case that the gain which would come from regulating the actions which give rise to the harmful effects will be less than the costs involved in government regulation.

The discussion of the problem of harmful effects in this section (when the costs of market transactions are taken into account) is extremely inadequate. But at least it has made clear that the problem is one of choosing the appropriate social arrangement for dealing with the harmful effects. All solutions have costs and there is no reason to suppose that government regulation is called for simply because the problem is not well handled by the market or the firm. Satisfactory views on policy can only come from a patient study of how, in practice, the market, firms, and governments handle the problem of harmful effects. Economists need to study the work of the broker in bringing parties together, the effectiveness of restrictive covenants, the problems of the large-scale real-estate development company, the operation of government zoning and other regulating activities. It is my belief that economists, and policy-makers generally, have tended to over-estimate the advantages which come from governmental regulation. But this belief, even if justified, does not do more than suggest that government regulation should be curtailed. It does not tell us where the boundary line should be drawn. This, it seems to me, has to come from a detailed investigation of the actual results of handling the problem in different ways. But it would be unfortunate if this investigation were undertaken with the aid of a faulty economic analysis. The aim of this article is to indicate what the economic approach to the problem should be.

VI. The Legal Delimitation of Rights and the Economic Problem

Of course, if market transactions were costless, all that matters (questions of equity apart) is that the rights of the various parties should be well-defined and the results of legal actions easy to forecast. But as we have seen, the situation is quite different when market transactions are so costly as to make it difficult to change the arrangement of rights established by the law. In such cases, the courts directly influence economic activity. It would therefore seem desirable that the courts should understand the economic consequences of their decisions and should, insofar as this is possible without creating too much uncertainty about the legal position itself, take these consequences into account when making their decisions. Even when it is possible to change the legal delimitation of rights through market transactions, it is obviously desirable to reduce the need for such transactions and thus reduce the employment of resources in carrying them out.

A thorough examination of the presuppositions of the courts in trying such cases would be of great interest but I have not been able to attempt it. Nevertheless it is clear from a cursory study that the courts have often recognized the economic implications of their decisions and are aware (as many economists are not) of the reciprocal nature of the problem. Furthermore, from time to time, they take these economic implications into account, along with other factors, in arriving at their decisions. The American writers on this subject refer to the question in a more explicit fashion than do the British. Thus, to quote Posser on Torts, a person may

> make use of his own property or . . . conduct his own affairs at the expense of some harm to his neighbors. He may operate a factory whose noise and smoke cause some discomfort to others, so long as he keeps within reasonable bounds. It is only when his conduct is unreasonable, *in the light of its utility and the harm which results* [italics added], that it becomes a nuisance. . . . As it was said in an ancient case in regard to candle-making in a town, "Le utility del chose excusera le noisomeness del stink."
>
> The world must have factories, smelters, oil refineries, noisy machinery and blasting, even at the expense of some inconvenience to those in the vicinity and the plaintiff may be required to accept some not unreasonable discomfort for the general good.

The standard British writers do not state as explicitly as this that a comparison between the utility and harm produced is an element in deciding whether a harmful effect should be considered a nuisance. But similar views, if less strongly expressed, are to be found. The doctrine that the harmful effect must be substantial before the court will act is, no doubt, in part a reflection of the fact that there will almost always be some gain to offset the harm. And in the reports of individual cases, it is clear that the judges have had in mind what would be lost as well as what would be gained in deciding whether to grant an injunction or award damages. . . .

The problem which we face in dealing with actions which have harmful effects is not simply one of restraining those responsible for them. What has to be decided is whether the gain from preventing the harm is greater than the loss which would be suffered elsewhere as a result of stopping the action which produces the harm. In a world in which there are costs of rearranging the rights established by the legal system, the courts, in cases relating to nuisance, are, in effect, making a decision on the economic problem and determining how resources are to be employed. It was argued that the courts are conscious of this and that they often make, although not always in a very explicit fashion, a comparison between what would be gained and what lost by preventing actions which have harmful effects. But the delimitation of rights is also the result of statutory enactments. Here we also find evidence of an appreciation of the reciprocal nature of the problem. While statutory enactments add to the list of nuisances, action is also taken to legalize what would otherwise be nuisances under the common law. The kind of situation which economists are prone to consider as requiring corrective government action is, in fact, often the result of government action. Such action is not necessarily unwise. But there is a real danger that extensive government intervention in the economic system may lead to the protection of those responsible for harmful effects being carried too far.

VII. Pigou's Treatment in "The Economics of Welfare"

The fountainhead for the modern economic analysis of the problem discussed in this article is Pigou's *Economics of Welfare* and, in particular, that section of Part II which deals with divergences between social and private net products which come about because

> one person A, in the course of rendering some service, for which payment is made, to a second person B, incidentally also renders services or disservices to other persons (not producers of like services), of such a sort that payment cannot be exacted from the benefited parties or compensation enforced on behalf of the injured parties.

Pigou tells us that his aim in Part II of *The Economics of Welfare* is

> to ascertain how far the free play of self-interest, acting under the existing legal system, tends to distribute the country's resources in the way most favorable to the production of a large national dividend, and how far it is feasible for State action to improve upon "natural" tendencies.

To judge from the first part of this statement, Pigou's purpose is to discover whether any improvements could be made in the existing arrangements which determine the use of resources. Since Pigou's conclusion is that improvements could be made, one might have expected him to continue by saying that he proposed to set out the changes required to bring them about. Instead, Pigou adds a phrase which contrasts "natural" tendencies with State action, which seems in some sense to equate the present arrangements with "natural" tendencies and to imply that what is required to bring about these improvements is State action (if feasible). That this is more or less Pigou's position is evident from Chapter 1 of Part II. Pigou starts by referring to "optimistic followers of the classical economists" who have argued that the value of production would be maximized if the government refrained from any interference in the economic system and the economic arrangements were those which came about "naturally." Pigou goes on to say that if self-interest does promote economic welfare, it is because human institutions have been devised to make it so. (This part of Pigou's argument, which he develops with the aid of a quotation from Cannan, seems to me to be essentially correct.) Pigou concludes:

> But even in the most advanced States there are failures and imperfections. . . . there are many obstacles that prevent a community's resources from being distributed . . . in the most efficient way. The study of these constitutes our present problem. . . . its purposes is essentially practical. It seeks to bring into clearer light some of the ways in which it now is, or eventually may become, feasible for governments to control the play of economic forces in such wise as to promote the economic welfare, and through that, the total welfare, of their citizens as a whole.

Pigou's underlying thought would appear to be: Some have argued that no State action is needed. But the system has performed as well as it has because of State action. Nonetheless, there are still imperfections. What additional State action is required?

If this is a correct summary of Pigou's position, its inadequacy can be demonstrated by examining the first example he gives of a divergence between private and social products.

> It might happen . . . that costs are thrown upon people not directly concerned, through, say, uncompensated damage done to surrounding woods by sparks from railway engines. All such effects must be included—some of them will be positive, others negative elements—in reckoning up the social net product of the marginal increment of any volume of resources turned into any use or place.

The example used by Pigou refers to a real situation. In Britain, a railway does not normally have to compensate those who suffer damage by fire caused by sparks from an engine. Taken in conjunction with what he says in Chapter 9 of Part II, I take Pigou's policy recommendations to be, first, that there should be State action to correct this "natural" situation and, second, that the railways should be forced to compensate those whose woods are burnt. If this a correct interpretation of Pigou's position, I would argue that the first recommendation is based on a misapprehension of the facts and that the second is not necessarily desirable.

Let us consider the legal position. Under the heading "Sparks from engines," we find the following in Halsbury's Laws of England:

> If railway undertakers use steam engines on their railway without express statutory authority to do so, they are liable, irrespective of any negligence on their part, for fires caused by sparks from engines. Railway undertakers are, however, generally given statutory authority to use steam engines on their railway; accordingly, if an engine is constructed with the precautions which science suggests against fire and is used without negligence, they are not responsible at common law for any damage which may be done by sparks. . . . In the construction of an engine the undertaker is bound to use all the discoveries which science has put within its reach in order to avoid doing harm, provided they are such as it is reasonable to require the

company to adopt, having proper regard to the likelihood of the damage and to the cost and convenience of the remedy; but it is not negligence on the part of an undertaker if it refuses to use an apparatus the efficiency of which is open to bona fide doubt.

To this general rule, there is a statutory exception arising from the Railway (Fires) Act, 1905, as amended in 1923. This concerns agricultural land or agricultural crops.

> In such a case the fact that the engine was used under statutory powers does not affect the liability of the company in an action for the damage. . . . These provisions, however, only apply where the claim for damage . . . does not exceed £200, [£100 in the 1905 Act] and where written notice of the occurrence of the fire and the intention to claim has been sent to the company within seven days of the occurrence of the damage and particulars of the damage in writing showing the amount of the claim in money not exceeding £200 have been sent to the company within twenty-one days.

Agricultural land does not include moorland or buildings and agricultural crops do not include those led away or stacked. I have not made a close study of the parliamentary history of this statutory exception, but to judge from debates in the House of Commons in 1922 and 1923, this exception was probably designed to help the smallholder.

Let us return to Pigou's example of uncompensated damage to surrounding woods caused by sparks from railway engines. This is presumably intended to show how it is possible "for State action to improve upon 'natural' tendencies." If we treat Pigou's example as referring to the position before 1905, or as being an arbitrary example (in that he might just as well have written "surrounding buildings" instead of "surrounding woods"), then it is clear that the reason why compensation was not paid must have been that the railway had statutory authority to run steam engines (which relieved it of liability for fires caused by sparks). That this was the legal position was established in 1860, in a case, oddly enough, which concerned the burning of surrounding woods by a railway, and the law on this point has not been changed (apart from the one exception) by a century of railway legislation, including nationalization. If we treat Pigou's example of "uncompensated damage done to surrounding woods by sparks from railway engines" literally, and assume that it refers to the period after 1905, then it is clear that the reason why compensation was not paid must have been that the damage was more than £100 (in the first edition of *The Economics of Welfare*) or more than £200 (in later editions) or that the owner of the wood failed to notify the railway in writing within seven days of the fire or did not send particulars of the damage, in writing, within twenty-one days. In the real world, Pigou's example could only exist as a result of a deliberate choice of the legislature. It is not, of course, easy to imagine the construction of a railway in a state of nature. The nearest one can get to this is presumably a railway which uses steam engines "without express statutory authority." However, in this case the railway would be obliged to compensate those whose woods it burnt down. That is to say, compensation would be paid in the absence of government action. The only circumstances in which compensation would not be paid would be those in which there had been government action. It is strange that Pigou, who clearly thought it desirable that compensation should be paid, should have chosen this particular example to demonstrate how it is possible "for State action to improve upon 'natural' tendencies."

Pigou seems to have had a faulty view of the facts of the situation. But it also seems likely that he was mistaken in his economic analysis. It is not necessarily desirable that the railway should be required to compensate those who suffer damage by fires caused by railway engines. I need not show here that, if the railway could make a bargain with everyone having property adjoining the railway line and there were no costs involved in making such bargains, it would not matter whether the railway was liable for damage caused by fires or not. This question has been treated at length in earlier sections. The problem is whether it would be desirable to make the railway liable in conditions in which it is too expensive for such bargains to be made. Pigou clearly thought it was desirable to force the railway to pay compensation and it is easy to see the kind of argument that would have led him to this conclusion. Suppose a railway is considering whether to run an additional train or to increase the speed of an existing train or to install spark-preventing devices on its engines. If the railway were not liable for fire damage, then, when making these decisions, it would not take into account as a cost the increase in damage resulting from the additional train or the faster train or the failure to install spark-preventing devices. This is the source of the divergence between private and social net products. It results in the railway performing acts which will lower the value of total production—and which it would not do if it were liable for the damage. This can be shown by means of an arithmetical example.

Consider a railway, which is *not* liable for damage by fires caused by sparks from its engines, which runs two trains per day on a certain line. Suppose that running one train per day would enable the railway to perform services worth $150 per annum and running two trains a day would enable the railway to perform services worth $250 per annum. Suppose further that the cost of running one train is $50 per annum and two trains $100 per annum. Assuming perfect competition, the cost equals the fall in the value of production elsewhere due to the employment of additional factors of production by the railway. Clearly the railway would find it profitable to run two trains per day. But suppose that running one train per day would destroy by fire crops worth (on an average over the year) $60 and two trains a day would result in the destruction of crops worth $120. In these circumstances running one train per day would raise the value of total production but the running of a second train would reduce the value of total production. The second train would enable additional railway services worth $100 per annum to be performed. But the fall in the value of production elsewhere would be $110 per annum; $50 as a result of the employment of additional factors of production and $60 as a result of the destruction of crops. Since it would be better if the second train were not run and since it would not run if the railway were liable for damage caused to crops, the conclusion that the railway should be made liable for the damage seems irresistible. Undoubtedly it is this kind of reasoning which underlies the Pigovian position.

The conclusion that it would be better if the second train did not run is correct. The conclusion that it is desirable that the railway should be made liable for the damage it causes is wrong. Let us change our assumption concerning the rule of liability. Suppose that the railway is liable for damage from fires caused by sparks from the engine. A farmer on lands adjoining the railway is then in the position that, if his crop is destroyed by fires caused by the railway, he will receive the market price from the railway; but if his crop is not damaged, he will receive the market price by sale. It therefore becomes a matter of indifference to him whether his crop is damaged by fire or not. The position is very different when the railway is *not* liable. Any crop destruction through railway-caused fires would then reduce the receipts of the farmer. He would therefore take out of cultivation any land for which the damage is likely to be greater than the net return of the land (for reasons explained at length in Section III). A change from a regime in which the railway is *not* liable for damage to one in which it *is* liable is likely therefore to lead to an increase in the amount of cultivation on lands adjoining the railway. It will also, course, lead to an increase in the amount of crop destruction due to railway-caused fires.

Let us return to our arithmetical example. Assume that, with the changed rule of liability, there is a doubling in the amount of crop destruction due to railway-caused fires. With one train per day, crops worth $120 would be destroyed each year and two trains per day would lead to the destruction of crops worth $240. We saw previously that it would not be profitable to run the second train if the railway had to pay $60 per annum as compensation for damage. With damage at $120 per annum the loss from running the second train would be $60 greater. But now let us consider the first train. The value of the transport services furnished by the first train is $150. The cost of running the train is $50. The amount that the railway would have to pay out as compensation for damage is $120. It follows that it would not be profitable to run any trains. With the figures in our example we reach the following result: if the railway is not liable for fire damage, two trains per day would be run; if the railway is liable for fire damage, it would cease operations altogether. Does this mean that it is better that there should be no railway? This question can be resolved by considering what would happen to the value of total production if it were decided to exempt the railway from liability for fire damage, thus bringing it into operation (with two trains per day).

The operation of the railway would enable transport services worth $250 to be performed. It would also mean the employment of factors of production which would reduce the value of production elsewhere by $100. Furthermore it would mean the destruction of crops worth $120. The coming of the railway will also have led to the abandonment of cultivation of some land. Since we know that, had this land been cultivated, the value of the crops destroyed by fire would have been $120, and since it is unlikely that the total crop on this land would have been destroyed, it seems reasonable to suppose that the value of the crop yield on this land would have been higher than this. Assume it would have been $160. But the abandonment of cultivation would have released factors of production for employment elsewhere. All we know is that the amount by which the value of production elsewhere will increase will be less than $160. Suppose that it is $150. Then the gain from operating the railway would be $250 (the value of the transport services) minus $100 (the cost of the factors of production) minus $120 (the value of crops destroyed by fire) minus $160 (the fall in the value of crop production due to the abandonment of cultivation) plus $150 (the value of production elsewhere of the released factors of production). Overall, operating the railway will increase the value of total production by $20. With these figures it is clear that it is better that the railway should not be liable for the damage it causes, thus enabling it to operate profitably. Of course, by altering the figures, it could be shown that there are other cases in which it would be desirable that the railway should be liable for the damage it causes. It is enough for my purpose to show that, from an economic point of view, a situation in which there is "uncompensated damage done to surrounding woods by sparks from railway engines" is not necessarily undesirable. Whether it is desirable or not depends on the particular circumstances.

How is it that the Pigovian analysis seems to give the wrong answer? The reason is that Pigou does not seem to have noticed that his analysis is dealing with an entirely different question. The analysis as such is correct. But it is quite illegitimate for Pigou to draw the particular conclusion he does. The question at issue is not whether it is desirable to run an additional train or a faster train or to install smoke-preventing devices; the question at issue is whether it is desirable to have a system in which the railway has to compensate those who suffer damage from the fires which it causes or one in which the railway does not have to compensate them. When an economist is comparing alternative social arrangements, the proper procedure is to compare the total social product yielded by these different arrangements. The comparison of private and social products is neither here nor there. A simple example will demonstrate this. Imagine a town in which there are traffic lights. A motorist approaches an intersection and stops because the light is red. There are no cars approaching the intersection on the other street. If the motorist ignored the red signal, no accident would occur and the total product would increase because the motorist would arrive earlier at his destination. Why does he not do this? The reason is that if he ignored the light he would be fined. The private product from crossing the street is less than the social product. Should we conclude from this that the total product would be greater if there were no fines for failing to obey traffic signals? The Pigovian analysis shows us that it is possible to conceive of better worlds than the one in which we live. But the problem is to devise practical arrangements which will correct defects in one part of the system without causing more serious harm in other parts.

I have examined in considerable detail one example of a divergence between private and social products and I do not propose to make any further examination of Pigou's analytical system. But the main discussion of the problem considered in this article is to be found in that part of Chapter 9 in Part II which deals with Pigou's second class of divergence and it is of interest to see how Pigou develops his argument. Pigou's own description of this second class of divergence was quoted at the beginning of this section. Pigou distinguishes between the case in which a person renders services for which he receives no payment and the case in which a person renders disservices and compensation is not given to the injured parties. Our main attention has, of course, centered on this second case. It is therefore rather astonishing to find, as was pointed out to me by Professor Francesco Forte, that the problem of the smoking chimney—the "stock instance" or "classroom example" of the second case—is used by Pigou as an example of the first case (services rendered without payment) and is never mentioned, at any rate explicitly, in connection with the second case. Pigou points out that factory owners who devote resources to preventing their chimneys from smoking render services for which they receive no payment. The implication, in the light of Pigou's discussion later in the chapter, is that a factory owner with a smoky chimney should be given a bounty to induce him to install smoke-preventing devices. Most modern economists would suggest that the owner of the factory with the smoky chimney should be taxed. It seems a pity that economists (apart from Professor Forte) do not seem to have noticed this feature of Pigou's treatment since a realization that the problem could be tackled in either of these two ways would probably have led to an explicit recognition of its reciprocal nature.

In discussing the second case (disservices without compensation to those damaged), Pigou says that they are rendered "when the owner of a site in a residential quarter of a city builds a factory there and so destroys a great part of the amenities of neighboring sites; or, in a less degree, when he uses his site in such a way as to spoil the lighting of the house opposite; or when he invests resources in erecting buildings in a crowded centre, which by contracting the air-space and the playing room of the neighborhood, tend to injure the health and efficiency of the families living there." Pigou is, of course, quite right to describe such actions as "uncharged disservices." But he is wrong when he describes these actions as "anti-social." They may or may not be. It is necessary to weigh the harm against the good that will result. Nothing could be more "anti-social" than to oppose any action which causes any harm to anyone.

The example with which Pigou opens his discussion of "uncharged disservices" is not, as I have indicated, the case of the smoky chimney but the case of the overrunning rabbits: "... incidental uncharged disservices are rendered to third parties when the game-preserving activities of one occupier involve the overrunning of a neighboring occupier's land by rabbits. ..." This example is of extraordinary interest, not so much because the economic analysis of the case is essentially any different from that of the other examples, but because of the peculiarities of the legal position and the light it throws on the part which economics can play in what is apparently the purely legal question of the delimitation of rights.

The problem of legal liability for the actions of rabbits is part of the general subject of liability for animals. I will, although with reluctance, confine my discussion to rabbits. The early cases relating to rabbits concerned the relations between the lord of the manor and commoners, since, from the thirteenth century on, it became usual for the lord of the manor to stock the commons with conies (rabbits), both for the sake of the meat and the fur. But in 1597, in *Boulston's* case, an action was brought by one landowner against a neighboring landowner, alleging that the defendant had made coney-burrows and that the conies had increased and had destroyed the plaintiff's corn. The action failed for the reason that

> ... so soon as the coneys come on his neighbor's land he may kill them, for they are ferae naturae, and he who makes the coney-boroughs has no property in them, and he shall not be punished for the damage which the coneys do in which he has no property, and which the other may lawfully kill.

As *Boulston's* case has been treated as binding—Bray, J., in 1919, said that he was not aware that *Boulston's* case has ever been overruled or questioned—Pigou's rabbit example undoubtedly represented the legal position at the time *The Economics of Welfare* was written. And in this case, it is not far from the truth to say that the state of affairs which Pigou describes came about because of an absence of government action (at any rate in the form of statutory enactments) and was the result of "natural" tendencies.

Nonetheless, *Boulston's* case is something of a legal curiosity and Professor Williams makes no secret of his distaste for this decision:

> The conception of liability in nuisance as being based upon ownership is the result, apparently, of a confusion with the action of cattle-trespass, and runs counter both to principle and to the medieval authorities on the escape of water, smoke and filth. ... The prerequisite of any satisfactory treatment of the subject is the final abandonment of the pernicious doc-

trine in *Boulston's* case. . . . Once *Boulston's* case disappears, the way will be clear for a rational restatement of the whole subject, on lines that will harmonize with the principles prevailing in the rest of the law of nuisance

The judges in *Boulston's* case were, of course, aware that their view of the matter depended on distinguishing this case from one involving nuisance:

> This cause is not like to the cases put, on the other side, of erecting a lime-kiln, dye-house, or the like; for there the annoyance is by the act of the parties who make them; but it is not so here, for the conies of themselves went into the plaintiff's land, and he might take them when they came upon his land, and make profit of them.

Professor Williams comments:

> Once more the atavistic idea is emerging that the animals are guilty and not the landowner. It is not, of course, a satisfactory principle to introduce into a modern law of nuisance. If A. erects a house or plants a tree so that the rain runs or drips from it on to B.'s land, this is A.'s act for which he is liable; but if A. introduces rabbits into his land so that they escape from it into B.'s, this is the act of the rabbits for which A. is not liable—such is the specious distinction resulting from *Boulston's* case.

It has to be admitted that the decision in *Boulston's* case seems a little odd. A man may be liable for damage caused by smoke or unpleasant smells, without it being necessary to determine whether he owns the smoke or the smell. And the rule in *Boulston's* case has not always been followed in cases dealing with other animals. For example, in *Bland v. Yates*, it was decided that an injunction could be granted to prevent someone from keeping an *unusual and excessive* collection of manure in which flies bred and which infested a neighbor's house. The question of who owned the flies was not raised. An economist would not wish to object because legal reasoning sometimes appears a little odd. But there is a sound economic reason for supporting Professor Williams' view that the problem of liability for animals (and particularly rabbits) should be brought within the ordinary law of nuisance. The reason is not that the man who harbors rabbits is solely responsible for the damage; the man whose crops are eaten is equally responsible. And given that the costs of market transactions make a rearrangement of rights impossible, unless we know the particular circumstances, we cannot say whether it is desirable or not to make the man who harbors rabbits responsible for the damage committed by the rabbits on neighboring properties. The objection to the rule in *Boulston's* case is that, under it, the harborer of rabbits can *never* be liable. It fixes the rule of liability at one pole: and this is as undesirable, from an economic point of view, as fixing the rule at the other pole and making the harborer of rabbits always liable. But, as we saw in Section VI, the law of nuisance, as it is in fact handled by the courts, is flexible and allows for a comparison of the utility of an act with the harm it produces. As Professor Williams says "The whole law of nuisance is an attempt to reconcile and compromise between conflicting interests. . . ." to bring the problem of rabbits within the ordinary law of nuisance would not mean *inevitably* making the harborer of rabbits liable for damage committed by the rabbits. This is not to say that the sole task of the courts in such cases is to make a comparison between the harm and the utility of an act. Nor is it to be expected that the courts will always decide correctly after making such a comparison. But unless the courts act very foolishly, the ordinary law of nuisance would seem likely to give economically more satisfactory results than adopting a rigid rule. Pigou's case of the overrunning rabbits affords an excellent example of how problems of law and economics are interrelated, even though the correct policy to follow would seem to be different from that envisioned by Pigou.

Pigou allows one exception to his conclusion that there is a divergence between private and social products in the rabbit example. He adds: ". . . unless . . . the two occupiers stand in the relation of landlord and tenant, so that compensation is given in an adjustment of the rent." This qualification is rather surprising since Pigou's first class of divergence is largely concerned with the difficulties of drawing up satisfactory contracts between landlords and tenants. In fact, all the recent cases on the problem of rabbits cited by Professor Williams involved disputes between landlords and tenants concerning sporting rights. Pigou seems to make a distinction between the case in which no contract is possible (the second class) and that in which the contract is unsatisfactory (the first class). Thus he says that the second class of divergences between private and social net product

> cannot, like divergences due to tenancy laws, be mitigated by a modification of the contractual relation between any two contracting parties, because the divergence arises out of a service or disservice rendered to persons other than the contracting parties.

But the reason why some activities are not the subject of contracts is exactly the same as the reason why some contracts are commonly unsatisfactory—it would cost too much to put the matter right. Indeed, the two cases are really the same since the contracts are unsatisfactory because they do not cover certain activities. The exact bearing of the discussion of the first class of divergence on Pigou's main argument is difficult to discover. He shows that in some circumstances contractual relations between landlord and tenant may result in a divergence between private and social products. But he also goes on to show that government-enforced compensation schemes and rent-controls will also produce divergences. Furthermore, he shows that, when the government is in a similar position to a private landlord, e.g., when granting a franchise to a public utility, exactly the same difficulties arise as when private individuals are involved. The discussion is interesting but I have been unable to discover what general conclusions about economic policy, if any, Pigou expects us to draw from it.

Indeed, Pigou's treatment of the problems considered in this article is extremely elusive and the discussion of his views raises almost insuperable difficulties of interpretation. Consequently it is impossible to be sure that one has understood what Pigou really meant. Nevertheless, it is difficult to resist the conclusion, extraordinary though this may be in an economist of

Pigou's stature, that the main source of this obscurity is that Pigou had not thought his position through.

VIII. A Change of Approach

It is my belief that the failure of economists to reach correct conclusions about the treatment of harmful effects cannot be ascribed simply to a few slips in analysis. It stems from basic defects in the current approach to problems of welfare economics. What is needed is a change of approach.

Analysis in terms of divergencies between private and social products concentrates attention on particular deficiencies in the system and tends to nourish the belief that any measure which will remove the deficiency is necessarily desirable. It diverts attention from those other changes in the system which are inevitably associated with the corrective measure, changes which may well produce more harm than the original deficiency. In the preceding sections of this article, we have seen many examples of this. But it is not necessary to approach the problem in this way. Economists who study problems of the firm habitually use an opportunity cost approach and compare the receipts obtained from a given combination of factors with alternative business arrangements. It would seem desirable to use a similar approach when dealing with questions of economic policy and to compare the total product yielded by alternative social arrangements. In this article, the analysis has been confined, as is usual in this part of economics, to comparisons of the value of production, as measured by the market. But it is, of course, desirable that the choice between different social arrangements for the solution of economic problems should be carried out in broader terms than this and that the total effect of these arrangements in all spheres of life should be taken into account. As Frank H. Knight has so often emphasized, problems of welfare economics must ultimately dissolve into a study of aesthetics and morals.

A second feature of the usual treatment of the problems discussed in this article is that the analysis proceeds in terms of a comparison between a state of laissez faire and some kind of ideal world. This approach inevitably leads to a looseness of thought since the nature of the alternatives being compared is never clear. In a state of laissez faire, is there a monetary, a legal, or a political system, and if so, what are they? In an ideal world would there be a monetary, a legal, or a political system, and if so, what would they be? The answers to all these questions are shrouded in mystery and every man is free to draw whatever conclusions he likes. Actually very little analysis is required to show that an ideal world is better than a state of laissez faire, unless the definitions of a state of laissez faire and an ideal world happen to be the same. But the whole discussion is largely irrelevant for questions of economic policy since whatever we may have in mind as our ideal world, it is clear that we have not yet discovered how to get to it from where we are. A better approach would seem to be to start our analysis with a situation approximating that which actually exists, to examine the effects of a proposed policy change, and to attempt to decide whether the new situation would be, in total, better or worse than the original one. In this way, conclusions for policy would have some relevance to the actual situation.

A final reason for the failure to develop a theory adequate to handle the problem of harmful effects stems from a faulty concept of a factor of production. This is usually thought of as a physical entity which the businessman acquires and uses (an acre of land, a ton of fertilizer) instead of as a right to perform certain (physical) actions. We may speak of a person owning land and using it as a factor of production but what the landowner in fact possesses is the right to carry out a circumscribed list of actions. The rights of a landowner are not unlimited. It is not even always possible for him to remove the land to another place, for instance, by quarrying it. And although it may be possible for him to exclude some people from using "his" land, this may not be true of others. For example, some people may have the right to cross the land. Furthermore, it may or may not be possible to erect certain types of buildings or to grow certain crops or to use particular drainage systems on the land. This does not come about simply because of government regulation. It would be equally true under the common law. In fact it would be true under any system of law. A system in which the rights of individuals were unlimited would be one in which there were no rights to acquire.

If factors of production are thought of as rights, it becomes easier to understand that the right to do something which has a harmful effect (such as the creation of smoke, noise, smells, etc.) is also a factor of production. Just as we may use a piece of land in such a way as to prevent someone else from crossing it, or parking his car, or building his house upon it, so we may use it in such a way as to deny him a view or quiet or unpolluted air. The cost of exercising a right (of using a factor of production) is always the loss which is suffered elsewhere in consequence of the exercise of that right—the inability to cross land, to park a car, to build a house, to enjoy a view, to have peace and quiet, or to breathe clean air.

It would clearly be desirable if the only actions performed were those in which what was gained was worth more than what was lost. But in choosing between social arrangements within the context of which individual decisions are made, we have to bear in mind that a change in the existing system which will lead to an improvement in some decisions may well lead to a worsening of others. Furthermore we have to take into account the costs involved in operating the various social arrangements (whether it be the working of a market or of a government department), as well as the costs involved in moving to a new system. In devising and choosing between social arrangements we should have regard for the total effect. This, above all, is the change in approach which I am advocating.

The Allocation of
Water Supplies

JACK HIRSHLEIFER, JAMES DeHAVEN,
and JEROME MILLIMAN

Jack Hirshleifer is Professor of Economics at the University of California at Los Angeles, James DeHaven is a staff member at the RAND Corporation, and Jerome Milliman is Professor of Economics at Indiana University. The following selection is from their book, Water Supply, *published in 1960.*

1. Efficiency Effects and Distribution Effects

The economic effects of any proposed policy can be divided under two headings: the effects on *efficiency* and the effects on *distribution*. Efficiency questions relate to the size of the pie available; distribution questions, to who gets what share. More formally, we can think of the pie as representing the national income or community income. Someone may propose reducing income taxes in the upper brackets on the ground that the high rates now effective there seriously deter initiative and enterprise and so reduce national income; he is making an efficiency argument that the present taxes reduce the size of the national pie. Someone else may point out that such a change will help large taxpayers as against small—a distributional consideration. In the field of water supply it is possible to find examples in the West where a certain amount of water could produce goods and services more highly valued in the market place if it were shifted from agricultural to industrial uses—this is an efficiency argument. On the other hand, this shift may hurt the interests of farmers or of their customers, employees, or suppliers while helping industrial interests—all distributional considerations.

Now economics can say something of the distributional consequences of alternative possible policies, but what it says stops short of any assertion that any man's interests or well-being can be preferred to another's. The fact that economics has nothing to say on such matters does not mean, of course, that nothing important can be said. Ethics as a branch of philosophy and the entire structure of law (which to some extent embodies or applies ethical thought) are devoted to the consideration of the rights and duties of man against man, and many propositions arising out of such thought may well command almost unanimous consent in our society. Ethics may say that no one should be permitted to starve, and law that no one should be deprived of property without due process, but these are propositions outside economics.

Most of what the existing body of economic thought has to say concerns the *efficiency* effects—the effects on size of the pie—of alternative possible policies or institutional arrangements. There is, of course, a sense in which enlarging the size of the pie may be said to be good for the eaters as a group irrespective of the distribution of shares. This sense turns upon the *possibility* of dividing the enlarged pie in such a way that everybody benefits. If such a distribution of the gain is not adopted, there may or may not be good reason for the failure to do so, but the reason is presumed to be legal or ethical and so outside the sphere of economic analysis. Economics alone cannot give us answers to policy problems; it can show us how to attain efficiency and what the distributional consequences are of attaining efficiency in alternative possible ways, but it does not tell us how to distribute the gain from increased efficiency.

It is true that it is often the case that the efficiency and distributional consequences of a proposed change cannot be so neatly separated. Any particular change in the direction of efficiency will involve a certain intrinsic distribution of gains and losses, and in practice it may be unfeasible to effect a redistribution such that everyone gains. Nevertheless, we feel that a presumption in favor of changes increasing the national income is justified, while conceding that this presumption can be defeated if there are irreparable distributive consequences that are sufficiently offensve on ethical or legal grounds.

Nothing is more common in public discussions of economic affairs, however, than a consideration of distributive effects of any change to the utter exclusion of the efficiency question. The agricultural price-support policy, for example, is usually and fruitlessly discussed pro and con in terms of the interests of farmers versus the interests of consumers and taxpayers. But a policy of expensive storage of perishing commodities to hold them out of human consumption is, obviously, inefficient. Concentration upon the efficiency question might readily suggest solutions that would increase the national income and would help consumers and taxpayers a great deal while hurting farmers relatively little or not at all.

2. *The Principle of Equimarginal Value in Use*

Suppose for simplicity we first assume that the stock or the annual flow of a resource like water becomes available without cost, the only problem being to allocate the supply among the competing uses and users who desire it. Economic theory asserts one almost universal principle which characterizes a good or efficient allocation—the principle we shall here call "equimarginal value in use." The *value in use* of any unit of water, whether purchased by an ultimate or an intermediate consumer, is essentially measured by the *maximum* amount of resources (dollars) which the consumer would be willing to pay for that unit. *Marginal* value in use is the value in use of the last unit consumed, and for any consumer marginal value in use will ordinarily decline as the quantity of water consumed in any period increases. The principle, then, is that the resource should be so allocated that all consumers or users derive equal value in use from the marginal unit consumed or used.

An example of the process of equating marginal values in use may be more illuminating than an abstract proof that this principle characterizes efficient allocations. Suppose that my neighbor and I are both given rights (ration coupons, perhaps) to certain volumes of water, and we wish to consider whether it might be in our mutual interest to trade these water rights between us for other resources—we might as well say for dollars, which we can think of as a generalized claim on other resources like clam chowders, baby-sitting services, acres of land, or yachts. My neighbor might be a farmer and I an industrialist, or we might both be just retired homeowners; to make the quantities interesting, we will assume that both individuals are rather big operators. Now suppose that the last acre-foot of my periodic entitlement is worth $10 at most to me, but my neighbor would be willing to pay anything up to $50 for that right—a disparity of $40 between our marginal values in use. Evidently, if I transfer the right to him for any compensation between $10 and $50, we will both be better off in terms of our own preferences; in other words, the size of the pie measured in terms of the satisfactions yielded to both of us has increased. (Note, however, that the question of whether the compensation should be $11 or $49 is purely distributional.)

But this is not yet the end. Having given up one acre-foot, I will not be inclined to give up another on such easy terms—water has become scarcer for me, so that an additional amount given up means foregoing a somewhat more urgent use. Conversely, my neighbor is no longer quite so anxious to buy as he was before, since his most urgent need for one more acre-foot has been satisfied, and an additional unit must be applied to less urgent uses. That is, for both of us marginal values in use decline with increases of consumption (or, equivalently, marginal value in use rises if consumption is cut back). Suppose he is now willing to pay up to $45, while I am willing to sell for anything over $15. Evidently, we should trade again. Obviously, the stopping point is where the last (or marginal) unit of water is valued equally (in terms of the greatest amount of dollars we would be willing to pay) by the two of us, based on the use we can make of or the benefit we can derive from the last or marginal unit. At this point no more mutually advantageous trades are available—efficiency has been attained.

Generalizing from the illustration just given, we may say that the principle of equimarginal value in use asserts that an efficient allocation of water has been attained when no mutually advantageous exchanges are possible between any pair of claimants, which can only mean that each claimant values his last or marginal unit of water equally with the others, measured in terms of the quantity of other resources (or dollars) that he is willing to trade for an additional unit of water.

What institutional arrangements are available for achieving water allocations that meet the principle of equimarginal value in use? Our example suggests that rationing out rights to the available supply will tend to lead to an efficient result if trading of the ration coupons is freely permitted; this is true so long as it can be assumed that third parties are unaffected by the trades. More generally, any such vesting of property rights, whether originally administrative, inherited, or purchased, will tend to an efficient solution if trading is permitted. (The question of the basis underlying the original vesting of rights is a serious and important one, but it is a distributional question.) A rather important practical result is derived from this conclusion if we put the argument another way: however rights are vested, we are effectively *preventing* efficiency from being attained if the law forbids free trading of those rights. Thus, if our ration coupons are not transferable, efficiency can be achieved only if the original distribution of rights was so nicely calculated that equimarginal value in use prevailed to begin with and that thenceforth no forces operated to change these values in use. As a practical matter, these conditions could never be satisfied. Nevertheless, legal limitations on the owner's ability to sell or otherwise transfer vested water rights are very common. While at times valid justification at least in part may exist for such limitations (one example is where third parties are injured by such transfers), it seems often to be the case that these prohibitions simply inflict a loss upon all for no justifiable reason. We shall examine some instances of limitations on freedom of transfer in a later section.

It is important to note here that the market price of water rights or ration coupons, if these can be freely traded, will tend to settle at (and so to measure) the marginal value in use of the consumers in the market. Any consumer who found himself with so many coupons that the marginal value in use to him was less than market price would be trying to sell some of his rights, while anyone with marginal value in use greater than market price would be seeking to buy. The process of trading equates marginal value in use to all, and the going market price measures this value. This proposition is of very broad validity, being in no way restricted to the commodity water. It is true, technical qualifications aside, that market price measures marginal value in use to its consumers for any commodity in which free trading is permitted and perfect rights can be conveyed.

Another possible institutional device for allocating water supplies of a community would be to establish, say, a municipal water-supply enterprise which would sell water, the customers being free to take any amount desired at the price set. The principle of equimarginal value in use then, setting aside possible complications, indicates a certain pattern of pricing: the price should be equal for all and at such a level that the customers in the aggregate use up all the supply. The reason for this pattern being the best is the same as that discussed earlier: if one individual had the privilege of buying units of water for $10 when another had to pay $50, mutually advantageous trading could take place if the water (or rights to it) could be transferred. If trading possibilities are ruled out, the marginal value in use would be $10 for the favored customer and $50 for the other—the former is taking so much in terms of his needs or desires that he is employing the marginal unit of water for very low-value purposes, while high-value uses are being deprived because water is so scarce to the other customer. The efficiency effects of trading can be achieved simply by setting the price to the two customers equal at such a level that the combined demands will take the supply in hand. Since the customer is permitted to purchase any desired amount, he will continue to buy additional units so long as the marginal value in use to him exceeds the price he must pay, marginal value in use being defined in terms of the price he is willing to pay for an additional unit. Evidently, he will stop purchasing where marginal value in use equals the price—and so, if the price is equal to all customers, marginal value in use will be equal to all. Then no mutually advantageous trading will be possible, so that we have achieved an efficient allocation of the water resource.

Note that there will be a distributional consequence of the removal of a privilege to buy water at a preferential price—the former holder of the privilege will lose as compared with all others. The attainment of efficiency in the new situation means that it is *possible* to insure that everyone is better off. But whether it is or is not desirable to provide the compensation required to balance the loss of the formerly preferred customers is a distributional question.

Our discussion of the principle of equimarginal value in use has led to two rules of behavior necessary if efficiency is to be achieved in different institutional contexts: (1) If rights to water are vested as property, there should be no restrictions on the purchase and sale of such rights, so long as third parties are unaffected. (2) If water is being sold, the price should be equal to all customers. This second rule was derived, however, under a special assumption that the water became available without cost. More generally, there will be costs incurred in the acquisition and transport of water supplies to customers; taking costs into account requires a second principle for pricing of water in addition to the principle of equimarginal value in use.

3. *The Principle of Marginal-Cost Pricing*

In our previous discussion we assumed that a certain volume or flow of water became available without cost, the problem being to distribute just that amount among the potential customers. Normally, there will not be such a definite fixed amount but rather a situation in which another unit could always be made available by expending more resources to acquire and transport it, that is, at a certain additional or marginal cost. The question of where to stop in increasing the supplies made available is then added to the question just discussed of how to arrange for the allocation of the supplies in hand at any moment of time.

From the argument developed earlier about the allocation of a certain given supply, we can infer that, whatever the price may be, it should be equal to all users (since otherwise employments with higher marginal values in use are being foregone in favor of employments with lower values). Suppose that at a certain moment of time this price is $30 per unit. Then, if the community as a whole can acquire and transport another unit of water for, say, $20, it would clearly be desirable to do so; in fact, any of the individual customers to whom the unit of water is worth $30 would be happy to pay the $20 cost, and none of the other members of the community is made worse off thereby. We may say that, on efficiency grounds, additional units should be made available so long as any members of the community are willing to pay the additional or marginal costs incurred. To meet the criterion of equimarginal value in use, however, the price should be made equal for all customers. So the combined rule is to make the price equal to the marginal cost and equal for all customers.

One important practical consideration is that, because of differing locations, use patterns, types of services, etc., the marginal costs of serving different customers will vary. It is of some interest to know in principle how this problem should be handled. The correct solution is to arrange matters so that for each class of customers (where the classes are so grouped that all customers *within* any single class can be served under identical cost conditions) the prices should be the same and equal to marginal cost. *Between* classes, however, prices should differ, and the difference should be precisely the difference in marginal costs involved in serving the two.

Consider, for example, a situation in which there are two customers, identical in all respects except that one can be served at a marginal cost of $10 per unit and the other at $40—perhaps because the latter has a hilltop location and requires pumped rather than gravity service. If they are both charged $10, the community will be expending $40 in resources to supply a marginal unit which the latter customer values at $10; if they both are charged $40, the former customer would be happy to lay out the $10 it costs to bring him another unit. The principle of equimarginal value in use which dictates equal prices was based on the assumption that costless transfers could take place between customers, but in this case any transfer from the gravity to the pumped customer involves a cost of $30. Another way to look at the matter is to say that the commodity provided is not the same: the customer who requires pumped water is demanding a more costly commodity than the gravity customer.

Where water is sold to customers, therefore, the principles we have developed indicate that customers served under identical cost conditions should be charged equal prices and that the commodity should be supplied and priced in such a way that the price for each class of service should equal the marginal cost of serving that class. Where marginal costs differ, therefore, prices should differ similarly.

4. Limitations on Voluntary Exchange of Water Rights

In our theoretical discussion we saw that, given any particular vesting of water rights an efficient allocation will tend to come about if free exchange of these rights between users is permitted. There is in practice, however, a wide variety of limitations upon the free exchange of water rights. Water rights are sometimes attached to particular tracts of land (i.e., the water cannot be transferred except as a package deal with the land), especially under the "riparian" principle; transfers of water rights or of uses within water rights also often must in a number of jurisdictions meet approval of some administrative agency. Some legal codes grant certain "higher" users priority or preference over other, "lower" users, transfers from "higher" to "lower" uses being hindered thereby. As a related point, "higher" uses sometimes have a right of seizure. While voluntary transfers can usually be presumed to make both parties better off, and so be in the direction of increased efficiency, no such presumption applies for compelled transfers through seizure.

The above are all instances of violation of a general proposition about property rights. If property is to be put to its most efficient use, there should be no uncertainty of tenure and no restrictions upon the use to which it may be put. When this is the case, voluntary exchange tends to make the property find the use where it is valued the highest, since this use can outbid all others on the market. Uncertainty of tenure interferes with this process, because people will be unwilling to pay much for property, however valuable, if a perfect right cannot be conveyed, and the existing holder will be wary about making those investments necessary to exploit the full value of the property if there is a risk of seizure. All restrictions upon free choice of use, whether the restriction is upon place, purpose, or transfers to other persons, obviously interfere with the market processes which tend to shift the resource to its most productive use.

The reasons underlying adoption of restrictions like those mentioned above are probably mixed, but at least one of them may have some validity: changes in water use may conceivably affect adversely the interests of third parties, such as complementary users downstream, for whom some protection seems needed. This protection should not, as it usually does, go beyond what is necessary to insure preservation of the rights of the third parties. Under California law, for example, a riparian user might attempt to sell water to a nonriparian user who can use the water more productively, none of the other riparian users being harmed thereby. However, the nonriparian purchaser gains no rights against the other riparian users, who can simply increase their diversions, leaving none for the would-be purchaser. Again, a holder of certain appropriate rights might attempt to sell his rights to another. This transfer in some cases requires approval of an administrative board which protects the rights of third parties but whose latitude goes beyond this and permits disapproval on essentially arbitrary grounds as well.

We may comment here that the growing trend to limitation of water rights to "reasonable use" is by no means a wholly obvious or desirable restriction. We might reflect on the desirability of legislation depriving people of their automobiles or their houses when it is determined in some administrative or judicial process that their use was "unreasonable." The purpose of such legislation is the prevention of certain wastes which, if only free voluntary exchange of water rights without unnecessary restrictions were permitted, would tend naturally to be eliminated by market processes (since efficient users can afford to pay more for water than it is worth to wasteful users).

The question of "higher" and "lower" uses has an interesting history. The California Water Code declares that the use of water for domestic purposes is the highest use of water and that the next highest use is for irrigation. Essentially the same statement has been attributed to the emperor Hammurabi (2250 B.C.), a remarkable demonstration of the persistence of error.

The correct idea underlying this thought seems to be that, if we had to do almost entirely without water, we would use the first little bit available for human consumption directly, and then, as more became available, the next use we would want to consider is providing food through irrigation. Where this argument goes wrong is in failing to appreciate that what we want to achieve is to make the *marginal* values in use (the values of the last units applied to any purpose) equal. It would obviously be mistaken to starve to death for lack of irrigation water applied to crops while using water domestically for elaborate baths and air conditioning; the domestic marginal value in use in such a case would be lower. Similar imbalances can make the marginal value in use in industry higher than it is in either domestic or irrigation uses. Actually, the principle of higher and lower uses is so defective that no one would for a moment consider using it consistently (first saturating domestic uses before using any water for other uses, then saturating irrigation uses, etc.). Rather, the principle enters erratically or capriciously in limiting the perfection of property rights in water applied to "lower" uses, however productive such uses may be.

5. Existing Pricing Practices in Water Supply

Our analysis of the principles of efficient allocation among competitive users led to the conclusion that prices should be equal for all customers served under equivalent cost conditions and that the price should be set at the marginal cost or the cost of delivering the last unit. Alternatively, we may say that the amount supplied should be such that the marginal cost equals the amount the customer is willing to pay for the marginal unit. There are considerable theoretical and practical complications in this connection which we are reserving for discussion in later chapters, but a general survey of the existing situation will be useful here for contrasting practice with the theoretical principles.

Examination of the allocation arrangements of local systems for domestic, commercial, and industrial water supply (primarily municipally owned) reveals that the great majority allocate water by charging a price for its use. The leading exceptions are in unmetered municipalities where, since water bills are not a function of consumption, water *deliveries* may be considered free to the consumer. While a certain amount is ordinarily charged as a water bill in such cities, this is a fixed sum (or "flat rate") and does not operate as a price does in leading consumers to balance the value of use against the cost of use. According to a report published by the *American City Magazine*, a survey made in 1949 of seventy-two cities discovered that 97.7 percent of the services in those cities were metered. The survey excluded, however, several of the largest cities which were partially under flat rates—New York, Chicago, Philadelphia, Buffalo, and others. Since that time, according to the report, Philadelphia has abandoned the fixed-bill system, and generally it may be said that in the United States a condition of universal metering has been approached. As of 1954, the report estimates that metering covered from 90 to 95 percent of all services. Since unmetered services usually represent the smaller domestic users, the proportion of *use* that is metered is even greater than the proportion of *services*.

In those cases, such as New York City, where some users (primarily domestic) are unmetered while other users are charged a price per unit of water used, our rule of prices equal to marginal cost is violated. An unmetered consumer will proceed to use water until its marginal value in use to him is nil to correspond to its zero price to him. This is of course wasteful, because the water system cannot provide the commodity costlessly, and hence society will lose (setting distributional considerations aside) by the excess of the cost of delivery over the value in use for such units of consumption.

It might be thought that the domestic consumers, who are the unmetered customers almost always (the only other substantial classes of use frequently unmetered are public agencies, such as park, sanitation, and especially fire departments), somehow deserve a priority or preference as compared with "intermediate" economic customers like industrial or commercial services. But an intermediate consumer is essentially a final consumer once removed. If consumers are required to pay more for water used in the production of food, clothing, and other items of value than they pay for water for direct consumption, an inefficient disparity in marginal values in use between the different uses will be created. Conversely, on efficiency grounds consumers should not be required to pay *more* for domestic water and for water used in industry than for water used to grow crops, such being the effect of existing policies which commonly grant the irrigation use of water a subsidy over all other uses.

A situation in which different prices are charge to different users, or to the same user for varying quantities of the same commodity, is called one of "price discrimination." While discrimination may under certain conditions be justified on one ground or another, it has the defect of preventing the marginal values in use from being made equal between the favored and the penalized uses or users. The only exception to this statement is where discrimination is applied within the purchases of a single individual—by, for example, a declining block rate. If there are no restrictions on use, the individual concerned will continue to equate all his marginal values in the various uses to the *marginal* price (the price for the last unit or for an additional unit) he must pay for the commodity purchased. So far as his own purchases are concerned, therefore, he will still equalize his marginal values in use for all his different uses. If such a block system is used for a number of individuals, however, marginal values in use will not in general be equated between individuals; some will tend to consume an amount such that they end up in the higher-priced block, and others will end up in the lower.

All price differences for the "same" commodity are not, however, evidence of price discrimination. In fact, there should be some difference of price where an extra delivery cost or processing cost must be incurred in serving certain users. These users can be considered as buying two commodities together—the basic commodity and the special delivery or processing. If the basic commodity is to be equally priced to all users, uses requiring such additional services must be charged more.

Turning to the practical side, we should mention at once that our earlier metering discussion neglected one important consideration: the cost of metering and the associated increase in billing costs. It is clear that the additional cost of meters (especially for a great many small users) may well exceed the possible gains from the rationalization of use which would following metering. (There would, in general, be an aggregate reduction of use as well.) While this question bears further investigation, the dominant opinion in the field of municipal water supply seems to be that universal metering produces gains that are worth the cost. By way of contrast, it appears that in Great Britain domestic use is never metered.

Even if we turn, however, to a consideration of that part of water supply that is metered, or to systems that are completely metered, we find that some non-uniform pattern of prices typically exists. There are some exceptions. In Chicago, for example, all metered users pay the same price per unit of water delivered. A more typical rate system is that of Los Angeles, where rates vary by type of use and also by amount of use (a declining or "promotional" block rate), with a service charge independent of use but based on size of connection. A rate distinction is also made in Los Angeles between firm service and service that the water department may at its convenience provide or refuse, and in some cases between gravity and pumped services.

Some of these rate differences may not be inconsistent with our theoretical discussion. The rate differential may reflect an extra cost or difficulty of delivering to the customer (or customer class, where it is not worthwhile distinguishing between individual customers) charged the higher price.

Where customers' demands vary in the degree to which they impose a peak load on the system, some differential service or demand charge can be justified. In a sense, the commodity delivered off-peak is not the same as that delivered on-peak. The common system of basing a fixed-sum demand charge on the size of service connection is, however, very crude; it provides no deterrent to the customer's contributing to the peak load. Charging a lower rate for interruptible service is somewhat more reasonable. Ideally, the situation might be handled by having differing on-peak and off-peak prices. In water enterprises storage in the distribution system usually smoothes out diurnal and weekly peaks. The seasonal peak in the summer is important, however. The Metropolitan Water District of Southern California has at times charged a premium price for summer deliveries.

Other differentiations can be justified by increased delivery costs necessary to reach certain classes of customers. A difference in rate between pumped and gravity service, for example, is eminently reasonable. We have not gone into the question of just how great the differences should be, but for the present we shall not consider such differences as violations of the principle of a common per-unit price to all.

Certain frequently encountered differences, which we may now properly call "price discrimination," are not based on any special cost of providing the service in question. In Los Angeles, for example, there is an exceptionally low rate for irrigation use. Domestic, commercial, and industrial services are not distinguished as such, but they are differentially affected by the promotional volume rates. More serious, because much more common, is the system of block rates, with reductions for larger quantities used. There is typically some saving in piping costs to large customers, since a main can be run directly to the service connection, whereas the same volume sold to many small customers would require a distribution network of pipes. Ideally, the cost of laying down the pipes to connect customers to the system should be assessed as one-time charge against the outlet served—or the lump sum could be converted into an annual charge independent of the amount of water consumed, to represent the interest and depreciation on the capital invested by the water system to serve the customer. The point is that, once the pipes are in, the unit marginal cost of servicing customers is almost independent of the volume taken. A lower block rate leads therefore to wasteful use of water by large users, since small users would value the same marginal unit of water more highly if delivered to them. We may say that the promotional or block-rate system in the case of water leads to a discrimination in favor of users of water that happen to find it convenient to use a great deal of the commodity and against users that do not need as much water. The customer paying the lower price will on the margin be utilizing water for less valuable purposes than it could serve if transferred to the customer paying the higher price.

Because of the enormous fraction of water being used for irrigational purposes unusual interest attaches to the method by which water suppliers of such projects are allocated to individual users. Not all irrigation water, of course, is distributed through an irrigation district or enterprise, a great deal being simply pumped or diverted by individual users. Such individual users can be considered to pay a price for water in the form of the costs actually incurred in its acquisition for irrigation purposes.

Reliable information is not available on the cost of water to irrigators, partly because of the differing methods of charging for water. The 1950 Census presented an over-all national average of $1.66 per acre-foot in 1949. This figure is not very meaningful, since it is the result of dividing water charges *per acre* by an estimate of average deliveries of water per acre. But the water charges per acre depend, for farmers served by an irrigation district or other supply enterprise, upon the terms of the "payment complex," which may include taxes and assessments, acreage charge, and service fees in addition to the water price.

Unfortunately, there do not seem to be any nationally compiled data on the methods used by irrigation enterprises to charge for water supplied. A tabulation by the Irrigation Districts Association of California indicates considerable variation in practice: some districts make no charge except by assessment of property; others charge a flat rate, either (1) a fixed amount per acre or (2), depending upon the crop, a variable amount per acre; still others charge a price per unit of water, either on a fixed or on a declining block (promotional) basis; still others have a mixture of pricing methods. Where no charge or only a flat-rate charge is made for water, the marginal price of water to the user would be zero if in fact the user can take unlimited quantities as a domestic consumer normally can (subject only to the limited size of his connection). But it seems to be fairly common practice in irrigation districts that the water is more or less rationed to the user; any "price" set is a fiscal measure to cover the operating and maintenance costs of the district and not a market price in the ordinary sense. We have seen that, with rationing of rights, efficiency can be achieved when trading is permitted. Purchase of water rights in irrigation districts normally takes place through purchase of land, which is usually freely possible (except for the so-called 160-acre limitation in Bureau of Reclamation projects), or through purchase of stock in mutual water companies. It may be remarked that a flat rate per acre varying by the type of crop grown is a kind of crude price, the higher flat rate generally corresponding to the more water-intensive crop. Irrigation districts may achieve reasonably efficient water allocations, but perhaps more often through the purchase of rights rather than the correct pricing of water itself. Where the water right cannot be detached from the land, this limitation on sale will create some inefficiency.

Some Implications of Marginal Cost Pricing for Public Utilities

WILLIAM VICKREY

William Vickrey is Professor of Economics at Columbia Univer-
sity. This well-known article appeared in the American Economic
Review *in 1955.*

As a preface to a discussion of the role of marginal cost pricing, it is perhaps well to state explicitly that in common with any other theoretical
principle, the principle of marginal cost pricing is not in practice to be followed absolutely and at all events, but is a principle that is to be followed
insofar as this is compatible with other desirable objectives, and from
which deviations of greater or lesser magnitude are to be desired when conflicting objectives are considered. On the other hand, I propose to maintain that marginal cost must play a major and even a dominant role in the
elaboration of any scheme of rates or prices that seriously pretends to have
as a major motive the efficient utilization of available resources and facilities.

Some of the conflicting considerations may be mentioned briefly. On a
mere mechanical level, there is always the cost involved in the determination, publication, and administration of a rate structure. The relative
importance of this consideration obviously declines as the value of the unit
of sale becomes larger, so that, for example, one could expect that more
refinement would be justifiable in the case of overseas airline fares than for
short-haul train trips. Ability of the consumer to respond intelligently is
also a limiting factor of a somewhat similar force. Thus a service used frequently by the same individual, such as local transit, will bear relatively
more complexity than a service used rarely, such as parcel checking. And
services used primarily by business firms, whose choices among alternatives
are in the hands of relatively expert specialists, will also bear more complexity. Thus freight tariffs can stand being fairly complex, though this is
by no means a justification of the present jumble.

Another consideration that may in some cases operate to require modification of pricing policies based on marginal cost is the desirability, other things being equal, of minimizing inequalities in income. In an ideal world where there existed an ideal income tax capable of producing any desired distribution of income without administrative expense or deleterious effects on incentives, it would be possible to leave to this measure all redistributions of income, and determine rates on the basis of securing the best possible allocation of resources. In practice, however, such measures of redistribution always have, at the margin, some deleterious effects, so that if modifications of the pricing scheme can be shown to have significant effects on the distribution of income, it will in general be desirable to depart at least to some extent from the strict marginal cost price system. For provided that the departure is small enough, it will in general be possible to provide for some improvement in the distribution of income with a cost in terms of impairment of incentives and misallocation of resources that is less than if the same improvement had been achieved through additional direct redistributive measures, such as increased income taxation. In many cases, however, the relation of the pricing structure of a particular utility service to the distribution of income will be slight or uncertain; in which case the distributional considerations will be correspondingly irrelevant. It is indeed likely that in most cases the magnitude of the modification that would be appropriate on this basis would be small. A major exception may be in the pricing of local transit services, where the incidence of a fare increase, regarded as a tax, is far more regressive than any substantial revenue for which it might be considered a substitute. This consideration would argue for pushing transit fares below the level that would otherwise be appropriate and even, possibly, below marginal cost.

Another point at which prices based on marginal cost may require modification in practice is where such prices come into too violent conflict with popular notions of equity. For example, it is clear that on marginal cost principles, transit fares should be substantially higher during rush hours than during off-peak hours. Yet a proposal of this sort is likely to be considered inequitable by many if not most of the lay population on such grounds as that rush-hour riding is less comfortable, is more of a necessity, is more heavily concentrated among low-income groups or at least among working people; or is, according to some naïve method of cost allocation (as by first computing a cost per vehicle-mile and then dividing this by the average load at various times), less costly. Some of these notions of equity may be considered to be valid in their own right, as the above consideration for the relative income level of the rush-hour riders would be if the facts as to the income distribution of riders actually bore out the assumption. Other notions of equity may be so strongly held as to require, as a matter of practical politics, some consideration in the design of rate structures if the proposals are to succeed. But while the economist may have a role to play in the design of such compromise measures, these compromises should in most cases be regarded as inferior solutions to be superseded by better ones as soon as public opinion can be educated to a more rational view.

Other considerations of a general nature, such as the desirability of promoting decentralization, health, intersectional and international enlightenment, and so on, may have a bearing on the selection of rate structures. But the modifications that might be justifiable on such grounds are in many cases minor and of an uncertain general direction, and as very little of the opposition to marginal cost pricing stems from such considerations, I will leave them with this brief acknowledgment.

By far the most important of the considerations that conflict with the strict application of marginal cost pricing is the need for revenues. Many of the more extreme advocates of marginal cost pricing for decreasing-cost industries seem tacitly to assume that the government has some perfectly costless and neutral source of revenue that is capable of very substantial expansion without ill effects. Such a state might be approached, for example, if we had an income tax free of its multiple defects, evasion proof, with no marginal costs of administration or compliance, and including in its base not only money income but all forms of direct income in kind, including an imputed value for leisure. Needless to say, this is far from the case. A convenient way to express the degree of departure from the ideal, for present purposes, is to estimate a marginal cost of public funds, which will be a percentage indicating the added administrative costs, compliance costs, and indirect losses through the misallocation of resources and the distortion of incentives that will result from increasing the level of public receipts. Such a cost will of course vary from one governmental unit to another. Purely as an offhand indication of the orders of magnitude involved, one may hazard the guess that in small units with a good community spirit or in large units operating with a good civil service and efficient administration, under favorable conditions and with low over-all tax levels, it is conceivable that the marginal cost of public funds might get below 10 per cent, while under unfavorable circumstances, say in a corruptly administered medium-to-large city, excessively circumscribed in its taxing powers, the figure might well exceed 50 per cent.

Obviously, it will not pay, on any concept of the public welfare, to carry a marginal cost pricing policy all the way to the limit, so that the last dollar of subsidy barely yields a dollar's worth of benefits to the using public, when the securing of this dollar for the subsidy imposes burdens of more than a dollar. In the simple case where all demands are perfectly independent, the indicated solution is to have all prices exceed marginal cost by a percentage equal to the marginal cost of public funds divided by the elasticity of the demand controlled by each particular price. Another way of arriving at substantially the same result is to consider prices made up of a base price at marginal cost plus an excise tax. Such excises on public utility rates would receive special consideration as possibly involving lower administrative costs, in the case where their imposition would take the form of the removal of a subsidy that might otherwise be indicated, or where administrative costs would be reduced by reason of the public ownership of the utility. But other than this there would be no justification for higher excise taxes on utility services than on other goods and services.

There is, however, very little to be said for the shibboleth that the rates should be above marginal cost by an amount just sufficient to produce revenues just covering average cost, however this may be defined. To be sure, there are often political and administrative advantages to having operations of a public utility carried on by independent agencies, whether private or public, rather than as governmental departments on a par with other non-revenue-producing agencies of government. It is often argued that this can only be done if the agencies are financially self-supporting. But to me this would be taking a far too defeatist attitude toward our ability to develop appropriate political institutions. Surely the fact that excise taxes are levied on a number of particular products, such as automobiles, gasoline, photographic equipment, and the like, will not be held to have seriously impaired the independence and efficiency of management of these industries, nor, conversely, if for good and sufficient reasons the taxes should be replaced by corresponding subsidies, would one expect the performance to be notably worse. To be sure, abuses occur in the distribution of subsidies, but except where the basis of the subsidy is ill-conceived, these abuses are but the obverse of tax evasion that occurs with excise taxes.

Similarly, if an independent public authority, instead of being required merely to meet its own expenses, is in addition required to turn over to the appropriate governmental unit a stipulated percentage of its gross receipts, either as an explicit excise tax or as an "in lieu" payment, I do not think anyone would imagine that this in and of itself would operate to impair the efficiency and independence of the agency, provided only that the amount is computed in a suitable manner and that the rates and methods of computation are fixed on a reasonably permanent basis. There seems to be no inherent reason why a subsidy cannot be handled in the same manner. There would, to be sure, be a somewhat greater temptation to attach conditions to the subsidy and thus open the door to interference with the independence of the management, and individuals may differ as to the extent to which and the occasions on which this would be desirable. But there is no necessity for this, and if independence is indeed considered a sufficiently important objective, there should be no great difficulty in specifying the manner of payment of the subsidy in such a way as to slam the door on such political interference. There need be no greater political bickering over the level of such a subsidy than over the rate of an excise tax.

This is not to say, however, that there are no impediments to the pursuit of a thoroughgoing marginal cost pricing policy by independent agencies. In particular, attempts to adjust prices to variations in marginal cost produced by the installation of large units of capacity or by unforeseen scarcity or surplus may, in the case of a public agency, produce financial difficulties of a sort that may well give rise to demands for revision of the subsidy provisions that would be too strong to resist. Even so, if this breakdown of independence could be resisted and the substantial fluctuations in earnings weathered by appropriate financial measures such as borrowing or the accumulation of reserves, such fluctuations would yield better resource utilization than a policy of keeping earnings as even as possible from year to year.

In the case of a regulated private utility, the incentives that would result from such a short-run marginal cost pricing policy for delaying expansion so as to raise marginal costs and with them the rates that would be warranted and consequently profits, would produce additional difficulties. If to prevent this the regulatory agency is empowered to dictate the installation of capacity, little discretion indeed would be left to private management, even if regulation could be kept from breaking down under the added administrative burden. Thus whether the agency be public or private, it does appear that it would be difficult to preserve political independence and still provide for the variations of rates in accordance with short-run excess or deficiency of capacity.

But whatever the conclusion as to the desirability of actual payment of subsidies, there can be little question that to require utility users to bear tax burdens in addition to paying the entire average costs is undesirable. The situation is bad enough when utilities must pay income taxes, property taxes, and other general taxes on the same basis as other industries. To impose in addition special discriminatory taxes and excises is completely unjustifiable under any but war emergency conditions. A first step in the direction of marginal cost pricing would be the removal of all such discriminatory tax burdens, such as the federal excises on transportation and telephone service. A second step would be the exemption of public utilities from the payment of such general taxes as can readily be abated without creating difficult administrative problems. This would include all in-lieu taxes, as well as property taxes on property improvements and movables specifically designed and used for utility service, and possibly taxes on land as well, though where property such as land is convertible to other uses, its exemption when normally devoted to utility uses might give rise to incentives for artificially extending the utility operation to cover an unnecessarily large area of land for the sake of extending the scope of such an exemption. Exemption from income taxes raises rather troublesome issues of allocation and accounting where utility companies carry on nonutility activities or otherwise compete directly in subsidiary operations with nonutility companies. But in general there is room for a very substantial step in the direction of marginal cost pricing through tax adjustments without getting involved in outright subsidy. Of course, such a program need not be carried out all the way to the limits suggested by the above considerations if for other reasons it is found desirable to keep prices further above marginal cost than this would make possible. Moreover, this argument would not preclude special taxation of utilities exploiting a scarce natural resource such as water power or natural gas, as a means of retaining for public use the pure economic rent arising in such situations.

Another argument that is often made for avoiding subsidies is that only by requiring customers in the aggregate to pay the full cost of the service can it be made absolutely certain that the service was worth providing. To do this, however, would be somewhat analogous to a playgoer who always rushes home before the end of the last act in order to see whether the TV show that he missed by going to the theater seemed better or worse than the play. Destructive testing is occasionally necessary, but to adopt a policy of applying an injurious test in every case is surely wasteful. Even if only those services are provided that could, it is estimated, pay for themselves, it will ordinarily be far better to operate such services at marginal cost. Even so, policy would err on the conservative side and many worth-while services would fail to be provided because they could not be made to pay for themselves in this way. There is no point in aiming at the wrong target merely because it is easier to tell if you hit it. Moreover, in practice, decisions as to whether to provide a service must be made fairly far in advance with a more or less permanent commitment of capital involved; so that, in practice, whether a service can be made to pay for itself must be estimated in advance and these estimates are almost as uncertain as estimates of whether the service is worth while on an over-all basis. Even if a service cannot pay for itself, this is no indication that it is not worth while. If a mistake is made in such forecasting, marginal cost pricing at least minimizes the resulting waste and salvages what can be retrieved, while an attempt to recover the full costs as nearly as may be often compounds the original error by allowing excess capacity provided in error to remain unused.

Another important consideration to be kept in mind is that marginal cost pricing will not be adopted everywhere simultaneously, and where closely competing services continue to be rendered at rates substantially above marginal cost, reduction of the rates under consideration to marginal cost might well produce a poorer allocation of resources than somewhat higher rates. Indeed, if the only consideration were the allocation of a given demand between two closely competitive forms of service, the proper price for the service under consideration would be one that makes the differential between the prices of the two services reflect the differential in marginal cost, at least where the application of this principle leads to a unique result. It should be noted that it is an equal absolute differential and not an equal percentage relationship that is sought. This may cause difficulty where the units are not directly comparable, especially where different consumers would have different substitution ratios and discrimination between them is not feasible For example, if air express rates are to be set so as to preserve the proper cost differential over established surface handling charges, some allowance should properly be made for the lighter packaging that would often be practiced for air shipment, and this allowance might vary considerably from customer to customer.

There may also be several competing services, differing in the degree to which their rates exceed marginal cost, in which case some sort of compromise will be necessary, with the influence of each competing service weighted according to the appropriate cross-elasticity of demand. For example, if rates for water transportation are to be set, it may not be possible to do this in such a way as to cause the rate differentials to agree with the marginal cost differentials for both rail and truck shipments, if the rates for these latter are not to be disturbed. Of course, where a single agency, such as the ICC, has control over the rates of all of the competing services, all of the rates can be adjusted together to a common margin above marginal costs and there is no difficulty in preserving the competitive relationships among the various services whatever the general level of rates decided upon, except possibly where it is necessary to distort the relationship in order to give the agency providing each service a fair return and no more on its investment. In such a case the problem might better be met by the imposition of appropriate discriminatory taxation on one or more of the operating agencies so as to bring their rates into an economical relationship with the highest rather than to permit traffic to be uneconomically diverted because of differing relationships between the marginal and average cost of the several competing services.

Of course, in a general sense every service competes with all other commodities and services for purchasing power and for the use of resources, and it is sometimes claimed that, since imperfect and monopolistic competition prevail fairly widely in the private sector of the economy, producing prices considerably above marginal cost on the average, therefore public utility prices should likewise be above marginal cost by a like percentage. This argument must be used with caution, however. At most, the presence in the economy of a substantial sector that appears to be genuinely competitive in the relevant sense would bring the average discrepancy between marginal cost and price down to a more moderate figure than would be thought of if attention is focused primarily on the imperfectly competitive sectors. Moreover, in applying such an argument it must not be forgotten that self-produced commodities and services, not produced through the market, also compete in this way. Such nonmarket production, including the utilization of leisure time, constitutes a very large area where there is no market friction, monopoly behavior, or taxation to drive a wedge between the marginal cost and the marginal value to the individual. Services that compete with such self-produced products would need to be priced particularly close to marginal cost if the best attainable allocation of resources is to be reached.

On the other hand, complementarity relations must be considered, also. It might be desirable to price at less than marginal cost a service that happens to be strongly complementary with services that have established prices unusually far above marginal cost. A somewhat inadvertent example of this is the practice of allowing the use of feeder highways at charges often substantially less than marginal cost, balanced in some instances by the charging of tolls substantially in excess of marginal cost on bridges, tunnels, and the like. Conversely, services that are strongly complementary with leisure or nonmarket production might warrantably be priced further above marginal cost than otherwise. This proposition might be held to indicate higher rates for recreational travel, amusements, and the like, except for the fact that there are also strong substitution relationships to be taken into consideration as well and that accordingly the demand for such services is often highly elastic.

The taking into consideration of complementarity and substitution relationships in the application of marginal cost pricing is thus an extremely complex matter that cannot be reduced to any simple rule of thumb. Except for a few special situations, however, it does not seem that complementarity relationships would in themselves require any but relatively minor modifications of marginal cost pricing practices.

But whatever arguments may be advanced for departing in various degrees from a strict marginal cost pricing policy, no sound pricing policy can be developed without using marginal cost as one of the principal determinants. Indeed, whiile marginal cost pricing has been discussed most frequently in a context of decreasing cost situations and subsidies, marginal cost has an important role to play even where economies of scale are absent and there is no problem of self-liquidating versus subsidized operation. Adequate consideration of marginal cost in the setting up of a price structure often leads to structures quite different from those in general use, wholly aside from the question of the proper general level of rates. Even where economies of scale are substantial, marginal cost considerations may be much more important in relation to the structure of rates than to the level.

To illustrate the structural importance of marginal cost pricing, let us consider the following example. A daily train is to be operated from A to B, and possibly to continue on to C, and return. Constant returns to scale prevail over the range of operations contemplated and costs are of three kinds: 20 cents per seat per day for capital and similar charges on the equipment, independent of the distance operated; 30 cents per seat for operating expenses for each leg of the trip; 10 cents per passenger for each leg of the trip for wear and tear on the equipment, cleaning, and service to passengers. It is assumed that equipment can be found to make the train up to any desired number of seats at strictly proportional costs but that it is impractical to change the consist of the train at B and that if it is to run through to C at all, the entire train must be run. Demand for the AB leg is linear, ranging from 2,000 at a price of zero to a maximum price of $2.00 that the most eager passenger is willing to pay; demand for the BC stretch is one-fourth as great, ranging up to 500 passengers at a zero price, with the same maximum price.

Some simple calculations will show that if the train is operated between A and B only, with the capacity exactly adjusted to the traffic, average and marginal costs are 50 cents per trip, and that at this fare there will be 1,500 riders each way, yielding a total consumer's surplus of $2,250.00 per day for the round trip. On the other hand, if the train is operated through to C, marginal cost for the BC portion of the trip is only 10 cents, since there will inevitably be empty seats, while the marginal cost for the AB trip will be 80 cents, the cost of providing additional seats for this trip having risen because the additional seats, if provided, will not have to be carried all the way to C. At fares equal to these marginal costs, there will be 475 BC passengers, whose consumer's surplus for the round trip will be $902.50, and 1,200 AB passengers, with consumer's surplus amounting to $1,440.00, or a total of $2,342.50. As this is a case of constant returns to scale, we can expect that revenues at marginal cost rates will just meet costs, and this is indeed the case. The net welfare product is thus in each case the consumer's surplus generated, and accordingly the second mode of operation is to be preferred to the first, and this is, indeed, the optimum mode of operation.

Now in principle, in a case where there are constant returns to scale, it should be possible to allocate costs in such a way as to produce allocated costs identical with marginal cost. And yet I venture to suggest that in a case such as the above the optimum result shown would not be reached by any of the usual cost allocation procedures unaided by marginal cost concepts. The concept of marginal cost cannot be dispensed with as a tool for making cost allocations even in the constant returns to scale case.

To be sure, the above example is a little unusual in that although. it is not strictly speaking a case of increasing returns, it is a case where indivisibilities enter through the assumption that it would not be possible to provide the service in two or more trains, with only some of the trains operating through to C. Thus the rather unusual result arrived at would not occur in a case where the production process is perfectly divisible and where accordingly competition is possible. But such cases do occur in varying degrees of complexity embedded in a context of decreasing costs. Yet in many cases the more dramatic results of the application of marginal cost pricing will not be a reflection of the degree of decreasing cost, but rather of the pattern of cost interrelationships produced by the indivisibilities.

Indeed, if the only implication of marginal cost pricing were that in decreasing-cost industries the price structure should be reduced more or less uniformly by a percentage reflecting the amount by which the elasticity of the long-run production function falls short of unity, one might be justified, in many cases, in feeling only a very restrained enthusiasm. For example, studies I have made of the marginal costs for railroad freight service indicate a level in the neighborhood of 80 per cent of average costs, on a long-run basis. Subsidies of the order of 2 billion dollars a year, which would be indicated in order to enable rates to be cut to a marginal cost level, would produce a net gain in national product of some 2.50 billions, assuming an elasticity of demand of about unity. In view of what has been said above concerning the marginal costs of public revenues, this would seem to have relatively little to promise. Actually, in such a case one could probably rest content with recommending that taxes bearing on freight transportation in one way or another be abated as far as administratively possible.

Passenger service is a somewhat different matter, however. While if we measure output of passenger service in terms of passenger car miles it is possible to arrive at a figure somewhat comparable to that for freight service, this is not the end of the story. The degree to which this service is actually utilized is positively correlated, to a considerable degree, with the density of traffic: a 10 per cent increase in traffic generally requires an increase of considerably less than 10 per cent in the space that must be provided to give an equivalent quality of service. Moreover, as traffic density increases, the quality of the service tends to increase, in terms of frequency, variety, speed, and sometimes in quality of equipment. Or to put it another way, the fact that passengers willl not wait as readily as will freight for the accumulation of trainloads of minimum cost size means that trainloads are generally smaller than would produce a minimum average cost per passenger and thus there are substantial economies of scale from increasing the number of passengers per train to be compounded with the economies of having more trains per year per route. All of this is rather difficult to evaluate, but it seems not impossible to place the marginal cost of passenger service as low as one-third of the average cost, particularly on lines where the density of traffic is fairly low and the average haul short. Some support for the more extreme point of view may be found in Gilbert Walker's figures comparing main line with local and branch line passenger service costs in England, given in an article in the *Oxford Economic Papers* for March, 1953.

It is fashionable in railroad circles to bemoan the present deficit shown for passenger operations as constituting one more unfair burden thrown upon railroad freight traffic, placing it at an improper disadvantage as compared with truck traffic. But if it is true that the elasticity of costs for passenger service is substantially lower than for freight, this would justify a substantial discrimination in favor of passenger service. The existing relation between passenger and freight rates may thus be more desirable, on the whole, than one where passenger service is required to meet all of the costs for which it is incrementally responsible as a whole, to say nothing of a share in the costs that are inextricably joint as between passenger and freight service. Of course, an even better allocation of resources could be obtained if railroad passenger services could be subsidized from general tax funds rather than, in effect, from a special tax on railroad freight service.

In another area, it is often claimed that telephone service is rendered under conditions of increasing rather than decreasing costs. It is claimed, with some justice, that the central office equipment required to furnish interconnections between subscribers increases more rapidly than in proportion to the number of subscribers. Comparisons of costs between large and small communities also seem to indicate increasing costs. But this is not the whole story. Much of the outside plant of telephone companies can be installed, under given outside conditions, at much lower unit costs at high densities of service than at low; long distance service in particular seems to have a strong decreasing cost characteristic. The economies of scale in the outside plant would seem to be sufficient in most cases to much more than offset the diseconomies of scale in the switching plant. Nor is the urban-rural or large town–small town comparison quite appropriate. While it is true that a large exchange will usually find that the conditions under which the outside plant must be installed are more costly than a small exchange, this is not caused by the size of the exchange but is only an associated condition. Actually, if in some given city such as Detroit, for example, one were to imagine that nine-tenths of the customers taken at random had never installed a telephone, I would be very much surprised if it would have been possible to design and construct a telephone system to serve the remaining tenth of the subscribers at as low a cost per subscriber as is obtainable with the existing pattern of service, particularly if the amount of use per telephone were to be held approximately the same. Moreover, even were it true that costs under given circumstances tended to go up more than in proportion to the number of subscribers, this might be considered offset by the increased value of the service rendered when a subscriber can reach a larger number of other phones in the community. Thus telephone service is by no means to be excluded from the candidates for subsidy if marginal cost pricing is adopted as a general principle.

One of the major characteristics of marginal cost structures is the rather marked variation in such costs as between-peak and off-peak demands, whether the peak be in terms of daily, weekly, or seasonal fluctuations, or even as between congested and uncongested sections of route. In the ideally simple case, where demand is exactly predictable and capacity is a sharp and rigid limit, the appropriate marginal cost price is one which covers only the utilization or service costs as long as demand at that price is below capacity, and which is at other times or places just sufficient to keep effective demand at the capacity level, capacity being in turn adjusted so that the amounts obtained over and above the service costs during such periods of capacity use are just enough to cover the marginal costs associated with an increase in capacity. The marginal cost of a peak period unit may be thought of as the opportunity cost involved in depriving the next most eager consumer of the service, or of a cost arrived at by taking the marginal cost of an increment of capacity and deducting as a credit the excess of the value of all other units of service which the increment of capacity makes it worth while to produce and sell over their respective direct variable costs.

The picture is of course often complicated by the fact that various different capacity limits often operate on the same service at different times and in different ways. In the very short run, for example, the number of seats scheduled to be operated on a given train may be fixed; with some advance notice, cars can be added or dropped, but perhaps only by shifting equipment from some other service; over a longer period, schedules can be adjusted and eventually adjustments to track layout can take place. The appropriate measure of the peak also varies: where the timing is crucial, as with transit service, limitations imposed by track or roadway capacity operate on the basis of a volume measured over an interval of say five or ten minutes; with respect to the availability of equipment, the peak is determined by integrating over a period equal to the time taken for a round trip, say ninety minutes.

Capacity limits on output of nonstorable services often operate to produce rather drastic fluctuations in marginal costs that are regular and predictable enough to be used as the basis for rate making. For subway service in New York, for example, it has been estimated that the marginal cost of a fairly long rush-hour trip would be on the order of 30 to 50 cents, while a comparable non-rush-hour trip would have a marginal cost of only 8 to 10 cents, and rush-hour trips in a direction opposed to the major flow of traffic would in most cases be a surplus by-product service with a marginal cost substantially zero. Costs per passenger mile will vary equally drastically for different portions of a single trip on a single train. An evening rush-hour trip from Coney Island to Bedford Park in the Bronx would have a zero marginal cost for the Brooklyn portion of the trip, a cost rising to about 5 cents per mile for the upper Manhattan portion of the trip and falling off to 1 or 2 cents per mile for the Bronx portion of the trip.

Capacity limits are, however, not always rigid. The usual way of expressing a somewhat elastic capacity limit is in terms of a more or less sharply rising marginal cost curve. In many cases, however, while the capacity limits on the volume of service offered are quite rigid, elasticity at the capacity limit is provided by impairment in the quality of the service offered. It may not be possible to run more trains or longer trains on a given route, at least in the short run, whether from lack of track capacity or of equipment; an increase in traffic will be accommodated by having a larger proportion of standees, or more intense crowding. Costs to the operating agency may be very little affected, and in this sense one might say that marginal cost is very low; the cost, however, is to be measured in terms of the deterioration in the value of the service to the former passengers. It is not often realized how great a marginal cost computed in this way can easily be. If the addition of 20 passengers to a car already containing 200 passengers creates increased crowding, that the original passengers would on the average pay 3 cents each to avoid, this is a cost of $6.00 to be divided among the 20 passengers causing it, resulting in a marginal cost of 30 cents each. Or as demand approaches the theoretical capacity, the slack necessary to insure taking care of customers as they apply may vanish, with the result of longer and longer queues or delays in getting service. The queue or the delay may operate to cut down to some extent the demand for service, but in general this will be an inadequate deterrent without substantial increases in the rate as well, since the operative deterrent for the individual is the average delay, not the much greater increment in total delays that will be caused by the addition of one person to the demand: not only will the additional customer have to wait while he works his way to the head of the queue, but all customers after him will have their waits increased by the time required to service the added customer, until such time as either the queue is entirely worked off or some potential customer is discouraged by the increased length of the queue.

In an extreme case where the control of the queue may require diversion of resources from the providing of the service, as for example may occur in some situations in telephone service, overload may even reduce the amount of service that can actually be rendered below what it would have been had demand been more moderate. For example, repeated attempts of thwarted subscribers to place calls may absorb the time of operators or of certain types of common equipment in an automatic exchange such as registers, senders, markers, and the like. Considerable additional complexity of central office equipment is often necessary to prevent paralysis in such contingencies.

Fairly extreme results also tend to occur in poorly controlled situations such as curb parking. Marked differences occur in the amount of time which a would-be parker will have to spend in finding a place to park, and also in the distance that he will have to walk to get to his ultimate destination, on the average, according to whether, out of say 1,000 parking spaces in a given area, 999 are, again on the average, occupied, or whether the average occupancy is only 995 or 990. Again, the deterrent to say the 990th parker is only the amount of time he will have to search, and he takes no account, ordinarily, of the added searching time that his occupancy of a space will impose on those who come after. Metering of curb parking space on marginal cost principles would thus require rather substantial fluctuations in the rate per hour as the degree of occupancy fluctuates in the neighborhood of 100 per cent.

In summary, then, marginal cost pricing must be regarded not as a mere proposal to lower rates generally below the average cost level but rather as an approach which implies a drastic rearrangement of the patterns and structures of rates. Indeed, it is this restructuring of rates that is likely to be the greatest contribution of marginal cost pricing to the improvement of the over-all efficiency of our economy, while the further gains that might be obtainable from the reduction of rates from a self-sustaining level to a marginal cost level, once the pattern of rates has been made to conform as closely as possible to marginal cost, are likely to be relatively small. The issue is thus not primarily one of subsidized versus nonsubsidized operation, though this is still an important issue. The dominant issue is one of whether the pattern of rates should be based on tradition, inertia, and happenstance, or whether it is to be developed by a careful weighing of the relevant factors with a view to guiding consumers to make an efficient use of the facilities that are available.

Perhaps some indication of the outstanding absurdities that occur in present utility rate structures may be worth while in conclusion. For example, in New York a new vehicular tunnel was opened a few years ago from the Battery to Brooklyn. Since it is a new facility and undoubtedly much more easy and pleasant to use than the old East River bridges, it must, forsooth, be made to pay for itself by the imposition of tolls starting at 35 cents, the practical consequence of which is to encourage continued heavy use of the Manhattan Bridge for all trips for which that route is shorter than the tunnel, with the result that the streets near the Manhattan end of the bridge are the scene of some of the worst traffic congestion in the city. Marginal cost considerations would call for the collection of a substantial toll on the old East River bridges, at least during hours of heavy congestion, and a smaller toll or none at all for the tunnel, even though this might mean that the users of the bridges might be "paying for" the tunnel.

In suburban railroad service, the lowest fares offered are almost invariably the weekly and monthly commutation tickets used predominantly by commuters who travel almost exclusively in the rush hour when marginal costs are highest; next highest are multiple-ride tickets used by family members, often at the rush hours, but somewhat less frequently so. Users of one-way or round-trip tickets, on the other hand, are more likely to be off-peak or even counter-rush riders with very low marginal cost. Nor can this pattern be defended on the basis of elasticity. The daily commuter rides from almost absolute necessity, in most cases, whereas the occasional trips of other family members are often dispensable trips; further, the use of the family car for such trips is much more often a strong competitor, since the car is then not needed at home, the schedules are less frequent and convenient than in the rush hour, and many persons may be riding together. To be sure, in the long run there is elasticity to the daily commuter traffic in that the fares influence the decision to move to the suburbs, but even to the extent that this is a significant factor, it will be some weighted average of the commutation and multi-trip ticket that would be the relevant rate to be considered by the prospective suburbanite. Political pressures seem to be partly responsible for this state of affairs: regular commuters have both a sufficient stake and a sufficient appeal to the public sentiments to bring effective pressure to bear on regulatory bodies. Some roads have been of late making tentative progress toward putting in a reduced rate type of ticket good only during the nonrush hours, but the attempt in most cases seems to have been rather half hearted, as the rate offered is usually still higher than that available in the multi-trip family ticket. Marginal cost pricing here would go much further than this and just about reverse the entire pricing structure.

The same delusion often gets a foothold in the local transit field. Philadelphia, probably on the basis of political pleas, has recently adopted a plan for selling strips of ten tickets, good for one week only, which of course are used predominantly by the high-cost rush-hour riders.

The rapid obsolescence of that great American institution, the open-section Pullman car, is in many ways the work of an inefficient pricing policy, itself in large measure the product of inefficient working arrangements between the Pullman Company and the railroads. No serious attempt seems ever to have been made to vary rates so as to balance the demand for upper and lower berths, so that what was and could still be a device for furnishing a satisfactory low-cost service is fast being relegated to the scrap heap.

And so it goes. One may, for various good and sufficient reasons, hesitate to embrace marginal cost pricing in all of its ramifications as an absolute standard. But no approach to utility pricing can be considered truly rational which does not give an important and even a major weight to marginal cost considerations. And when adequate weight is given to such consideration, important changes in present pricing practices will be indicated in many areas.

Efficiency and Amenity

BERTRAND DE JOUVENEL

Bertrand de Jouvenel is a well-known French economist. The following article is the Earl Grey Memorial Lecture, given at King's College in 1960.

I

Men have ever desired to improve their material lot. But the idea that year after year the material lot of all or most members of a nation can and should be increased is new. Medieval radicals called for the rejection of the burdens laid upon the workers for the benefit of the privileged classes, but looked no further than the once-for-all improvement procured thereby. The thought that practically everybody can get somewhat richer continuously could not have arisen but for the gradual progress achieved over time and the awareness that it was due to successive gains in the productivity of labor. Awareness of the process has fostered a demand that it be accelerated. Accountancy has become a major criterion of our judgments.

We find nothing strange in the grading of nations according to their National Product per inhabitant, estimated in dollars, never mind how imperfectly. Those which lie in the lower ranges we call "underdeveloped": they are to be pitied, spurred, and helped up. Those which stand on the higher rungs we call "advanced." Such classification is common ground for leaders of opinion in both "Capitalist" and "Communist" countries. Indeed for more than thirty years, the avowed objective of Soviet planning has been "to overtake the American standard of life." Further, the vast increase in the worldwide prestige of Communism is due to the very high rates of growth achieved, and paradoxically enough the poorer countries are tempted to follow the Communist path as that which leads fastest to the way of life of the Capitalist countries.

In the advanced countries themselves the yearly rate of growth is a subject of great interest: if high it redounds to the credit of the Government, if low it affords an argument to the Opposition. Such focusing of attention upon economic growth should lead to the acceleration of the process.

May I quote just a few figures? The United States have amazed the world by multiplying real product per inhabitant almost sevenfold since 1839, according to the estimate of Raymond W. Goldsmith; that is a pace of 1.64 percent per year; in France during the last decade (i.e., 1949–1959), real product per inhabitant has increased by more than one half, growing at a rate of 3.5 percent a year. If such a rate were sustained, it would *treble* the flow of goods and services per inhabitant in 32 years. This would imply a metamorphosis of life in the course of a generation. The British rate of increase has been a good deal lower, about 2.1 percent yearly (1948–1958), which if sustained would imply *doubling* the flow of goods and services per inhabitant within a generation. May I be so indiscreet as to say that I hope to see the British rate of growth increased by British entry into the faster growing Common Market? I must stress that the figures quoted all refer to progress of Gross National Product per inhabitant, not to the progress of production per man-hour, which is higher.

My figures serve no other purpose than to indicate the magnitude or speed of change. Surely if all the children now being born can, when reaching the age of 32, find themselves two or three times better off than their parents are now, it is worth thinking what to make of this opportunity. This is the problem I wish to raise. As we shall find, it is by no means an easy one to discuss.

II

The statement of the problem contains by implication two value judgments which should be made explicit. Firstly, I have assumed that people could obtain more and more goods and services and implied that it is a good thing; I so believe. Secondly, I have said that we should think of increasing riches as an increasing opportunity and implied that we can make thereof a better or worse use. These two assumptions may well pass unchallenged because they agree with current common sense. But however trivial the position taken, it has to be noted that it contradicts two strongly entrenched schools of thought, one ancient the other modern. The ancient moralists have all held that Man should limit his desires, that the pursuit of ever more goods and services is folly, bound to make men wicked and miserable. By reason of our first premise therefore we run foul of their venerable wisdom, and indeed we shall find that our wealth-mindedness brings us into conflict with many values which deserve respect. The second premise clashes with the relativist school, so powerful nowadays, which holds that there are no values other than subjective. If every man be the only judge of his own interest, if we can ascertain what makes him better off *solely* by observation of the *preferences* his actions *reveal*, then however Society develops under free individual choices, we must assume that whatever is, is the best possible world at the moment.

The position sketched out therefore is *modern* in opposition to the ancient moralists, and if you will it is progressive. It is however *classical* in opposition to the relativists, in its assumption that the judgments we pass upon the quality of life are not mere expressions of individual fancy but tend to objective value, however approximately attained.

III

To approach our problem, let us firstly ask ourselves how much good has come out of the economic progress already achieved and how near it has brought us to a Golden Age. A great deal of good has come out of economic progress up to date. Among these goods some figure in our statistics and some do not—housing does, and so does the labor-saving equipment provided to housewives; in the case of the latter however, mere statistics fail to do justice to a major boon, which has transformed the life of the better part of Mankind. The shortening of the workweek figures in our statistics as well as the holidays, but what cannot figure is the great lessening of the physical labor involved in work. Indeed if we could draw two curves, one of them describing the shortening of the work-time and the other the lessening of the intensity of muscular effort per hour, we would find the second falling far more than the first.[1] Some changes such as Full Employment which spares men the anxiety and indignity of being unwanted do not arise directly out of the progress of Productivity but are closely linked with it, and so are the social measures for the relief of misery which we could not have afforded but for our enrichment. Some effects figure in statistics but have connotations which do not so figure; for instance the great transformation of workers' clothing has erased a visible distinction. If I may add a light note, when I see two drivers locked in conflict, I reflect that but for the automobile, one of them might be on horseback the other on foot, while now they are on the same footing.

It is idle to say that all have benefited from economic progress. Obviously the class which had servants cannot afford them any more due to the up-pricing of labor; and this by itself involves for the class mentioned a great decline in the ease of life; but also it makes for greater similarity of situations, and presumably for readier understanding.

We could of course say more about the benefits of progress but some shall be stressed in due time. On the other hand, can we say that our progress has brought us anywhere near the Golden Age? I fear not.

In writing and image, many glimpses of the Golden Age have been vouchsafed to us; they concur quite remarkably. *Homo Felix* moves against a background of beauty, delights in his workmanship, is benefited by the company he keeps, and his song of joy praises his Creator. Most

---

[1] Note that I speak of muscular effort; nervous fatigue is quite a different business.

often he is shown in a landscape mellowed by the human hand, with a nice balance of trees, meadows, and stream; a graceful temple, however, testifies to urbanity. Contrariwise, if *Homo Felix* happens to be painted in a public place, then the greenery of the surroundings shows through the monuments of the town. The latter is no more than a meeting place for worship and conviviality. *Homo Felix* is not idle, but the enjoyment of doing things so overcomes the awareness that they must be done as to exclude any sense of drudgery. His associates move his heart and quicken his wit, expecting the best of him, they help him to achieve it. He opens his eyes at dawn, eager for the activities of the day, and closes them at dusk; free from worry, he exerts no pressure on any other man nor does he endure any.

Such, in brief, is the picture of *Homo Felix*. As against it the man of our day lives steeped in ugliness, injured, whether he be aware of it or not, by ugly sights, ugly sounds, ugly smells. His labors, in the great majority of cases, give little scope for his talents, and he can seldom forget that they are done solely for the sake of the reward. He is exceptionally fortunate if the company he keeps induces him to reach the excellence of which he is inherently capable.

It is a long way indeed to the Golden Age. Maybe the picture drawn thereof was a fanciful one. But surely there is some way of life which would be an improvement upon that which we find.

IV

An opinion which enjoys great currency is that the productivity gains we may look to, will for the greater part, translate themselves into a very rapid shortening of the time of work, so that we may expect in a few years the thirty-hour week or even the twenty-eight-hour week, i.e., three days and a half. Minds which start with this assumption then find themselves faced with the "problem of leisure"; what shall the people do, with all that spare time? They will be half workers, half gentlemen of leisure. Now it is no easy thing to be a gentleman of leisure, and not so many gentlemen have made a good showing at it. So runs the argument.

I happen to doubt very strongly that the working-week shall be shortened as much or as fast as people imagine. A lot of things can be reckoned out on paper which can not happen in reality. For instance, we may picture, say a 3.5 percent increase in production per man-hour, of which 2 percent would be taken out in the shortening of the time of work and 1.5 percent in the increase of production per worker. Under such conditions a thirty-hour week could easily be achieved within twenty years, while presumably production per inhabitant would be stable or declining, due to the reduction in the proportion of workers relatively to population, of which more anon.

This can be worked out with closer arithmetic than mine, but it simply would not work out in life. It is inconceivable that a 3.5 percent increase in productivity per year could occur with a slow expansion of production. High rates of productivity gain are linked to high rates of expansion. High overall rates of expansion are themselves linked with the introduction of new products in the production of which, or thanks to the production of which, the great productivity gains are achieved.

Some people reason as if we could nicely immobilize needs and then take out all our productivity gains in leisure. Let us follow this fancy. Suppose that our needs in lighting had been assessed in 1760, and that the candle industry had been asked to work down the time necessary for the provision of that much amount of lighting. Under such circumstances, the electricity industry could never have appeared, as it required a rapidly expanding market. That example has been chosen because lighting is of all goods and services that in which labor-saving has been greatest, but it has also been that for which the expansion of the market has been greatest.

The nature of productivity gains is best grasped if one traces over time the cost in minutes of labor of the several goods and services. Nearly all these costs decline, but at very different rates. What makes for a great gain in the collection of goods and services obtained per average hour is the presence, in the "mix," of an increasing variety of products intervening with increasing weights; such presence will be felt the more, the greater the overall expansion. Therefore, if, counting upon a high rate of productivity gains, we proposed to apply them mostly to shortening the time of work, and only to a lesser degree to the increase of production, we might find that the expected productivity gains withered away.

According to Moses Abramovitz, over the last seventy-five years, the productivity increase obtained in the U.S. has been cashed in to the proportion of three-fourths in the increase of production per man, to the proportion of one-fourth in the decrease of work-time per man. Should we assume that progress continued at just the same rate and was allocated according to the same proportions, it would take another seventy years to bring the U.S. to the thirty-hour week. Now of course one should shun such extrapolations. On the one hand productivity gains can be stepped up, considerably. On the other hand we should take into account that cutting down the workweek from very high levels certainly does not cut down pro rata the effective input of labor, because the effective input per hour then rises; it is very doubtful whether this same phenomenon would remain operative when cutting down the work-time from lower levels.

I do not pretend to know at what rate through the years the workweek can be shortened. But it seems very necessary to point to the demographic phenomena which shall militate against any very great and rapid shortening of the workweek. We can easily perceive that the workweek of the adult shall have to support an increasing proportion of weeks of existence of nonlaboring population.

We tend to live longer, and every year more that we live beyond working age is an added charge upon the worker. To an increasing degree the poor of an advanced society are its aged, and if we wish, as I feel we should, to pursue our effort for the relief of poverty, we must give to the aged a greater share of the proceeds of our work because of their increasing proportion and in order to raise their relative status. In the same manner, every year more which an adolescent spends at school is an added charge upon the adult workers. And surely nothing is more desirable than the successive prolongation of education. This can endow youths both with a better capacity for production and, what seems to me more important, with a better capacity for the right use of life and leisure, of which more anon.

Indeed I strongly feel that we should think of giving less time to productive work, not in terms of less hours per week but in terms of coming later to gainful employment and remaining longer in existence after retirement. Speaking very roughly, delaying entry into the labor market by one year is the arithmetic equivalent of shortening the workweek by two hours for a period of twenty years.[2] Shown that the change in labor input arising from the one or the other change is the same, and given the choice, what father would hesitate to prefer longer schooling for his child or shorter hours for himself? Whatever the choice of the individual, the choice to be made in the name of Society can give rise to no hesitation. Our opportunities for labor-saving should be applied by preference to the longer and more elaborate formation of our citizens.

This is not to say that the normal workweek shall not be shortened, but the effective workweek need not evolve in the same manner except for those who are the least employable. There exists already a clearly marked tendency for the duration of work to be longest for the most able—which is a quite natural feature of an expansive economy, which presses harder upon its most scarce resources, human as well as material.

V

People are apt to confuse the two notions of "time not spent at work" and of "free time," this is a mistake; it neglects the time spent in getting to the work place and back home. While such time is not spent in productive processes, it is not available to the individual. Such transport time was nil in the case of the artisan, negligible in the case of a factory hand of a nineteenth century mill-town. Nowadays it is very seldom less than five hours a week, frequently ten, sometimes fifteen. This is a subject which our passion for surveys has left untouched. Yet it would be very interesting to have a distribution of the working population according to the number

---

[2] Assuming a typical year of 48 weeks of 44 hours, it shall take 22 years at a rate of two hours per week to retrieve one year of delay in entry.

of hours spent on transport to and from work, and the evolution of this distribution over time. It would not be at all astonishing if we found that in recent times average transport time has risen a good deal more than the average workweek has shrunk. Indeed in some countries, such as Britain and France, there has been of late no visible trend toward the reduction of the effective workweek while there has been a clear trend toward the rise of transport time. I know quite a few workers to whom it costs twelve hours a day to do an eight hour spell. This great waste of time, attended by nervous fatigue, does not figure in our statistics. We say that John Smith makes so much for, say, 44 hours of presence; in fact, he gets so much, less fares, for 44 hours of presence involving n hours of transport.

National Accounting constitutes a great intellectual advance but its best experts are least prone to believe that it offers a comprehensive picture of the human situation. We know that rapid progress in National Income involves a ceaseless process of shifting men from A positions to B positions where they contribute more to overall product and are better rewarded. Talking of such Labor Mobility, we stress the increase in market power which it brings to the subject, and we are apt to forget the psychological costs which may be incurred in the process. The very fact that Labor Mobility has to be preached testifies that men are often reluctant to break off their links with a given place, a given job, given work associates. Instances of such reluctance are often enough noted in our newspapers, and testify to psychological costs. Economists will say that when people do move, thereby they reveal a preference for the B position—the gain in market power is subjectively superior to the cost of uprooting. True enough if the man has the choice of remaining in the A position or of moving to the B position; but such is not always the case; it may well be that the A position folds up and that he is left no choice. If a professor of Greek becomes an employee of an advertising firm, it may be by reason of the superior reward offered, and then he has indeed revealed a subjective preference; not so if the teaching of Greek is being discontinued in the institution which employed him.

While taking into account the increase in a man's real earnings we fail to take into account the unpleasantness of his uprooting. Nor is this only a subjective cost. It has ever been accepted that there is value in attachment to a place, a skill, and a fellowship. Indeed the Good Society as it was traditionally pictured was one in which such loyalties were strong; but they must be weak for the proper working of our Progressive Society. The point deserves to be pondered.

The bias of our accounting is most strikingly reflected in our assessment of what occurs when a tannery or paper factory is set up. Its product—in terms of value added—is registered as a positive increment to National Product. But the discharge from the factory pollutes the river. Nobody would deny that this is to be deplored; but such an incidental effect is regarded as alien to the realm which we agree to consider in earnest.

Nobody says that on the one hand the factory produces *goods*, but that on the other, quite as concretely, it produces *bads*. I would argue that this is what we should state: there are two forms of production, one of positive value, the other of negative value. Most economists are very unwilling to speak in this manner; they would say that the positive values produced are proved and measured by the prices paid for them in the open market, while what I call negative values cannot be so proved and measured. True enough, because people can buy leather or paper by the yard, while they can not buy a yard of unpolluted river. The factory produces its *goods* in divisible form; it produces its *bads* as indivisible nuisances. There are no economic means of stating their negative values, yet this exists, and it is proved by the fact that we become increasingly disposed to vast public expenditures to remove such nuisances. Incidentally the champions of free private enterprise would be well inspired to force upon firms measures for the prevention of nuisances, for want of which the removal of nuisances must inevitably lead to the development of a great new field of public activities. Indeed in any case, important "Utilities" of the future will be the industries designed to remove nuisances.

Looking upon our rivers today one thinks of the times when they were personified into semideities. Such Pagan fancies can only be allegories to Christians, but not useless allegories. The Renaissance made much of the river figures in poetry and sculpture; what poor bedraggled figures we should paint today if we returned to such allegories! With this suggestion we touch upon the *Amousia* of modern civilization.

VI

In an economic policy-making committee I recently happened to suggest that the Parthenon was an addition to the wealth of Athenians, and its enjoyment an element of their standard of life. This statement was regarded as whimsical. When I had made it clear that it was seriously meant, I was told that the standard of life is expressed by per capita Private Consumption of goods and services acquired on the market. Meekly accepting this correction, I asked my colleague whether when he drove out to the country on weekends, his satisfaction was derived from the costly consumption of gasoline, or from the free sight of trees and possibly the free visit of some cathedral. At this point people are wont to make a distinction between the useful and the pleasant. I would certainly not deny that there is a stark utility in being so clad as to be protected against the cold, but I fail to see any difference in kind between enjoying a variety of clothes and enjoying a variety of flowers, and happen to prefer the latter.

Until quite recently the laborer meant the agricultural laborer. Throughout the millennia, Production would be equated with Agriculture. The business of procuring food undoubtedly has a prior claim upon our attention, and I feel no doubt that growing food is more important business than Art. Strangely enough, while Production had this vital character, it was looked down upon. In all the civilizations of the past the producer was a mean person and his concerns mean concerns. Paradoxically, Production has acquired an unprecedented moral status while less and less of it caters to indispensable needs, to whit the precipitous fall in the agricultural labor force. I have no quarrel with the enhanced status of Production; indeed I feel certain that modern Society's great success in Production is mainly due to our thinking better and thinking more of Production. It is not a matter I propose to discuss here, but in my view the great contrast offered by our civilization with the civilizations of the past lies in that *their* social leaders would have deemed it *improper* to think of Production, a concern of underlings, while *our* social leaders are recruited on the basis of their *interest* in and contribution to the heightening of *efficiency* in Production, a change which occurred in our own Society within a small number of generations.

But if I do not at all object to the much enhanced status of Production, I may point out that Production has come to embrace so much that it would be foolish to grant any and every productive activity the moral benefit of an earnestness not to be found in so called "nonproductive activities." When popular newspapers propose to bring out their comic strips in color, I find it hard to regard such "progress in production" as something more earnest than planting flowering shrubs along the highways. I am quite willing to regard poetry as a frivolous occupation as against the tilling of the soil but not as against the composing of advertisements.

When organizers of production have to relieve a situation of hunger, efficiency is the one and only virtue. But when this virtue has been thoroughly developed and comes to be applied to less and less vital objects, the question surely arises of the right choice of objects.

VII

Most economists, among whom the masters of the science, would deny that there is any real problem here. They would stress that individuals, in the handling of their family budgets, display their preferences, and that therefore the allocation of total consumer expenditures, subject to the existing distribution of incomes, reveals the preferences of the public as a whole; that therefore also the collection of goods and services obtained at present is presently the best possible, the right one. They would go on to say: "You personally may think that a different collection would be better, but in so stating all you do is to pit your single subjective preference against the aggregate of individual subjective preferences."

However powerful this argument, it is not decisive. We can point out, firstly, that current choices are made between currently available goods and services, secondly, that they are a function of the consumer's own past.

Speaking to the first point, it is not true that the buyer is the sole author of his choices. These of course depend upon what is offered. Let us turn our minds, not without shame, to the goods which were first offered by colonial traders to American Indians and African Negroes. What were they? Trinkets and liquor, objects useless or harmful, the market for which could be rapidly expanded because emulation fostered the demand for baubles and habit the demand for liquor. In the case of our own laboring populations the initial exploitation of the popular market was little better. The first industries which really benefited the people were the cotton and glass industries, both conducive to neatness and hygiene.

As our working classes got richer, a great obstacle stood in the way of selling them anything worthwhile. There was a fatter weekly pay envelope, but accumulating out of this weekly pay the wherewithal to acquire, say, a house required an inordinate strength of character. In my own country the point was made *ad nauseam* that people would rather spend on drink, the movies, and other evanescent goods and services than upon getting a proper home. This was a most unfair judgment; the situation altered radically as soon as housing could be made available, to be paid consecutively out of incoming pay.

The order in which goods come to be offered is also important. The American economy was characterized after World War I by the great upsurge of the motor car and the movie, after World War II by the comparable upsurge of household equipment and television. It is at least plausible that if the second set of goods had become available before the first, their home-binding influence would have colored the American way of life.

The second point is of course that consumer choices are a function of the consumer's own past. For instance, in my library there is not a single book in Russian; this of course is because I can not read the Russian language. Now suppose that there were no books left or published in any other language than Russian. Then I would have no books at all, which, by the reasoning which is now current, would establish that I do not like reading. Presumably I would take pains to learn Russian, but, starting at my time of life, I would not become proficient at it; it would take me a great deal of time to work through a book; possibly I would then turn to comic strips; this would triumphantly reinforce the proof that "people prefer" comic strips. Revealed preferences in fact reveal *ignorances*, the lack of intellectual and aesthetic formation.

VIII

I suspect that our Society is the most deficient in Culture which has ever been seen. It is a natural need of man to express himself in oratory, poetry, song, dance, music, sketching, sculpture, and painting. If Culture has any meaning, it means that the aptitudes which all children have, in diverse degrees, for some or other of these pleasurable activities should be cultivated. This can not harm the development of another and more scarce aptitude, that for understanding and conveying such understanding in the language either of philosophy or of mathematics. But the aesthetic pleasures should naturally be the most common. Their lack makes us properly Barbarians, if the Barbarian be the man without powers of appreciation or expression.

Strangely enough, anything which lies in the realm of aesthetic enjoyment is regarded in our wealthy Society as nonessential. Nonessential and "distinguished"; no doubt we think highly of "works of art" which the rich may possess and which the poor are invited to admire in a museum. But this treatment of works of art by itself displays their "eccentricity" in the literal sense of the word, with regard to our Civilization.

In my opinion, it is the very definition of Philistinism to think of Art with a capital A, no matter indeed whether this way of thinking is that of the much-blamed bourgeois or of the artist himself. In the epochs of Culture, the term "the arts" corresponded to our present notion of "the industries." Thus in Florence the *arte di la lana* meant the industry of woolens. One did not think that turning out woolens was one thing, concerning oneself with beauty another. One did not think that building edifices of worship, or public edifices, or private houses was one thing entirely distinct from any preoccupation for beauty. The nineteenth century, which was basically Philistine, developed the notion of the *objet d'art*, the small thing of beauty which the rich, having turned out goods without beauty, could thus afford to lodge in their houses built without beauty.

The dizzy height of prestige to which painting had risen in the last two generations is, I feel, the true index to the Philistinism of our Society. In an age of Culture, painting is not a thing in itself, it is an element of decoration fitting into a general pattern of beauty.

The fact that there are objects of beauty in the museums of London and Paris does not acquit us of the fact that London and Paris are not beautiful; within them any combination of buildings we can point to with pride is at least a century and a half old. Since then we have done nothing to improve; everything which has been done has tended to degrade.

It is claimed that people do not care. It seems to me that their behavior testifies to the contrary. How do people spend their holidays? In escaping from the setting in which they are forced to live; they go to the country to see what the world was meant to look like, and they go to ancient cities whose inhabitants were concerned, however poor, to achieve a beauty which in our wealth we neglect. Indeed when on weekends one sees people teeming out of London one is tempted to think that the word *Sunday* has been restored to its primitive meaning; it is now the day without smog.

From people's behavior it seems apparent that as individuals we attach far more importance to beauty than we do collectively as a Society. Why do we, as a Society, set so little importance upon it? My own feeling is that the preoccupation with Beauty is always associated with the feeling that life centers upon singing the glory of God; were I to discuss how Puritanism has divorced the Good from the Beautiful, and how the secularist concern for man alone has become a concern for the "functional," I would be treading upon ground which would be controversial and moreover using big words in an elliptic manner which is apt not only to mislead the audience but to muddle the speaker. Such investigation of causes is indeed not relevant at this time and for the purpose on hand.

IX

I find it hard to agree that the man of our Society has a high standard of life. The life of modern man seems to me unstructured; it flexes to embrace the new good which is offered; possession thereof alters the shape of life which is therefore a function of what happens to be put on the market. This is an invertebrate, amoeba-like progress of the way of life. If anyone were to furnish a house by accumulating "good buys" wherever and whenever encountered, that house would be a meaningless clutter, without style or personality. This is to me the aspect offered by our life.

Imagine that an eighteenth century philanthropist, say the Marquis de Mirabeau or Thomas Jefferson, were resurrected and briefed as to the increase in labor productivity and wealth which has occurred since his day. He would certainly imagine a world where beauty and culture prevailed, where the setting of life would immediately manifest the social wealth; in poorer societies the edifices of God, the palaces of rulers, and the mansions of the rich had been made beautiful. An epoch of general wealth would surely be one where the houses of the people and their work places would be built with the same loving care, that we were on the threshold of such an age was assumed already by Ledoux (1736–1806) in the last third of the eighteenth century.[3] Also it had previously been the good fortune of the artisans serving a rich market that they could work with delight. When the mass market had become a rich market this would seem destined to be the lot of all workers; finally it had been the privilege of the well-to-do that they could enjoy good company, with pleasant manners and interesting topics. Presumably, with a society wealthy throughout, this sort of company would be that of everyman.

Now of these three goals relating to the setting, the work, and the company, which seemed natural outcomes of growing wealth, the first—setting—and the last—good company—have not been achieved merely, as it seems to me, through an inexplicable lack of attention to them; the second, which is possibly the most important, deserves special attention.

It does seem true, up to date, that we have had to pay a price for the

[3] The industrial city of Chaux, then designed and built by Ledoux, testifies to the preoccupation.

increasing productivity of labor in the sense that the Industrial Revolution from its very beginning has created a new phenomenon which I would call "pure labor." In order to live, men have ever needed to perform certain activities, be it hunting, fishing, tilling, building, weaving, etc. It seems to me, however, that in the case of those folk we call "primitive" the activities devoted to the material sustenance of life have been admired with play, sport, devotion, as we can still see it in the case of vine harvesting, which is all suffused with joking, laughing, its brief spells of matching speeds interspersed with episodes of bantering and courting. As against this, modern work has become an altogether bleaker thing, purely a task to be performed for the result, under the sign of efficiency alone. It is by no means different in the so-called Socialist countries where "norms" of work are successively raised. I have noted that work has become in the last generations very much less exacting in a physical sense, but as against this we must set, I think, the bleakness of work. The lessening of the physical strain of work is a recent phenomenon, its bleakness is an altogether more ancient phenomenon. It is probably as old as the regimentation of work, which has existed for a long time (think of the galley slaves) but which has become a far more extensive phenomenon.

It is, I think, the bleakness of work which has led to our current dichotomy of man, of whom it is expected that he be purely efficient in his hours of work, while he is allowed, nay, encouraged, to satisfy his wants in his hours of leisure. From which it naturally follows that nothing seems more important than to successively whittle down the hours of work. But work is so essential that the psychological deprivation experienced by man at work colors, I believe, his whole life. It can be observed that the men who in fact seem to have a good life are not those who work few hours (in which case the good life would have been that of the rentier who had no hours of work at all) but those who can take pleasure in their work. And therefore I believe that we should regard the amenity of work as a much more interesting goal than the shortening of work hours.

X

There are many other points I would like to touch upon, one of them is the following. Those out of work on a pension by reason of age shall form an increasing proportion of our population. This shall constitute a very large "leisure class" of a very different complexion from the "leisure class" of the nineteenth century; much more numerous on the one hand, and on the other, distinguished from the working class to which all adults now belong, not by *greater* incomes but by *smaller* incomes. Our society now comprises no "leisure class" at the top of the income ladder, but a large "leisure class" at the bottom of the income ladder: the aged.

This phenomenon of a very large population combining a great deal of leisure with very little money poses the problem of its way of life. I think it is very miserable in the present day. Surely it deserves to be given some thought, and the problem is not insoluble since the combination new to us of a great deal of leisure with scant material means is the very condition under which Greek culture flourished. The aged may be the Greek among us, if we attack the problem in that way.

This is but one of the points I wished to raise. I would deem myself fortunate indeed if I had found it possible to contribute toward the crystallization of a concern to induct our increasing wealth in the service of a greater amenity of life.

The Anatomy of Market Failure

FRANCIS M. BATOR

Francis M. Bator is Professor of Economics at Harvard University. This paper appeared in the Quarterly Journal of Economics *in 1958.*

What is it we mean by "market failure"? Typically, at least in allocation theory, we mean the failure of a more or less idealized system of price-market institutions to sustain "desirable" activities or to stop "undesirable" activities.[1] The desirability of an activity, in turn, is evaluated relative to the solution values of some explicit or implied maximum-welfare program.

It is the central theorem of modern welfare economics that under certain strong assumptions about technology, tastes, and producers' motivations, the equilibrium conditions which characterize a system of competitive markets will exactly correspond to the requirements of Paretian efficiency.[2] Further, if competitively imputed incomes are continuously redistributed in costless lump-sum fashion so as to achieve the income-distribution implied by a social welfare function, then the competitive market solution will correspond to the one electronically calculated Pareto-efficient solution which maximizes, subject only to tastes, technology and initial endowments, that particular welfare function.[3]

[1] "Activities" broadly defined, to cover consumption as well as production.

[2] I.e., to the conditions which define the attainable frontier of maximal utility combinations with given preference functions, resource endowments and technology. A community is on its Paretian frontier if it is impossible to make anyone better off (in terms of his own ordinal preference function) without making someone else worse off. Associated with the utility possibility frontier, in turn, is a production possibility frontier denoting maximal alternative output combinations. (Cf. my "Simple Analytics of Welfare Maximization," *American Economic Review*, XLVII (Mar. 1957), 22–59, and references therein.)

[3] In other words, given the "right" lump-sum taxes, markets will match the allocation called for by the point of tangency of the relevant W-function with the utility-

425

Many things in the real world violate such correspondence: imperfect information, inertia and resistance to change, the infeasibility of costless lump-sum taxes, businessmen's desire for a "quiet life," uncertainty and inconsistent expectations, the vagaries of aggregate demand, etc. With most of these I am not here concerned: they have to do with the efficiency of "real life" market institutions operated by "real life" people in a nonstationary world of uncertainty, miscalculation, etc.

What follows is an attempt, rather, to explore and order those phenomena which cause even errorless profit- and preference-maximizing calculation in a stationary context of perfect (though limited) information and foresight to fail to sustain Pareto-efficient allocation. I am concerned, in other words, with the decentralizing efficiency of that regime of signals, rules, and built-in sanctions which defines a price-market system.[4]

Specifically, Section I sets out the necessary conditions for efficiency of decentralized price-profit calculations both in a "laissez-faire" and in a "socialist" setting of Lange-Lerner civil servants. Section II is a brief digression on an often discussed mode of failure in these conditions: neoclassical external economies. It is concluded that the modern formulation of the doctrine, in terms of "direct interaction," begs more questions than it answers; further, that the usual emphasis on "divorce of scarcity from effective ownership" is misplaced. Section III, then, suggests a comprehensive ordering of types of market failure, with generalized indivisibility, public goods, and, last and least, nonappropriability as the villains of the piece. Section IV consists of some comments on the Meade and Scitovsky classifications of external economies; on the analytical link between indivisibility and public goods; on the significance of "exclusion"; on organizational arrangements designed to offset externality; and on blends of the various types of market failure. Section V concludes with some cautionary notes on the relevance of market-efficiency for choice of institutions.

I. The Conditions of Market Efficiency

The central theorem of modern welfare economics, the so-called *duality theorem*, asserts a correspondence between Pareto efficiency and market

---

possibility frontier, i.e., by the "bliss point." The W-function need not, of course, be explicit—it could be implicit in the political power-configuration which characterizes a community. On the other hand, it cannot be just any kind of function. It has to have some special characteristics which reflect a number of ethic-loaded restrictions, e.g., that individuals' preference functions are to count, and to count positively (cf., *ibid.*, and Section V below).

[4] In most of what follows, I shall assume that individual preferences, though not necessarily sensitive only to own-consumption, are representable by strictly convex indifference surfaces (i.e., by an ordering (one for each individual) such that all points on a straight line connecting two equivalent points x and y are preferred to x (hence to y)). But convexity is too restrictive. It excludes not only such characteristics of man's psyche as violate the "usual" regularities—these I do want to exclude—but also such physical and

performance. Its analytical essence lies in the remarkable fact that with all-round convexity, independence of tastes, etc., the technocratically formulated, institutionally neutral, Paretian maximum-of-welfare problem has embedded within it a set of constants: "duals," Lagrangean multipliers, shadow-prices, which have all the analytical characteristics of prices, wages, rents, interest rates.[5] Correspondence between Pareto-efficiency and market performance implies, at the least, that decentralized decisions in response to these "prices" by atomistic profit- and satisfaction-maximizers sustain just that constellation of inputs, outputs and commodity-distribution, that the maximum of the specified social welfare function calls for. It implies, in other words, that decentralized market calculations correctly account for all "economic" costs and benefits to which the relevant W-function is sensitive.[6]

Duality can fail in many ways. Specifically, and in a statical and "laissez-faire" context:[7]

(1) Duality will fail unless the Pareto-efficient (a) input-output points (production) and (b) associated commodity distribution points (exchange) which associate with the maximum of the welfare function in hand are characterized by a complete set of marginal-rate-of-substitution (MRS) equalities (or limiting inequalities) which, in turn, yield a set of price-like constants. Where no such constants exist, reference will be to *failure of existence*.[8]

---

topographical facts as lumpy consumption-goods. Rather than attempt a specification of preferences with convex-like properties where choice must be made among discrete bundles, I dodge the problem by attributing lumpiness only to inputs (including, however, inputs that are intermediate outputs).

[5] The theorem holds for the statical steady-state flow model of the Walrasian sort where the solution values are stationary time-rates; it holds, also, for dynamical systems involving capital formation (given, still, convexity throughout). For these last, the solution values are time paths of inputs, outputs, prices, etc. (A set of points is convex if, and only if, the straight lines connecting all possible pairs do not anywhere pass outside the set. The set of feasible output points bounded by a production possibility curve is convex, for instance, if the curve itself is concave-to-the-origin or a straight line. On all this, see Section V of "Simple Analytics," *ibid.*)

[6] Given, again, optimal lump-sum redistribution of as-imputed incomes. While I make use of the lump-sum transfer device throughout this paper to abstract from the income distribution problem and permit exclusive attention to Pareto efficiency, it is well to note that this involves a measure of sleight-of-hand. No decentralized price-market type "game" can reveal the pattern of taxes and transfers that would maximize a particular welfare function. "Central" calculation—implicit if not explicit—is unavoidable. Moreover, since distribution (hence correct redistribution) of numeraire-incomes interdepends with allocation in production and exchange, the supposedly automatic, non-political character of market mediation is a myth on the strictest neoclassical assumptions. This is not to say, even on our stratospheric levels of abstraction, that markets are "useless." Where they do compute well we are saved an awful lot of calculation.

[7] With optimal redistribution.

[8] We could consider, instead, the configuration which associates with the initial pattern of ownership of endowment. Or we could play it safe and extend the conditions to cover each and every Pareto efficient configuration. But this would be overly strict, since many efficient situations have no relevance either to any interesting W-functions or in terms of the initial distribution of scarcities.

(2) Should such an associated set of Lagrangean parameters exist, duality would nevertheless fail, specifically in production, unless the bliss configuration of inputs and outputs, evaluated in terms of these price parameters, will yield: (a) a local profit-maximum position for each producer, rather than, as possible, a profit minimum; (b) non-negative profits for all producers from whom production is required; (c) maximum profits-in-the-large for each producer. Failure on counts (a) and (c) will be labeled *failure by signal*, that on count (b) *failure by incentive*.[9]

(3) Even if all efficient production configurations, or the one which maximizes a particular welfare-function, coincide with points of maximum and non-negative producers' profits, market mediation may fail in production. If prices are determined by market forces, they will not correspond to a Paretian maximum unless self-policing perfect competition obtains in all markets. Self-policing competition requires "very many" producers in every market.[10] If, then, for whatever reason, some markets are saturated by a few firms of "efficient" scale, the full welfare-maximum solution of inputs, outputs *and prices* will not be sustained. There will be *failure by structure*.

(4) Finally, even if all above is satisfied, market performance could still fail, and fail in a statical sense, due to arbitrary legal and organizational "imperfections," or feasibility limitations on "keeping book," such as leave some inputs or outputs "hidden," or preclude their explicit allocation or capture by market processes (e.g., the restriction, unless I go into baseball, on the sale of the capitalized value of my lifetime services). Failure is *by enforcement*.

All the above are germane to duality in its usual sense, to the statical Pareto-efficiency of laissez-faire markets with genuine profit- and satisfaction-seekers.[11] Conditions (1), (2) and (4) are relevant, also, to the decentralizing efficiency of a Lange-Lerner type organizational scheme. In its "capitalist" version, with profit-motivated operation of privately-owned means of production where it is simply an anti-monopoly device to assure parametric take-prices-as-given behavior, conditions (1), (2) and (4) are

---

It may be worth noting, incidentally, that "existence," as used above, is not the same as existence in the sense of, e.g., Arrow and Debreu (in "Existence of an Equilibrium for a Competitive Economy," *Econometrica*, Vol. 22 (July 1954), pp. 265–90). They use the term to denote the complete set of conditions which defines competitive equilibrium, and this includes, in addition to all that is implied by (1) above, conditions akin to my conditions (2), and some analogous conditions on consumers.

[9] This is slightly misleading: as we shall see, failure on count (c) leads both to signaling and to incentive troubles. Anyway, the labels are only for expository convenience.

[10] Or at least the potentiality of very many producers, ready and able to "enter the fray" instantaneously. This may be sufficient in the constant-cost case, where the equilibrium number of firms per industry is indeterminate.

[11] The mathematically minded will object that (3) and (4), at least, do not really violate "duality" in its strict mathematical sense; the dual minimum problem still yields Lagrangean constants. True, yet I think it suggestive to use "duality" rather more loosely as a label for the general welfare theorem, particularly as this does not lead, in this context, to any ambiguity.

all necessary for efficiency. Of course condition (3): self-policing competition, no longer matters.

In its true socialist version, a Lange-Lerner system can afford to "fail" also "by incentive," (2b). Socialist civil servants, under injunction to maximize profit (in the small) in terms of fixed centrally-quoted prices, care or should care not at all about absolute profitability. By assumption the scheme can dispense with the built-in incentive of positive profit: the lure of bureaucratic advancement, the image of Siberia, or the old school tie presumably substitute for the urge to get rich. But if prices and the injunction to maximize profit are to be used to decentralize, condition (1): existence, and (2a) and (2c): correct and unambiguous signals, remain crucial.[12] So does condition (4): the solution of quantities and prices need not be profitable and self-enforcing, but it does have to be enforceable. If the nectar in apple blossoms is scarce and carries a positive shadow price, it must be possible to make every beekeeper pay for his charges' meals.

It warrants repetition that this has to do with whether a decentralized price-market game will or will not *sustain* a Pareto-efficient configuration. The word sustain is critical. There exists a host of further considerations which bear on dynamical questions of adjustment, of "how the system gets there." (E.g., will some "natural" price-market type computational routine of price-quantity responses with a meaningful institutional counterpart tend to track the solution?) These are not here at issue. We shall be concerned only with the prior problem of whether a price-market system which finds itself at the maximum-welfare point will or will not tend to remain there.[13]

The relevant literature is rich but confusing. It abounds in mutually reinforcing and overlapping descriptions and explanations of market failure:

[12] It is tempting, but wrong, to suggest that in a true Lange-Lerner world totals do not matter and only margins count. It is true that the non-negativeness of profits is immaterial. Where there is any sharing of shadow-price sets by two or more production points, however, totals necessarily become a part of the signaling system and if 2(c) does not hold they may lead down the garden path.

[13] More precisely, whether the point of maximum welfare is or is not a point of self-policing and "enforceable" market equilibrium, where, following common usage, equilibrium is defined to subsume both the first-order and the second-order inequalities for a maximum. A firm, for instance, is taken to be in equilibrium only at a point of maximum profit. This way of defining equilibrium does bring in issues of stability, hence some implicit dynamics. In particular, the word "sustain" is taken to imply some scanning or reconnaissance by producers and consumers at least in the neighborhood of equilibrium. But I do not think it does any harm to subsume this much stability in the equilibrium notion. The possibility of a firm in *unstable* "equilibrium," i.e., in equilibrium at a point of minimum profit, is hardly likely to be of import.

On the other hand, correspondence between Pareto-efficiency and the equilibrium state of perfectly competitive markets is not sufficient to insure market efficiency. It is the burden of "failure by structure" that markets may fail to be competitive, and of "failure by enforcement" that legal or institutional constraints may prevent competitive markets from allocating efficiently, even though there does exist a competitive equilibrium for each Pareto-efficient configuration. "Existence" in the sense of Arrow and Debreu (*op. cit.*) is necessarily but not sufficient for market-efficiency in the present context.

external economies, indivisibility, nonappropriability, direct interaction, public goods, atmosphere, etc. In a sense, our problem is simply to sort out the relations among these. In doing so, it is appropriate and useful to begin with a brief review of the neoclassical doctrine of external economies and of its modern formulation in terms of "direct interaction."

II. Neoclassical External Economies: A Digression

BY WAY OF SOME HISTORY

Marshall, as has often been pointed out, proposed the external economy argument to explain, without resort to dynamics, the phenomenon of a negatively sloped ("forward falling") long-run industry supply curve in terms consistent with a horizontal or rising marginal cost curve (MC) in the "representative" firm. The device permits—in logic, if not in fact— long-run competitive equilibrium of many firms within an industry, each producing at its profit-maximum price-equal-to-a-rising-MC position, without foreclosing the possibility of a falling supply price with rising industry output.[14]

The mechanism is simple. It is postulated that an expansion in the output of the industry as a whole brings into play economies which cause a downward shift of the cost curves of all the component firms. These economies, however, are not subject to exploitation by any one of the myriad of tiny atomized firms. Their own MC curves, at $p = MC$, rise both before and after the shift, due, presumably, to internal diseconomies associated with the entrepreneurial function which defines the firm. Even the modern formulation is not entirely without ambiguity—institutional ambiguity is intrinsic to the device of parametrization: how many firms does it take for the demand curve of each to be perfectly horizontal?—but it does provide a means for "saving" the competitive model, of ducking the monopoly problem.

Marshall, and also Professor Pigou, "preferred," as it were, the other horn of what they perhaps saw as a dilemma. The external economy device, while saving competition, implies a flaw in the efficacy of the "invisible hand" in guiding production.[15] "Price equal to MC" is saved, but wrong. Market forces, they argued, will not give enough output by industries enjoying external economies and will cause industries with rising supply curves to overexpand. Hence the Marshall-Pigou prescription: to harmonize private production decisions with public welfare, tax the latter set of industries and subsidize the former.

It took the better part of thirty years, and the cumulative powers of

[14]This refers to a so-called Marshallian supply curve. It has nothing whatever to do with the Walrasian "maximum quantity supplied at a given price" type schedule.

[15]That there are difficulties also with income distribution was by that time generally recognized.

Allyn Young, and Messrs. Robertson, Knight, Sraffa, and Viner, to unravel the threads of truth and error which run through the Marshall-Pigou argument.[16] The crucial distinction, which provides the key to it all, is between what Viner labeled technological external economies, on the one hand, and pecuniary external economies on the other. The latter, if dominant, cause the long-run supply curve of an industry, say A, to decline because the price of an input, B, falls in response to an increase in A's demand for it. The technological variety, on the other hand, though also a reversible function of industry output, consists in organizational or other improvements in efficiency which do not show up in input prices.[17]

As regards pecuniary external economies, Robertson and Sraffa made it clear that in a sense both the Marshall-Pigou conclusions were wrong. For one thing, no subsidy is called for. The implied gains in efficiency are adequately signaled by the input price, and profit-maximizing output levels by the A-firms are socially efficient. Second, monopoly troubles may be with us, via, as it were, the back door. For what causes the price of B to drop in response to increased demand? We are back where we started: a declining long-run supply curve.

In the end, then, if *internal* technological economies of scale are ruled out, we are left with only *technological* external economies. All pecuniary external economies must be due to technological economies somewhere in the system.[18] It is true—and this is what remains of the original Marshall-Pigou proposition—that technological externalities are not correctly accounted for by prices, that they violate the efficiency of decentralized market calculation.

THE MODERN FORMULATION [19]

In its modern version, the notion of external economies—external economies proper that is: Viner's technological variety—belongs to a more general doctrine of "direct interaction." Such interaction, whether it involves producer-producer, consumer-consumer, producer-consumer, or employer-employee relations, consist in interdependences that are external to the

[16] The strategic articles, with the exception of Young's ("Pigou's *Wealth and Welfare*," *Quarterly Journal of Economics*, XXVII (1913), 672–86), as well as Ellis and Fellner's 1943 treatment, have all been reprinted in American Economic Association, *Readings in Price Theory*, ed. Stigler & Boulding. For an excellent modern discussion, see R. L. Bishop, *Economic Theory* (to appear).

[17] Note, however, that there need be nothing about an organizational improvement to make it obvious in advance whether it will turn out to be technological or, through "internalization," pecuniary. Many trade-association type services which are justified by the scale of an industry could as well be provided commercially, and vice versa.

[18] Pecuniary diseconomies, in contrast, need have no technological counterpart. Finite-elastic supplies of unproduced inputs are a sufficient cause. Recall, incidentally, that only narrowly statical reversible phenomena are admissible here.

[19] While this section makes some slight use of elementary calculus, the reader uninterested in technicalities may avoid, without loss of continuity, all but some simple notation.

price system, hence unaccounted for by market valuations. Analytically, it implies the nonindependence of various preference and production functions. Its effect is to cause divergence between private and social cost-benefit calculation.

That this is so, is easily demonstrated by means of a simplified variant of a production model suggested by J. E. Meade.[20] Assume a world of all-round perfect competition where a single purchasable and inelastically supplied input, labor (L), is used to produce two homogeneous and divisible goods, apples (A) and honey (H), at nonincreasing returns to scale. But while the output of A is dependent only on $L_A : A = A(L_A)$, honey production is sensitive also to the level of apple output: $H = H(L_H, A(L_A))$. (Professor Meade makes pleasurable the thought of apple blossoms making for honey abundance.)[21]

By solving the usual constrained maximum problem for the production-possibility curve, it can be shown that Paretian production efficiency implies

$$p_H \frac{\partial H}{\partial L_H} = w \tag{1}$$

$$p_A \frac{dA}{dL_A} + p_H \frac{\partial H}{\partial A} \frac{dA}{dL_A} = w \tag{2}$$

where p_H, p_A, and w represent the prices, respectively, of honey, apples and labor.[22] Equation (1) is familiar enough and consistent with profit maximizing. Each competitive honey producer will do for profit what he must for efficiency: hire labor until the value of its social as well as private marginal product equals the wage rate. Not so the apple producers; unless $\frac{\partial H}{\partial A} = 0$—unless the cross effect of apples on honey is zero—their profit-maximizing production decision will be nonefficient. Specifically, if apples have a positive external effect on honey output, market-determined L_A will be less than is socially desirable.[23]

---

[20] *Economic Journal*, LXII (Mar. 1952). Meade uses a two factor model and, while he does not explicitly solve the Paretian maximum problem, shows that market imputed rates of remuneration will not match marginal social product.

[21] Both functions are assumed homogeneous of degree one. Moreover, apple blossoms (or the nectar therein) are exhaustible, rationable "private" goods; more nectar to one bee means less to another. On the need for this assumption, see Section III-3 below.

[22] Assuming internal tangencies and all-round convexity (the last is implicit in constant returns to L: the A-effect on H reinforces convexity), as well as nonsatiation and nonredundancy $(L = L_A + L_H)$, the maximization of $p_A A + p_H H$, subject to the production functions and the supply of labor, is equivalent to finding a critical value for the Lagrangean expression, $F = p_A A(L_A) + p_H H[L_H; A(L_A)] + w(L - L_A - L_H)$. To do so, differentiate F with respect to L_A and L_H, treating p_A, p_H and w as arbitrary constants and set the resulting first order partial derivatives equal to zero. This will give exactly (1) and (2). (Needless to say, the value weights can be varied at will, or taken as given.)

[23] To see this, rewrite (2) to read $\dfrac{dA}{dL_A} = \dfrac{w}{p_A + p_H \dfrac{\partial H}{\partial A}}$ and match it against the profit-

A different way to see this is to examine the relations of private to social marginal cost. The marginal money cost of apples to the competitive apple producer is $\dfrac{w}{dA/dL_A}$; that of honey to a beekeeper, $\dfrac{w}{\partial H/\partial L_H}$. It is the ratio of the two: $\dfrac{\partial H/\partial L_H}{dA/dL_A}$, that competitive market-mediation brings into equality with the equilibrating configuration of relative prices. Markets will be efficient if, and only if, this *private* marginal cost ratio reflects the true marginal cost to society of an extra apple in terms of foregone honey: the marginal rate of transformation between H and A.

What is MRT in the model? Differentiating (totally) the two production functions and dividing the value of one derivative into the other, we get, in absolute (cost) terms:

$$MRT \equiv \left| \frac{dH}{dA} \right| = \frac{\partial H/\partial L_H}{dA/dL_A} - \frac{\partial H}{\partial A}.$$

If, then, $\dfrac{\partial H}{\partial A} > 0$, the true marginal *social* cost of an "extra" apple, in terms of honey foregone, is less than the market-indicated private cost. It is less precisely by the amount of positive "feed-back" on honey output due the "extra" apple.

By combining (1) and (2), eliminating w, and dividing through by p_H and $\dfrac{dA}{dL_A}$, we get the condition for Pareto efficiency in terms of private MC's:

$$\frac{\partial H/\partial L_H}{dA/dL_A} = \frac{p_A}{p_H} + \frac{\partial H}{\partial A}.$$

Clearly, price equal to private marginal cost will not do. Further, if prices are market-determined, they will diverge from true, *social* marginal cost.

Any number of variations on the model suggest themselves. As Meade pointed out, interactions can be mutual and need not be associated with the outputs. Even in the above case, it is perhaps more suggestive to think of L_A as producing some social value-product both in the A industry and the H industry. In the most general formulation, one can simply think of each production function as containing all the other variables of the system, some perhaps with zero weight. Moreover, by introducing two or more nonproduced inputs one can, as Meade does, work out the consequences for income distribution and input proportions.[24]

---

maximizing rule, $\dfrac{dA}{dL_A} = \dfrac{w}{p_A}$. Clearly, $\dfrac{\partial H}{\partial A} \gtrless 0 \longrightarrow$

$$\left(\frac{dA}{dL_A} \right)_{\text{Private}} \gtrless \left(\frac{dA}{dL_A} \right)_{\text{Social}}$$

[24] The question of whether technological external economies involve shifts of each other's production functions, or mutually induced movements along such functions, is purely definitional. If one chooses so to define each producer's function as to give axes only to inputs and outputs that are purchased and sold, or at least "controlled," and the effects of everything else impinging on production (e.g., of humidity, apple blos-

SOME QUERIES

The modern formulation of the doctrine of external economies, in terms of direct interaction, is not only internally consistent: it also yields insight. Yet one may well retain about it some dissatisfaction. There is no doubt that the Robertson-Sraffa-Viner distinction between the technological and the pecuniary sort gets to the nub of what is the matter with the original Marshallian analysis. It ρuts right through the confusion which led Marshall and Pigou to conclude that the price mechanism is faulty in situations where in truth it is at its best: in allocating inputs in less than infinitely elastic supply between alternative productive uses. It also facilitates unambiguous formulation of the more difficult "falling supply price" case. But in a sense it only begs the fundamental question: what is it that gives rise to "direct interaction," to short circuit, as it were, of the signaling system?

Most modern writers have let matters rest with the Ellis-Fellner type explanation: "the divorce of scarcity from effective ownership."[25] Does nonappropriability then explain all direct interaction? In a sense it does, yet by directing attention to institutional and feasibility considerations which make it impracticable for "real life" market-institutions to mimic a price-profit-preference computation, it diverts attention from some deeper issues. Surely the word "ownership" serves to illuminate but poorly the phenomenon of a temperance leaguer's reaction to a hard-drinking neighbor's (sound insulated and solitary) Saturday night, or the reason why a price system, if efficient, will not permit full "compensation," in an age of electronic scramblers, for an advertisement-less radio program, or for the "services" of a bridge.[26]

It may be argued, of course, that at least the two latter examples are out of order, that radio programs and bridges do not involve "direct," i.e., non-price, interaction. But is this really so? Does not the introduction of a new program directly affect my and your consumption possibilities, in ways other than by a change in relative prices? Does not a bridge, or a road, have a direct effect on the production possibilities of neighboring producers, in

---

soms, etc.) are built into the curvature of the function, then it follows that externalities will consist in shifts of some functions in response to movements along others. On the other hand, if, as in our apple-honey case, it seems useful to think of the production function for H as having an A-axis, then, clearly, induced movement along the function is a signal of externality.

[25] *Op. cit.*

[26] Moreover, in the one sense in which nonappropriability fits all cases of direct interaction, it explains none. If all it denotes is the failure of a price-market game properly to account for (to appropriate) all relevant costs and benefits, then it is simply a synonym for market failure (for generalized externality), and cannot be used to explain what causes any particular instance of such failure. I use it in a much narrower sense, to mean the inability of a producer of a good or service physically to exclude users, or to control the rationing of his produce among them. In my sense not only bridges but also, say, television programs are fully appropriable: it is always possible to use scramblers.

precisely the sense in which apples affect the possibility of beekeepers?[27]

True, perhaps bridges and roads are unfair: they violate the neoclassical assumption of perfect divisibility and nonincreasing returns to scale. But they surely do involve non-price interaction. In fact, lumpiness and increasing returns are perhaps the most important causes of such interaction. Are they to be denied status as externalities? More generally, are we to exclude from the class of externalities any direct interaction not due to difficulties with "effective ownership," any failures other than "by enforcement"?

It would be, of course, perfectly legitimate to do so—tastes are various. But I think it more natural and useful to broaden rather than restrict, to let "externality" denote any situation where some Paretian costs and benefits remain *external* to decentralized cost-revenue calculations in terms of prices.[28] If, however, we do so, then clearly nonappropriability[29] will not do as a complete explanation. Its concern with the inability of decentralized markets to sustain the solution-prices and quantities called for by a price-profit-preference type calculation, as computed by a team of mathematicians working with IBM machines, tends to mask the possibility that such machine-calculated solution q's may well be nonefficient.[30] It explains failure "by enforcement," but leaves hidden the empirically more important phenomena which cause failure by "nonexistence," "signal," and "incentive." Section III is designed to bring these deeper causes of generalized externality into the foreground.

III. Statical Externalities: An Ordering

If nonappropriability is, by itself, too flimsy a base for a doctrine of generalized (statical) externality, what broader foundation is there? Section I's hierarchy of possible modes of market failure suggests a fivefold classifica-

---

[27] It is possible, of course, to interpret these examples as involving very large changes in price: from infinity to zero. But it does not help to do so. The shared characteristic of bridges and programs is that there is no price which will efficiently mediate both supply and demand.

I have puzzled over ways of limiting the notion of "direct interaction" to something less than all instances where there is some interaction not adequately signaled by price. Robert Solow has suggested to me that this might be done by distinguishing situations where something is not subject to a market test at all from instances where no single price constitutes a correct test for both sides of a transaction (e.g., where the correct ration price for the services of an expensive facility is zero). I am inclined, rather, to drop the attempt to use "direct interaction" as an explanation of market failure; it is best used, if at all, as yet another synonym for such failure.

[28] Recall that it is the existence of such "externality," of residue, at the bliss-point, of Pigouvian "uncompensated services" and "incidental uncharged disservices" that defines market failure. It may be objected that to generalize the externality notion in this way is to rob it of all but descriptive significance. But surely there is not much to rob; even in its strictest neoclassical formulation it begs more than it answers. In its generalized sense it at least has the virtue of suggesting the right questions.

[29] As defined in fn. 8, above.

[30] Or that the algorithm may break down for lack of a consistent set of p's.

tion. If, however, one looks for an organizing principle not to modes of failure but to causes, there appear to be three polar types: (1) Ownership Externalities, (2) Technical Externalities,[31] and (3) Public Good Externalities. These are not mutually exclusive: most externality phenomena are in fact blends. Yet there emerges a sufficient three-cornered clustering to warrant consolidation.[32]

TYPE (1): OWNERSHIP EXTERNALITIES

Imagine a world which exhibits generalized technological and taste convexity, where the electronically calculated solution of a Paretian maximum-of-welfare problem yields not only a unique set of inputs, outputs and commodity-distribution, but where initial endowments plus lump-sum transfers render income distribution optimal in terms of the community's social welfare function. Assume, further, that everything that matters is divisible, conventionally rationable, and either available in inelastic total supply,[33] or producible at constant returns to scale; also that tastes are sensitive only to own-consumption. We know, then, from the duality theorem, that the bliss point implies a unique[34] set of prices, wages and rents, such as would cause atomistic profit- and preference-maximizers to do exactly what is necessary for bliss. In particular, all required production points give maximum and non-negative producer's profits.

This is an Adam Smith dream world. Yet it is possible that due to more or less arbitrary and accidental circumstances of institutions, laws, customs, or feasibility, competitive markets would not be Pareto-efficient. Take, for instance, the Meade example of apples and honey. Apple blossoms are "produced" at constant returns to scale and are (we assumed) an ordinary, private, exhaustible good: the more nectar for one bee, the less for another. It is easy to show that if apple blossoms have a positive effect on honey production (and abstracting from possible satiation and redundancy) a maximum-of-welfare solution, or any Pareto-efficient solution, will associate with apple blossoms a positive Lagrangean shadow-price.[35] If, then, apple

[31] I should much prefer "technological," but since this would necessarily confuse my Type (2) with Professor Viner's "technological" I fixed on "technical."

[32] In effect, we end up with a five-by-three ordering of types of "failure": five "modes" vs. three "causes." Its relation to Meade's categories (*op. cit.*) and to Tibor Scitovsky's classification (in "Two Concepts of External Economies," *Journal of Political Economy*, LXII, April 1954) is discussed in Section IV below. I have had the benefit of reading, also, William Fellner's "Individual Investment Projects in Growing Economies," *Investment Criteria and Economic Growth* (Proceedings of a Conference, Center for International Studies, Massachusetts Institute of Technology, 1955) and an unpublished paper by Svend Laursen, "External Economies and Economic Growth."

[33] The supply of such nonproduced scarcities need not, of course, remain constant. On the other hand, their ownership distribution must not be so concentrated as to preclude competitive rationing. There must exist no "indivisible" lake full of fish, etc., such as might be subject to monopolization, but thousands of lakes, all perfect substitutes.

[34] Or, where there are corners, only inessentially indeterminate.

[35] Set up a variant of the Apple-Honey model of Part II, introducing apple blossoms, B, explicitly. Add a production function, $B = B(L_A)$, and substitute $B(L_A)$ for $A(L_A)$ as

producers are unable to protect their equity in apple-nectar and markets do not impute to apple blossoms their correct shadow value, profit-maximizing decisions will fail correctly to allocate resources (e.g., L) at the margin. There will be failure "by enforcement."

This is what I would call an *ownership* externality. It is essentially Meade's "unpaid factor" case. Nonappropriation, divorce of scarcity from effective ownership, is *the* binding consideration. Certain "goods" (or "bads") with determinate non-zero shadow-values are simply not attributed. It is irrelevant here whether this is because the lake where people fish happens to be in the public domain, or because "keeping book" on who produces, and who gets what, may be impossible, clumsy, or costly in terms of resources.[36] For whatever legal or feasibility reasons, certain variables which have positive or negative shadow value are not "assigned" axes. The beekeeper thinks only in terms of labor, the orchard-owner only in terms of apples.

The important point is that the difficulties reside in institutional arrangements, the feasibility of keeping tab, etc. The scarcities at issue are rationable and finely divisible and there are no difficulties with "total conditions": at the bliss-configuration every activity would pay for itself. Apple nectar has a positive shadow price, which would, if only payment were enforceable, cause nectar production in precisely the right amount and even distribution would be correctly rationed. The difficulty is due exclusively to the difficulty of keeping accounts on the nectar-take of Capulet bees as against Montague bees.[37]

Many of the few examples of interproducer external economies of the reversible technological variety are of this type: "shared deposits" of fish, water, etc.[38] Much more important, so are certain irreversible dynamical examples associated with investment. For instance, many of Pigou's first category of externalities: those that arise in connection with owner-tenant relationships where durable investments are involved, have a primarily organizational quality.[39] Perhaps the most important instance is the training of nonslave labor to skills—as distinct from education in a broader sense (which partakes more of Type (3)). In the end, however, and in particular

---

the second input in honey production. The solution will give out a positive Lagrangean shadow price for B, and the profit-maximizing producers of the joint products: A and B, will push L_A to the socially desirable margin.

[36] Though on this last, see Section IV, first paragraph.

[37] More generally, it could as well be due to difficulty in knowing who "produced" the "benefit"—oil wells drawing on the same pool are an example. The owner cannot protect his own; in fact it is difficult to know what one means by "his own." Moreover, in the case of *diseconomies*, at least, it may be that both the source and the recipient of the "bad" are identified: one factory producing soot and nothing but one laundry in the neighborhood, yet it is difficult to see how a price can be brought to bear on the situation. Presumably the laundry can pay for negative units of smoke.

[38] Though indivisibility elements enter into some of these. Why can't somebody "own" part of a lakeful of fish?

[39] When not simply due, in a world of uncertainty, to inconsistent expectations.

if restricted to reversible statical cases, it is not easy to think of many significant "ownership externalities" pure and simple. Yet it turns out that only this type of externality is really due to nonappropriability.

TYPE (2): TECHNICAL EXTERNALITIES

Assume, again, that all goods and services are rationable, exhaustible, scarcities, that individual ordinal indifference maps are convex and sensitive only to own-consumption and that there exist no ownership "defects" of Type (1). If, then, the technology exhibits indivisibility or smooth increasing returns to scale in the relevant range of output, these give rise to a second and much more important type of market failure: "technical externality."[40]

The essential analytical consequence of indivisibility,[41] whether in inputs, outputs or processes, as well as of smooth increasing returns to scale, is to render the set of feasible points in production (input-output space) nonconvex. A connecting straight line between some pairs of feasible points will pass outside the feasible set. Nonconvexity, in turn, has a devastating effect on duality.[42]

In situations of pure "technical externality" there does, of course, still exist a maximal production possibility frontier (FF); and with a Samuelson-type social indifference map (SS)—i.e., a map "corrected" for income distribution which provides a ranking for the community as a whole of all

---

[40] Again, this is not the same as Viner's "technological." Note, incidentally, that the above formulation unabashedly begs the question of whether smooth increasing returns to scale could or could not arise without indivisibility somewhere. The issue is entirely definitional: it is conceptually impossible to disprove either view by reference to empirical evidence. (Cf. "Simple Analytics," *loc. cit.*, fn. 37 and references.)

The pioneer work on decreasing cost situations is Jules Dupuit's remarkable 1844 essay, "On the Measurement of Utility of Public Works," translated in *International Economic Papers*, No. 2, ed. A. T. Peacock, *et al.* Harold Hotelling's "The General Welfare in Relation to Problems of Taxation and of Railway and Utility Rates," in the July 1938 issue of *Econometrica*, is the originating modern formulation. Cf., also, references to work by R. Frisch; J. E. Meade, W. A. Lewis and others in Nancy Ruggles' excellent survey articles on marginal cost pricing (*Review of Economic Studies*, XVII (1949–50), 29–46, and 107–26).

[41] Indivisibility means lumpiness "in scale" and not the kind of indivisibility-in-time we call durability. (Durability, as such, does not violate convexity.) Lumpiness has to do with the impossibility to vary continuously, e.g., the capacity service-yield per unit time of such things as bridges.

[42] The best known and perhaps most important variety of nonconvexity occurs where isoquants are properly convex, but returns to scale are increasing, hence the full set of feasible input-output points is nonconvex. (In a two-input, one-output situation, slices by (vertical) planes through the origin perpendicular to the input plane will cut the production surface in such a way as to give a nonconvex boundary.) A production point lying in an "increasing returns" region of a production function implies that (1) the associated average cost curve (AC) is downward sloping at that level of output; (2) the associated marginal cost curve (MC), while it may be rising, could as well be falling and will certainly lie below AC; and (3) the production possibility curve of the community may be nonconvex. On all this, see Part V of "Simple Analytics," *loc. cit.*

conceivable output combinations[43]—it is possible, in concept, to define a bliss point(s).[44] Also, where indivisibility is exhibited by outputs, and only outputs, or, stronger, where smoothly increasing returns to scale is the only variety of nonconvexity—isoquants for one, are properly convex—the locus of efficient output combinations can be defined in terms of conditions on marignal-rates-of-input-substitution.[45] Moreover, bliss could possibly occur at a point where SS is internally tangent to FF, perhaps to a convex FF. But even in the least "pathological," most neoclassically well-behaved case, where there exists a meaningfully defined set of shadow prices associated with the bliss point, genuinely profit-seeking competitive producers, responding to that set of prices, would fail to sustain optimal production. At best, even if at the bliss-configuration all MC's are rising, some producers would have to make continuing losses, hence would go out of business; market calculations would necessarily fail "by incentive." If, in turn, prices are not centrally quoted but permitted to set themselves, monopoly behavior will result. There will be failure "by structure."

Further, bliss may require production at levels of output where losses are not only positive, but at a constrained maximum,[46] $p = MC$ may be correct, though MC at that point is falling. If so, the embedded Lagrangean constants may still retain meaning as marginal rates of transformation, but they will fail to sustain efficient production even by Lange-Lerner civil servants who care only about margins and not about absolute totals. There will be failure "by signal": producers under injunction to maximize profit (in the small) will not remain where they ought to be.

If, moreover, we drop the assumption of smooth increasing returns to scale and permit indivisibilities such as give scallop-like effects and kinks in cost curves and in the production-possibility curve, things get even more complicated. Bliss could require production at points of positive but locally minimum profit, where MC exceeds AC but is falling. Worse, even if bliss should occur at points where production functions are locally convex and MC (greater than AC) is rising, prequoted prices may still not sustain the solution unless production functions are in fact convex throughout. Though positive and at a local maximum, profits may not be at their maximum-maximorum: other hills with higher peaks may induce producers with vision at a distance to rush away from bliss. Alternatively, if prices are not administered, competition may not be self-policing and markets could fail "by structure."[47]

[43] Cf. P. A. Samuelson, "Social Indifference Curves," this *Journal*, LXX (Feb. 1956), 1–22. Such a function presumes that *numeraire*-incomes are continuously redistributed so as to maximize in utility space over the community's operative social welfare function.

[44] This is saying very little, of course, except on the level of metaphysics.

[45] Inequalities due to kinks and corners are as good as equalities where all is smooth.

[46] Subject to the requirement that total cost for that level of output be a minimum, i.e., that each producer be on his least-cost expansion path.

[47] Where sharp indivisibility gives a nonconvex production possibility curve with corners and kinks, duality may fail even if there exists a price vector in terms of which decen-

On the other hand, given our assumptions, the Paretian contract locus of maximal (ordinal) utility combinations which is associated with any one particular output point is defined, as in the trouble-free neoclassical model, by the usual subjective, taste-determined, marginal-rate-of-substitution equalities (or, at corners, inequalities). These *MRS* equalities, in turn, imply a set of shadow-prices which, if centrally quoted, would efficiently ration among consumers the associated (fixed) totals of goods. In the sphere of exchange, then, a decentralized price system works without flaw.

In what sense do these Type (2) situations exhibit "externality"? In the (generalized) sense that some social costs and benefits remain external to decentralized profitability calculations. With Type (1) externalities, though it is not feasible to police the bliss values of all quantities and prices, there exists embedded in the solution a set of prices whose use for purposes of decentralized signaling would sustain, if only appropriation or exclusion were feasible, both itself and the maximum welfare configuration of inputs, outputs, and distribution. This is not the case here. In Type (1) situations, at the bliss point there is complete correspondence between social and private pay-off, both at the margin and in totals.[48] Profits are at their maxima and non-negative throughout. Here there is no such correspondence; there may well be divergence, either at the margin: bliss-profits may be at a "minimum," or in *totals*. The private totals in terms of which producers in an (idealized) market calculate—total revenue minus total cost—will not reliably signal the social costs and benefits implied by the relevant social indifference curves.[49] Hence at the set of prices which would correctly ration the bliss point bill of goods, that bill of goods may not be produced by profit seekers, or even by Lange-Lerner civil servants.[50]

---

tralized producer-calculations would sustain the bliss-point output mix. The existence of such a vector does not assure that it will coincide with the price-vector which would efficiently ration that bill of goods among consumers. The point is that there may not exist a *single* set of prices which will at the same time keep both consumers and producers from rushing away from where they ought to be. The prices which will effectively mediate production may cause consumers' calculations to go wrong and vice versa.

It should be noted, incidentally, that none of the above takes space and distance considerations into account. For some interesting effects of plant-indivisibility where there are interplant flows and transport takes resources, see T. C. Koopmans and M. Beckmann, "Assignment Problems and the Location of Economic Activities," *Econometrica*, Vol. 25 (Jan. 1957).

[48] More correctly, there would be such correspondence, if only the p's could be policed.

[49] This is particularly awkward since the very nonconvexities which cause a divergence between private and social total conditions render output-mix calculations based on margins alone wholly inadequae. Even if bliss gives all local profit maxima, there may be several such open to any one producer, hence he must make total calculations in order to choose.

[50] There is one qualification to be made to the above. It may be that the bliss configuration gives unique and positive profit maxima throughout, though some production functions exhibit nonconvexities at a distance. It was to exclude this case that we assumed that increasing returns or indivisibility obtain in the "relevant ranges." Should this happen, no "externality" divergence of social and private calculation will occur, at

A point to note, in all this, is that in relation to "technical externalities" the nonappropriability notion, as generally conceived, tends to miss the point. Strictly speaking, it is, of course, true that price mediation, if efficient, cannot be counted on to "appropriate" the full social benefits of activities showing increasing returns to scale or other types of indivisibility to those engaged in them. But the existence of such "uncompensated services" has in this case nothing whatever to do with "divorce of scarcity from ownership," with feasibility on "exclusion." It is entirely feasible to own a bridge and profitably ration crossings; indeed, a private owner would do so. The point is, rather, that such profitable rationing, such "compensation" for services rendered, would inefficiently misallocate the "output" of bridge crossings. If in terms of scarce resource inputs the marginal cost of an additional crossing is zero, any positive toll will, in general, have the usual monopolistic effect: the resulting output configuration will not be efficient.[51]

This, incidentally, is where most pecuniary external economies lead: a supplier is required to produce in a range of declining AC due to internal technological economies of scale and hence cannot make "ends meet" at the socially correct price. The crucial associated difficulty at the level of social organization is monopoly.

Can we leave matters at that? Not quite. There is a third kind of externality, recently emphasized by Professor Samuelson, caused by so-called "public goods."

TYPE (3): PUBLIC GOOD EXTERNALITIES

In some recent writings on public expenditure theory, Samuelson has reintroduced the notion of the collective or public good. The defining quality of a pure public good is that "each individual's consumption of such a good leads to no subtractions from any other individual's consumption of that good . . . ,"[52] hence, "it differs from a private consumption good in that each man's consumption of it, X_2^1 and X_2^2 respectively, is related to the total X_2 by a condition of *equality* rather than of summation. Thus, by definition, $X_2^1 = X_2$ and $X_2^2 = X_2$."[53]

As Samuelson has shown, the form of the marginal rate of substitution conditions which define the Pareto-efficient utility possibility frontier in a

---

least in a statical context. But unless all is convex throughout, the existence of such a locally stable tangency cannot be taken as evidence that the point is in fact the bliss-point—a difficulty of considerable significance for dynamical efficiency.

[51] Of course, if at bliss the bridge were to be used "to capacity," it is possible that the Lagrangean ration price (now positive) would make commercial operation profitable. If so, an administered price setup would efficiently mediate the demand and supply of crossings. But while a Lange-Lerner system would work fine, laissez-faire markets would fail "by structure."

[52] P. A. Samuelson, *Review of Economics and Statistics*, XXXVI (Nov. 1954), 387.

[53] P. A. Samuelson, *Review of Economics and Statistics*, XXXVII (Nov. 1955), 350.

world where such public goods exist, or at least where there are outputs with important "public" qualities, renders any kind of price-market routine virtually useless for the computation of output-mix and of distribution, hence, also, for organizational decentralization. Where some restraints in the maximum problem take the form: total production of X *equals* consumption by Crusoe of X *equals* consumption of X by Friday, Pareto efficiency requires that the marginal rate of transformation in production between X and Y equal not the (equalized) MRS of each separate consumer, but rather the algebraic *sum* of such MRS's. This holds, of course, in what in other respects is a conventionally neoclassical world: preference and production functions are of well-behaved curvature, all is convex.

If, then, at the bliss point, with Y as numeraire, p_x is equated to the marginal Y-cost of X in production (as is required to get optimal production), and X is offered for sale at that p_x, preference-maximizing consumers adjusting their purchases so as to equate their individual MRS's to p_x will necessarily under-use X. Moreover, a pricing game will not induce consumers truthfully to reveal their preferences. It pays each consumer to understate his desire for X relative to Y, since his enjoyment of X is a function only of total X, rather than, as is true of a pure private good, just of that fraction of X he pays for.

The two Samuelson articles[54] explore both the analytics and the general implications of "public goods." Here the notion is of relevance because much externality is due precisely to the "public" qualities of a great many activities. For example, the externality associated with the generation of ideas, knowledge, etc., is due in good part to the public character of these "commodities." Many interconsumer externalities are of this sort: my party is my neighbor's disturbance, your nice garden is any passerby's nice view, my children's education is your children's good company, my Strategic Air Command is your Strategic Air Command, etc. The same consumption item enters, positively or negatively, both our preference functions. The consumptions involved are intrinsically and essentially joint.

This kind of externality is distinct from either of the other two pure types. Here technological nonconvexities need in no way be involved. In fact the $MRT = \Sigma MRS$ condition is certain to hold true precisely where production takes place at constant or nonincreasing returns, and hence where the production possibility set is necessarily convex. Further, there are no decentralized organizational rearrangements, no private bookkeeping devices, which would, if only feasibility were not at issue, eliminate the difficulty. It is the central implication of the Samuelson model that where public good phenomena are present, there does not exist a set of prices associated with the (perfectly definable) bliss point, which would sustain

---

[54] And a third unpublished paper, which was read at the 1955 American Economic Association meetings and to a copy of which I came to have access while this paper was being written. For earlier writings on public goods, by Wicksell, Lindahl, Musgrave, Bowen and others see references in the above cited Samuelson articles.

the bliss configuration. The set of prices which would induce profit-seeking competitors to produce the optimal bill of goods, would be necessarily inefficient in allocating that bill of goods. Moreover, even abstracting from production, no single set of relative prices will efficiently ration any fixed bill of goods so as to place the system on its contract locus, except in the singular case where at that output and income-distribution MRS's of every individual are identically the same (or zero for all but one). There is failure "by existence."

IV. Comments

Type (1). In a sense, Type (1) is not symmetrical with the other two categories. One can think of some nontrivial instances where the institutional element does appear to be "binding": skill-training of people, for example. But even there, it could be argued that the crucial elements are durability, uncertainty, and the fact that slavery as a mode of organization is itself in the nature of a public good which enters people's preference functions, or the implicit social welfare function, inseparably from the narrowly "economic" variables. In those instances, in turn, where bookkeeping feasibility appears to be the cause of the trouble, the question arises why bookkeeping is less feasible than where it is in fact being done. In the end, it may be that much of what appears to partake of Type (1) is really a compound of Types (2) and (3), with dynamical durability and uncertainty elements thrown in. At any rate, a deeper analysis of this category may cause it substantially to shrink.

Nonproduced scarcities. One particular instance where what appears like Type (1) is really Type (2) warrants special mention. Public ownership of nonproduced resources, e.g., the lakes and mountains of national parks, may make it appear that externality is due to statutory barriers to private ownership and commercial rental. But this is missing the point. Take, for instance, a community which has available a single source of fresh water of fixed capacity. Assume that the bliss solution gives out a positive ration-price per gallon such as would make sale of the water commercially profitable. Yet a laissez-faire system would fail, "by structure," to sustain bliss. A private owner of the single indivisible well, if given his head, would take advantage of the tilt in the demand curve. The real cause of externality is not the arbitrary rapaciousness of public authority but the indivisibility of the source of supply. This case, by the way, is akin to where indivisibility or increasing returns to scale within a range allow profitable scope for one or a few efficient producers, but for no more. At the bliss price all will do the right thing, but if prices are not administered, oligopoly or monopoly will result. A capitalist Lange-Lerner system with private ownership but administered prices would work fine, but laissez-faire markets would fail.

Meade's "atmosphere." The relation of my tri-cornered ordering to Meade's polar categories is of interest.[55] His first category, "unpaid factors," is identical to my Type (1). But his second, labeled "atmosphere," is a rather curious composite. Meade's qualitative characterization of "atmosphere": e.g., of afforestation-induced rainfall, comes very close to the public good notion.[56] He links this, however, as necessarily bound up with increasing returns to scale in production to society at large, hence a J. B. Clark-like overexhaustion, adding-up problem.[57]

If, following Meade, one abstracts from shared water-table phenomena (let rain-caused water input be rigidly proportional to area) then Farmer Jones' rain is Farmer Smith's rain and we have my Type (3). But nothing in this situation requires that either farmer's full production function (with an axis for rain) need show increasing returns to scale. It may be that returns to additional bundles of non-rain inputs, with given constant rainfall, diminish sharply, and that it takes proportional increases of land, labor *and* *rain* to get a proportional effect on output. If so, Meade's overexhaustion problem will not arise. But all would not be well: the public good quality of rainfall would cause an independent difficulty, one that Meade, if I understand him correctly, does not take into account, i.e., that rain ought to be "produced" by timber growers until its MC is equal to the sum of all the affected farmers MRS's for rain as an input, whatever may be the curvature of the latters' production functions.[58]

On the other hand, Meade's formal mathematical treatment of "atmosphere," as distinct from his verbal characterization and his example, suggests that it is a nonappropriable, and therefore unpaid, factor which gives rise to increasing returns to scale to society though not to the individual producer. At least this is all he needs for the effect he is looking for: a self-

---

[55] *Op. cit.* (This and the next section can be omitted without loss of continuity.)

[56] See esp. bottom of p. 61 and top of p. 62, *op cit.*

[57] Since his argument is restricted to competitive situations, hence necessarily excludes increasing-returns-to-paid-factors such as would require production at a loss, Meade specifies constant returns to proportional variation of labor and land in wheat farming, though the full production function for wheat, including the atmosphere input (rain), exhibits increasing returns to scale. But the individual farmer does not pay for rain, hence his factor payments just match his sales revenue, by the Euler Theorem.

[58] Formally, Meade denotes "atmosphere" as a situation where the production function, e.g., of farmers takes the form $X_1 = H_1(L_1,C_1)A_1(X_2)$, with L as labor, C as capital and A the atmosphere effect on X_1 of X_2. The full function exhibits increasing returns to scale but the H function alone, with A constant, is homogeneous of first degree. But why can't this be put in terms of Meade's unpaid factor type function where $X_1 = H_1$ (L_1,C_1,X_2)? Example: $X_1 = L_1^a C_1^{1-a} X_2$. All this has nothing to do with whether $A = A_1 + A_2$ or rather $A = A_1 = A_2$. Unfortunately, the example itself tends to mislead. The fact that exclusion of rain-users (farmers) by producers (timber-growers) is hardly feasible, i.e., that rain is like Type (1), distracts attention from the important point that *if* rain is, as Meade tells us, a public good, then rationing it by price would be inefficient even if it were feasible. (It should be said that Meade concludes his article: "But, in fact, of course, external economies or diseconomies may not fall into either of these precise divisions and may contain features of both of them.")

policing though nonoptimal competitive situation, where, because the full production functions (i.e., with an axis for rain) are of greater than first degree, the correction of externality via subsidies to promote the creation of favorable atmosphere requires net additions to society's fiscal burden. If this is the crucial consequence of "atmosphere," then it need have no "public" quality. All this would happen even though Smith and Jones were "competing" for the water from the shared water-table under their subsoil, just like bees competing for nectar.

Scitovsky's "two concepts."[59] Professor Scitovsky, in turn, in his suggestive 1954 article, distinguishes between the statical direct interactions of equilibrium theory and the kinds of pecuniary external economies emphasized in the economic development literature. He classifies the former as consumer-consumer, producer-consumer, and producer-producer interactions, labels the last as external economies and asserts that they are rare and, on the whole, unimportant.

While Scitovsky does not raise the question of what gives rise to such producer-producer interactions, both his examples, and his conclusion that they are of little significance, suggest that he is thinking primarily of Type (1): nonappropriabiilty. But this is to ignore public goods—surely a more important cause of interaction. Moreover, by taking full account of these, Scitovsky's "fifth and important case, which, however, does not quite fit into . . . (his) . . . classification . . . , where society provides social services through communal action and makes these available free of charge to all persons and firms," can be made nicely to fall into place.[60]

Samuelson on Types (2) *and* (3). While the public good model helps to sort out the phenomena Meade lumped under "atmosphere," Samuelson himself emphasizes the analytical bond between indivisibility and public good situations. In both an explicit "summing in" is required of "all direct and indirect utilities and costs in all social decisions."[61] In Type (2) situations it is the intramarginal consumer's and producer's surpluses associated with various all or nothing decisions "in-the-lump" that have to be properly (interpersonally) weighted and summed, while in Type (3) it is only utilities and costs at the margin that require adding. But, and this is the crucial

---

[59] *Op. cit.*

[60] *Ibid.,* fn. 3, p. 144. Scitovsky, following Meade, restricts his "first concept" of external economies to phenomena consistent with competitive equilibrium. He treats indivisibilities and increasing returns to scale as belonging to his "second concept" which has to do with disequilibrium, investment decisions, and growth. It is, of course, entirely legitimate to restrict analysis to competitive situations. But the Scitovsky treatment must not be taken to imply that lumpiness is irrelevant to statical analysis of stationary solution points. If one is interested in the statical efficiency of decentralized price calculations, they are crucial. But this is carping. Scitovsky's important contribution lies in emphasizing and clarifying the point first hinted at by P. N. Rosenstein-Rodan that in a world of disequilibrium dynamics pecuniary external economies may play an independent role—one distinct, that is, from simply being an unreliable signal of monopoly troubles (*Economic Journal*, LIII, 1943, 202–11).

[61] *Ibid.,* p. 9.

shared quality of the two categories, both make it necessary to sum utilities over many people.[62]

Exclus 1. One more comment may be warranted on the significance, in a public good type situation, of nonappropriability. "Exclusion" is almost never impossible. A recluse can build a wall around his garden, Jones can keep his educated children away from those of Smith, etc. But if thereby some people (e.g., the recluse) are made happier and some (e.g., the passers-by) less happy, any decision about whether to "exclude" or not implies an algebraic summing of the somehow-weighted utilities of the people involved. And if the wall requires scarce resources, the final utility sum must be matched against the cost of the wall. When Type (3) blends with indivisibility in production, as it does in the case of the wall, or in the case of a lighthouse, the comparison has to be made between intramarginal totals. Where no lumpiness is involved (e.g., the decibels at which I play my radio) only *MRS* and perhaps *MC* calculations are called for. But the really crucial decision may well be about how much perfectly feasible appropriation and exclusion is desirable.

Arrangements to offset. It is of interest to speculate what, if any, organizational rearrangements could offset the three categories of externality and avoid the need for centrally calculated tax-subsidy schemes.[63] In concept, Type (1) can be offset by rearrangements of ownership and by "proper" bookkeeping, such as need not violate the structural requirements of decentralized competition. Further, no resort to nonmarket tests would be required.[64]

Types (2) and (3) are not so amenable to correction consistent with decentralized institutions. The easiest possible case occurs where increasing returns obtain on the level of single producers'-good plants, much of whose production can be absorbed by a single user firm. Here vertical integration takes care of the problem. Not every process inside a well-run firm is expected to cover its cost in terms of the correct set of internal accounting (shadow) prices. Total profits are the only criterion, and it may pay a firm to build a private bridge between its two installations on opposite sides of a river yet charge a zero accounting price for its use by the various decentralized manufacturing and administrative divisions; the

---

[62] There is one qualification to be made: if all public good and increasing returns to scale industries produce only intermediate products, all externalities may cancel out in intra-business-sector transactions. If so, only total revenues and total costs have to be summed. Incidentally, the exposition may misleadingly suggest another symmetry between Types (2) and (3). In a pure Type (3) situation, *if* there are no public producers' goods, then while prices cannot be used to ration the bliss point output-mix, they can be used efficiently to mediate production. In Type (2), on the other hand, *if* all final consumables are divisible, price calculations, while failing in production, will work in exchange. This symmetry breaks down, of course, as soon as one violates, as does the real world, the two "if's."

[63] For illustrative derivation of the formulas for corrective taxes and subsidies in Type (1) situations, see Meade (*op. cit.*).

[64] The Emancipation Proclamation could constitute, of course, a substantial barrier.

bridge would make accounting losses, yet total company profits will have increased. As long, then, as such integration is consistent with the many-firms requirement for competition, no extra-market tests are required.[65] The private total conditions: TR less TC, correctly account for social gain.

Where a producers'-good firm, required to produce at a stage of falling AC, sells to many customer firms and industries, an adding up of all the associated TR's and TC's at the precalculated "as if" competitive prices associated with the bliss point would again effectively "mop up" all social costs and benefits.[66] But the institutional reorganization required to get correct decentralized calculation involves horizontal and vertical integration, and the monopoly or oligopoly problem looms large indeed. The Type (3) case of a pure *producers'* public good belongs here: only input MRS's along production functions require summing.

In the general case of a mixed producer-consumer good (or of a pure consumer good) which is "public" or is produced under conditions of increasing returns to scale, it is impossible to avoid comparison of multiperson utility totals. Explicit administrative consideration must be given, if you like, to consumer's and producer's surpluses for which no market-institution tests exist short of that provided by a perfectly discriminating monopolist. But to invoke perfect discrimination is to beg the question. It implies knowledge of all preference functions, while as Samuelson has emphasized,[67] the crucial game-theoretical quality of the situation is that consumers will not correctly reveal their preferences: it will pay them to "cheat."

Blends. Examination is needed of various blends of Types (2) and (3), such as Sidgwick's lighthouse,[68] or, for that matter, and as suggested by Samuelson, of blends of public and private goods even where all production functions are fully convex. There are many puzzling cases. Do bridge crossings differ in kind from radio programs? Both involves indivisibility and, where variable cost is zero for the bridge, zero MC's. The correct price for an extra stroller, as for an extra listener, is clearly zero. Yet bridge crossings have a distinctly private quality: bridges get congested, physical ca-

---

[65] If, however, the "break even" scale of operation of the integrated firm (i.e., where MC cuts AC from below) is much greater than if the river had not been there to span, or could be spanned by some means of a lower fixed-cost-to-variable-cost ratio, the monopoly problem may simply be "pushed forward" to consumer markets.

[66] Assuming that all consumer goods are finely divisible and require no lumpy decisions by consumers.

[67] Cf. any of the three "Public Expenditure" articles (*supra*).

[68] Sidgwick, by the way, as also Pigou, thought of a lighthouse as of Type (1). It is, of course, "inconvenient" to levy tolls on ships, but it is hardly impossible to "exclude," for instance by means of "scrambling" devices (though poor Sidgwick could hardly have known about such things). The point is, rather, that it would be inefficient to do so: the marginal cost to society of an additional ship taking directional guidance from the beacon atop the Statue of Liberty is zero, *ipso* price should be zero. In the case of a lighthouse this is twice true: because the beacon is in the nature of a public good: more for the Queen Mary means no less for the Liberté; and because a lighthouse is virtually an all-fixed-cost, zero variable-cost facility.

pacity is finite. This is not true of a broadcast. There is no finite limit to the number of sets that can costlessly tune in.[69] Radio programs, then, have a public dimension. Yet, in a sense, so do bridges. While your bridge crossing is not my bridge crossing, in fact could limit my crossings, your bridge is my bridge. What is involved here is that most things are multi-dimensional and more than one dimension may matter.

V. Efficiency, Markets and Choice of Institutions

All the above has to do with the statical efficiency of price-directed allocation in more or less idealized market situations. Relevance to choice of institutions depends, of course, on the prevalence of the phenomena which cause externality and on the importance to be attached to statical efficiency. Space precludes extensive discussion of these important issues, but a few casual comments, in the form of *dicta*, are perhaps warranted.

How important are nonappropriability, nonconvexity and public goods? I would be inclined to argue that while nonappropriability is of small import,[70] the same cannot be said of the other two. True enough, it is difficult to think of many examples of pure public goods. Most things—even battleships, and certainly open air concerts and schools (though not knowledge)—have an "if more for you then less for me" quality. But this is of little comfort. As long as activities have even a trace of publicness, price calculations are inefficient.[71] And it is surely hard to gainsay that some degree of public quality pervades much of even narrowly "economic" activity.

Lumpiness, in turn, and nonlinearity of the increasing returns sort, while in most instances a matter of degree, and, within limits, of choice, are also in the nature of things. The universe is full of singularities, thresholds and nonproportionalities: speed of light, gravitational constant, the relation of circumference to area, etc. As economists we can cajole or bully engineers into designing processes and installations that save on congealed inputs and give smaller maximal service yields, especially when designing for low-income communities. But the economically perhaps arbitrary, not completely physics-imposed quality of indivisibilities associated with standard designs and ways of doing things should not blind. Nonlinearity and lumpiness are evident facts of nature.[72]

---

[69] Richard Eckaus has suggested to me that it is possible to exhaust the space to which the broadcast is limited and that this makes the situation a little more like that of a bridge. Neither of us is entirely satisfied, however.

[70] Except for labor skills—and these would take us beyond the bounds of reversible statics.

[71] This is not to say that there exist other feasible modes of social calculation and organization which are more efficient.

[72] Their quantitative significance is, of course, very sensitive to scale, to "size" of markets. This explains the particular emphasis on the role of "social overheads" in low income countries.

More important, at this level of discourse[73]—though perhaps it hardly need be said—is that statical market efficiency is neither sufficient nor necessary for market institutions to be the "preferred" mode of social organization. Quite apart from institutional considerations, Pareto efficiency as such may not be necessary for bliss.[74] If, e.g., people are sensitive not only to their own jobs but to other people's as well, or more generally, if such things as relative status, power, and the like, matter, the injunction to maximize output, to hug the production-possibility frontier, can hardly be assumed "neutral" and points on the utility frontier may associate with points inside the production frontier.[75] Furthermore, there is nothing preordained about welfare functions which are sensitive only to individual consumer's preferences. As a matter of fact, few people would take such preferences seriously enough to argue against any and all protection of individuals against their own mistakes (though no external effects be involved).

All this is true even when maximization is subject only to technological and resource limitations. Once we admit other side relations, which link input-output variables with "noneconomic" political and organizational values, matters become much more complicated. If markets be ends as well as means, their nonefficiency is hardly sufficient ground for rejection.[76] On the other hand, efficient markets may not do, even though Pareto-efficiency is necessary for bliss. Even with utopian lump-sum redistribution, efficiency of the "invisible hand" does not preclude preference for other efficient modes of organization, if there be any.[77]

[73] Where recourse to strategic considerations of feasibility, crucial though they be, is quite out of order.

[74] That it is never sufficient is, of course, well known. Of the infinite Pareto-efficient configurations at best only one: that which gives the "right" distribution of income in terms of the W-function that is to count, has normative, prescriptive significance. Moreover, most interesting W-functions are likely to be sensitive to "noneconomic" factors, such as are, if not inconsistent, at least extraneous to Paretian considerations. Where such additional values of a political or social nature are separable from input-output values (i.e., where the two sets can be varied independently of each other) one "can" of course separate the overall W-function into a "political" and an "economic" component and maximize separately over each.

[75] This is different from the usual case of consumer sensitivity to the input-output configuration of producers, e.g., factory soot or a functional but ugly plant spoiling the view. Such joint-product "bads" can be treated as inputs and treated in the usual Paretian fashion. It is a different matter that their public quality will violate duality, hence render market calculation inefficient.

[76] This is too crude a formulation. It is not necessary that markets as such be an "ultimate" value. Political and social (non-output) values relating to the configuration of power, initiative, opportunity, etc., may be so much better served by some form of non-efficient market institutions than by possible alternative modes of more efficient organization as to warrant choice of the former. The analytical point, in all this, is that the outcome of a maximization process and the significance of "efficiency" are as sensitive to the choice of side-conditions as to the welfare-function and that these need be "given" to the economist in the same sense that a welfare function has to be given.

[77] The above is still strictly statical. For related dynamical problems, e.g., possible conflict between one-period and intertemporal efficiency, cf., "On Capital Productivity, Input Allocation and Growth," *Quarterly Journal of Economics*, LXXI (Feb. 1957).

Yet when all is said, and despite the host of crucial feasibility considerations which render choice in the real world inevitably a problem in the strategy of "second best," it is surely interesting and useful to explore the implications of Paretian efficiency. Indeed, much remains to be done. There is need, in particular, for more systematic exploration of the inadequacies of market calculation in a setting of growth.[78]

[78] The development literature on market failure, while full of suggestive insight, is in a state of considerable confusion. Much work is needed to exhaust and elucidate the seminal ideas of Young, Rosenstein-Rodan, Nurkse and others. For important beginnings, see Scitovsky (*op. cit.*), M. Fleming, "External Economies and the Doctrine of Balanced Growth," *Economic Journal*, LXV (June 1955), and Fellner (*op. cit.*).

The view that we should not turn social historian or what not, that the logic of economizing has some prescriptive significance, rests on the belief that narrowly "economic" efficiency is important in terms of many politically relevant W-functions, and consistent with a wide variety of power and status configurations and modes of social organization. On the other hand, some may feel that the very language of Paretian welfare economics: "welfare function," "utility-frontier," in relation to choice of social institutions, is grotesque. What is at stake, of course, is not the esthetics of language, on which I yield without demur, but abstraction and rigorous theorizing.

Part Six

PUBLIC GOODS AND SOCIAL WELFARE

Social choice is a central topic in welfare economics and political theory. In the opening paper of this section, Kenneth Arrow summarizes his famous thesis that it is impossible to make a choice among all sets of alternatives without violating some of the conditions that social choices must satisfy to reflect the preferences of the individuals comprising the society. Arrow's paper is a classic in this important area of economics. In the next article, Paul Samuelson presents a theory of public expenditure which has received considerable attention from economists, here and abroad. In addition, he goes on "to demonstrate the fatal inability of any decentralized market or voting mechanism to attain or compute . . . [the social] optimum." His paper is both important and controversial. After describing his theory, Samuelson discusses some of the criticisms and comments that have been directed at it.

Mancur Olson, Jr., in the following paper, describes the nature of public goods and explains why small groups may provide such goods without relying on coercion or any other positive inducements other than the good itself. However, even in the smallest groups, a public good will generally not be provided on an optimal scale. Kenneth Arrow, in the next essay, analyzes the set of activities in which the private sector should properly be engaged.

Then he takes up conditions under which nonmarket allocating mechanisms may be superior to the price system.

The last two papers in this part of the book deal with cost-benefit analysis, a technique that is used frequently to evaluate government projects. Roland McKean defines cost-benefit analysis, as an attempt "to estimate certain costs and gains that would result from alternative courses of action," and he describes the elements involved. In addition, he is careful to point out the limitations of cost-benefit analysis. A. R. Prest and Ralph Turvey provide an extensive discussion of applications of cost-benefit analysis to public-policy concerns—water projects, transport projects, land usage, and health.

A Difficulty in the Concept
of Social Welfare

KENNETH J. ARROW

*Kenneth J. Arrow is Professor of Economics at Stanford University.
This classic article appeared in the* Journal of Political Economy
in 1950.

I. Introduction

In a capitalist democracy there are essentially two methods by which social
choices can be made: voting, typically used to make "political" decisions,
and the market mechanism, typically used to make "economic" decisions.
In the emerging democracies with mixed economic systems, Great Britain,
France, and Scandinavia, the same two modes of making social choices
prevail, though more scope is given to the method of voting and to decisions based directly or indirectly on it and less to the rule of the price
mechanism. Elsewhere in the world, and even in smaller social units
within the democracies, the social decisions are sometimes made by single
individuals or small groups and sometimes (more and more rarely in this
modern world) by a widely encompassing set of traditional rules for
making the social choice in any given situation, e.g., a religious code.

The last two methods of social choice, dictatorship and convention,
have in their formal structure a certain definiteness absent from voting or
the market mechanism. In an ideal dictatorship, there is but one will
involved in choice; in an ideal society ruled by convention, there is but the
divine will or perhaps, by assumption, a common will of all individuals
concerning social decisions, so that in either case no conflict of individual
wills is involved. The methods of voting and of the market, on the other
hand, are methods of amalgamating the tastes of many individuals in the
making of social choices. The methods of dictatorship and convention are,
or can be, rational in the sense that any individual can be rational in his

453

choice. Can such consistency be attributed to collective modes of choice, where the wills of many people are involved?

It should be emphasized here that the present study is concerned only with the formal aspects of the foregoing question. That is, we ask if it is formally possible to construct a procedure for passing from a set of known individual tastes to a pattern of social decision-making, the procedure in question being required to satisfy certain natural conditions. An illustration of the problem is the following well-known "paradox of voting." Suppose there is a community consisting of three voters and this community must choose among three alternative modes of social action (e.g., disarmament, cold war, or hot war). It is expected that choices of this type have to be made repeatedly, but sometimes not all of the three alternatives will be available. In analogy with the usual utility analysis of the individual consumer under conditions of constant wants and variable price-income situations, rational behavior on the part of the community would mean that the community orders the three alternatives according to its collective preferences once for all and then chooses in any given case that alternative among those actually available which stands highest on this list. A natural way of arriving at the collective preference scale would be to say that one alternative is preferred to another if a majority of the community prefer the first alternative to the second, i.e., would choose the first over the second if those were the only two alternatives. Let A, B, and C be the three alternatives, and 1, 2, and 3 the three individuals. Suppose individual 1 prefers A to B and B to C (and therefore A to C), individual 2 prefers B to C and C to A (and therefore B to A), and individual 3 prefers C to A and A to B (and therefore C to B). Then a majority prefers A to B, and a majority prefers B to C. We may therefore say that the community prefers A to B and B to C. If the community is to be regarded as behaving rationally, we are forced to say that A is preferred to C. But, in fact, a majority of the community prefers C to A.[1] So the method just outlined for passing from individual to collective tastes fails to satisfy the condition of rationality as we ordinarily understand it. Can we find other methods of aggregating individual tastes which imply rational behavior on the part of the community and which will be satisfactory in other ways?

If we adopt the traditional identification of rationality with maximization of some sort, then the problem of achieving a social maximum derived from individual desires is precisely the problem which has been central to the field of welfare economics. However, the search for a clear definition of optimum social welfare has been plagued by the difficulties of interpersonal comparisons. The emphasis, as is well known, has shifted to a weaker definition of optimum, namely, the determination of all social

[1] It may be added that the method of decision sketched above is essentially that used in deliberative bodies, where a whole range of alternatives usually comes up for decision in the form of successive pairwise comparisons. The phenomenon described in the text can be seen in a pure form in the disposition of the proposals before recent Congresses for federal aid to state education, the three alternatives being no federal aid, federal aid to public schools only, and federal aid to both public and parochial schools.

states such that no individual can be made better off without making someone worse off. As Professors Bergson, Lange, and Samuelson have argued, though, the weaker definition cannot be used as a guide to social policy; the second type of welfare economics is only important as a preliminary to the determination of a genuine social maximum in the full sense. E.g., under the usual assumptions, if there is an excise tax imposed on one commodity in the initial situation, it can be argued that the removal of the tax accompanied by a suitable redistribution of income and direct tax burdens will improve the position of all individuals in the society. But there are, in general, many redistributions which will accomplish this end, and society must have some criterion for choosing among them before it can make any change at all. Further, there is no reason for confining the range of possible social actions to those which will injure no one as compared with the initial situation, unless the status quo is to be sanctified on ethical grounds. All we can really say is that society ought to abolish the excise tax and make some redistribution of income and tax burdens; but this is no prescription for action unless there is some principle by which society can make its choice among attainable income distributions, i.e., a social indifference map.

Voting can be regarded as a method of arriving at social choices derived from the preferences of individuals. Another such method of more specifically economic content is the compensation principle, as proposed by Mr. Kaldor:[2] in a choice between two alternative economic states x and y, if there is a method of paying compensations under state x such that everybody can be made better off in the state resulting from making the compensations under x than they are in state y, then x should be chosen in preference to y, *even if the compensation is not actually paid.* Apart from the ethical difficulties in the acceptance of this principle, there is a formal difficulty which was pointed out by Professor Scitovsky:[3] it is possible that simultaneously x should be preferred to y and y be preferred to x. Just as in the case of majority voting, this method of aggregating individual preferences may lead to a pattern of social choice which is not a linear ordering of the social alternatives. Note that in both cases the paradox need not occur; all that is said is that there are preference patterns which, if held by the individual members of the society, will give rise to an inconsistent pattern of social choice. Unless the trouble-breeding individual preference patterns can be ruled out by a priori assumption, both majority voting and the compensation principle must be regarded as unsatisfactory techniques for the determination of social preferences.

The aim of the present paper is to show that these difficulties are general. For any method of deriving social choices by aggregating individual

[2] N. Kaldor, "Welfare Propositions of Economics and Interpersonal Comparisons of Utility," *Economic Journal*, XLIX (1939), 549–652; see also J. R. Hicks, "The Foundations of Welfare Economics," *Economic Journal*, XLIX (1939), 698–701 and 711–12.
[3] T. Scitovsky, "A Note on Welfare Propositions in Economics," *Review of Economic Studies*, IX (1942), 77–88.

preference patterns which satisfies certain natural conditions, it is possible to find individual preference patterns which give rise to a social choice pattern which is not a linear ordering. In particular, this is very likely to be the case if, as is frequently assumed, each individual's preferences among social states are derived purely from his personal consumption-leisure-saving situation in each. It is assumed that individuals act rationally, in the sense that their behavior in alternative situations can be described by an indifference map. It is further assumed that utility is not measurable in any sense relevant to welfare economics, so that the tastes of an individual are completely described by a suitable preference pattern or indifference map.

II. Definitions and Notation

1. A NOTATION FOR PREFERENCES AND CHOICE

In this paper I shall be interested in the description of preference patterns both for the individual and for society. It will be found convenient to represent preference by a notation not customarily employed by economics, though familiar in mathematics and particularly in symbolic logic. We assume that there is a basic set of alternatives which could conceivably be presented to the chooser. In the theory of consumers' choice, each alternative would be a commodity bundle; in the theory of the firm, each alternative would be a complete decision on all inputs and outputs; in welfare economics, each alternative would be a distribution of commodities and labor requirements. These alternatives are mutually exclusive; they are denoted by small letters, x, y, z. . . . On any given occasion the chooser has available to him a subset S of all possible alternatives, and he is required to choose one out of this set. The set S is a generalization of the well-known opportunity curve; thus, in the theory of consumers' choice under perfect competition, it would be the budget plane. It is assumed further that the choice is made in this way: Before knowing the set S, the chooser considers in turn all possible pairs of alternatives, say x and y, and for each pair he makes one and only one of three decisions: x is preferred to y, x is indifferent to y, or y is preferred to x. The decisions made for different pairs are assumed to be consistent with one another, so that, for example, if x is preferred to y and y to z, then x is preferred to z; similarly, if x is indifferent to y and y to z, then x is indifferent to z. Having this ordering of all possible alternatives, the chooser is now confronted with a particular opportunity set S. If there is one alternative in S which is preferred to all others in S, then the chooser selects that one alternative.[4]

[4] It may be that there is a subset of alternatives in S, such that the alternatives in the subset are each preferred to every alternative not in the subset, while the alternatives in the subset are indifferent to one another. This case would be one in which the highest indifference curve which has a point in common with a given opportunity curve has at least two points in common with it (the well-known case of multiple maxima). In this case, the best thing to say is that the choice made in S is the whole subset; the first case discussed is one in which the subset in question, the choice, contains a single element.

Preference and indifference are relations between alternatives. Instead of working with two relations, it will be slightly more convenient to use a single relation, "preferred or indifferent." The statement, "x is preferred or indifferent to y," will be symbolized by xRy. The letter R, by itself, will be the name of the relation and will stand for a knowledge of all pairs such that xRy. From our previous discussion, we have, for any pair of alternatives x and y, either that x is preferred to y or y to x or that the two are indifferent. That is, we have assumed that any two alternatives are comparable. But this assumption may be written symbolically,

Axiom I: For all x and y, either xRy or yRx.

Note that Axiom I is presumed to hold when $x = y$, as well as when x is distinct from y, for we ordinarily say that x is indifferent to itself for any x, and this implies xRx. Note also that the word "or" in the statement of Axiom I does not exclude the possibility of both xRy and yRx. That word merely asserts that at least one of the two events must occur; both may.

The property mentioned above of consistency in the preferences as between different pairs of alternatives may be stated more precisely, as follows: if x is preferred or indifferent to y and y is preferred or indifferent to z, then x must be either preferred or indifferent to z. In symbols,

Axiom II: For all x, y, and z, xRy and yRz imply xRz.

A relation satisfying both Axiom I and Axiom II is termed a weak ordering or sometimes simply an ordering. It is clear that a relation having these two properties taken together does create a ranking of the various alternatives. The adjective "weak" refers to the fact that the ordering does not exclude indifference, i.e., Axioms I and II do not exclude the possibility that for some distinct x and y, both xRy and yRx.

It might be held that the two axioms in question do not completely characterize the concept of a preference pattern. For example, we ordinarily feel that not only the relation R but also the relations of (strict) preference and of indifference satisfy Axiom II. It can be shown that, by defining preference and indifference suitably in terms of R, it will follow that all the usually desired properties of preference patterns obtain.

Definition 1: xPy is defined to mean not yRx.

The statement "xPy" is read, "x is preferred to y."

Definition 2: xIy means xRy and yRx.

The statement "xIy" is read, "x is indifferent to y." It is clear that P and I, so defined, correspond to the ordinary notions of preference and indifference, respectively.

Lemma: a) For all x, xRx.
  f) If xPy and yRz, then xPz.
  b) If xPy, then xRy.
  c) If xPy and yPz, then xPz.
  d) If xIy and yIz, then xIz.
  e) For all x and y, either xRy or yPx.

All these statements are intuitively self-evident from the interpretations placed on the symbols.

For clarity, we shall avoid the use of the terms "preference scale" or "preference pattern" when referring to R, since we wish to avoid confusion with the concept of preference proper, denoted by P. We shall refer to R as an "ordering relation" or "weak ordering relation" or, more simply, as an "ordering" or "weak ordering." The term "preference relation" will refer to the relation P.

Suppose that we know the choice which would be made from any given pair of alternatives; i.e., given two alternatives x and y from which the chooser must select, we know whether he would take x or y or remain indifferent between them. Since choosing x from the pair x, y implies that x is preferred to y, and similarly with a choice of y, a knowledge of the choice which would be made from any two given alternatives implies a knowledge of the full preference scale; from earlier remarks this, in turn, implies a knowledge of the choice which would be made from any set of alternatives actually available. Hence, one of the consequences of the assumption of rational behavior is that the choice from any collection of alternatives can be determined by a knowledge of the choices which would be made from pairs of alternatives.

2. THE ORDERING OF SOCIAL STATES

In the present study the objects of choice are social states. The most precise definition of a social state would be a complete description of the amount of each type of commodity in the hands of each individual, the amount of labor to be applied by each individual, the amount of each productive resource invested in each type of productive activity, and the amounts of various types of collective activity such as municipal services, diplomacy and its continuation by other means, and the erection of statues to famous men. It is assumed that each individual in the community has a definite ordering of all conceivable social states in terms of their desirability to him. It need not be assumed here that an individual's attitude toward different social states is determined exclusively by the commodity bundles which accrue to his lot under each. The individual may order all social states by whatever standards he deems relevant. A member of Veblen's leisure class might order the states solely on the criterion of his relative income standing in each; a believer in the equality of man might order them in accordance with some measure of income equality. Indeed, since as mentioned above, some of the components of the social state, considered as a vector, are collective activities, purely individualistic assumptions are useless in analyzing such problems as the division of the national income between public and private expenditure. The present notation permits perfect generality in this respect. Needless to say, this generality is not without its price. More information would be available for analysis if the generality were restricted by a prior knowledge of the nature of individual orderings of social states.

In general, then, there will be a difference between the ordering of social states according to the direct consumption of the individual and the ordering when the individual adds his general standards of equity (or perhaps his standards of pecuniary emulation). We may refer to the former ordering as reflecting the *tastes* of the individual and the latter as reflecting his *values*. The distinction between the two is by no means clear cut. An individual with aesthetic feelings certainly derives pleasure from his neighbor's having a well-tended lawn. Under the system of a free market, such feelings play no direct part in social choice; yet, psychologically, they differ only slightly from the pleasure in one's own lawn. Intuitively, of course, we feel that not all the possible preferences which an individual might have ought to count; his preferences for matters which are "none of his business" should be irrelevant. Without challenging this view, I should like to emphasize that the decision as to which preferences are relevant and which are not is itself a value judgment and cannot be settled on an a priori basis. From a formal point of view, one cannot distinguish between an individual's dislike of having his grounds ruined by factory smoke and his extreme distaste for the existence of heathenism in Central Africa. There are probably not a few individuals in this country who would regard the former feeling as irrelevant for social policy and the latter as relevant, though the majority would probably reverse the judgment. I merely wish to emphasize here that we must look at the entire system of values, including values about values, in seeking for a truly general theory of social welfare.

It is the ordering according to values which takes into account all the desires of the individual, including the highly important socializing desires, and which is primarily relevant for the achievement of a social maximum. The market mechanism, however, takes into account only the ordering according to tastes. This distinction is the analogue, on the side of consumption, of the divergence between social and private costs in production which has been developed by Professor Pigou.[5]

As for notation, let R_i be the ordering relation for alternative social states from the standpoint of individual i. Sometimes, when several different ordering relations are being considered for the same individual, the symbols will be distinguished by adding a superscript. Corresponding to the ordering relation R_i, we have the (strict) preference relation P_i and the indifference relation I_i. If the symbol for the ordering has a prime or second attached (thus, R'_i, R''_i), then the corresponding symbols for preference and indifference will have the prime or second attached, respectively.

Similarly, society as a whole will be considered provisionally to have a social ordering relation for alternative social states, which will be desig-

[5] A. C. Pigou, *The Economics of Welfare* (London: Macmillan & Co., 1920), Part II, chap. vi.

nated by R, sometimes with a prime or second. Social preference and indifference will be denoted by P and I, respectively, primes or seconds being attached when they are attached to the relation R, respectively.

Throughout this analysis, it will be assumed that individuals are rational, by which is meant that the ordering relations R_i satisfy Axioms I and II. The problem will be to construct an ordering relation for society as a whole which is also to reflect rational choice-making, so that R also will be assumed to satisfy Axioms I and II.

III. The Social Welfare Function

1. FORMAL STATEMENT OF THE PROBLEM OF SOCIAL CHOICE

I shall largely restate Bergson's formulation of the problem of making welfare judgments[6] in the terminology here adopted. The various arguments of his social welfare function are the components of what I have here termed the "social state," so that essentially he is describing the process of assigning a numerical social utility to each social state, the aim of society then being described by saying it seeks to maximize the social utility or social welfare subject to whatever technological or resource constraints are relevant, or, put otherwise, it chooses the social state yielding the highest possible social welfare within the environment. As with any type of behavior described by maximization, the measurability of social welfare need not be assumed; all that matters is the existence of a social ordering satisfying Axioms I and II. As before, all that is needed to define such an ordering is to know the relative ranking of each pair of alternatives.

The relative ranking of a fixed pair of alternative social states will vary, in general, with changes in the values of at least some individuals; to assume that the ranking does not change with any changes in individual values is to assume, with traditional social philosophy of the Platonic realist variety, that there exists an objective social good defined independently of individual desires. This social good, it was frequently held, could be best apprehended by the methods of philosophic inquiry. Such a philosophy could be and was used to justify government by elite, secular or religious, although the connection is not a necessary one.

To the nominalist temperament of the modern period the assumption of the existence of the social ideal in some Platonic realm of being was meaningless. The utilitarian philosophy of Jeremy Bentham and his followers sought instead to ground the social good on the good of individuals. The hedonist psychology associated with utilitarian philosophy was further used to imply that each individual's good was identical with his desires.

---

[6] A. Bergson (Burk), "A Reformulation of Certain Aspects of Welfare Economics," *Quarterly Journal of Economics*, LII (1938), 310–34.

Hence, the social good was in some sense to be a composite of the desires of individuals. A viewpoint of this type serves as a justification of both political democracy and laissez faire economics or at least an economic system involving free choice of goods by consumers and of occupations by workers.

The hedonist psychology finds its expression here in the assumption that individuals' behavior is expressed by individual ordering relations R_i. Utilitarian philosophy is expressed by saying for each pair of social states that the choice depends on the ordering relations of all individuals, i.e., depends on $R_1, \ldots, R_n$, where n is the number of individuals in the community. Put otherwise, the whole social ordering relation R is to be determined by the individual ordering relations for social states, $R_1, \ldots, R_n$. We do not exclude here the possibility that some or all of the choices between pairs of social states made by society might be independent of the preferences of certain particular individuals, just as a function of several variables might be independent of some of them.

> *Definition 3:* By a "social welfare function" will be meant a process or rule which, for each set of individual orderings $R_1, \ldots, R_n$ for alternative social states (one ordering for each individual), states a corresponding social ordering of alternative social states, R.

As a matter of notation, we shall let R be the social ordering corresponding to the set of individual orders $R_1, \ldots, R_n$, the correspondence being that established by a given social welfare function; if primes or seconds are added to the symbols for the individual orderings, primes or seconds will be added to the symbol for the corresponding social ordering.

There is some difference between the concept of social welfare function used here and that employed by Bergson. The individual orderings which enter as arguments into the social welfare function as defined here refer to the values of individuals rather than to their tastes. Bergson supposes individual values to be such as to yield a social value judgment leading to a particular rule for determining the allocation of productive resources and the distribution of leisure and final products in accordance with individual tastes. In effect, the social welfare function described here is a method of choosing which social welfare function of the Bergson type will be applicable, though of course I do not exclude the possibility that the social choice actually arrived at will not be consistent with the particular value judgments formulated by Bergson. But in the formal aspect the difference between the two definitions of social welfare function is not too important. In Bergson's treatment the tastes of individuals (each for his own consumption) are represented by utility functions, i.e., essentially by ordering relations; hence, the Bergson social welfare function is also a rule for assigning to each set of individual orderings a social ordering of social states. Further, as already indicated, no sharp line can be drawn between tastes and values.

A special type of social welfare function would be one which assigns the same social ordering for every set of individual orderings. In this case, of course, social choices are completely independent of individual tastes, and we are back in the Platonic case.

For simplicity of exposition, it will be assumed that the society under study contains only two individuals and that the total number of alternatives which are conceivable is three. Since the results to be obtained are negative, the latter restriction is not a real one; if it turns out to be impossible to construct a social welfare function which will define a social ordering of three alternatives, it will a fortiori be impossible to define one which will order more alternatives. The restriction to two individuals may be more serious; it is conceivable that there may be suitable social welfare functions which can be defined for three individuals but not for two, for example. In fact, this is not so, and the results stated in this paper hold for any number of individuals. However, the proof will be considerably simplified by considering only two.

We shall not ask, in general, that the social welfare function be defined for every logically possible set of individual orderings. On a priori grounds we may suppose it known that preferences for alternative social states are formed only in a limited set of ways, and the social welfare function need only be defined for individual orderings formed in those ways. For example, we may suppose (and will later on) that each individual orders social alternatives according to his own personal consumption under each (the purely individualistic case). Then the social welfare function need be defined only for those sets of individual orderings which are admissible, in the sense of being consistent with our a priori assumptions about the empirical possibilities.

Condition 1: The social welfare function is defined for every admissible pair of individual orderings, R_1, R_2.

Condition 1, it should be emphasized, is a restriction on the form of the social welfare function, since we are requiring that for some sufficiently wide range of sets of individual orderings, the social welfare function give rise to a true social ordering.

2. POSITIVE ASSOCIATION OF SOCIAL AND INDIVIDUAL VALUES

Since we are trying to describe social "welfare" and not some sort of "illfare," we must assume that the social welfare function is such that the social ordering responds positively to alterations in individual values or at least not negatively. Hence, we may state the following condition:

Condition 2: If an alternative social state x rises or does not fall in the ordering of each individual without any other change in those orderings and if x was preferred to another alternative y before the change in individual orderings, then x is still preferred to y.

3. THE INDEPENDENCE OF IRRELEVANT ALTERNATIVES

Just as for a single individual, the choice made by society from any given set of alternatives should be independent of the very existence of alternatives outside the given set. For example, suppose an election system has been devised whereby each individual lists all the candidates in order of his preference, and then, by a preassigned procedure, the winning candidate is derived from these lists. (All actual election procedures are of this type, although in most the entire list is not required for the choice.) Suppose an election is held, with a certain number of candidates in the field, each individual filing his list of preferences, and then one of the candidates dies. Surely, the social choice should be made by taking each of the individual's preference lists, blotting out completely the dead candidate's name, and considering only the orderings of the remaining names in going through the procedure of determining the winner. That is, the choice to be made among the set of surviving candidates should be independent of the preferences of individuals for the nonsurviving candidate. To assume otherwise would be to make the result of the election dependent on the obviously accidental circumstance of whether a candidate died before or after the date of polling. Therefore, we may require of our social welfare function that the choice made by society from a given set of alternatives depend only on the orderings of individuals among those alternatives. Alternatively stated, if we consider two sets of individual orderings such that, for each individual, his ordering of those particular alternatives under consideration is the same each time, then we require that the choice made by society be the same if individual values are given by the first set of orderings as if they are given by the second.

> *Condition 3*: Let R_1, R_2, and R'_1, R'_2 be two sets of individual orderings. If, for both individuals i and for all x and y in a given set of alternatives S, xR_iy if and only if xR'_iy, then the social choice made from S is the same whether the individual orderings are R_1, R_2, or R'_1, R'_2. (Independence of irrelevant alternatives.)

The reasonableness of this condition can be seen by consideration of the possible results in a method of choice which does not satisfy Condition 3, the rank-order method of voting frequently used in clubs. With a finite number of candidates, let each individual rank all his candidates, i.e., designate his first-choice candidate, second-choice candidate, etc. Let preassigned weights be given first, second, etc., choices, the higher weight to the higher choice, and then let the candidate with the highest weighted sum of votes be elected. In particular, suppose there are three voters and four candidates, x, y, z, and w. Let the weights for first, second, third, and fourth choices be 4, 3, 2, and 1, respectively. Suppose that individuals 1 and 2 rank the candidates in the order x, y, z, and w, while individual 3 ranks them in the order z, w, x, and y. Under the given electoral system, x

is chosen. Then, certainly, if *y* is deleted from the ranks of the candidates, the system applied to the remaining candidates should yield the same result, especially since, in this case, *y* is inferior to *x* according to the tastes of every individual; but, if *y* is in fact deleted, the indicated electoral system would yield a tie between *x* and *z*.

The condition of the independence of irrelevant alternatives implies that in a generalized sense all methods of social choice are of the type of voting. If *S* is the set consisting of the two alternatives *x* and *y*, Condition 3 tells us that the choice between *x* and *y* is determined solely by the preferences of the members of the community as between *x* and *y*. That is, if we know which members of the community prefer *x* to *y*, which are indifferent, and which prefer *y* to *x*, then we know what choice the community makes. Knowing the social choices made in pairwise comparisons in turn determines the entire social ordering and therewith the social choice made from any set of alternatives. Condition 2 guarantees that voting for a certain alternative has the usual effect of making surer that that alternative will be adopted.

Condition 1 says, in effect, that, as the set of alternatives varies and individual orderings remain fixed, the different choices made shall bear a certain type of consistent relation to one another. Conditions 2 and 3, on the other hand, suppose a fixed set of alternatives and say that for certain particular types of variation in individual values, the various choices made have a certain type of consistency.

4. THE CONDITION OF CITIZENS' SOVEREIGNITY

We certainly wish to assume that the individuals in our society be free to choose, by varying their values, among the alternatives available. That is, we do not wish our social welfare function to be such as to prevent us, by its very definition, from expressing a preference for some given alternative over another.

> *Definition 4:* A social welfare function will be said to be *imposed* if for some pair of distinct alternatives *x* and *y*, xRy for any set of individual orderings R_1, R_2, where *R* is the social ordering corresponding to R_1, R_2.

In other words, when the social welfare function is imposed, there is some pair of alternatives *x* and *y* such that the community can never express a preference for *y* over *x* no matter what the tastes of both individuals are, indeed even if both individuals prefer *y* to *x*; some preferences are taboo. (Note that, by Definition 1, asserting that xRy holds for all sets of individual orderings is equivalent to asserting that yPx never holds.) We certainly wish to require of our social welfare function the condition that it not be imposed in the sense of Definition 4; we certainly wish all choices to be possible if unanimously desired by the group.

> *Condition 4:* The social welfare function is not to be imposed.

Condition 4 is stronger than need be for the present argument. Some decisions, as between given pairs of alternatives, may be assumed to be imposed. All that is required really is that there be a set S of three alternatives such that the choice between any pair is not constrained in advance by the social welfare function.

It should also be noted that Condition 4 excludes the Platonic case discussed in section 1 of Part III above. It expresses fully the idea that all social choices are determined by individual desires. In conjunction with Condition 2 (which insures that the determination is in the direction of agreeing with individual desires), Condition 4 expresses the same idea as Professor Bergson's Fundamental Value Propositions of Individual Preference, which state that of two alternatives between which all individuals but one are indifferent, the community will prefer one over the other or be indifferent between the two according as the one individual prefers one over the other or is indifferent between the two.[7] Conditions 2 and 4 together correspond to the usual concept of consumers' sovereignty; since we are here referring to values rather than to tastes, we might refer to them as expressing the idea of citizens' sovereignty.

5. THE CONDITION OF NONDICTATORSHIP

A second form of social choice not of a collective character is the choice by dictatorship. In its pure form this means that social choices are to be based solely on the preferences of one man. That is, whenever the dictator prefers x to y, so does society. If the dictator is indifferent between x and y, presumably he will then leave the choice up to some or all of the other members of society.

> *Definition 5:* A social welfare function is said to be "dictatorial" if there exists an individual i such that for all x and y, xP_iy implies xPy regardless of the orderings of all individuals other than i, where P is the social preference relation corresponding to those orderings.

Since we are interested in the construction of collective methods of social choice, we wish to exclude dictatorial social welfare functions.

> *Condition 5:* The social welfare function is not to be dictatorial (nondictatorship).

We have now imposed five apparently reasonable conditions on the construction of a social welfare function. These conditions are of course value judgments and could be called into question; taken together, they express the doctrines of citizens' sovereignty and rationality in a very general form, with the citizens being allowed to have a wide range of values. The question is that of constructing a social ordering of all conceivable alternative

[7] Bergson, *op. cit.*, pp. 318–20. The Fundamental Value Propositions of Individual Preference are not, strictly speaking, implied by Conditions 2 and 4 (in conjunction with Conditions 1 and 2), although something very similar to them is so implied; see Consequence 1 in Part IV, section 2 below. A slightly stronger form of Condition 2 than that stated here would suffice to yield the desired implication.

social states from any given set of individual orderings of those social states, the method of construction being in accordance with the value judgments of citizens' sovereignty and rationality as expressed in Conditions 1–5.

IV. The Possibility Theorem for Social Welfare Functions

1. THE RANGE OF POSSIBLE INDIVIDUAL ORDERINGS

For simplicity we shall impose on the individual preference scales two conditions which in fact have almost invariably been assumed in works on welfare economics: (1) each individual's comparison of two alternative social states depends only on the commodities that he receives (and labor that he expends) in the two states, i.e., he is indifferent as between any two social states in which his own consumption-leisure-saving situations are the same or at least indifferent to him; (2) in comparing two personal situations in one of which he receives at least as much of each commodity (including leisure and saving as commodities) and more of at least one commodity than in the other, the individual will prefer the first situation. Suppose that among the possible alternatives there were three, none of which gave any individual at least as much of both commodities as any other. For example, suppose that there are two individuals and a total of ten units of each of two commodities. Consider three alternative distributions described by the accompanying tabulation. The individualistic restrictions imposed do not tell us anything about the way either individual

| Alternative | Individual 1 | | Individual 2 | |
	Commodity 1	Commodity 2	Commodity 1	Commodity 2
1.........	5	1	5	9
2.........	4	2	6	8
3.........	3	3	7	7

orders these alternatives. Under the individualistic assumptions there is no a priori reason to suppose that the two individuals will not order the alternatives in any given way. In the sense of Part III, section 1, above, all individual orderings of the three alternatives are admissible. Condition 1 therefore requires that the social welfare function be defined for all pairs of individual orderings, R_1, R_2.

2. THE POSSIBILITY THEOREM

Some consequences will be drawn from Conditions 1–5 for the present case of a social welfare function for two individuals and three alternatives.

It will be shown that the supposition that there is a social welfare function satisfying those conditions leads to a contradiction.

Let x, y, and z be the three alternatives among which choice is to be made, e.g., three possible distributions of commodities. Let x' and y' be variable symbols which represent possible alternatives, i.e., range over the values x, y, z. Let the individuals be designated as 1 and 2, and let R_1 and R_2 be the orderings by 1 and 2, respectively, of the alternatives x, y, z. Let P_1 and P_2 be the corresponding preference relations; e.g., $x'P_1y'$ means that individual 1 strictly prefers x' to y'.

Consequence 1: If $x'P_1y'$ and $x'P_2y'$, then $x'Py'$.

I.e., if both prefer x' to y', then society must prefer x' to y'.

PROOF.—By Condition 4 there are orderings R'_1 and R'_2, for individuals 1 and 2, respectively, such that, in the corresponding social preference $x'P'y'$. Form R''_1 from R'_1 by raising x', if need be, to the top, while leaving the relative positions of the other two alternatives alone; form R''_2 from R'_2 in the same way. Since all we have done is raise alternative x' in everyone's esteem, while leaving the others alone, x' should still be preferred to y' by society in accordance with Condition 2, so that $x'P''y'$. But, by construction, both individuals prefer x' to y' in the orderings R''_1, R''_2, and society prefers x' to y'. Since, by Condition 3, the social choice between x' and y' depends only on the individual orderings of those two alternatives, it follows that whenever both individuals prefer x' to y', regardless of the rank of the third alternative, society will prefer x' to y', which is the statement to be proved.

Consequence 2: Suppose that for some x' and y', whenever $x'P_1y'$ and $y'P_2x'$, $x'Py'$. Then, for that x' and y', whenever $x'P_1y'$, $x'Py'$.

I.e., if in a given choice, the will of individual 1 prevails against the opposition of 2, then individual 1's views will certainly prevail if 2 is indifferent or if he agrees with 1.

PROOF.—Let R_1 be an ordering in which $x'P_1y'$, R_2 be any ordering. Let R'_1 be the same ordering as R_1, while R'_2 is derived from R_2 by depressing x' to the bottom while leaving the relative positions of the other two alternatives unchanged. By construction, $x'P'_1y'$, $y'P'_2x'$. By hypothesis, $x'P'y'$, where P' is the social preference relation derived from the individual orderings R'_1, R'_2. Now the only difference between R'_1, R'_2 and R_1, R_2 is that x' is raised in the scale of individual 2 in the latter as compared with the former. Hence, by Condition 2 (interchanging the R_i's and the R'_i's) it follows from $x'P'y'$ that $x'Py'$. I.e., whenever R_1, R_2 are such that $x'P_1y'$, then $x'Py'$.

Consequence 3: If $x'P_1y'$ and $y'P_2x'$, then $x'Iy'$.

I.e., if the two individuals have exactly opposing interests on the choice between two given alternatives, then society will be indifferent between the alternatives.

PROOF—Suppose the consequence is false. Then, for some orderings R_1 and R_2 and for some pair of alternatives x' and y', we would have $x'P_1y'$, $y'P_2x'$, but not $x'Iy'$. In that case, either $x'Py'$ or $y'Px'$. We will suppose $x'Py'$ and show that this supposition leads to a contradiction; the same reasoning would show that the assumption $y'Px'$ also leads to a contradiction.

Without loss of generality it can be assumed that x' is the alternative x, $y' = y$. Then we have, for the particular orderings in question, xP_1y, yP_2x, and xPy. Since the social choice between x and y depends, by Condition 3, only on the individual choices as between x and y, we must have

$$(1) \qquad \text{whenever } xP_1y \text{ and } yP_2x, xPy.$$

It will be shown that (1) leads to a contradiction.

Suppose individual 1 prefers x to y and y to z, while individual 2 prefers y to z and z to x. Individual 2 then prefers y to x. By (1) society prefers x to y. Also, both prefer y to z; by Consequence 1, society prefers y to z. Since society prefers x to y and y to z, it must prefer x to z. Therefore, we have exhibited orderings R_1, R_2 such that xP_1z, zP_2x, but xPz. Since the social choice between x and z depends only on the individual preferences for x and z,

$$(2) \qquad \text{whenever } xP_1z \text{ and } zP_2x, xPz.$$

Now suppose R_1 is the ordering y, x, z, and R_2 the ordering z, y, x. By Consequence 1, yPx; by (2) xPz, so that yPz. By the same reasoning as before,

$$(3) \qquad \text{whenever } yP_1z \text{ and } zP_2y, yPz.$$

If R_1 is the ordering y, z, x, and R_2 the ordering z, x, y, it follows from Consequence 1 and (3) that zPx and yPz, so that yPx. Hence,

$$(4) \qquad \text{whenever } yP_1x \text{ and } xP_2y, yPx.$$

If R_1 is the ordering z, y, x, and R_2 the ordering x, z, y, then from Consequence 1 and (4), zPy and yPx, so that zPx.

$$(5) \qquad \text{Whenever } zP_1x \text{ and } xP_2z, zPx.$$

If R_1 is the ordering z, x, y, and R_2 x, y, z, then, using (5), zPx and xPy, so that zPy.

$$(6) \qquad \text{Whenever } zP_1y \text{ and } yP_2z, zPy.$$

From (1) it follows from Consequence 2 that whenever xP_1y, xPy. Similarly, from (1) to (6) it follows that for any pair of alternatives x', y', whenever $x'P_1y'$, then $x'Py'$. That is, by Definition 5, individual 1 would be a dictator. This is prohibited by Condition 5, so that (1) must be false. Therefore, Consequence 3 is proved.

Now suppose individual 1 has the ordering x, y, z, while individual 2 has the ordering z, x, y. By Consequence 1,

(7) $$xPy.$$

Since yP_1z, zP_2y, it follows from Consequence 3 that

(8) $$yIz.$$

From (7) and (8), xPz. But, also xP_1z, zP_2x, which implies xIz by Consequence 3. It cannot be that x is both preferred and indifferent to z. Hence the assumption that there is a social welfare function compatible with Conditions 1–5 has led to a contradiction.

Put another way, if we assume that our social welfare function satisfies Conditions 2–3 and we further suppose that Condition 1 holds, then either Condition 4 or Condition 5 must be violated. Condition 4 states that the social welfare function is not imposed; Condition 5 states that it is not dictatorial.

Possibility Theorem.—If there are at least three alternatives among which the members of the society are free to order in any way, then every social welfare function satisfying Conditions 2 and 3 and yielding a social ordering satisfying Axioms I and II must be either imposed or dictatorial.[8] The Possibility Theorem shows that, if no prior assumptions are made about the nature of individual orderings, there is no method of voting which will remove the paradox of voting discussed in Part I, neither plurality voting nor any scheme of proportional representation, no matter how complicated. Similarly, the market mechanism does not create a rational social choice.

[8] The negative outcome expressed in this theorem is strongly reminiscent of the intransitivity of the concept of domination in the theory of multiperson games; see John von Neumann and Oskar Morgenstern, *Theory of Games and Economic Behavior* (2d ed.; Princeton University Press, 1947), pp. 38–39.

Diagrammatic Exposition of a Theory of Public Expenditure

PAUL A. SAMUELSON

Paul A. Samuelson is Institute Professor of Economics at Massachusetts Institute of Technology. This paper appeared in the Review of Economics and Statistics *in 1955.*

In 1954 I presented a mathematical exposition of a public expenditure theory that goes back to Italian, Austrian, and Scandinavian writers of the last 75 years. After providing that theory with its needed logically-complete optimal conditions, I went on to demonstrate the fatal inability of any decentralized market or voting mechanism to attain or compute this optimum. The present note presents in terms of two-dimensional diagrams an essentially equivalent formulation of the theory's optimum conditions and briefly discusses some criticisms.

A Polar-Case Model of Government

Doctrinal history shows that theoretical insight often comes from considering strong or extreme cases. The grand Walrasian model of competitive general equilibrium is one such extreme polar case. We can formulate it so stringently as to leave no economic role for government. What strong polar case shall the student of public expenditure set alongside this pure private economy?

One possibility is the model of a group-mind. Such a model, which has been extensively used by nationalists and by Romantic critics of classical economics, can justify any, and every, configuration of government. So there is perhaps little that an economic theorist can usefully say about it.

My alternative is a slightly more sophisticated one, but still—intentionally—an extreme polar case. It is consistent with individualism, yet at the same time it explicitly introduces the vital external interdependencies that no theory of government can do without. Its basic assumption is an over-sharp distinction between the following two kinds of goods:

(i) A *private* consumption good, like bread, whose total can be parcelled out among two or more persons, with one man having a loaf less if another gets a loaf more. Thus if X_1 is total bread, and X^1_1 and X^2_1 are the respective private consumptions of Man 1 and Man 2, we can say that the total equals the sum of the separate consumptions—or $X_1 = X^1_1 + X^2_1$.

(ii) A *public* consumption good, like an outdoor circus or national defense, which is provided for each person to enjoy or not, according to his tastes. I assume the public good can be varied in total quantity, and write X_2 for its magnitude. It differs from a private consumption good in that each man's consumption of it, X^1_2 and X^2_2 respectively, is related to the total X_2 by a condition of *equality* rather than of summation. Thus, by definition, $X^1_2 = X_2$, and $X^2_2 = X_2$.

Obviously, I am introducing a strong polar case. We could easily lighten the stringency of our assumptions. But on reflection, I think most economists will see that this is a natural antipodal case to the admittedly extreme polar case of traditional individualistic general equilibrium. The careful empiricist will recognize that many—though not all—of the realistic cases of government activity can be fruitfully analyzed as some kind of a blend of these two extreme polar cases.

Graphical Depiction of Tastes and Technology

The first three charts summarize our assumptions about tastes and technology. Each diagram has a private good, such as bread, on its vertical axis; each has a public good on its horizontal axis. The heavy indifference curves of Chart 1 summarize Man 1's preferences between public and private goods. Chart 2's indifference curves do the same for Man 2; and the relative flatness of the contour shows that, in a sense, he has less liking for the public good.

The heavy production-possibility or opportunity-cost curve AB in Chart 3 relates the total productions of public and private goods in the usual familiar manner; the curve is convex from above to reflect the usual assumption of increasing relative marginal costs (or generalized diminishing returns).[1]

---

[1] Even though a public good is being compared with a private good, the indifference curves are drawn with the usual convexity to the origin. This assumption, as well as the one about diminishing returns, could be relaxed without hurting the theory. Indeed, we could recognize the possible case where one man's circus is another man's poison, by permitting indifference curves to bend forward. This would not affect the analysis, but would answer a critic's minor objection. Mathematically, we could without loss of generality set $X^1_2 =$ any function of X_2, relaxing strict equality.

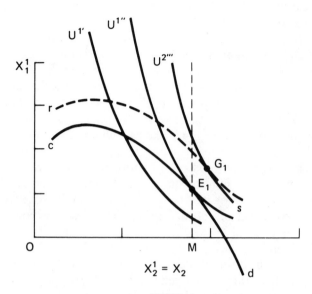

CHART 1.
INDIFFERENCE CONTOURS RELATING MAN 1'S CONSUMP-
TION OF PUBLIC AND PRIVATE GOODS

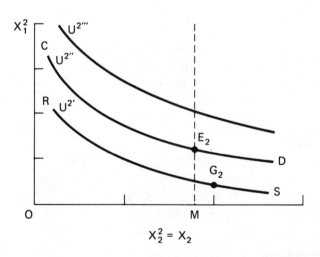

CHART 2.
INDIFFERENCE CONTOURS RELATING MAN 2'S CONSUMP-
TION OF PUBLIC AND PRIVATE GOODS

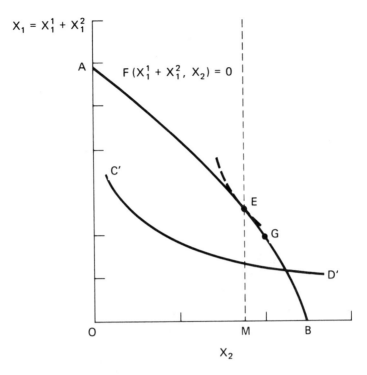

CHART 3.
TRANSFORMATION SCHEDULE RELATING TOTALS OF PUBLIC
AND PRIVATE GOODS

Because of our special definition of a public good, the three diagrams are not independent. Each must be lined up with *exactly the same horizontal scale*. Because increasing a public good for society simultaneously increases it for each and every man, we must always be simultaneously at exactly the same longitude in all three figures. Moving an inch east in one diagram moves us the same amount east in all.

The private good on the vertical axis is subject to no new and unusual restrictions. Each man can be moved north or south on his indifference diagram independently. But, of course, the third diagram does list the total of bread summed over the private individuals; so it must have a larger vertical axis, and our momentary northward position on it must correspond to the sum of the independent northward positions of the separate individuals.

Tangency Conditions for Pareto Optima

What is the best or ideal state of the world for such a simple system? That is, what three vertically-aligned points corresponding to a determination of a given total of both goods and a determinate parcelling out of them among all separate individauls will be the ethically preferred final configuration?

To answer this ethical, normative question we must be given a set of norms in the form of a *social welfare function* that renders interpersonal judgments. For expository convenience, let us suppose that this will be supplied later and that we know in advance it will have the following special individualistic ·property: leaving each person on his same indifference level will leave social welfare unchanged; at any point, a move of each man to a higher indifference curve can be found that will increase social welfare.

Given this rather weak assurance about the forthcoming social welfare function, we can proceed to determine tangency conditions of an "efficiency" type that are at least necessary, though definitely not sufficient. We do this by setting up a preliminary maximum problem which will eventually necessarily have to be satisfied.

Holding all but one man at specified levels of indifference, how can we be sure that the remaining man reaches his highest indifference level?

Concretely, this is how we define such a tangency optimum: Set Man 2 on a specified indifference curve, say his middle one CD. Paying attention to Mother Nature's scarcity, as summarized in Chart 3's AB curve, and following Man 1's tastes as given by Chart 1's indifference curves, how high on those indifference curves can we move Man 1?

The answer is given by the tangency point E_1, and the corresponding aligned points E_2 and E.

How is this derived? Copy CD on Chart 3 and call it $C'D'$. The distance between $C'D'$ and AB represents the amounts of the two goods that are physically available to Man 1. So subtract $C'D'$ vertically from AB and plot the algebraic result as cd in Chart 1. Now where on cd would Man 1 be best off? Obviously at the tangency point E_1 where cd touches (but does not cross) his highest attainable indifference contour.

How many such Pareto-optimal points are there? Obviously, for each of the infinite possible initial indifference curves to put Man 2 on, we can derive a new highest attainable tangency level for Man 1. So there are an infinity of such optimal points—as many in number as there are points on the usual contract curve. All of these Pareto-optimal points have the property that from them there exists no physically-feasible movement that will make every man better off. Of course we cannot compare two different Pareto points until we are given a social welfare function. For a move from one Pareto point to another must always hurt one man while it is helping another, and an interpersonal way of comparing these changes must be supplied.

Chart 4 indicates these utility possibilities on an ordinal diagram. Each axis provides an indicator of the two men's respective indifference curve levels. The utility frontier of Pareto-optimal points is given by *pp*: the double fold infinity of "inefficient," non-Pareto-optimal points is given by the shaded area; the *pp* frontier passes from northwest to southeast to reflect the inevitable conflict of interests characterizing any contract locus; the curvature of the *pp* locus is of no particular type since we have no need to put unique cardinal numbers along the indifference contours and can content ourselves with east-west and north-south relationships in Chart 4 without regard to numerical degree and to uneven stretchings of either utility axis.

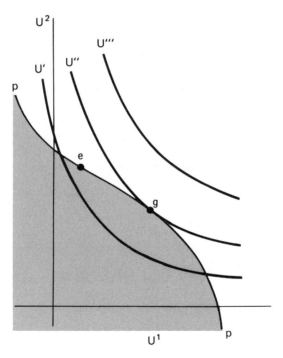

CHART 4.
UTILITY FRONTIER OF PARETO-OPTIMAL EFFICIENCY POINTS
AND ITS TANGENCY TO HIGHEST ATTAINABLE SOCIAL WEL-
FARE CONTOUR

The Optimum of All the Pareto Optima

Now we can answer the fundamental question: what is the best configuration for this society?

Use of the word "best" indicates we are in the ascientific area of "welfare economics" and must be provided with a set of norms. Economic science cannot deduce a social welfare function; what it can do is neutrally interpret any arbitrarily specified welfare function.

The heavy contours labelled U', U'', and U''' summarize all that is relevant in the provided social welfare function (they provide the needed ordinal scoring of every state of the world, involving different levels of indifference for the separate individuals).[2]

Obviously society cannot be best off inside the utility frontier. Where then on the utility frontier will the "best obtainable bliss point" be? We will move along the utility frontier pp until we touch the highest social indifference curve: this will be at g where pp tangentially touches, without crossing, the highest obtainable social welfare level U''. In words, we can interpret this final tangency condition in the following terms:

(i) The social welfare significance of a unit of any private good allocated to private individuals must at the margin be the same for each and every person.

(ii) The Pareto-optimal condition, which makes relative marginal social cost equal to the sum of all persons' marginal rates of substitution, is already assured by virtue of the fact that bliss lies on the utility frontier.

Relations with Earlier Theories

This completes the graphical interpretation of my mathematical model. There remains the pleasant task of relating this graphical treatment to earlier works of Howard R. Bowen and others.

To do this, look at Chart 5, which gives an alternative depiction of the optimal tangency condition at a point like E. I use the private good X_1 as numeraire, measuring all.values in terms of it. The MC curve is derived from the AB curve of Chart 3: it is nothing but the absolute slope of that production-possibility schedule plotted against varying amounts of the public good; it is therefore a marginal cost curve, with MC measured in terms of the numeraire good.

The marginal rate of substitution curves MRS^1 and MRS^2 are derived in a similar fashion from the respective indifference curves of Man 1 and Man 2: thus, MRS^1 is the absolute slope of the $u^{1'''}$ indifference curve plotted against varying amounts of the public good; MRS^2 is the similar

---

[2] These social welfare or social indifference contours are given no particular curvature. Why? Again because we are permitting any arbitrary ordinal indicator of utility to be used on the axes of Chart 4.

An ethical postulate ruling out all "dog-in-the-manger phenomena" will make all partial derivatives of the social welfare function $U(u^1,u^2, \ldots)$ always positive. This will assure the usual negative slopes to the U contours of Chart 4. However, without hurting the Pareto part of the new welfare economics, we can relax this assumption a little and let the contours bend forward. If, at every point there can be found at least one positive partial derivative, this will be sufficient to rule out satiation points and will imply the necessity of the Pareto-optimal tangency condition of the earlier diagrams.

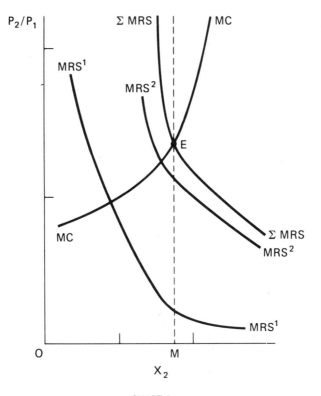

CHART 5.
INTERSECTION OF PUBLIC GOOD'S MARGINAL COST
SCHEDULE AND THE VERTICALLY-SUMMED INDIVIDUAL'S
MARGINAL RATES OF SUBSTITUTION, AS ENVISAGED BY
LINDAHL AND BOWEN

slope function derived from Man 2's indifference curve CD. (All three are "marginal" curves, bearing the usual relationship to their respective "total" curves.)

These schedules look like demand curves. We are accustomed to adding horizontally or laterally the separate demand curves of individuals to arrive at total market demand. But this is valid only for private goods. As Bowen rightly says, *we must in the case of public goods add different individuals' curves vertically.*

This gives us the heavy Σ*MRS* curve for the whole community. Where is equilibrium? It is at *E*, where the community *MC* curve intersects the community Σ*MRS* curve. Upon reflection the reader will realize that the equality $MC = \Sigma MRS = MRS^1 + MRS^2$ is the precise equivalent of my mathematical equation (2) and of our Pareto-type tangency condition at E_1, E_2, or E. Why? Because of the stipulated requirement that Chart 5's curves are to depict the absolute slopes of the curves of Charts 1–3.

Once the economic theorist has related my graphical and mathematical analysis to the Lindahl and Bowen diagrams, he is in a position, I believe, to discern the logical advantage of the present formulation. For there is something circular and unsatisfactory about both the Bowen and Lindahl constructions: they show what the final equilibrium looks like, but by themselves they are not generally able to find the desired equilibrium. To see this, note that whereas we might know MC in Chart 5, we would not know the appropriate MRS schedules for *all* men until we already were familiar with the final E intersection point. (We might know MRS^2 from the specification that Man 2 is to be on the AB level; but then we wouldn't know MRS^1 until Chart 1's tangency had given us Man 1's highest attainable level, $u^{1\prime\prime\prime}$.) Under conditions of general equilibrium, Charts 1–3 logically contain Chart 5 inside them, but not vice versa. Moreover, Charts 1–3 explicitly call attention to the fact that there is an infinite number of different diagrams of the Lindahl-Bowen type, one for each specified level of relative interpersonal well-being.[3]

Concluding Reflections

I hope that the analytic model outlined here may help make a small and modest step toward understanding the complicated realities of political economy. Much remains to be done. This is not the place to discuss the wider implications and difficulties of the presented economic theory. However, I should like to comment briefly on some of the questions about this theory that have been raised.

(i) On the deductive side, the theory presented here is, I believe, a logically coherent one. This is true whether expressed in my original mathematical notation or in the present diagrammatic form. Admittedly, the latter widens the circle of economists who can understand and follow what is being said. The present version, with its tangencies of methodologically the same type as characterize Cournot-Marshall marginal theory and Bergson-Pigou welfare theory, should from its easily recognized equivalence with the mathematical version make clear my refusal to agree with Dr. Stephen Enke's view that my use of mathematics was limited "to notation."

(ii) In terms of the history of similar theories, I hope the present paper

---

[3] The earlier writers from Wicksell on were well aware of this. They explicitly introduce the assumption that there is to have been a *prior* optimal interpersonal distribution of income, so what I have labelled E might better be labelled G. But the general equilibrium analyst asks how can the appropriate distribution of income be decided on a prior basis *before* the significant problems of public consumptions have been determined? A satisfactory general analysis can resist the temptation to assume (i) the level of government expenditure must be so small as not to affect appreciably the marginal social significance of money to the different individuals; (ii) each man's indifference curves run parallel to each other in a vertical direction so that every and all indifference curves in Chart 1 (or in Chart 2) give rise to the same MRS^1 (or MRS^2) curve in Chart 5. The modern theorist is anxious to free his analysis from the incubus of unnecessarily restrictive partial equilibrium assumptions.

will make clear relationships to earlier writers. (In particular, see the above discussion relating my early diagrams and equations to the Bowen-Lindahl formulation.) I shall not bore the reader with irrelevant details of independent rediscoveries of doctrine that my ignorance of the available literature may have made necessary. Yet is it presumptuous to suggest that there does not exist in the present economic literature very much in the way of "conclusions and reasoning" that are "familiar"? Except for the writers I have cited, and the important unpublished thoughts of Dr. Richard A. Musgrave, there is much opaqueness in the literature. Much of what goes by the name of the "voluntary exchange theory of public finance" seems pure obfuscation.

(iii) Far from my formulation's being, as some have thought, a revival of the voluntary exchange theory—it is in fact an attempt to demonstrate how right Wicksell was to worry about the inherent political difficulty of ever getting men to reveal their tastes so as to attain the definable optimum. I may put the point most clearly in terms of the familiar tools of modern literary economics as follows:

Government supplies products jointly to many people. In ordinary market economics as you increase the number of sellers of a homogeneous product indefinitely, you pass from monopoly through indeterminate oligopoly and can hope to reach a determinate competitive equilibrium in the limit. It is sometimes thought that increasing the number of citizens who are jointly supplied public goods leads to a similar determination result. This is reasoning from an incorrect analogy. A truer analogy in private economics would be the case of a bilateral-monopoly supplier of joint products whose number of joint products—meat, horn, hide, and so on—is allowed to increase without number: such a process does not lead to a determinate equilibrium of the harmonistic type praised in the literature. My simple model is able to demonstrate this point—which does have "policy implications."

(iv) Admittedly, public expenditure and regulation proceed from considerations other than those emphasized in my models. Here are a few:

a. Taxes and expenditure aim at redistributing incomes. I am anxious to clear myself from the understandable suspicion that I am the type of liberal who would insist that all redistributions take place through tax policies and transfer expenditures: much public expenditure on education, hospitals, and so on, can be justified by the feasibility consideration that, even if these are not 100 percent efficient in avoiding avoidable deadweight loss, they may be better than the attainable imperfect tax alternatives.

b. Paternalistic policies are voted upon themselves by a democratic people because they do not regard the results from spontaneous market action as optimal. Education and forced paces of economic development are good examples of this.

c. Governments provide or regulate services that are incapable of being produced under the strict conditions of constant returns that go to characterize optimal self-regulating atomistic competition.

d. Myriad "generalized external economy and diseconomy" situations, where private pecuniary interest can be expected to deviate from social interests, provide obvious needs for government activity.

I am sure this list of basic considerations underlying government expenditure could be extended farther, including even areas where government probably ought not to operate from almost anyone's viewpoint.

(v) This brief list can end with the most important criticism put forth: "Is it factually true that most—or any!—of the functions of government can be properly fitted into your extreme category of a public good? Can education, the courts, public defense, highway programs, police and fire protection be put into this rigid category of a 'public good available to all'? In practically every one of these cases isn't there an element of variability in the benefit that can go to one citizen *at the expense* of some other citizens?"

To this criticism, I fully agree. And that is why in the present formulation I have insisted upon the polar nature of my category. However, to say that a thing is not located at the South Pole does not logically place it at the North Pole. To deny that most public functions fit into my extreme definition of a public good is not to grant that they satisfy the logically equally-extreme category of a private good. To say that your absence at a concert may contribute to my enjoyment is not to say that the elements of public services can be put into homogeneous additive packages capable of being optimally handled by the ordinary market calculus.

Indeed, I am rash enough to think that in almost every one of the legitimate functions of government that critics put forward there is to be found a blending of the extreme antipodal models. One might even venture the tentative suspicion that any function of government not possessing any trace of the defined public good (and no one of the related earlier described characteristics) ought to be carefully scrutinized to see whether it is truly a legitimate function of government.

(vi) Whether or not I have overstated the applicability of this one theoretical model to actual governmental functions, I believe I did not go far enough in claiming for it relevance to the vast area of decreasing costs that constitutes an important part of economic reality and of the welfare economics of monopolistic competition. I must leave to future research discussions of these vital issues.

Economic theory should add what it can to our understanding of governmental activity. I join with critics in hoping that its pretentious claims will not discourage other economic approaches, other contributions from neighboring disciplines, and concrete empirical investigations.

Groups and Public Goods

MANCUR OLSON, JR.

Mancur Olson, Jr., is Professor of Economics at the University of Maryland. This is an excerpt from his book, The Logic of Collective Choice.

The Purpose of Organization

Since most (though by no means all) of the action taken by or on behalf of groups of individuals is taken through organizations, it will be helpful to consider organizations in a general or theoretical way. The logical place to begin any systematic study of organizations is with their purpose. But there are all types and shapes and sizes of organizations, even of economic organizations, and there is then some question whether there is any single purpose that would be characteristic of organizations generally. One purpose that is nonetheless characteristic of most organizations, and surely of practically all organizations with an important economic aspect, is the furtherance of the interests of their members. That would seem obvious, at least from the economist's perspective. To be sure, some organizations may out of ignorance fail to further their members' interests, and others may be enticed into serving only the ends of the leadership. But organizations often perish if they do nothing to further the interests of their members, and this factor must severely limit the number of organizations that fail to serve their members.

The idea that organizations or associations exist to further the interests of their members is hardly novel, nor peculiar to economics; it goes back at least to Aristotle, who wrote, "Men journey together with a view to particular advantage, and by way of providing some particular thing needed for the purposes of life, and similarly the political association seems to have come together originally, and to continue in existence, for the sake of the *general* advantages it brings." More recently, Professor Leon Festinger, a social psychologist, pointed out that "the attraction of group membership

481

is not so much in sheer belonging, but rather in attaining something by means of this membership." The late Harold Laski, a political scientist, took it for granted that "associations exist to fulfill purposes which a group of men have in common."

The kinds of organizations that are the focus of this study are *expected* to further the interests of their members. Labor unions are expected to strive for higher wages and better working conditions for their members; farm organizations are expected to strive for favorable legislation for their members; cartels are expected to strive for higher prices for participating firms; the corporation is expected to further the interests of its stockholders; and the state is expected to further the common interests of its citizens (though in this nationalistic age the state often has interests and ambitions apart from those of its citizens).

Notice that the interests that all of these diverse types of organizations are expected to further are for the most part *common* interests: the union members' common interest in higher wages, the farmers' common interest in favorable legislation, the cartel members' common interest in higher prices, the stockholders' common interest in higher dividends and stock prices, the citizens' common interest in good government. It is not an accident that the diverse types of organizations listed are all supposed to work primarily for the *common* interests of their members. Purely personal or individual interests can be advanced, and usually advanced most efficiently, by individual, unorganized action. There is obviously no purpose in having an organization when individual, unorganized action can serve the interests of the individual as well as or better than an organization; there would, for example, be no point in forming an organization simply to play solitaire. But when a number of individuals have a common or collective interest—when they share a single purpose or objective—individual, unorganized action (as we shall soon see) will either not be able to advance that common interest at all, or will not be able to advance that interest adequately. Organizations can therefore perform a function when there are common or group interests, and though organizations often also serve purely personal, individual interests, their characteristic and primary function is to advance the common interests of groups of individuals.

The assumption that organizations typically exist to further the common interests of groups of people is implicit in most of the literature about organizations, and two of the writers already cited make this assumption explicit: Harold Laski emphasized that organizations exist to achieve purposes or interests which "a group of men have in common," and Aristotle apparently had a similar notion in mind when he argued that political associations are created and maintained because of the "general advantages" they bring. R. M. MacIver also made this point explicitly when he said that "every organization presupposes an interest which its members all share."

Even when unorganized groups are discussed, at least in treatments of "pressure groups" and "group theory," the word "group" is used in such a way that it means "a number of individuals with a common interest." It would of course be reasonable to label even a number of people selected at random (and thus without any common interest or unifying characteristic) as a "group"; but most discussions of group behavior seem to deal mainly with groups that do have common interests. As Arthur Bentley, the founder of the "group theory" of modern political science, put it, "there is no group without its interest." The social psychologist Raymond Cattell was equally explicit, and stated that "every group has its interest." This is also the way the word "group" will be used here.

Just as those who belong to an organization or a group can be presumed to have a common interest, so they obviously also have purely individual interests, different from those of the others in the organization or group. All of the members of a labor union, for example, have a common interest in higher wages, but at the same time each worker has a unique interest in his personal income, which depends not only on the rate of wages but also on the length of time that he works.

Public Goods and Large Groups

The combination of individual interests and common interests in an organization suggests an analogy with a competitive market. The firms in a perfectly competitive industry, for example, have a common interest in a higher price for the industry's product. Since a uniform price must prevail in such a market, a firm cannot expect a higher price for itself unless all of the other firms in the industry also have this higher price. But a firm in a competitive market also has an interest in selling as much as it can, until the cost of producing another unit exceeds the price of that unit. In this there is no common interest; each firm's interest is directly opposed to that of every other firm, for the more other firms sell, the lower the price and income for any given firm. In short, while all firms have a common interest in a higher price, they have antagonistic interests where output is concerned. This can be illustrated with a simple supply-and-demand model. For the sake of a simple argument, assume that a perfectly competitive industry is momentarily in a disequilibrium position, with price exceeding marginal cost for all firms at their present output. Suppose, too, that all of the adjustments will be made by the firms already in the industry rather than by new entrants, and that the industry is on an inelastic portion of its demand curve. Since price exceeds marginal cost for all firms, output will increase. But as all firms increase production, the price falls; indeed, since the industry demand curve is by assumption inelastic, the total revenue of the industry will decline. Apparently each firm finds that with price exceeding marginal cost, it pays to increase its output, but the result is that each firm gets a smaller profit. Some economists in an earlier day may have questioned this result, but the fact that profit-maximizing firms in a perfectly competitive industry can act contrary to their interests as a group is now widely understood and accepted. A group of profit-maximizing firms can act to reduce their aggregate profits because in perfect competition each firm is, by definition, so small that it can ignore the effect of its output on price. Each firm finds it to its advantage to increase output to the point where marginal cost equals price and to ignore the effects of its extra output on the position of the industry. It is true that the net result is that all firms are worse off, but this does not mean that every firm has not maximized its profits. If a firm, foreseeing the fall in price resulting from the increase in industry output, were to restrict its own output, it would lose more than ever, for its price would fall quite as much in any case and it would have a smaller output as well. A firm in a perfectly competitive market gets only a small part of the benefit (or a small share of the industry's extra revenue) resulting from a reduction in that firm's output.

For these reasons it is now generally understood that if the firms in an industry are maximizing profits, the profits for the industry as a whole will be less than they might otherwise be. And almost everyone would agree that this theoretical conclusion fits the facts for markets characterized by pure competition. The important point is that this is true because, though all the firms have a common interest in a higher price for the industry's product, it is in the interest of each firm that the other firms pay the cost—in terms of the necessary reduction in output—needed to obtain a higher price.

About the only thing that keeps prices from falling in accordance with the process just described in perfectly competitive markets is outside intervention. Government price supports, tariffs, cartel agreements, and the like may keep the firms in a competitive market from acting contrary to their interests. Such aid or intervention is quite common. It is then important to ask how it comes about. How does a competitive industry obtain government assistance in maintaining the price of its product?

Consider a hypothetical, competitive industry, and suppose that most of the producers in that industry desire a tariff, a price-support program, or some other government intervention to increase the price for their product. To obtain any such assistance from the government, the producers in this industry will presumably have to organize a lobbying organization; they will have to become an active pressure group. This lobbying organization may have to conduct a considerable campaign. If significant resistance is encountered, a great amount of money will be required. Public relations experts will be needed to influence the newspapers, and some advertising may be necessary. Professional organizers will probably be needed to organize "spontaneous grass roots" meetings among the distressed producers in the industry, and to get those in the industry to write letters to their congressmen. The campaign for the government assistance will take the time of some of the producers in the industry, as well as their money.

There is a striking parallel between the problem the perfectly competitive industry faces as it strives to obtain government assistance, and the problem it faces in the marketplace when the firms increase output and bring about a fall in price. *Just as it was not rational for a particular producer to restrict his output in order that there might be a higher price for the product of his industry, so it would not be rational for him to sacrifice his time and money to support a lobbying organization to obtain government assistance for the industry. In neither case would it be in the interest of the individual producer to assume any of the costs himself. A lobbying organization, or indeed a labor union or any other organization, working in the interest of a large group of firms or workers in some industry, would get no assistance from the rational, self-interested individuals in that industry.* This would be true even if everyone in the industry were absolutely convinced that the proposed program was in their interest (though in fact some might think otherwise and make the organization's task yet more difficult).

Although the lobbying organization is only one example of the logical analogy between the organization and the market, it is of some practical importance. There are many powerful and well-financed lobbies with mass support in existence now, but these lobbying organizations do not get that support because of their legislative achievements. The most powerful lobbying organizations now obtain their funds and their following for other reasons, as later parts of this study will show.

Some critics may argue that the rational person will, indeed, support a large organization, like a lobbying organization, that works in his interest, because he knows that if he does not, others will not do so either, and then the organization will fail, and he will be without the benefit that the organization could have provided. This argument shows the need for the analogy with the perfectly competitive market. For it would be quite as reasonable to argue that prices will never fall below the levels a monopoly would have charged in a perfectly competitive market, because if one firm increased its output, other firms would also, and the price would fall; but each firm could foresee this, so it would not start a chain of price-destroying increases in output. In fact, it does not work out this way in a competitive market; nor in a large organization. When the number of firms involved is large, no one will notice the effect on price if one firm increases its output, and so no one will change his plans because of it. Similarly, in a large organization, the loss of one dues payer will not noticeably increase the burden for any other one dues payer, and so a rational person would not believe that if he were to withdraw from an organization he would drive others to do so.

The foregoing argument must at the least have some relevance to economic organizations that are mainly means through which individuals attempt to obtain the same things they obtain through their activities in the market. Labor unions, for example, are organizations through which workers strive to get the same things they get with their individual efforts in the market—higher wages, better working conditions, and the like. It would be strange indeed if the workers did not confront some of the same problems in the union that they meet in the market, since their efforts in both places have some of the same purposes.

However similar the purposes may be, critics may object that attitudes in organizations are not at all like those in markets. In organizations, an emotional or ideological element is often also involved. Does this make the argument offered here practically irrelevant?

A most important type of organization—the national state—will serve to test this objection. Patriotism is probably the strongest non-economic motive for organizational allegiance in modern times. This age is sometimes called the age of nationalism. Many nations draw additional strength and unity from some powerful ideology, such as democracy or communism, as well as from a common religion, language, or cultural inheritance. The state not only has many such powerful sources of support; it also is very important economically. Almost any government is economically beneficial to its citizens, in that the law and order it provides is a prerequisite of all civilized economic activity. But despite the force of patriotism, the appeal of the national ideology, the bond of a common culture, and the indispensability of the system of law and order, no major state in modern history has been able to support itself through voluntary dues or contributions. Philanthropic contributions are not even a significant source of revenue for most countries. Taxes, *compulsory* payments by definition, are needed. Indeed, as the old saying indicates, their necessity is as certain as death itself.

If the state, with all of the emotional resources at its command, cannot finance its most basic and vital activities without resort to compulsion, it would seem that large private organizations might also have difficulty in getting the individuals in the groups whose interests they attempt to advance to make the necessary contributions voluntarily.

The reason the state cannot survive on voluntary dues or payments, but must rely on taxation, is that the most fundamental services a nation-state provides are, in one important respect, like the higher price in a competitive market: they must be available to everyone if they are available to anyone. The basic and most elementary goods or services provided by government, like defense and police protection, and the system of law and order generally, are such that they go to everyone or practically everyone in the nation. It would obviously not be feasible, if indeed it were possible, to deny the protection provided by the military services, the police, and the courts to those who did not voluntarily pay their share of the costs of government, and taxation is accordingly necessary. The common or collective benefits provided by governments are usually called "public goods" by economists, and the concept of public goods is one of the oldest and most important ideas in the study of public finance. A common, collective, or public good is here defined as any good such that, if any person X_i in a group $X_1, \ldots, X_i, \ldots, X_n$ consumes it, it cannot feasibly be withheld from the others in that group. In other words, those who do not purchase or pay for any of the public or collective good cannot be excluded or kept from sharing in the consumption of the good, as they can where noncollective goods are concerned.

Students of public finance have, however, neglected the fact that *the achievement of any common goal or the satisfaction of any common interest means that a public or collective good has been provided for that group.* The very fact that a goal or purpose is *common* to a group means that no one in the group is excluded from the benefit or satisfaction brought about by its achievement. As the opening paragraphs of this chapter indicated, almost all groups and organizations have the purpose of serving the common interests of their members. As R. M. MacIver puts it, "Persons . . . have common interests in the degree to which they participate in a cause . . . which indivisibly embraces them all." It is of the essence of an organization that it provides an inseparable, generalized benefit. It follows that the provision of public or collective goods is the fundamental function of organizations generally. A state is first of all an organization that provides public goods for its members, the citizens; and other types of organizations similarly provide collective goods for their members.

And just as a state cannot support itself by voluntary contributions, or by selling its basic services on the market, neither can other large organizations support themselves without providing some sanction, or some attraction distinct from the public good itself, that will lead individuals to help bear the burdens of maintaining the organization. The individual member of the typical large organization is in a position analogous to that of the firm in a perfectly competitive market, or the taxpayer in the state: his own efforts will not have a noticeable effect on the situation of his organization, and he can enjoy any improvements brought about by others whether or not he has worked in support of his organization.

There is no suggestion here that states or other organizations provide *only* public or collective goods. Governments often provide noncollective goods like electric power, for example, and they usually sell such goods on the market much as private firms would do. Moreover, as later parts of this study will argue, large organizations that are not able to make membership compulsory *must also* provide some noncollective goods in order to give potential members an incentive to join. Still, collective goods are the characteristic organizational goods, for ordinary noncollective goods can always be provided by individual action, and only where common purposes or collective goods are concerned is organization or group action ever indispensable.

Provision of Public Goods by Small Groups

. . . Certain small groups can provide themselves with collective goods without relying on coercion or any positive inducements apart from the collective good itself. This is because in some small groups each of the members, or at least one of them, will find that his personal gain from having the collective good exceeds the total cost of providing some amount of that collective good; there are members who would be better off if the collective good were provided, even if they had to pay the entire cost of providing it themselves, than they would be if it were not provided. In such situations there is a presumption that the collective good will be provided. Such a situation will exist only when the benefit to the group from having the collective good exceeds the total cost by more than it exceeds the gain to one or more individuals in the group. Thus, in a very small group, where each members gets a substantial proportion of the total gain simply because there are few others in the group, a collective good can often be provided by the voluntary, self-interested action of the members of the group. In smaller groups marked by considerable degrees of inequality—that is, in groups of members of unequal "size" or extent of interest in the collective good—there is the greatest likelihood that a collective good will be provided; for the greater the interest in the collective good of any single member, the greater the likelihood that that member will get such a significant proportion of the total benefit from the collective good that he will gain from seeing that the good is provided, even if he has to pay all of the cost himself.

Even in the smallest groups, however, the collective good will not ordinarily be provided on an optimal scale. That is to say, the members of the group will not provide as much of the good as it would be in their common interest to provide. Only certain special institutional arrangements will give the individual members an incentive to purchase the amounts of the collective good that would add up to the amount that would be in the best interest of the group as a whole. This tendency toward suboptimality is due to the fact that a collective good is, by definition, such that other individuals in the group cannot be kept from consuming it once any individual in the group has provided it for himself. Since an individual member thus gets only part of the benefit of any expenditure he makes to obtain more of the collective good, he will discontinue his purchase of the collective good before the optimal amount for the group as a whole has been obtained. In addition, the amounts of the collective good that a member of the group receives free from other members will further reduce his incentive to provide more of that good at his own expense. Accordingly, *the larger the group, the farther it will fall short of providing an optimal amount of a collective good.*

This suboptimality or inefficiency will be somewhat less serious in groups composed of members of greatly different size or interest in the collective good. In such unequal groups, on the other hand, there is a tendency toward an arbitrary sharing of the burden of providing the collective good. The largest member, the member who would on his own provide the largest amount of the collective good, bears a disproportionate share of the burden of providing the collective good. The smaller member by definition gets a smaller fraction of the benefit of any amount of the collective good he provides than a larger member, and therefore has less incentive to provide additional amounts of the collective good. Once a smaller member has the amount of the collective good he gets free from the largest member, he has more than he would have purchased for himself, and has no incentive to obtain any of the collective good at his own expense. In small groups with common interests there is accordingly *a surprising tendency for the "exploitation" of the great by the small.*

The argument that small groups providing themselves with collective goods tend to provide suboptimal quantities of these goods, and that the burdens of providing them are borne in an arbitrary and disproportionate way, does not hold in all logically possible situations. Certain institutional or procedural arrangements can lead to different outcomes. The subject cannot be analyzed adequately in any brief discussion. For this reason, and because the main focus of this book is on large groups, many of the complexities of small-group behavior have been neglected in this study. An argument of the kind just outlined could, however, fit some important practical situations rather well, and may serve the purpose of suggesting that a more detailed analysis of the kind outlined above could help to explain the apparent tendency for large countries to bear disproportionate shares of the burdens of multinational organizations, like the United Nations and NATO, and could help to explain some of the popularity of neutralism among smaller countries. Such an analysis would also tend to explain the continual complaints that international organizations and alliances are not given adequate (optimal) amounts of resources. It would also suggest that neighboring local governments in metropolitan areas that provide collective goods (like commuter roads and education) that benefit individuals in two or more local government jurisdictions would tend to provide inadequate amounts of these services, and that the largest local government (e.g., the one representing the central city) would bear disproportionate shares of the burdens of providing them. An analysis of the foregoing type might, finally, provide some additional insight into the phenomenon of price leadership, and particularly the possible disadvantages involved in being the largest firm in an industry.

The most important single point about small groups in the present context, however, is that they may very well be able to provide themselves with a collective good simply because of the attraction of the collective good to the individual members. In this, small groups differ from larger ones. The larger a group is, the farther it will fall short of obtaining an optimal supply of any collective good, and the less likely that it will act to obtain even a minimal amount of such a good. In short, the larger the group, the less it will further its common interests.

The Organization of Economic Activity: Issues Pertinent to the Choice of Market Versus Nonmarket Allocation

KENNETH J. ARROW

Kenneth Arrow is Professor of Economics at Stanford University. This paper was published by the Joint Economic Committee of Congress in 1969.

Introduction

The concept of public goods has been developed through a process of successive refinement over a long period of time. Yet surprisingly enough there does not seem to exist anywhere in the literature a clear general definition of this concept or the more general one of "externality." The accounts given are usually either very general and discursive, difficult of interpretation in specific contexts, or else they are rigorous accounts of very special situations. What exactly is the relation between externalities and such concepts as "appropriability" or "exclusion"?

Also, there is considerable ambiguity in the purpose of the analysis of externalities. The best developed part of the theory relates to only a single question: the statement of a set of conditions, as weak as possible, which insure that a competitive equilibrium exists and is Pareto efficient. Then the denial of any of these hypotheses is presumably a sufficient condition for considering resort to non-market channels of resource allocation—usually thought of as Government expenditures, taxes, and subsidies.

At a second level the analysis of externalities should lead to criteria for nonmarket allocation. We are tempted to set forth these criteria in terms analogous to the profit-and-loss statements of private business; in this form, we are led to benefit-cost analysis. There are, moreover, two possible aims for benefit-cost analysis; one, more ambitious but theoretically simpler, is specification of the nonmarket actions which will restore Pareto efficiency; the second involves the recognition that the instruments available to the Government or other nonmarket forces are scarce resources for one reason or another, so that all that can be achieved is a "second-best."

Other concepts that seem to cluster closely to the concept of public goods are those of "increasing returns" and "market failure." These are related to Pareto inefficiency on the one hand and to the existence and optimality of competitive equilibrium on the other; sometimes the discussions in the literature do not adequately distinguish these two aspects. I contend that market failure is a more general category than externality; and both differ from increasing returns in a basic sense, since market failures in general and externalities in particular are relative to the mode of economic organization, while increasing returns are essentially a technological phenomenon.

Current writing has helped bring out the point that market failure is not absolute; it is better to consider a broader category, that of transaction costs, which in general impede and in particular cases completely block the formation of markets. It is usually though not always emphasized that transaction costs are costs of running the economic system. An incentive for vertical integration is replacement of the costs of buying and selling on the market by the costs of intrafirm transfers; the existence of vertical integration may suggest that the costs of operating competitive markets are not zero, as is usually assumed in our theoretical analysis.

Monetary theory, unlike value theory, is heavily dependent on the assumption of positive transaction costs; the recurrent complaint about the difficulty of integrating these two branches of theory is certainly governed by the contradictory assumptions made about transaction costs. The creation of money is in many respects an example of a public good.

The identification of transaction costs in different contexts and under different systems of resource allocation should be a major item on the research agenda of the theory of public goods and indeed of the theory of resource allocation in general. Only the most rudimentary suggestions are made here. The "exclusion principle" is a limiting case of one kind of transaction cost, but another type, the costliness of the information needed to enter and participate in any market, has been little remarked. Information is closely related on the one hand to communication and on the other to uncertainty.

Given the existence of Pareto inefficiency in a free market equilibrium, there is a pressure in the market to overcome it by some sort of departure from the free market; i.e., some form of collective action. This need not be undertaken by the Government. I suggest that in fact there is a wide variety of social institutions, in particular generally accepted social norms of behavior, which serve in some means as compensation for failure or limitation of the market, though each in turn involves transaction costs of its own. The question also arises how the behavior of individual economic agents in a social institution (especially in voting) is related to their behavior on the market. A good deal of theoretical literature has arisen in recent years which seeks to describe political behavior as analogous to economic, and we may hope for a general theory of socioeconomic equilibrium. But it must always be kept in mind that the contexts of choice are radically different, particularly when the hypotheses of perfectly costless action and information are relaxed. It is not accidental that economic analysis has been successful only in certain limited areas.

Competitive Equilibrium and Pareto Efficiency

A quick review of the familiar theorems on the role of perfectly competitive equilibrium in the efficient allocation of resources will be useful. Perfectly competitive equilibrium has its usual meaning: households, possessed of initial resources, including possibly claims to the profits of firms, choose consumption bundles to maximize utility at a given set of prices; firms choose production bundles so as to maximize profits at the same set of prices; the chosen production and consumption bundles must be consistent with each other in the sense that aggregate production plus initial resources must equal aggregate consumption. The key points in the definition are the parametric role of the prices for each individual and the identity of prices for all individuals. Implicit are the assumptions that all prices can be known by all individuals and that the act of charging prices is not itself a consumer of resources.

A number of additional assumptions are made at different points in the theory of equilibrium, but most are clearly factually valid in the usual contexts and need not be mentioned. The two hypotheses frequently not valid are (C), the convexity of household indifference maps and firm production possibility sets, and (M), the universality of markets. While the exact meaning of the last assumption will be explored later at some length, for the present purposes we mean that the consumption bundle which determines the utility of an individual is the same as that which he purchases at given prices subject to his budget constraint, and that the set of production bundles among which a firm chooses is a given range independent of decisions made by other agents in the economy.

The relations between Pareto efficiency and competitive equilibrium are set forth in the following two theorems:

1. *If (M) holds, a competitive equilibrium is Pareto-efficient.* This theorem is true even if (C) does not hold.

2. *If (C) and (M) hold, then any Pareto-efficient allocation can be*

achieved as a competitive equilibrium by a suitable reallocation of initial resources.

When the assumptions of proposition 2 are valid, then the case for the competitive price system is strongest. Any complaints about its operation can be reduced to complaints about the distribution of income, which should then be rectified by lump-sum transfers. Of course, as Pareto already emphasized, the proposition provides no basis for accepting the results of the market in the absence of accepted levels of income equality.

The central role of competitive equilibrium both as a normative guide and as at least partially descriptive of the real world raises an analytically difficult question: does a competitive equilibrium necessarily exist?

3. *If (C) holds, then there exists a competitive equilibrium.* This theorem is true even if (M) does not hold.

If both (C) and (M) hold, we have a fairly complete and simple picture of the achievement of desirable goals, subject always to the major qualification of the achievement of a desirable income distribution. The price system itself determines the income distribution only in the sense of preserving the status quo. Even if costless lump-sum transfers are possible, there is needed a collective mechanism reallocating income if the status quo is not regarded as satisfactory.

Of course (C) is not a necessary condition for the existence of a competitive equilibrium, only a sufficient one. From proposition 1, it is possible to have an equilibrium and therefore efficient allocation without convexity (when (M) holds). However, in view of the central role of (C) in these theorems, the implications of relaxing this hypothesis have been examined intensively in recent years by Farrell (1959), Rothenberg (1960), Aumann (1966), and Starr (1969). Their conclusions may be summarized as follows: Let (C') be the weakened convexity assumption that there are no indivisibilities large relative to the economy.

4. *Propositions 2 and 3 remain approximately true if (C) is replaced by (C').*

Thus, the only nonconvexities that are important for the present purposes are increasing returns over a range large relative to the economy. In those circumstances, a competitive equilibrium cannot exist.

The price system, for all its virtues, is only one conceivable form of arranging trade, even in a system of private property. Bargaining can assume extremely general forms. Under the assumptions (C') and (M), we are assured that not everyone can be made better off by a bargain not derived from the price system: but the question arises whether some members of the economy will not find it in their interest and within their power to depart from the perfectly competitive price system. For example, both Knight (1921, pp. 190–194) and Samuelson (1967, p. 120) have noted that it would pay all the firms in a given industry to form a monopoly. But in fact it can be argued that unrestricted bargaining can only settle down to a resource allocation which could also be achieved as a perfectly competitive equilibrium, at least if the bargaining itself is costless and each agent is small compared to the entire economy. This line of argument originated with Edgeworth (1881, pp. 20–43) and has been developed recently by Shubik (1959), Debreu and Scarf (1963), and Aumann (1964).

More precisely, it is easy to show:

5. *If* (M) *holds and a competitive equilibrium prevails, then no set of economic agents will find any resource allocation which they can accomplish by themselves* (*without trade with the other agents*) *which they will all prefer to that prevailing under the equilibrium.*

Proposition 5 holds for any number of agents. A deeper proposition is the following converse:

6. *If* (C′) *and* (M) *hold, and if the resources of any economic agent are small compared with the total of the economy, then, given any allocation not approximately achievable as a competitive equilibrium, there will be some set of agents and some resource allocation they can achieve without any trade with others which each one will prefer to the given allocation.*

These two propositions, taken together, strongly suggest that when all the relevant hypotheses hold, (*a*) a competitive equilibrium, if achieved, will not be upset by bargaining even if permitted, and (*b*) for any bargain not achievable by a competitive equilibrium there is a set of agents who would benefit by change to another bargain which they have the full power to enforce.

The argument that a set of firms can form a monopoly overlooks the possibility that the consumers can also form a coalition, threaten not to buy, and seek mutually advantageous deals with a subset of the firms; such deals are possible since the monopoly allocation violates some marginal equivalences.

In real life, monopolizing cartels are possible for a reason not so far introduced into the analysis: bargaining costs between producers and consumers are high, those among producers low—a point made most emphatically by Adam Smith (1937, p. 128); "People of the same trade seldom meet together, even for merriment or diversion, but the conversation ends in a conspiracy against the public, or in some contrivance to raise prices." *It is not the presence of bargaining costs per se but their bias that is relevant.* If all bargaining costs are high, but competitive pricing and the markets are cheap, then we expect the perfectly competitive equilibrium to obtain, yielding an allocation identical with that under costless bargaining. But if bargaining costs are biased, then some bargains other than the competitive equilibrium can be arrived at which will not be upset by still other bargains if the latter but not the former are costly.

Finally, in this review of the elements of competitive equilibrium theory, let me repeat the obvious and well-known fact that in a world where time is relevant, the commodities which enter into the equilibrium system include those with future dates. In fact, the bulk of meaningful future transactions cannot be carried out on any existing present market, so that assumption (M), the universality of markets, is not valid.

Imperfectly Competitive Equilibrium

There is no accepted and well-worked out theory corresponding to the title of this section. From the previous section it is clear that such a theory is forcibly needed in the presence of increasing returns on a scale large relative to the economy (hereafter, the phrase "increasing returns" will always be understood to include the prepositional phrase just employed), and is superfluous in its absence.

There are two approaches to a theory of general equilibrium in an imperfectly competitive environment; most writers who touch on public policy questions implicitly accept one or the other of these prototheories without always recognizing that they have made a choice. One assumes all transactions are made according to the price system, i.e., the same price is charged for all units of the same commodity; this is the *monopolistic competition* approach. The alternative approach assumes unrestricted bargaining; this is the *game theory* approach. The first might be deemed appropriate if the costs of bargaining are high relative to the costs of ordinary pricing, while the second assumes costless bargaining.

It cannot be too strongly emphasized that neither approach is, at the present stage, a fully developed theory, and it is misleading to state any implications about the working of these systems. Chamberlin's (1933), purpose was certainly the incorporation of monopoly into a general equilibrium system, together with a view that the commodity space should be viewed as infinite-dimensional, with the possibility of arbitrarily close substitutes in consumption; Triffin (1941) emphasized this aspect, but the only completely worked-out model of general monopolistic equilibrium is that of Negishi, (1960–61), and he made the problem manageable by regarding the demand functions facing the monopolists as those preceived by them, with only loose relations to reality. Such a theory would have little in the way of deducible implications (unless there were a supplementary psychological theory to explain the perceptions of demand functions) and certainly no clear welfare implications.

Of course, whatever a monopolistic competitive equilibrium means, it must imply inefficiency in the Pareto sense if there are substantial increasing returns. For a firm can always make zero profits by not existing; hence, if it operates, price must at least equal average cost which is greater than marginal cost. Kaldor (1935) and Demsetz (1964), however, have argued that in the "large numbers" case, the welfare loss may be supposed very small. I would conjecture that this conclusion is true, but it is not rigorously established, and indeed the model has never been formulated in adequate detail to discuss it properly.

With unrestricted bargaining it is usual to conclude that the equilibrium, whatever it may be, must be Pareto-efficient for, by definition, it is in the interest of all economic agents to switch from a Pareto-inefficient allocation to a suitably chosen Pareto-efficient one. This argument seems plausible, but is not easy to evaluate in the absence of a generally accepted concept of solution for game theory. Edgeworth (1881) held the outcome of bargaining to be indeterminate within limits, and von Neumann and Morgenstern (1944) have generalized this conclusion. But when there is indeterminacy, there is no natural or compelling point on the Pareto frontier at which to arrive. It is certainly a matter of common observation, perhaps most especially in the field of international relations, that mutually advantageous agreements are not arrived at because each party is seeking to engross as much as possible of the common gain for itself. In economic affairs a frequently cited illustration is the assembly of land parcels for large industrial or residential enterprises whose value (net of complementary costs) exceeds the total value of the land in its present uses. Then each owner of a small parcel whose acquisition is essential to the execution of the enterprise can demand the entire net benefit. An agreement may never be reached or may be long delayed; at positive discount rates even the latter outcome is not Pareto-efficient. It is to avoid such losses that the coercive powers of the state are invoked by condemnation proceedings.

There is, however, another tradition within game theory which argues for the determinacy of the outcome of bargaining. Zeuthen (1930, ch. IV) had early propounded one such solution. After von Neumann and Morgenstern, Nash (1950, 1953) offered a solution, which Harsanyi (1956) later showed to be identical with that of Zeuthen. Nash's analysis of bargaining has been extended by Harsanyi (1959, 1963, 1966); variant but related approaches have been studied by Shapley (1953) and Selten (1964). The analysis has proceeded at a very general level, and its specific application to resource allocation has yet to be spelled out. In the simplest situation, bargaining between two individuals who can cooperate but cannot injure each other except by withholding cooperation and who can freely transfer benefits between them, the conclusion of the theories is the achievement of a joint optimum followed by equal splitting of the benefits of cooperation net of the amounts each bargainer could obtain without cooperation. Thus, in a land assembly, if the participation of all parcels is essential, each owner receives the value of his parcel in its present (or best alternative) use plus an equal share of the net benefits of the project. Without further analytic and empirical work it is not easy to judge the acceptability of this conclusion.

An elementary example may bring out the ambiguities of allocation with unrestricted bargaining. Since the perfectly competitive equilibrium theory is satisfactory (in the absence of marketing failures and costs) when increasing returns on a substantial scale are absent, the problem of imperfectly competitive equilibrium arises only when substantial increasing returns are present. In effect, then, there are small numbers of effective participants. Suppose there are only three agents. Production is assumed to take place in coalitions; the output of each coalition depends only on the number of members in it. If the average output of the members of a coalition does not increase with the number of members, then the equilibrium outcome is the perfectly competitive one, where each agent produces by himself and consumes his own product. If the average output of a coalition increases with the number of members, then clearly production will take place in the three-member coalition; but the allocation is not determined by the threats of individuals to leave the coalition and go on their own, nor by threats of pairs to form coalitions (for any one member can claim more than one-third of the total output and still leave the other two more than they could produce without him). But perhaps the most interesting case is that where the average output is higher for two individuals than for either one or three; i.e., increasing returns followed by diminishing returns. For definiteness, suppose that one agent can produce one unit, two agents can produce four units, and all three together can produce five units. Clearly, Pareto efficiency requires the joint productive activity of all three. Since each pair can receive four units by leaving the third agent out, it would appear that each pair must receive at least four units. But this implies that the total allocated to keep the three-man coalition together must be at least six, more than is available for distribution.

(Theories of the Nash-Harsanyi type arrive at solutions in cases like this by assuming that the economic agents foresee these possible instabilities and recognize that any attempt by any pair to break away from the total coalition can itself be overturned. If each is rational and assumes the others are equally rational, then they recognize, in the completely symmetric situation of the example, that only a symmetric allocation is possible.)

The point of this lengthy discussion of possible game theory concepts of equilibrium is to suggest caution in accepting the proposition that bargaining costs alone prevent the achievement of Pareto efficiency in the presence of increasing returns, as Buchanan and Tullock (1962, p. 88) and Demsetz (1968, p. 61) assert.

Risk and Information

The possible types of equilibria discussed in the previous two sections are not, in principle, altered in nature by the presence of risk. If an economic agent is uncertain as to which of several different states of the world will obtain, he can make contracts contingent on the occurrence of possible states. The real-world counterparts of these theoretical contingent contracts include insurance policies and common stocks. With these markets for contingent contracts, a competitive equilibrium will arise under the same general hypotheses as in the absence of uncertainty. It is not even necessary that the economic agents agree on the probability distribution for the unknown state of the world; each may have his own subjective probabilities.

Further, the resulting allocation is Pareto-efficient if the utility of each individual is identified as his expected utility according to his own subjective probability distribution.

But, as Radner (1968) has pointed out, there is more to the story. Whenever we have uncertainty we have the possibility of information and, of course, also the possibility of its absence. No contingent contract can be made if, at the time of execution, either of the contracting parties does not know whether the specified contingency has occurred or not. This principle eliminates a much larger number of opportunities for mutually favorable exchanges than might perhaps be supposed at first glance. A simple case is that known in insurance literature as "adverse selection." Suppose, for example, there are two types of individuals, A and B, with different life expectancies, but the insurance company has no way to distinguish the two; it cannot in fact identify the present state of the world in all its relevant aspects. The optimal allocation of resources under uncertainty would require separate insurance policies for the two types, but these are clearly impossible. Suppose further that each individual knows which type he belongs to. The company might charge a rate based on the probability of death in the two types together, but the insurance buyers in the two types will respond differently; those in the type with the more favorable experience, say A, will buy less insurance than those in type B, other things (income and risk aversion) being equal. The insurance company's experience will be less favorable than it intended, and it will have to raise its rates. An equilibrium rate will be reached which is, in general, between those corresponding to types A and B separately but closer to the latter. Such an insurance arrangement is, of course, not Pareto-efficient. It is not *a priori* obvious in general that this free market arrangement is superior to compulsory insurance even though the latter is also not Pareto-efficient because it typically disregards individual differences in risk aversion.

As the above example shows, the critical impact of information on the optimal allocation of risk bearing is not merely its presence or absence but its inequality among economic agents. If neither side knew which type the insured belonged to, then the final allocation would be Pareto-efficient if it were considered that the two types were indistinguishable; but in the above example the market allocation is Pareto-efficient neither with the types regarded as indistinguishable nor with them regarded as distinguishable.

There is no particular case of the effect of differential information on the workings of the market economy (or indeed any complex economy) which is so important as to deserve special comment: one agent can observe the joint effects of the unknown state of the world and of decisions by another economic agent, but not the state or the decision separately. This case is known in the insurance literature as "moral hazard," but because the insurance examples are only a small fraction of all the illustrations of this case and because, as Pauly (1968) has argued, the adjective "moral" is not always appropriate, the case will be referred to here as the "confounding of risks and decisions." An insurance company may easily observe that a fire has occurred but cannot, without special investigation, know whether the fire was due to causes exogenous to the insured or to decisions of his (arson, or at least carelessness). In general, any system which, in effect, insures against adverse final outcomes automatically reduces the incentives to good decisionmaking.

In these circumstances there are two extreme possibilities (with all intermediate possibilities being present): full protection against uncertainty of final outcome (e.g., cost-plus contracts for production or research) or absence of protection against uncertainty of final outcome (the one-person firm; the admiral shot for cowardice "pour encourager les autres"). Both policies produce inefficiency, though for different reasons. In the first, the incentive to good decisionmaking is dulled for obvious reasons; in the second, the functions of control and risk bearing must be united, whereas specialization in these functions may be more efficient for the workings of the system.

The relations between principals and agents (e.g., patients and physicians, owners and managers) further illustrate the confounding of risks and decisions. In the professions in particular they also illustrate the point to be emphasized later: that ethical standards may to a certain extent overcome the possible Pareto inefficiencies.

So far we have taken the information structure as given. But the fact that particular information structures give rise to Pareto inefficiency means that there is an economic value in transmitting information from one agent to another, as well as in the creation of new information. J. Marschak (1968), Hirshleifer (unpublished), and others have begun the study of the economics of information, but the whole subject is in its infancy. Only a few remarks relevant to our present purpose will be made here.

(1) As both communications engineering and psychology suggest, the transmission of information is not costless. Any professor who has tried to transmit some will be painfully aware of the resources he has expended and, perhaps more poignantly, of the difficulties students have in understanding. The physical costs of transmission may be low, though probably not negligible, as any book buyer knows; but the "coding" of the information for transmission and the limited channel capacity of the recipients are major costs.

(2) The costs of transmitting information vary with both the type of information transmitted and the recipient and sender. The first point implies a preference for inexpensive information, a point stressed in oligopolistic contexts by Kaysen (1949, pp. 294–295) and in other bargaining contexts by Schelling (1957). The second point is relevant to the value of education and to difficulties of transmission across cultural boundaries (so that production functions can differ so much across countries).

(3) Because the costs of transmission are nonnegligible, even situations which are basically certain become uncertain for the individual; the typical

economic agent simply cannot acquire in a meaningful sense the knowledge of all possible prices, even where they are each somewhere available.
Markets are thus costly to use, and therefore the multiplication of markets,
as for contingent claims as suggested above, becomes inhibited.

Externalities Illustrated

After this long excursus into the present state of the theory of equilibrium and optimality it is time to discuss some of the standard concepts of
externality, market failure, and public goods generally. The clarification of
these concepts is a long historical process, not yet concluded, in which the
classic contributions of Knight (1924), Young (1913 pp. 676–684), and
Robertson (1924) have in more recent times been enriched by those of
Meade (1952), Scitovsky (1954), Coase (1960), Buchanan and Stubblebine (1962), and Demsetz (1966). The concept of externality and the
extent to which it causes nonoptimal market behavior will be discussed
here in terms of a simple model.

Consider a pure exchange economy. Let x_{ik} be the amount of the kth
commodity consumed by the ith individual ($i = 1, \ldots, n; k = 1, \ldots,$
m) and x_k be the amount of the kth commodity available. Suppose in general that the utility of the ith individual is a function of the consumption
of all individuals (not all types of consumption for all individuals need
actually enter into any given individual's utility function); the utility of
the ith individual is $U_i(x_{11}, \ldots, x_{mn})$. We have the obvious constraints:

$$(1) \qquad\qquad \sum_i x_{ik} \leqq x_k.$$

Introduce the following definitions:

$$(2) \qquad\qquad x_{jik} = x_{ik}.$$

With this notation a Pareto-efficient allocation is a vector maximum of
the utility functions $U_j(x_{j11}, \ldots, x_{jmn})$, subject to the constraints (1) and
(2). Because of the notation used, the variables appearing in the utility
function relating to the jth individual are proper to him alone and appear
in no one else's utility function. If we understand now that there are n^2m
commodities, indexed by the triple subscript jik, then the Pareto-efficiency
problem has a thoroughly classical form. There are n^2m prices, p_{jik}, attached
to the constraints (2), plus m prices, q_k, corresponding to constraints (1).
Following the maximization procedure formally, we see, much as in Samuelson [1954], that Pareto efficiency is characterized by the conditions:

$$(3) \qquad\qquad \lambda_j(\partial U_j/\partial x_{ik}) = p_{jik},$$

and

$$(4) \qquad\qquad \sum_j p_{jik} = q_k,$$

where λ_j is the reciprocal of the marginal utility of income for individual j. (These statements ignore corner conditions, which can easily be supplied.)

Condition (4) can be given the following economic interpretation: Imagine each individual i to be a producer with m production processes, indexed by the pair (i.k). Process (i,k) has one input namely commodity k, and n outputs, indexed by the triple (j,i,k). In other words, what we ordinarily call individual i's consumption is regarded as the production of joint outputs, one for each individual whose utility is affected by individual i's consumption.

The point of this exercise is to show that by suitable and indeed not unnatural reinterpretation of the commodity space, externalities can be regarded as ordinary commodities, and all the formal theory of competitive equilibrium is valid, including its optimality.

It is not the mere fact that one man's consumption enters into another man's utility that causes the failure of the market to achieve efficiency. There are two relevant factors which cannot be discovered by inspection of the utility structures of the individual. One, much explored in the literature, is the appropriability of the commodities which represent the external repercussions; the other, less stressed, is the fact that markets for externalities usually involve small numbers of buyers and sellers.

The first point, Musgrave's "exclusion principle," (1959, p. 86) is so well known as to need little elaboration. Pricing demands the possibility of excluding nonbuyers from the use of the product, and this exclusion may be technically impossible or may require the use of considerable resources. Pollution is the key example; the supply of clean air or water to each individual would have to be treated as a separate commodity, and it would have to be possible in principle to supply to one and not the other (though the final equilibrium would involve equal supply to all). But this is technically impossible.

The second point comes out clearly in our case. Each commodity (j,i,k) has precisely one buyer and one seller. Even if a competitive equilibrium could be defined, there would be no force driving the system to it; we are in the realm of imperfectly competitive equilibrium.

In my view, the standard lighthouse example is best analyzed as a problem of small numbers rather than of the difficulty of exclusion, though both elements are present. To simplify matters, I will abstract from uncertainty so that the lighthouse keeper knows exactly when each ship will need its services, and also abstract from indivisibility (since the light is either on or off). Assume further that only one ship will be within range of the lighthouse at any moment. Then exclusion is perfectly possible; the lighthouse need only shut off its light when a nonpaying ship is coming into range. But there would be only one buyer and one seller and no competitive forces to drive the two into a competitive equilibrium. If in addition the costs of bargaining are high, then it may be most efficient to offer the service free.

If, as is typical, markets for the externalities do not exist, then the allocation from the point of view of the "buyer" is determined by a rationing process. We can determine a shadow price for the buyer: this will differ from the price, zero, received by the seller. Hence, formally, the failure of markets for externalities to exist can also be described as a difference of prices between buyer and seller.

In the example analyzed, the externalities related to particular named individuals; individual i's utility function depended on what a particular individual, j, possessed. The case where it is only the total amount of some commodity (e.g., handsome houses) in other people's hands that matters is a special case, which yields rather simpler results. In this case, $\partial U_j / \partial x_{ik}$ is independent of i for $i \neq j$, and hence, by (3), p_{jik} is independent of i for $i \neq j$. Let

$$p_{iik} = p_{ik}, p_{jik} = \bar{p}_{jk} \text{ for } i \neq j.$$

Then (4) becomes,

$$p_{ik} + \sum_{j \neq i} \bar{p}_{jk} = q_k,$$

or,

$$(p_{ik} - \bar{p}_{ik}) + \sum_j \bar{p}_{jk} = q_k,$$

from which it follows that the difference, $p_{ik} - \bar{p}_{ik}$, is independent of i. There are two kinds of shadow prices, a price $\bar{p}_{ik}$, the price that individual i is willing to pay for an increase in the stock of commodity k in any other individual's hands, and the premium, $p_{ik} - \bar{p}_{ik}$, he is willing to pay to have the commodity in his possession rather than someone else's. At the optimum, this premium for private possession must be the same for all individuals.

Other types of externalities are associated with several commodities simultaneously and do not involve named individuals, as in the case of neighborhood effects, where an individual's utility depends both on others' behavior (e.g., esthetic, criminal) and on their location.

There is one deep problem in the interpretation of externalities which can only be signaled here. What aspects of others' behavior do we consider as affecting a utility function? If we take a hard-boiled revealed preference attitude, then if an individual expands resources in supporting legislation regulating another's behavior, it must be assumed that that behavior affects his utility. Yet in the cases that students of criminal law call "crimes without victims," such as homosexuality or drug-taking, there is no direct relation between the parties. Do we have to extend the concept of externality to all matters that an individual cares about? Or, in the spirit of John Stuart Mill, is there a second-order value judgement which excludes some of these preferences from the formation of social policy as being illegitimate infringements of individual freedom?

Market Failure

The problem of externalities is thus a special case of a more general phenomenon, the failure of markets to exist. Not all examples of market failure can fruitfully be described as externalities. Two very important examples have already been alluded to; markets for many forms of risk-bearing and for most future transactions do not exist and their absence is surely suggestive of inefficiency.

Previous discussion has suggested two possible causes for market failure: (1) inability to exclude; (2) lack of necessary information to permit market transactions to be concluded.

The failure of futures markets cannot be directly explained in these terms. Exclusion is no more a problem in the future than in the present. Any contract to be executed in the future is necessarily contingent on some events (for example, that the two agents are still both in business), but there must be many cases where no informational difficulty is presented. The absence of futures markets may be ascribed to a third possibility: (3) supply and demand are equated at zero; the highest price at which anyone would buy is below the lowest price at which anyone would sell.

This third case of market failure, unlike the first two, is by itself in no way presumptive of inefficiency. However, it may usually be assumed that its occurrence is the result of failures of the first two types on complementary markets. Specifically, the demand for future steel may be low because of uncertainties of all types; sales and technological uncertainty for the buyer's firm, prices and existence of competing goods, and the quality specification of the steel. If, however, adequate markets for risk-bearing existed, the uncertainties could be removed, and the demand for future steel would rise.

Transaction Costs

Market failure has been presented as absolute, but in fact the situation is more complex than this. A more general formulation is that of transaction costs, which are attached to any market and indeed to any mode of resource allocation. Market failure is the particular case where transaction costs are so high that the existence of the market is no longer worthwhile. The distinction between transaction costs and production costs is that the former can be varied by a change in the mode of resource allocation, while the latter depend only on the technology and tastes, and would be the same in all economic systems.

The discussions in the preceding sections suggest two sources of transaction costs. (1) exclusion costs; (2) costs of communication and information, including both the supplying and the learning of the terms on which transactions can be carried out. An additional source is (3) the costs of disequilibrium; in any complex system, the market or authoritative allocation, even under perfect information, it takes time to compute the optimal allocation, and either transactions take place which are inconsistent with the final equilibrium or they are delayed until the computations are completed (see T. Marschak, 1959).

These costs vary from system to system; thus, one of the advantages of a price system over either bargaining or some form of authoritative allocation is usually stated to be the economy in costs of information and communication. But the costs of transmitting and especially of receiving a large number of price signals may be high; thus, there is a tendency not to differentiate prices as much as would be desirable from the efficiency viewpoint; for example, the same price is charged for peak and offpeak usage of transportation or electricity.

In a price system, transaction costs drive a wedge between buyer's and seller's prices and thereby give rise to welfare losses as in the usual analysis. Removal of these welfare losses by changing to another system (for example, governmental allocation on benefit-cost criteria) must be weighed against any possible increase in transaction costs (for example, the need for elaborate and perhaps impossible studies to determine demand functions without the benefit of observing a market).

The welfare implications of transaction costs would exist even if they were proportional to the size of the transaction, but in fact they typically exhibit increasing returns. The cost of acquiring a piece of information, for example, a price, is independent of the scale of use to which it will be put.

Collective Action: The Political Process

The State may frequently have a special role to play in resource allocation because, by its nature, it has a monopoly of coercive power, and coercive power can be used to economize on transaction costs. The most important use of coercion in the economic context is the collection of taxes; others are regulatory legislation and eminent domain proceedings.

The State is not an entity but rather a system of individual agents, a widely extensive system in the case of a democracy. It is appealing and fruitful to analyze its behavior in resource allocation in a manner analogous to that of the price system. Since the same agents appear in the two systems, it becomes equally natural to assume they have the same motives. Hotelling (1929, pp. 54–55) and Schumpeter (1942, ch. XXII) had sketched such politicoeconomic models, and von Neumann and Morgenstern's monumental work is certainly based on the idea that all social phenomena are governed to essentially the same motives as economics. The elaboration of more or less complete models of the political process along the lines of economic theory is more recent, the most prominent contributors being Black (1958), Downs (1957), Buchanan and Tullock (1962), and Rothenberg (1965).

I confine myself here to a few critical remarks on the possibilities of such theories. These are not intended to be negative but to suggest problems that have to be faced and are raised by some points in the preceding discussion.

1. If we take the allocative process to be governed by majority voting, then, as we will know, there are considerable possibilities of paradox. The possible intransitivity of majority voting was already pointed out by Condorcet (1785). If, instead of assuming that each individual votes according to his preferences it is assumed that they bargain freely before voting (vote-selling), the paradox appears in another form, a variant of the bargaining problems already noted in section 2. If a majority could do what it wanted, then it would be optimal to win with a bare majority and take everything; but any such bargain can always be broken up by another proposed majority.

Tullock (1967) has recently argued convincingly that if the distribution of opinions on social issues is fairly uniform and if the dimensionality of the space of social issues is much less than the number of individuals, then majority voting on a sincere basis will be transitive. The argument is not, however, applicable to income distribution, for such a policy has as many dimensions as there are individuals, so that the dimensionality of the issue space is equal to the number of individuals.

This last observation raises an interesting question. Why, in fact, in democratic systems has there been so little demand for income redistribution? The current discussion of a negative income tax is the first serious attempt at a purely redistributive policy. Hagström (1938) presented a mathematical model predicting on the basis of a self-interest model for voters that democracy would inevitably lead to radical egalitarianism.

2. Political policy is not made by voters, not even in the sense that they choose the vector of political actions which best suits them. It is in fact made by representatives in one form or another. Political representation is an outstanding example of the principal-agent relation. This means that the link between individual utility functions and social action is tenuous, though by no means completely absent. Representatives are no more a random sample of their constituents than physicians are of their patients.

Indeed, the question can be raised: to what extent is the voter, when acting in that capacity, a principal or an agent? To some extent, certainly, the voter is cast in a role in which he feels some obligation to consider the social good, not just his own. It is in fact somewhat hard to explain otherwise why an individual votes at all in a large election, since the probability that his vote will be decisive is so negligible.

Collective Action: Social Norms

It is a mistake to limit collective action to State action; many other departures from the anonymous atomism of the price system are observed regularly. Indeed, firms of any complexity are illustrations of collective action, the internal allocation of their resources being directed by authoritative and hierarchical controls.

I want, however, to conclude by calling attention to a less visible form of social action: norms of social behavior, including ethical and moral codes. I suggest as one possible interpretation that they are reactions of society to compensate for market failures. It is useful for individuals to have some trust in each other's word. In the absence of trust, it would become very costly to arrange for alternative sanctions and guarantees, and many opportunities for mutually beneficial cooperation would have to be foregone. Banfield (1958) has argued that lack of trust is indeed one of the causes of economic underdevelopment.

It is difficult to conceive of buying trust in any direct way (though it can happen indirectly, for example, a trusted employee will be paid more as being more valuable); indeed, there seems to be some inconsistency in the very concept. Nonmarket action might take the form of a mutual agreement. But the arrangement of these agreements and especially their continued extension to new individuals entering the social fabric can be costly. As an alternative, society may proceed by internalization of these norms to the achievement of the desired agreement on an unconscious level.

There is a whole set of customs and norms which might be similarly interpreted as agreements to improve the efficiency of the economic system (in the broad sense of satisfaction of individual values) by providing commodities to which the price system is inapplicable.

These social conventions may be adaptive in their origins, but they can become retrogressive. An agreement is costly to reach and therefore costly to modify; and the costs of modification may be especially large for unconscious agreements. Thus, codes of professional ethics, which arise out of the principal-agent relation and afford protection to the principals, can serve also as a cloak for monopoly by the agents.

REFERENCES

Aumann, R. J. 1964. Markets with a continuum of traders. *Econometrica* 32:39–50.
Aumann, R. J. 1966. The existence of competitive equilibria in markets with a continuum of traders. *Econometrica* 34:1–17.
Aumann, R. J. and Maschler, M. 1964. The bargaining set for cooperative games. In M. Dresher, L. S. Shapley, A. W. Tucker (eds). *Advances in Game Theory. Annals of Mathematics Study.* Princeton, New Jersey: Princeton, University Press, 52:443–476.

Banfield, E. C. 1958. *The Moral Basis of a Backward Society.* The Free Press.

Black, D. 1958. *The Theory of Committees and Elections.* Cambridge, U.K.: Cambridge University Press.

Buchanan, J. and W. C. Stubblebine. 1962. Externality. *Economica* 29:371–384.

Buchanan, J. and G. Tullock. 1962. *The Calculus of Consent,* Ann Arbor, Michigan: University of Michigan Press.

Chamberlin, E. H. 1933. *The Theory of Monopolistic Competition.* Cambridge, Mass. Eighth edition, 1965.

Coase, R. H. 1960. The problem of social cost. *Journal of Law and Economics* 3:1–44.

Condorcet, Marquis de. 1785. *Essai sur l'application de l'analyse à la probabilitié des décisions rendues à la pluralité des voix.* Paris.

Debreu, G. and H. Scarf. 1963. A limited theorem on the core of an economy. *International Economic Review* 4:235–246.

Demsetz, H. 1964. The welfare and empirical implications of monopolistic competition. *Economic Journal* 74:623–641.

Demsetz, H. 1966. Some aspects of property rights. *Journal of Law Economics* 9:61–70.

Demsetz, H. 1968. Why regulate utilities. *Journal of Law and Economics* 11:55–66.

Downs, A. 1957. *An Economic Theory of Democracy.* New York: Harper.

Edgeworth, F. Y. 1881. *Mathematical Psychics: An Essay on the Application of Mathematics to the Moral Sciences.* London: C. Kegan Paul & Co.

Farrell, M. J. 1959. The convexity assumption in the theory of competitive markets. *Journal of Political Economy* 67:377–391.

Hagstrom, K. G. 1938. A mathematical note on democracy. *Econometrica* 6:381–383.

Harsanyi, J. C. 1956. Approaches to the bargaining problem before and after the theory of games: A critical discussion of Zeuthen's, Hicks', and Nash's Theories. *Econometrica* 24:144–157.

Harsanyi, J. C. 1959. A bargaining model for the cooperative n-person game. In A. W. Tucker and R. D. Luce (eds.) *Contributions to the Theory of Games IV. Annals of Mathematics Study,* Princeton, New Jersey: Princeton University 40:325–355.

Harsanyi, J. C. 1963. A simplified bargaining model for the n-person cooperative game. *International Economic Review* 4:194–220.

Harsanyi, J. C. 1966. A general theory of rational behavior in game situations. *Econometrica.* 34:613–634.

Hotelling, H. 1929. Stability in competition. *Economic Journal* 39:41–57.

Kaldor, N. 1935. Market imperfection and excess capacity. *Economica, N.S.* 2:35–50.

Kaysen, Carl. 1949. Basing point pricing and public policy. *Quarterly Journal of Economics* 63:289–314.

Knight, F. H. 1921. *Risk, Uncertainty, and Profit.* Boston and New York: Houghton-Mifflin. Reprinted by London School of Economics and Political Science 1948.

Knight, F. H. 1924. Some fallacies in the interpretation of social cost. *Quarterly Journal of Economics* 38:582–606.

Luce, R. D. 1954. A definition of stability for n-person games. *Annals of Mathematics* 59:357–366.

Luce, R. D. 1955a. Ψ-stability: a new equilibrium concept for n-person game theory. In *Mathematical Models of Human Behavior.* Stamford, Conn.: Dunlap and Associates, pp. 32–44.

Luce, R. D. 1955b. k-stability of symmetric and quota games. *Annals of Mathematics* 62:517–555.

Marschak, J. 1968. Economics of inquiring, communicating, deciding. *American Economic Review Papers and Proceedings* 58:1–18.

Marschak, T. 1959. Centralization and decentralization in economic organizations. *Econometrica* 27:399–430.

Meade, J. E. 1952. External economies and diseconomies in a competitive situation. *Economic Journal* 62:54–67.

Musgrave, R. A. 1959. *The Theory of Public Finance: A Study in Public Economy.* New York: McGraw-Hill Book Company.

Nash, J. F. Jr. 1950. The bargaining problem. *Econometrica* 18:155–162.

Nash, J. F. Jr. 1953. Two person cooperative games. *Econometrica* 21:128–140.

Negishi, T. 1960–1. Monopolistic competition and general equilibrium. *Review of Economic Studies* 28:196–201.

von Neumann, J., and O. Morgenstern. 1944. *Theory of Games and Economic Behavior.* Princeton, N. J.: Princeton University Press. Second edition. 1947.

Pauly, M. V. 1968. The economics of moral hazard: comment *American Economic Review* 58:531–537.

Radner, R. 1968. Competitive equilibrium under uncertainty. *Econometrica* 36:31–58.

Robertson, D. H. 1924. Those empty boxes. *Economic Journal* 34:16–30.

Rothenberg, J. 1960. Non-convexity, aggregation, and Pareto optimality. *Journal of Political Economy* 68:435–468.

Rothenberg, J. 1965. A model of economic and political decision-making. In J. Margolis (ed.) *The Public Economy of Urban Communities.* Washington, D.C.: Resources for the Future.

Samuelson, P. A. 1954. The pure theory of public expenditures. *Review of Economic Statistics* 36:387–389.

Samuelson, P. A. 1967. The monopolistic competition revolution. In R. E. Kuenne (ed.) *Monopolistic Competition Theory: Studies in Impact.* New York, London, and Sydney: Wiley, pp. 105–138.

Schelling, T. 1957. Bargaining, communication, and limited war. *Journal of Conflict Resolution* 1:19–36.

Schumpeter, J. 1942. *Capitalism, Socialism, and Democracy.* New York: Harper. Third Edition, 1950.

Scitovsky, T. 1954. Two concepts of external economies. *Journal of Political Economy* 62:143–151.

Selten, R. 1964. Valuation of n-person games. In M. Dresher, L. S. Shapley, A. W. Tucker (eds.) *Advances in Game Theory.* Princeton, New Jersey; Princeton University Press, 52:577–626.

Shapley, L. S. 1953. A value for n-person games. In H. W. Kuhn and A. W. Tucker (eds.) *Contributions to the Theory of Games II. Annals of Mathematics Study.* Princeton, New Jersey: Princeton University Press, 28:307–317.

Shapley, L. S., and M. Shubik. 1967. Ownership and the production function. *Quarterly Journal of Economics* 81:88–111.

Shubik, M. 1959. Edgeworth market games. In A. W. Tucker and R. D. Luce (eds.) *Contributions to the Theory of Games IV. Annals of Mathematics Study.* Princeton, New Jersey: Princeton University Press, 40:267–278.

Smith, A. 1937. *An Enquiry Concerning the Causes of the Wealth of Nations.* New York: Modern Library.

Starr, R. 1969. Quasi-equilibria in markets with nonconvex preferences. *Econometrica* 37:25–38.

Triffin, R. 1941. *Monopolistic Competition and General Equilibrium Theory.* Cambridge, Mass.: Harvard University Press.

Tullock, G. 1967. *Toward a Mathematics of Politics.* Ann Arbor, Michigan: University of Michigan Press.

Young, A. A. 1913. Pigou's Wealth and Welfare. *Quarterly Journal of Economics* 27:672–686.

Zeuthen, F. 1930. *Problems of Monopoly and Economic Warfare.* London, George Routledge & Sons Ltd.

The Nature of Cost-Benefit Analysis

ROLAND N. McKEAN

Roland N. McKean is Professor of Economics at the University of Virginia. The following item is from his book, Public Spending, *published in 1968.*

"Cost-benefit analyses" are attempts to estimate certain costs and gains that would result from alternative courses of action. For different applications, other names are often used: "cost-effectiveness analysis" when courses of action in defense planning are compared; "systems analysis" when the alternatives are relatively complex collections of interrelated parts; "operations research" when the alternatives are modes of operation with more or less given equipment and resources; or "economic analysis" when the alternatives are rival price-support or other economic policies. The term "cost-benefit analysis" was originally associated with natural-resource projects but has gradually come to be used for numerous other applications. The basic idea is not new: individuals have presumably been weighing the pros and cons of alternative actions ever since man appeared on earth; and in the early part of the nineteenth century, Albert Gallatin and others put together remarkably sophisticated studies of proposed U.S. government canals and turnpikes. But techniques have improved, and interest has been growing. All these studies might well be called economic analyses. This does not mean that the economist's skills are the only ones needed in making such analyses or, indeed, that economists are very good at making them. It merely means that this analytical tool is aimed at helping decision makers—consumers, businessmen, or government officials—economize.

In recent years, the Bureau of the Budget, the National Bureau of Standards, many other U.S. agencies, and governments and agencies in other nations have been exploring possible uses of cost-benefit analysis. Sometimes the analyses are essentially simple arithmetic. Sometimes high-speed computers are used—as they were, for instance, in the search by a Harvard group for the best way to use water in the Indus River basin in Pakistan. One of the major applications of cost-benefit analysis will continue to be the comparison of alternative natural-resources policies—proposals to reduce air and water pollution, to divert water from the Yukon to regions further south, to do something about the rapidly declining water level in the Great Lakes, and so on. But other applications are appearing with growing frequency—comparisons of such things as alternative health measures, personnel policies, airport facilities, education practices, transportation systems, choices about the management of governmental properties, and antipoverty proposals.

All such analyses involve working with certain common elements: (1) objectives, or the beneficial things to be achieved; (2) alternatives, or the possible systems or arrangements for achieving the objectives; (3) costs, or the benefits that have to be foregone if one of the alternatives is adopted; (4) models, or the sets of relationships that help one trace out the impacts of each alternative on achievements (in other words, on benefits) and costs; and (5) a criterion, involving both costs and benefits, to identify the preferred alternative. In connection with each of these elements there are major difficulties. Consider a personal problem of choice that an individual might try to analyze—selecting the best arrangements for his family's transportation. Spelling out the relevant objectives, that is, the kind of achievements that would yield significant benefits, is no simple task. The objectives may include commuting to work, getting the children to school, travel in connection with shopping, cross-country trips, and so on. Part of this travel may be across deserts, along mountain roads, in rainy or icy or foggy conditions. The family may attach a high value to the prestige of traveling in style (or of being austere, or of simply being different from most other people). Another objective that is neglected all too often is a hard-to-specify degree of flexibility to deal with uncertainties. Adaptability and flexibility are particularly important objectives if one is examining alternative educational programs, exploratory research projects, or R & D policies. Overlooking any of the relevant objectives could lead to poor choices.

The second element, the alternative ways of achieving the benefits, also deserves careful thought, for selecting the best of an unnecessarily bad lot is a poor procedure. In choosing a family's transportation system, the alternatives might include various combinations of a compact automobile, a luxury automobile, a pickup truck, a jeep, a motor scooter, an airplane, a bicycle, the use of a bus system, and the use of taxicabs.

In many problems of choice, the alternatives are called "systems," and the analyses are called "systems analyses." This terminology is quite appropriate, because the word "system" means a set of interrelated parts, and the alternative ways of achieving objectives usually are sets of interrelated parts. At the same time, the word "system" is so general that this usage is often confusing. In defense planning, for example, the term "system" can be used to refer to such sets of interrelated parts as the following:

All three of these systems are collections of interrelated parts. How large should systems be for their comparison to be called a "systems analysis" or for their comparison to be a useful aid? There are no correct answers; one must exercise judgment in deciding how large the systems should be to provide worthwhile assistance in tracing out the costs and benefits. (In effect, one must weigh the costs against the benefits of preparing alternative cost-benefit analyses.) Where interrelationships are relatively important, one is usually driven to consider large systems. Thus to choose between two engines for a supersonic airliner, one can hardly compare thrusts alone and make an intelligent selection, for weight, reliability, cost, noise, etc., may have diverse effects on overall desirability. The power plants must be fitted (at least on paper) into rival aircraft designs, and thence into airline and airport systems to see their net impact on the real objectives and the full costs. Moreover, other components of the projected systems may have to be modified so as not to use either engine stupidly. Suppose one engine would make possible the use of relatively short runways. To use an aircraft with this power plant in an intelligent way, one might have to modify many parts of the proposed airports, traffic patterns, ground installations for instrument-landing systems, and even proposed airline schedules. Hence one would end up comparing rather broad systems having many common components but also having several components that differed.

So much for the alternative systems to be compared. The third element of cost-benefit analysis, cost, is crucial because it really reflects the alternative benefits that one might obtain from the resources. It is just as foolish to measure costs incorrectly or to neglect part of them as it is to measure benefits incorrectly or neglect part of them. If selecting a luxury car entails building a new garage or paying higher insurance premiums, these are part of the costs of choosing that alternative. If one already has an adequate garage, the value foregone by using it (but *not* the cost of building a garage) is the relevant cost.

"Models," the fourth element of cost-benefit analysis, are simply crude representations of reality that enable one to estimate costs and benefits. If a person figures, "With the bus I could average 10 miles per hour, traverse the 5 miles to work in one-half hour, spend five hours per week commuting to work, and would stand up 50 percent of the distance on 50 percent of the trips," he is using a model. If he says, "With Automobile X, I would get a motor tune-up every 5,000 miles and would therefore spend $50 per year on that item," he visualizes these events and uses a set of relationships, that is, a model, to estimate this cost. When one tries to perceive how something would work, it has become convenient and fashionable to say, "Let's build a model," though one could simply say, "Let's devise a way to predict what would happen (or a way to estimate costs and benefits)."

The fifth element of cost-benefit analysis is the criterion or test of preferredness by means of which one points to the best choice. People tend to make a variety of criterion errors. One error, the use of the ratio of benefits to costs, is such a perennial favorite that it merits a brief discussion. Suppose at first that both benefits and costs can be measured *fully and correctly* in monetary terms and that one must choose among the following three discrete (and not mutually exclusive) alternatives:

	A	B	C
Cost	$100	$100	$200
Benefit one year later	$150	$105	$220
Ratio of benefits to costs	1.5	1.05	1.10

Suppose further that the constraint is that funds can be borrowed at 6 percent. Which projects should be undertaken, and what is the criterion? A and C, both of which yield more than 6 percent, should be undertaken, and the proper criterion is to maximize the present value of net worth or, its surrogate, to undertake projects wherever the marginal benefit exceeds the marginal cost. Note that the criterion is *not* to maximize the ratio of benefits to costs, which would restrict one to Project A. If the constraint is a fixed budget of $200, Projects A and B should be selected. Again, maximizing the ratio of benefits to costs would limit one to Project A.

Or consider two discrete and mutually exclusive alternatives (for example, two sizes of a dam):

	A	B
Cost	$100	$200
Benefit one year later	$150	$260
Ratio of benefits to costs	1.50	1.30

If funds can be borrowed at 6 percent, Project B should be undertaken. One should not choose A simply because the benefit-cost ratio is larger. Ratios are not irrelevant—every marginal productivity is a ratio—for one often seeks to *equalize* certain ratios as a condition for achieving a desired maximum. But the ratio itself is not the thing to be maximized.

The issue takes on a good deal of importance when the benefits can only be suggested by physical products or capabilities. In these circumstances, presumably in desperation, people frequently adopt as a criterion the maximization of some such ratio as satellite payload per dollar, hours of student instruction per dollar, or target-destruction capability per dollar. But the benefit-cost ratios of rival proposals simply cover up the relevant information. Take another example from the choices that confront the individual. If one is selecting a hose with which to sprinkle his lawn, one may have the following options:

	⅝-*in. Diameter*	1-*in. Diameter*
Cost	$3	$5
Benefit (water put on lawn per hour)	108 gallons	150 gallons
Ratio of benefits to costs	36/1	30/1

The ratios are irrelevant. The pertinent question is whether or not the extra capability is worth the extra $2. Less misleading than showing the ratio would be showing the physical capabilities and the costs à la Consumers' Research. Or, where it makes sense to do so, one can adjust the scale of the alternatives so that each costs the same or achieves the same objectives. Then one can see which system achieves a specified objective at minimum cost, or achieves the greatest benefit for a specified budget. This is not a perfect criterion, for someone has to decide if the specified budget (or objective) is appropriate. But at least this sort of test is less misleading than a benefit-cost ratio.

With regard to this fifth element of cost-benefit analysis, discussing the correct way to design criteria may seem like discussing the correct way to find the Holy Grail. In a world of uncertainty and individual utility functions, judgments must help shape choices, and no operational test of preferredness can be above suspicion. Moreover, analyses vary in their quality, which is hard to appraise, and in their applicability to different decisions. For these reasons, responsible decision makers must treat cost-benefit analyses as "consumers' research" and introduce heroic judgments in reaching final decisions. In a sense, then, it may be both presumptuous and erroneous to discuss having a test of preferredness in these quantitative analyses.

Criteria should be considered, nonetheless, in connection with such analysis. First, cost-benefit analysts do apply criteria, especially in designing and redesigning the alternatives to be compared. They delete features that appear to be inefficient, add features that appear to be improvements, and probe for alternative combinations that are worth considering. This screening of possibilities and redesign of alternative systems entails the use of criteria, and these should be explicitly considered and exhibited. Second, whether or not they ought to, analysts often present the final comparisons in terms of a criterion. Thus while it may be wrong to talk as if a definitive criterion is an element of every analysis, these warnings about criterion selection should be emphasized.

Needless to say, in reaching decisions, one should attempt to take into account *all* gains and *all* costs. Some people feel that there are two types of gain or cost, economic and noneconomic, and that economic analysis has nothing to do with the latter. This distinction is neither very sound nor very useful. People pay for—that is, they value—music as well as food, beauty or quiet as well as aluminum pans, a lower probability of death as well as garbage disposal. The significant categories are not economic and noneconomic items but (1) gains and costs that can be measured in monetary units (for example, the use of items like typewriters that have market prices reflecting the marginal evaluations of all users); (2) other commensurable effects (impacts of higher teacher salaries, on the one hand, and of teaching machines, on the other hand, on students' test scores); (3) incommensurable effects that can be quantified but not in terms of a common denominator (capability of improving science test scores and capability of reducing the incidence of ulcers among students); and (4) nonquantifiable effects. Examples of the last category are impacts of alternative policies on the morale and happiness of students, on the probability of racial conflicts, and on the probability of protecting individual rights. In taking a position on an issue, each of us implicitly quantifies such considerations. But there is no way to make quantifications that would necessarily be valid for other persons. This sort of distinction between types of effects does serve a useful purpose, especially in warning us of the limitations of cost-benefit analysis.

One should recognize, too, that cost-benefit analysis necessarily involves groping and the making of subjective judgments, not just briskly proceeding with dispassionate scientific measurements. Consider the preparation of such analyses to aid educational choices. No one says, "This is the educational objective, and here are the three alternative systems to be compared. Now trace out the impacts of each on cost and on achievement of the objective, and indicate the preferred system." What happens is that those making the analysis spend much time groping for an *operational* statement of the objective, such as a designated improvement in specific test scores without an increase in the number of dropouts or nervous breakdowns. A first attempt is made at designing the alternative ways of realizing this objective. Preliminary costs are estimated. Members of the research team perceive that the systems have differential impacts on other objectives, such as flexibility, or student performance on tests two years later, or student interest in literature. Or the rival arrangements may elicit different reactions from teachers, parents, and school boards, affecting the achievement of other objectives. The analysts redesign the alternatives in the light of these impacts, perhaps so that each alternative performs at least "acceptably" with respect to each objective. Next it appears that certain additional features, such as extra English-composition courses, might add greatly to capability but not much to cost. Or the research team's cost group reports that certain facilities are extremely expensive and that eliminating them might reduce costs greatly with little impairment of effectiveness. In both cases the systems have to be modified again. This cut-and-try procedure is essential. Indeed, this process of redesigning the alternatives is probably a more important contribution than the final cost-effectiveness exhibits. In any event, the preparation of such an analysis is a process of probing—and not at all a methodical scientific comparison following prescribed procedures.

An appreciation of cost-benefit analysis also requires an awareness that incommensurables and uncertainties are pervasive. Consider the impacts of alternative educational policies that were mentioned above. These effects can perhaps be described, but not expressed in terms of a common denominator. Judgments about the extent of these effects and their worth have to be made. Some costs, such as the monetary measures of foregone benefits, perhaps additional sacrifices in terms of personality adjustment and ultimate effectiveness, or undesirable political repercussions that yield costs, cannot validly be put in terms of a common denominator. Furthermore, because of uncertainties, whatever estimates can be prepared should in principle be probability distributions rather than unique figures for costs and gains. The system that performs best in one contingency may perform worst in another contingency. Finally, costs and gains occur over a period of time, not at a single point in time, and there is no fully acceptable means of handling these streams of costs and gains in analyzing many options.

These difficulties are present because life is complex, and there is no unique correct choice. The difficulties are not created by cost-benefit analysis. Moreover, they do not render quantitative economic analysis useless. They simply mean that one has to be discriminating about when and how to use various tools. In general, the broader choices made by higher-level officials pose relatively great difficulties regarding what value judgments to make and what the physical and social consequences of alternative actions would be. Consider, for example, the allocation of the U.S. budget among various departments or the allocation of funds among such functions as the improvement of health, education, or postal service. Cost-benefit analysis gives relatively little guidance in making these choices, for in the end the decision maker's task is dominated by difficult personal judgments. Cost-benefit analysis may help somewhat, for it is the appropriate framework in terms of which to *think* about these broad choices, and it can usually provide *some* improved information. When personal judgments must play such a huge role, however, the improved information may not be worth much.

Consider another example of such broad choices: the government's allocation of its R & D effort between basic research and applied development. To choose between these two alternatives, officials must rely heavily on personal judgments about the consequences and judgments concerning the value of those consequences. Values cannot be taken as agreed upon, and physical-sociological effects cannot be predicted with confidence. Quantitative analysis can probably contribute only a little toward the sharpening of intuition here. Or consider the allocation of effort between improving medical care for the aged and improving it for the young. Suppose one could make extremely good predictions of the effects, which would of course aid decision makers. The final choice would be dominated in this instance by value judgments about the worth of prolonging the lives of elderly persons, the worth of lengthening the lives of persons in great pain, the worth of saving the lives of weakened or physically handicapped children, the relief of different kinds of distress, and so on.

Another broad or high-level choice that brings out these difficulties is the allocation of funds to, or for that matter within, the State Department. In the tasks of diplomacy it is hard to visualize taking a set of value tags as being clearly stated, let alone agreed upon. And disagreement is quite understandable in predicting the effects of alternative courses of action on the probabilities of stable alliances, provocations, little wars, nuclear wars, and so on. Positive science has provided few tested hypotheses about these relationships.

As one proceeds to narrower or lower-level problems of choice, these difficulties frequently, though not always, become less severe. (Actual decisions, of course, vary continuously in the extent to which they present these difficulties, but it is often economical to think in terms of such categories as broad and narrow or high-level and low-level choices.) Within such tasks as education and health improvement, there are lower-level choices for which quantitative analysis may be very helpful, but there are also many middle-level choices that are fraught with difficulties. Should more effort be placed on the improvement of mental health even if it means less emphasis on the treatment of conventional ailments? Should effort be reallocated from higher education toward the improvement of elementary-school training, or vice versa? Or, as an alternative policy, should government leave such allocative decisions more than at present to the uninfluenced choices of individual families? Cost-benefit analysis cannot do much to resolve the uncertainties about the consequences of such decisions, about their relative worths to individual citizens, or about whose value judgments should be given what weights.

Within applied research and development, a choice between specific projects might appear to be a low-level choice that economic analysis could greatly assist. In such instances, it is true that values can sometimes be taken as agreed upon. In selecting research and development projects for new fuels, for instance, the values to be attached to various outcomes are not obvious, yet they are probably not major sources of divergent views.

Perhaps the principal difficulty is the inability to predict the physical consequences, including "side effects," of alternative proposals. Here too, cost-benefit analysis may be destined to play a comparatively small role.

One can list many problems of choice that seem to fall somewhere in this middle ground—that is, where cost-benefit analysis can be helpful but not enormously so. It would appear, for instance, that the selection of anti-poverty and welfare programs depends heavily on consequences that one cannot predict with confidence and on value judgment about which there is much disagreement. Similar statements apply also to the selection of foreign-aid programs, urban-development proposals, or law-enforcement programs—the comparison of different methods of curbing the use of narcotics, say, or of different penal institutions and procedures. In education, many decisions that may appear to be low-level or relatively simple—for example, the selection among alternative curricula or teaching methods or disciplinary rules—are inevitably dominated by judgments about the consequences of these policies and about the value tags to be attached to those consequences.

It is in connection with comparatively narrow problems of choice that cost-benefit analysis can sometimes play a more significant role. In these instances, as might be expected, the alternatives are usually rather close substitutes. Science can often predict the consequences of governmental natural-resource investments or choices affecting the utilization of water or land, and people can often agree on the values at stake—at least to a sufficient extent to render analyses highly useful. Competing irrigation plans, flood-control projects, swamp drainage and land reclamation ventures, and water-pollution control measures are examples of narrow problems of choice in which cost-benefit analysis can help.

Cost-benefit analysis also promises to be helpful in comparing certain transportation arrangements. The interdependencies of transportation networks with other aspects of life are formidable, yet with ingenuity extremely useful studies of some transportation alternatives can be produced. Numerous transportation alternatives have been the subject of such studies: highways, urban systems, inland waterways, modified railway networks, the utilization of a given amount of sea transport, air transport fleets, and of course many lower-level choices, such as alternative road materials, construction practices, airport facilities, and loading arrangements. In some instances, of course, the interdependencies may be too complex for analyses to be very valuable; transportation alternatives that affect a large region and its development yield chains of consequences that are extremely difficult to trace out.

At best, the difficulties of providing *valuable* information are awesome. There can always be legitimate disagreement about any of these policy decisions, and analyses must be regarded as inputs to decisions, not as oracular touchstones. Nonetheless, to think systematically about the costs and gains from alternative policies is surely more sensible than to rely on haphazard thought or intuition. Such analyses can bring out the areas of disagreement so that people can see where their differences lie. Even with considerable divergence in judgments, they can screen out the absurdly inferior alternatives, focusing the debate on subsets of relatively good alternatives. For some choices, cost-benefit analysis provides information that can help officials agree upon a course of action that is preferred or accepted by most citizens. And for all choices, it is the right framework to use in organizing the evidence and one's thoughts and intuitions regarding alternatives. Even in deciding which research project to undertake, or how much time to spend on it, a researcher consults rough cost-benefit T-accounts. In deciding anything, a person should weigh costs and gains. Preliminary weighing may suggest that the use of a tentative rule of thumb or "requirement" is preferable to further or repeated analyses, but he should not initially pull some mythical requirement out of the air.

Applications of Cost-Benefit Analysis

A. R. PREST and RALPH TURVEY

A. R. Prest and Ralph Turvey are well-known British economists. The following article is from their paper in the Economic Journal, *1965.*

We shall first look at some water projects and then turn to transport—these being the two areas where cost-benefit studies have been most common. Subsequently, we shall survey the application and applicability of these techniques in land-usage schemes (urban renewal, recreation, and land reclamation) [and] health. Throughout, we shall be illustrative rather than comprehensive—both in the sense that we are concerned only with the main features of, say, irrigation schemes rather than detailed case studies, and in that we shall emphasize the differences in treatment rather than the similarities. This means that we examine general techniques for enumerating and evaluating costs and benefits rather than "standard" items, such as the choice of appropriate discount rates, the exclusion of superogatory secondary benefits, etc.

1. Water Projects

Water projects take many different forms. They may differ enormously in respect of their engineering characteristics, *e.g.*, an estuarine barrage or a dam in the hills. Similarly, the purposes of water investment are many—provision of more water for an industrial area, provision of irrigation water, prevention of flood damage, and so on. In some cases there may be only one such purpose in a particular scheme; in others it may be a case of multipurpose development. The details of cost-benefit analysis inevitably differ from project to project, and we can only cover a sample. We shall look at irrigation, flood control, and hydroelectric schemes in turn, and in this way

519

hope to catch the smell even if not the flavor of the ingredients. Finally, we shall have a few words to add on the particular characteristics of multipurpose schemes.

(A) IRRIGATION

Since it is seldom possible to ascertain directly the price at which water could be sold upon the completion of a proposed irrigation project, and since this price would in any case give no indication of consumers' surplus, the *direct* benefits of a project have to be estimated by:

(i) forecasting the change in the output of each agricultural project, leaving out those outputs which, like the cattle feed, are also inputs;

(ii) valuing and summing these changes;

(iii) deducting the opportunity cost of the change in all farming inputs other than the irrigation water;

in order to get, as a result, the value of the net change in agricultural output consequent upon the irrigation of the area.

We now discuss each of these steps in turn.

(i) Forecasts of additional output, whether sold in the market or consumed on the farm, can be made in countries with well-developed agricultural advisory services. But this is only the beginning of the story. Even if there were no delay in the response of farmers to new conditions, it will often be the case that the full effects of irrigation will take some years to be felt. Since, in addition, farmers will take time to adapt, it is clear that what is required here is not just a simple list of outputs but a schedule showing the development of production over time. Yet this is too complicated in practice, and usually the best that can be done is to make estimates for one or two benchmark dates and extrapolate or, alternatively, postulate a discrete lag in the response of farmers.

The forecast is difficult as well as complicated (in principle), because it is the behavior of a group of people that is involved, behavior which may depend upon peasant conservatism, superstition, political tensions, and so on just as much or more than it depends upon any nice agronomic calculus. Thus, an Indian study reports that the peasants in an area irrigated by the Hirakud dam erroneously believed that planting a second crop on the valley-bottom land would lead to waterlogging and salinization. The authors explicitly assumed that in the first ten years after irrigation began the area would settle down to irrigated agriculture with the least possible change in techniques and capital investment.

The probability that farmers will not follow an income-maximizing course of action is one reason why a farm-management or programming approach may be of little use—except in setting an outside limit to outputs. Another is that the requisite information may be lacking. Thus, it is frequently necessary either to substitute or supplement the projections based upon the assumption of maximizing behavior with projections based upon the assumption that the behavior of other farmers elsewhere constitutes a useful precedent. The effect of irrigation in A is then forecast by comparing an irrigated area B either with B before irrigation or with an unirrigated area, C. There is obviously scope for judgment (and bias) here.

(ii) The amount the farmer gets for his crops may differ markedly from their value to the community where agriculture is protected or subsidized, as in the United States or the United Kingdom. In fact, some United States calculations have allowed for this by making an arbitrary 20% deduction in the prices of major commodities in surplus or receiving federal support. This is one example of the point that when the conditions for optimal resource allocation are not fulfilled in the rest of the economy market prices may prove a poor guide to project costs and benefits. Another general problem arises when the increment in the output of any crop is large enough to affect its price, so that there is no unique price for valuation purposes. There is the further point that output should be valued at a given price-level, consistent with the valuations of other benefits and of costs, but that future changes in price relativities need to be taken into account. Thus, price projections are required, and once again there is scope for judgment, as anything from simple extrapolation to highly sophisticated supply and demand studies may be utilized. Finally, there is the old problem, much aired in social accounting literature, about the appropriate valuation of subsistence output.

(iii) The principles for valuing farm inputs are the same as those for valuing outputs, while the forecast of input quantities is clearly related to the forecast of output quantities. In an elaborate income-maximizing analysis inputs and outputs would be simultaneously determined, while in a simpler approach inputs per acre of irrigated land or per unit of output will be taken as being the same as on comparable irrigated land elsewhere. In either case, costs include the opportunity earnings, if any, of any additional farmers who come to work in the irrigated area.

The *secondary* benefits which have sometimes been regarded as appropriately included in irrigation benefit calculations reflect the impact of the project on the rest of the economy, both via its increased sales to farmers and via its increased purchases from them. More important is the technological interdependence which is likely to be found in many irrigation schemes, such as when the effects on the height of the water-table in one area spill over to another district.

Any irrigation project will have a number of *minor* effects not obviously covered in the categories so far discussed. As these will vary from case to case, and no general list is possible, some examples may be of use. They are taken from an *ex-post* study of the Sarda Canal in India:

Canal water is also used for washing, bathing, watering cattle.

Silt is deposited at the outlet heads, which necessitates constant and laborious cleaning of the channels.

Some plots of land have been made untillable by unwanted water.

The canal divides the area (and sometimes individual fields) into two parts, but has few bridges, so that much time is wasted in circumnavigating it.

Many such effects will be unquantifiable, but must nevertheless be remembered in any analysis.

(B) FLOOD CONTROL

Ever since the River and Harbor Act of 1927 the United States Army Corps of Engineers has had the responsibility of preparing plans for improving major rivers for flood-control purposes—as well as irrigation, hydroelectric power, and navigation. On the flood-control side, the major benefits which have been categorized in this—and other—work have been the losses averted. Losses of this sort can refer to different types of assets—property, furnishings, crops, etc.; or to different types of owners—individuals, business firms, government, and so on. In all these cases the general principle is to estimate the mathematical expectation of annual damage (on the basis of the likely frequency of flood levels of different heights) and then regard such sums as the maximum annual amounts people would be willing to pay for flood-control measures.

Other benefits which must be taken into account are as follows:

(i) Avoidance of deaths by drowning. We shall deal with the general principles relevant in such cases in connection with health improvements.

(ii) Avoidance of temporary costs, e.g., evacuation of flood victims, emergency sand-bag work, etc., risks of sanitation breakdowns, epidemics, etc.

(iii) Possibilities of putting flood land to higher uses if the risk of inundation is eliminated.

The costs involved in flood-control calculations are relatively straightforward. Obviously, the initial costs of the flood-control works and their repair and maintenance charges must be included. The most difficult point in any such compilation is likely to be the cost of land acquisition for reservoirs, etc. In the absence of anything remotely approaching a free land market in a country such as the United Kingdom there is bound to be an arbitrary element in such items.

There are some obvious reasons why private investment principles are insufficient in the case of flood-control measures. Protection for one inhabitant in a district inevitably implies protection for another, and so one immediately runs into the collective goods problem; protection for one district may worsen flood threats to another, and so this inevitably brings up technological externalities; finally, flood works often have to be on a large scale and of a complex nature, and so this brings up non-marginal and imperfect competition problems. So one simply has to try to estimate willingness to pay for flood protection by the roundabout devices described above. There is no simple short-cut appeal to market principles.

(c) HYDROELECTRIC POWER SCHEMES

The standard way of measuring the value of the extra electricity generated by a public hydroelectric scheme is to estimate the savings realized by not having to buy from an alternative source. This sounds simple, but in fact raises all sorts of complicated issues: we shall look at these by, first, considering the simple alternative of a single hydroelectric source versus a single private steam plant, and secondly, by considering the implications of adding another source to a whole supply system.

In the first case the general point is to say that benefits can be measured by the costs of the most economical private alternative. This raises a number of issues, *e.g.*, a private sector station will not be working under competitive conditions, and so its charges may not coincide with opportunity costs; private sector charges will not be directly relevant to public sector circumstances in that they will reflect taxes, private sector interest rates, etc.; as we need the pattern of future, as well as current, benefits, we have to allow for the effects of future technological changes in reducing alternative costs, and hence benefits, through time. A further point arises when a new hydroelectric station provides a proportionately large net addition to the supply in a region. In this case the alternative-cost principle would produce an over-estimate of benefits, and we are forced back to a measure of what the extra output would sell for plus the increased consumers' surplus of its purchasers. Presumably a survey of the potential market for the power will provide some of the needed information, but the difficulties of making reliable estimates are clearly enormous.

We now turn to the case where a new hydroelectric station has to be fitted into a whole system.

The amount of power produced by a new hydroelectric station and the times of year at which it will be produced depend not only upon the physical characteristics of the river providing the power but also upon the cost characteristics of the whole electricity supply system and upon the behavior of the electricity consumers. The supply system constitutes a unity which is operated so as to minimize the operating costs of meeting consumption whatever its time pattern happens to be. Hence the way in which the hydroelectric station is operated may be affected by alterations in the peakiness of consumption, the bringing into service of new thermal stations, and so on.

If we now try to apply the principle of measuring benefits by the cost savings of not building an alternative station it follows from the system interdependence just described that the only meaningful way of measuring this cost saving is to ascertain the difference in the present value of total system operating costs in the two cases and deduct the capital cost of the alternatives. A simple comparison of the two capital costs and the two running costs, that is to say, will only give the right answer if the level and time pattern of the output of each would be exactly the same. In general, therefore, a very complicated exercise involving the simulation of the operation of the whole system is required, as, for that matter, may be the case for other water-resource analysis.

Finally, there is another point. Even if two or more hydroelectric stations are not linked in the same distribution and consumption network, there may be production interdependence. The clearest example is that when upstream stations in a river basin have reservoirs for water storage, this is highly likely to affect water flows downstream, and hence the generating pattern of stations in that area. If technological interdependence of this type is not internalized by having both types of station under the same authority it will be necessary to have some system of compensatory arrangement if we want to cut down resource misallocation.

(D) MULTIPURPOSE SCHEMES

In practice, many river developments have a number of purposes in mind—not only those we have dealt with above but also transport improvements, etc., as well. Obviously, the range of choice now becomes much wider. Not only does one have to look at the cost-benefit data for, say, different sized hydroelectric stations, but one also has to take different combinations of, say, irrigation and navigation improvements. The calculations will also be more complicated, in that the possibilities of interdependence are clearly multiplied, and so the warnings we have already uttered about the feasibility of some calculations will be even more applicable. We shall have no more to say at this stage on multistage projects, but simply make the final point that these reflections are highly apposite in the case of projects such as the Morecambe Bay and Solway Firth barrage schemes (providing for industrial and domestic water supplies, transport improvements, land reclamation, improved recreation facilities, etc.), which are receiving a good deal of attention at the time of writing (in 1965).

2. Transport Projects

(A) ROADS

A great deal of work has now accumulated on the principles and methods of application of cost-benefit techniques in this field, ever since the first experiments in the state of Oregon in 1938. We shall illustrate the arguments by references to the work done on the M1 in the United Kingdom, this being a typical example of what one finds in this field.

The calculation of net annual savings was classified under four heads:

(i) those relating to diverted traffic; (ii) those to generated traffic; (iii) savings in non-business time; and (iv) the effects of the growth of G.N.P. Under (i) (diverted traffic) estimates were made of the likely net savings of the traffic diverted from other routes to the M1, *i.e.*, positive items, such as working time savings of drivers, vehicle-usage economies, petrol savings, accident reductions, etc., together with negative items in respect of additional mileages traveled on faster roads and maintenance costs of the motorway.

In respect of generated traffic the argument is that the opening of the motorway would in effect reduce the "price" (in terms of congestion and inconvenience of motoring) and enable demand which had hitherto been frustrated to express itself in motorway usage. As it must be assumed that benefits per vehicle-mile to frustrated consumers are of less consequence than those to actual consumers (if not, they would not remain frustrated), they were rated as half as great as the latter in the M1 calculations.

Savings in non-business time were the third main ingredient. This calculation involves many complications, to which we shall return in a moment. The fourth component was the introduction of a trend factor, to allow for the long-term growth of G.N.P. and the effects on the demand for road travel—an obvious ingredient of any calculation, whether relating to private or public investment. The upshot of the combined calculations was that the rate of return was of the order of 10–15%.

A number of comments can be made on these calculations. First, there are the obvious statistical shortcomings which are recognized by everyone, including the authors. Second, there are a number of minor omissions, such as allowances for police and administrative costs, the benefits accruing to pedestrians and cyclists, etc., the advantages of more reliable goods deliveries. Thirdly, there are some inconsistencies in these particular calculations, in that on some occasions a long-period view seems to be taken (*e.g.*, when calculating the savings resulting from reductions in road vehicle fleets) and on others a short-period one (*e.g.*, in assessing the benefits of diversion of traffic from the railways). Much more important than these points are the savings due to accident reduction and to economies in travel time, where important logical and practical issues arise. On the first of these, the economic benefits of a fall in the amount of damage to vehicles and to real property, the work done by insurance companies, the work of the police and the courts are simple enough. It is the loss of production due to death or, temporarily, to accident or illness which raises complications. However, these complications are exactly the same as those raised in cost-benefit studies of health programs, and so it will be convenient to leave discussion of this general topic until we reach that heading.

This leaves us with the problem of valuing time savings; as these savings often form a very high proportion of total estimated benefits of road improvements, they are extremely important. Unfortunately, these calculations have not so far been very satisfactory.

Whatever the valuation procedure followed, it is necessary to assume that one time saving of sixty minutes is worth the same as sixty savings each lasting one minute, since estimates of the value of time savings of different lengths are unobtainable. One the one hand, it is clear that some short-time savings are valueless, since nothing can be done in the time saved. On the other hand, however, there are cases where the extra time makes possible some activity which would otherwise be precluded, as, for instance, when arriving a little earlier at a theater means that one does not have to wait until the interval to gain one's seat. Similarly, the value of an hour gained may depend partly upon when it is gained. *Faute de mieux*, such variations have to be ignored and an average treated as meaningful.

It is customary to distinguish between working time saved and leisure time saved, valuing the former at the relevant wage-rate, *e.g.*, drivers' wages in the case of buses and lorries. The argument is simply that this is what the worker's time is worth to his employer. This raises certain difficulties: if the driver does the same work as before, the gain is a matter of his having more leisure, while if he works the same hours as before and does more work, the value of his marginal net product may fall. The first point matters only if leisure time is valued differently from working time, but the second is awkward, if only in principle.

The various methods that have been proposed for valuing leisure time all rest upon the observation of choices which involve the substitution of leisure for some other good which, in contrast to leisure, does have a market price. Leisure can be substituted:

(i) for wages, net of tax, by workers;

(ii) for transport expenditure, by those who travel in their own time and are able to choose between alternative speeds of travel either directly (as drivers) or indirectly (*e.g.*, train versus bus);

(iii) for housing and transport expenditure, by people who can choose the location of their dwelling in relation to that of their place of work, and hence determine the length of the journey to work.

Each of these approaches has its difficulties. One difficulty which is common to all of them is that the substitution rarely involves just leisure and money; for example:

(i) A man may refuse to work an extra hour for an extra £1, yet value leisure at less than £1 because extra work involves missing a bus.

(ii) The driver who pays a toll and alters the running cost he incurs in order to get to his destination faster by using a toll-road is buying not only a time-saving but also the pleasure of driving along a restricted access highway. (A separate and trickier problem is that he may not know the true effect of the change in route and speed upon his car's running costs.)

(iii) A house nearer work may be in a less or more attractive environment.

These problems are surveyed in Winch; Mohring presents the theory underlying the approach via land values and shows how difficult it is to apply in practice; and Moses and Williamson discuss the related problem of passengers' choice between alternative modes of transport and list American applications of the approach via toll-road utilization. A recent piece of research in the United Kingdom produces valuations of time savings on journeys by public transport on the basis of comparing different combinations of cash and time outlays for given journeys; by substituting this result into the comparison of public and private transport opportunities, an estimate of the valuation of time savings by private transport is obtained. It might be noted that those investigations yield markedly lower estimates than those quoted on previous occasions in the United Kingdom. So, at the very least, one can say that there are major unknowns which may or may not prove tractable to further analysis.

So far we have made no mention of the many American studies of the impact of road improvements on by-passed shopping centers, on the value of adjacent property, and on the pattern of land use. This is because, as Mohring and Harwitz explain, these "studies suffer from either or both of two shortcomings: (1) they have concentrated on measuring benefits to specific population groups, and have done so in such a way that *net* benefits to society as a whole cannot be estimated from their results; and/or (2) they have concentrated on measuring highway-related changes in the nature and locus of economic activity and have not isolated those aspects of change that reflect net benefits."

We have concentrated on the application of cost-benefit analysis to a major motorway construction. The same general principles apply in other types of road investment, ranging from the "simple" kind of case such as the Channel Tunnel or the Forth Bridge to the far more complex network problems such as the whole transport system of a metropolitan area. If one wishes to include the *Buchanan Report* notion of "environment" in the calculus for urban road improvements the estimation process is likely to become very complex and laborious, if indeed it is feasible at all. The Report's own attempt to give an empirical filling to the idea is perfunctory in the extreme, but Beesley and Kain have proposed the principle of "environmental compensation" as an operational way of taking some account of environmental benefits and disbenefits in allocating budgeted expenditure on urban roads.

Finally, one might take note of the work of Bos and Koyck. They construct a complete general equilibrium model of a simple economy with three geographical areas and four goods. This involves a series of demand equations, technical equations, supply equations, and definitional equations. They show that a reduction in transport costs between two of these areas will raise national income by much more than the customary estimate of benefits, *i.e.*, the saving of transport costs of existing traffic between these areas plus half the cost of saving for the generated traffic. The essential point is that there is a much fuller allowance for ramifications, *e.g.*, they not only allow for the effects on goods transported but also on goods not transported. This system, of course, requires knowledge of all the demand and supply equations in the economy, so is scarcely capable of application by road engineers. It does, however, serve to remind us of the limitations of partial analysis.

(B) RAILWAYS

Railways have received a great deal less attention than roads from cost-benefit analysts, perhaps because they have, relatively if not absolutely, been a contracting sector of the transport industry in many countries. However, there have been two railway projects which have attracted attention in the United Kingdom in the last few years, and brief reference to them may be sufficient to illustrate the general principles.

In their well-known study of the New Victoria underground line in London, Foster and Beesley followed much the same principles as those employed in cost-benefit studies on the roads. The main benefits were time savings, cost savings (*e.g.*, private vehicle operating costs), extra comfort and convenience, and a variety of gains to Central London resulting from an effective widening of the catchment area. These benefits were distributed among the traffic diverted to the Victoria line, the traffic not so diverted, and generated traffic. But by and large, gains by generated traffic were unimportant compared with the other two categories; and of the various categories of savings, time savings amounted to almost half the total. When compared with the totality of costs involved in constructing and maintaining the line over a fifty-year period it was found that there was a "social surplus rate of return" of something of the order of 11%, the precise figure depending on the rate of interest chosen. The reasons why this rate of return is much greater than any financial or accounting return were said to be twofold: first, that London Transport's policy of averaging fares over different modes of traveling from one place to another meant that potential money receipts would underestimate benefits, and second, that potential revenue was reduced by the fact that road users are not charged the full social cost of the resources they absorb.

Although the proposals in the Beeching Report for closing down sections of the United Kingdom main-line railway system were not couched in cost-benefit terms, various commentators have looked at these aspects. The financial savings of the measures in view can be classified under four heads: improved methods of working, increased charges to some particular users (*e.g.*, National Coal Board), the savings from closing commuter lines, and the savings from rural closures. The first of these clearly represents a social as well as a financial saving, and need not detain us further. The second is more debatable; raising charges does not as such save any real resources, but it is possible that it would stimulate some savings of cost, and so to that extent would involve a social gain. In so far as the closure of commuter lines leads to further road congestion in large cities, the social saving is likely to be very small indeed, if anything at all. Finally, the closure of rural lines involves questions such as redundancies of specialist labor in out-of-the-way areas, extra road maintenance, more road accidents, lengthier journeys, etc. We are not concerned with the details of such calculations, but it might be noted that the overall result of Beeching would seem to be a substantial saving in real terms, even if not quite as large as the financial one. This does, however, leave out many intangibles, such as the more indirect and longer-term effects on particular regions, *e.g.*, the north of Scotland; and no one, to our knowledge, has suggested any unique and convincing way of quantifying and incorporating such repercussions in the analysis.

To summarize, the principles developed in the analysis of road improvements can fairly readily be applied to railway investment and in the assessment of the overall consequences of railway closures. As before, time savings are an important item in many cases, and to the extent that we are still very ignorant of how to crack this hardest of nuts, we are still in a position of intellectual discomfort.

(c) INLAND WATERWAYS

A good deal of work has been done in the United States on the estimation of benefits from new canals or from rendering an existing river channel navigable. This is of interest both for its own sake and for the light it throws on other transport fields.

Let us start with some points first made by Dupuit and raised diagrammatically by Renshaw. Let DD in Figure 1 be the demand curve for transport of a given commodity along a specified route and OF_r be the present

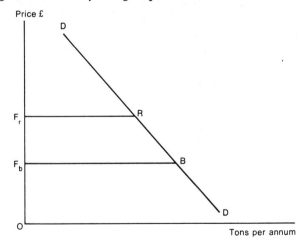

FIGURE 1. INLAND WATERWAYS.

rail freight rate. Then F_rR will be the existing volume of traffic. If a canal were built and the barge freight rate were OF_b traffic would expand to F_bB and the gain to shippers would be F_rRBF_b. This can be approximated by multiplying the existing volume of traffic F_rR by the unit freight saving F_rF_b, and this is the procedure followed in practice, *e.g.*, by the United States Corps of Engineers.

We now bring in complications.

1. The gain to shippers will not measure social gain unless freight rates adequately reflect marginal social costs. The main reason why this may not be so is that railways are frequently subject to regulation. Thus, if the freight receipts of the railway from the traffic in question exceed its avoidable costs, part of the gain to shippers is merely a transfer from the railway's owners, and must be deducted to obtain a measure of the social benefit from the canal.

2. The single demand curve of the diagram is a legitimate construction only when neither canal nor railway are part of a network and only when they both link exactly the same points. If neither of these conditions is fulfilled a more complicated construction is required, since total system rail traffic and total system barge traffic are both functions of both rail and barge freight rates (including shippers' terminal costs). The net gain to shippers who direct traffic from rail to a canal joining points A and B will differ from the simple product of the freight rate differential between A and B and the number of tons of freight diverted to the canal because:

(i) There may be a saving or gain in transport costs beyond A and B. Consider, for example, traffic from A to C; this may previously have gone by rail all the way without going through B.

(ii) There may be a saving or gain in costs other than freight. Thus, if canal is slower than rail more working capital will be required.

(iii) The railway may cut its freight rate in response to competition from the canal, so reducing the amount of traffic diverted.

Taking these three complications into account we find that the social benefit from the canal (gross of its costs) equals:

The saving in railway system costs

Less barge costs

Less increase in shippers' other costs

Plus the value to shippers of generated traffic on the canal.

This amount will be less than the product of the diverted traffic volume and the rail—canal freight rate differential unless the consumers' surplus on generated canal traffic outweighs any excess of railway rates over avoidable costs, any deficit between canal freight rates and barge costs, and any increase in shippers' other costs. Thus, except where traffic generation is expected to be large, multiplying the rate differential by traffic diversion may exaggerate benefits.

An example of the application of these techniques in a particular case relates to a cross-Florida barge canal. The following figures were produced:

$000 per annum

Item	Corps of Engineers	Consultants' Evaluation
Amortization, interest, maintenance	5,960	8,235
Transportation savings	6,980	1,102
Commercial fishing boats' benefits	70	0
Contractor's floating equipment benefits	30	0
New vessel delivery benefits	110	0
Recreational boating benefits	110	0
Flood-control benefits	240	0
Enhancement of waterfront land values	590	0
Benefit–cost ratio	1.20	0.13

To what extent the divergence is due to the facts that the Corps likes to build canals and that the consultants were retained by the railroads, and to what extent it is due to the intrinsic impossibility of making accurate estimates is left entirely to the reader to decide!

3. Land Usage

(A) URBAN RENEWAL

The application of cost-benefit analysis to proposals for redevelopment projects in towns has been discussed by Rothenberg and by Lichfield, both of whom have provided partial examples. The problem is complicated by the large number of types of people or institutions involved in urban development. Thus, the public acquisition of all private property in a slum area which is then redeveloped may involve more than one public agency, the dispossessed property owners, dispossessed tenants, owners and tenants of property adjacent to the redevelopment area, owners and tenants in other areas affected by the search for alternative accommodation on the part of the dispossessed tenants, potential developers and tenants of the cleared area, and, finally, the population of the town at large, both as taxpayers who meet some of the cost and (more indirectly) in so far as they suffer any adverse social consequence from the slum.

Lichfield is primarily concerned to show how all the costs and benefits to all affected parties can be systematically recorded in a set of accounts. The arguments in favor of proceeding this way instead of by simply listing and evaluating the net amount of each type of cost or benefit are threefold. First, starting on an all-inclusive gross basis and then canceling out to obtain net social benefits and costs insures against omissions. Second, the financial consequences of any project are sometimes important, and it may need to be redesigned in the light of the distribution of benefits and costs so as to compensate parties who would otherwise stand to lose from it, securing their support for it. The notion of compensation is familiar enough in welfare economics; here is a case where it can be important in practice. Third, whether or not financial transfers are used to affect the final distribution of net gains, that distribution will often be relevant to choice. In practice, that is to say, for good or bad reasons, the attitude of a county council or similar body toward a scheme will depend upon who gains as well as upon how much they gain. As the client of the cost-benefit analyst, it will therefore want to know more than just the total net figures.

Rothenberg discusses those types of benefits from urban development projects which involve slum clearance (mentioning other, aesthetic, considerations in a footnote). The first is the "internalization of market externalities," which we discuss in a moment, the second is the effect on real income distribution, and the third consists of the reduction in fire risks, crime, and other social consequences of slum living.

By internalizing market externalities, Rothenberg is thinking of the improvement of efficiency in resource allocation which can be achieved when a neighborhood is regarded as a unit where previously each of the separate owners in it had paid no regard to the adverse effects upon other owners' property of the inadequate maintenance of his own. Leaving aside a property tax complication which arises in the United States, Rothenberg's basic suggestion is that the social gain is measured by the increase in the total site value of the redevelopment area ("the value of the increased productivity of the land on the redevelopment site") corrected for any change in locational advantages brought about by redevelopment plus any increase in the value of properties adjacent to the redevelopment area resulting from its physical improvement (*i.e.*, technological externalities). The nature of the locational advantages is not very clear, and the convenient assumption that the sum of locational effects in the town as a whole is zero requires a good deal of justification.

Another difficulty relates to the increment of site values. The relevance of site values after slum clearance is obvious enough, since these values are the capitalized values of the rents to be had from the new buildings which are most appropriate, less the present value of the costs of erecting and maintaining those buildings. But the relevance of site values in the absence of a redevelopment scheme is not so clear.

A second difficulty with Rothenberg's expositions is that the illustrative example of his technique is an *ex-post* one. This introduces problems which are irrelevant to the *ex-ante* calculations that are required if the technique is ever to be of use. How different an actual past change in land value would have been if things had been different, that is to say, is no concern of the man making forward-looking estimates. His problem is to estimate how much the site would sell for if not only it but also all the surrounding sites were to be redeveloped. The way to answer this question is surely to start with an estimate of the rental or selling value of new accommodation in the improved area and then deduct for building costs.

But does this not require the art of the valuer as much as the science of the economist or econometrician?

(B) RECREATION

The problem of estimating and valuing recreational gains or losses due to projects has received a good deal of attention in the United States, where much of the discussion has been usefully surveyed by Clawson. An example of the problem is provided by the conflict between the provision of hydroelectric power and the preservation of the salmon runs in the Pacific Northwest (though this involves commercial fishing as well as sports fishing), while the gain to pleasure-boating from harbor improvements constitutes another case.

The principle is clear enough: what is needed in any particular case, on the benefit side, is measurement of the demand curve for access to the recreational facility in question. In practice, however, the choice has often lain between getting a figure by the wrong method and not getting one by the right method. Thus, Crutchfield lists four invalid techniques that have been used in the case of sports fishing.

(a) The argument that recreational facilities should not, in principle, be measured in money terms and that some level of provision should thus be arbitrarily set regardless of competing demands.

(b) Expenditure on providing and using the fishery. This merely measures the size of the sport fishing industry, but provides no indication of the loss that would be sustained if it disappeared.

(c) Imputing to sport fishing the market value of the fish caught, which implies that the angler is simply out to get some food.

(d) Valuing anglers' fishing time at the earnings the anglers could have acquired by working. This implies, among other things, that every hour spent in any kind of recreation is equally valuable.

The method proposed by Clawson and Trice and Wood, though statistically dubious, in practice does at least attempt to get at an imputed demand curve. The basic idea is to deduce the amount of usage at different "prices" from data of differential travel (and other) costs actually incurred in utilizing recreational facilities. If visitors to a recreation area come from a series of concentric zones one can reasonably postulate that anyone coming from the nearest zone enjoys a consumer's surplus which can be measured by the difference between his travel costs and those incurred by a man coming from the farthest zone. (There is an implicit assumption that the inner-zone resident derives as much satisfaction from a visit as the outer-zone man, but in a situation where approximations have to be made this does not seem too wild a one.) It is understood that this notion is due basically to Hotelling, and that use has been made of it in an Upper Feather River basin study. Unfortunately, it ignores the point that part of the consumers' surplus derived from proximity may be swallowed up in residential rent.

(C) LAND RECLAMATION

A Dutch paper describes the use of cost-benefit analysis for evaluating land-reclamation schemes. The particular points singled out are the insistence that one must not overlook related investment expenditure (*e.g.*, for the manufacture of raw materials for use on reclaimed land or for processing) and the corresponding returns, the use of foreign exchange shadow prices for such calculations as the expected saving in imports, allowances for harm done to fisheries and for benefits to road traffic, and a general recognition of the widespread nature and importance of intangible ("indeterminables" in Dutch–English). This is in no sense a complete listing of the relevant variables, but may be sufficient to savor the flavor of the dish.

4. Health

The major purpose of health programs is to save lives and reduce illness, and on this score there is some overlap with flood-prevention and road-improvement measures. There are no special problems which relate to the estimate of the costs of such programs, and the special problem of quantifying their effects is a matter for engineers and doctors rather than for economists. The interest of the latter is thus concentrated on the problem of valuing the benefits per life saved or per illness avoided, and this is all we shall consider here. And even within this limited area, we shall devote most of our time to the former. Our task is aided by the work of Weisbrod, and the useful surveys of Mushkin and Klarman. It might be further noted that this subject is a well-established one, having attracted the attention of Irving Fisher many years ago.

Before exploring the conceptual problems, it should be noted that some of the differences between authors in the way they estimate benefits stem from differences in the availability of statistics rather than from differences in what the authors would like to measure if they could. Thus, some of the simplifications in Reynolds' classic paper on the cost of road accidents were surely dictated by statistical exigencies rather than by considerations of high principle. This paper at least has the merit that after calculating the average costs in 1952 of various consequences of accidents (death, injury, property damage, insurance, administrative costs) the author went on, in an appendix, to show how his results could be used to estimate the purely economic benefits that would have accrued from new pedestrian crossing regulations and from adequate rear lighting on all vehicles and cycles.

A death avoided means that a loss of production may be avoided. Thus the present value of this is an economic benefit to be credited to the measure responsible for saving life. The first step in estimating it is to ascertain what the average person whose life is made safer will earn over the rest of his life. This depends upon age at death, the probability of survival to each higher age, the proportion of people at each age who will both be in the labor force and employed, and their contribution to production at each age.

(*a*) Age at death of those whose lives would be saved can be assumed to equal the average age of all those who die from whatever it is, unless the proposed life-saving expenditure obviously discriminates between age groups.

(*b*) The probability of survival to each age can be calculated from a life table for the group at risk, which should be amended to take account of any projected changes in its age-specific death-rates.

(*c*) Participation rates have to be forecast. It is generally agreed that the appropriate unemployment percentage to assume is that corresponding to "full employment."

(*d*) The earnings of a person are usually taken as a measure of the value of his marginal product, average product being obviously too high. Since it is future earnings which are relevant, the trend of growth in earnings should be allowed for if the analysis starts with figures of current earnings.

In practice, Weisbrod was able to construct estimates only for all men and all women and not for any particular group at risk, on account of data limitations. He and Reynolds both took earnings in a recent year without making any addition for future productivity increases.

The question whether housewives' services should be included as lost production has produced some discussion. Since there can be no question but that the loss of these services does impose a cost upon the survivors, it would sometimes bias choice to disregard the services of housewives in calculating production loss. As Klarman points out, the distribution of diseases between the sexes is not uniform, so that the relative economic benefits of different health programs will be affected by the weight given to housewives' services. What is really at issue, therefore, is how to measure their value, not whether to measure it. One possibility is to estimate their opportunity cost, *i.e.*, what housewives could earn in paid jobs (net of taxes and extra expenses), since this provides a minimum estimate of what the services are worth to the family. Alternatively, replacement cost, *i.e.*, the cost of a housekeeper, could be used. Weisbrod develops a very ingenious measure along these lines, where the value of a housewife's services is an increasing function of the number of other persons in her family. Neither measure can be accurately estimated in practice.

An even larger question is that of consumption. If society loses the production of the decedent, does it not also gain by not having to supply his own consumption? The answer is a matter of definition. If society is defined to exclude the decedent, the loss is confined to the wealth he would have accumulated and the taxes he would have paid less the transfers he would have received, and would be borne partly by his heirs and partly by the Government on behalf of all other taxpayers. It thus constitutes the amount which society so defined would find it worthwhile to pay to save his life (leaving aside all non-materialistic considerations for later discussion). Now the society whose representatives decide whether or not to undertake a measure which would save lives includes those people who may lose their lives if the proposed measure is not undertaken. Hence, so the argument might run, society is relevantly defined as including the prospective decedent, and his consumption is part of the social loss contingent upon his death.

Those, like Weisbrod, who take the line that consumption should be deducted have to face the problem of estimating it, and Weisbrod does so with commendable ingenuity. He argues that marginal rather than average consumption is relevant, and measures this as the change in family consumption with a change in family size, given income. Using family budget data, he calculates for each age bracket a weighted mean of the marginal consumption of persons in mean-income families of all sizes. It is only fair to add that he is far from dogmatic about the virtues of this approach.

Whether or not consumption is deducted, the economic value of a life saved varies according to a variety of factors, including age (it rises during childhood and falls after a certain age because of the twin influences of life earning patterns and discounting). Other things being equal, therefore, these calculations are worth undertaking only if we believe that more resources should be devoted to saving a more "productive" life than a less "productive" life—e.g., the average man in preference to the average woman of the same age, a white Protestant American in preference to a colored one, the average Englishman rather than the average Scot, a young worker rather than a baby.

To put the question this way outrages many people's feelings who do not see that the "other things" which are here assumed "equal" include one's estimate of the moral worth and human value of the different people and of the sorrow caused by their death. Without taking any position, therefore, we pass on to consider the non-economic value of a human life. By this we mean merely the amount which it is worth sacrificing in economic terms to save a life. It is less than infinity (since there are avoidable deaths), it exceeds zero (since money is spent to save lives) and it is worth ascertaining (in so far as consistent decision-making implies such a value).

The problem has been discussed by two French authors (Thedié and Abraham) with a certain Gallic elegance which does not entirely conceal the (necessary) arbitrariness of their procedure. They speak of "affective" loss and distinguish: affective injury to the family, affective injury to the rest of the nation, *pretium doloris* and *pretium vivendi*, the last two corresponding to the prospective decedent's aversion to suffering and death respectively. Court judgments, they consider, "should . . . make it possible in each country to obtain an average opinion as regards the sums to be spent to avoid the various affective losses."

Estimates of the benefits to be had from reducing illness, relating to particular diseases, offer no new problems of principle but involve great statistical difficulties. Mushkin discusses some of the principles, making the useful distinction between the effects of disability (*e.g.*, loss of working time) and debility (*e.g.*, loss of capacity while at work). Weisbrod and Klarman also raise valuable pointers. But the fundamental difficulty—and this affects the loss through deaths arguments too—is that of the multiplicity of variables—when there are manifold influences at work on life-expectancy, productivity, and the like, how can one hope to sort out the unambiguous influence of a particular health program or any other single causative factor?

Finally, mention should be made of a different approach to all those problems, even though, as far as we are aware, it is not one which has been pursued. This stresses that the problem is essentially the *ex-ante* one of deciding how much to spend in reducing various kinds of risk. Since people in their private capacities do incur costs to reduce risks to which they and their children are exposed, it is conceivable that their valuation of diminutions in risk could be inferred from their behavior.

Part Seven

INTERTEMPORAL CHOICE AND TECHNOLOGICAL CHANGE

Microeconomics is concerned with choices regarding investment projects. Such choices are among the most important decisions facing corporate executives and government officials. In the first article in this part of the book, James Lorie and Leonard Savage discuss the solution to three basic problems of this sort: (1) Given a firm's cost of capital, which group of investment proposals should a firm accept? (2) Given a fixed sum of money to be used for capital investment, what group of investment proposals should be undertaken? (3) How should the firm select the best among mutually exclusive alternative projects? These problems are of obvious importance to firms of any size, type, or industry.

In the next paper, William Baumol discusses the discount rate that should be used for public projects. He points out that: "At stake in the choice of an acceptable discount rate is no less than the allocation of resources between the private and public sectors of the economy." When a public activity draws resources from a number of sectors of the economy, he argues that "the correct social discount rate . . . will be a weighted average of the opportunity cost rate for the various sectors from which the project would draw its resources." Then he discusses the difficulties in applying these principles and in determining in practice what the social discount rate should be.

Technological change is one of the most important factors, if not the most important one, determining the rate of economic growth. Microeconomics has been concerned, particularly in recent years, with the determinants of the rate of technological change and with public policy toward science and technology. In the next paper, Zvi Griliches summarizes some of the available studies of the returns from investments in research and development. He concludes that: "Investment in research, both private and public, has clearly been one of the major sources of growth in output per man in this century. It has been a good investment both in the sense that it yielded a positive rate of return, and in the sense that this rate of return has been as good and often better than the rate of return on other private and public investments."

In the final paper in this part of the book, the editor discusses a number of aspects of public policy toward civilian technology in the United States. There is evidence that the United States may be under-investing in civilian technology. This evidence, as well as a variety of measures that might be adopted in an attempt to remedy this underinvestment, is described. In addition, some principles are put forth which may be useful in deciding whether or not to establish such a program, and in avoiding a number of pitfalls in this area. During 1978 and 1979, the Carter administration was engaged in an extensive evaluation of its policies toward civilian technology, due in part to the significant slowdown in the rate of productivity growth in the United States. Microeconomics played an important role in this policy discussion.

Three Problems in Rationing Capital

JAMES H. LORIE AND LEONARD J. SAVAGE

James Lorie is a professor at the Graduate School of Business of the University of Chicago. The late Leonard J. Savage was Professor of Statistics at Yale University. This paper appeared in the Journal of Business.

I. Introduction

Corporate executives face three tasks in achieving good financial management. The first is largely administrative and consists in finding an efficient procedure for preparing and reviewing capital budgets, for delegating authority and fixing responsibility for expenditures, and for finding some means for ultimate evaluation of completed investments. The second task is to forecast correctly the cash flows that can be expected to result from specified investment proposals, as well as the liquid resources that will be available for investment. The third task is to ration available capital or liquid resources among competing investment opportunities. This article is concerned with only this last task; it discusses three problems in the rationing of capital, in the sense of liquid resources.

1. Given a firm's cost of capital and a management policy of using this cost to identify acceptable investment proposals, which group of "independent" investment proposals should the firm accept? In other words, how should the firm's cost of capital be used to distinguish between acceptable and unacceptable investments? This is a problem that is typically faced by top management whenever it reviews and approves a capital budget.

Before presenting the second problem with which this paper deals, the use of the word "independent" in the preceding paragraph should be explained. Investment proposals are termed "independent"—although not completely accurately—when the worth of the individual investment proposal is not profoundly affected by the acceptance of others. For example, a proposal to invest in materials-handling equipment at location A may not profoundly affect the value of a proposal to build a new warehouse in location B. It is clear that the independence is never complete, but the degree of independence is markedly greater than for sets of so-called "mutually exclusive" investment proposals. Acceptance of one proposal in such a set renders all others in the same set clearly unacceptable—or even unthinkable. An example of mutually exclusive proposals would be alternative makes of automotive equipment for the same fleet or alternative warehouse designs for the same site. The choice among mutually exclusive proposals is usually faced later in the process of financial management than is the initial approval of a capital budget. That is, the decision as to which make automotive equipment to purchase, for example, typically comes later than the decision to purchase some make of equipment.

2. Given a fixed sum of money to be used for capital investment, what group of investment proposals should be undertaken? If a firm pursues a policy of fixing the size of its capital budget in dollars, without explicit cognizance of, or reference to, its cost of capital, how can it best allocate that sum among competing investment proposals? This problem will be considered both for proposals which require net outlays in only one accounting period and for those which require outlays of more than one accounting period. In the latter case, special difficulties arise.

3. How should a firm select the best among mutually exclusive alternatives? That is, when the management of an enterprise, in attempting to make concrete and explicit proposals for expenditures of a type which is included in an approved capital budget, develops more than one plausible way of investing money in conformance with the budget, how can it select the "best" way?

After presenting our solutions to these three problems, we shall discuss the solutions implied by the rate-of-return method of capital budgeting.[1] These solutions are worthy of special attention, since they are based on a different principle from the solutions that we propose and since the rate-of-return method is the most defensible method heretofore proposed in the business literature for maximizing corporate profits and net worth.

II. The Three Problems

A. GIVEN THE COST OF CAPITAL, WHAT GROUP OF INVESTMENTS SHOULD BE SELECTED?

The question of determining the cost of capital is difficult, and we, happily, shall not discuss it. Although there may be disagreement about meth-

[1] This method was developed by Joel Dean, who has probably done more than anyone else in applying the formal apparatus of economics to the solution of capital budgeting problems in their business context.

ods of calculating a firm's cost of capital, there is substantial agreement that the cost of capital is the rate at which a firm should discount future cash flows in order to determine their present value.[2] The first problem is to determine how selection should be made among "independent" investment proposals, given this cost or rate.

Assume that the firm's objective is to maximize the value of its net worth—not necessarily as measured by the accountant but rather as measured by the present value of its expected cash flows. This assumption is commonly made by economists and even business practitioners who have spoken on the subject. It is equivalent to asserting that the corporate management's objective is to maximize the value of the owner's equity or, alternatively, the value of the owner's income from the business. Given this objective and agreement about the significance of the firm's cost of capital, the problem of selecting investment proposals becomes trivial in those situations where there is a well-defined cost of capital; namely, proposals should be selected that have positive present values when discounted at the firm's cost of capital. The things to discount are the net cash flows resulting from the investments, and these cash flows should take taxes into account.

There is nothing unusual or original about this proposed solution. It is identical with that proposed by Lutz and Lutz[3] and is an economic commonplace. Joel Dean in his writings has developed and recommended a method which typically yields the same results for this problem, although the principle of solution is somewhat different, as is discussed later in this article.

The principle of accepting all proposals having positive present value at the firm's cost of capital is obvious, since the failure to do so would clearly mean foregoing an available increment in the present value of the firm's net worth. The principle is discussed here only because it seems a useful introduction to the somewhat more complicated problems that follow. An interesting property of this principle is that adherence to it will result in the present value of the firm's net worth being at a maximum at all points in time.

B. GIVEN A FIXED SUM FOR CAPITAL INVESTMENT, WHAT GROUP OF INVESTMENT PROPOSALS SHOULD BE UNDERTAKEN?

Some business firms—perhaps most—do not use the firm's cost of capital to distinguish between acceptable and unacceptable investments but,

[2] One of the difficulties with the concept of cost of capital is that in complicated circumstances there may be no one rate that plays this role. Still worse, the very concept of present value may be obscure.

[3] Friederich and Vera Lutz, *The Theory of Investment of the Firm* (Princeton: Princeton University Press, 1951). The solution proposed here is identical with the maximization of V−C, where V is the present value of future inflows and C is the present value of future outflows. This is discussed in chap. ii of the Lutz book.

instead, determine the magnitude of their capital budget in some other way that results in fixing an absolute dollar limit on capital expenditures. Perhaps, for example, a corporate management may determine for any one year that the capital budget shall not exceed estimated income after taxes plus depreciation allowances, after specified dividend payments. It is probable that the sum fixed as the limit is not radically different from the sum that would be expended if correct and explicit use were made of the firm's cost of capital, since most business firms presumably do not long persist in policies antithetical to the objective of making money. (The profit-maximizing principle is the one that makes use of the firm's cost of capital, as described previously.) Nevertheless, there are probably some differences in the amount that would be invested by a firm if it made correct use of the firm's cost of capital and the amount that would be invested if it fixed its capital budget by other means, expressing the constraint on expenditures as being a maximum outlay. At the very least, the differences in the ways of thinking suggest the usefulness to some firms of a principle that indicates the "best" group of investments that can be made with a fixed sum of money.

The problem is trivial when there are net outlays in only one accounting period—typically, one year. In such cases, investment proposals should be ranked according to their present value—at the firm's cost of capital—per dollar of outlay required. Once investment proposals have been ranked according to this criterion, it is easy to select the best group by starting with the investment proposal having the highest present value per dollar of outlay and proceeding down the list until the fixed sum is exhausted.[4]

The problem can become more difficult when discontinuities are taken into account. For large firms, the vast majority of investment proposals constitute such a small proportion of their total capital budget that the problems created by discontinuities can be disregarded at only insignificant cost, especially when the imprecision of the estimates of incomes is taken into account. When a project constitutes a large proportion of the capital budget, the problem of discontinuities may become serious, though not necessarily difficult to deal with. This problem can become serious because of the obvious fact that accepting the large proposal because it is "richer" than smaller proposals may preclude the possibility of accepting two or more smaller and less rich proposals which, in combination, have a greater value than the larger proposal. For example, suppose that the total amount available for investment were $1,000 and that only three investment proposals had been made: one requiring a net outlay of $600 and creating an increment in present value of $1,000 and two others, each requiring a net

[4] We mention, for completeness, that the outlay or the present value or both for a proposal can be negative. Proposals for which the outlay alone is negative—something for nothing—are always desirable but almost never available. Proposals for which both the outlay and present value are negative can sometimes be acceptable if something sufficiently profitable can be done with ready cash expressed by the negative outlay. The rules which we shall develop can be extended to cover such cases.

outlay of $500 and each creating an increment in present value of $600. Under these circumstances, the adoption of the richest alternative, the first, would mean foregoing the other two alternatives, even though in combination they would create an increment in present value of $1,200 as compared with the increment of $1,000 resulting from the adoption of the richest investment alternative. Such discontinuities deserve special attention, but the general principles dealing with them will not be worked out here, primarily because we do not know them.

We shall, however, deal with the more serious difficulties created by the necessity to choose among investment proposals some of which require net cash outlays in more than one accounting period. In such cases a constraint is imposed not only by the fixed sum available for capital investment in the first period but also by the fixed sums available to carry out present commitments in subsequent time periods. Each such investment requires, so to speak, the use of two or more kinds of money—money from the first period and money from each subsequent period in which net outlays are required. We shall discuss only the case of investments requiring net outlays in two periods, for simplicity of exposition and because the principle—although not the mechanics—is the same as for investments requiring net outlays in more than two periods.

Let us start with a very simple case. Suppose that all the available opportunities for investment that yield a positive income can be adopted without exceeding the maximum permitted outlay in either time period one or time period two. Clearly, no better solution can be found, because all desirable opportunities have been exhausted. This simple case is mentioned not because of its practical importance, which is admittedly slight, but because it may clarify the more complicated cases that follow.

Next, consider a slightly more complicated case. Suppose that the opportunities available require more funds from either time period one or two than are permitted by the imposed constraints. Under these circumstances the problem becomes somewhat more complicated, but it still may not be very complicated. It is still relatively simple if (a) the best use of money available in period one does not exhaust the money available in period two or (b) the best use of money available in period two does not exhaust the money available in period one. In either case the optimum solution—that is, the solution which results in the greatest increment in the net worth of the firm, subject to the two stated constraints—is the one that makes the best possible use of the funds available for investment in one of the two time periods.

This statement is justified by the following reasoning. The imposition of additional restrictions upon the freedom of action of any agency can obviously never increase the value of the best opportunity available to that agency. In the problem at hand, this means that the imposition of an absolute dollar constraint or restriction in time period two can never make it possible to make better use of dollars available in time period one than would have been possible in the absence of that constraint. Thus, if the best possible use is made of the dollars available in time period one, the imposition of a restriction relating to time period two can never mean increased possibilities of profit from the use of funds available in time period one. Therefore, the maximization of the productivity of dollars available in time period one will constitute a maximization of productivity subject to the two constraints as well as to the one constraint. The reasoning is equally valid if we start with the constraint referring to time period two and maximize productivity of money available in that time period and then think of the effect of the additional constraint imposed for time period one.

Unfortunately, typical circumstances will probably make the relatively simple solutions unavailable. The solution to the relatively complex problem will—abstracting from discontinuities—require expending the full amount available for investment in each period. To illustrate how the solution is to be reached, consider the average actual net outlay of the two periods as being an outlay in a single "virtual" period and consider the average net outlay that is permitted by the constraints as being the average permitted outlay for the "virtual" period. Plan a budget for this "virtual" period according to the method of the one-period problem with which this section begins. That is, ration the capital available in the "virtual" period among the available investment opportunities so as to maximize the firm's net worth according to the principles stated in the discussion of the one-period problem. If, by accident, this budget happens to require precisely those outlays which are permitted for the first and second periods, it is easy to see that the problem has been solved. No other budget with a higher present value can be devised within the stated constraints for periods one and two.

Typically, the happy accident referred to in the preceding paragraph will not occur. The optimum use of the average amount available for investment in the two periods will typically result in expending too much in one period and not so much as is permitted in the other. Indeed, the happy accident was mentioned only as a step in explaining one method that will work. Though a simple average will almost never work, there is always some weighted average that will, and it can be found by trial and error. We shall describe in some detail a method that is mathematically equivalent to this method of weighted averages. In this method the solution is found by choosing, for suitable positive constants p_1 and p_2, those, and only those, proposals for which the following quantity is positive: $y - p_1c_1 - p_2c_2$. Here y is the present value of the proposal; c_1 and c_2 are the present values of the net outlays required in the first and second periods, respectively; and the multipliers p_1 and p_2 are auxiliary quantities for which there does not seem to be an immediate interpretation but that nonetheless help in solving the problem.[5]

Initially, the values of p_1 and p_2 will be determined by judgment. Subse-

[5] The multipliers, p_1 and p_2, are closely related to what are known in mathematics and in economics as "Lagrange multipliers."

quently, they will be altered by trial and error until the amounts to be expended in the first and second period, according to the rule just enunciated, are precisely the amounts permitted by the constraints. The initial choice of values for p_1 and p_2 is not very important, since a graphical process can usually lead rapidly to the correct values.

TABLE 1

Investment	Outlay— Period 1 (c_1)	Outlay— Period 2 (c_2)	Present Value of Investment
a...........	$12	$ 3	$14
b...........	54	7	17
c...........	6	6	17
d...........	6	2	15
e...........	30	35	40
f...........	6	6	12
g...........	48	4	14
h...........	36	3	10
i...........	18	3	12

Certain special possibilities are worth noting. Proposals of positive present value may have negative cost, that is, release cash, for either period. Some proposals of zero or negative present value may be acceptable because they release cash for one period or both. All such possibilities are automatically covered by the rule as stated and by the rules to be given for later problems.

Finding the correct values for p_1 and p_2 is sometimes not easy—especially when combined with the problem of selecting among mutually exclusive alternatives—but the task is usually as nothing compared to the interests involved or compared to many everyday engineering problems.[6] The following example may clarify the process.

Nine investments have been proposed. The present value of the net outlays required in the first and second time periods and the present values of the investments are as shown in Table 1. The finance committee has stated that $50 and $22 will be available for capital investment in the first and second periods, respectively. We shall consider these amounts to have present values of $50 and $20, respectively. According to the principle stated above, we must now find appropriate multipliers, p_1 and p_2.

Multipliers p_1 and p_2 were initially set at 1 and 3, respectively. With these values, only for investment d was the expression $(y - p_1 c_1 - p_2 c_2)$ positive and therefore acceptable. This would have resulted in net outlays of only $6 and $2 in periods one and two, respectively. Clearly, the values initially chosen for p_1 and p_2 were too great. On the other hand, values of 0.1 and 0.5 for p_1 and p_2 respectively, are too low, resulting in a positive

---

[6] It is true, however, that the numbers in engineering problems are less conjectural; hence the cost of calculation is more likely to be considered worth while.

value of $(y - p_1c_1 - p_2c_2)$ for all investments and required outlays in periods one and two far exceeding the permitted outlays.

Values of 0.33 and 1 for p_1 and p_2 result in a near-perfect fit. The expression $(y - p_1c_1 - p_2c_2)$ is postive for investments a, c, d, f, and i. These investments require outlays of $48 and $20 in the first and second periods, as near the permitted outlays of $50 and $20 as discontinuities permit. No other group of investments that is possible within the stated constraints has a greater present value than $70, the present value of this group.[7]

C. SELECTING THE BEST AMONG MUTUALLY EXCLUSIVE ALTERNATIVES

Before moneys are actually expended in fulfillment of an approved capital budget, the firm usually considers mutually exclusive alternative ways of making the generally described capital investment. When the firm is operating without an absolute limit on the dollars to be invested, the solution to the problem of selecting the best alternative is obvious. (Throughout this article, it is assumed that decisions regarding individual investment proposals do not significantly affect the firm's cost of capital.) The best alternative is the one with the greatest present value at the firm's cost of capital.

When the firm is operating subject to the constraint of an absolute dollar limit on capital expenditures, the problem is more difficult. Consider, first, the case in which there are net outlays in only one time period. The solution is found by the following process:

1. From each set of mutually exclusive alternatives, select that alternative for which the following quantity is a maximum: $y - pc$. Here y is the present value of the alternative; c is the net outlay required; and p is a constant of a magnitude chosen initially according to the judgment of the analyst. (Remember that the alternative of making no investment—that is accepting $y = 0$ and $c = 0$—is always available, so that the maximum in question is never negative.)

2. Compute the total outlays required to adopt all the investment proposals selected according to the principle just specified.

3. If the total outlay required exceeds the total amount available, p should be increased; if the total amount required is less than the amount available for investment, p should be reduced. By trial and error, a value for p can be found that will equate the amount required for investment with that available for investment.

It should be clear that, as the value of p is increased, the importance of the product, pc, increases, with a consequent increase in the probability that in each set of mutually exclusive alternatives, an alternative will be selected that requires a smaller net outlay than is required with a smaller value for p. Thus increasing p tends to reduce the total amount required

[7] For the three-period problem, the relevant quantity is $(y - p_1c_1 - p_2c_2 - p_3c_3)$ rather than $(y - p_1c_1 - p_2c_2)$.

to adopt the investment proposals selected according to the principle indicated in (1) above. Conversely, reducing p tends to increase the outlay required to adopt the investment proposals selected according to this principle.

When there are net outlays in more than one period, the principle of solution is the same. Instead of maximizing the quantity $(y - pc)$, it is necessary to maximize the quantity $(y - p_1c_1 - p_2c_2)$, where again c_1 and c_2 are the net outlays in the first and second periods and p_1 and p_2 are auxiliary multipliers.

Up to this point, we have not discussed the problem of rationing capital among both independent investment proposals and sets of mutually exclusive investment proposals. Superficially, this problem seems different from the one of rationing among mutually exclusive proposals only, but in fact the problems are the same. The identity rests upon the fact that each so-called "independent" proposal is and should be considered a member of the set of proposals consisting of the independent proposal and of the always present proposal to do nothing. When independent proposals are viewed in this way, it can be seen that the case of rationing simultaneously among independent proposals and sets of mutually exclusive proposals is really just a special case of rationing among mutually exclusive proposals according to the principles outlined in the preceding paragraph.

The mechanics of solution are easily worked out. All that is required in order to make the solution the same as the solution for what we have called "mutually exclusive" sets of alternatives is that each so-called "independent" proposal be treated as a member of a mutually exclusive set consisting of itself and of the alternative of doing nothing. Once this is done, it is possible to go into the familiar routine of selecting from each set that proposal for which the expression $(y - pc)$, or its appropriate modification to take account of constraints existing in more than one time period, is a maximum. Again, of course, that value of p will have to be found which results in matching as nearly as discontinuities permit the outlays required by the accepted proposals with the outlays permitted by the stated budgetary constraints.

III. Some Comparisons with the Rate-of-Return Method of Capital Rationing[8]

Since the rate-of-return method of capital rationing is fully described elsewhere, we shall describe it only briefly.[9] As in the methods described

[8] Joel Dean has pioneered in the development of methods of capital rationing that have an understandable relationship to profit maximization, in contrast to methods still quite widely used in business that rely on such criteria as pay-back, average return on book investment, etc. The method that he advocates is called the "rate-of-return" method.
[9] See Joel Dean, *Capital Budgeting* (New York: Columbia University Press, 1951); "Measuring the Productivity of Capital," *Harvard Business Review*, January–February, 1954.

previously, attention is focused exclusively on net cash flows rather than on the data produced by conventional accounting practices. Investment proposals are ranked according to their "rate of return," defined as that rate of discounting which reduces a stream of cash flows to zero, and selected from this ranking, starting with the highest rate of return.

The rate-of-return solution to the three problems that are the subject of this paper is discussed below.

A. GIVEN THE COSTS OF CAPITAL, WHAT GROUP OF INVESTMENTS SHOULD BE SELECTED?

The rate-of-return solution to the problem of selecting a group of independent proposals, given the firm's cost of capital, is to accept all investment proposals having a rate of return greater than the firm's cost of capital. This solution is necessarily identical with the solution proposed previously, except when the present value of some of the proposals is other than a steadily decreasing function of the cost of capital. An intuitive substantiation of this statement is achieved by an understanding of Figure 1.

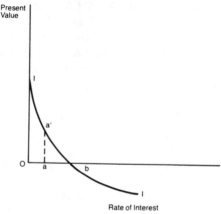

FIGURE 1

In Figure 1, *I–I* indicates the present value of an investment at different rates of interest; *Oa* is the firm's cost of capital; *Ob* is the rate of return on the investment; and *aa'* is the present value of the investment at the firm's cost of capital. It should be clear from the diagram that any proposal that has a positive ordinate (present value) at the firm's cost of capital will also have a rate of return (*x*-intercept) greater than the cost of capital. (However, it usually takes a little longer to find an intercept than to determine the value of an ordinate at one point.)

Under what circumstances can the present value of an investment proposal be something other than a steadily decreasing function of the cost of capital? Some investment proposals can intersect the *x*-axis at more than one point. In particular, investment proposals having initial cash outlays, subsequent net cash inflows, and final net cash outlays can intersect the x-axis more than once and have, therefore, more than one rate of return. Investments of this nature are rare, but they do occur, especially in the extractive industries. For example, an investment proposal might consist of an investment in an oil pump that gets a fixed quantity of oil out of the ground more rapidly than the pump currently in use. Making this investment would require an initial net outlay (for the new pump), subsequent net incremental cash inflow (larger oil production), and final net incremental cash outlay (the absence of oil production, because of its earlier exhaustion with the use of the higher-capacity new pump).[10] The present value of an investment in such a pump could look like Figure 2. In Figure 2, *I–I* indicates the present value of the investment; *Oa* is the firm's cost of capital; *Ob* and *Oc* are the two rates of return on the investment; and *aa'* is the present value of the investment at the firm's cost of capital.

The reasoning behind this apparent paradox of the double rate of return is as follows:

a) As the cost of capital of the firm approaches zero, the present value of the investment proposal approaches the algebraic sum of net cash flow and will be negative if this sum is negative.

b) As the cost of capital increases, the present value of the final net cash out-flow diminishes in importance relative to the earlier flows, and this diminution can cause the present value of the entire proposal to become positive.

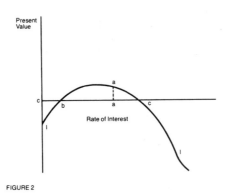

FIGURE 2

c) If the cost of capital continues to increase, the significance of all future cash flows tends to diminish, causing the present value of the proposal to approach the initial outlay as a limit.

The rate-of-return criterion for judging the acceptability of investment

[10] These incremental flows are measured with reference to the flows that would have resulted from the use of the smaller pump. Thus the final net outlay is not absolute but rather by comparison with oil (money) that would have produced had the smaller pump been in use.

proposals, as it has been presented in pubished works, is then ambiguous or anomalous. This is in contrast to the clarity and uniform accuracy of the decisions indicated by the principle proposed earlier, which relates to the present value of an investment at the cost of capital rather than to a comparison between the cost of capital and the rate of return.[11]

B. GIVEN A FIXED SUM FOR CAPITAL INVESTMENT, WHAT GROUP OF INVESTMENT PROPOSALS SHOULD BE UNDERTAKEN?

The rate-of-return solution to the problem of allocating a fixed sum of money—without reference to cost of capital—among competing proposals is to order the proposals according to their rate of return and to proceed down the ladder thus created until the available funds are exhausted. The

TABLE 2

Period	Net Cash Flows Investment A	Investment B
0– year.......	−$ 85	−$ 90
0–1 year.......	+ 17	+ 21
1–2 years	+ 35	+ 33
2–3 years	+ 68	+ 57
3–4 years	+ 131	+ 94
4–5 years	+ 216	+ 155
5–6 years	+ 357	+ 255
6–7 years	+ 546	+ 420
7–8 years	+ 555	+ 695
8–9 years	+ 345	+ 1,150
Present value at 20%	+ 606	+ 853
Rate of return.....	66%	62%

group of investment proposals selected by the use of this principle can be different, and probably would usually be different, from the group selected when the criterion is present value rather than rate of return. A difference between the two groups would not exist if the available capital funds were just equal to that amount which would permit investment in all those proposals having a rate of return at least equal to the firm's cost of capital and only those proposals, and if the anomalies mentioned under Section A were not present.

The preceding statements are equivalent to saying that the groups of

---

[11] The rate-of-return rule could be easily modified to remove this ambiguity or anomaly by specifying that the relevant rate of return is the one at which the investment is a decreasing function of the rate of interest.

investments that would be chosen by the use of the two principles or criteria would necessarily be the same only if the fixed sum to be invested happened to be the optimum sum and that investment of any other sum could result in selection of different groups of proposals by use of the two principles. This difference would result from the fact that the different principles can result in a different ranking of proposals within the group that would be accepted if the optimum amount were invested. Table 2 indicates the validity of the statement that the ordering of two investment proposals according to their rate of return can be contrary to their ordering according to their present value per dollar of outlay.

The example of Table 2 illustrates that a proposal with a higher rate of return can have a lower present value and that, therefore, the two rules can conflict. The present-value rule maximizes the present value of the firm's net worth—by definition—and the rate-of-return rule therefore may not.

This discrepancy is undoubtedly of small practical significance. In the first place, firms that ration their capital rationally use the firm's cost of capital as the constraint rather than an absolute dollar sum, and under such rational behavior the two rules yield the same results, with the exception noted previously. (Undoubtedly, no firms long persist in setting absolute dollar constraints that differ significantly in their effects from the cost of capital constraint.) In the second place, the present values of investment proposals, expressed as functions of the cost of capital, are often thoughtful enough not to intersect above the *x*-axis (the rate-of-interest axis), a necessary condition for a conflict between the rate-of-return and present-value principles.

C. SELECTING THE BEST AMONG MUTUALLY EXCLUSIVE ALTERNATIVES

The rate-of-return solution to the problem of selecting the "best" among mutually exclusive investment alternatives, although occasionally tricky in practice, is simply explained as follows:

1. Compute the rate of return for that investment proposal, among the set of mutually exclusive proposals, requiring the least initial net outlay.

2. If the rate of return on the investment requiring the smallest outlay exceeds the firm's cost of capital (or other cutoff rate), tentatively accept that investment. Next compute the rate of return on the incremental outlay needed for the investment requiring the second lowest outlay. If that rate exceeds the firm's cutoff rate, accept the investment requiring the greater outlay in preference to that requiring the lesser. Proceed by such paired comparisons (based on rates of return on incremental outlay) to eliminate all but one investment.

3. If the rate of return on the proposal requiring the least outlay does not exceed the firm's cutoff rate, drop it from further consideration, and

compute the rate of return for the proposal requiring the next least outlay. If that rate exceeds the firm's cutoff rate, that investment proposal becomes the bench mark for the first paired comparison. If that rate does not exceed the firm's cutoff rate, drop that proposal from further consideration. The process just described is to be repeated until either a proposal is found with a rate of return exceeding the cost of capital or until all proposals have been eliminated because their rates of return do not exceed the cutoff rate.

The rate-of-return solution to the problem of selecting the best among mutually exclusive investment alternatives is especially subject to the ambiguities and anomalies mentioned under Section A, because the costs and revenues associated with incremental investments required for proposals included in mutually exclusive sets are much more likely to have unusual time shapes and reversals than are the costs and revenues associated with independent investments.

SUMMARY

We have given solutions to three problems in bugeting capital so as to maximize the net worth of the firm. The solutions that we have given differ in principle from those implied by the rate-of-return method of capital rationing. The difference in principle can lead to differences in behavior. Differences in behavior will be rare in coping with problems of the first and third sorts and will be relatively frequent for problems of the second sort. When differences do exist, the rate-of-return solution does not result in maximizing the present worth of the firm's net worth.

On the Discount Rate for Public Projects

WILLIAM J. BAUMOL

William Baumol is Professor of Economics at Princeton and New York Universities. This paper was published by the Joint Economic Committee of Congress in 1969.

1. Significance of the Discount Rate

It is generally recognized that the discount rate is a critical datum for the evaluation of any proposed Government project. Even where there is little basic disagreement about the investment's prospective costs and benefits, the choice of discount rate figure may make the difference between acceptance and rejection. A project which seems to yield substantial net benefits when evaluated at a 3 percent rate may well appear extremely wasteful if the rate is 5 percent.

Yet, despite the critical nature of this parameter, in some calculations it is assigned a value almost cavalierly, with little attempt to show that the selected figure is not chosen arbitrarily and capriciously. One sometimes encounters discount figures in cost-benefit calculations whose sole justification seems to be that similar figures were used in the past. Of course that can never be an acceptable argument, first because the earlier figure may have had as little justification as the one presently employed and, second, because changing circumstances change the appropriate value of the discount rate.

At stake in the choice of an acceptable discount rate is no less than the allocation of resources between the private and the public sectors of the economy. The discount rate, by indicating what Government projects should be undertaken, can determine the proportion of the economy's activity that is operated by governmental agencies, and hence, the proportion that remains in the hands of private enterprise.

Moreover, even given the decision on resource allocation between the private and the public sectors, the choice of discount rate can affect profoundly the type of projects undertaken by Government agencies. When the discount rate is low this will encourage highly durable investments, the bulk of whose benefits will become available only in the distant future. Thus, when the economy is beset by urgent and immediate investment needs a relatively high discount rate will tend to be appropriate.

With so much at issue it is well worth exploring in some detail the principles that should be employed in arriving at a discount figure, and the rationale that underlies them. This paper undertakes to do so without heavy reliance on the jargon of technical economics.

2. The Basic Criterion: Opportunity Cost

The observation that the discount rate is the arbiter of the allocation of resources between private and public enterprise is the key to the principles which underlie the choice of an acceptable discount figure. The right discount rate becomes that number which indicates correctly when resources should be transferred from one sector to another.

More specifically, suppose one is considering the construction of a dam which will employ x man-hours of labor, y tons of cement, and z kilowatt hours of electricity. In an economy in which the level of employment is high, if those resources are made available to the Government they must be transferred out of the private sector. Just as in the guns versus butter case, each item added to the public sector involves some corresponding reduction in the volume of resources in private hands.

We may now establish a rather obvious criterion to test the desirability of the proposed resource transfer. If the resources in question produce a rate of return in the private sector which society evaluates at r percent, then the resources should be transferred to the public project if that project yields a return greater than r percent. They should be left in private hands if their potential earnings in the proposed government investment is less than r percent. The logic of this criterion is self-evident. It states no more than the minimal dictate of efficiency: Never take resources out of a use where they bring in (say) 9 percent in order to utilize them in a manner which yields only 6 percent!

The standard which has just been described is the concept economists call *opportunity cost*. We have stated, in effect, that the proper criterion on which to judge the desirability of a governmental project, from the point of view of the general welfare, is the value of the opportunities which the private sector must pass by when the resources are withdrawn from that sector. A government project is desirable if and only if the value of the net benefits which it promises exceeds the cost of the lost productive opportunities which that investment causes.

It follows almost immediately that *the correct discount rate for the evaluation of a government project is the percentage rate of return that the resources utilized would otherwise provide in the private sector.* That is, the correct discount rate is the opportunity cost in terms of the potential rate of return in alternative uses on the resources that would be utilized by the project. An example will readily show why this must be so. Suppose these resources are capable of returning our hypothetical 9 percent in the private sector. Consider three proposed government projects: Project A which offers an average rate of return of 12 percent, project B whose expected return is 9 percent, and project C whose anticipated yield is 7 percent. It should be obvious that if we discount the returns of project C at the opportunity rate of 9 percent we will end up with a negative net present value figure (i.e., 7 percent discounted at 9 percent comes out to less ⁀n the principal invested). If we discount project B's expected returns at 9 percent we will obtain a zero figure for the present value of net benefits (the returns will just cover the cost of the investment). Only project A, when discounted at 9 percent, will be assigned a positive net benefit figure. Thus the discount rate calculated at the opportunity rate works just as it should: it passes projects whose yield is greater than its resources could earn in the private sector and turns down projects whose benefits are not ⁀qual to the earnings the resources could provide in private hands.

The same illustration also shows immediately how an incorrect choice of discount figure—one not equal to the opportunity rate—can result in decisions harmful to the general welfare. For example, consider two extreme possibilities in terms of our hypothetical figures—a discount rate that is much too high (say, 15 percent) and one that is much too low (say, 5 percent). At the excessive 15 percent figure the usual cost-benefit criterion would reject all three projects, even project A. The Government would then fail to undertake an investment that clearly represents an efficient use of society's resources. On the other hand, a 5 percent discount rate would, on a cost-benefit criterion, lead to the construction of all three projects. Thus even investment C would be undertaken even though it uses resources that should better be left in private hands. For it takes resources from employments in which they return 9 percent and puts them into an occupation in which they bring in only 7 percent, a palpable 2 percent net loss to the community.

The upshot is perfectly clear. Any discount rate that is clearly above or clearly below the opportunity cost rate is indefensible because either of these will lead to decisions that reduce the general welfare. We must turn therefore to an investigation of the opportunity cost rate of resources, for once we have determined this we will have the requisite information for the choice of discount rate to be used in the evaluation of Government projects.

3. Reasons for Differences in Opportunity Costs

Matters would be relatively simple if any batch of resources withdrawn from the private sector were to incur the same (percentage) opportunity cost as any other batch. If an opportunity cost of r percent were to apply throughout the economy, to determine the social discount rate one would simply proceed to estimate this number, r, and the resulting figure would then be the discount rate.

Unfortunately, for a variety of reasons, the magnitude of the opportunity cost varies with the source from which a project's resources are obtained. As we will see, resources which might otherwise have been used by a corporation will generally incur a higher opportunity cost than do resources drawn from direct consumer use.

In some sense, differences in opportunity costs of resources taken from different sectors of the economy are all a manifestation of imperfections in the market. In principle, if capital could flow without restriction to any sector of the economy where its earnings would be increased and all returns on capital were to accrue to its investors, resources would be forced by the market process to yield the same rate of return in every use. The standard argument is easily summarized. Suppose in such an economy that there were two industries, one of which returned k percent on capital while the other yielded some higher return, say $2k$. In that case investors would find it profitable to withdraw funds from the first of these industries and put them to work in the second. But the growing scarcity of capital in the first industry would tend to reduce its outputs, raising its prices and (therefore) its rate of return. Similarly, in the second industry the influx of capital would expand production, and force prices and returns downward. This transfer of capital would continue so long as any substantial difference in the two rates of return persisted. The flow of capital would cease only when the rate of return in the first industry had risen sufficiently and that in the second had fallen enough to make the two rates of return equal. At that point, clearly, capital withdrawn from the one sector would have exactly the same rate of return as capital withdrawn from the other—their opportunity cost rates would be identical.

Why does such equalization generally not occur in practice? There are two broad reasons: First, part of the return to capital may not accrue to the investor. A prime example of this is provided by taxation which siphons part of that return off to the Government, and since the burden of taxation varies from industry to industry, from the corporate to the noncorporate sector, and so forth, it means that opportunity costs will vary accordingly. A second broad reason for such variation lies in impediments, such as monopoly, to the influx of capital into some productive activities. Specifically, we will consider three broad sources of such divergence because they must be taken into explicit account in the determination of the social rate of discount. These elements are the following: (a) taxes, (b) risk, (c) divergence between private and social benefits (externalities). Let us examine them in turn.

4. *The Role of Taxes: Analysis*

As already indicated, the burden of taxes will vary from industry to industry, from one class of producer to another, depending on its mode of organization—that is, corporation, partnership, or do-it-yourself production by the consumer himself.

However, let us, to begin with, assume for simplicity that there are only two classes of producer: The corporation, which pays a 50 percent corporate income tax, and the private individual who produces certain items for his own use, and who pay no taxes on this production process. Assume also that there are available for sale riskless Government bonds offering a rate of return of, say, 5 percent.

In our example, it is easy to determine the opportunity cost of resources withdrawn from the corporate sector. Corporations must yield to their investors an after-tax return of 5 percent. For otherwise investors would be unwilling to provide any funds to the corporations and would instead put all their money into the safe Government bonds. But the required after-tax return of 5 percent on corporate capital means that these firms must earn 10 percent on capital *before* payment of the 50 percent corporate profit tax. In other words, the presence of special taxes on the output of this sector means that resources invested in it must produce goods and services valued at a level sufficiently high to yield a 10 percent return. The corporation can then engage only in the production of consumers' or producers' goods whose purchasers value them sufficiently to pay a price that yields a 10 percent return on corporate investment. A withdrawal of resources from the corporation, then, will cause a reduction in output whose opportunity cost in terms of consumer valuation is given by that figure: 10 percent.

Notice in evaluating resources from the corporate sector in this way, it does not matter whether the resources are used by the firm to produce consumers' goods or producers' goods (e.g., machinery). So long as the output in question is supplied by a corporation, the resources used in its manufacture will have a 10 percent opportunity cost. The relevance of this consideration will be clear presently.

Let us turn now to the more difficult problem, the opportunity cost of resources withdrawn from the other productive sector in our imaginary economy, the do-it-yourself consumers.

Since goods produced by consumers for their own use do not provide a rate of return that is measurable directly it is necessary to find some indirect means by which their opportunity cost can be inferred. Fortunately there is a straightforward way in which this can be done. When a consumer voluntarily purchases one of the bonds available in our imaginary economy he is indicating that their 5 percent rate of return compensates him for giving up the use of that money in his do-it-yourself operation. Put another way, if this investment in his own production were worth more than 5 percent to him he would not buy the bond, while if his investment in his own work were worth less than 5 percent to him he would purchase more bonds than he does. Thus without any conscious calculation on his part, a consumer's security purchases reveal something about what the rate of return of investment in the production of goods for his own consumption is worth to him—the opportunity cost incurred when a dollar's worth of resources is prevented from going to him and is transferred to a Government investment project.

What about consumers who do not buy any bonds? It follows from the preceding discussion that their opportunity cost must be at least as high and probably higher than it is for bond purchasers. To a man who chooses *not* to purchase bonds at 5 percent, the purpose for which he uses his money must by definition be worth more than 5 percent. This is no less true for a man who fails to purchase bonds because "he cannot afford them." That phrase merely implies that his consumption dollar means a great deal to him—perhaps even survival itself, and is therefore certainly more valuable than 5 percent.

We may summarize by saying that the opportunity cost of present consumption to nonbondholders must be at least as great as the figure for bondholders, and that to bondholders the opportunity cost of resources is indicated by the rate of return on their bondholdings.

In practice, of course, there is a broad spectrum of earnings tax conditions, among which are included the untaxed do-it-yourself productive process and corporate production with its (roughly) 50 percent profits tax. We have seen that the opportunity cost of resources from the untaxed sector (assuming the absence of risk and other such complications) is, roughly, r percent. In the corporation, half of whose earnings are taxed away the opportunity cost rate is $2r$, where r is the bond rate of interest. Similarly, if the earnings of a partnership in a particular industry were reduced by, say, one-fourth through taxation, that firm would also have to earn enough before taxes to yield r percent after taxes to its investors. This company's pretax rate of return, call it s percent, must then satisfy the relationship

$$s - (1/4)s = r, \text{ that is, } (3/4)s = r \text{ or } s = (4/3)r.$$

This figure, which obviously lies between r and $2r$, will then be the opportunity cost rate for resources withdrawn from a firm paying 1/4 of its earnings in taxes.

5. Taxes and the Social Discount Rate: General Principles

We may then generalize our results as follows:

(a) For production that is not subject to taxation the opportunity cost rate will generally be no lower than, and as an approximation, be equal to the r percent rate of return on riskless bonds.

(b) For production whose returns are taxed at a rate such that the fraction $1/k$ of the returns *remains* after taxes, then the opportunity cost rate for resources withdrawn from this sector will be kr percent. Thus, in the preceding example, $1/k$, the fraction of the partnership's pretax returns remaining after taxes, is ¾. Therefore, the opportunity cost rate for its resources is $kr = 4/3r$ percent.

What can be done with the diverse opportunity cost figures for resources drawn from different sectors in calculating a single discount rate for the evaluation of a Government project? The answer is simple. Suppose the Government is to withdraw some resources from the one type of productive activity and some from the other. Suppose, for example, 20 percent of these resources would have come from do-it-yourself production yielding a 5 percent return, and 80 percent from the corporate sector with its 10 percent opportunity cost yield. Then the Government project will offer a net benefit to society if on the whole it can produce a rate of return equal to their weighted average:

$$(20/100) \times 5\% + (80/100) \times 10\% = 9\%.$$

More generally, we have as a third rule:

(c) The correct social discount rate for a project will be a weighted average of the opportunity cost rate for the various sectors from which the project would draw its resources, and the weight for each such sector in this average is the proportion of the total resources that would come from that sector.[1]

---

[1] The weighted average expression for the social discount rate can be derived by the following elementary argument. Let k dollars be invested in the Government project and let v be its value (including benefit flow) one year later. Suppose, if the project had not been built, that the proportion p of the investment would have been employed in an activity yielding r percent, and that the remainder, $(1-p)$, would have been used in an investment with an s percent yield. In total, at the end of the year the alternative use would then have yielded the total value.

$$pk(1+r) + (1-p)k(1+s) = k[1 + pr + (1-p)s].$$

The Government's use of the k dollar investment will therefore be socially preferable to the private use if and only if

$$v > k[1 + pr + (1-p)s], \text{ i.e., } k < \frac{v}{1 + [pr + (1-p)s]}.$$

Thus, the discount rate is given by $pr + (1-p)s$, the weighted average of the returns in the two sectors described in rule (c) in the text. This argument obviously also

The preceding rule, incidentally, will be seen to hold where there are differences in opportunity cost rates whatever their origin, whether produced by variation in the tax treatment of different economic sectors, or differences arising from any other source. The three rules (*a*), (*b*), and (*c*) also hold for an economy with many more than the two sectors in our simple illustration.

Before turning to the next general topic, it should be emphasized that the preceding analysis was couched entirely in terms of productive sectors and had nothing to do with the distinction between consumption and investment goods. A corporation can produce either or both of these two types of output and the same opportunity cost rate will apply to both. This means, if the analysis is valid, that the correct social discount rate will tend to be considerably higher than it would appear to be on the basis of some of the more standard modes of calculation[2] which, in terms of our simple example again, would employ the bond rate *r* for the discounting of all relevant consumers' goods production and the corporate rate only to (corporate) investment. An illustration will make the difference clear. Suppose the opportunity cost rates for our two sectors were the figures in our previous illustration (5 and 10 percent), and suppose the resources to be employed in the proposed project would otherwise have been divided into the following proportions:

	Percent
Consumers' goods production by consumer sector	20
Consumers' goods production by corporate sector	70
Producers' goods production by corporate sector	10

Since the conventional calculation applies the 5 percent bond discount rate to all consumers' goods, its weighted average calculation of the social discount rate would be

$$[(20 + 70)/100] \times 5\% + [10/100] \times 10\% = 5.5\%.$$

But, as has been shown, even consumers' goods produced by the corporate sector must yield a 10 percent return on investment, and hence the correct weighted opportunity cost rate must be (as before)

$$[20/100] \times 5\% + [(70 + 10)/100] \times 10\% = 9\%,$$

---

applies directly to the case where resources are taken from more than two economic sectors.

[2] See, for example, Krutilla and Eckstein [8] and Eckstein [3]. On the other hand, I suspect that the radically different discount rate calculation recommended by Harberger [4] will yield results very similar to those that would be obtained by the methods proposed in the text. There also seems to be no conflict between these methods and the views expressed in the Joint Economic Committee's report ([7], pp. 13–14), which are deliberately (and, no doubt, wisely) vague on this issue, stating "while advocating the opportunity cost of displaced private spending as a correct conceptual basis for the Government discount rate, the subcommittee does not presume to advocate a precise method for calculating this rate. . . . We agree with the Bureau of the Budget's reluctance to 'adopt . . . the rate of return on private investment foregoing alone be-

a very substantial difference.[3] It may be noted, incidentally, that the orders of magnitude of the figures are not totally unrealistic.

A final conclusion to be derived from the analysis is the implication that the appropriate discount rate may vary from one proposed Government project to another. If they derive their resources from different sectors or vary in the proportions in which they draw upon the different sectors, then their opportunity costs may vary. Consequently, it may sometimes be possible to reduce the opportunity cost rate for the project by careful planning of the means by which its resources are obtained. In particular, as has already been noted, a project designed to draw heavily on resources which would otherwise be unemployed will for this reason incur an opportunity cost that is particularly low.

6. The Role of Risk

Risk will also typically vary from industry to industry and from firm to firm. This produces further differences in reported rates of return. A risky industry may be expected to offer comparatively high profit prospects in order to be attractive to investors. That is why returns on stocks are typically higher than bond yields and why the rate of interest on a corporate bond is normally higher than that on a comparable Government security.

The nature of the issue this poses for the calculation for a social discount

---

cause government funds are withdrawn from both consumption and investment.' " The text of this paper obviously recognizes the relevance of the distinction between consumption and investment but maintains that the proper role of consumption in the discount rate of calculation is not quite what it is sometimes taken to be.

[3] The recommended procedure does of course conflict with the approach that has been taken in a number of highly reputable studies. It is therefore important to be very clear about the case for taking the opportunity cost of consumers' goods produced by a corporation to be dependent on the corporate income tax. The argument can be put very simply: assume that without a corporation tax all consumers' goods are associated with an r percent opportunity cost rate. Then the imposition of such a tax will lead the corporate sector to reduce its outputs and hence to raise the marginal utility of these goods to their consumers. Therefore a reduction of c units of corporate output of consumers' goods after the tax has gone into effect will incur a greater loss of consumer utility than the same c units of decrease in output would have caused before the tax. Hence if the opportunity cost was r when there was no tax it *must* exceed r percent after the tax has taken effect.

The argument clearly runs into all sorts of complications in practice in a world of risk and imperfect competition. But if the corporations were perfect competitors in a riskless economy it would apply precisely. Then the imposition of a tax would lead a sufficient number of firms to leave the production of any consumers' good to raise the pretax rate of return to $2r$ where r is the pure rate of interest. The marginal cost of a unit of output (excluding marginal return to capital) would, in equilibrium, equal price minus $2r\Delta k$ where Δk is the incremental capital needed to produce the output, and hence the opportunity cost per unit of capital moved out of this productive activity must then be $2r$.

Note that this argument is independent of the incidence of the tax, i.e., it must hold whether or not price has gone up by the amount of the tax, or has even gone up at all.

rate as well as its resolution can be brought out clearly with another simple example. Suppose two firms which are in all other aspects alike produce respective rates of return before taxes of 10 and 12 percent. The 2 percent excess in the return of the riskier firm is, in effect, an insurance premium to compensate investors for the greater gamble involved in offering funds to the less safe of the two companies. The question then is whether resources withdrawn from the second firm incur an opportunity cost of 12 percent, or whether the true (riskless) opportunity cost is merely 10 percent as it is for the other firm.

One may argue that in fact the two companies yield the same real rate of return to their investors. Since the latter's 2 percent higher return merely covers investors' risk, as already noted, the real loss to investors of withdrawal of a unit of resources will therefore be equal.

However, a number of noted economists (see, e.g., Arrow [1], Hirshleifer [6] and Samuelson [14]) have argued with considerable cogency that the risk for the investment in an individual project taken by itself does not necessarily correspond to the risk it contributes to society's investment as a whole. A bankrupt firm which continues to operate in the hands of its receivers is a loss to its investors but not to society. More important, because in the economy a very large number of projects are underway at any given time, the insurance principle, that is, the statistical "law" of large numbers, applies to them if their prospects for success are largely independent. It is true that because a recession can produce serious consequences for a large number of investment projects simultaneously, the prospects for their success are not completely unrelated. But if, as an approximation, we ignore this complication it can be shown that the larger number of projects involved the smaller the risk contributed to total social return by any one of them. Taken as a whole, from the viewpoint of society, they become virtually riskless.

This is essentially the principle on which a life insurance company operates. It cannot tell when any one of its policyholders will expire and, taken by itself, the risk of insuring him is enormous. But when it insures a large body of policyholders the operation becomes *virtually riskless*. That is, barring calamities such as epidemics or wars, the insurance company can forecast with virtual certainty how many of its policyholders will die in any given year, and the residual risk approaches zero as the number of policyholders increases.

Viewed in this way, we must conclude that while the risk involved in any individual investment project is apt to be substantial for the supplier of capital, it may be negligible from the point of view of society as a whole.

Only one more step is needed to see what these considerations imply for the role of risk in the evaluation of the social discount rate. Going back to our illustration, consider once again the 12 percent rate of return of our riskier firm. The 2 percent differential between this return and that of the safe company represents, as we saw, no net gain to the investor who is merely compensated thereby for his risk relative to investment in the other company. But since to society either firm's investment program is virtually riskless, it follows that the social rates of return of the two are *not* equal. One produces a riskless 12 percent while the other yields a riskless 10 percent. This means that the corresponding social discount rate of resources drawn from these two firms would be a weighted average of these two rates, in accord with rule (c) of the preceding section.

Specifically, it means that in the social discount rate calculation there should be no deductions for a risk component in the rates of return observed in practice. When a corporation produces a before-tax yield of 16 percent, 6 percent of which might be judged as a risk premium, from the point of view of the social discount rate the corresponding opportunity cost rate is 16 and not 10 percent. For here risk plays the same role as taxation in its effects on the social rate of return. Private risk forces the firm to invest only in opportunities which offer a yield of 16 percent. The social opportunity cost is therefore correspondingly high.

We conclude that the correct discount rate is a weighted average, over all tax and risk circumstances, of the rates of return that would otherwise be earned by the resources to be used in a Government project. As already stated, rule (c) then holds, at least approximately, for variations in rates of return resulting from differences in risk as well as from disparities in tax rates.

7. Externalities

There is one other element important for the social discount rate calculation, though we may treat it rather briefly. It is a matter that has been given considerable emphasis in the economic literature, and justly so. This is the issue of externalities—the differences between social and private costs and benefits of an investment program, of which risk compensation is a special case, as we have just seen.

The point is easily made with the aid of the most standard of illustrations of an externality. The firm whose output pollutes the atmosphere obviously provides a net social return significantly lower than the figure given by the yield on its capital. Similarly, the company that produces external benefits; perhaps training of the underprivileged, yields a social product greater than is indicated by its financial returns. In calculating the social discount rate, corresponding adjustments naturally have to be made in the discount figure. The polluting firm's rate of return figure has to be adjusted downward in order to base the calculation on its true social yield, and a corresponding upward adjustment is required to obtain the true social opportunity cost of the company whose operations provide training to the unskilled.

This principle is one that would no doubt be accepted by virtually all economists. Yet one must not overlook some reservations relating to its implementation. First, one must recognize difficulties that beset the evaluation of externalities. The cases where investigators have succeeded in providing some quantification of external costs and benefits are extremely rare. Many types of externality (that is, the impairment of health that is caused by pollutants) simply are not readily translated into financial terms; for example, into a numerical evaluation of their consequences for the social rate of return. Even where such a translation is possible, the effects are typically so widely diffused among the population that an estimate of their aggregate value becomes very difficult. These remarks are of course not meant to question the validity of the principle under discussion—the need to adjust the discount rate for the *social* costs and benefits of the resources concerned. It does however suggest that anything but the roughest sort of implementation of this principle will not be very easy.

A second comment on the externalities issue is the fact, not often alluded to in the literature, that governmental projects can also produce externalities. Army trucks pollute the air as effectively as private vehicles, and government work also can, as a byproduct, teach skills to ghetto residents. This means that in judging the desirability of a proposed Government project adjustments for externalities must be made on both sides of the ledger— the estimated yields of both the private and the governmental projects competing for resources must be revised in order to arrive at *net* social contribution.

8. Subsidy for the Future

There is one argument in the literature which has been used to maintain that the weighted average rate of return such as that proposed in rule (c) yields too high a social discount rate. This view maintains that private citizens tend systematically not to invest enough from the viewpoint of the Nation's future. It concludes that the discount rate should be kept very low in order to induce an increase in investment today, as a contribution to the Nation's welfare tomorrow. A low discount rate will clearly lead to approval of a large number of governmental investment projects, and the greater the number of investment projects undertaken, the greater is the contribution to the Nation's prosperity.

Such a position is, however, questionable in several respects. First of all, there is no basis for the presumption that a transfer of resources from the private to the public sector will necessarily produce a net increase in the amount of investment undertaken by the economy. The increase in the amount of government capital construction is very likely to be offset, at least in part, by a decline in private investments in plant and equipment.

Surely, if society's investment for the future is considered to be inadequate the appropriate remedy is to institute simultaneous inducements to both private and public capital formation. As we have seen, an arbitrarily low discount rate on public projects is certainly not the instrument for that purpose. Such artificially low discount rates on public projects introduce serious inefficiencies into the investment process by causing the withdrawal of resources from areas of use in which their yield is high and leading to their transfer to areas in which their return is low. This is a most peculiar way to encourage more effective investment in the future.

In any event, those who maintain that there is inadequate provision for the future draw incorrect general inferences from irrelevant particular cases. It is difficult to quarrel with the conservationist's view that the destruction of irreplaceable natural resources imposes a heavy cost on our posterity. The destruction of a portion of a canyon, the extinction of a species of wildlife, the erosion of soil are all matters of serious concern because once done they cannot be undone, and this is precisely the legitimate ground on which conservationists urge increased care in avoiding depletion of our resources.

But it is not legitimate to jump from the valid point that one generation has no right to use up wastefully the resources that cannot be replaced by its successors, to the questionable conclusion that each generation is constrained to engage in overall efforts to support its posterity beyond the level that is indicated by the free market. For that is precisely what is involved in a program of low discount rates or any other program of special inducements to investment.

The basic issue is whether it is desirable to subsidize in this way the commitment to the future of resources which could otherwise serve society today. Considerable real investment is already provided by the private sector and by the program of government projects which can pass the standard cost-benefit test utilizing the discount rate that has already been described. Is there any justification for a program of subsidies designed to produce an even greater overall commitment of resources to the future?

A little thought shows that the grounds for such a program are tenuous at best. Our economy is characterized by a long run rate of growth of GNP of the order of 3 to 4 percent per year, compounded, and in recent years the growth rate has been even greater. Per capita income has risen persistently throughout our history and there is every reason to expect the rise to continue. We are therefore wealthier than our predecessors and it can quite safely be predicted that our successors will be richer than we. In effect, then, the subsidization of a program of added investment amounts to an inducement for the transfer of additional resources from the poor to the rich. It would take inputs whose product would be available for consumption today and make them available tomorrow when the supply of consumer goods is likely to be so much more abundant than it is at present.

It should be made clear that the preceding discussion is not meant to imply that there is no need for increased activity by the public sector. The crisis of our cities, the problems of the impoverished and the underprivileged minorities and a variety of other critical issues may well require for their resolution governmental activity on an increased scale. But these all call for investments whose yield is obtainable quickly, not long-term investments, the bulk of whose benefits will become available in the more distant future. Advocacy of a very low discount rate in these circumstances is tantamount to the view that these immediate problems are not very pressing, and that society's resources are better transferred to the service of the future generations who in any case will surely be wealthier than we.

9. The Problem of the Second Best

One technical problem besets the analysis of the social discount rate presented in this paper. This is the well-known problem of the second best. We have seen how taxes, risk, and externalities produce discrepancies in the rates of return earned by various parts of the private sector. This means that capital simply is not allocated optimally within that sector. Society could obviously benefit by a transfer of capital from areas in which its social rate of return is relatively low to other parts of the economy offering a higher social return.

It is, then, not necessarily true that the rules of optimal investment procedure for the public sector are applicable, unless they are simultaneously put into operation in the private portion of the economy as well. For it has long been shown (see [9]) that if an optimality rule is enforced in one sector of the economy alone it can actually make matters worse.

In the present case, however, it does not seem plausible that this problem will be very serious. By the nature of the opportunity cost test, it calls for a transfer of resources only from a use in which its yield is relatively low to one where its return is comparatively high. This implies that the social welfare can be expected to increase in the process, assuming of course that there has been adequate adjustment for differences between private and social returns, so that the yield and opportunity cost figures take into account the more indirect contributions of the resources in question.

10. Concluding Comment

There always remains a formidable task of implementing even after the basic principles in an area have been enunciated. But a rational decision process does require examination of those principles. It is primarily to this task that this paper has addressed itself. It has proposed what is, in appearance, a relatively simple formula for the evaluation of the social discount rate, the weighted average of the rates of return in the various productive sectors from which resources would be withdrawn for the government project under consideration.

But the simplicity of this expression is deceptive. It is not easy to determine in practice from what productive sector a given project will be drawn, or even from where governmental investment as a whole obtains its resources. What one seeks in trying to obtain this information is the catalog of the decrements in the outputs of the various portions of the private sector which would result from a governmental investment program. When the matter is put in this way, its difficulties should be obvious.

Nor is it easy to judge the rate of return figures for the various sectors of the economy. A corporation offers different nominal rates of return on its various types of debt and equity and, as the recent literature on corporation finance has brought out so forcefully, it is not easy to arrive on the basis of these figures at a single number representing the rate of return on the company's capital. Perhaps a reasonable rule of thumb is the traditional weighted average of the rates of return on a firm's stocks, its bonds, and its other securities, where each of these sources of funds is weighted by the proportion of the company's total finances which it contributes.

In sum, the calculation of the social rate of discount is not something that can be left simply to traditional practices and conventions. The underlying principles should enable us, by a reasonable process of approximation to arrive at operational procedures that represent a significant improvement over current procedures. I have sought to emphasize the complications in order to avoid the impression that all the issues have been settled and can readily be reduced to routine. But I believe firmly that with the help of the principles and the data now available one should be able to arrive at reasonable approximations to the social rate of discount. Certainly it should be possible to derive figures considerably more defensible than the conventional calculations that are all too often utilized to justify projects not all of which are clear in their economic merit.

REFERENCES

[1] K. J. Arrow, "Discounting and Public Investment Criteria," in A. V. Kneese and S. C. Smith, eds., *Water Research*, Baltimore, 1966.
[2] W. J. Baumol, "On the Social Rate of Discount," *American Economic Review*, September 1968, pp. 788–802.
[3] Otto Eckstein, *Water Resources Development: The Economics of Project Evaluation*, Cambridge, Mass., 1961.
[4] Arnold Harberger, "Statement," in *Hearings Before the Subcommittee on Economy in Government of the Joint Economic Committee of the Congress of the United States*, July 30–August 1, 1968, Washington, 1968.
[5] R. Haveman and J. V. Krutilla, "Unemployment, Excess Capacity, and Benefit-Cost Investment Criteria," *Review of Economics and Statistics*. Vol 49, No. 3, August 1967.
[6] Jack Hirshleifer, "Investment Decisions Under Uncertainty: Applications of the State-Preference Approach," *Quarterly Journal of Economics*, May 1966. 80, 252–77.
[7] Joint Economic Committee, *Economic Analysis of Public Investment Decisions: Interest Rate Policy and Discounting Analysis*, Washington, 1968.
[8] J. V. Krutilla and O. Eckstein, *Multiple Purpose River Development, Studies in Applied Economic Analysis*, Baltimore, 1958.

[9] R. Lipsey and K. Lancaster, "The General Theory of the Second Best," *Review of Economic Studies*, 1956, 24, 11–32.

[10] S. A. Marglin, "The Social Rate of Discount and the Optimal Rate of Investment," *Quarterly Journal of Economics*, February 1963, 77, 95–112.

[11] ———, "The Discount Rate in Public Investment Evaluation" (unpublished) December 1968.

[12] A. C. Pigou, *The Economics of Welfare*, 4th ed., London, 1932.

[13] D. D. Ramsey, "On the Social Rate of Discount: Comment," 1968 (unpublished).

[14] P. A. Samuelson, "Principles of Efficiency: Discussion," *American Economic Review*, Proc., May 1964, 54, 93–96.

[15] Gordon Tullock, "The Social Rate of Discount and the Optimal Rate of Investment: Comment," *Quarterly Journal of Economics*, May 1964, 78, 331–36.

Research and Economic Growth

ZVI GRILICHES

Zvi Griliches is Professor of Economics at Harvard University. This paper appeared in Research and Development and Economic Growth/Productivity, *published by the National Science Foundation in 1972.*

1. The Scattered Evidence

Investment in research, both private and public, has clearly been one of the major sources of growth in output per man in this century. It has been a good investment both in the sense that it yielded a positive rate of return, and in the sense that this rate of return has been as good and often better than the rate of return on other private and public investments. The evidence for these statements is scattered; much of it is secondhand; but it is still quite strong.

This evidence is of three kinds: individual invention returns calculations, industry studies, and aggregate residual attribution calculations. Examples of individual invention calculations include Griliches (1958) for hybrid corn and hybrid sorghum, by Peterson (1967) for poultry breeding research, and by Weisbrod (1970) for polio vaccines. In such studies, the total social returns from a particular invention are estimated and compared *with all* the research costs in the particular area of research, not just the costs of the successful part of the research. The internal rates of return implied by these estimates are quite high (10 to 50 percent per annum), even though they are usually based on conservative assumptions, and even at their lower end (such as the 12 percent estimate for polio vaccines by Weisbrod) are at a level worth considering investing more if the opportunity to do so were to arise again.

A major objection to such studies is that they are not "representative," having concentrated on the calculation of rates of return only for "successful" inventions or fields. This objection can be met by econometric studies of productivity growth in specific industries. Here all of the productivity growth is related to all of the research costs and an attempt is made to estimate the part of productivity growth that is related to the past investments in research. The list of detailed studies is longer here; the most prominent are Mansfield's studies of the private rate of return to research for chemical and petroleum firms (1965); Minasian's study of private return to drug research (1962); Griliches' (1964) and Evenson's (1968) studies of the social rate of return to public investments in research in agriculture, and Mansfield's study of the social rate of return to private research investments in manufacturing industries (1965). While each of these studies is subject to a variety of separate reservations, together they all point to relatively high (30–50 percent) rates of return *on average to both* public and private investments in research.

Finally, a number of studies having measured as well as they could the contribution of other sources to economic growth, attribute the rest (the "residual") to research and compute the implied rate of return. Such calculations have been performed in the past by Schultz (1953) and Griliches (1958) for total research in agriculture, and by Denison (1962) and Fellner (1970) for the total economy. Again, the implied rates of return have been very high.

Perhaps it is not surprising that different studies yield rather high estimates for the rate of return to research in the private sector. After all, research is an investment and like other investments should yield a positive return. Given the great uncertainties associated with it (including the uncertainty about the degree of appropriability of its results) it is plausible that the ex post returns should be rather high on the average. They include a nonnegligible risk premium. What is more surprising is that public investments in research, which are not constrained or guided by the profit motive do seem to yield not only a positive but actually rather high rate of return. This, while not unexpected, is heartening.

There are two other noteworthy points to be drawn from the above mentioned studies: First, there appears to be a significant lag between the time that the investments in research are made and the time that the products of such research activity begin to affect the average productivity of an industry or economy. The average lag appears to be on the order of 5 to 8 years. Thus, although we are unlikely to observe the effects of the current drought in research support on productivity growth soon, the results of this drought may plague us in the late 70's. Second, research investments both depreciate and become obsolete. They depreciate in the sense that much of knowledge would be forgotten and rendered useless without continued efforts at exercising, retrieving, and transmitting it. This is what much of higher education is about. Also, some of the newer findings displace or make obsolete large parts of previously acquired knowledge; thus, their net contribution is smaller than would appear at first sight. In short, a nonnegligible rate of investment in research may be required just to keep us where we are and to prevent us from slipping back.

II. The Arguments

A major objection to drawing policy conclusions from such findings is that they are all based on "average" rates of return, while decisions have to be made on the margin. This objection contains an important half-truth: the next research project in the stack may turn out to be unsuccessful ex post and this, perhaps, could even be clear ex ante. But this is only a *half-truth*. *Any one* research project may be wasteful without the same being true for other potential research endeavors in this and other fields.

Perhaps some analogies will help here. An economist can examine the accounts and experience of the wildcat oil prospecting and drilling industry and conclude that on the whole investments in this industry appear to have been profitable and that the people running it seem to know what they are doing. He could not guarantee, however, that the next well drilled would not turn out to be dry, and much less tell them where to drill it.

Consider that historically the private financial returns from investment in real estate or equities have been higher than those from investments in bonds or other fixed debt assets. This information may be of some use to you even though this relationship is not guaranteed to persist into the future and even though the particular uranium mine investment that you are contemplating may turn out quite badly. Such knowledge is of some use, but clearly we'd like to know more. In any case we will have to make more specific choices and take more specific risks in any actual choice situation.

At the more abstract level there is another answer to this objection. There doesn't seem to be any evidence that the *average* rate of return to research is declining and hence there is no presumption that the average and marginal rates of return are far apart.

Most economists, if queried, would assert that there is underinvestment in research by private firms because much of its product is not capturable (appropriable) by the private firm (see Arrow, 1962 and Nelson, 1959). This is the major argument for the patent system and for government support of this activity. There are only few contrary voices. In a recent paper Hirschleifer (1970) points out that to the extent that the new knowledge may provide a firm (or an individual) with a competitive advantage, there may be a private incentive to invest in it even in excess of its social return. His point is well taken but seems to be irrelevant for most types of research supported by the government. Their results are unlikely to be of a form directly translatable into a market advantage. In any case, government supported research is rarely directly competitive with private research in the same area. Usually, if it is a flourishing private research area, there will be little public support for research in the same field.

Not all research contributes to growth or to the capacity of the economy to produce goods and services and to consume them wisely. Some of it, as pointed out by Johnson (1965), is a kind of public consumption like mountain climbing. We investigate certain secrets of Nature because they are there, not just, and not even primarily because their solution may prove "useful." That some of research is of this type does not mean that it shouldn't be supported; only that it has to compete for the scarce public dollar with other public consumption activities such as the architecture of public buildings and the support of fine arts.

Both the empirical and the theoretical literature provide some arguments why public investment in science and research may be a good thing. They also provide some evidence, in the form of higher average rates of return in this sector relative to other sectors of the economy, for the argument that more investment might be even better, but almost no information on where particular investments should be made and no assurances that any particular set of investments will in fact pay off. There is no reason, however, to expect that a well diversified public research portfolio should yield a lower rate of return in the future than such investments have yielded in the past.

III. Hunches

The Inadvisability of Variability. In most cases research is a long term investment. A field has to be learned, special equipment has to be designed. Also, it takes quite a bit of time and moving back and forth across known territory before a new way out occurs and the various pieces fall into place. The research process can be rendered very inefficient and wasteful if support is turned on and off at random intervals. A steady lower rate of support is preferable to a higher but more variable rate.

Thus, when cuts in research support occur, in allocating them one should also take into account not only the quality of the new research that will not get done but also of the old that won't get finished.

Similarly, when cuts are contemplated, account should be taken of the specific human capital that they may waste. Many scientists have been trained, at great length and great expense, for a very specific field or purpose. Rendering them unemployed, or transferring them to alternative much less specific uses, may involve a significant waste of resources and should be allowed for. Thus, to the extent that these resources will not be actually employed in the civilian economy, the budget costs overestimate the real savings to be had from cutting down on certain lines of activity.

The Usefulness of a Hard Look. While the economist has no panaceas for the problem of allocating social resources, more rational thinking can be done on these problems than seems usually the case. Major budget allocations pose the following questions: (1) If the project is successful, would it be useful or interesting? (2) Is it likely to succeed? (3) What are the alternative uses for this money?

In general, scientists and administrators have not wanted to face such hard questions. Nor is it clear that good answers will be forthcoming. But something will be learned from the process of asking the questions themselves. For example, investments to prolong life may not be as valuable, even if successful, as investments to improve the quality of life. Similarly, a new large-scale econometric model would have to justify itself in terms of "What questions could it answer that we cannot answer now?", "Are these interesting questions?", "Is it likely actually to answer them?", "Are these answers worth the costs?". One should not pretend that all or even any such questions can be answered today. Only that trying to ask them and trying to figure out how one might go about answering them is likely to be a very useful exercise. If the current funding stringency forces us into doing more along these lines, that may be one of its few positive products.

"Applied" is Often Bad. In the fields I am familiar with most of the "applied" research is bad. I mean by "applied," research that promises a solution to some pressing economic or social problem. First of all, because granting offices like "relevance," there occurs a substantial substitution of "relevance" for competence and quality of the researcher. It attracts lower quality people and it forces some of us to "repackage" our research interests under new labels. Either we cheat, in which case the results are no more "applied" than they would have been otherwise, or the project is wrenched from its natural scientific framework and has a tendency to flounder.

Most of the "real" problems are either not scientific but political and economic or are not amenable to the type of small-scale attack that characterizes university based research. For example, issues such as the disposal of the garbage of New York City, or a better tax system, do not require really very much new scientific work. What they require is a political and economic power base and a willingness to pay the price of solving such problems. If one were willing to spend the resources and ride roughshod over the entrenched interests of unions, zoning laws, and smaller scale political units, one could solve the garbage problem or design and build lower cost housing.

The solution to many of our current economic and social problems, such as public transport, housing, or even race relations, are as much "within the state of the arts" as were the bomb and the trip to the moon when they were first seriously thought of. What is lacking is the will to allocate the resources to their solution and the willingness to take the political consequences of attempting it. What will not solve them is "more research."

Good applied research benefits from a sense of mission and a large-scale commitment of resources and from pressure. A good example, whatever its shortcomings, is the "Coleman Report." A need was felt, a much larger amount of money than ever before was allocated to collecting a new set of data, and good people were brought in to design the survey and analyze the results. It is fair to say that it revitalized a whole field of research bringing new standards and new questions into it. I am sure that the same amount of money distributed according to previous patterns in thirty grants for various studies of the interrelationships between schooling, achievement, race, social class, and segregation would have led to much less tangible results. Once we know what we want there are economies of scale and pressure in research. If we really have a clear "applied" goal, there is little use in "smearing" and dribbling away the resources on scattered projects. If there is something we want to get done, let's do it, but let us not confuse it with basic "research." Another example of this type would be the wheat and rice improvement programs of the Rockefeller Foundation. I doubt that the same amount of money spread over various plant breeding programs in a dozen universities would have produced anywhere near the same results. An applied goal needs concentration and leadership.

The Scientific Community as a Self-Policing Instrument. In spite of some of the things said above, I am rather impressed with how well the scientific community operates in allocating resources and encouraging talent. As long as there are several centers of power and some competition among them, the system seems to work rather well. In periods of "easy money" it tends to get soft, though, and the current shakeout may do it some good, provided the scientific panels are given enough room to maneuver and are allowed to reallocate the scarce funds according to merit rather than history.

Education and research. It is quite clear that much of the publicly supported research and our higher education system are intimately interwoven. Much of the "research" dollar really went to supporting graduate teaching at the major universities. Any attempt to change this, cut it, or reform it will have very serious consequences for the way graduate education is carried on in this country. Such "externalities" should be taken into account in any serious decisionmaking. The higher education system may need reforming, but this should be undertaken deliberately as the result of some thought, not as a byproduct of a short-term funding crisis.

IV. Some Research Topics

We really know very little about how research output is generated. What can one get on demand and what not? It seems to me that the experience of the DOD in commissioning various "desired" breakthroughs in technology deserves more study. (Little has been done since the early RAND studies. See Klein, 1962 and Marshall and Meckling, 1962.) There are now ten more years of experience. What type of technological breakthrough can be commissioned and at what cost?

We also know very little about how "specific" is the human capital that is embodied in the scientific community. What does it cost to produce a physicist? What is the best that he can do if he will not be employed as a physicist? What is the associated social loss? How malleable are the talents of aeronautical or electrical engineers? What else can they do? What do we want them to do?

We know very little, really, what the private industry does with scientists. What do they produce? How do they get paid, how much and for what? And who pays for it?

Note: I have not commented on the recent attacks on science and growth as the sources of all evil. I believe that they are largely misguided and misinformed. Most of our problems are due not to per capita growth, but to growth in numbers. To the extent that growth has brought *new* problems with it, these are "the problems of the rich." These problems are real and we will not solve them until we are willing to pay a much higher price for their solution. In the process, we may become, by conventional yardsticks, poorer. But we will not solve them by making ourselves poorer.

REFERENCES

Kenneth J. Arrow, "Comment," in *The Rate and Direction of Inventive Activity*. National Bureau of Economic Research. (Princeton: Princeton University Press, 1962), pp. 353-358.

Department of Health, Education, and Welfare, Office of Education, *Equality of Educational Opportunity* by James S. Coleman and others. Washington, D.C. 20402: Supt. of Documents, U.S. Government Printing Office, 1966.

Edward F. Denison, *The Sources of Economic Growth in the United States and the Alternatives Before Us*. Supplementary Paper No. 12. (New York: Committee for Economic Development, 1962).

Robert Evenson, "The Contribution of Agricultural Research and Extension to Agricultural Production." Unpublished Ph.D. thesis. (Chicago: University of Chicago, 1968).

William Fellner, "Trends in the Activity Generating Technological Progress," *American Economic Review* (March 1970).

Zvi Griliches, "Research Costs and Social Returns: Hybrid Corn and Related Innovations," *Journal of Political Economy*, Vol. 66 (October 1958).

———. "Research Expenditures, Education, and the Aggregate Agricultural Production Function," *American Economic Review*, Vol. 54 (December 1964).

J. Hirschleifer, *The Private and Social Value of Information and the Reward to Inventive Activity*. Working Paper No. 158. (Los Angeles: University of California, Western Management Science Institute, 1970).

H. G. Johnson, "Federal Support of Basic Research: Some Economic Issues," in *Basic Research and National Goals* (Washington: Supt. of Documents, U. S. Government Printing Office, 1965).

Burton H. Klein, "The Decision Making Problem in Development," in *The Rate and Direction of Inventive Activity*. National Bureau of Economic Research. (Princeton: Princeton University Press, 1962).

Edwin Mansfield, "Rates of Return from Industrial Research and Development," *American Economic Review*, Vol. 55, No. 2 (May 1965).

———. *Industrial Research and Technological Innovation*. (New York: W. W. Norton & Co., 1967).

A. W. Marshall and W. H. Meckling, "Predictability of the Costs, Time, and Success of Development," in *The Rate and Direction of Inventive Activity*. National Bureau of Economic Research. (Princeton: Princeton University Press, 1962).

Jora R. Minasian, "The Economics of Research and Development," in *The Rate and Direction of Inventive Activity*. National Bureau of Economic Research. (Princeton: Princeton University Press, 1962).

Richard R. Nelson, "The Simple Economics of Basic Scientific Research—A Theoretical Analysis," *Journal of Political Economy*, Vol. 67 (June 1959).

Willis L. Peterson, "Return to Poultry Research in the United States," *Journal of Farm Economics* (August 1967).

Theodore W. Schultz, *The Economic Organization of Agriculture*. (New York: McGraw-Hill, 1953).

Burton A. Weisbrod, "Polio Research and Its Application: Costs and Returns." Working Paper No. 9. Madison: University of Wisconsin, Workshop on the Econommics of Human Resources, 1969).

Public Policy Toward Civilian Technology

EDWIN MANSFIELD

Edwin Mansfield is Professor of Economics at the University of Pennsylvania. This is part of his paper, "Federal Support of R and D Activities in the Private Sector," published by the Joint Economic Committee of Congress in 1976.

The Basic Economics of Government Support of Civilian Technology

In recent years, economists have made some attempt to determine, on the basis of general economic theory, whether it is likely that existing Federal programs in support of civilian technology are adequate. In this section, we summarize some of the arguments bearing on this question. To begin with, it is generally agreed that, because it is often difficult for firms to appropriate the benefits that society receives from new technology, there may be a tendency for too few resources to be devoted to the development of new technology. It is also generally agreed that the extent to which these benefits are appropriable is probably related to the extent of competition faced by the potential innovator and to the kind of research or development activity in question. In particular, the more competition there is and the more basic the information, the less appropriable it is likely to be. However, this argument is blunted somewhat by the obvious fact that some inventive activity is carried on with little or no economic motive. Clearly, inventors and technologists are not motivated solely by dollars and cents.

Economists seem to agree that, because R. & D. is a relatively risky activity, there may be a tendency for firms to invest too little in it, given that many firms seem to be averse to risk and that there are only limited and imperfect ways to shift risk. On the one hand, if firms are big enough so that their R. & D. program is reasonably large compared to particular projects, uncertainty is likely to be handled more effectively. On the other hand, since the threat of competitive innovation is an important stimulus to make firms more willing to accept the uncertainties involved in R. & D., there are obvious disadvantages in firms becoming too large relative to the total market. In any event, it seems to be generally agreed that the riskiness of R. & D. is likely to result in less R. & D. than may be socially optimal.

Still another reason why there may be an under investment in particular kinds of R. & D. is that they may be characterized by significant indivisibilities. In other words, they may be characterized by economies of scale that prevent small organizations from undertaking them efficiently. This argument seems much more applicable to development than to research. It is important to recognize that, while firms may have to be a certain minimum scale to do many kinds of R. & D. effectively, this scale may be a relatively small share of the market. Furthermore, it is important to recognize that small firms have been responsible for many important innovations, while many big firms have concentrated on more minor improvement innovations. Nonetheless, bearing these qualifications in mind, it is often argued that some industries are so fragmented that they cannot do the proper amount of R. & D.

While the preceding arguments have a considerable amount of force, they by no means prove that there is presently an under investment in civilian technology. For one thing, these arguments generally are based on the supposition that markets are perfectly competitive, whereas in fact many important markets are oligopolistic. In oligopolistic markets, many economists believe that firms often stress product improvement as a form of rivalry, rather than direct price competition. Because of tacit agreement among the firms, this may be the principal form of rivalry, with the result that more may be spent on research and development than is socially optimal. One industry in which this is sometimes claimed to be true is the ethical drug industry. This is not, however, a proposition that is easy to prove or disprove.

Despite the arguments listed above, another reason why there may be no under investment in various forms of civilian technology is that the government is already intervening in a large number of ways to support civilian technology. For example, there are already some general tax incentives that encourage R. & D. Beyond this, in particular industries like aircraft, there are a host of government influences promoting R. & D. and technological change. For example, the Government has paid for R. & D. related to aircraft. It has increased the demand for new airplanes by providing subsidies to the airlines and by regulating the airlines in such a way as to discourage price competition. Of course, the aircraft industry is hardly typical in this regard, but, as we have seen, there is considerable government support for R. & D. of various kinds in the private sector, and it is not obvious, on *a priori* grounds, that the Government has not already offset whatever latent under investment in R. & D. was present in particular parts of the economy.

Going a step further, some economists have argued that, even in the absence of oligopoly or government intervention, a private enterprise economy might not under invest in R. & D. For example, it has been pointed out that the inventor might be in a position to predict and thus speculate on price changes resulting from the release of his new technology. In principle at least, this might offset the fact that he could not appropriate all of the benefits directly. But it is important to recognize how difficult it is to foretell what price changes will be, particularly since there are many factors other than the technology to be considered.

In sum, there are several important factors, related to the inappropriability, uncertainty, and indivisibility of R. & D. that seem likely to push toward an under investment in R. & D. by the private sector. But these factors may be offset, partially or fully, by oligopolistic emphasis on non-price competition, by existing government intervention, or by other considerations. Thus, on *a priori* grounds, it is impossible to say with any reasonable degree of certainty whether there is an under investment in R. & D. in particular parts of the private sector.

Measurement of Social Benefits From New Technology: Agriculture

Since we cannot rely solely on *a priori* theorizing to tell us whether there is an under investment in R. & D. in the private sector (and if so, where it is most severe), we must turn to the available empirical studies of the returns from R. & D. of various types. These results should provide some information concerning what society has received from various forms of R. & D. investment in the past. Of course, there are a variety of problems in measuring the social benefits from new technology. Any innovation, particularly a major one, has effects on many firms and industries, and it obviously is difficult to evaluate each one and sum them up properly. Nonetheless, economists have devised techniques that should provide at least rough estimates of the social rate of return from particular innovations, assuming that the innovations can be regarded as basically resource-saving in nature.

To estimate the social benefits from an innovation, economists have used a model of the following sort. If the innovation results in a shift downward in the supply curve for a product (such as from S_1 to S_2 in figure 1), they have used the area under the product's demand curve (DD^1) between the two supply curves—that is, ABCE in figure 1—as a measure of the social benefit during the relevant time period from the innovation. If all other prices remain constant, this area equals the social value of the additional quantity of the product plus the social value of the resources saved as a consequence of the innovation. Thus, if one compares the stream of R. & D. inputs relating to the innovation with the stream of social benefits measured in this way, it is possible to estimate the social rate of return from the R. & D. investment.

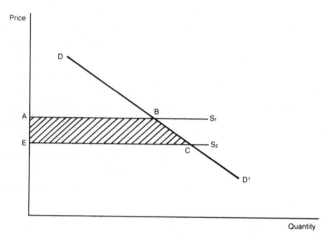

FIGURE 1. MEASUREMENT OF SOCIAL BENEFITS FROM TECHNOLOGICAL INNOVATION.

One of the first studies to use this approach was Griliches's study of hybrid corn. Based on data concerning the increase in yields resulting from hybrid corn, the value of corn output each year, and the price elasticity of demand for corn, he could estimate the area corresponding to ABCE in figure 1 each year. Then using data concerning the amount spent each year on hybrid corn research, he could estimate the rate of return from the investment in hybrid corn research, which turned out to be 37 percent. Clearly, a 37 percent rate of return is high. However, in evaluating this result, it is important to bear in mind that this is the rate of return from an investment which was known in advance to have been very successful. Thus, it is not surprising that it is high.

Another study, based on much the same principles, was carried out by Peterson to estimate the rate of return from poultry research. This study, unlike the previous one, looked at the rate of return from all research in this particular area, successful or not. In other words, it included the failures with the successes. The resulting rate of return was 18 percent, which again is a rather high figure. However, as would be expected, this figure is lower than that for hybrid corn. A further study, by Schmitz and Seckler, used basically the same kind of techniques to estimate the social rate of return from the investment in R. & D. pertaining to the tomato harvester. The result depends on how long workers displaced by the tomato harvester remained unemployed, but the authors report that, even if the tomato workers received compensation of $2 to $4 million per year for lost jobs, the net social rate of return from the harvester would still have far exceeded 100 percent.

It is important to recognize that all of the rates of return cited so far are average rates of return. That is, they are the average rate of return from all of the amounts spent on the relevant R. & D. For many purposes, a more interesting measure is the marginal rate of return, which is the rate of return from an additional dollar spent. This is the measure that is most relevant in determining whether there is an under investment in civilian technology. If the marginal rate of return from investment in civilian technology is higher than the marginal rate of return from using the extra resources in other ways, more resources should be devoted to civilian technology. Thus, a very high marginal rate of return from investments in civilian technology is a signal of an under investment in civilian R. & D.

Using econometric techniques, a number of studies have estimated the marginal rate of return from agricultural R. & D. One study, by Griliches, investigated the relationship in various years between output per farm in a state and the amount of land, labor, fertilizer, and machinery per farm, as well as average education and expenditures on research and extension in a State. The results indicate that holding other inputs constant, output was related in a statistically significant way to the amount spent on research and extension. Assuming a 6-year lag between research input and its returns, these results indicate a marginal rate of return from agricultural R. & D. of 53 percent. Another study, by Evenson, uses time-series data to estimate the marginal rate of return from agricultural R. & D., the result being 57 percent. Also, Peterson's study of poultry R. & D. indicates that the marginal rate of return for this type of agricultural R. & D. is about 50 percent. Schultz's study indicates a marginal rate of return of 42 percent.

In sum, every study carried out to date seems to indicate that the average social rate of return from agricultural R. & D. tends to be very high. The marginal social rate of return from agricultural R. & D. also seems to be high, generally in the neighborhood of 40 to 50 percent. Of course, as stressed above, these studies are based on a number of simplifications, and it would be very risky to attach too much significance to them, since they are rough at best. All that can be said is that the available evidence, for what it may be worth, suggests that the rate of return from agricultural R. & D. has been high.

Measurement of Social Benefits From New Technology: Industry

Having summarized the available results concerning the social rate of return from R. & D. in agriculture, we must now provide the same information for industry. Recently, a study was made by Mansfield, Rapoport, Romeo, Wagner, and Beardsley of the returns from 17 specific industrial innovations. These innovations occurred in a variety of industries, including primary metals, machine tools, industrial controls, construction, drilling, paper, thread, heating equipment, electronics, chemicals, and household cleaners. They occurred in firms of quite different sizes. Most of them are of average or routine importance, not major breakthroughs. Although the sample cannot be regarded as randomly chosen, there is no obvious indication that it is biased toward very profitable innovations (socially or privately) or relatively unprofitable ones.

To obtain social rates of return from the investments in each of these innovations, my colleagues and I used a model somewhat like that described in figure 1, except that we extended the analysis to include the pricing behavior of the innovator, the effects on displaced products, and the costs of uncommercialized R. & D. and of R. & D. done outside the innovating organization. The results indicate that the median social rate of return from the investment in these innovations was 56 percent, a very high figure. On the other hand, the median private rate of return was 25 percent. (In interpreting the latter figure, it is important to note that these are before-tax returns and that innovation is a risky activity.)

In addition, my colleagues and I obtained very rich and detailed data concerning the returns from the innovative activities (from 1960 to 1972) of one of the Nation's largest firms. For each year, this firm has made a careful inventory of the technological innovations arising from its R. & D. and related activities, and it has made detailed estimates of the effect of each of these innovations on its profit stream. We computed the average rate of return from this firm's total investment in innovative activities during 1960–72, the result being 19 percent, which is not too different from the median private rate of return given in the previous paragraph. Also, we computed lower bounds for the social rate of return from the firm's investment, and found that they were about double its private rate of return, which also agrees with the results in the previous paragraph.

The foregoing results pertain to the average rate of return. In earlier investigations .based on econometric estimation of production functions, Mansfield and Minasian estimated the marginal rate of return from R. & D. in the chemical and petroleum industries. Mansfield's results indicated that the marginal rate of return was about 40 percent or more in the petroleum industry, and about 30 percent in the chemical industry if technical change was capital embodied (but much less if it was disembodied). Minasian's results indicated about a 50 percent marginal rate of return on investment in R. & D. in the chemical industry.

In a more recent study, Terleckyj has used econometric techniques to analyze the effects of R. & D. expenditures on productivity change in 33 manufacturing and nonmanufacturing industries during 1948–66. In manufacturing, the results seem to indicate about a 30 percent rate of return from an industry's R. & D. based only on the effects of an industry's R. & D. on its own productivity. In addition, his findings show a very substantial effect of an industry's R. & D. on productivity growth in other industries, resulting in a social rate of return greatly exceeding that of 30 percent. No evidence was found, however, demonstrating that government contract

R. & D. has any effect on the productivity increase of the industries performing it.

Griliches has carried out an econometric study, based on data for almost 900 firms, to estimate the rate of return from R. & D. in manufacturing. His results pertain only to the private, not the social, rate of return. He finds that the private rate of return is about 17 percent. It is much higher than this in chemicals and petroleum, and much lower than this in aircraft and electrical equipment. He finds that the returns from R. & D. seem to be lower in industries where much R. & D. is federally financed.

Based on computations for the economy as a whole, Denison concluded that the rate of return from R. & D. was about the same as the rate of return from investment in capital goods. His estimate of the returns from R. & D. was lower than the estimates of other investigators, perhaps due to his assumptions regarding lags. In his presidential address to the American Economic Association, Fellner estimated the average social rate of return from technological-progress activities, his conclusion being that it is "substantially in excess" of 13 or 18 percent, depending on the cost base, and that this is much higher than the marginal rate of return from physical investment at a more or less given level of knowledge.

To sum up, practically all of the studies carried out to date indicate that the average social rate of return from industrial R. & D. tends to be very high. Moreover, the marginal social rate of return also seems high, generally in the neighborhood of 30–50 percent. As in the case of agriculture, there are a variety of very important problems and limitations inherent in each of these studies. Certainly, they are very frail reeds on which to base policy conclusions. But recognizing this fact, it nonetheless is remarkable that so many independent studies based on so many types of data result in so consistent a set of conclusions.

Advantages and Disadvantages of Various Mechanisms For Federal Support

As stressed above, existing evidence is too weak to indicate with any degree of certainty whether there is an underinvestment in civilian R. & D. of various sorts. All that can be said is that practically all of the studies carried out to date conclude that the average and marginal social rate of return from R. & D. have tended to be very high. Nonetheless, most economists who have studied the question seem to feel, on the basis of the existing evidence, that it is likely that some underinvestment of this sort exists. If so, it is important to consider the various means by which Federal support for civilian R. & D. might be increased. In this section, we discuss the major advantages and disadvantages associated with each of a number of mechanisms for Federal support of private sector R. & D.

First, consider tax incentives for privately financed R. & D. Perhaps the most important advantages of this mechanism are that it involves less direct Government control than some of the other techniques, and that it would be relatively easy to administer. Its most important disadvantages are that it would reward firms for doing R. & D. that they would have done anyhow, that it would not help firms that have no profits, and that it would be likely to encourage the same kind of R. & D. that is already being done (rather than the more radical and risky work where the shortfall, if it exists, is likely to be greatest). Furthermore, according to estimates made by former Secretary Peterson of the Department of Commerce, a 25 percent tax credit for R. & D. would mean that the Treasury would lose about $2–3 billion annually. Also, any program of this sort might run into difficulties in defining R. & D., since firms would have an incentive to use as wide a definition as possible.

Second, consider Federal contracts and grants in support of civilian technology. This, of course, is the route taken by the Department of Defense and the National Aeronautics and Space Administration in much of their work. This is the route also taken by the National Research and Development Corporation in Britain and by some proposals in the United States. It has the advantage of being direct and selective, but it can involve political problems in the choice of contractors, as well as problems relative to the disposition of patents resulting from such contracts and grants. At present, different Government agencies have adopted different policies with respect to patents. Some, notably the Department of Defense, allow the title to the patent to remain with the contractor; others, like the Atomic Energy Commission, have retained title to the patents. There has been a longstanding argument over the relative merits of these different patent policies. Still another, more fundamental difficulty with this mechanism for supporting private sector R. & D. is that it is so difficult to estimate the social costs and benefits of a proposed R. & D. project in advance.

Third, the Federal Government could support additional civilian R. & D. by initiating and expanding work of the relevant sorts in government laboratories. This technique has the advantage of being direct and selective. But there are great problems in having R. & D. conducted by organizations that are not in close touch with the marketing and production of the product. It is very important that there be unimpeded flows of information and good coordination of R. & D. on the one hand, and marketing and production, on the other. Otherwise, the R. & D. is likely to be misdirected, or even if it is not, it may be neglected or resisted by potential users. This is a difficult enough problem for various divisions of a firm, and it would seem to be made worse if the R. & D. is done in government laboratories. In the last decade, many governments have tended to convert government laboratories and to increase the amount of government-financed R. & D. done in industrial firms in order to bring R. & D. into closer contact with application and commercialization.

Fourth, the Federal Government could insure a portion of private credit to firms for R. & D. and innovation costs. It is frequently claimed that the reluctance of lenders to extend credit to risky and long term projects is an undesirable barrier to innovation. To the extent that this is the case, such a program might help to remedy the situation. The government could, for a fee, share the risk with the private lender for loans for R. & D. and related purposes. The advantages of such a program are that it would not commit the government to large expenditures, the administrative costs would be low, and there would be little federal interference in the lending decision. The disadvantages are that it results in a contingent liability for the Treasury, political problems could arise in awarding the loan insurance, and, most important of all, there is very little hard evidence that the capital markets operate so inefficiently (from a social point of view) that such a program is needed.

Fifth, the Federal Government could use its own purchasing procedures to encourage technological change in the private sector. As shown in table 1, the Federal Government's purchases of many kinds of goods and services are very substantial. The Federal Government could encourage innovation by using performance criteria, which specify the desired end result without limiting the design to existing products, rather than product specifications. Proponents of performance-based Federal procurement argue that it will free industry to innovate (limited only by the requirement that it perform certain specified functions), encourage cost reduction for the Government, and encourage the Government to serve as a pilot customer for technical innovations in areas where it represents a big enough market or a market sufficiently free from local restrictions or codes to make it worth industry's while to innovate. The disadvantages of this mechanism are that performance criteria may be expensive to develop and administer, and that the procurement process may be made less efficient by adding innovation to the list of socioeconomic objectives that already influence this process. Another suggestion is that the Government could make greater use of life cycle costs in purchasing decisions.

Sixth, the Federal Government could use its regulatory policies to try to encourage R. & D. in the private sector. According to some observers, some (but by no means all) of the Federal regulatory agencies have, through their policies and procedures, tended to restrain or distort technological innovation in the industries they regulate. Because so little is known about the effects of regulation on technological change, it is hard to specify exactly what changes might be effective (and cost-effective). Among the suggested alternatives are that technology advisers be located in the regulatory agencies, and that a technology impact statement be appended to all major regulatory decisions. Based on existing knowledge, it is hard to say whether such actions would be worthwhile.

Seventh, the Federal Government might establish prizes for important industrial innovations and developments. Such prizes would of course, make privately financed R. & D. more attractive; if a firm or individual felt

TABLE 1.   Government sales as a percent of total sales, 1967

Product line	Percent sold to Federal Government
Food and kindered products	1.86
Tobacco manufactures	3.53
Textile mill products	1.13
Lumber and wood products	0.96
Furniture and fixtures	1.99
Paper and allied products	0.82
Chemicals and allied products	1.53
Petroleum and coal products	1.45
Rubber and miscellaneous plastics products	2.57
Leather and leather goods	4.19
Stone, clay, and glass products	0.83
Primary metal industries	1.08
Fabricated metal products	3.20
Machinery except electrical	3.39
Electrical machinery and supplies	14.05
Transportation equipment	28.01
Instruments	11.05
Miscellaneous manufacturing	1.97
Wholesale trade	1.60

SOURCE: Study Group 13A on Commercial Products, *Final Report to the Commission on Government Procurement*, Washington, February 1972, p. 42.

that a prospective R. & D. project might lead to results worthy of such a prize, the rewards would appear higher than without the prize. An important disadvantage of this mechanism is that it is so difficult to figure out which innovations are worthy of prizes and which are not. Given the enormous problems in measuring the social importance of an innovation, this mechanism may not be as feasible as might appear at first glance.

General Versus Selective Support Mechanisms

With the foregoing material as background, we turn now to a discussion of some of the major considerations that probably should be kept in mind in appraising the policy options in this area. To begin with, it seems fair to say that most economists who have studied this problem have come away with the impression that our nation's programs in support of civilian technology are *ad hoc*, and that it is difficult to understand why we have allocated this support in the way that we have. For example, an enormous amount of support has been provided for civilian aviation technology, but very little has been provided for railroad technology; an enormous amount of support has been provided for agricultural technology, but very little has been provided for construction technology; and so on. (Perhaps this allocation of support can be defended, but I know of no serious attempt to do so.) Also, many economists who have written on this topic seem somewhat uncomfortable about the extent to which federal support of R. & D. in the private sector is related to a relatively few high technology areas. When one looks at federal expenditures for R. & D. performed in the private sector, the data indicate that the lion's share goes to industries like aircraft, electrical equipment, and instruments. Yet the marginal rate of return from R. & D. may be higher in less exotic areas like textiles or machine tools than in these high-technology fields.

If these misgivings are close to correct, it is likely that a general tax credit for R. & D. would be a relatively inefficient way of increasing federal support for R. & D. in the private sector. This is because, as pointed out above, it would reward many firms for doing what they would have done anyway, and it would be likely to encourage the same sorts of R. & D. that are already being done. A tax credit for increases in R. & D. spending would be less objectionable on these grounds, but it too is frequently regarded as inefficient because it is not sufficiently selective. To get the most impact from a certain level of Federal support, it seems to be generally agreed that a more selective technique would be desirable.

However, to utilize more selective techniques, some way must be found to determine where the social payoff from additional federal support is greatest (or at least relatively high). The way that most economists would approach this problem is to use some form of benefit-cost analysis to evaluate the pay-off from additional Federal support of various kinds of R. & D. Unfortunately, although such methods are of some use, they are not able to provide very dependable guidance as to how additional Federal support for civilian technology should be allocated, due in large part to the fact that the benefits and costs from various kinds of R. & D. are very hard to forecast. As the Department of Defense knows so well, it is difficult indeed to forecast R. & D. costs. And even major corporations have difficulty in using various forms of benefit-cost analysis for R. & D. project selection, even though they have a much easier benefit concept to estimate than most Government agencies do.

Thus, the choice between the general and more selective forms of support is not as simple as it may seem at first. And when one recognizes that the estimates constructed to guide the selective forms of support may be biased for parochial, selfish, or political reasons, the choice becomes even more difficult. As Eads has pointed out, the organizations and individuals that benefit from, or have a positive interest in, a certain R. & D. program may inflate the benefits estimate by claiming various "secondary" or "external" benefits that in fact are spurious or at least exaggerated. Given that it is so hard to estimate with reasonable accuracy the true social benefits of various R. & D. programs, the result could be a distortion of social priorities, if the estimates are taken seriously. And if they are not taken seriously, it would be difficult to prove them wrong.

Another consideration also bears on this choice. As noted above, some studies have concluded that an industry's R. & D. expenditures have a significant effect on its rate of productivity increase, but that the amount of federally financed R. & D. performed by an industry seems to have little or no such effect. In part, this may be due to the possibility that output measures in industries like aircraft are not reliable measures of social value. But it may also be due to a difference in the effectiveness of federally financed and privately financed R. & D. At present, there is no way to tell how much of the observed difference is due to the latter effect; but if it turns out to be substantial, this would seem to favor tax credits rather than increased Federal contracts and grants.

To sum up, although selective forms of support have obvious advantages (where they are at all appropriate), it would seem that they might well be supplemented with more general forms of support. Tax credits for increases in R. & D. spending are less objectionable than a tax credit for R. & D. spending. Although there are problems in defining R. & D. (and thus in measuring increases in R. & D. expenditures), a tax credit for increases in R. & D. spending might be considered, if it seems desirable to increase federal support for civilian technology. If adequate measures were available to guide more selective forms of support, perhaps they alone could do the job; but such measures are presently in their infancy.

Major Considerations in Formulating Programs

The choice of the general type (or types) of program is only one of many decisions that would have to be made, if some new federal support for R. & D. in the private sector were deemed desirable. This section takes up five additional points concerning the formulation of such a program. First, to the extent that such a program were selective, there seems to be a considerable amount of agreement among economists that it should be neither large scale nor organized on a crash basis. Instead, it should be characterized by flexibility, small-scale probes, and parallel approaches. In view of the relatively small amount of information that is available and the great uncertainties involved, it should be organized, at least in part, to provide information concerning the returns from a larger program. On the basis of the information that results, a more informed judgment can be made concerning the desirability of increased or, for that matter, perhaps decreased amounts of support.

Second, any temptation to focus the program on economically beleaguered industries should be rejected. The fact that an industry is in trouble, or that it is declining, or that it has difficulty competing with foreign firms is, by itself, no justification for additional R. & D. More R. & D. may not have much payoff there, or even if it does, the additional resources may have a bigger payoff somewhere else in the economy. It is important to recall the circumstances under which the government is justified in augmenting private R. & D. Practically all economists would agree that such augmentation is justifiable if the private costs and benefits derived from R. & D. do not adequately reflect the social costs and benefits. But in many industries there is little or no evidence of a serious discrepancy of this sort between private and social costs and benefits. Indeed, some industries may spend too much, from society's point of view, on R. & D.

Third, except in the most unusual circumstances, the government should avoid getting involved in the latter stages of development work. In general, this is an area where firms are far more adept than government agencies. As Pavitt has put it, government programs in support of civilian technology "should be managed on an incremental, step-by-step basis, with the purpose of reducing key scientific and technical uncertainties to a degree that private firms can use the resulting knowledge to decide when (with their own money) they should move into full-scale commercial development." Although there may be cases where development costs are so high that private industry cannot obtain the necessary resources, or where it is so important to our national security or well-being that a particular technology be developed that the government must step in, these cases do not arise very often. Instead, the available evidence seems to indicate that, when governments become involved in what is essentially commercial development, they are not very successful at it.

Fourth, in any selective government program to increase support for civilian technology, it is vitally important that a proper coupling occur between technology and the market. Recent studies of industrial innovations point repeatedly to the key importance of this coupling. In choosing areas and projects for support, the government should be sensitive to market demand. To the extent that it is feasible, potential users of new technology should play a role in project selection. Information transfer and communication between the generators of new technology and the potential users of new technology are essential if new technology is to be successfully applied. As evidence of their importance, studies show that a sound coupling of technology and marketing is one of the characteristics that is most significant in distinguishing firms that are relatively successful innovators from those that are relatively unsuccessful innovators.

Fifth, in formulating any such program, it is important to recognize the advantages of pluralism and decentralized decisionmaking. If the experience of the last 25 years in defense R. & D. and elsewhere has taught us anything, it has taught us how difficult it is to plan technological development. Technological change, particularly of a major or radical sort, is marked by great uncertainty. It is difficult to predict which of a number of alternative projects will turn out best. Very important concepts and ideas come from unexpected sources. It would be a mistake for a program of this sort to rely too heavily on centralized planning. Moreover, it would be a mistake if the government attempted to carry out work that private industry can do better or more efficiently.

Part Eight

POLLUTION, ENERGY, AND LAW ENFORCMENT: SOME MAJOR PROBLEMS OF THE EIGHTIES

Microeconomics is not an art, like music or ballet, that is practiced for its own sake. Although some practitioners regard microeconomics as a thing of beauty, few would pit its aesthetic appeal against that of Beethoven or Bach—or even Lerner and Loewe. Microeconomics is a body of knowledge that is helpful in solving problems in both the private and public sectors of the economy. Much of its importance—and its interest to students— stems from its usefulness in shedding light on pressing social problems. In this final part of this book, we present a number of papers and reports dealing with major questions facing American society in the eighties and showing how microeconomics bears on the relevant issues.

The first two papers deal with one of the primary social problems of our time—pollution of air and water. Everyone who reads the newspapers, even occasionally, knows that the degradation of the environment is becoming a nuisance and a potential threat to man's comfort and existence. In the first paper, Larry Ruff describes the reasons for pollution, and some measures that can be taken to reduce its incidence and costs. He emphasizes that the "divergence between private and social costs is the fundamental cause of pollution of all types." In the next paper, Allen Kneese considers the nature of the problem of water pollution, the approaches adopted by governments to deal with this problem, the deficiencies in these approaches, and possible improvements that might be made in public policy in this area.

Anyone who read the newspapers or listened to television in recent years is aware of the so-called "energy crisis," which involves a shortage of fuel. The next two papers are concerned with some reasons for this shortage. Morris Adelman argues that the oil producing countries have maintained a monopoly price at 10 to 20 times the long-run marginal cost of producing oil, and that the big oil companies are essentially "tax collectors" for the oil producing countries. In his view, a "world energy crisis" is a fiction. Paul MacAvoy and Robert Pindyck state that a shortage of natural gas has developed in this country because the Federal Power Commission (now the Federal Energy Regulatory Commission) has established ceiling prices below the equilibrium level. They explore the effects of various regulatory policies on the size of this shortage in the future. (In late 1978, after a long fight in the Congress, legislation was passed which will deregulate the price of new gas, as of January 1, 1985.)

Another extremely important set of social problems involves drugs and crime. In the following article, Simon Rottenberg applies microeconomic concepts to the problem of clandestine heroin distribution, and discusses ways in which its distribution can be discouraged. George J. Stigler discusses the optimum enforcement of laws, and concludes that there may be two reasons for the widespread failure to adopt rational criteria of enforcement: lack of understanding, and the desire· of the public not to enforce the laws. These papers demonstrate that microeconomics can be, and is being, applied to a very wide range of social problems.

The Economic Common Sense of Pollution

LARRY E. RUFF

Larry E. Ruff is Chief of the Systems Evaluation Branch of the Implementation Research Division of the Environmental Protection Agency. This article appeared in the Public Interest *in 1970.*

We are going to make very little real progress in solving the problem of pollution until we recognize it for what, primarily, it is: an economic problem, which must be understood in economic terms. Of course, there are *noneconomic* aspects of pollution, as there are with all economic problems, but all too often, such secondary matters dominate discussion. Engineers, for example, are certain that pollution will vanish once they find the magic gadget or power source. Politicians keep trying to find the right kind of bureaucracy; and bureaucrats maintain an unending search for the correct set of rules and regulations. Those who are above such vulgar pursuits pin their hopes on a moral regeneration or social revolution, apparently in the belief that saints and socialists have no garbage to dispose of. But as important as technology, politics, law, and ethics are to the pollution question, all such approaches are bound to have disappointing results, for they ignore the primary fact that pollution is an economic problem.

Before developing an economic analysis of pollution, however, it is necessary to dispose of some popular myths.

First, pollution is not new. Spanish explorers landing in the sixteenth century noted that smoke from Indian campfires hung in the air of the Los Angeles basin, trapped by what is now called the inversion layer. Before the first century B.C., the drinking waters of Rome were becoming polluted.

Second, most pollution is not due to affluence, despite the current popularity of this notion. In India, the pollution runs in the streets, and advice against drinking the water in exotic lands is often well taken. Nor can pollution be blamed on the self-seeking activities of greedy capitalists. Once-beautiful rivers and lakes which are now open sewers and cesspools can be found in the Soviet Union as well as in the United States, and some of the world's dirtiest air hangs over cities in Eastern Europe, which are neither capitalist nor affluent. In many ways, indeed, it is much more difficult to do anything about pollution in noncapitalist societies. In the Soviet Union, there is no way for the public to become outraged or to exert any pressure, and the polluters and the courts there work for the same people, who often decide that clean air and water, like good clothing, are low on their list of social priorities.

In fact, it seems probable that affluence, technology, and slow-moving, inefficient democracy will turn out to be the cure more than the cause of pollution. After all, only an affluent, technological society can afford such luxuries as moon trips, three-day weekends, and clean water, although even our society may not be able to afford them all; and only in a democracy can the people hope to have any real influence on the choice among such alternatives.

What *is* new about pollution is what might be called the *problem* of pollution. Many unpleasant phenomena—poverty, genetic defects, hurricanes—have existed forever without being considered problems; they are, or were, considered to be facts of life, like gravity and death, and a mature person simply adjusted to them. Such phenomena become problems only when it begins to appear that something can and should be done about them. It is evident that pollution had advanced to the problem stage. Now the question is what can and should be done?

Most discussions of the pollution problem begin with some startling facts: Did you know that 15,000 tons of filth are dumped into the air of Los Angeles County every day? But by themselves, such facts are meaningless, if only because there is no way to know whether 15,000 tons is a lot or a little. It is much more important for clear thinking about the pollution problem to understand a few economic concepts than to learn a lot of sensational-sounding numbers.

Marginalism

One of the most fundamental economic ideas is that of *marginalism*, which entered economic theory when economists became aware of the differential calculus in the nineteenth century and used it to formulate economic problems as problems of "maximization." The standard economic problem came to be viewed as that of finding a level of operation of some activity which would maximize the net gain from that activity, where the net gain is the difference between the benefits and the costs of the activity. As the level of activity increases, both benefits and costs will increase; but because of diminishing returns, costs will increase faster than benefits. When a certain level of the activity is reached, any further expansion increases costs more than benefits. At this "optimal" level, "marginal cost"—or the cost of expanding the activity—equals "marginal benefit," or the benefit from expanding the activity. Further expansion would cost more than it is worth, and reduction in the activity would reduce benefits more than it would save costs. The net gain from the activity is said to be maximized at this point.

This principle is so simple that it is almost embarrassing to admit it is the cornerstone of economics. Yet intelligent men often ignore it in discussion of public issues. Educators, for example, often suggest that, if it is better to be literate than illiterate, there is no logical stopping point in supporting education. Or scientists have pointed out that the benefits derived from "science" obviously exceed the costs and then have proceeded to infer that their particular project should be supported. The correct comparison, of course, is between *additional* benefits created by the proposed activity and the *additional* costs incurred.

The application of marginalism to questions of pollution is simple enough conceptually. The difficult part lies in estimating the cost and benefits functions, a question to which I shall return. But several important qualitative points can be made immediately. The first is that the choice facing a rational society is *not* between clean air and dirty air, or between clear water and polluted water, but rather between various *levels* of dirt and pollution. The aim must be to find that level of pollution abatement where the costs of further abatement begin to exceed the benefits.

The second point is that the optimal combination pollution control methods is going to be a very complex affair. Such steps as demanding a 10 percent reduction in pollution from all sources, without considering the relative difficulties and costs of the reduction, will certainly be an inefficient approach. Where it is less costly to reduce pollution, we want a greater reduction, to a point where an additional dollar spent on control anywhere yields the same reduction in pollution levels.

Markets, Efficiency, and Equity

A second basic economic concept is the idea—or the ideal—of the self-regulating economic system. Adam Smith illustrated this ideal with the example of bread in London: the uncoordinated, selfish actions of many people—farmer, miller, shipper, baker, grocer—provide bread for the city dweller, without any central control and at the lowest possible cost. Pure self-interest, guided only by the famous "invisible hand" of competition, organizes the economy efficiently.

The logical basis of this rather startling result is that, under certain conditions, competitive prices convey all the information necessary for making the optimal decision. A builder trying to decide whether to use brick or concrete will weigh his requirements and tastes against the prices of the materials. Other users will do the same, with the result that those whose needs and preferences for brick are relatively the strongest will get brick. Further, profit-maximizing producers will weigh relative production costs, reflecting society's productive capabilities, against relative prices, reflecting society's tastes and desires, when deciding how much of each good to produce. The end result is that users get brick and cement in quantities and proportions that reflect their individual tastes and society's production opportunities. No other solution would be better from the standpoint of all the individuals concerned.

This suggests what it is that makes pollution different. The efficiency of competitive markets depends on the identity of *private* costs and *social* costs. As long as the brick-cement producer must compensate somebody for every cost imposed by his production, his profit-maximizing decisions about how much to produce, and how, will also be socially efficient decisions. Thus, if a producer dumps wastes into the air, river, or ocean; if he pays nothing for such dumping; and if the disposed wastes have no noticeable effect on anyone else, living or still unborn; then the private and social costs of disposal are identical and nil, and the producer's private decisions are socially efficient. *But if these wastes do affect others, then the social costs of waste disposal are not zero. Private and social costs diverge, and private profit-maximizing decisions are not socially efficient.* Suppose, for example, that cement production dumps large quantities of dust into the air, which damages neighbors, and that the brick-cement producer pays these neighbors nothing. In the social sense, cement will be over-produced relative to brick and other products because users of the products will make decisions based on market prices which do not reflect true social costs. They will use cement when they should use brick, or when they should not build at all.

This divergence between private and social costs is the fundamental cause of pollution of all types, and it arises in any society where decisions are at all decentralized—which is to say, in any economy of any size which hopes to function at all. Even the socialist manager of the brick-cement plant, told to maximize output given the resources at his disposal, will use the People's Air to dispose of the People's Wastes; to do otherwise would be to violate his instructions. And if instructed to avoid pollution "when possible," he does not know what to do: how can he decide whether more brick or cleaner air is more important for building socialism? The capitalist manager is in exactly the same situation. Without prices to convey the needed information, he does not know what action is in the public interest, and certainly would have no incentive to act correctly even if he did know.

Although markets fail to perform efficiently when private and social costs diverge, this does not imply that there is some inherent flaw in the idea of acting on self-interest in response to market prices. Decisions based on private cost calculations are typically correct from a social point of view; and even when they are not quite correct, it often is better to accept this inefficiency than to turn to some alternative decision mechanism, which may be worse. Even the modern economic theory of socialism is based on the high correlation between managerial self-interest and public good. There is no point in trying to find something—some omniscient and omnipotent *deus ex machina*—to replace markets and self-interest. Usually it is preferable to modify existing institutions, where necessary, to make private and social interest coincide.

And there is a third relevant economic concept: the fundamental distinction between questions of efficiency and questions of equity or fairness. A situation is said to be efficient if it is not possible to rearrange things so as to benefit one person without harming any others. That is the *economic* equation for efficiency. *Politically*, this equation can be solved in various ways; though most reasonable men will agree that efficiency is a good thing, they will rarely agree about which of the many possible efficient states, each with a different distribution of "welfare" among individuals, is the best one. Economics itself has nothing to say about which efficient state is the best. That decision is a matter of personal and philosophical values, and ultimately must be decided by some political process. Economics can suggest ways of achieving efficient states, and can try to describe the equity considerations involved in any suggested social policy; but the final decisions about matters of "fairness" or "justice" cannot be decided on economic grounds.

Estimating the Costs of Pollution

Both in theory and practice, the most difficult part of an economic approach to pollution is the measurement of the cost and benefits of its abatement. Only a small fraction of the costs of pollution can be estimated straightforwardly. If, for example, smog reduces the life of automobile tires by 10 percent, one component of the cost of smog is 10 percent of tire expenditures. It has been estimated that, in a moderately polluted area of New York City, filthy air imposes extra costs for painting, washing, laundry, etc., of $200 per person per year. Such costs must be included in any calculation of the benefits of pollution abatement, and yet they are only a part of the relevant costs—and often a small part. Accordingly it rarely is possible to justify a measure like river pollution control solely on the basis of costs to individuals or firms of treating water because it usually is cheaper to process only the water that is actually used for industrial or municipal purposes, and to ignore the river itself.

The costs of pollution that cannot be measured so easily are often called "intangible" or "noneconomic," although neither term is particularly appropriate. Many of these costs are as tangible as burning eyes or a dead fish, and all such costs are relevant to a valid economic analysis. Let us therefore call these costs "nonpecuniary."

The only real difference between nonpecuniary costs and the other kind lies in the difficulty of estimating them. If pollution in Los Angeles harbor is reducing marine life, this imposes costs on society. The cost of reducing commercial fishing could be estimated directly: it would be the fixed cost of converting men and equipment from fishing to an alternative occupation, plus the difference between what they earned in fishing and what they earn in the new occupation, plus the loss to consumers who must eat chicken instead of fish. But there are other, less straightforward costs: the loss of recreation opportunities for children and sportsfishermen and of research facilities for marine biologists, etc. Such costs are obviously difficult to measure and may be very large indeed; but just as surely as they are not zero, so too are they not infinite. Those who call for immediate action and damn the cost, merely because the spiney starfish and furry crab populations are shrinking, are putting an infinite marginal value on these creatures. This strikes a disinterested observer as an overestimate.

The above comments may seem crass and insensitive to those who, like one angry letter-writer to the Los Angeles *Times*, want to ask: "If conservation is not for its own sake, then what in the world *is* it for?" Well, what *is* the purpose of pollution control? Is it for its own sake? Of course not. If we answer that it is to make the air and water clean and quiet, then the question arises: what is the purpose of clean air and water? If the answer is, to please the nature gods, then it must be conceded that all pollution must cease immediately because the cost of angering the gods is presumably infinite. But if the answer is that the purpose of clean air and water is to further human enjoyment of life on this planet, then we are faced with the economists' basic question: given the limited alternatives that a niggardly nature allows, how can we best further human enjoyment of life? And the answer is, by making intelligent marginal decisions on the basis of costs and benefits. Pollution control is for lots of things: breathing comfortably, enjoying mountains, swimming in water, for health, beauty, and the general delectation. But so are many other things, like good food and wine, comfortable housing and fast transportation. The question is not which of these desirable things we should have, but rather what combination is most desirable. To determine such a combination, we must know the rate at which individuals are willing to substitute more of one desirable thing for less of another desirable thing. Prices are one way of determining those rates.

But if we cannot directly observe market prices for many of the costs of pollution, we must find another way to proceed. One possibility is to infer the costs from other prices, just as we infer the value of an ocean view from real estate prices. In principle, one could estimate the value people put on clean air and beaches by observing how much more they are willing to pay for property in nonpolluted areas. Such information could be obtained; but there is little of it available at present.

Another possible way of estimating the costs of pollution is to ask people how much they would be willing to pay to have pollution reduced. A resident of Pasadena might be willing to pay $100 a year to have smog reduced 10 or 20 percent. In Barstow, where the marginal cost of smog is much less, a resident might not pay $10 a year to have smog reduced 10 percent. If we knew how much it was worth to everybody, we could add up these amounts and obtain an estimate of the cost of a marginal amount of pollution. The difficulty, of course, is that there is no way of guaranteeing truthful responses. Your response to the question, how much is pollution costing *you*, obviously will depend on what you think will be done with this information. If you think you will be compensated for these costs, you will make a generous estimate; if you think that you will be charged for the control in proportion to these costs, you will make a small estimate.

In such cases it becomes very important how the questions are asked. For example, the voters could be asked a question of the form: Would you like to see pollution reduced x percent if the result is a y percent increase in the cost of living? Presumably a set of questions of this form could be used to estimate the costs of pollution, including the so-called "measurable" costs. But great care must be taken in formulating the questions. For one thing, if the voters will benefit differentially from the activity, the questions should be asked in a way which reflects this fact. If, for example, the issue is cleaning up a river, residents near the river will be willing to pay more for the cleanup and should have a means of expressing this. Ultimately, some such political procedure probably will be necessary, at least until our more direct measurement techniques are greatly improved.

Let us assume that, somehow, we have made an estimate of the social cost function for pollution, including the marginal cost associated with various pollution levels. We now need an estimate of the benefits of pollution—or, if you prefer, of the costs of pollution abatement. So we set the Pollution Control Board (PCB) to work on this task.

The PCB has a staff of engineers and technicians, and they begin working on the obvious question: for each pollution source, how much would it cost to reduce pollution by 10 percent, 20 percent, and so on. If the PCB has some economists, they will know that the cost of reducing total pollution by 10 percent is *not* the total cost of reducing each pollution source by 10 percent. Rather, they will use the equimarginal principle and find the pattern of control such that an additional dollar spent on control of any pollution source yields the same reduction. This will minimize the cost of achieving any given level of abatement. In this way the PCB can generate a "cost of abatement" function, and the corresponding marginal cost function.

While this procedure seems straightforward enough, the practical difficulties are tremendous. The amount of information needed by the PCB is staggering; to do this job right, the PCB would have to know as much about each plant as the operators of the plant themselves. The cost of gathering these data is obviously prohibitive, and, since marginal principles apply to data collection too, the PCB would have to stop short of complete information, trading off the resulting loss in efficient control against the cost of better information. Of course, just as fast as the PCB obtained the data, a technological change would make it obsolete.

The PCB would have to face a further complication. It would not be correct simply to determine how to control existing pollution sources given their existing locations and production methods. Although this is almost certainly what the PCB would do, the resulting cost functions will overstate the true social cost of control. Muzzling existing plants is only one method of control. Plants can move, or switch to a new process, or even to a new product. Consumers can switch to a less-polluting substitute. There are any number of alternatives, and the poor PCB engineers can never know them all. This could lead to some costly mistakes. For example, the PCB may correctly conclude that the cost of installing effective dust control at the cement plant is very high and hence may allow the pollution to continue, when the best solution is for the cement plant to switch to brick production while a plant in the desert switches from brick to cement. The PCB can never have all this information and therefore is doomed to inefficiency, sometimes an inefficiency of large proportions.

Once cost and benefit functions are known, the PCB should choose a level of abatement that maximizes net gain. This occurs where the marginal cost of further abatement just equals the marginal benefit. If, for example, we could reduce pollution damages by $2 million at a cost of $1 million, we should obviously impose that $1 million cost. But if the damage reduction is only $½ million, we should not and in fact should reduce control efforts.

This principle is obvious enough but is often overlooked. One author, for example, has written that the national cost of air pollution is $11 billion a year but that we are spending less than $50 million a year on control; he infers from this that "we could justify a tremendous strengthening of control efforts on purely economic grounds." That *sounds* reasonable, if all you care about are sounds. But what is the logical content of the statement? Does it imply we should spend $11 billion on control just to make things even? Suppose were were spending $11 billion on control and thereby succeeded in reducing pollution costs to $50 million. Would this imply we were spending too *much* on control? Of course not. We must compare the *marginal* decrease in pollution costs to the *marginal* increase in abatement costs.

Difficult Decisions

Once the optimal pollution level is determined, all that is necessary is for the PCB to enforce the pattern of controls which it has determined to be optimal. (Of course, this pattern will not really be the best one, because the PCB will not have all the information it should have.) But now a new problem arises: how should the controls be enforced?

The most direct and widely used method is in many ways the least efficient: direct regulation. The PCB can decide what each polluter must do to reduce pollution and then simply require that action under penalty of law. But this approach has many shortcomings. The polluters have little incentive to install the required devices or to keep them operating properly. Constant inspection is therefore necessary. Once the polluter has complied with the letter of the law, he has no incentive to find better methods of pollution reduction. Direct control of this sort has a long history of inadequacy; the necessary bureaucracies rarely manifest much vigor, imagination, or devotion to the public interest. Still, in some situations there may be no alternative.

A slightly better method of control is for the PCB to set an acceptable level of pollution for each source and let the polluters find the cheapest means of achieving this level. This reduces the amount of information the PCB needs, but not by much. The setting of the acceptable levels becomes a matter for negotiation, political pull, or even graft. As new plants are built and new control methods invented, the limits should be changed; but if they are, the incentive to find new designs and new techniques is reduced.

A third possibility is to subsidize the reduction of pollution, either by subsidizing control equipment or by paying for the reduction of pollution below standard levels. This alternative has all the problems of the above methods, plus the classic shortcoming which plagues agricultural subsidies: the old joke about getting into the not-growing-cotton business is not always so funny.

The PCB will also have to face the related problem of deciding *who* is going to pay the costs of abatement. Ultimately, this is a question of equity or fairness which economics cannot answer; but economics can suggest ways of achieving equity without causing inefficiency. In general, the economist will say: if you think polluter A is deserving of more income at polluter B's expense, then by all means give A some of B's income; but do *not* try to help A by allowing him to pollute freely. For example, suppose A and B each operate plants which produce identical amounts of pollution. Because of different technologies, however, A can reduce his pollution 10 percent for $100, while B can reduce his pollution 10 percent for $1,000. Suppose your goal is to reduce total pollution 5 percent. Surely it is obvious that the best (most efficient) way to do this is for A to reduce his pollution 10 percent while B does nothing. But suppose B is rich and A is poor. Then many would demand that B reduce his pollution 10 percent while A does nothing because B has a greater "ability to pay." Well, perhaps B does have greater ability to pay, and perhaps it is "fairer" that he pay the costs of pollution control; but if so, B should pay the $100 necessary to reduce A's pollution. To force B to reduce his own pollution 10 percent is equivalent to taxing B $1,000 and then blowing the $1,000 on an extremely inefficient pollution control method. Put this way, it is obviously a stupid thing to do; but put in terms of B's greater ability to pay, it will get considerable support though it is no less stupid. The more efficient alternative is not always available, in which case it may be acceptable to use the inefficient method. Still, it should not be the responsibility of the pollution authorities to change the distribution of welfare in society; this is the responsibility of higher authorities. The PCB should concentrate on achieving economic efficiency without being grossly unfair in its allocation of costs.

Clearly, the PCB has a big job which it will never be able to handle with any degree of efficiency. Some sort of self-regulating system, like a market, is needed, which will automatically adapt to changes in conditions, provide incentives for development and adoption of improved control methods, reduce the amount of information the PCB must gather and the amount of detailed control it must exercise, and so on. This, by any standard, is a tall order.

Putting a Price on Pollution

And yet there is a very simple way to accomplish all this. *Put a price on pollution.* A price-based control mechanism would differ from an ordinary market transaction system only in that the PCB would set the prices, instead of their being set by demand-supply forces, and that the state would force payment. Under such a system, anyone could emit any amount of pollution so long as he pays the price which the PCB sets to approximate the marginal social cost of pollution. Under this circumstance, private decisions based on self-interest are efficient. If pollution consists of many components, each with its own social cost, there should be different prices for each component. Thus, extremely dangerous materials must have an extremely high price, perhaps stated in terms of "years in jail" rather than "dollars," although a sufficiently high dollar price is essentially the same thing. In principle, the prices should vary with geographical location, season of the year, direction of the wind, and even day of the week, although the cost of too many variations may preclude such fine distinctions.

Once the prices are set, polluters can adjust to them any way they choose. Because they act on self-interest they will reduce their pollution by every means possible up to the point where further reduction would cost more than the price. Because all face the same price for the same type of pollution, the marginal cost of abatement is the same everywhere. If there are economies of scale in pollution control, as in some types of liquid waste treatment, plants can cooperate in establishing joint treatment facilities. In fact, some enterprising individual could buy these wastes from various plants (at negative prices—i.e., they would get paid for carting them off), treat them, and then sell them at a higher price, making a profit in the process. (After all, this is what rubbish removal firms do now.) If economies of scale are so substantial that the provider of such a service becomes a monopolist, then the PCB can operate the facilities itself.

Obviously, such a scheme does not eliminate the need for the PCB. The board must measure the output of pollution from all sources, collect the fees, and so on. But it does not need to know anything about any plant except its total emission of pollution. It does not control, negotiate, threaten, or grant favors. It does not destroy incentive because development of new control methods will reduce pollution payments.

As a test of this price system of control, let us consider how well it would work when applied to automobile pollution, a problem for which direct control is usually considered the only feasible approach. If the price system can work here, it can work anywhere.

Suppose, then, that a price is put on the emissions of automobiles. Obviously, continuous metering of such emissions is impossible. But it should be easy to determine the average output of pollution for cars of different makes, models, and years, having different types of control devices and using different types of fuel. Through graduated registration fees and fuel taxes, each car owner would be assessed roughly the social cost of his car's pollution, adjusted for whatever control devices he has chosen to install and for his driving habits. If the cost of installing a device, driving a different car, or finding alternative means of transportation is less than the price he must pay to continue his pollution, he will presumably take the necessary steps. But each individual remains free to find the best adjustment to his particular situation. It would be remarkable if everyone decided to install the same devices which some states currently require; and yet that is the effective assumption of such requirements.

Even in the difficult case of auto pollution, the price system has a number of advantages. Why should a person living in the Mojave desert, where pollution has little social cost, take the same pains to reduce air pollution as a person living in Pasadena? Present California law, for example, makes no distinction between such areas; the price system would. And what incentive is there for auto manufacturers to design a less polluting engine? The law says only that they must install a certain device in every car. If GM develops a more efficient engine, the law will eventually be changed to require this engine on all cars, raising costs and reducing sales. But will such development take place? No collusion is needed for manufacturers to decide unanimously that it would be foolish to devote funds to such development. But with a pollution fee paid by the consumer, there is a real advantage for any firm to be first with a better engine, and even a collusive agreement wouldn't last long in the face of such an incentive. The same is true of fuel manufacturers, who now have no real incentive to look for better fuels. Perhaps most important of all, the present situation provides no real way of determining whether it is cheaper to reduce pollution by muzzling cars or industrial plants. The experts say that most smog comes from cars; but *even if true, this does not imply that it is more efficient to control autos rather than other pollution sources.* How can we decide which is more efficient without mountains of information? The answer is, by making drivers and plants pay the same price for the same pollution, and letting self-interest do the job.

In situations where pollution outputs can be measured more or less directly (unlike the automobile pollution case), the price system is clearly superior to direct control. A study of possible control methods at the Delaware estuary, for example, estimated that, compared to a direct control scheme requiring each polluter to reduce his pollution by a fixed percentage, an effluent charge which would achieve the same level of pollution abatement would be only half as costly—a saving of about $150 million. Such a price system would also provide incentive for further improvements, a simple method of handling new plants, and revenue for the control authority.

In general, the price system allocates costs in a manner which is at least superficially fair: those who produce and consume goods which cause pollution, pay the costs. But the superior efficiency in control and apparent fairness are not the only advantages of the price mechanism. Equally important is the ease with which it can be put into operation. It is not necessary to have detailed information about all the techniques of pollution reduction, or estimates of all costs and benefits. Nor is it necessary to determine whom to blame or who should pay. All that is needed is a mechanism for estimating, if only roughly at first, the pollution output of all polluters, together with a means of collecting fees. Then we can simply pick a price—any price—for each category of pollution, and we are in business. The initial price should be chosen on the basis of some estimate of its effects but need not be the optimal one. If the resulting reduction in pollution is not "enough," the price can be raised until there is sufficient reduction. A change in technology, number of plants, or whatever, can be accommodated by a change in the price, even without detailed knowledge of all the technological and economic data. Further, once the idea is explained, the price system is much more likely to be politically acceptable than some method of direct control. Paying for a service, such as garbage disposal, is a well-established tradition, and is much less objectionable than having a bureaucrat nosing around and giving arbitrary orders. When businessmen, consumers, and politicians understand the alternatives, the price system will seem very attractive indeed.

Who Sets the Prices?

An important part of this method of control obviously is the mechanism that sets and changes the pollution price. Ideally, the PCB could choose this price on the basis of an estimate of the benefits and costs involved, in effect imitating the impersonal workings of ordinary market forces. But because many of the costs and benefits cannot be measured, a less "objective," more political procedure is needed. This political procedure could take the form of a referendum, in which the PCB would present to the voters alternative schedules of pollution prices, together with the estimated effects of each. There would be a massive propaganda campaign waged by the interested parties, of course. Slogans such as "Vote NO on 12 and Save Your Job," or "Proposition 12 Means Higher Prices," might be overstatements but would contain some truth, as the individual voter would realize when he considered the suggested increase in gasoline taxes and auto registration fees. But the other side, in true American fashion, would respond by overstating *their* case: "Smog Kills, Yes on 12," or "Stop *Them* From Ruining *Your* Water." It would be up to the PCB to inform the public about the true effects of the alternatives; but ultimately, the voters would make the decision.

It is fashionable in intellectual circles to object to such democratic procedures on the ground that the uncultured masses will not make correct decisions. If this view is based on the fact that the technical and economic arguments are likely to be too complex to be decided by direct referendum, it is certainly a reasonable position; one obvious solution is to set up an elective or appointive board to make the detailed decisions, with the expert board members being ultimately responsible to the voters. But often there is another aspect to the antidemocratic position—a feeling that it is impossible to convince the people of the desirability of some social policy, not because the issues are too complex but purely because their values are "different" and inferior. To put it bluntly: many ardent foes of pollution are not so certain that popular opinion is really behind them, and they therefore prefer a more bureaucratic and less political solution.

The question of who should make decisions for whom, or whose desires should count in a society, is essentially a noneconomic question that an economist cannot answer with authority, whatever his personal views on the matter. The political structures outlined here, when combined with the economic suggestions, can lead to a reasonably efficient solution of the pollution problem in a society where the tastes and values of all men are given some consideration. In such a society, when any nonrepresentative group is in a position to impose its particular evaluation of the costs and benefits, an inefficient situation will result. The swimmer or tidepool enthusiast who wants Los Angeles Harbor converted into a crystal-clear swimming pool, at the expense of all the workers, consumers, and businessmen who use the harbor for commerce and industry, is indistinguishable from the stockholder in Union Oil who wants maximum output from offshore wells, at the expense of everyone in the Santa Barbara area. Both are urging an inefficient use of society's resources; both are trying to get others to subsidize their particular thing—a perfectly normal, if not especially noble, endeavor.

If the democratic principle upon which the above political suggestions are based is rejected, the economist cannot object. He will still suggest the price system as a tool for controlling pollution. With any method of decision—whether popular vote, representative democracy, consultation with the nature gods, or a dictate of the intellectual elite—the price system can simplify control and reduce the amount of information needed for decisions. It provides an efficient, comprehensive, easily understood, adaptable, and reasonably fair way of handling the problem. It is ultimately the only way the problem will be solved. Arbitrary, piecemeal, stop-and-go programs of direct control have not and will not accomplish the job.

Some Objections Aren't an Answer

There are some objections that can be raised against the price system as a tool of pollution policy. Most are either illogical or apply with much greater force to any other method of control.

For example, one could object that what has been suggested here ignores the difficulties caused by fragmented political jurisdictions; but this is true for any method of control. The relevant question is: what method of control makes interjurisdictional cooperation easier and more likely? And the answer is: a price system, for several reasons. First, it is probably easier to get agreement on a simple schedule of pollution prices than on a complex set of detailed regulations. Second, a uniform price schedule would make it more difficult for any member of the "cooperative" group to attract industry from the other areas by promising a more lenient attitude toward pollution. Third, and most important, a price system generates revenues for the control board, which can be distributed to the various political entities. While the allocation of these revenues would involve some vigorous discussion, any alternative methods of control would require the various governments to raise taxes to pay the costs, a much less appealing prospect; in fact, there would be a danger that the pollution prices might be considered a device to generate revenue rather than to reduce pollution, which could lead to an overly-clean, inefficient situation.

Another objection is that the Pollution Control Board might be captured by those it is supposed to control. This danger can be countered by having the board members subject to election or by having the pollution prices set by referendum. With any other control method, the danger of the captive regulator is much greater. A uniform price is easy for the public to understand, unlike obscure technical arguments about boiler temperatures and the costs of electrostatic collectors versus low-sulfur oil from Indonesia; if pollution is too high, the public can demand higher prices, pure and simple. And the price is the same for all plants, with no excuses. With direct control, acceptable pollution levels are negotiated with each plant separately and in private, with approved delays and special permits and other nonsense. The opportunities for using political influence and simple graft are clearly much larger with direct control.

A different type of objection occasionally has been raised against the price system, based essentially on the fear that it will solve the problem. Pollution, after all, is a hot issue with which to assault The Establishment, Capitalism, Human Nature, and Them; any attempt to remove the issue by some minor change in institutions, well within The System, must be resisted by The Movement. From some points of view, of course, this is a perfectly valid objection. But one is hopeful that there still exists a majority more concerned with finding solutions than with creating issues.

There are other objections which could be raised and answered in a similar way. But the strongest argument for the price system is not found in idle speculation but in the real world, and in particular, in Germany. The Rhine River in Germany is a dirty stream, recently made notorious when an insecticide spilled into the river and killed millions of fish. One tributary of the Rhine, a river called the Ruhr, is the sewer for one of the world's most concentrated industrial areas. The Ruhr River valley contains 40 percent of German industry, including 80 percent of coal, iron, steel and heavy chemical capacity. The Ruhr is a small river, with a low flow of less than half the flow on the Potomac near Washington. The volume of wastes is extremely large—actually exceeding the flow of the river itself in the dry season! *Yet people and fish swim in the Ruhr River.*

This amazing situation is the result of over forty years of control of the Ruhr and its tributaries by a hierarchy of regional authorities. These authorities have as their goal the maintenance of the quality of the water in the area at minimum cost, and they have explicitly applied the equimarginal principle to accomplish this. Water quality is formally defined in a technological rather than an economic way; the objective is to "not kill the fish." Laboratory tests are conducted to determine what levels of various types of pollution are lethal to fish, and from these figures an index is constructed which measures the "amount of pollution" from each source in terms of its fish-killing capacity. This index is different for each source, because of differences in amount and composition of the waste, and geographical locale. Although this physical index is not really a very precise measure of the real economic *cost* of the waste, it has the advantage of being easily measured and widely understood. Attempts are made on an *ad hoc* basis to correct the index if necessary—if, for example, a non-lethal pollutant gives fish an unpleasant taste.

Once the index of pollution is constructed, a price is put on the pollution, and each source is free to adjust its operation any way it chooses. Geographical variation in prices, together with some direct advice from the authorities, encourage new plants to locate where pollution is less damaging. For example, one tributary of the Ruhr has been converted to an open sewer; it has been lined with concrete and landscaped, but otherwise no attempt is made to reduce pollution in the rivet itself. A treatment plant at the mouth of the river processes all these wastes at low cost. Therefore, the price of pollution on this river is set low. This arrangement, by the way, is a rational, if perhaps unconscious, recognition of marginal principles. The loss caused by destruction of *one* tributary is rather small, if the nearby rivers are maintained, while the benefit from having this inexpensive means of waste disposal is very large. However, if *another* river were lost, the cost would be higher and the benefits lower; one open sewer may be the optimal number.

The revenues from the pollution charges are used by the authorities to measure pollution, conduct tests and research, operate dams to regulate stream flow, and operate waste treatment facilities where economies of scale make this desirable. These facilities are located at the mouths of some tributaries, and at several dams in the Ruhr. If the authorities find pollution levels are getting too high, they simply raise the price, which causes polluters to try to reduce their wastes, and provides increased revenues to use on further treatment. Local governments influence the authorities, which helps to maintain recreation values, at least in certain stretches of the river.

This classic example of water management is obviously not exactly the price system method discussed earlier. There is considerable direct control, and the pollution authorities take a very active role. Price regulation is not used as much as it could be; for example, no attempt is made to vary the price over the season, even though high flow on the Ruhr is more than ten times larger than low flow. If the price of pollution were reduced during high flow periods, plants would have an incentive to regulate their production and/or store their wastes for release during periods when the river can more easily handle them. The difficulty of continuously monitoring wastes means this is not done; as automatic, continuous measurement techniques improve and are made less expensive, the use of variable prices will increase. Though this system is not entirely regulated by the price mechanism, prices are used more here than anywhere else, and the system is much more successful than any other.[1] So, both in theory and in prac-

---

[1] For a more complete discussion of the Ruhr Valley system, see Allen V. Kneese, *The Economics of Regional Water Quality Management* (Baltimore, Md.: Johns Hopkins Press, 1964).

tice, the price system is attractive, and ultimately must be the solution to pollution problems.

"If We Can Go to the Moon, Why . . . etc?"

"If we can go to the moon, why can't we eliminate pollution?" This new, and already trite, rhetorical question invites a rhetorical response: "If physical scientists and engineers approached their tasks with the same kind of wishful thinking and fuzzy moralizing which characterizes much of the pollution discussion, we would never have gotten off the ground." Solving the pollution problem is no easier than going to the moon, and therefore requires a comparable effort in terms of men and resources and the same sort of logical hard-headedness that made Apollo a success. Social scientists, politicians, and journalists who spend their time trying to find someone to blame, searching for a magic device or regulation, or complaining about human nature, will be as helpful in solving the pollution problem as they were in getting us to the moon. The price system outlined here is no magic formula, but it attacks the problem at its roots, and has a real chance of providing a long-term solution.

Public Policy Toward
Water Pollution

ALLEN KNEESE

Allen Kneese is Professor of Economics at the University of New Mexico. The following item presents his testimony before the Senate Subcommittee on Air and Water Pollution in 1965.

As you well know, interest in the problem of water quality is at a high pitch. Several sets of congressional hearings on the matter have been recently held, a special Senate committee has in the past few years completed a monumental study of water resources, and the daily press carries articles on one or another aspect of water pollution with great frequency. A number of national laws dealing with Federal participation in pollution control activities have been passed in the past decade. Others are now pending. The U.S. Public Health Service has started to conduct comprehensive water quality investigations which will eventually include all of the river basins in the United States.

State and interstate activities have been accelerated, and research pertinent to water quality in the natural sciences and engineering has expanded greatly in the past several years.

The pollution control efforts have already borne some fruit. Over the past ten years or so the condition of the main stems of some of our most heavily used streams has improved markedly. This is true, for example, of the Delaware, the Ohio, and the Potomac; many of the highly offensive materials that once floated down these rivers are now removed from the effluents before they enter the stream.

Nevertheless, serious problems of water quality still confront the nation. One of our major challenges is to devise an optimal balance between the valuable use of watercourses for waste disposal and the external or downstream costs which this inevitably imposes.

Economic institutions on which we customarily rely to balance costs and returns—the interaction of market forces in a private enterprise system—do not perform this function satisfactorily for waste disposal. In deciding how to dispose of its wastes, an upstream firm or city is not forced by the market to take into account the costs imposed upon downstream water users or the value of water use opportunities foreclosed by its effluent discharge.

The upstream papermill which dumps its wastes into water without bearing any of the downstream costs produces paper which is artificially cheap. In effect, it pays nothing for the use of a valuable resource; for example, the waste, dilution, stabilization, and carriage capacity of the watercourse.

From a social point of view the value of this resource is measured by the alternate uses which can be made of the water. Failure of the waste discharger to consider the reduced value of water in other uses which are made more expensive or foreclosed entirely by his pollution is a basic element of the pollution problem.

Because the waste discharger does not consider the social cost of his actions, he is induced to use the waste carriage capacity of the stream excessively. Because he may dispose of waste material at a cost to others, not to himself, he makes a lesser effort to design and operate industrial processes in such a way as to reclaim valuable residues than if the full social costs of waste disposal were met.

The effectiveness of process engineering and materials recovery processes in reducing waste loads has been richly demonstrated in the United States and perhaps even more strikingly in West Germany by the *Genossenschaften* (regional water resources authorities in the main industrial area of West Germany).

Moreover, studies of waste loads generated per unit of physical output by plants producing identical goods but with different productive processes suggest the degree to which wastes can be engineered away. This emphasizes the importance of water resources management authorities providing the appropriate incentives for such procedures. A society which neglects the off-site costs of waste disposal or undervalues them will waste too much. Furthermore, if downstream costs are not reflected in the decisions of the upstream waste dischargers there will be no treatment of waste water effluents even when such treatment is less costly than downstream water supply treatment or the value of water use opportunities forgone downstream.

What have been our approaches in the United States to this first major problem of water quality management—optimal control of waste discharges from individual waste disposers?

Market forces are supplemented in a variety of ways. Appeals are made to civic responsibility to minimize waste contribution to watercourses. Damaged parties may resort to adversary proceedings in courts of law. Recognition of the limits of these devices has caused us to go beyond them to administrative regulations of waste discharges from cities and industries usually on the basis of some sort of general standards. In more recent years, the Federal Government has provided financial assistance to local communities for the construction of waste treatment facilities.

I would like to comment on the economic implications of these devices—regulation and financial support to local communities—as a means of achieving an optimum degree of waste discharge reduction.

The control of waste discharges through administrative orders regulating individual waste disposers has been a useful device and cannot be abandoned until we have a better substitute. However, regulation of individual discharges has been based on general, across-the-board standards, not on a systematic balancing of benefits to downstream users and cost to the waste discharger, and this is a limitation. If the regulatory agency is to achieve such a balance, using the traditional tool of effluent standards, it will require extremely large amounts of information—perhaps more than an administrative organization could be expected to secure and handle effectively.

Of particular significance, this agency must know how much it would cost the water user to reduce the effluent contribution to streams by specified amounts. In other words, the regulatory agency must have a detailed knowledge of the costs of using water in different ways in the manufacturing process as well as of the cost of treating residual materials.

Reducing industrial waste discharge into streams is not a simple question of treating waste. There are such issues as whether potential waste materials can be recovered or whether some change in industrial processes would alter the quality of the effluent. The food and pulp and paper industries are the greatest generators of degradable organic wastes, and in some instances emit massive loads. For example, a single sugarbeet processing plant, during its seasonal period of operation, may produce organic wastes equivalent to the sewage flow of a city of half a million people. Yet careful examination of technology in this industry leads to the conclusion that even now it would be possible to design a plant with no waste discharges at all.

Moreover, it is almost always possible to achieve any desired level of waste load reduction more economically by process changes and waste recovery procedures than by treatment. To evaluate these alternatives would entail a measure of public inquiry into private business activities which is not readily accepted in the United States. Yet, in seeking economical methods to reduce industrial waste loads, we are addressing an extremely important issue.

The U.S. Public Health Service reports that industrial waste water effluents presently carry at least twice as much degradable organic material into U.S. watercourses as the sewage effluents of all our municipalities combined. Needless to say, they carry a still larger proportion of most other types of pollutants.

The other frequently used device, Federal subventions to local communities, has helped to improve water quality in many areas. The Federal Water Pollution Control Act, amended in 1961 and again in 1965, authorized grants to municipalities for construction of sewage treatment works. A grant of 30 percent of the estimated reasonable cost of construction, or $600,000—whichever is less—may be made for a single project, and a joint project to serve two or more communities may receive $2.4 million.

Federal funds authorized to be appropriated for this are currently $100 million per year. It is frequently proposed in the Congress that industry be accorded some tax relief when it installs waste treatment facilities. Such financial support tends to reduce waste loads discharged, but a question arises as to whether the existing and proposed procedures produce the greatest results at a given cost.

If we were to make the best use of public funds in dealing with pollution, public financial support would have to be strategically supplied. To achieve the highest net returns from a system of financial support, the payments to the city or firm would have to be designed to accomplish a degree of reduction in waste discharge which, incrementally speaking, would not cost more than the downstream benefits society would realize from such reduction. In particular, payments would be made for waste reduction, not treatment, and geared to differences in regional situations and to the timing of streamflows. Since process and waste recovery adjustments are often more efficient ways to reduce industrial waste discharge, payments would have to be framed so as to take advantage of these alternatives rather than to be simply linked to treatment. Needless to say, proposals for rapid writeoffs of industrial treatment facilities could well lead to the use of costly and inefficient devices to reduce waste.

It might be difficult, of course, to obtain agreement on a subsidy system capable of efficient results. Moreover, many members of both political parties have become quite cognizant of the perverse and distorting effects which the existing tax structure frequently has. To load that structure further, through additional subsidy measures or further erosion of the base, as would occur if proposed rapid tax writeoffs of pollution reducing industrial investments come into existence, can only increase these difficulties.

If we are to cope with water pollution problems both effectively and economically, we must look beyond direct regulatory practices to new, perhaps revolutionary approaches.

A most promising possibility in this connection is a charge on waste discharge reflecting the offsite costs associated with the discharge. If all the downstream opportunity costs of pollution, including increased costs of water supply treatment, lost recreation values, et cetera, could be identified, expressed as monetary values, and levied upon the effluent of waste dischargers, private incentives could be relied upon to come up with proper levels of treatment, optimal process and product adjustments by manufacturers, and appropriate industrial location decisions.

All these decisions would have reflected in them the real costs of waste disposal just as they do the wages of labor, outlays for materials, and other costs.

Industrial plants would then tend to take steps to reduce waste loads by all relevant means—treatment, process, and product changes—until the costs of all these measures were equated incrementally with the reduction in damages which they produce. In other words, until the manufacturer could no longer profitably "trade off" an additional dollar spent to reduce wastes discharged into the water for more than an additional dollar in reduced effluent levies or charges.

In effect, a situation would prevail in which attempts to minimize private costs, for example, to produce output efficiently, would also produce a minimization of costs to society. Similarly a system of assessing downstream costs on communities would give them an incentive to treat their wastes to the point at which the damage avoided downstream, for example, the effluent charge avoided, is just equal to the cost of producing a further increment of treatment.

These adjustments would mean that the sum of the costs associated with waste disposal alternatives, including pollution damage, would be minimized. It may seem strange to include downstream damages as a sensible alternative because such damages use up resources, that is, cause a social cost, but so do abatement measures. The problem is to achieve an optimal balance between damages and abatement. It would seldom, if ever, minimize social costs to eliminate from use entirely the waste degradation capacity of the stream.

This technique can utilize the incentive for private gain to achieve the social purpose of reducing waste discharge in an optimal manner. Moreover, it can usually do this with much less information than would be needed to achieve the same end by means of direct regulation of individual waste discharges. To the degree that the authority does not itself find it desirable to operate a waste disposal system, merely imposing the downstream costs of waste dischargers upon them would accomplish desired results without such extensive knowledge of all the details of plant operations.

In effect, many of the most difficult decisions would be imposed on individual manufacturers who are more likely to possess the requisite information about their operations. The individual firm would find it necessary to decide upon levels of production and optimum waste reduction methods, including process adjustments, waste recovery, lagooning of wastes, etc. These decisions would have to be made in view of the full costs of using the waste assimilative capacity of the stream.

The charge on effluents has a firm theoretical foundation. There is every reason to believe it will lessen the distortion in resources allocation caused by the side effects of water resource use. At the same time, it will yield revenue which can be used for various public purposes, thereby lessening pressures for taxes which are known to have perverse effects.

As I have already implied, frequently public or collective agencies can do more than provide the proper level of incentive for reducing waste discharge by industries and municipalities. The improvement of water quality by various large-scale, collectively provided measures is among the purposes to which the revenues resulting from charges could be devoted.

This is the case when collective facilities like reservoirs for flow regulation, treatment in the stream itself, or treatment of waste transported to a collective plant are economical alternatives to discharge reduction at the individual outfall. Let us turn then to this second aspect of the problem of water quality management, the optimum provision of large-scale collective facilities for water quality improvement.

Low-flow augmentation (use of reservoirs to provide additional flow during dry periods) is an appropriate technique for helping to maintain water quality in an overall system of water quality management. However, present institutional arrangements in general do not provide an appropriate mechanism for identifying, evaluating, and implementing relevant alternatives which might provide the same returns at lower cost.

These include collective treatment of waste, measures for improving water quality in the stream such as instream detention ponds or mechanical reaeration, and stream specialization.

It is existing policy to provide flow augmentation for multipurpose Federal reservoir projects with funds that do not have to be repaid provided certain specified standards of treatment are met. For municipal wastes this is interpreted to be so-called secondary or biological treatment. In the case of industry, where the notion of the character of secondary treatment is frequently not very meaningful in view of the character of the wastes involved, the treatment required is that level deemed "adequate."

Several points may be made concerning these policies and the likelihood that they will actually result in a least-cost combination of flow augmentation with other alternatives.

First, the secondary treatment requirement for municipal wastes and the much more vague "adequacy" requirements for industrial wastes are essentially arbitrary—they do not result from a weighing off of comparative costs. This may be justifiable as a matter of administrative convenience in the absence of resources to make systematic studies of appropriate management institutions, but in terms of precise management of water quality, it must be deemed an arbitrary restriction.

Second, there is no provision in the Federal procedures for a systematic identification, evaluation, balancing off, and implementation of other alternatives, such as collective treatment of wastes, direct reaeration of streams, provision of retention ponds in the streams themselves to produce degradation of residual wastes, and artificial recharge of ground waters to improve quality before use.

Third, the nonreimbursable feature of present policy does not provide an appropriate incentive for the optimum use of methods for controlling waste discharges into streams. Unless waste dischargers, particularly industry, must bear the cost of, for example, providing low-flow augmentation—a cost that can be avoided by reducing waste discharge—they will not tend to substitute alternatives such as process adjustments and byproduct recovery in appropriate measure. It is true that attempting to assess waste discharges with the cost of flow augmentation would entail an additional administrative cost, but especially in highly developed basins this may prove richly worthwhile in terms of the increased efficiency achieved.

Fourth, it is important to realize that nonreimbursable features of Federal programs lead to pressures tending toward inefficiency. If beneficiaries of a program bear none of its costs, they will favor it even though it is in fact worth less to them than it costs. Also, they will tend to favor it over less costly alternatives for which they have to bear the cost. Let me just illustrate how such pressure could arise. The Corps of Engineers is proposing a costly system of reservoirs in the Potomac Basin whose primary function is to dilute the waste at the Washington metropolitan area. It has been suggested that a less costly alternative would be to conduct the treated wastes of the area by pipeline to the Chesapeake Bay where copious amounts of dilution water are naturally available. Let us, for the sake of argument, grant that this is the case. The Washington metropolitan area would then have to bear most, if not all, of the cost of the more efficient alternative and none of the cost of the less efficient one.

Thus, an incentive is given for beneficiaries to favor the alternative which is financially less expensive from their point of view, but which in fact is socially more costly. The conflict between socially efficient and locally advantageous decisions is particularly serious if we wish to use regional agencies for water resource management to a more far reaching extent.

In recent years, public agencies, both state and Federal, have made substantial progress in dealing with the pollution problem. However, my brief examination of existing approaches to pollution abatement reveals that there are inherent limitations in the techniques upon which we have relied. These limitations may be summarized briefly as follows:

(1) For the direct regulation of individual waste discharges to be fully effective, the regulatory agency would require a knowledge of economics of water use within the individual plant which would be difficult to obtain as well as to utilize effectively.

(2) Federal financial aid is not as effective as it might be because it is not geared to different regional situations and different streamflow conditions.

(3) Low-flow augmentation policies offer an incentive to use this technique as opposed to alternatives which may be more economical but which are not eligible for Federal financial support.

(4) The industrial firm disposing of wastes to streams has no systematic

economic incentive to adopt industrial process changes, including materials and byproduct recovery, which might result in substantial reduction in waste contribution when these processes involve a lesser cost than the side effects they tend to produce.

We have generally not evolved arrangements for realizing economies of large-scale treatment and management of waste disposal. It is evident that large plants which will process the wastes of a number of communities or plants often will be more economical than individual waste treatment facilities.

Substantial economies also can be realized through development of regional waste disposal systems which utilize alternatives such as the direct improvements of water quality in the stream, the specialization of streams, diversion channels for wastes, and a whole host of other possible alternatives.

Present procedures are not well adapted for day-to-day, well-articulated operation of waste disposal faciles in a region as a whole. In many instances, this is fully as important as finding an efficient system in the first place.

I do not mean that precise, optimizing approaches would necessarily be appropriate in all areas. It is, of course, essential that attention be given to the costs of implementing such approaches in the various regions. In some cases, points of pollution are scattered and more systematic approaches may not yield large dividends.

It should be noted, however, that already some 40 percent of our urban population and a higher portion of our industrial activity is located in only four of our twenty-two major river basins. These basins frequently contain huge megalopolitan complexes and intensively developed watersheds where the gains from systematic approaches are likely to be large.

It is my strong conviction that in our more heavily populated industrialized regions, we should move toward the creation of regional agencies with far-reaching powers to plan, construct, operate, and finance regional systems of waste disposal. Emphasis should be on the use of effluent charges by these organizations both to control waste loads delivered to the system and to provide the financial support for large-scale efforts aimed at improving water quality to the extent that incremental benefits are deemed to exceed incremental costs.

There is one area of the world where problems of the intensity we are beginning to face in the United States have existed for a long time and where they have, in my view, been effectively and efficiently handled: the Ruhr region of Germany. The Ruhr region is approximately half the size of the Delaware River Basin. The streams which serve it have a very low flow during the summer season. It is, for example, approximately one-quarter of the lowest flow ever recorded on the Delaware River.

The population of the area is around eight million and it is perhaps the world's most heavily industrialized area. Forty percent of the industrial production of Germany occurs in this region, including over 80 percent of the heavy industrial output.

Because of the density of population and enormous industrial output, the waste disposal demands within this region are immense. Yet, major sections of the Ruhr River are so managed that the stream itself is suitable for recreation purposes, including swimming and boating. Moreover, prices of unsubsidized publicly supplied water are as low as, or lower than, any of the major urban areas of Germany. The following features are central to the success of these organizations:

(1) The system that has developed has been specifically designed to meet the needs of the Ruhr region. It is a unique system within Germany.

(2) Waste disposal is managed on a regionwide basis in which advantage is taken of economies resulting from flow regulation and large-scale treatment and recovery of potential waste products. The regenerative capacity of the streams is utilized to the extent consistent with water quality standards which are based on a variety of water uses in the area.

(3) One stream in the region is used in a completely specialized way, being dedicated to waste disposal use only.

(4) Industries and cities pay a charge for the effluent they contribute to the waste disposal system based upon periodic tests of the quality and quantity of their effluent.

The charge which is levied is not contingent upon whether the wastes are directly handled in treatment plants or not. This independence of effluent charges from the provision of specific facilities is essential if potential gains in efficiency from system design are to be realized.

This can perhaps best be illustrated. Economics of scale and treatment may mean that wastes from factory A are given far-reaching treatment because it has a large effluent volume and costs per unit of waste removed are comparatively low.

Say plant B has only a very small effluent volume and treatment would be very expensive. Desirable (cost minimizing) stream conditions may be attainable by treating only factory A's waste at low cost and not treating B's at all. If an appropriate method of assessing costs exists, part of the cost will be paid by B and both A and B can benefit because total costs are lower than they would be if the same results had been achieved by two smaller plants. The Ruhr area associations have worked out rather sophisticated cost assessment procedures along these lines.

The results that have been obtained in the Ruhr region are impressive. The system of effluent charges is an effective means of motivating industries to reduce the contribution of their waste to rivers. The firm decides on the basis of the schedule of charges the extent to which it should treat its wastes or alter its industrial process to minimize costs. The administrative agency decides upon a level of charges consistent with what it considers to be the overall cost of dealing with the wastes.

It would seem appropriate that we begin moving toward regional systems adopted to the needs of particular areas in the United States. A start has already been made. The Delaware River Basin Commission has the authority to experiment with new techniques and devices for dealing with the pollution problem and the obligation to plan and implement systems of water resources management tailored to the Delaware region.

Further institutional development along these lines might well be carried on in smaller river basins within individual states where the difficulties attendant to the formation of interstate compacts with rather extensive powers are not an obstacle. The more highly developed tributaries of the Ohio suggest themselves as likely candidates, for instance.

Full-scale development of regional approaches to the water quality problem will probably depend upon some national policy changes which would encourage the development of regional agencies, both by removing existing obstacles and by providing positive aid. One possibility would, of course, be for the Federal Government to take direct action.

It could set up regional water quality management agencies or overall regional water resources agencies with water quality management responsibilities. These could be separate entities such as TVA or units of a regionalized Federal agency such as proposed by the first Hoover Commission.

There has been much opposition to such arrangements and even if deemed desirable, it seems quite doubtful that the Federal Government would be willing to move in this direction.

An alternative would be for the Federal Government to establish incentives for the organization and operation of regional agencies either under state law or through interstate compacts. Such incentives might be provided in the following manner: Upon creation of an agency with adequate authority to institute an optimizing system, the agency would be eligible for a grant of funds to support a share of its operating costs while it assembled and analyzed pertinent data and designed its specific program. If the Federal Government is satisfied that the proposed program would meet reasonable optimizing objectives, the agency might be eligible for a grant to assist it with its operating expenses. Such assistance might appropriately be limited to the implementation period such as five years. The regional agency might also be made eligible for Federal loans for investment in large-scale facilities where scale economies can be achieved.

If the regional agency has general water resources development and management responsibilities—as seems highly desirable—Federal Government could provide support through the agency for flood control, navigation, irrigation, power, and recreation facilities on the same terms as such support is now provided through the Federal agencies.

Unless this were done, regional agencies would operate at a serious disadvantage and it is doubtful that regions would willingly impose such disadvantages upon themselves. A partial or complete alternative to the extension of subsidy arrangements to regional agencies would be a concerted effort to impose the cost of Federal agency water programs upon beneficiaries. The latter would have desirable general consequences in terms of the efficiency of water resource use.

Finally, and perhaps most importantly, the Federal Government could establish minimum standards for the entire country, and a policy of levying charges upon effluents. This would help to eliminate the relative disadvantage in competing for new industry, under which regional agencies levying charges would otherwise labor. It would provide acceptable performances even in instances where regional authorities do not become established, while opening opportunities for establishment of such agencies and flexible planning on their part. Once a regional agency were duly established the authority and responsibility for levying the charges could be turned over to it. The regional agency could refine the system of charges as a tool of management since in areas without regional agencies having continuing responsibilities for water quality management the charge might, for administrative reasons, need to be based upon rather crude rules of thumb and self-monitoring by waste dischargers.

In both cases, however, it would be very important that assessment be made in such a way that the waste discharger could reduce or avoid the charge by reducing his waste discharge, otherwise the incentive effect would be lost.

For the established regional agency, the charge would provide a source of revenue which could be used to operate a system making full and flexible use of the full array of efficient means for dealing with the problem.

If we are to develop management tools and skills commensurate with the increasingly challenging problems of environmental quality we confront, bold thought and imaginative experimentation are fully as essential in the realms of economics, institutions, and laws as are science and engineering.

Is the Oil Shortage Real? Oil Companies as OPEC Tax-Collectors

MORRIS A. ADELMAN

Morris Adelman is Professor of Economics at Massachusetts Institute of Technology. This article appeared in Foreign Policy *in 1970.*

The multinational oil companies have become, in the words of the board chairman of British Petroleum, the "tax collecting agency" of the producing nations. In 1972, the companies operated the greatest monopoly in history and transferred about $15 billion from the consuming countries to their principals. If the arrangement continues, a conservative estimate for 1980 collection is over $55 billion per year. Much of that wealth will be available to disrupt the world monetary system and promote armed conflict. Oil supply is now much more insecure. Monopoly, the power to overcharge, is the power to withhold supply. Among nations, an embargo is an act of war, and the threat of an oil embargo ushered in the Organization of Petroleum Exporting Countries (OPEC) cartel.

The oil companies are now the agents of a foreign power. They will be blamed for impairing the sovereignty of the consuming countries, and quite unjustly. They only did the will of the OPEC nations and of the consuming countries themselves, notably the United States. The consumers' "strange and self-abuse" is the key to how the events of 1970–71 turned a slowly retreating into a rapidly advancing monopoly.

The most important player in the game is the American State Department. This agency is deplorably poorly informed in mineral resource economics, the oil industry, the history of oil crises and the participation therein of the Arabs with whom it is obsessed; in fact, State cannot even give an accurate account of its own recent doings.

Prediction is unavoidable but risky. In 1963 I thought that, abstracting from inflation, a price of $1 per barrel at the Persian Gulf was not unlikely fairly soon. In terms of 1963 dollars it did go to 92 cents by early 1970. As predicted, supply remained excessive, and the companies could not control the market. But on the political side, the prediction went all wrong in 1970–71. Although I had warned that the producing countries might threaten a cutoff of supply, and urged insurance against it, I was much mistaken to call it an unlikely event. Nor did I expect the consuming countries, especially the United States, to cooperate so zealously. I may be equally wrong to expect that consuming countries will continue this way for most or all of the 1970's.

The unanimous opinion issuing from companies and governments in the capitalist, Communist, and Third Worlds is that the price reversal of 1970 and 1971 resulted from a surge in demand, or change from surplus to scarcity, from a buyers' to a sellers' market. The story has no resemblance to the facts. The 1970 increase in consumption over 1969 was somewhat below the 1960–70 average in all areas. The increase in 1971 over 1970, in Western Europe and Japan, was about half the decade average. In the first quarter of 1972, Western European consumption was only 1.5 percent above the previous year. By mid-1972, excess producing capacity, a rarity in world oil (i.e. outside North America) was almost universal and had led to drastic government action, especially in Venezuela and Iraq. The industry was "suffering from having provided the facilities for an increase in trade which did not materialize." A drastic unforeseen slowdown in growth and unused capacity would make prices fall, not rise, in any competitive market.

Some powerful force has overridden demand and supply. This force did not enter before the middle of 1970, at the earliest. Up to that time the trend of prices had been downward, and long-term contracts had been at lower prices than short-term, indicating that the industry expected still lower prices in the future, even as far as 10 years ahead.

If demand exceeds supply at current prices, sellers and buyers acting individually make new bargains at higher prices. When supply exceeds demand yet prices are raised, the conclaves, joint actions, and "justifications" are strong evidence of collusion, not scarcity.

More precisely: in a competitive market, a surge in demand or shrinkage in supply raises price because it puts a strain on the productive apparatus. To produce additional output requires higher costs; unless compensated by higher prices, the additional output will not be supplied.

If there were increasing long run scarcity at the Persian Gulf, discoveries falling behind consumption, the reservoirs would be exploited more intensively to offset decline, and to maintain and expand production. More capital and more labor would be required per additional barrel of producing capacity. In fact, between 1960 and 1970 (the last year available), the investment needed per unit of new crude oil capacity fell by over 50 percent, despite a rising general price level. Labor requirements (which are both for construction and operation) have fallen even more drastically. Supply has not only not tightened, it has been getting easier.

The world "energy crisis" or "energy shortage" is a fiction. But belief in the fiction is a fact. It makes people accept higher oil prices as imposed by nature, when they are really fixed by collusion. And sellers of all fuels, whatever their conflicts, can stand in harmony on the platform of high oil prices.

Twenty years ago, the Paley Commission made the classic statement of the problem:

> Exhaustion is not waking up to find the cupboard is bare but the need to devote constantly increasing efforts to acquiring each pound of materials from natural resources which are dwindling both in quality and quantity. . . . The essence of the materials problem is costs.

It is worth assuming arbitrarily that in the future supply will tighten. The worst that can happen is zero new discoveries. The table shows Persian Gulf production and reserves in the zero-discoveries model, recognizing that reserves in fields known in 1971 can be expanded by development and discoveries of new pools in the old fields. The assumption of 50 percent expansion is highly conservative in the light of American experience, considering also that probably most Persian Gulf reserves (like most production) are in fields discovered in the last 20 years.

In 1950, Persian Gulf reserves were estimated at 42 billion barrels, mostly in eight large fields still producing today at ever-higher rates with

Persian Gulf Production and Reserves, Zero Discoveries Model, 1971–85.

1971			
Production		6	BBY
Reserves		367	BB
Production/Reserves		1.6	%
Reserves plus 50 percent		550	BB
1971–85			
Average Growth per year	8	11	%
1985			
Production	17	25	BBY
Cumulative 1972–85	143	178	BB
Remaining	407	372	BB
Production/Reserves	4.0	6.7	%

BB = billion barrels
BBY = billion barrels per year; a billion = one thousand million.

SOURCE: 1971 production and reserves, from *Oil & Gas Journal*, December 31, 1971.

no peaking out. In 1951–71 inclusive, 47 billion barrels were extracted. At end-1971 reserves were 367 billions, mostly in 26 large fields, including the original eight. On the basis of production, one may estimate that nearly half the reserves are in fields operating in 1950, nearly a fourth in fields discovered in 1950–59, between a fourth and a third in 1960–69 discoveries, which have the greatest expansion potential (reserve data from *BP Statistical Review of the World Oil Industry* and *Oil & Gas Journal*).

Production growth in 1971–85 is estimated first according to a recent BP forecast of 7.7 percent, which takes account of rising U.S. imports, to come mostly from the Persian Gulf. Doubtless also it registers, as does a Shell forecast, the cessation of growth in European imports as North Sea oil and gas takes over. Indeed, Persian Gulf shipments to Europe will probably be lower in 1980 than in 1972—rising and then falling in the interim. But to be on the safe side, we also estimate 1972–85 production by extrapolating the long time growth rate.

The cumulated production 1972–85 is subtracted from expanded end-1971 reserves. The higher the production-reserve ratio, the higher is cost, all else being equal. The zero-discoveries model is drastic to the point of absurdity. Moreover, it sets to zero the reserves of African and Persian Gulf natural gas, which at current prices are worth producing, and which equate to an additional 90 billion barrels oil equivalent. Even so, the 1985 production-reserve percent is much lower than is planned for similar, i.e. high capacity, reservoirs in the North Sea or Alaska, which are usually in the range of 7 to 11 percent.

Depletion of reserves at the Persian Gulf is only about 1.5 percent a year. It is uneconomic to turn over an inventory so slowly. But Persian Gulf operators have not been free to expand output and displace higher cost production from other areas because this would wreck the world price structure. Therefore, it is meaningless to average production-reserve ratios for the whole world, as is too often done. A barrel of reserves found and developed elsewhere in the world is from five to seven times as important in terms of productive capacity as a barrel at the Persian Gulf. In other words, one could displace production from the entire Persian Gulf with reserves from one-fifth to one-seventh as large. And this is perhaps the only constructive aspect of the current drive for self-sufficiency in oil. This zero-discoveries model yields a much higher production-reserves percent, hence a substantial increase in investment requirements and current operating costs per barrel. Today at the Persian Gulf, capital and operating costs are each about 5 cents per barrel; under our extreme assumptions, they are roughly double. The difference between 10 and 20 cents measures the value of discovering new fields: it takes the strain off the old.

No Basis for Fears

The zero-discoveries model only estimates the worst that could happen; it is not a prediction of what will happen. When the procedure was applied in 1965, current and projected costs were higher than they are now, since many new discoveries have freshened the mix, not to speak of improvements in technology.

There is no more basis for fears of acute oil scarcity in the next 15 years than there was 15 years ago—and the fears were strong in 1957. The myth that rising imports (of the United States) will "turn the market around" is only the latest version of the myth that rising imports (of Europe and Japan) would "dry out the surplus in 1957–70."

More generally: supply and demand are registered in incremental cost, which is and long will be a negligible fraction of the current crude oil price of about $1.90 per barrel. Hence *supply and demand are irrelevant to the current and expected price of crude oil.* All that matters is whether the monopoly will flourish or fade.

In Europe and Japan, there was a mild and temporary shortage of refining capacity in early 1970. At the same time, a tanker shortage put rates at the highest level since shortly after the closing of the Suez Canal, and raised product prices.

In May 1970 the trans-Arabian pipeline was blocked by Syria to obtain higher payments for the transit rights, while the Libyan government began to impose production cutbacks on most of the companies operating there, to force them to agree to higher taxes. Although the direct effect of the cutback and closure was small, the effect on tanker rates was spectacular, and product prices and profits shot up.

The companies producing in Libya speedily agreed to a tax increase. The Persian Gulf producing countries then demanded and received the same increase, whereupon Libya demanded a further increase and the Persian Gulf countries followed suit. Finally, agreements were signed at Tehran in February 1971, increasing tax and royalty payments at the Persian Gulf as of June 1971 by about 47 cents per barrel, and rising to about 66 cents in 1975. North African and Nigerian increases were larger. In Venezuela the previous 1966 agreement was disregarded and higher taxes were simply legislated. These taxes are in form income taxes, in fact excise taxes, in cents per barrel. Like any other excise tax they are treated as a cost and become a floor to price. No oil company can commit for less than the sum of tax-plus-cost per barrel.

Government-Company Harmony

The multinational companies producing oil were amenable to these tax increases because as was openly said on the morrow of Tehran, they used the occasion to increase their margins and return on investment in both crude and products. In Great Britain the object was stated: to cover the tax increase "and leave some over," and the February 1971 tax increase was matched by a product price increase perhaps half again as great. The best summary of the results was by a well known financial analyst, Kenneth E. Hill, who called the agreements "truly an unexpected boon for the worldwide industry."

Mr. Hill rightly emphasized product price increases, but arm's length crude prices also increased by more than the tax increases. When the producing countries made fresh demands later in 1971, an American investment advisory service (United Business Services) remarked that tax increases were actually favorable to oil company profits. And 1971 was easily the best year for company profits since 1963, although there was a profit slide off later in the year, as competition in products though not yet in crude again reasserted itself.

The price pattern is set for the 1970's. From time to time, either in pursuance or in violation of the Tehran-Tripoli "aggreements," the tax is increased, whereupon prices increase as much or more, but then tend to erode as the companies compete very slowly at the crude level and less slowly at the products level. Thus prices increase in steps, yet at any given moment there is usually a buyer's market, i.e. more is available than is demanded at the price, which is under downward pressure.

The companies' margin will therefore wax and wane, but they benefit by the new order. They cannot, even if they would, mediate between producing and consuming nations. As individual competitors, they are vulnerable to producing-nation threats to hit them one at a time. As a group, they can profit by a higher tax through raising prices in concert, for the higher tax is that clear signal to which they respond without communication. The Secretary General of OPEC, Dr. Nadim Pachachi, said truly that there is no basic conflict between companies and producing nations. The then head of Shell, Sir David Barran, spoke of a "marriage" of companies and producing governments. Most precise of all was Sir Eric Drake, the chairman of BP, who called the companies a "tax collecting agency," for both producing and consuming country governments. There is, however, a difference in kind between serving a government in its own country to collect revenue from its own citizens, and serving a government to collect revenue from other countries.

Leading Role of the United States

Without active support from the United States, OPEC might never have achieved much. When the first Libyan cutbacks were decreed, in May 1970, the United States could have easily convened the oil companies to work out an insurance scheme whereby any single company forced to shut down would have crude oil supplied by the others at tax-plus-cost from another source. (The stable was possibly locked a year after the horse was stolen.) Had that been done, all companies might have been shut down, and the Libyan government would have lost all production income. It would have been helpful but not necessary to freeze its deposits abroad. The OPEC nations were unprepared for conflict. Their unity would have been severely tested and probably destroyed. The revenue losses of Libya would have been gains to all other producing nations, and all would have realized the danger of trying to pressure the consuming countries. Any Libyan division or brigade commander could consider how he and friends might gain several billions of dollars a year, and other billions deposited abroad, by issuing the right marching orders.

Failure to oppose does not necessarily imply that the United States favored the result. But there was unambiguous action shortly thereafter. A month after the November agreements with Libya, a special OPEC meeting in Caracas first resolved on "concrete and simultaneous action," but this had not been explained or translated into a threat of cutoff even as late as January 13, nor by January 16, when the companies submitted their proposals for higher and escalating taxes.

Then came the turning point: the United States convened a meeting in Paris of the Organization for Economic Cooperation and Development (OECD) nations (who account for most oil consumption) on January 20. There is no public record of the meeting, but—as will become clear below—there is no doubt that the American representatives and the oil companies assured the other governments that if they offered no resistance to higher oil prices they could at least count on five years' secure supply at stable or only slightly rising prices.

The OECD meeting could have kept silent, thereby keeping the OPEC nations guessing, and moderating their demands for fear of counteraction. Or they might have told the press they were sure the OPEC nations were too mature and statesmanlike to do anything drastic, because after all the OECD nations had some drastic options open to them too . . . but why inflame opinion by talking about those things? Instead an OECD spokesman praised the companies' offer, and declined to estimate its cost to the consuming countries. He stated that the meeting had not discussed "contingency arrangements for coping with an oil shortage." This was an advance capitulation. The OPEC nations now had a signal to go full speed ahead because there would be no resistance.

Before January 20, an open threat by the OPEC nations would not have been credible, in view of the previous failure of even mild attempts at production regulation in 1965 and 1966. But after the capitulation, threats were credible and were made often. (This is clear from a careful reading of the press in January and February 1971.) They culminated in a resolution passed on February 7 by nine OPEC members, including Venezuela but not Indonesia, providing for an embargo after two weeks if their demands were not met. The Iranian Finance Minister, chief of the producing nations' team, said: "There is no question of negotiations or resuming negotiations. It's just the acceptance of our terms." The companies were resigned to this, but wanted assurances that what they accepted would not be changed for five years.

The United States had been active in the meantime. Our Under Secretary of State arrived in Tehran January 17, publicly stating his government's interest in "stable and predictable" prices, which in context meant higher prices. He told the Shah of Iran the damage that would be done to Europe and Japan if oil supplies were cut off. Perhaps this is why the Shah soon thereafter made the first threat of a cutoff of supply. It is hard to imagine a more effective incitement to extreme action than to hear that this will do one's opponents great damage.

Resistance to the OPEC demands would have shattered the nascent cartel. As late as January 24, the Shah told the press: "If the oil producing countries suffer even the slightest defeat, it would be the death-knell for OPEC, and from then on the countries would no longer have the courage to get together."

When the Tehran agreement was announced, another State Department special press conference hailed it, referring many times to "stability" and "durability." They "expected the previously turbulent international oil situation to calm down following the new agreements." They must really have believed this! Otherwise they would not have claimed credit for Mr. Irwin or for Secretary Rogers, or induced President Nixon's office to announce that he too was pleased. They must have said this in Paris in January and again at an OECD meeting in May. We now live with the consequences.

State Department representative James Atkins told a Senate Committee in February 1972: "The approach we made in the Persian Gulf [was] primarily because of the threat to cut off oil production. . . . We informed the countries that we were disturbed by their threats, and these were withdrawn very shortly after our trip." The public record outlined above shows that the threats of embargo began after the Under Secretary's arrival, culminated in OPEC Resolution XXII.131 on February 7, *and were never withdrawn.*

Scraps of Paper

The oil companies knew better than to take the "agreements" seriously; they had been there before. To be sure, one could cite many a statement by an oil executive about the "valuable assurances of stability," but this was ritual. The London *Economist*, always in close touch with the industry, expected any agreements to last only a few months, given the "persistent bad faith." The best summary was made by *Petroleum Intelligence Weekly*: "If such agreements were worth anything the present crisis wouldn't exist."

This was borne out in August of 1971. Devaluation of the dollar, the occasion for new demands, was of course an incident in the worldwide price inflation to which the Tehran and Tripoli agreements had adjusted by providing for periodic escalation. Moreover, Persian Gulf revenues were mostly not payable in dollars. The new element in the situation was not the increased dollar cost of imports to the producing countries, but the fact that prices in dollars increased, especially in Germany and Japan. This was another windfall gain to the companies, just as in early 1970. Again the producing countries were able to take most of that gain in the consuming countries because the multinational companies were the producers of oil as well as sellers of refined products.

The "oil companies had hailed the agreements as guaranteeing a semblance of stability in oil prices . . . they would seek to pass on the impact of any new cost [tax] increases." The new demands, said the chairman of Jersey Standard (Esso, or now Exxon), were a violation of the Tehran agreements, but "the industry will solve these problems just as our differences with them were reconciled earlier this year and before," i.e. higher taxes and higher prices. This was precisely correct both as to substance and as to ritual. The OPEC governments made their demands. The companies made an offer. The governments refused it and broke off the talks. The companies made a better offer, taxes were raised again, and crude oil prices with them.

Even before this deal, the producing nations had already made an additional demand, for so-called "participation." The companies said they were distressed that the agreements "have not led to the long peace . . . that they had anticipated." They would resist the demands as a violation of the agreements. Whereupon the governments "announced that they would take part in a 'combined action' if they didn't receive 'satisfaction,'" and the companies agreed to negotiate. In March, the Aramco companies who account for nearly all output in Saudi Arabia conceded participation "in principle."

"Participation," by recently negotiated companies and various Arabian governments, is a misnomer. "Pseudo-participation" would be more apt.

"Participation" does not mean that the government actually produces or sells oil, or transfers it downstream for refining and sale. As we will see later, selling oil is what Saudi Arabia wisely aims to avoid. "Participation" is simply an ingenious way of further increasing the tax per barrel without touching either posted prices or nominal tax rates, thus apparently respecting the Tehran agreements. Once the tax increase is decided, everything can be cut to fit. The same oil is still sold or transferred by the same companies. On the terms discussed early in 1972, "participation" would mean about 9 cents more tax per barrel. Those who believe that this assures supply, stable prices and a solution to the balance of payments problem will believe anything.

There has been unparalleled turbulence since the State Department special conference. Venezuela dispensed with the elaborate sophistry of "agreements," and legislated: an additional tax increase in 1971 and again in early 1972 with another expected in early 1973; nationalization of natural gas; the requirement that companies deposit increasing sums of money lest they permit properties to run down before the national take-over in 1984; and the extension of this "reversion" to all facilities rather than only producing facilities. Confronted with declining production because it was cheaper for the companies to lift additional output from the Persian Gulf, Venezuela set minimum production rates, with fines for insufficient output.

In Libya, the government followed the Persian Gulf countries in demanding and getting an increase on the same pretext of monetary adjustment; and also in demanding participation, whether "participation" or the real thing is not yet clear. In December 1971, when Iran seized two islands near the mouth of the Persian Gulf, Libya seized the properties of British Petroleum in "retaliation"; any stick is good enough to beat a dog.

The Algerian government took two-thirds of the output of the French companies, who were "compensated" with what little remained after deducting newly calculated taxes.

In Iraq, the operating Iraq Petroleum Company (IPC) cut back output sharply during 1972 for the same reason as everywhere else in the Mediterranean (where the main field delivers via pipeline)—costs plus taxes were lower at the Persian Gulf, where capacity was being quickly and cheaply expanded. Iraq demanded that production be restored, and that IPC make a long-term commitment to expand output by 10 percent per year. The IPC counter-offer not being acceptable, Iraq made headlines by seizing the Kirkuk field June 1, then offered forthwith to sell at "reduced and competitive prices," for spot delivery or long-term contracts. This threat was aimed at the most sensitive point of the world oil industry: the permanent potential over-supply which in Iraq (and other countries) had already been made actual. Price-cutting is intolerable in a cartel; to avoid it, a flurry of complex negotiations began. A loan was soon made by other Arab

OPEC members. "Behind the Arab nations' action . . . lies an offer by Iraq to sell its newly nationalized oil at a cut rate, which would have driven down the revenues received by the other countries for their oil." This may also explain the gentlemanlike behavior of the expropriated IPC, which did not attempt to blacklist Iraq oil to be sold in non-Communist markets.

Onward and Upward with Taxes and Prices

The genie is out of the bottle. The OPEC nations have had a great success with the threat of embargo and will not put the weapon away. The turbulence will continue as taxes and prices are raised again and again. The producing nations are sure of oil company cooperation and consuming-country nonresistance. This is a necessary condition. There are two purely economic reasons why the situation cannot be stable.

1. The crude oil price can go much higher before it reaches the monopoly equilibrium or point of greatest profit.

The average price in Europe of a barrel of oil products in 1969–70 was about $13 per barrel. It is higher today. If the new tax rates were doubled, say from $1.50 to $3 per barrel at the Persian Gulf, a straight pass-through into product prices would be an increase of only 10–14 percent. It is doubtful that such an increase would have any noticeable effect on oil consumption. Moreover, about half of the European price consists of taxes levied by the various consuming-country governments. The producing nations have long insisted that in justice they *ought* to receive some or most of this amount. Be that as it may, most or all of this tax *can* be transferred from consuming to producing nations, with help from consuming to producing nations, with help from consuming-country governments who dislike unpopularity through higher fuel prices. The Italian government collaborated early in 1971.

The current price of oil, however far above the competitive level, is still much less than alternatives. The producing nations are not a whit displeased by big expensive projects to produce oil or gas from coal or shale or tar sands, which are a constant reminder of what a bargain crude is, even at higher prices. Particularly outside the United States, nuclear power sets a high ceiling, coal a much higher ceiling. The price of British coal has long and well served sellers of fuel oil in Britain, who priced at or slightly below coal-equivalent. Small wonder that the head of Shell appealed in October 1971 for the maintenance of a British coal industry.

There has therefore been much discussion, mostly oral, of the goal for the Persian Gulf nations being the U.S. price; or $5 per barrel, etc. These are attainable goals, and we must therefore expect attempts to reach them.

2. The producing nations cannot fix prices without using the multinational companies. All price-fixing cartels must *either* control output *or* detect and prevent individual price reductions, which would erode the

price down toward the competitive level. The OPEC tax system accomplishes this simply and efficiently. Every important OPEC nation publishes its taxes per barrel; they are a public record, impossible to falsify much. Outright suppression would be a confession of cheating. Once the taxes are set by concerted company-government action, the price floor of taxes-plus-cost is safe, and the floor can be jacked up from time to time, as in early 1971, or early 1972, or by "participation."

It is essential for the cartel that the oil companies continue as *crude oil marketers*, paying the excise tax before selling the crude or refining to sell it as products.

Were the producing nations the sellers of crude, paying the companies in cash or oil for their services, the cartel would crumble. The floor to price would then be not the tax-plus-cost, but only bare cost. The producing nations would need to set and obey producing quotas. Otherwise, they would inevitably chisel and bring prices down by selling incremental amounts at discount prices. Each seller nation would be forced to chisel to retain markets because it could no longer be assured of the collaboration of all the other sellers. Every cartel has in time been destroyed by one then some members chiselling and cheating; without the instrument of the multinational companies and the cooperation of the consuming countries, OPEC would be an ordinary cartel. And national companies have always been and still are price cutters.

Chiselling will accelerate if national companies go "downstream" into refining and marketing. One can transfer oil to downstream subsidiaries or partners at high f.o.b. prices, but with fictitious low tanker rates or generous delivery credits. The producing nation can put up most of the money or take a minority participation, or lend at less than market interest rates. One can arrange buy-back deals, barter deals, and exchanges of crude in one part of the world for availability elsewhere. The world oil cartel in the 1930's was eroded by this kind of piecemeal competition, and so will the new cartel of the 1970's if the individual producing nations become the sellers of oil.

The Saudi Arabian petroleum minister, Sheik Yamani, who designed "participation," warned in 1968 against nationaliizng the oil companies, and making them "buyers and brokers" of crude oil. This would, he argued truly, lead to "collapse" of oil prices and benefit only the consuming countries. The experts retained by OPEC also warned in 1971 that "participation" must not interfere with marketing of the oil through the companies. More recently, in 1971, Sheik Yamani warned that "participation" had to provide the right kind of "marketing operations." In 1972 he added: "We are concerned that prices in world markets do not fall down."

OPEC has come not to expel but to exploit. And if the excess crude oil supply were not permanent, Sheik Yamani would have no cause for the "concern" he rightly feels.

We may therefore conclude: the producing countries can raise prices and revenues further by jacking up the excise tax floor, in concert. Conversely, if and when the consuming countries want to be rid of the cartel, they can take their companies out of crude oil marketing. To avoid taxation, they can decommission the tax collecting agents who are their own creation.

So far, the consuming countries have gone in precisely the opposite direction. As they develop high cost substitutes, and strive to get their respective companies, public or "private," into crude oil production and marketing, they will rivet the tax collection agency more firmly on their necks. It is time to ask why they do this, and whether the policy may change.

One can only guess at the unstated reasons why the United States has put OPEC in the driver's seat. First, American companies have a large producing interest in the world market. In 1971, American companies produced about 6.5 billion barrels outside the United States. For every cent of increase in prices above that in tax, there is an additional $65 million in profit. Second, the higher energy costs will now be imposed on competitors in world markets; and in petrochemicals, higher raw material costs as well. Third, the United States has a large domestic oil producing industry. The less the difference between domestic and world prices, the less the tension between producing and consuming regions.

Fourth, the United States desired to appease the producing nations, buying popularity with someone else's money and trying to mitigate the tension caused by the Arab-Israeli strife, which, however, is irrelevant to oil. If the Arab-Israeli dispute were settled tomorrow, the producing nations would not slow down for one minute their drive for ever-higher prices and taxes. The acknowledged leader of the Persian Gulf nations in early 1971 was Iran, which has in one important respect—the Trans-Israel Pipe Line—actually cooperated with Israel more than the United States, which in 1957 and 1968 discouraged the pipeline.

The State Department View

In a recent speech—to the West Texas Oil and Gas Association—the director of the State Department Office of Fuels and Energy, James Akins, professed he could not sleep for worry over the possibility of a "supply crisis" caused by even one Arab nation stopping oil production. Such a "crisis" is a fantasy. Five Arab countries produce an aggregate of *one* MBD; they would never be missed. In 1951, Iran, producing nearly 40 percent of Persian Gulf output, shut down; yet 1951 Persian Gulf output actually rose. No Arab or non-Arab country is nearly that important today. In the winter of 1966–67, Iraq—about 10 percent then as now—shut down, and there was not even a ripple on the stream.

If any proof were needed that an Arab boycott will hurt only the Arabs and soon collapse, the 1967 experience should suffice. The *Wall Street Journal*, for example, said that the former Secretary General of OPEC, Francisco R. Parra, "can't conceive of any political situation arising in the Middle East that would lead to confiscation of investments held by the oil companies. Should another Arab-Israeli war break out, Mr. Parra doesn't expect any repetition of the unsuccessful attempt by the Arab nations to embargo oil shipments to some Western nations. 'I don't believe oil can effectively be used as a political weapon by withholding supplies from market—there just can't be an effective selective embargo,' he asserted."

The Oil Import Task Force report, signed by the Secretary of State and not contested on this point by the minority, explained why partial shutdowns or boycotts could not be sustained, concluding: "Thus to have a problem one must postulate something approaching a total denial to all markets of all or most Arab oil." It might help if State explained why it no longer agrees.

Along with warnings about "the Arabs," the State Department has taken to warnings of oil scarcity. Thus Under Secretary Irwin warned the OECD in May 1972 of a worldwide "shortage" of 20 MBD by 1980, because of rising consumption. Mr. Irwin's speech was widely noted and commented on. Three weeks later, Iraq moved at Kirkuk, confident of eventual success because of the "growing energy requirements of the industrialized countries," and growing U.S. imports.

Mr. Akins had already outdone Mr. Irwin in a speech to the Independent Petroleum Association of America, warning that "by 1976 our position could be nothing short of desperate," and that Perisan Gulf reserves would decline after 1980. The basis of these fears is a well kept secret which the economist cannot penetrate. But the prediction of a Persian Gulf price of $5 by 1980 must be taken seriously. There was not even a perfunctory disclaimer of expressing only personal opinions in the speech or one to the National Coal Association. He is voicing government policy. In another speech, he spoke of the "widespread recognition . . . that it is not in the Arabs' interests to allow the companies to continue expansion of production at will, and that the producing countries, most notably Saudi Arabia, must [sic] follow Libya's and Kuwait's leads in imposing production limitations."

It seems odd to have an American official telling "the Arabs" they should restrict output. Kuwait has found the argument persuasive and has limited output. But this is the only clear example. Libyan oil is overpriced, i.e. overtaxed, and better bargains are available elsewhere. In fact, the expulsion of British Petroleum in December was seen as a "windfall" to the industry because of excessive supply. According to Platt's Oilgram News Service: "Companies have been anxious to reduce production in Libya but 'no company had the courage to do it and now Libya is making BP do it 100 percent,' one observer said." No other Arab country has restricted, and "few . . . are likely to follow Kuwait's lead," despite the State Department telling them they "must." Saudi Arabia is engaged in a record expansion of capacity. So is Iran, whose Finance Minister directly rejected the argument in March of 1972. For the whole Middle East, 1972 drilling was expected in February to exceed 1971 by a massive 74 percent.

Akins also makes the baffling statement (in the IPAA speech) that "the sellers' market" arrived in June 1967. Yet prices continued to slide for three years more, and Mr. Akins himself notes that neither buyers nor sellers know the "sellers' market" had come. He never explains it. Almost surely he refers to the Suez Canal closure, which by raising transport costs should somewhat *weaken* the demand for crude oil. But the effect of the Suez closure is negligible either way. Reopening of the Canal would equate to a 9 percent addition to the world tanker fleet, which has been growing at nearly 13 percent per year: loss of the Canal is a loss of eight and one-half months growth. Indeed the presence or absence of the Suez Canal is less than the error of estimate of the tankers available at any given time.

The same State Department source feared a world shortage because "the Arabs" [sic] would find it difficult or impossible to raise the "enormous sums of capital" needed for new production. In 1970 (most recent year available), total production expenditures in the "Middle East," i.e. Persian Gulf *plus* some substantial expenditures in Turkey, Israel, and Syria, *plus* some payments to governments, amounted to $300 million. In 1972, the revenues of the Persian Gulf nations will amount to about $9 billion. The expenditures are less than two weeks' revenues. The Kirkuk field just confiscated in Iraq requires less than $4 million annually to maintain the rate of output—revenues from one day's capacity output.

If the producing nations had to spend $300 million in order to obtain $600 million in revenue, i.e. a 100 percent return, they would spend that money; the alternative would be to receive nothing at all. And the $300 million net revenue would be about 3 percent of the tribute they obtain today by using the multinational companies. In other words, to talk about their "needs" and "plans" is totally irrelevant to how much they can get before they can spend.

Perhaps the OPEC countries (including the non-Arabs who do not exist for State but do produce 45 percent of OPEC oil) may be convinced they should restrict output in concert because oil in the ground will appreciate faster than money in the bank. Perhaps too there will be discussion in the United States: why our government is so poorly informed on oil economics; why it repeats "Arabs-oil . . . oil-Arabs" as though slogans proved something logic could not; whether the national interest is well served by sponsoring, supporting, and urging on the cartel; and whether our interests may change when, as is generally expected, our imports are substantially larger.

The Changing American Interest

First, security has been greatly impaired for all importing countries by the cohesion of the OPEC nations which made an embargo feasible.

Second, the balance of payments impact will soon turn unfavorable to us, as it is to all other importers.

The fact will slowly be recognized, that nearly all of the oil deficit could be abolished by getting American companies out of crude oil marketing, to produce on contract for the producing countries, who could then compete the price way down. The companies' profits (and contribution to the balance of payments) would not be much less, and in the long run they might be greater, as the experience in Venezuela proves: the companies producing there are at or over the loss line.

Larger American imports will if anything tend to put the world price down. The process was seen on a small scale after 1966, when quotas on (heavy) residual fuel imports were lifted. Imports increased considerably, and the price *decreased*. Moreover, concern over air pollution was growing rapidly, and alarm was felt over possible loss of markets for residual fuel oil. Hence the Venezuelan government made agreements with Esso and Shell granting them lower taxes on production of low-sulfur oil. This bit of history was too rapidly forgotten.

The declining price of fuel oil in the face of greater demand would be inexplicable in a competitive market, but is to be expected when the price is far above cost. It is exactly what happened in Europe to embarrass coal. The hope of greater profits on increased sales, and the knowledge that large buyers have now an incentive to roam the market and look for every chance of a better deal, means that one must reduce the price before one's rivals tie up the good customers. As American quotas are relaxed, refiners who have a crude deficit will become exactly the kind of large-scale buyer whom Sheik Yamani rightly fears.

The prospect of world prices rising because of large-scale American imports has alarmed Europe and Asia, and the United States government has gladly fanned those fears. But they have no basis in theory or experience.

Let the reader excuse our saying again what needs to be said often: larger consumption only raises price in a competitive market, by raising marginal cost. In so awesomely noncompetitive a market, cost is not relevant because price is 10 to 20 times cost. Supply and demand have nothing to do with the world price of oil: only the strength of the cartel matters.

Alternative Regulatory Policies for Dealing with the Natural Gas Shortage

PAUL W. MACAVOY AND
ROBERT S. PINDYCK

Paul MacAvoy is Professor of Economics at Yale University. Robert Pindyck is a faculty member at the Sloan School at Massachusetts Institute of Technology. This article appeared in the Bell Journal *of Economics and Management Science in 1973.*

A substantial shortage of natural gas has been developing over the last few winter heating seasons. Reports of the Federal Power Commission indicate that in the winters of 1970 to 1972 gas supplies were cut off with increasing frequency, and for longer periods of time, throughout the Northern and Eastern portions of the United States. This has been a matter not only of cutting off supplies in peak periods to industry—as occurred in Cleveland in January 1970 when 30,000 employees of 700 companies were laid off for 10 days as a result of gas interruptions—but of systematic curtailments of deliveries to certain classes of consumers. During 1971 to 1972, seven major interstate pipelines curtailed service throughout the winter season to existing customers. Service entering the Northeastern part of the country from Texas Eastern Transmission Corporation was curtailed by 18 percent, from Transcontinental Gas Pipeline by 9 percent, and from Trunkline Gas Company by 27 percent. Service throughout the region from New Mexico to Southern California was curtailed by El Paso Natural Gas Company by 15 percent. The FPC staff has shown deliveries falling short of the amount of gas demanded for consumption by 3.6 percent in 1971 and by 5.1 percent in 1972, and has predicted that production will fall short of demand by 12.1 percent by 1975.

These estimates encompass recent and expected future *production* shortages. The amounts do not, however, include anywhere near all of the unsatisfied demands for gas. The "markets" for natural gas are not spot markets for production, but rather center on sales of reserves. The pipeline buyer offers to take new gas deposits out of the ground, and pays for this production, so as to deliver gas to residential, commercial, and industrial consumers throughout the United States. The transaction involves the dedication of reserves by oil and gas discovery companies to pipelines, and this is followed by a transaction in which the pipelines make commitments to deliver production to final consumers over a ten- to twenty-year period. The reserves markets have experienced shortages to a much greater extent than shown by recent production shortages (according to one estimate, new reserves have been more than 50 percent short since 1961). Also, it has been estimated that demands for new production by old and new potential buyers exceeded the total supply of new production available by more than 50 percent. These unsatisfied demands were never registered by curtailment proceedings because most of the new potential buyers simply were refused service from the pipelines. This shortage resulted in additional demands for other fuels.

Production curtailments have immediate effects on the consumer. They may require him to use stand-by heating facilities or possibly to do without heating entirely. The larger shortage of new production contract commitments has more diverse effects. Some consumers are required to go to other fuels—with the result that their consumption costs are increased or that pollution is greater, so that social costs are increased. Other consumers can work their way around the shortage by changing locations or by offering various premia to be put at the head of the queue. In general, the economic and locational effects of the shortage are likely to be significant.

The political consequences are another matter of import. The contract sales of gas at the wellhead and at the city gate are closely regulated by the Federal Power Commission, so that the FPC, the Congress, and the Office of the President become focal points for complaints that regulatory policies have either caused or failed to ameliorate the shortages. With neither producers nor consumers supporting the regulatory process—neither clearly benefiting from the shortage—the possibility of significant political losses for legislators or regulators is substantial.

Reactions to the potential adverse political effects have been along two lines. The first has been to call for the loosening of regulation of contractual agreements at the wellhead. President Nixon in April 1973 called for deregulation of wellhead prices on new contracts; the Chairman of the FPC at the same time argued that "gas supplies are short . . . and the way to encourage more drilling and discoveries may be to let prices rise." Proposals for deregulation are based on the argument that FPC rulings have restricted price increases, despite the fact that cost increases have reduced supplies at the same time that demand has increased. Thus, decontrol would allow higher prices which would clear the market of excess demand and would be an inducement to take on increased exploration and development so as to add to reserve supply.

The second reaction has been to the opposite effect. Proposals have been made to put stronger controls over wellhead contracts. The argument, in part at least, is that producers have been holding back reserves in anticipation of relaxed price controls—and tighter controls would cause them to see the futility of holding back. Draft bills proposed by staff of the Senate Interior and Commerce Committees extend FPC jurisdiction to cover not only interstate sales to pipelines, but all intrastate sales now outside the jurisdiction of the Federal Power Commission. The requirement that the FPC set "just and reasonable rates" on the basis of historical average costs of exploration and development is reaffirmed. Proposals are made to further the development of artificial gas or liquefied natural gas to replace the short supplies of inground natural gas reserves within the domestic United States. In effect, prices are held constant, and price controls are extended to encompass all relevant sources of supply and demand under this policy.

Another rationale for strengthened regulation is that, "given the relatively large unsatisfied demand for gas, deregulation of natural gas prices would lead to massive increases in wellhead prices to abnormally high levels." There would be little increase in supply—"there is evidence that gas supplies are relatively inelastic in the short run." There is also asserted to be some basis for arguing that present regulation is not the cause for the present shortage. At least, "although cost based regulation was slow in getting started, it is an adequate method of regulation that has been developed in the 1960s. Many of the uncertainties have been worked out. . . . The system of regulation can meet the needs of the 1970s to elicit the necessary supply of natural gas at the lowest reasonable price."

These proposals will be evaluated in this paper. After a more explicit rendition of alternative policies, the industry into which these policies are to be introduced is discussed in some detail. Then an econometric model is used to evaluate the policy options. This evaluation is in terms of the extent to which the alternative options are likely to ameliorate the shortage.

Three Policy Alternatives

Frequent asessments of the size of the gas shortage bring forth even more frequent changes in Congress and the Office of the President in proposals for dealing with the gas shortage. Each of these new policies could be catalogued and evaluated—but the results would be so specific as to be relevant only to that policy, and the duration of the policy might well be rather short. Alternatively, the policies can be characterized along two or three dimensions; this is attempted here, in the expectation that the characterizations will approximate the many specific alternatives to be considered, accepted, or rejected by the Government in the coming three or four years.

The first alternative policy is that of deregulation of wellhead prices of natural gas. The Federal Power Commission sets regional limits on prices for gas dedicated to interstate pipelines; these limits would be loosened or eliminated in a number of specific policy proposals. In general, the FPC price ceilings would be eliminated only after a number of years, by taking controls only off prices in all new contracts signed in each year (the time lag in price increases would be extensive, since most of the flowing gas is under old contracts signed in previous years). Even these prices would not be free to rise to a level that would clear out all the excess immediately, since most proposals—including President Nixon's Energy Message of April 1973—decree that there be some national ceiling imposed on new prices in keeping with gradual elimination of the deficit and with anti-inflationary price controls. The gradual loosening of price controls is coupled with "short-term" rationing schemes that may involve the extension of regulatory jurisdiction to presently unregulated companies that are bidding up prices. This class of policies can be evaluated in terms of (1) elimination of price controls under new contracts, (2) an overall price ceiling in keeping with a 50-percent increase in *average* wholesale price over five years, and (3) some regulatory jurisdiction over all field sales by the Federal Power Commission.

The second alternative class of proposals centers on more rather than less regulation by the FPC. Prices would be set regionally or nationally on the basis of "cost of service." The cost of service is found by Commission and Court judgment of historical records on average exploration and development costs in the region. All production in the region would come under the jurisdiction of the Commission (except perhaps for the smallest producers, who would be exempt in order to cut down on the number of case reviews). Production under these conditions would admittedly be short of demands; holding prices to historical averages essentially limits reserves or production to amounts equal to or less than historical levels, and these historical levels were not sufficient to meet demands in the past. As a result, attention has to be centered on inducements under regulation for the development of alternative gas supplies, either through manufacture or import in liquefied form. These alternative supplies would be regulated as well. As a result, the second class of policies would (1) set price ceilings close to 1972 to 1973 price levels, with perhaps a one cent per annum increase as historical average costs rise slowly with inflation, (2) place all dedications of reserves and production of gas under the jurisdiction of the FPC, and (3) set the regulated price on manufactured or liquefied gas according to the specific cost of providing these products.

These first two alternatives are basically contradictory, and it does not seem likely that amendments could be made to either that would capture the loyalty of those supporting the other. If neither can be made politically effective, then the relevant alternative—the third—is the status quo, which consists of regulation according to rulings in recent cases at the Federal Power Commission. In recent years the Commission has followed policies of allowing field price increases in keeping with "changes in average historical costs"; but wide variation in the estimate of such costs has occurred—and the Commission has probably chosen the estimate to be as large as permissible by Court review. Area ceilings reached by negotiated settlements between producers and consumers have been proposed to the Commission, and the Commission has found them to be "reasonable ceiling prices" not outside the range of possible average costs. Comparisons with costs could be made in the near future that would justify higher future prices, if the Commission so willed—comparisons of cost on the most recent contracts for sale of intrastate (unregulated) gas, rather than of interstate (regulated) gas sold over the last few years. The Commission, in the 1970 to 1973 period, allowed prices on new contracts to increase each year by two-and-one-half cents per thousand cubic feet, after having held prices to one-half cent increases each year over the 1960s; the regulator can continue to find estimates of historical average costs that would allow further relatively large price increases. But there are limits to the extent of price increases in keeping with *some* estimate of costs—Court appeals by buyers could lead to rejection of FPC decisions unless there were some justification on cost grounds given in the decisions. Thus, the third class of policies, which can be characterized as maintaining the status quo, includes (1) prices that increase from two to four cents per Mcf in each of the next five years, (2) limited regulatory jurisdiction over intrastate sales, and (3) manufactured and liquefied gas with regulated price ceilings in keeping with their respective costs.

Characteristics of an Economic Model of Natural Gas Reserves and Production

In order to analyze the effects of these alternative policies, a model of natural gas markets with explicit policy controls has been constructed. The model provides a vehicle for performing simulations using different policy options, so as to indicate the effects of the options on the size of shortages. Thus, its formulation stresses prices, reserve quantities, production quantities, and associated demands for production.

The model, which will be described below, treats simultaneously the field market for reserves (gas producers dedicating new reserves to pipeline companies at the wellhead price) and the wholesale market for production (pipeline companies selling gas to retail utilities and industrial consumers). The linking of these two markets by interstate pipeline companies is an important characteristic of the natural gas industry. Delivery in the wholesale market is a determinant of pipelines' demands for gas reserves in the field market, and wholesale delivered prices are determined in part by the prices on new reserve contracts in the field market.

In surveying the interaction of these two markets, we shall consider their behavior in the rather complex case when there are excess demands for production. Pricing policies, under both regulation and deregulation, are briefly reviewed for their impact on the size of the shortage. Pricing will be quantitatively analyzed at the end of this paper.

FIELD MARKETS

These markets are the locus of transactions between oil and gas producers having volumes of newly discovered reserves and pipeline buyers seeking to obtain by contract the right to take production from these reserves. The amounts of reserves committed by the oil and gas companies are based primarily on the amounts of inground deposits of oil and gas. Additions to reserves come about from additions in (1) gas associated with newly discovered or developed oil reserves—"associated" gas reserves—and (2) gas volumes found in reservoirs not containing oil—or "nonassociated" reserves; both result from new discoveries and from extensions of previous discoveries or revisions of earlier estimates of previous discoveries. The amounts actually in place in the producing reservoirs limit the amounts of both associated and nonassociated new gas reserves that can be "supplied" or dedicated to the pipelines.

Needless to say, there is a finite amount of gas in the ground that can be discovered, and thus we should observe a depletion effect on volumes dedicated. It is not our objective to predict how much gas there actually is remaining to be discovered, or when this finite resource will be depleted. But an economic model of the gas industry should at least take this depletion effect into account; we shall do this by using indicators of depletion or of decreasing returns that occurred over the past decade as variables explaining "supply."

There are important economic determinants of the amount of reserves available for commitment as well, and these include prices of new contracts signed by producers, expected future prices under possibly forthcoming new contracts in subsequent years, and changes in average and marginal costs of exploration and development. These factors are widely believed to have substantial effects upon reserve availability, although with considerable time lags. Commitments today to higher prices for new contract volumes might lead to immediate increased planning activities for further exploratory or developmental work; this might lead in a year or two to additional drilling activity and, in a subsequent year or two, to the offering of additional reserves for sale to pipeline buyers.

Production of gas into the pipelines, termed short-run or annual supply, is limited by the amount of reserves available. Production cannot take place at rates greater than some fixed percent of reserves per annum because sandstone contained in the reservoirs is impermeable or because faster rates by "channeling" and sealing off parts of the reservoir may reduce the economic value of the remaining reserves. But up to that limit, more production in this period can take place at higher short-run costs. This is justified if prices are higher. Thus, for both technical and economic reasons, the supply of production out of reserves will be less the lower is the volume of reserves and the lower is the price in the contract commitment.

The demands for new reserves in the field market are manifest in the willingness to buy on the part of pipeline companies and local (direct) consumers. They seek to obtain long-term contracts for the extraction of the reserves. Demand determinants in the field markets include the wellhead price that pipelines and others are willing to pay for additions to their reserve holdings, the amount of reserves available at a specific location, the location of these reserves, and the final demands for new production by the buyers repurchasing the gas from the pipelines. These demands would be "registered" in the market only so long as there was no regulatory price control which set regional field prices below those at which total demands were equal to the available supplies of new reserves. After 1961, when ceiling prices were put into effect, the demand variable became the exogenous FPC-determined price, since it was lower than the price that would have equilibrated markets.

These characteristics of field markets are found in many futures markets in which raw materials are dedicated for production and refining. The important characteristics of these particular markets are that (1) more will be made available for sale if the buyers offer higher prices (in rough approximation to the competitive "supply" mechanism), (2) the lag adjustment process bringing forth additional supplies of reserves is likely to be long and possibly quite complex, (3) production out of reserves is determined by a combination of technical and economic circumstances, but is likely to be greater the larger the volume of reserves available and the higher the contract prices pipelines are paying for the gas they are taking, and (4) demands depend on prices, but are also derived from final residential, industrial, and commercial consumption.

WHOLESALE MARKETS

Pipelines provide gas deliveries, usually under long-term contract, to industrial consumers taking gas right off the line and to retail public utility companies for resale to industrial, residential, and commercial consumers. The amounts of gas demanded by direct (mainline) industrial consumers and retail gas utilities are believed to depend upon the prices for whole-sale gas contracts, the prices for alternative fuels consumed by final buyers, and economy-wide variables that determine the overall size of energy markets. If the consumers are industrial companies seeking gas as boiler fuel or process material, the "market size" variables relate to the demands for these companies' outputs and to their investment in capacity to burn fuel or to utilize energy. If the final consumers are households and commercial building owners, then the "market size" variables relate to total population and income.

Wholesale markets also operate with lags. Changes in wholesale prices quoted by pipeline sellers of gas production feed through as changes in final consumer prices and then feed back as changes in final consumer demand quantities; the feedback may take some time because of consumers' commitment to gas burning equipment and the necessity for that equipment to wear out before demands are reduced. As a result, the effects of price changes may be felt only in reduced demands for more gas in subsequent years.

The amount of production provided to industrial and public utility buyers is not determined by a fixed "supply schedule" of quantities at various prices. The pipelines offer service in the form of delivered gas supplies at a markup over the field purchase price for the reserves backing up that production. The price markups are determined by the cost of transmission and add-on profits limited by FPC regulation (following orthodox public utility procedures of finding cost of capital by taking a "fair return" on "fair value" of original investment outlay for pipeline equipment). They vary widely in level among wholesale markets—there are one to four sources of transmission capacity in most wholesale buying regions—but in most regions the process seems to be to set the markup and then to provide production out to the limit of either reserves or pipeline capacity.

Markup pricing has been formulated to build in significant lags from changes in field contracts. The Commission has followed the policy of allowing the markup for historical average transmission costs plus profit for the pipelines over historical average field prices for gas at the wellhead. This "rolled-in" price at wholesale is thus changed by an increased field price only to the extent that new contract prices change the historical average of all field prices. The full impact of a field price change on wholesale prices would occur only after that change had been in effect for roughly ten years (assuming 10 percent of contracts in each year are new contracts).

There is considerable simultaneity in the behavior of production, reserves, and prices in field and wholesale markets. Field prices determine the availability of new reserves and the production conditions under new contracts at the same time. Changes in field prices are reflected, albeit slowly, in changing wholesale prices and demands for quantities of production at wholesale. This two-level industry can thus be modeled by simultaneous equations estimates of production and prices as they depend upon reserves and conditions in the final markets for energy.

THE BEHAVIOR OF GAS MARKETS WHEN THERE ARE SHORTAGES

The behavior of this "mixed" set of markets—some of which exhibit competitive characteristics of supply while others follow noncompetitive patterns—may be rather complex when there are significant excess demands for production. Let us examine how shortages resulting from regulatory policy move through the different layers of transactions for gas reserves and production.

In the field market for natural gas, proved reserves are incremented through the discovery process and depleted through production. The amount of additions to reserves is positively related to some extent to the field price of gas contracts being signed at the locations close to where that volume of new reserves is available. The demands for new reserves by pipelines could be specified in terms of field prices, but under conditions of shortage, the regulated ceiling price P_c prevails rather than the market demand price P^*. This is illustrated in Figure 1. Under conditions

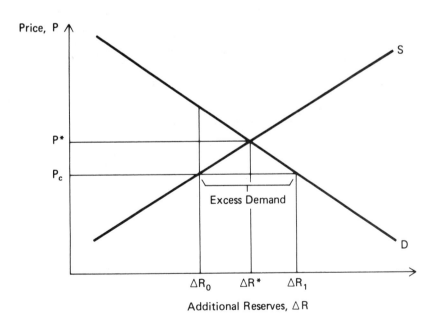

FIGURE 1. SUPPLY AND DEMAND FOR ADDITIONAL RESERVES

of shortage, the quantity realized is on the supply but not on the demand function, with the result that the demand function is not observable. At the same time, production out of reserves is affected by the reserve shortage. The supply curve for gas production consists of a marginal development cost curve which represents the cost of incrementing gas production (by running existing gas development wells at higher capacity or by drilling new development wells). The demands for gas production consist of wholesale volumes taken by final buyers from the pipeline systems at prices equal to field prices plus the pipeline markups. The final demands could conceivably still be satisfied at the beginning of the reserve shortage, as a result of the pipelines' calling on existing reserves to produce at a higher rate.

Sufficient production under a condition of reserve depletion cannot be had indefinitely. Eventually, the amount of reserves available to back production is reduced, and supply of production at ceiling prices is reduced. As the reserve backing becomes smaller, production tends to fall, and a gap is opened between the demands for production and the supplies that will be made available.

The marginal cost curves, the price markup, and a wholesale demand curve are all shown in Figure 2. In this diagram, the ceiling price is suffi-

FIGURE 2. SUPPLY AND DEMAND FOR PRODUCTION

cient to bring forth production Q^* which clears the market at wholesale price P^*, which is just the field price plus the pipeline's markup. Under these conditions, the demand curve for production is "registered in the market" or observable as a total quantity demand at one specific price level. However, if the regulated field price is reduced at a level P_c', excess demand will result equal to $(Q_1 - Q_0)$. The supply of production is reduced by price disincentives to a level below the demands put on the pipeline system by retail gas utility companies serving final residential, industrial, and commercial consumers. There are shortages in both field reserve and final production markets.

How would an increase in the ceiling price eventually cause a reduction in the production shortage? Consider, for example, an increase in wellhead ceiling prices under FPC regulation. When the ceiling price is increased, the production cost curve remains fixed initially, since reserve levels would not change immediately, and therefore marginal production costs would not change. The higher price, however, would soon elicit more production out of given reserves Q_0' and also reduce demands for production from Q_1 to Q_1' (as shown in Figure 3). Thus, even within the short run, excess demand would be decreased by a price change from $(Q_1 - Q_0)$ to $(Q_1' - Q_0')$, although the change may not be substantial because the

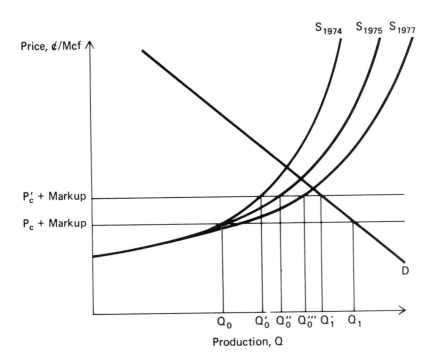

FIGURE 3. SUPPLY AND DEMAND FOR PRODUCTION

"roll-in" pricing practices of the Commission would dampen the demand effect.

After a few years, however, it is likely that reserve levels will have been increased as a result of the higher level of new contract prices. Higher ceiling prices would stimulate more exploratory drilling which, in turn, should result in new discoveries of gas that would add to reserve levels. At that point in time, a given level of production could be induced at lower marginal development costs because of the presence of higher reserve levels. The supply of production curve would have shifted to the right. Even if demand were to remain at Q_1', an increase in supply to Q_0'' would reduce the extent of the shortage. After a few more years, the full effects of the ceiling price increase would have occurred, with the supply of production shifting farther to the right so that excess demand would fall to the even lower level of $(Q_1' - Q_0''')$.

Of course, if we could increase the ceiling price by just the right amount —to shift the supply curve enough to make up for past excess demand and the present and independent shifts in the demand curve (stemming from increased population, national income, etc.)—we would reach a situation where there was no excess demand in 1977. This is shown in Figure 4.

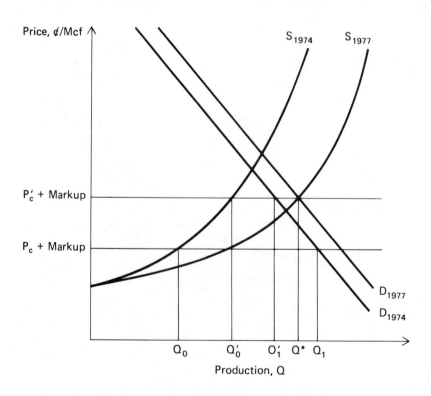

FIGURE 4. LONG-RUN EQUILIBRIUM

Note, however, that *until* 1977, there would still be some amount of excess demand. In the first year after the price increase, for example, excess demand will be $(Q_1' - Q_0')$; not until 1977, when the supply curve, demand curve, and price line all intersect at the same point, would there be a level of production, Q^*, that resulted in no excess demand.

What if the field price of all gas were immediately and completely deregulated? This would result in a field price increase to the level P_f^* which, when the pipeline markup is added on, would clear the production market immediately (as shown in Figure 5, the supplies and demands for production are both equal in one year to Q^*). This substantial price increase would not be the end of the story, however. After three or four years, the supply curve would have shifted to the right, again because increased exploration and discoveries in response to the price increase would have added substantially to the reserve base. The demand curve would perhaps have shifted to the right after three or four years, but the net result would probably be a decrease in price and further increase in quantity of production over the four-year period. This is illustrated in Figure 5

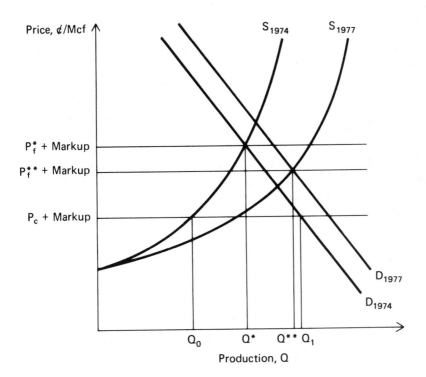

FIGURE 5. EQUILIBRIUM UNDER COMPLETE DEREGULATION

where the 1974 equilibrium quantity Q^* is increased over time to Q^{**} as the equilibrium field price P_f^* falls to P_f^{**}.

These examples indicate that pricing policies have a three- or four-step effect upon the size of the shortage, and it may take several years before the full effects of a price change become apparent. Our econometric model allows us to analyze these dynamic effects of alternative price changes quantitatively.

EFFECT OF PARTIAL DEREGULATION OF FIELD PRICES:
ECONOMETRIC RESULTS

A large number of alternative proposals have been made under the rubric of "deregulation of field prices." These have included complete and instantaneous deregulation on the one hand, and a slightly higher rate of increase of FPC-controlled prices on the other hand. But the central proposal is probably to allow new contract prices to seek their own levels, subject to a national ceiling on all new prices that would keep average wholesale prices from increasing by more than 50 percent over the subsequent five-year period. This policy has been simulated as a price increase of 15 cents per Mcf on all new contracts in 1974 over a 29.6 cents per Mcf price level on new contracts in 1973. Prices would increase an additional 3.0 cents per year after 1974, as part of the (allowed) response to rising drilling and operating costs.

The impact of the price increases on new discoveries of reserves would not occur in 1974, but rather would be spread over the period 1975 to 1978. It is expected that 1975 new discoveries would be slightly more than 9 trillion cubic feet—almost 30 percent more than the previous year. By 1976 new discoveries would increase to the level of 11 trillion cubic feet, and by 1979 would be 19 trillion cubic feet. Total additions to reserves (including new discoveries, extensions, and revisions) would track new discoveries rather closely. A major part of the impact of price increases would be felt within four years, as an increase in annual additions 10 trillion cubic feet greater than previously experienced. The full impact would not be felt, however, until 1980, when total additions had leveled off at 34 trillion cubic feet, an amount approximately 21 trillion cubic feet greater than the 13 trillion realized before this series of price increases.

The results of this policy of "partial deregulation" are to raise prices [to about 60 cents per Mcf] and to reduce greatly the magnitude of the gas shortage. Price increases, while substantial, eliminate the production shortage after five years, so that by 1979, the supply of production and the demand for production are both approximately 31 trillion cubic feet. In subsequent years, supplies again match demands rather closely; in fact, the small excess supplies (or negative deficits) would probably lead to rebuilding of the reserves base and to some price softening on new field contracts.

EFFECT OF "COST OF SERVICE" REGULATION OF FIELD PRICES: ECONOMETRIC RESULTS

One criticism of regulation is that prices have been allowed to creep up at the rate of 2.5 cents per annum on new contracts, when there has been little "cost justification" for this to occur. It is argued that the Federal Power Commission should follow traditional procedures for setting prices—that is, full reviews of the historical costs of providing gas should be undertaken and prices should be limited to these costs. It is expected that under this regimen, price increases under new contracts would be limited to one cent per annum. This would result in average wholesale prices limited to the 40 to 48 cent range over the rest of the 1970s.

The effects of such limited price increases on reserve and production supply would be substantial. New discoveries would increase by little more than one trillion cubic feet per year for the remainder of this decade, and total additions to reserves would be limited in 1980 to 26 trillion cubic feet per year. The supply of production out of reserves would range from 23 trillion cubic feet in 1974 to close to 28 trillion cubic feet in 1980. Altogether, additions to reserves are approximately 3.7 trillion cubic feet less per year than under the "deregulation" policy.

The demands for production would be much greater when prices are held within this range. Total demands for new production increase by 1.3 to 2.5 trillion cubic feet per annum. Total new demands by 1980 are expected to be more than 37 trillion cubic feet, 5 trillion cubic feet greater than under price increases associated with "deregulation."

Excess demands persist over the remainder of the decade. Indeed, the gap between supply and demand for production increases as time passes, from approximately 3 trillion cubic feet in 1974 to 9 trillion cubic feet by 1980. The impact of this "cost of service regulation" policy is to exacerbate the excess demands that already exist, so that the shortage would be close to 25 percent of the total demands for production by 1980.

EFFECT OF MAINTAINING THE STATUS QUO: ECONOMETRIC RESULTS

Continuation of present regulation is envisioned as maintenance of the 1970 to 1972 policy of allowing price increases on new contracts of 2 to 4 cents per Mcf each year. The cases on field pricing brought before the Commission for the rest of the decade would be decided on any number of "cost" bases, as long as the result would be a price series for new commitments of reserves with annual increments of approximately 3 cents per Mcf per year leading to new contract prices in 1980 of more than 50 cents per Mcf. Such price changes would not be easy to put into effect—each requiring multiple applications for certification of new contracts under conditions different from the previous year's certification and each requiring estimates of (increased) costs of providing the new contract production. The allowed increases—if the best that can be provided by a commission trying to reduce the shortage, but operating within orthodox regulatory "cost-pricing" procedures—would raise average wholesale prices from 37 cents to 55 cents by 1980. They would have a perceptible effect on both supplies of reserves and production, and demands for production.

Supplies of reserves are expected to increase at a slower rate under these conditions than under "deregulation." The combination of successive 3-cent increments leading to a higher final price, and of near-certainty of the occurrence of these increments, leads to some additions to both reserves and production. But these are not enough to eliminate the shortage.

Demands for production on the other hand are greater than under "deregulation." The successive increments of 3-cent new contract field price increases pass through as average wholesale price increases only gradually. The new contract field price is approximately 16 cents per Mcf higher in 1980 than in 1974, and the average wholesale price is about 15 cents higher. As a result, demands for production increase from 25 trillion cubic feet in 1974 to 35 trillion cubic feet in 1980. These demands at the end of the decade are 8 trillion cubic feet per annum greater than under the higher-priced "deregulation."

As a result of lower additions to supply and higher additions to demand, the shortage increases. In the mid-1970s the total supply of production would be from 2.5 to 3.5 trillion cubic feet less than the demand. By 1979 or 1980, further net increments of demand increase the shortage each year until it levels off at 5.3 trillion cubic feet. This short fall is a lower percentage of demand than under strict "cost-of-service" regulation (and the increments of supply are larger under the "status quo" than under "cost of service" in 1974 to 1980).

The Clandestine Distribution of Heroin, Its Discovery and Suppression

SIMON ROTTENBERG

Simon Rottenberg is Professor of Economics at the University of Massachusetts. This article appeared in the Journal of Political Economy *in 1968.*

Heroin that is illegally consumed in the United States derives, for the most part, from opium produced in Turkey which is converted there or in Lebanon to morphine base and which is, in turn, shipped through Istanbul or Beirut to France. In France it is transformed to heroin in small laboratories and is transported to the United States, either directly or via Italy, Canada, or Mexico. A distribution system in the United States puts the product into the hands of consumers. There are said to be between 45,000 and 100,000 narcotics addicts in this country, about half of whom are in New York City.

The trade is illegal, and various federal agencies (mainly the Bureaus of Customs and Narcotics and the Food and Drug Administration) and state and local law enforcement authorities are charged with the responsibility of the execution of the law. The prevention of the contraband introduction of narcotics into the country is apparently very difficult because narcotics are easily transported and concealed and have great value relative to their weight and volume. It is estimated that one and one-half tons of heroin are brought into the country illegally each year; only a small fraction of this quantity is intercepted and seized by the authorities.

The Organization of Clandestine Enterprise

Clandestine enterprises consist of two parts: one that produces the service or good which is the nominal product of the enterprise and another that conceals the activities done in the pursuit of the first object. Both activities consume resources. The firm will, in the fulfilment of the second object, choose among alternative strategies for security on optimizing principles. That is to say, it will seek to minimize security costs per unit of concealment achieved, and it will carry the security operations of the enterprise to a scale that will fulfil the condition that the marginal cost of that activity will equal its marginal revenue.

A unit of revenue in the firm's security operations is the magnitude by which the probability of detection diminishes times the "loss" suffered (the costs incurred) if detected. Thus 0.4 probability of detection may be reduced, by incurring additional security or concealment costs, to 0.3 probability. The incremental revenue derived from the additional expenditure would be 0.1 times, say, the negative value put on five years in prison—which might be lost earnings—net of consumption while in prison, plus the negative value put on the state of being shut away from society and being deprived of the freedom to move, both discounted, minus the capitalized value of the income stream produced by schooling in criminal business skills while in prison and by business associations formed there.

The probability of discovery of someone engaged in the narcotics trade is a partial function of the number of transactions in which he engages. Thus one kilo of heroin sold in a single one-kilo transaction is to be preferred by those engaged in the trade to one kilo sold in two half-kilo transactions. This suggests that the risk of discovery is largest at the point in the chain of distribution where the quantum of heroin transferred in any given transaction is smallest at the mean and where, therefore, the number of transactions is largest. Since the mean of the magnitude of transactions becomes successively smaller as heroin makes its way from importing to retailing, and the number of transactions engaged in by any operators becomes larger in the same process, the risks of detection are, other things being equal, smaller for the importer and larger for the retailer.

The narcotics distribution system may be long or short. In principle, the importer can do his own retailing; or his own wholesaling, selling to other retailers; or he may sell to jobbers who, in turn, sell to wholesalers who sell to retailers. The length of the system will depend, in part, on the extent of the market, since this, in turn, affects the degree of specialization in the trade. If the organization of the trade is managed—if, that is to say, a central director (say the importer or a factor) determines the number of transaction points—then the length of the system may be greater than that indicated by efficiency criteria. This is because the narcotics trade is illegal, and, therefore, those who engage in it operate clandestinely. A clandestine enterprise can be expected to be organized so as to minimize the probability of discovery of its organizer.

The larger the number of transaction points, the smaller the quantity of information possessed by any participant at any point. By elongating the chain, therefore, the organizer of the trade creates a buffer between himself and any point on the chain. The risk he runs of being discovered is inversely proportional to the number of informants who must be successively broken in order that he be found out.

The narcotics trade in some territory may be that of a single monopoly firm which organizes a chain of dealers of some number, or the trade may be carried on by a number of complementary monopolists. If it were a single firm, then the organizer (manager) would determine the magnitude of the difference in prices of heroin between each pair of links in the chain of distribution. This magnitude would be just what is sufficient to attract the relevant number of people to the trade at each link. The compensation of the traders would be determined by the differences between their buying and their selling prices net of the costs of doing business, including the cost of being thought odious by the community and the cost of punishment for engaging in an illegal trade, in a probability sense. If the trade is carried on by complementary monopolists, the price at each transaction link will be indeterminate, since this would simulate Edgeworth's classic duopoly case; the price would depend upon the relative shrewdness of the monopoly traders, within some range.

The magnitudes of differences in prices of narcotics between successive pairs of transaction points will be primarily affected by differences, between successive pairs of points, in the cost of doing business. In this trade, the largest single cost is that associated with discovery, apprehension, conviction, and punishment. The quantity of law enforcement resources and its allocation along the distribution chain would seem to be the primary determinant of the structure of narcotics prices.

Sellers of drugs, when they hold inventories, possess commodities which, if they are discovered, constitute incriminating evidence. There will be a strong incentive to "unload" rapidly and to refrain from holding inventories. As with other stored commodities, inventories may be held in expectation of a price rise; there is an optimal storage policy that takes account of the cost of storage. In the case of an illegal commodity (that is, one whose mere possession, or whose possession with intent to sell, is illegal), the cost of storage is pre-eminently the negative value associated with discovery.

Law enforcement would be advantaged by any change that induced sellers to hold larger inventories and for longer periods. Can enforcement policy be designed to bring this about? Would it be helpful in this connection if possession were not illegal, nor presumptive evidence of illegal activities accepted by the courts? If this induced illegal operators to hold inventories and, in turn, provided information to the authorities about the persons to watch (for *other* kinds of activities than possession—which activities *would* be illegal), would the incidence of discovery rise? But, if possession, even if legal, were found to have secondary adverse consequences, operators would still have an incentive to refrain from storing.

The distribution of opiates is apparently done by "organized criminals," and the distribution of LSD and marijuana is done largely by amateurs. Presumably, this is because the rate of return, adjusted for the cost of doing business, is higher in the opiate trade than in the others. This must be because opiate traders are able to enforce a monopoly which produces rents for them. But why do they not also enforce a monopoly in the other drug trades? Is it because (a) opiate distribution is considered to be the more odious trade; therefore, "amateurs" are less willing to engage in it; therefore, "professionals" have a monopoly of "talent," and it is from this that their rents derive?

Or is it because (b) the costs imposed upon discovered and apprehended opiate distributors are higher than the costs put on traders in LSD and marijuana; these costs are differentially valued by different classes of persons; the amateurs believe a five-year prison sentence is a high price to pay for the monetary gains derived from the trade, but the professionals believe the price is not so high. Therefore, only a small number will engage in the trade (if there were no monopoly and given the relative, adjusted earnings in the opiate trade), and the enforcement costs of a monopoly— which must exclude only a small number of aspirants to the trade—will be low. The costs imposed upon LSD and marijuana distributors are lower (the prison sentences are shorter); therefore, for given rewards, more will engage in these trades; the enforcement of monopolies in these trades would require the exclusion of many disposed to enter; the cost of enforcement of the monopoly would, therefore, be high in them. Presumptively, since we do not observe monopolies in these trades, the cost of making a monopoly effective is high enough so that such an undertaking is not worth while.

What are the expected consequences of more energetic enforcement of the laws against the trade in narcotics?

Crimes are of three classes: (1) They may destroy part of the capital stock of society, as murder and arson; (2) they may involve coercive transfer payments, as theft; (3) they may involve the sale and purchase of commodities that society believes reprehensible, as prostitution and narcotics.

Some crimes damage society more than others. Society can affect the product mix of the crime industry by allocating law enforcement resources among crimes, thus determining the distribution among crimes of the costs of criminal activity paid by criminals. It is assumed that criminals will choose that criminal career which will maximize their net revenues. If, other things being equal, some crimes are made more costly for those who perpetrate them, criminals will, at the margin, move to other crimes. The degree of enforcement of the law against the trade in narcotics will, therefore, enlarge the cost to society from other crimes.

Society's indifference curve between crimes can be assumed to be concave to the origin so that the increment of other crimes than the trade in narcotics that it is willing to suffer, in exchange for the reduction by one unit of the narcotics trade, will be small, if the narcotics trade is of relatively small volume and other crimes of relatively large volume; and it will be large if the volume of narcotics trade is relatively large and the volume of other crimes is relatively small. Criminals now diversify their output to some extent. That is to say, they engage in a number of different criminal activities. This is a form of hedging. If one criminal activity is made relatively more costly to engage in, other things being equal, the quantity of that crime tends to shrink, and that activity becomes inferior as a hedge to what it had been before the cost change occurred. The failure rate of criminal enterprises will rise as a consequence.

As heroin moves forward toward the consumer in the distribution chain it is successively diluted, usually by milk sugar or quinine hydrochloride. The consumer finally buys a combination of heroin and inert materials that may be 1.5-33.0 percent heroin by weight. Why does narcotics dilution take place? As with any other commodity, it is not necessary to dilute in order to effect a rise in price. Two alternative hypotheses are suggested: (1) Consumers will offer less resistance to a price rise produced by additional adulteration of the product and will be less likely to search out alternative sources of supply than if the price rise were outright and open. This seems like a questionable hypothesis, since users can apparently tell the intensity of their experience in the consumption of drugs and do adjust by increasing the number of bags used in a single dose when adulteration occurs. On the other hand, adulteration simulates the behavior of, say, the candy manufacturers who kept the price of candy bars constant while shrinking their sizes. (2) Adulteration is a rationing device employed when heroin is in short supply. This hypothesis would explain variance in the degree of dilution but not the apparent secular tendency for dilution to occur.

Another possible hypothesis is that dilution opens options for consumers. It permits users to choose between small (say one bag) doses and large (say three bag) doses. But this hypothesis gives no clue as to why the extent of dilution has increased with time; it suggests only that dilution will always occur in order to provide a lower "quality" product for those whose preference functions make it desirable to ingest small quantities. It is like explaining why Falcon automobiles will be manufactured, as well as Continentals, but would not explain why the fraction of Falcons rises and the fraction of Continentals falls.

The Market for the Service of Police Inaction

An increase in the probability of interception of illegally imported heroin would have the expected effects of raising its price and of shrinking the trade. These effects can also be achieved in other ways. Anything that increases the expected costs of engaging in this trade will have the same results. Thus, if the fraction of illegally imported heroin that is intercepted does not rise, but if there were an increase in the probability of discovery, apprehension, and/or conviction of smugglers, the trade would also tend to decline. Conversely, of course, anything that diminishes the expected cost of doing business in the trade will diminish the price of its product and enlarge the trade.

The narcotics trade, like many other criminal activities, is probably cartellized, and it produces monopoly rents. Those engaged in the trade have earnings which are superior to those they could earn in alternative competitive employments, and they might be disposed to use these differential earnings to buy the "services" of law enforcement officers. Even if the trade were competitive, the earnings of the traders would be higher than those in alternative employments by some quantity just sufficient to compensate them for the higher risks they run of having fine, imprisonment, deportation, and other costs imposed upon them; these are risks they would not run in legal employments. It would pay them, therefore, to use part of their differential earnings to reduce, in a probability sense, the magnitude of the expected costs for which the differential compensates them. Competitive traders, too, therefore, would be disposed to buy law enforcement officers' services. They will do so only if the price of these services is less than the "value" of the fraction by which the risk of the trader is diminished.

The quantity of discovery and apprehension can be expected to be a function of the quantity of information that comes into the possession of the law enforcement officers charged with the execution of the narcotics laws and of the officers' willingness to use that information to proceed against violators of the law. The information that comes into the possession of these officers may be suppressed. It is reported that "the importation and distribution at wholesale levels, and frequently at retail levels, is likely to flourish only under some form of police protection."

This protection can occur, however, only if the administration of law enforcement activity has the properties of a monopoly industry. Law enforcement officers are employed in something like a competitive labor market. They are paid the market wage for performing the services of their craft. For this wage, they are expected, among other things, to receive information or to search it out, to develop information that will be acceptable in the criminal courts, and to report this information to their relevant superior officers. The officer may, however, be in a position to extract some of the monopoly rents of monopoly illegal traders or to share with them the differential earnings for superior risk of competitive illegal traders. The officer can do this only if he, himself, monopolizes access to the relevant information and the initial "right" to report information. If other officers "compete" with him in the performance of these services and if there are enough of them so that coalitions cannot be formed among them at low cost, then the officer is without monopoly power and has nothing to sell to the illegal trader. For if the trader should buy inaction from one officer, he still runs the risk of discovery and action by another.

This problem can perhaps be solved by contriving arrangements in the administration of the law enforcement function so that administrative monopolies of the kind here suggested do not exist, and administrative competition is substituted for it. Another possible solution is to install incentive-compensation systems for law enforcement officers that will pay off for the delivery of information. There are, of course, problems associated with this form of the solution; the system may generate larger police earnings to patrols which are in crime-prone areas than others; and, if not done with care, it may produce the formation of coalitions of criminals and policemen whose object is the promotion of criminal activities which, in turn, produce incentive earnings.

A nominal rule of police administration is that officers will execute the orders of their superiors and, ultimately, that the police will be administratively responsive to the behavioral implications of the law—that they will do those things which they must do, if the law is to be effectively applied. The law imposes costs upon criminals in some probability sense, but these costs can be diminished by purchasing inaction from a police officer. To the extent that these costs are reduced, the incidence of crime and the cost of crime borne by the community rises.

The propensity to sell the services of inaction varies among police officers so that some will fail to act (refrain from enforcing the law) if they are given, say, $100, while others would require $1,000 for the same (non)act. If it were possible to identify the class with respect to which the propensity to be dutiful (to do only those things which are consistent with nominal and relevant rules or, perhaps, to do only those things which the community does not think odious) is high, police recruitment and selection procedures ought to be biased in favor of that class.

Given the magnitude of these propensities in a given police force, it should be possible to organize the activity of the police so as to minimize the quantity of police inaction. If the probability of buying non-performance at a given price by one officer is 0.1 and by another also 0.1, then the probability of doing so for two independently deciding officers is the product of these probabilities, or 0.01. If these were the magnitudes involved, there would be great advantage in organizing the law enforcement machinery in such a way that inaction, to be effective in a given case (to have value to someone), would require that more than one officer be bought off. If the individual propensities to sell non-performance were much larger than this, the advantage of such an organization would be much smaller. For example, if the corresponding probabilities were 0.9 for each officer, then the probability of securing inaction from two of them would be reduced to only 0.81, and there may be other costs associated with such an organization of police acivity that would cause this arrangement to produce net disbenefits.

On the assumption that the probability numbers are small, the clear advantage associated with an organization such that inaction requires that non-performance be bought from more than one officer will occur, as has been mentioned, only if each officer makes his decision with respect to whether he will sell his (non)services independently of the decisions of other officers. If the decision of one affects the decision of the other, the factor by which the joint probability is reduced is smaller. The organization of police activity ought, therefore, to take account, also, of joint decision effects. There is an advantage, that is to say, in refraining from establishing regular pairs or teams of officers that encourages the formation of coalitions among them.

Corrupt behavior by a police officer may be either known or not known to his colleagues on the force. If known, others who possess the knowledge may either divulge it to their superiors or they may not. Non-divulgence may imply the imposition of costs upon those who conceal information about the malfeasance of their fellow officers, and these costs may be of different magnitudes rising from the polar case of zero cost. Or divulgence may be rewarded, and the gains may be of different magnitudes. Whatever increases the cost of concealment or increases the gains from non-concealment will increase the quantity of information about corrupt behavior that passes to superior officers.

An increase in the quantity of information on the corrupt behavior of an officer that is transmitted to higher echelons of the force will increase the probability of discovery and punishment of the corrupt officer. This will increase the price of corrupt behavior. Corrupt behavior purchased from the police officer is an input of a criminal activity. If the price of this input rises, the cost of doing criminal business rises, and the price of the product (narcotics-selling services) also rises. If there is any demand elasticity, the quantity (of narcotics, and narcotics-selling services) transacted falls.

A bribe paid to a police officer is different in detail, but similar in effect, to the payment of an insurance premium. If one insures against disaster, he does not diminish the probability that the disaster will occur but reduces the cost of the disaster to *him* to the magnitude of the premium payments. Bribes paid to officers *do* reduce the probability of the occurrence of the disaster and, in doing so, reduce the disaster cost to the payer of the bribes. If the probability of occurrence is reduced to zero, then the disaster cost is the cost of its avoidance and is equal to the magnitude of the bribes paid. A criminal may self-insure by running the whole risk that disaster will strike and by bearing the whole cost associated with it. If he pays the bribe-premium instead, it is because his costs are lower this way.

The purchase of police inaction can be thought of in another context. If the state prohibits the sale of narcotics and executes, say, a punishment of three years of imprisonment or a fine of $500 upon offenders, it is saying, substantially, that the value of that punishment is the price for a license to engage in the trade. A police officer who accepts a private payment made to him for failing to charge an offender is selling the license— the right to enter the trade—for some other price. The officer's price must be lower than the state's or the offender would not consent to transact the license with him; he would prefer to purchase it from the state by paying the state's (punishment) price. The officer's behavior shifts traders' marginal cost curves to the right and enlarges the trade.

The Allocation of Police Resources

Even if corruption tends to be most common at the lowest level of police administration: with the man on the beat—it may be that the more uncommon cases at higher levels, when properly weighted, turn out to be more important in the aggregate. In any case, detected information tends to grow by a chain process, and the suppression of a seemingly trivial bit of information discovered "on the street" may forestall the coming into possession of more important pieces some links away. A large fraction of law enforcement activity is that subset of activity which generates information. Information is of a number of classes, for example, information that a crime has been committed, information about the identity of the criminal and his whereabouts, and information of an evidentiary nature that will pass muster in a criminal court proceeding.

Information-generating resources are commanded by the police, and they are scarce goods that ought to be economized. The police have options in the allocation of these resources along the narcotics distributional chain. This allocation is optimal when the information outputs at every link, which are produced by the final units of information-generating resources employed at each link, are themselves equal. The fulfilment of this condition undoubtedly requires the use of more of the resources at some links than at others. It seems reasonable to suppose that a larger expenditure at middle links than at polar links is appropriate, since the former may produce information which, in turn, produces a second generation of information about occurrences both forward and backward in the chain of distribution, while information produced at the poles can have only unidirectional second-generation consequences.

This is complicated by the fact that the cost of acquiring a bit of information is less at the retail end of the chain than elsewhere along its length; concealment seems to be more difficult at the retail end. This is probably because retailers advertise their wares more than do distributors at other parts of the system. If a large part of the cost of doing business is the imprisonment cost imposed upon discovered operators, this cost becomes successively larger. Margins between buying and selling prices can be expected to cover the full cost of doing business. This explains why margins become progressively larger as heroin moves toward the consumer.[1]

In seeking information that is necessary to law enforcement, it is appropriate that information-collecting resources be employed preferentially at the points (*a*) where information is concentrated and (*b*) where the cost of concealment of information is high. Customs personnel and search resources are not sufficiently large to permit intensive inspection of all entries of persons and cargo. If these resources *were* large enough for this purpose, intensive inspection would apparently prolong the time consumed in entry beyond permissible limits. Except for persons and cargo which are suspect because U.S. Customs possess incriminating information about them (all of which should presumably be intensively examined), Customs has the options of extensive examination of all entrants, or intensive examination of a sample of entrants, or some combination of these two. The sample that is examined intensively may be randomly selected. It is not clear whether there would be any advantage in the intensive inspection of a randomly selected sample of the universe of entrants.

Narcotics agents work overseas, infiltrating, producing information, standing at the ready to receive information, and offering payments for information. Is the price paid for information sufficient to draw forth the optimal quantity of it?[2] Information is non-homogeneous with respect to its value in enforcement of the law. Is the structure of rewards or payoffs to informers appropriate from the standpoint of maximizing information (adjusted for quality) received by the law enforcement agencies for given expenditures for this purpose?

The narcotics trade is now apparently a monopoly trade. We assume that, as in other monopoly cases, the net revenue position of the narcotics trader is maximized when the prices he charges are higher and the output he produces is lower than they would be if this were a competitive trade. The enforcement authorities are in a position to re-enforce the monopoly or to make the trade more competitive. They do the former if they are more energetic in the enforcement of the law against new entrants than

[1] It is reported that, in the spring of 1966, the price of a gram of heroin (at 10 per cent purity) was a little less than $0.05 in Turkey (in the form of illegal opium), $1.40 at the point of importation in New York, $35 at wholesale in Chicago, and $295 at retail in Chicago.

[2] It is reported that the U.S. Treasury Department pays $500 for information leading to the seizure of a kilo of narcotics; that this is less than the payment for information that leads to other kinds of contraband goods, where the payment is 25 per cent of the value of the contraband recovered and may be as much as $50,000; and that the Treasury's "standing offer" to informers of narcotics smuggling is a weak incentive for disclosure.

against the monopolist incumbent in the trade. They do the latter if they are equally energetic in enforcement against all.

If consumer expenditure for narcotics were of income earned from the performance of services or from the ownership of assets, it would clearly be in the community interest to re-enforce the monopoly on the ground that a smaller noxious industry is preferable to a larger one. Since it is known, however, that income spent for this purpose is derived largely from clandestine or coercive extraction of unwilling transfer payments from others (that is, from theft), it is not so certain that a smaller industry is always to be preferred. This is because the demand schedule for narcotics, if relatively inelastic, causes a smaller industry to impose higher larcenous transfer payment costs upon the community than would a larger industry.

The optimal allocation of enforcement resources will be affected by the mechanism by which addiction spreads. Two possible hypotheses are: (1) There are constant "returns" to scale, and (2) there are increasing "returns" to scale. If the first of these characterizes the world, one addict will infect x number of non-addicts (causing them to become addicts), and a cluster of ten addicts will infect $10x$ non-addicts. If the second is true, then if one addict will infect x non-addicts, a cluster of ten addicts will infect some number of non-addicts which is larger than $10x$. If the second hypothesis is correct, it suggests that critical mass of some magnitude is necessary for infection to occur. The process would be analogous to the spread of fire. If a matchstick burns, the probability of neighborhood fires is less than if a house burns. Or if ten houses burn, each of which is separated from any other burning house by ten miles, the probability of disastrous spread of fire is less than if the ten burning houses were in the same neighborhood.

Suppose non-addicts experiment with drugs for a number of reasons, say: (a) they are told by an addict that it produces pleasurable experiences, or, by observing a user, they can see that it produces these experiences; (b) they admire another whom they know to be a user because of other qualities he possesses (he is an accomplished playwright, or poet, or musician); and (c) they desire to be a member of a community they believe to be congenial, and the consumption of drugs is a necessary condition of entry into this community. Of this small catalogue of motivations for experimentation, (a) and (b) would be operative whether the observed addict is isolated or one of a cluster of addicts. However, (c) would be operative only when there were clusters. As long as there is one additional incentive associated with a cluster which is absent in the case of the isolated addict, the cluster will be a stronger focus of infection than the individual; and a cluster will have stronger infecting consequences than an equal number of isolated individuals.

This suggests that the quantity of enforcement per addict should be larger where clusters occur than where there are no clusters and addicts are isolated; that clusters should be broken up and their members diffused more thinly in the population and in space; that clusters, where they are not broken, should be isolated; that devices should be employed to cause that segment of the non-addict population which is on the margin of experimentation to believe, given the values they presently hold, that the addict cluster community is not congenial (this may require either the exposition of the truth, or systematic misrepresentation of fact, or some combination of them); and that devices be employed to alter the values of the sector that is on the margin of experimental drug consumption so that the probability diminishes that experiments occur.

Maximizing individuals seeking euphoric utilities will prefer those instruments for securing it that are cheapest.[3] Can the substitutes for dangerous drugs (either in the form of drugs that are not dangerous or other [non-drug] commodities) be ranked in the order of their goodness as substitutes? If so, policy can perhaps reduce their prices, relative to the prices of dangerous drugs. The authorities charged with the enforcement of the narcotics laws are faced with a set of alternative strategies among which they exercise options. This paper has touched upon some of the variables that affect optimizing behavior by those authorities.

[3] Juveniles arrested in Los Angeles told the police there that they turned from marijuana to barbiturates "because they are cheaper."

The Optimum Enforcement of Laws

GEORGE J. STIGLER

George J. Stigler is Walgreen Professor of American Institutions at the University of Chicago. This article appeared in the Journal of Political Economy *in 1970.*

All prescriptions of behavior for individuals require enforcement. Usually the obligation to behave in a prescribed way is entered into voluntarily by explicit or implicit contract. For example, I promise to teach certain classes with designated frequency and to discuss matters which I, and possibly others, believe are relevant to the course titles. By negotiation, and in the event of its failure, by legal action, I and my employer seek to enforce the contract of employment against large departures from the promised behavior. Performance of some kinds of behavior is difficult or impossible to enforce—such as promises to be creative, noble, or steadfast in crisis—and as a result such contractual promises are either not made or enforced only when there is an uncontroversially flagrant violation. The influence upon contract, and upon economic organization generally, of the costs of enforcing various kinds of contracts has received virtually no study of economists, despite its immense potential explanatory power.

When the prescribed behavior is fixed unilaterally rather than by individual agreement, we have the regulation or law, and enforcement of these unilateral rules is the subject of the present essay. Departures of actual from prescribed behavior are crimes or violations, although one could wish for a less formidable description than "criminal" to describe many of the trifling offenses or the offenses against unjust laws. My primary purpose is to construct a theory of rational enforcement, a theory which owes much to Gary Becker's major article on the subject (1968).

In the conclusion the problem of explanation, as distinguished from prescription, will be commented upon.

The Goal of Enforcement

The goal of enforcement, let us assume, is to achieve that degree of compliance with the rule of prescribed (or proscribed) behavior that the society believes it can afford. There is one decisive reason why the society must forego "complete" enforcement of the rule: enforcement is costly.

The extent of enforcement of laws depends upon the amount of resources devoted to the task. With enough policemen almost every speeding automobile could be identified. The success of tenacious pursuit of the guilty in celebrated crimes (such as the great English train robbery and the assassination of Martin King) suggests that few crimes of sane men could escape detection. We could make certain that crime does not pay by paying enough to apprehend most criminals. Such a level of enforcement would of course be enormously expensive, and only in crimes of enormous importance will such expenditures be approached. The society will normally give to the enforcement agencies a budget which dictates a much lower level of enforcement.

The cost limitation upon the enforcement of laws would prevent the society from forestalling, detecting, and punishing all offenders, but it would appear that punishments which would be meted out to the guilty could often be increased without using additional resources. The offender is deterred by the expected punishment, which is (as a first approximation) the probability of punishment times the punishment—$100 if the probability of conviction is $\frac{1}{10}$ and the fine $1,000. Hence, increasing the punishment would seem always to increase the deterrence. Capital punishment is cheaper than long term imprisonment; and seizure of all the offender's property may not be much more expensive than collecting a more moderate fine.

To escape from this conclusion, Becker introduces as a different limitation on punishment the "social value of the gain to offenders" from the offense. The determination of this social value is not explained, and one is entitled to doubt its usefulness as an explanatory concept: what evidence is there that society sets a positive value upon the utility derived from a murder, rape, or arson? In fact the society has branded the utility derived from such activities as illicit. It may be that in a few offenses some gain to the offender is viewed as a gain to society,[1] but such social gains seem too infrequent, small, and capricious to put an effective limitation upon the size of punishments.

Instead we take account of another source of limitation of punishment,

[1] For example, the thief reduces the welfare expenditures of the state, or the arsonist warms the neighboring houses.

which arises out of the nature of the supply of offenses. It is no doubt true that the larger the punishment, the smaller will be the expected net utility to the prospective offender from the commission of a given offense. But marginal decisions are made here as in the remainder of life, and the marginal deterrence of heavy punishments could be very small or even negative. If the offender will be executed for a minor assault and for a murder, there is no marginal deterrence to murder. If the thief has his hand cut off for taking five dollars, he had just as well take $5,000. Marginal costs are necessary to marginal deterrence. The marginal deterrence to committing small crimes is also distorted if an otherwise appropriate schedule of penalties is doubled or halved.

One special aspect of this cost limitation upon enforcement is the need to avoid overenforcement. The enforcement agency could easily apprehend most guilty people if we placed no limits upon the charging and frequent conviction of innocent people. In any real enforcement system, there will in fact be conviction and punishment of some innocent parties, and these miscarriages of justice impose costs of both resources and loss of confidence in the enforcement machinery. The costs of defense of innocent parties, whether borne by themselves or by the state, are part of the costs of enforcement from the social viewpoint. The conviction of innocent persons encourages the crime because it reduces the marginal deterrence to its commission.

The significance of an offense to society—the quantity of resources that will be used to "prevent" the offense—will in general increase with the gravity of the offense. The increase in resources, however, will not manifest itself only in an increase in punishments. The state will pursue more tenaciously the offender who commits a larger crime (or repetitive crimes) and thus increase also the probability of apprehending him.

There is a division of labor between the state and the citizen in the prevention of virtually every offense. The owner of large properties is required to do much of his direct policing: there are surely more watchmen and guards than policemen in a typical city. The larger accumulations of wealth, moreover, are to be guarded by the owner through devices such as nonnegotiability and custody of funds by specialists. Accordingly, the *public* punishments for crimes against property do not increase in proportion to the value of the property. In the protection of people, as distinguished from their property, the individual is required to protect himself from minor offenses or at least to detect their occurrence and assume a large part of the burden of prosecution (for example, shoplifting, insults, simple trespass), but he is allowed less discretion in prosecution for major assaults.

The relationship of duration and nature of penalties to age and sex of offender, frequency of previous offenses, and so forth is also explicable in terms of cost of enforcement. The first-time offender may have committed the offense almost accidentally and (given any punishment) with negligible probability of repetition, so heavy penalties (which have substantial costs to the state) are unnecessary. The probability of a repetition of an offense by a seasoned offender is also zero during his imprisonment, so the probability of repetition of an offense is relevant to the penalty also in his case.

Indeed, the problem of determining the efficient penalty may be viewed as one is statistical inference: to estimate the individual's average, durable propensity to offend (the population value) on the basis of a sample of his observed behavior and how this propensity responds to changes in penalties. As in other sequential sampling problems, one can estimate this propensity more accurately, the longer the individual's behavior is observed.

The society will be more concerned (because each individual is more concerned) with major than minor offenses in the following sense: There is increasing marginal disutility of offenses, so a theft of $1,000 is more than twice as harmful as a theft of $500. In the area of offenses to property, this result is implied by diminishing marginal utility of income. In the area of offenses to persons, it is more difficult to measure damage in any direct way, but a similar rule probably holds.

So much for prevention and punishment; let us turn to the offenses.

The Supply of Offenses

The commission of offenses will be an act of production for income or an act of consumption. A consumption offense would be illustrated by speeding in an automobile used for recreation or assaulting a courtship rival (when the girl is poor). A production offense would be illustrated by theft, smuggling, and the violation of economic regulations. In the realm of offenses to property, income objectives are of course paramount, and we may recall Adam Smith's emphasis upon the economic nature of crime:

> The affluence of the rich excites the indignation of the poor, who are often both driven by want, and prompted by envy, to invade his possessions. It is only under the shelter of the civil magistrate that the owner of that valuable property, which is acquired by the labour of many years, or perhaps of many successive generations, can sleep a single night in security. He is at all times surrounded by unknown enemies, whom, though he never provoked, he can never appease, and from whose injustice he can be protected only by the powerful arm of the civil magistrate continually held up to chastise it. The acquisition of valuable and extensive property, therefore, necessarily requires the establishment of civil government. Where there is no property, or at least none that exceeds the value of two or three days labour, civil government is not so necessary.

The professional criminal seeks income, and for him the usual rules of occupational choice will hold. He will reckon the present value of the expected returns and costs of the criminal activity and compare their difference with the net returns from other criminal activities and from legitimate activities. The costs of failure in the execution of the crime correspond to the costs of failure in other occupations. The costs of injuries to a professional athlete are comparable to the costs to the offender of apprehension, defense, and conviction, but normally legal occupations have only monetary costs of failure.

The details of occupational choice in illegal activity are not different from those encountered in the legitimate occupations. One must choose the locality of maximum income expectation (and perhaps, like a salesman, move from area to area). One must choose between large, relatively infrequent crimes and smaller, more frequent crimes. One must reckon in periods of (involuntary) unemployment due to imprisonment. Earnings can be expected to rise for a time with experience.

The probability of apprehension (and therefore of conviction) is an increasing function of the frequency of commission of offenses. If the probability of detection is p for one offense, it is $1 - (1 - p)^n$ for at least one conviction in n offenses, and this expression approaches unity as n becomes large. In fact the probability of detection (p) rises after each apprehension because the enforcement agency is also learning the offender's habits. On this score alone, there is a strong incentive to the criminal to make very infrequent attempts to obtain very large sums of money. The probability of success is also affected by the precautions of the prospective victim: For Knox is more difficult to enter than a liquor store. The efforts of detection will also increase with the size of the offense.

We may postulate, in summary, a supply of offenses which in equilibrium has the following properties:

1. Net returns are equalized, allowance being made for risk and costs of special equipment required for various activities.
2. The determinants of supply which are subject to the control of society are: (a) the structure of penalties by offense; (b) the probability of detection for each offense; (c) certain costs of the conduct of the offending activity; for example, the cost of making successful counterfeit money can be increased by complicating the genuine money.
3. The penalties and chances of detection and punishment must be increasing functions of the enormity of the offense.

Although it smacks of paradox, it may be useful to reinterpret the offending activity as providing a variety of products (offenses). These offenses are in a sense demanded by the society: My wallet is an invitation to the foot pad, my office funds to the embezzler. The costs of production of the offenses are the ordinary outlays of offenders plus the penalties imposed by the society. The industry will operate at a scale and composition of output set by the competition of offenders and the cost of producing offenses.

The structure of rational enforcement activities will have these properties:

1. Expected penalties increase with expected gains so there is no marginal net gain from larger offenses. Let the criminal commit in a year S crimes of size Q, where Q is the monetary value to the criminal of the successful completion of the crime. The fraction (p) of crimes completed successfully, (or the probability of successful completion of one crime) is a decreasing function of the amount of expenditure (E) undertaken by society to prevent and punish the crime. (Punishment is used for deterrence, and is only a special form of prevention.) Hence $p = p(E, Q)$, or possibly $p = p(E, Q, S)$. The expected punishment is the fraction of crimes apprehended (and punished) times the punishment, F. The condition for marginal deterrence is, for all Q, $d(pSQ)/dQ \leq d(1 - p)SF/dQ$.
2. The expenditures on prevention and enforcement should yield a diminution in offenses, at the margin, equal to the return upon these resources in other areas. An increment of expenditures yields a return in reduced offenses,

$$\sum_{Q'} d(pSQ')/dE = \text{marginal return on expenditures elsewhere,}$$

where Q' is the monetary value of the offense to society.[2]
I do not include foregone lawful services of the criminal in the cost of his activity to society ($=$ noncriminals) since he, not others, would receive the return (taxes aside!) if he shifted from crime to a lawful occupation.

The Enforcement Agency: A Normative Approach

A law is enforced, not by "society," but by an agency instructed to that task. That agency must be given more than a mandate (an elegant admonition) to enforce the statute with vigor and wisdom: It must have incentives to enforce the law efficiently. There are at least two deficiencies in the methods by which most agencies are induced to enforce the laws properly.

The first deficiency is that the enforcement agency does not take into account, at least explicitly and fully, the costs it imposes upon the activity or persons regulated. In the area of ordinary criminal offenses, the society will, if anything, wish to increase (at no expense to itself) the costs of defense for guilty persons but it should not impose costs (and certainly

---

[2] Currency has the same value to the criminal as to society, so $Q' = Q$. But for any commodity which does not have a market price independent of ownership, $Q < Q'$.

not unnecessary costs) upon innocent parties. In fact, the administration of criminal justice should in principle include as a cost the reimbursement of the expenses of defense of people charged and acquitted. The compensation actually paid will not exactly compensate injured persons, because of the administrative costs of ascertaining exact compensation, but the taking of an innocent person's personal wealth, including foregone income, differs in no respect from the taking of some of his real estate (for which under eminent domain it is necessary to compensate him fully).[3]

In the area of economic regulation, guilt is often an inappropriate notion, and when it is inappropriate all costs of compliance must be reckoned into the social costs of enforcement. The utility's costs in preparing a rate case or Texas Gulf Sulfur's costs in defending itself against the Securities and Exchange Commission are social costs of the regulatory process. Reimbursement is now achieved by charging the consumers of the products and the owners of specialized resources of these industries: They bear the private costs of the regulatory process. This is at least an accidental allocation of costs, and when the regulation seeks to aid the poorer consumers or resource owners, a perverse allocation.

The second deficiency in the design of enforcement is the use of inappropriate methods of determining the extent of enforcement. The annual report of an enforcement agency is in effect the justification of its previous expenditures and the plea for enlarged appropriations. The Federal Trade Commission will tell us, for example, that in fiscal 1966 as part of its duty to get truthful labeling of furs and textiles, it inspected 12,625 plants and settled 213 "cases" for $1,272,000 plus overhead. The agency may recite scandals corrected or others still unrepressed, but it neither offers nor possesses a criterion by which to determine the correct scale of its activities.

A rational measure of enforcement procedure could in principle be established in almost any area. Consider the fraudulent labeling of textiles. We could proceed as follows:

1. The damage to the consumer from the purchase of a mislabeled textile could be estimated, and will obviously vary with the mislabeling (assuming that the legal standards are sensible!). The difference between market value of the true and alleged grades is one component of the damage. A second and more elusive component is the additional cost of deception (earlier replacement, skin irritation, and so forth): The consumer who would not have purchased the inferior quality at a competitive price had he known its inferiority has suffered additional damage. Thus the measure of damage is the amount a consumer would pay to avoid the deception, that is, the value of

---

[3] It is an interesting aspect of our attitudes in this area that many people believe that acquitted persons are probably guilty.

the *insured* correct quality minus the value of the actual quality.

2. As a matter of deterrence, the penalties on the individual mislabeler should be equal to a properly taken sum of the following items: (a) The damage per yard times the number of yards, say per year. Let this be H. (b) The costs of the enforcement agency, say E, per year. This sum should include reimbursement of the costs of those charged and acquitted. (c) The costs of defense (if detected) for the mislabeler, D. Where guilt is an appropriate notion, as presumably in the case of mislabeling, the society may wish to ignore these costs, which is to say, resources devoted to this end deserve no return. Where guilt is inappropriate, these costs should be reckoned in. The sum of these penalties must be multiplied by $1/p$, where p is the probability of detection of the offense within the year. This probability is a function of E and H.

3. The enforcement agency should minimize the sum of damages plus enforcement costs, $(\sum H + E)$ or $(\sum H + \sum D + E)$.

This goal will serve two functions. The first is to set the scale of enforcement, namely where marginal return equals marginal cost. If the scale of enforcement is correct, society is not spending two dollars to save itself one dollar of damage, or failing to spend one dollar where it will save more than that amount of damage. The second function is to guide the selection of cases: The agency will not (as often now) seek numerous, easy cases to dress up its record, but will pursue the frequent violator and the violator who does much damage.

This sort of criterion of enforcement is readily available in certain areas. The secret service, for example, reports that in fiscal 1967 the loss to the public from counterfeit money was $1,658,100.75 (an excellent instance of counterfeit accuracy). Perhaps half of the $17 million spent by this agency was devoted to the suppression of counterfeiting, and to this one must add the costs of legal actions, imprisonment, and so forth. The secret service should be asking whether the amount of counterfeit money passed would fall by a dollar if a dollar more were spent on enforcement costs minus the corresponding fines collected.

The penalty structure should incorporate the social appraisal of the importance of the suppression of the offenses. The law does not in general provide this scale of values, as can be shown by the list of maximum penalties for the violations of economic regulations listed in Table 1.

The use of criminal sanctions is erratic, and the implicit equivalence of fines and imprisonment varies from $1,000 per year to $10,000 per year. Many of the penalties are not even stated in the statutes: The penalty for drinking (industrial) alcohol which has not paid its beverage tax is sometimes blindness or death. The penalties for the essentially similar offense (if such it must be called) of reducing freight rates can be ten times as much for a barge operator as for a trucker. Of course these maximum

TABLE I.

Offense	Enforcement Agency	Maximum Penalty	Statute
Restraint of trade.	Antitrust Division	$50,000 + 1 year (+ triple damages and costs)	Sherman (1890, 1955)
Unfair methods of competition	FTC	Cease and desist order	FTC (1914)
Refusal to testify, or testify falsely, under same	FTC	$1,000–$5,000 + 1 year	Same
Price discrimination	FTC	Cease and desist (+ triple damages and costs)	Clayton (1914)
False advertisements of foods, drugs, or cosmetics	FTC	$5,000 + 6 months	Wheeler-Lea (1938)
Adulteration or misbranding of food	Secretary of Health, Education, and Welfare	$1,000 + 1 year, first offense; $10,000 + 3 years, later offense	Copeland Act (1938)
Exporting apples and pears without certificate of quality	Dept. of Agriculture	Denial of certificate for 10 days $100–$1,000 for knowing violation	Apples and Pears for Export (1933)
Exporting apples in improper barrels	Dept. of Agriculture	$1 barrel	Standard Barrels and Standard Grades of Apples Act (1912)
Exporting other fruit or vegetables in improper barrels	Dept. of Agriculture	$500 or 6 months if willful	Standard Barrels . . . for Fruits, Vegetables and Other Dry Commodities (1915)
Exporting grapes in improper baskets	Dept. of Agriculture	$25	Standard Baskets Act (1916)

TABLE I. (*Continued*)

Offense	Enforcement Agency	Maximum Penalty	Statute
Giving rebates in freight charges (trucks)	ICC	$200–$500 first offense; $250–$5,000 repeated offense	Motor Carrier Act (1935)
Same, water carriers	ICC	$5,000 if willful	Transportation Act (1940)
Failure to disclose interest charges	FRB	Twice finance charge, within $100–$1,000; $5,000 and/or 1 year if willful	Consumer Credit Protection Act (1968)
Falsely certify a check	FBI	$5,000 and/or 5 years	62 Stat. 749 (June 25, 1948)
Failure to deliver gold or certificates to FR Bank when ordered	FRB	Twice the number of dollars	Federal Reserve Act (1913)
Evasion of excise taxes	Treasury	$10,000 and/or 5 years if willful; forfeiture of goods and conveyance	Revenue Act (1954)
Security Act violation	SEC	$5,000 and/or 5 years	Securities Act (1934)
Misbrand hazardous substances	Secretary of Health, Education, and Welfare	$500 and 90 days; $3,000 or 1 year if willful or repeated	Hazardous Substances Act (1960)

penalties are not actual penalties, but one is not entitled to hope for much more rationality or uniformity in the fixing of penalties for specific offenses. (The lawyers have apparently not studied in adequate detail the actual sanctions for economic offenses.)

One may conjecture that two features of punishment of traditional criminal law have been carried over to economic regulation: the attribution of a substantial cost to the act of conviction itself, and the related belief that moral guilt does not vary closely with the size of the offense. Whatever the source, the penalty structure is not well designed for either deterrence or guidance of enforcement.

Conclusion

The widespread failure to adopt rational criteria of enforcement of laws has been due often and perhaps usually to a simple lack of understanding of the need for and nature of rational enforcement. The clarification of the logic of rational enforcement, and the demonstration that large gains would be obtained by shifting to a rational enforcement scheme, are presumably the necessary (and hopefully sufficient) conditions for improving public understanding of enforcement problems.[4]

There is, however, a second and wholly different reason for the use of what appear to be inappropriate sanctions and inappropriate appropriations to enforcement bodies: the desire of the public *not* to enforce the laws. The appropriations to the enforcement agency and the verdicts of juries are the instruments by which the community may constantly review public policy. If the society decides that drinking alcoholic beverages or speeding in automobiles is not a serious offense in their ordinary forms, they may curtail resources for enforcement and so compel the enforcement agency to deal only with a small number of offenses (perhaps offenses of larger magnitude, such as chronic drunkenness or driving at extremely high speeds). There is considerable inertia in the legislative process—inertia that serves highly useful functions—and it is much easier to make continuous marginal adjustments in a policy through the appropriations committee by varying the resources for its enforcement than it is to modify the statute. Variation in enforcement provides desirable flexibility in public policy.

[4] The peculiarities of the structure of sanctions in economic regulation are partially due also to the response of the regulated businesses. They may effectively lobby to limit appropriations to the regulatory body, but they can also impose costly activities upon the regulatory body which force it to curtail other controls.